A Companion to Alfred Hitchcock

Wiley-Blackwell Companions to Film Directors

The Wiley-Blackwell Companions to Film Directors survey key directors whose work together constitutes what we refer to as the Hollywood and world cinema canons. Whether Haneke or Hitchcock, Bigelow or Bergman, Capra or the Coen brothers, each volume, comprised of 25 or more newly commissioned essays written by leading experts, explores a canonical, contemporary and/or controversial *auteur* in a sophisticated, authoritative, and multi-dimensional capacity. Individual volumes interrogate any number of subjects – the director's *oeuvre*; dominant themes, well-known, worthy, and under-rated films; stars, collaborators, and key influences; reception, reputation, and above all, the director's intellectual currency in the scholarly world.

Published
A Companion to Michael Haneke, edited by Roy Grundmann
A Companion to Alfred Hitchcock, edited by Thomas Leitch and Leland Poague

Forthcoming
A Companion to Rainer Fassbinder, edited by Brigitte Peucker

A Companion to
Alfred Hitchcock

Edited by

Thomas Leitch and Leland Poague

A John Wiley & Sons, Ltd., Publication

This edition first published 2011

© 2011 Blackwell Publishing Ltd except for editorial material and organization © 2011 Thomas Leitch and Leland Poague

Blackwell Publishing was acquired by John Wiley & Sons in February 2007. Blackwell's publishing program has been merged with Wiley's global Scientific, Technical, and Medical business to form Wiley-Blackwell.

Registered Office
John Wiley & Sons Ltd, The Atrium, Southern Gate, Chichester, West Sussex, PO19 8SQ, United Kingdom

Editorial Offices
350 Main Street, Malden, MA 02148-5020, USA
9600 Garsington Road, Oxford, OX4 2DQ, UK
The Atrium, Southern Gate, Chichester, West Sussex, PO19 8SQ, UK

For details of our global editorial offices, for customer services, and for information about how to apply for permission to reuse the copyright material in this book please see our website at www.wiley.com/wiley-blackwell.

The right of Thomas Leitch and Leland Poague to be identified as the author(s) of the editorial material in this work has been asserted in accordance with the UK Copyright, Designs and Patents Act 1988.

Library of Congress Cataloging-in-Publication Data

A companion to Alfred Hitchcock / edited by Thomas Leitch and Leland Poague.
    p.   cm. – (Wiley-Blackwell companions to film directors)
   Includes bibliographical references and index.
   ISBN 978-1-4051-8538-7 (hardback)
1. Hitchcock, Alfred, 1899–1980–Criticism and interpretation.   I. Leitch, Thomas M.   II. Poague, Leland A., 1948–
   PN1998.3.H58C63 2011
   791.43 0233 092–dc22

                              2010051052

A catalogue record for this book is available from the British Library.

This book is published in the following electronic formats: ePDFs 9781444397307; Wiley Online Library 9781444397321; ePub 9781444397314

Set in 11/13pt Dante by SPi Publisher Services, Pondicherry, India

1   2011

In memoriam
Robin Wood
1931–2009

Contents

Notes on Contributors

Richard Allen is Professor of Cinema Studies at New York University. He is author of *Hitchcock's Romantic Irony* and co-editor of three anthologies dealing with Hitchcock's work. With Sidney Gottlieb, he is co-editor of the *Hitchcock Annual*.

Charles Barr taught for many years at the University of East Anglia, helping to develop one of the pioneer British programs in Film Studies at undergraduate and graduate level. Since then, he has held Visiting Professorships at Washington University in St. Louis and at University College Dublin. His many publications on cinema include books on *Ealing Studios, English Hitchcock,* and *Vertigo.*

Janet Bergstrom, Professor of Cinema and Media Studies at UCLA, specializes in archivally-based, cross-national studies of such émigré directors as F.W. Murnau, Jean Renoir, Fritz Lang, and Josef von Sternberg. She pursues the same approach as Associate Editor of *Film History*, as curator of retrospectives and events (Cinema Ritrovato, Bologna), and in documentaries created for DVD –*Murnau's* 4 Devils: *Traces of a Lost Film* (2003), *Introduction to* Phantom (2006), *Murnau and Borzage at Fox – The Expressionist Heritage* (2008), and Underworld: *How It Came to Be* (2010). She edited the anthology *Endless Night: Cinema and Psychoanalysis, Parallel Histories* and co-founded *Camera Obscura: A Journal of Feminism and Film Theory.*

Lesley Brill is the author of *The Hitchcock Romance: Love and Irony in Hitchcock's Films* (1988) and of numerous essays on film and photography. His latest book is *Crowds, Power, and Transformation in Cinema* (2006). He teaches at Wayne State University in Detroit.

Paula Marantz Cohen is Distinguished Professor of English at Drexel University. She is the author of four nonfiction works, including *Alfred Hitchcock: The Legacy of Victorianism,* and four novels, including, most recently, *What Alice Knew: A Most Curious Tale of Henry James and Jack the Ripper.* Her essays, stories, and reviews have appeared in *The Yale Review, The American Scholar, Raritan, The Southwest Review, The Times Literary Supplement*, and other publications. She is the host of the Drexel InterView, a cable television show out of Philadelphia, and a co-editor of *jml: Journal of Modern Literature*.

Alexander Doty is a professor in the Department of Gender Studies and the Department of Communication and Culture at Indiana University–Bloomington. He has written *Making Things Perfectly Queer* and *Flaming Classics*, and co-edited *Out in Culture: Essays on Gay, Lesbian, and Queer Popular Culture*. He was recently the editor for two special issues of *Camera Obscura* titled "Fabulous! The Diva Issues." His favorite (queer) Hitchcock film is *Marnie*, closely followed by *Shadow of a Doubt*.

Richard Gilmore is Associate Professor of Philosophy at Concordia College in Moorhead, MN. He is the author of *Philosophical Health: Wittgenstein's Method in "Philosophical Investigations"* (1999) and *Doing Philosophy at the Movies* (2005).

Sidney Gottlieb is Professor of Media Studies at Sacred Heart University, in Fairfield, Connecticut. His publications on film include *Hitchcock on Hitchcock* (1995), *Alfred Hitchcock: Interviews* (2005), and Roberto Rossellini's *Rome Open City* (2004). With Richard Allen, he edits the *Hitchcock Annual*.

Ina Rae Hark is Distinguished Professor Emerita of English and Film and Media Studies at the University of South Carolina. Among her twenty-five articles and chapters on film and media are five other pieces on Hitchcock. She is the author of *Star Trek* in the BFI Television Classics series and the forthcoming *Deadwood* for Wayne State UP's *TV Milestones* series. She has also edited or co-edited *Screening the Male, The Road Movie Book, Exhibition: the Film Reader*, and *American Cinema of the 1930s*.

Thomas Hemmeter is Associate Professor of English at Arcadia University (Glenside, PA), where he teaches courses in British and American literature and in film studies. He has published on Hitchcock in various essay collections as well as film journals, including *The Journal of Film and Video, PostScript*, and the *Hitchcock Annual*, and devoted concerted attention to Robert Altman, Martin Scorsese, and recent Irish film.

Florence Jacobowitz teaches film and cultural studies at York University in Toronto and is an editor of *CineAction* magazine.

Noel King teaches in the Department of Media, Music, Communication and Cultural Studies at Macquarie University, Sydney, Australia. His current research includes Don DeLillo and film, Richard Hugo and film, and an ongoing study of "cultures of independence" in contemporary fiction and poetry publishing.

Thomas Leitch teaches English and directs the Film Studies program at the University of Delaware. His books include *Find the Director and Other Hitchcock Games, The Encyclopedia of Alfred Hitchcock*, and, most recently, *Film Adaptation and Its Discontents: From* Gone with the Wind *to* The Passion of the Christ.

Joe McElhaney teaches in the Department of Film and Media Studies at Hunter College and the Ph.D. program in Theatre at the City University of New York Graduate Center. He is the author of *The Death of Classical Cinema: Hitchcock, Lang, Minnelli* and *Albert Maysles*, and the editor of *Vincente Minnelli: The Art of Entertainment*. He is currently editing *A Companion to Fritz Lang* for Blackwell.

Todd McGowan teaches critical theory and film at the University of Vermont. He is the author of *The Impossible David Lynch* (2007), *The Real Gaze: Film Theory After Lacan* (2007), and *Out of Time: Desire in Atemporal Cinema* (2011), among other works. His work brings together psychoanalysis and Hegel as a way of thinking about the subject's encounter with culture.

Toby Miller works in the Department of Media and Cultural Studies at the University of California, Riverside. His latest books are *The Contemporary Hollywood Reader* and *Television Studies: The Basics*.

Tania Modleski is Florence R. Scott Professor of English at the University of Southern California. Her *The Women Who Knew Too Much: Hitchcock and Feminist Theory* first appeared in 1988; a second edition came out in 2005. Among her other books are *Loving with a Vengeance* (1982, 2008) and *Feminism without Women* (1991).

Ken Mogg is a lifelong admirer, teacher, and proponent of Hitchcock's films. His monograph "The Day of the Claw: A Synoptic Account of *Alfred Hitchcock's The Birds*" has been published online in *Senses of Cinema*, issue 51, "Toward an Ecology of Cinema" (2009).

Richard R. Ness is Associate Professor of Film and Media Studies at Western Illinois University. He is the author of *Alan Rudolph: Romance and a Crazed World* and *From Headline Hunter to Superman: A Journalism Filmography*. His articles and reviews have appeared in *Cinema Journal*, the *Hitchcock Annual, Quarterly Review of Film and Video*, and the anthology *Print the Legend: Cinema and Journalism*.

Harry Oldmeadow is Coordinator of Religion and Spirituality Studies at La Trobe University Bendigo, where he also teaches Cinema Studies. He has published on a wide range of subjects, including the Australian cinema, John Ford, and postmodernist theory. His particular interests include classical Hollywood genres, especially the Western and the noir crime film, and the history of film criticism.

Brigitte Peucker is the Elias Leavenworth Professor of German and Professor of Film Studies at Yale University. She has published extensively on matters of film and the other arts. Her latest book is *The Material Image* (2007).

Leland Poague is Professor of English at Iowa State University. He is the author of books on Frank Capra, Ernst Lubitsch, and Howard Hawks, of the "Hollywood Professionals" volume on Billy Wilder and Leo McCarey, and the co-author, with William Cadbury, of *Film Criticism: A Counter Theory* (1982). He has edited books on Susan Sontag and Frank Capra, and with Marshall Deutelbaum co-edited *A Hitchcock Reader*, which recently appeared in its second edition (2009) from Wiley-Blackwell.

Murray Pomerance is Professor in the Department of Sociology at Ryerson University. His books include *Magia D'Amore* (1999), *An Eye for Hitchcock* (2004), *Savage Time* (2005), *Johnny Depp Starts Here* (2005), *The Horse Who Drank the Sky: Film Experience Beyond Narrative and Theory* (2008), *Edith Valmaine* (forthcoming), and *Michelangelo Red Antonioni Blue: Eight Reflections on Cinema* (forthcoming). He is editor of the Techniques of the Moving Image series at Rutgers University Press and the Horizons of Cinema series at SUNY Press, as well as co-editor, with Lester D. Friedman and Adrienne L. McLean respectively, of the Screen Decades and Star Decades series at Rutgers.

Angelo Restivo is the author of *The Cinema of Economic Miracles: Visuality and Modernization in the Italian Art Film*, as well as a number of essays on Hitchcock. He is currently working on two book projects on the relationship of modernization to formal questions of cinema and media. He is Associate Professor and Graduate Director of the Program in Moving Image Studies, Department of Communication, Georgia State University.

William Rothman is Professor of Motion Pictures and Director of the Graduate Program in Film Study at the University of Miami. He is the author of *Hitchcock— The Murderous Gaze* (1982), *The "I" of the Camera: Essays in Film Criticism, History, and Aesthetics* (1988; second edition, 2004), and *Documentary Film Classics* (1997). With Marian Keane, he co-authored *Reading Cavell's* The World Viewed: A Philosophical Perspective on Film (2000) and has recently edited *Cavell on Film* (2005), *Jean Rouch: A Celebration of Life and Film* (2007), and *Three Documentary Filmmakers: Errol Morris, Ross McElwee, Jean Rouch* (2009).

Tom Ryall is Emeritus Professor of Film History at Sheffield Hallam University. His books include *Alfred Hitchcock and the British Cinema* (1986), *Blackmail* (1993), *Britain and the American Cinema* (2001), and *Anthony Asquith* (2005). He has contributed various articles on British and American cinema to such collections as *The Oxford Guide to Film Studies* (1998), *The Cinema of Britain and Ireland* (2005), and *The British Cinema Book* (2009).

David Sterritt is chair of the National Society of Film Critics, adjunct professor at Columbia University and the Maryland Institute College of Art, and professor emeritus at Long Island University. He is the film critic of *Tikkun*, chief book critic of *Film Quarterly*, and an editorial board member of *Cinema Journal* and *Quarterly Review of Film and Video*. He has been film and cultural critic of *The Christian Science Monitor*, co-chair of the Columbia University Seminar on Cinema and Interdisciplinary Interpretation, and a member of the New York Film Festival selection committee. His books include *The Films Of Alfred Hitchcock* (1993).

Jack Sullivan, Professor of English and Director of American Studies at Rider University, is the author most recently of *New World Symphonies* and *Hitchcock's Music*, the winner of the ASCAP–Deems Taylor Award for best book of 2006 in the concert music category. His articles and reviews have appeared in *The New York Times, The Wall Street Journal, Opera, The Chronicle Review* and others.

George Toles is Distinguished Professor of Literature and Film and Chair of Film Studies at the University of Manitoba. He is the author of *A House Made of Light: Essays on the Art of Film*. For twenty-five years, he has been the screenwriting collaborator of director Guy Maddin. He has recently written an original screenplay for Maddin's feature film *Keyhole* (2011).

James M. Vest is Professor Emeritus of French, Film Studies, and Interdisciplinary Humanities at Rhodes College. He has authored books and articles on topics ranging from the French origins and reception of Shakespeare's Ophelia to French poetry and Hitchcock's French connections. His current research centers on Hitchcock's earliest films.

Susan White is Associate Professor of Literature and Film Studies in the Department of English at the University of Arizona. She is the author of *The Cinema of Max Ophuls: Magisterial Vision and the Figure of Woman*, and of numerous articles on gender and cinema, focusing especially on the works of Hitchcock, Kubrick, and Nicholas Ray. She has also produced several commentary tracks on Ophuls's films for Criterion and Second Sight.

Introduction

Thomas Leitch and Leland Poague

Our dedication of this volume to the late Robin Wood honors one of the founding practitioners of Hitchcock studies. In looking backward to a departing generation of Hitchcock scholars that now sadly includes Raymond Durgnat, Eric Rohmer, and Claude Chabrol, it seeks to root the present volume in a rich tradition of Hitchcock commentary that now numbers hundreds of books and essays. Alfred Hitchcock and his films have been the subject of biographies, thematic surveys of his entire career, scholarly monographs on aspects ranging from Hitchcock's Victorianism to his bi-textuality, case studies of individual films and even sequences from particular films, catalogues of Hitchcockian motifs, reference books, quiz books, and books for readers still too young to know what monster lurks in Norman Bates's fruit cellar.

In considering our place in this tradition of Hitchcockiana, we are especially mindful of other collections of essays on the Master of Suspense. If Hitchcock has commanded vastly more scholarly attention than any other filmmaker, he has also been incomparably well served by the anthologies that have done so much to set the course of Hitchcock studies. Albert J. LaValley's *Focus on Hitchcock* (Englewood Cliffs, NJ: Prentice-Hall, 1972), whose editor provided a masterful introduction to a potpourri of interviews, reviews, analyses, and polemics, went a long way toward consolidating Hitchcock's position in film studies. The two editions of Marshall Deutelbaum and Leland Poague's *A Hitchcock Reader* (Ames: Iowa State UP, 1986; Chichester, UK: Wiley-Blackwell, 2009), addressed alike to students in the university-level Hitchcock courses that LaValley's anthology clearly anticipated, proposed the director's work and its reception as embodiments of cinema's leading traditions and developments. Walter Raubicheck and Walter Srebnick's *Hitchcock's Rereleased Films: From* Rope *to* Vertigo (Detroit: Wayne State UP, 1991) made a case for the centrality of five Hitchcock films – *Rope* (1948), *Rear Window* (1954), *The Trouble*

A Companion to Alfred Hitchcock, First Edition. Edited by Thomas Leitch and Leland Poague.

with Harry (1955), *The Man Who Knew Too Much* (1956), and *Vertigo* (1958) – long kept from audiences by contractual negotiations that outlived the director himself. Slavoj Žižek's *Everything You Always Wanted to Know about Lacan (But Were Afraid to Ask Hitchcock)* (London: Verso, 1992) placed the director, who had already played a leading role in Žižek's shotgun wedding of Lacan and pop culture, front and center in debates about cultural signification. Later in the same decade, Jonathan Freedman and Richard Millington's *Hitchcock's America* (New York: Oxford UP, 1999) joined Žižek and company in shifting the grounds of Hitchcock studies from formal and thematic studies that focused on mining each film for meaning to a cultural-studies perspective that took each film, and Hitchcock in general, as symptoms of larger signifying patterns. The two anthologies with which Richard Allen and Sam Ishii-Gonzáles bookended the 1999 Hitchcock centennial conference – *Alfred Hitchcock: Centenary Essays* (London: BFI, 1999) and *Hitchcock: Past and Future* (New York: Routledge, 2004) – sought to reclaim film studies from the flattening sterility of reception studies, which too often saw the films as value-neutral or even pathologically symptomatic, and reestablish them as works of art. The two volumes of essays reprinted from the *Hitchcock Annual* – *Framing Hitchcock: Selected Essays from the Hitchcock Annual*, edited by Sidney Gottlieb and Christopher Brookhouse (Detroit: Wayne State UP, 2002), and *The Hitchcock Annual Anthology: Selected Essays from Volumes 10–15*, edited by Gottlieb and Allen (London: Wallflower, 2009) – offered specific suggestions for the responsible care and feeding of Hitchcock studies in light of the worrisome rise of "Big-Time Hitchcock" (*Framing* 15). And of course the venue in which the essays collected in these two volumes originally appeared, the *Hitchcock Annual*, is itself, like *The MacGuffin*, its sister publication edited by Ken Mogg, a constant source of new essays on Hitchcock.

Given such a long and varied tradition, not only of Hitchcock scholarship but of Hitchcock anthologies, why do we now extend the list with still another volume? Each of these earlier anthologies was organized more or less explicitly around a controversy. Was Hitchcock an artist or an entertainer? Did Hitchcock's American films represent his crowning achievement or a falling-off from a series of faster-paced English films more immediately grounded in wit, brio, and social observation? How did the re-release of five long unavailable films reshape received wisdom about the shape of his career? What role did this most popular of genre filmmakers play in the commodification of meaning and the challenge to meaning-making systems? Could Hitchcock's films more fruitfully be studied from aesthetic perspectives or when taken as symptomatic of the cultural pathologies of postmodern America or of global postmodernism more generally? How exactly was Big-Time Hitchcock to be managed?

Because Hitchcock always seems to be at the center of some controversy swirling around film studies or semiology or cultural studies, he has been incomparably useful in providing an accessible laboratory in which to test ideas about filmmakers, films, filmmaking, and popular culture. Even if there is always a Hitchcock controversy, however, the nature of the controversy is always shifting.

In particular, each Hitchcock anthology has taken previous Hitchcock criticism as an indispensable part of its subject. Every one of these anthologies, even those that rely entirely on previously published material, uses the retrospective force of its survey of Hitchcock scholarship as the basis for an argument about how Hitchcock studies can shape the disciplinary future of film studies or cultural studies or new media studies and so forth.

So part of our purpose here has been to provide a retrospective overview of some of the leading controversies that have shaped Hitchcock studies, establishing and confirming it as a discipline and marking the principal stages in its development. These controversies begin long before Robin Wood's pioneering interventions. They leave their traces in the extended 1950s debate in *Cahiers du cinéma* over Hitchcock's status as a film artist, and in Lindsay Anderson's even earlier dismissal of Hitchcock's American films as "heavy, tedious, glossed, at their best, ingenious, expert, synthetically entertaining" ("Alfred Hitchcock," in *Focus on Hitchcock*, LaValley, 1972, 48–59, at 59). But they are given their definitive articulation by the question with which Wood first called *Hitchcock's Films* to order in 1965: "Why should we take Hitchcock seriously?" (*Hitchcock's Films Revisited*. Rev. ed. New York: Columbia UP, 2002, 55) – a question that was enormously influential because it provided a primary impetus not only for Hitchcock studies but for cinema studies in general as it fought to establish its cultural and academic credentials by asserting that its subject, though originating as popular entertainment, could also have the power of art.

The present collection extends the tradition of anthologies that have sought to characterize Hitchcock studies by providing a retrospective snapshot, a time capsule of the debates that have shaped Hitchcock scholarship. But it differs from earlier collections in several important ways. The most obvious of these is its scope. Because we had the freedom to plan the collection on a generous scale, we sought to include as many approaches to Hitchcock, as many different Hitchcocks, as possible instead of focusing on a single aspect of Hitchcock's work or a single definitive Hitchcock. Moreover, we planned the collection from the top down. Instead of asking potential contributors what they most wanted to write about, we approached them with specific topics in mind in hopes of producing a volume that would be at once comprehensive and integrated. We commissioned virtually every contribution expressly for this volume, and the few exceptions were extensively revised for their appearance here. Although James Vest and Jack Sullivan were obvious choices to write on the French reception of Hitchcock and on the director's use of music, their essays extend rather than simply recapitulating their earlier work.

Our abiding concern was to nurture and extend the kind of productive debate that has been the lifeblood of Hitchcock studies. From its beginnings, the field has been driven by a series of antinomies that have allowed notable critics to weigh in on either side of the question. *Cahiers* contributors debated Hitchcock's status as maker and artist, and Durgnat developed his reading of Hitchcock in direct response to Wood's question, "Why should we take Hitchcock seriously?" Hitchcock studies ever since has developed through a series of theses and antitheses that have led to syntheses capable of generating new antitheses. This collection continues this Hegelian pattern by emphasizing questions capable of generating a range of useful answers. Is Hitchcock inimitable, or is he everywhere imitated? Richard Allen contends that his influence has been extensive and multifarious, but by no means indiscriminate. Is Hitchcock fundamentally a creator of original works or the leading member of a production team? Leland Poague, Tania Modleski, and Susan White develop an impressively wide range of models for discussing Hitchcockian collaboration. Should Hitchcock's films be studied for their own virtues and values, or for what they can tell us about cultural currents, industry practices, and the nature of narrative suspense? Half a dozen different contributors show that his films can be at once admired and pressed into serving larger intellectual or cultural programs. Indeed, even those essays most overtly concerned with Hitchcock's status as auteur director – those by James Vest, Janet Bergstrom, and Harry Oldmeadow – observe how thoroughly his reputation was constructed, by his detractors as well as his partisans, though they focus alike on the crucial role played by critics associated with *Cahiers du cinéma*, especially François Truffaut and Robin Wood.

In soliciting contributions, we have aimed for a balance between established and emerging scholars, notable Hitchcockians and contributors from outside Hitchcock studies who could bring a fresh perspective to familiar material. An earlier policy we set proved still more decisive. Because we had no desire to build our collection out of authorized readings of canonical films, we chose to organize our contributions in terms of topics and approaches instead of soliciting new readings of individual films. This decision had the effect of subordinating each contributor's departures from scholarly consensus – how many of the numberless essays on *Psycho* (1960) cite earlier commentators on the film only to mark the given essay's distance from them? – to potential disagreements among the present contributors, who felt free to range outside the individual preserve of *The 39 Steps* (1935) or *Rear Window* to which assignments to write on individual films might have safely confined them.

In lieu of essays devoted to individual films that offer interpretations explaining what the films mean, we sought contextual essays on the circumstances under which Hitchcock's films have been produced and received, especially essays on topics most likely to lend themselves to productive debate. Ken Mogg and Charles Barr investigate the influence of earlier writers and filmmakers on a director notorious for the highly selective list of literary and cinematic influences he acknowledged. Thomas Hemmeter and Angelo Restivo consider Hitchcock's credentials as an exemplary modernist and postmodernist in a pair of essays whose relation to each other is far more complex than simple opposition.

Although we gave each contributor a specific topic, the inevitably serendipitous development of essays as they moved from topics through premises and examples to conclusions led to a wealth of unexpected results. We anticipated a good deal of emphasis on *Vertigo*, but not nearly so much on *Waltzes from Vienna* (1933) or *Under Capricorn* (1949). Imagine our surprise, then, when Richard Ness announced his intention to focus on both of these neglected films in his essay on Hitchcockian melodrama. We were equally surprised by the number of contributors who wrote at length about *Marnie* (1964). In view of the fascinating differences that emerge from the considerations of *Marnie* in the essays by Tania Modleski, Brigitte Peucker, William Rothman, and Florence Jacobowitz, however, we were happy to be surprised, and we trust that readers will share our pleasure.

Enterprising readers might well imagine a collection using alternative topics for section headings or individual essays. To an extent, so did we, in that our table of contents shifted considerably as essays began to arrive and we saw how different authors treated their assigned topics, sometimes in ways we could not have anticipated. Our one obligatory section, the longest of our nine sections and the central one in the structure of the volume, surveys the historical development of Hitchcock's career. But this section is more notable than any other for its variety of approaches. Sidney Gottlieb contends that Hitchcock's silent films establish themselves as Hitchcockian years before he became identified with the thriller. Tom Ryall traces the relation between Hitchcock's films for Gaumont British and other contemporaneous English films. Ina Rae Hark, adopting a more thematic approach to Hitchcock's first American films, offers some highly original conclusions about Hitchcock and American masculine heroism. David Sterritt considers the ways in which Hitchcock's brief period as an independent producer laid the groundwork for his subsequent films. Joe McElhaney's emphasis on Hitchcock's distinctive mise-en-scène provides new insight into his years at Paramount. And William Rothman, emphasizing the disappointments of Hitchcock's last years at Universal, balances a sense of Hitchcock's compromises and missteps with his achievements in films from *The Birds* (1963) through *Family Plot* (1976). Since Gottlieb begins with an account of *The Blackguard* (Graham Cutts, 1925), on which Hitchcock worked as assistant director, art director, and screenwriter before he directed *The Pleasure Garden* (1925), and Rothman provides an extended consideration of *The Short Night*, Hitchcock's unproduced last project, this section on Hitchcock's development is as comprehensive as it is varied.

Both inside and outside this section on Hitchcock's development, there are many readings of individual films. McElhaney analyzes the ways *Psycho* marks a decisive turn in Hitchcock's mise-en-scène. Paula Marantz Cohen uses *Shadow of a Doubt* (1943) to anchor a notion of "conceptual suspense" that sheds new light on Hitchcock and narrative suspense generally. George Toles's meditation on the nature of moral experience in Hitchcock follows the affective itinerary of the cigarette lighter in *Strangers on a Train* (1951). In every case, the analysis of individual films illustrates a larger argument about Hitchcock, cinema, or storytelling.

Although we have not encouraged contributors to argue with each other directly, we must plead guilty as accessories before the fact in arranging categories and juxtapositions that would foster implicit controversy. Many of these essays, for example, dramatize a fundamental schism in Hitchcock studies between retrospective views that seek to consolidate Hitchcock's position as an auteur, a brand name, an ascription of value, an historical function, or an otherwise privileged signifier, and prospective views that seek to expose ruptures in Hitchcock commentary in order to address a perceived absence. Lesley Brill looks backward at the enduring myths of Hitchcock romance; Thomas Leitch looks forward to ask whether Hitchcock's biography has been exhausted and how it might be replenished. What is more surprising is how many of these essays embody both impulses in different combinations. Brigitte Peucker and Murray Pomerance both argue for a fundamental reassessment of Hitchcock's visuals that would break sharply with earlier analyses. Yet their procedures – Peucker's motivic examination of Hitchcock's aestheticized public spaces versus Pomerance's cornucopia of isolated visual moments that break free of their films' narrative discipline – could not be more different from one another, even as they root themselves in earlier studies by Alenka Zupančič and Michel Mourlet respectively. No debate in contemporary cinema studies would seem more likely to divide conservatives from progressives than the question of whether films posed ethical dilemmas devised by individual filmmakers or were everywhere informed by deeper ideological commitments outside the control of any individual. Even so, both Toby Miller and Noel King's take on the ideology of Hitchcock's English spy films and Alexander Doty's interrogation of the term "queer Hitchcock" illustrate a far more nuanced conception of ideology than the earlier commentary they consider. And if Richard Gilmore's Socratic Hitchcock is a traditional ethicist in postmodern garb, Todd McGowan presents a director every bit as deeply invested in the ethical dimensions of experience who is still absolutely different from every other filmmaker.

Our effort to locate this anthology in the sequence of similar Hitchcock compendiums is, among other things, an acknowledgement of indebtedness to the larger critical tradition of Hitchcock scholarship. But many more specific debts require acknowledgment. Most of all, we are indebted to our contributors. This was a labor of love all around, in the sense that the main reward for participating in the project was the participation, the chance to contribute to an unprecedentedly compendious reassessment of Hitchcock's crucial role in film culture and modern culture. We were deeply gratified at the generous responses we received to our initial queries and for the wonderful essays we finally received. Not only were contributors generous with their time and their words, they had reason to be generous with their patience as well, given the editorial necessity we encountered to urge economy. To each and all, we offer heartfelt thanks.

Warm thanks are also due our Wiley-Blackwell editor Jayne Fargnoli, who suggested the project in the first place. Jayne was also the lead editor on the second edition of Marshall Deutelbaum and Leland Poague's *A Hitchcock Reader*, and it was midway through that effort that she posed the question to Marshall and Lee regarding their interest in joining her in yet another editorial project. Having recently retired, Marshall declined the opportunity while offering Lee steadfast encouragement. (Thanks, Marshall!) Lee Poague recruited Thomas Leitch to share editorial duties, and we soon confirmed our suspicion that there was work aplenty to go around. Though Jayne Fargnoli's encouragement and sage counsel were exceptionally helpful, we are also eager to acknowledge and applaud the professionalism of Wiley-Blackwell editorial assistants Margot Morse and Matthew Baskin and production manager Lisa Eaton, and Revathy Kaliyamoorthy of SPi. Copyeditor Gillian Andrews did much to improve the volume, and we gladly express our gratitude for her conscientious editorial stewardship.

Portions of James Vest's essay "French Hitchcock, 1945–1955" are based upon materials published in Vest's earlier scholarship on Hitchcock and France, including his essay "The Emergence of an Auteur: Hitchcock and French Film Criticism, 1950–1954" in *Hitchcock Annual* (2001–02): 108–24 and his chapter "To Catch a Liar: Bazin, Chabrol, and Truffaut Encounter Hitchcock," which appeared in *Hitchcock: Past and Future*, edited by Richard Allen and Sam Ishii-Gonzáles (London: Routledge, 2004, 109–18), both used and modified here with permission of the copyright holder and publishers. Portions are also derived from *Hitchcock and France: The Forging of an Auteur*, by James M. Vest. Copyright © 2003 by James M. Vest. Reproduced with permission of Greenwood Publishing Group, Inc., Westport, CT.

Toby Miller and Noel King's essay "Accidental Heroes and Gifted Amateurs: Hitchcock and Ideology" borrows from Toby Miller's "39 Steps to 'The Borders of the Possible': Alfred Hitchcock, Amateur Observer and the New Cultural History," which appeared in *Alfred Hitchcock: Centenary Essays*, edited by Richard Allen and S. Ishii-Gonzáles (London: BFI, 1999): 316–31. The passages are reproduced here with the kind permission of Palgrave Macmillan. These involve Non-exclusive Print and Electronic rights in the English language for distribution in the following territory: World for one edition.

A shorter version of George Toles's essay "Occasions of Sin: The Forgotten Cigarette Lighter and Other Moral Accidents in Hitchcock" appeared in *Raritan* 28.4 (2009). The material in this shorter version was published by arrangement with Wiley-Blackwell.

Between its initial publication as *Hitchcock's Films* (London: A. Zwemmer; New York: A.S. Barnes, 1965) and its most recent iteration as *Hitchcock's Films Revisited*, revised edition, no book has proven more essential to Hitchcock studies than Robin Wood's. We are especially grateful to Columbia University Press for allowing us to quote extensively from *Hitchcock's Films Revisited*, revised edition, by Robin Wood. Copyright © 2002, 1989 Columbia University Press. Reprinted with permission of the publisher.

Lee Poague is grateful to Iowa State University's Center for Excellence in the Arts and Humanities for supporting both his research on Hitchcock's writers and his editorial efforts, as did the ISU Department of English, especially former chair Charlie Kostelnick and former assistant chair Debra Marquart. For research assistance, he is indebted to the Interlibrary Loan staff at the Parks Library, to Dan Coffey of the Parks Library faculty, and to Amy Poague, who ran down obscure periodical sources in the library of the University of Iowa. His admiration of Thomas Leitch as a discerning and eloquent Hitchcock scholar occasioned the

hope that Tom would agree to collaborate, and he is grateful that their collaboration proved so happily productive. Susan Poague has been patient beyond measure
as the process of writing and editing has gone forward, but sympathetic and loving
all the same, after all these years and Hitchcock books! Some debts defy repayment.

Thomas Leitch offers special thanks to Lee Poague for his example, wisdom,
and patience, to Sidney Gottlieb and Ken Mogg for help above and beyond the
duty of the most exemplary Hitchcockians, and to Lisa Elliott for her understanding, support, and love.

A word about style. Though we have done our best to follow the style mandates
of the most recent *MLA Handbook* – still another way of trying the patience of our
contributors – we have made no attempt to iron out all stylistic inconsistencies by
making our contributors sound more like us. In addition, we have settled on several
idiosyncratic or volume-specific usages. In honor of Robin Wood, for example, we
spell *CineAction* with two capitals, though MLA style is clear about disregarding such
accidentals. We have followed our contributors' practice of referring to foreign language films by the titles most often used in the English-speaking film community,
though we have on occasion given the original title followed by an English translation. Where foreign language articles are cited, we have followed a similar practice,
especially in James Vest's chapter. Except for the first film Hitchcock directed,
The Pleasure Garden, which some authorities date to 1925, the year it was shot, and
others to 1927, the year it was finally released, we have made every attempt to be
consistent in providing the release date for each film (and the name of its director, if
the director is not Hitchcock) and the name of the performer when a given film or
character is first mentioned in a given essay.

In reviewing the contents of this volume, we are keenly aware of its omissions.
There is nothing on Hitchcock's collaboration with cinematographers, costume
designers, or other visual artists; nothing on *Bon Voyage* (1944) or *Aventure Malgache*
(1944); very little on Hitchcock's work for television (though see Ness's provocative
remarks on "Incident at a Corner" [1960]); and hardly anything on the non-musical
elements of his soundtracks. The neglect of Hitchcockian comedy that Gottlieb
lamented in 1995 (*Hitchcock on Hitchcock: Selected Writing and Interviews*, Berkeley:
U of California P, xxiii) continues here. And of course the same antinomies that
have made films like *North by Northwest* (1959) and *Psycho* so central to the
Hitchcock canon continue to marginalize films as different as *Rich and Strange*
(1931), *Jamaica Inn* (1939), and *The Trouble with Harry*. Given our decision to avoid
the close-reading format, we are proud of the comprehensive (dare we say catholic)
treatment of Hitchcock's work. We are well aware that this is not the ultimate
Hitchcock anthology. But we hope the very omissions that make it less than definitive will help drive the continuing development of Hitchcock studies by provoking its readers to productive response. Although we are proud to salute the
achievements of Hitchcock scholars past and present, we are convinced that the
most exciting work on Hitchcock has yet to appear, and we hope that this collection will play a part in bringing it to birth.

PART I

Background

1

Hitchcock's Lives

Thomas Leitch

The appearance of Donald Spoto's *Spellbound by Beauty* (2008) marks a turning point in Hitchcock studies, though hardly for the reasons the author indicates. The dust-jacket description of the book as "the final volume in master biographer Donald Spoto's Hitchcock trilogy" will not be taken seriously by anyone who has read *The Art of Alfred Hitchcock*, the formal and thematic study of Hitchcock's films distinguished from other film-by-film surveys largely by Spoto's access to the production of *Family Plot* (1976), or *The Dark Side of Genius* (1983), the full-dress biography that cast Hitchcock as a tormented loner who delighted in sadistically teasing and sometimes torturing audiences and colleagues alike. Despite publisher claims of a volume "[r]ich with fresh revelations based on previously undisclosed" testimony or with materials offering "important insights into the life of a brilliant, powerful, eccentric and tortured artist," Spoto's new book, accurately subtitled *Alfred Hitchcock and His Leading Ladies*, does not complete a trilogy because it is neither a sequel nor a complement to his earlier volumes. It is something altogether more interesting.

Spoto is admirably direct in explaining the reasons he returned to Hitchcock after *The Dark Side of Genius* launched his career as a celebrity biographer whose subjects have included Marilyn Monroe, Princess Diana, Joan of Arc, and Jesus of Nazareth. Several of the collaborators he interviewed in preparation for the earlier volume asked him "to omit certain comments either for some years or until after their own deaths" (xxi). So much of Hitchcock's conduct toward his actresses "can only be called sexual harassment" that "his biography remains a cautionary tale of what can go wrong in any life" (xxi). Spoto felt particularly obliged to respond to legions of Hitchcock fans "who will not hear a syllable spoken against" him (xx). For Spoto, however, "the craft of biography requires that the shadow side of subjects be set forth and comprehended" (xx). Armed with previously withheld

A Companion to Alfred Hitchcock, First Edition. Edited by Thomas Leitch and Leland Poague.
© 2011 Thomas Leitch and Leland Poague. Published 2011 by Blackwell Publishing Ltd.

confidences and a more comprehensive sense of Hitchcock's life, Spoto intends by focusing on the most problematic aspect of the director's professional life – his relationships with the actresses "for whom he had a strange amalgam of adoration and contempt" (xviii) – to rescue Hitchcock in all his dark complexity from a horde of uncritical admirers by offering "new insights into Hitchcock the filmmaker – in particular, how he understood the element of collaboration" (xxiii).

But these claims ring just as hollow as the publisher's claim that *Spellbound by Beauty* completes a trilogy. The new material at Spoto's disposal is of five kinds: new interviews he conducted with Alida Valli, Gregory Peck, Ann Todd, Diane Baker, and especially Tippi Hedren; previously withheld comments from interviews with a somewhat wider array of sources; the interviews with and writings by Hitchcock that Sidney Gottlieb collected in *Hitchcock on Hitchcock* and *Alfred Hitchcock: Interviews*; critical studies of Hitchcock's life, films, and working habits by Leonard J. Leff, Bill Krohn, and Ken Mogg published since *The Dark Side of Genius*; and intervening biographies of Hitchcock by Patrick McGilligan and Charlotte Chandler, as well as Patricia Hitchcock O'Connell's biography of her mother, Alma Reville, Hitchcock's wife.

All but the first two of these, of course, have been equally at the disposal of other commentators for years, but Spoto treats them as if they were his own private preserve. It is sadly ironic to see an author who so regularly castigates Hitchcock for his well-known inability to credit any of his collaborators for the success of his films – he shrewdly suggests that Hitchcock resented his screenwriters because "he wanted to write the script entirely on his own but could not" (50) – display an equal lack of generosity toward his own sources. Chandler is never identified by name outside Spoto's notes, for example, while John Russell Taylor is referred to by name only thrice in Spoto's text. Though Spoto cites McGilligan a dozen times in his notes, the only time he mentions McGilligan by name in his text is in his disapproving reference to McGilligan's account of a sexual liaison between Alma Reville and screenwriter Whitfield Cook, the single most salacious revelation in McGilligan's 864-page biography.

Just as he takes pains to correct the title of the 1936 film *Secret Agent* (57) – though this error has not appeared in Hitchcock commentary for years – Spoto treats Leonard J. Leff's long-ago-published revelations (*Hitchcock and Selznick*, 1987) about Hitchcock's bullying treatment of Joan Fontaine on and off the set of *Rebecca* (1940) and Bill Krohn's more recent account (*Hitchcock at Work*, 2000) of Hitchcock's often serendipitous collaborative working methods as if they were breaking news. Though biographers commonly depend on the work of earlier biographers and interpreters and scholars, it is surprising to see Spoto, who certainly was under no obligation to return to the subject of Hitchcock after 26 years, offer so little new material of his own. Apart from repeated denunciations of Hitchcock's misogynist cruelty and toilet humor, the most substantial additions Spoto makes here to the portrait of the director he presented in *The Dark Side of Genius* are a series of supplementary portraits, interpolated biographical sketches of leading ladies from

Virginia Valli to Madeleine Carroll to Ingrid Bergman to Tippi Hedren. In order to flesh out the Sardou motto – "Torture the women!" (xix) – that Hitchcock applied to plot construction and Spoto to Hitchcock's life in *The Dark Side of Genius*, he adds a catalog of variously vulnerable young actresses Hitchcock either adoringly sought to dominate (Ingrid Bergman, Grace Kelly, Vera Miles) or tormented (June Howard-Tripp, Lilian Hall-Davis, Jessie Matthews, Madeleine Carroll, Joan Fontaine, Kim Novak) or both (Tippi Hedren), while passing hastily over his collaborations with actresses who fell into neither category (Isabel Jeans, Betty Balfour, Anny Ondra, Norah Baring, Joan Barry, Edna Best, Sylvia Sidney, Nova Pilbeam, Margaret Lockwood, Maureen O'Hara, Laraine Day, Carole Lombard, Priscilla Lane, Teresa Wright, Tallulah Bankhead, Marlene Dietrich, Ruth Roman, Shirley MacLaine, Eva Marie Saint, Janet Leigh, Julie Andrews, and Barbara Harris, the last of whom Spoto curiously fails to mention even in passing). The obvious conclusion, that Hitchcock tormented all his actresses except for the ones he didn't, adds nothing compelling or new to the case Spoto documented so persuasively in *The Dark Side of Genius*.

In the years since Spoto's influential biography was first published, many commentators, as he accurately notes, have taken exception to its portrait of Hitchcock as dominated by dark fantasies he felt compelled to play out onscreen. Except at book signings, however, it is hard to imagine where Spoto has run into fans quite as obtuse about either Hitchcock or sexual harassment as his description of "the consensus" would indicate. In *The Dark Side of Genius*, Spoto had revealingly noted the labored attempts of "Hitchcock's admirers (this author among the most defensive of them)" to justify the "sloppy technique" of Hitchcock's 1964 film, *Marnie* (476). In *Spellbound by Beauty*, his principal antagonist still seems to be the Spoto who wrote *The Art of Alfred Hitchcock*. On the whole, however, he redirects his unhappiness with uncritical defenses of Hitchcock onto other targets, like Patricia Hitchcock O'Connell's reticence about her childhood in England, her relation to her father, and her mother's contribution to Hitchcock's films. Of O'Connell's early days, he concludes that "her life sounded thumpingly dull – nothing stands out at all" (75). He disputes her recollection of her parents as "ordinary people. I know a lot of people insist that my father must have had a dark imagination. Well, he did not. He was a brilliant filmmaker and he knew how to tell a story. That's all" (76).

Most characteristic of all is Spoto's response to O'Connell's claims that "her father 'made all the important decisions with Alma as his closest collaborator' and that 'Alma's participation was constant'" (89). These claims would seem to support Spoto's view of Hitchcock, based on Bill Krohn's research, as "a senior supervising collaborator" rather than "the sole creative force behind his pictures" (84). But Spoto remains curiously unconvinced: "The idea may provide a tender revisionist history in praise of a supposedly underrated wife, but it does not stand up to scrutiny, and Alma herself would swiftly have deflected such hyperbolic praise (indeed, she did when it was implied over the years)" (89–90). More curious yet is the fact that the contentious issue of Alma's collaboration with her husband surfaces in

Spoto's discussion of *Rebecca*, where Alma's participation in the scripting process is frequently attested to, despite the lack of a formal screen credit. And the evidence Spoto does adduce to discount Patricia Hitchcock's suggestion that Hitchcock depended on his wife's collaboration seems just as ephemeral as Patricia Hitchcock O'Connell's familial perspective.

In fact, so few verifiable details are available concerning the extent of Reville's influence on Hitchcock's films that commentators are unlikely to reach a consensus on the subject anytime soon. Attempting to rise above this debate rather than entering into it, Spoto mostly reiterates the position he had taken in *The Dark Side of Genius*. So it is throughout *Spellbound by Beauty*. Although Spoto's avowed purpose in returning to Hitchcock is to set the record straight, he offers no compelling new evidence that would refute the biographers, critics, or scholars who have the temerity to present Hitchcocks different from his own. In the end, his decision to revisit Hitchcock produces nothing more than another visit, an invitation to reconsider Hitchcock directed toward a politically insensitive, art-for-art's-sake audience that in all likelihood no longer exists.

Even so, *Spellbound by Beauty* is much more interesting than a more successful book would have been because its very failure suggests a remarkable possibility: the depletion of Hitchcock's biography. Just because Spoto cannot find anything new to say about Hitchcock's life, of course, is no reason to conclude that there is nothing new to be said. But *Spellbound by Beauty* seems to mark a point of exhaustion in the course of Hitchcock biography. When it appeared in 1978, Taylor's authorized biography, *Hitch: The Life and Times of Alfred Hitchcock*, had presented an official, public life that focused on the director's career, larded with the sorts of anecdotes Hitchcock had been sharing with interviewers for years. Taylor's Hitchcock was an inveterate practical joker, but his pranks – inventive, good-humored, and often enough repaid in kind by "like-minded friends" (121) who knew that "if Hitch felt he had gone a little too far ... he always made generous amends" (121–22) – simply "kept his units cheery and ready for anything" (122) and incidentally provided leavening for a blow-by-blow chronicle of his public life, since Taylor provided little insight into Hitchcock's private life except the tacit implication that it was not eventful enough to be worth examining. Taylor's Hitchcock was neurotically fearful and obsessive in his professional habits, but urbanely, even comically so.

Five years later, Spoto, taking his cue from interviews with Hitchcock's collaborators rather than restricting his point of view to the director himself, portrayed a dramatically different Hitchcock in *The Dark Side of Genius: The Life of Alfred Hitchcock*. This filmmaker was still a practical joker, but in Spoto's telling the jokes did not provide relief from the tedious routine of filmmaking. Beginning with a prophetic childhood prank in which he and "an accomplice" dragged their younger schoolmate Robert Goold to the basement boiler room at St. Ignatius College, pinned "a string of firecrackers ... to his underwear and ignited" them (32), Spoto charts the way Hitchcock's pranks became "carefully controlled antisocial gestures"

(112) that revealed "a cruder and crueler streak" (111) even as they "exterioriz[ed] his own deepest fears" (112) in the same way Hitchcock's films did. Spoto's Hitchcock, an intensely private person, was sexually repressed, voyeuristic, possessive, defensive, often sadistic, ungenerous and mean-spirited to collaborators, and addicted to playing Svengali to a series of ingénues he sought to mold into Hitchcock blondes, especially Joan Fontaine, Grace Kelly, Vera Miles, and Tippi Hedren. Like Edmund Wilson, whose 1941 study *The Wound and the Bow* had posited a generation earlier "the conception of superior strength as inseparable from disability" (468), Spoto presented a Hitchcock who could shape the nightmares of so many filmgoers because of his success in putting his own private torment onscreen. The result was to recast Taylor as remaining on the surface that Spoto dared to go beneath. The genial raconteur whom Taylor had taken to be the author of Hitchcock's films became in Spoto a public mask that concealed dark dreams of lust and power, dreams that became more explicitly rendered onscreen with the eclipse of the 1930 Production Code and the director's advancing age, so that the climactic attack on Melanie Daniels in *The Birds* (1963) and the murder sequences in *Psycho* (1960), *Frenzy* (1972), and the unproduced *The Short Night* became "the last expression of the darkest desire that had occupied Hitchcock's imagination for decades" (544).

If Spoto's controversial biography – was it true? and if it was true, should it be published? – posed an antithesis to Taylor's Hitchcock, Patrick McGilligan's *Alfred Hitchcock: A Life in Darkness and Light* (2003) might have been expected to provide a synthesis. And in some ways, that is exactly what it did provide. McGilligan's Hitchcock had all the dark complexity of Spoto's. En route to terrifying audiences around the world, he deceived scriptwriters, humiliated technicians, and tyrannized actresses. He never outgrew an adolescent sense of humor, and professional success only accentuated his mania for complete control over his films. But the public behavior Spoto dismissed as a mask McGilligan took to be equally authentic, representative of the radically divided nature indicated by his subtitle. McGilligan's Hitchcock was a devoted son, a faithful if undersexed husband, a tender and affectionate father, and a colleague as capable of unexpected generosity as of cruelty. If Spoto's Hitchcock struggled his whole life to repress a sociopathic side that sprang to life in a series of films that chart the return of the repressed, McGilligan's Hitchcock, whose weight fluctuated wildly throughout his adult life, struggled as well to balance the conflicting sides of his nature.

According to Hegelian dialectics, McGilligan's attempted synthesis of Taylor and Spoto should have led to a new antithesis. But neither of the biographies produced more recently by a pair of professional journalists revealed anything like a new Hitchcock. Despite lengthy and sometimes revealing quotations from many interviews with Hitchcock's surviving colleagues, Charlotte Chandler's aptly titled *It's Only a Movie: Alfred Hitchcock: A Personal Biography* (2005), which reads like an extended magazine profile, retreats into Taylor territory. Chandler's gossipy tone, virtually indistinguishable from that of her interviewees, normalizes the anecdotes and revelations about Hitchcock's working habits but works against integration. She offers no new insight into Hitchcock's private life, no rationale of his career, and no explanation of how the witty, mischievous Hitchcock his colleagues describe, voluble yet withdrawn, came to make the films that made his name. The result is that although almost everyone Chandler quotes attempts to encapsulate Hitchcock's life or work – from Ronald Neame's "Hitchcock wasn't ever ruffled by anything" (73) to Melanie Griffith's "He was a motherfucker. And you can quote me" (272) – she never does. Nor does Quentin Falk in *Mr. Hitchcock* (2007), which begins with a guileless warning not to "expect … anything startlingly new in terms of original research" (2). Like Chandler's montage of interviews, Falk's brisk survey of Hitchcock's career, framed by new interviews with Hitchcock's collaborators on *Frenzy*, uses that career as a familiar story that can be retold with charm and profit.

Both Chandler and Falk, like Spoto in *Spellbound by Beauty*, invite their readers to revisit Hitchcock rather than offering any major new revelations about him. In doing so, they present Hitchcock's life as a known quantity that can still give pleasure even after repeated doses if it is repackaged or approached from a slightly different angle or with new details filled in. In retrospect, they suggest that McGilligan's Hitchcock was not so much a synthesis as a compromise, his biographer less interested in presenting a new Hitchcock than in judiciously correcting the record. McGilligan gets Robert Goold, who "entered St. Ignatius a full term after Hitchcock departed," to admit that "he 'was wrong in ascribing the [firecracker prank] to him [Hitchcock]'" (20). He corrects Peter Bogdanovich's report that "Hitchcock 'taught' photography" to Jack Cox on the 1927 film *The Ring* (95). He disputes "the myth that Hitchcock ate up inordinate time" in filming *Rebecca*, whose "most taxing delays weren't the director's fault" (252). He notes that Czenzi Ormonde, who with Barbara Keon wrote the final version of the screenplay for *Strangers on a Train* (1951), "wasn't aware of the slightest homoerotic undercurrent between Bruno and Guy; Hitchcock certainly didn't mention it, and in her opinion it didn't exist in the script or the film" (449). He quotes Ron Miller, a Pulitzer-winning reporter who interviewed Hitchcock as a student journalist just before the release of *Psycho*: "Hitchcock was 'far from boastful and, in fact, suggested that many of the innovations he was credited with on screen were not original with him'" (638). He challenges Spoto's assertion that after she refused his demand for sex, "he refused to address Tippi Hedren personally. He never even uttered her name, referring only to 'that girl'" (*Dark* 476). Instead, McGilligan suggests, "the record is far from clear. Hitchcock had always referred to Hedren, outside her own presence, as 'the Girl' (it was how many silent-film directors referred to the leading lady's role, and it was the established nickname of the character Hedren had played in *The Birds*)." In addition, "his logbook indicates that he met with Hedren several times over the next year, trying to bridge the gulf between them" (648–49).

McGilligan's differences with Spoto have done nothing to discourage the proliferation of Hitchcock biographies, but they have not yet had the power to generate new Hitchcocks. If Taylor presents a smiling public Hitchcock, Spoto a tormented and tormenting private Hitchcock, and McGilligan a Hitchcock somewhere in the middle, then all possible positions concerning the director's life would seem to have been taken. Apart from filling in the details, there is nothing new to say.

This curious exhaustion would seem less curious if commentators on Taylor, Spoto, and McGilligan did not focus so intently on their differences, which are indeed striking, that they overlooked their similarities, which are much more fundamental. The essential premise shared by all biographers of Hitchcock is that Hitchcock's life *matters*, that it is interesting and important enough to attract at least a significant proportion of the vast audience for his films, and that knowing the facts of his life allows readers to watch his films in new and better informed ways. The director's life is assumed to serve a vital function for a significant reading public: It is valuable because it helps them do things (in this case, watch Hitchcock's films) better.

Taylor, the one biographer to make a point of disclaiming this intention, defines it better than any of the others when he observes that "for one so enormously publicized and so aware of the value and uses of publicity he has managed to remain [so] astonishingly private … [that] in an important sense the dictum of another film-maker who has known him well for forty years is true: 'There is no real Alfred Hitchcock outside his movies.'" Because "Hitchcock is not so much in his films: he *is* his films," Taylor concludes, whatever autobiographical motifs have found their way into his work "have been precipitated into art which needs no external explanation. … So ultimately it does not matter what sort of man Hitchcock is" (17–19). Although he is convinced that Hitchcock's life is too private, too unknowable, to illuminate his films, Taylor proposes a more modest goal for his own exploration: "[E]ven if such questions make no noticeable difference to our appreciation of the films, there is still human curiosity that impels us to unravel the puzzle. And puzzle Hitchcock undoubtedly remains" (19–20). So instead of treating Hitchcock's life as a source of privileged information about his work, Taylor treats it as a work itself, a puzzle to be unraveled.

The truism that artists' lives inform their work and its corollary that their lives raise questions that can best be answered either by recourse to their work or by treating the life as if it were a work of art have been at the heart of biographies of writers and artists since Samuel Johnson's *Lives of the Most Eminent English Poets* (1779–81). As the creator's art reflects his or her life, so a study of the life can inform a study of the art. But three distinctive features of Hitchcock's life and work complicate this apparently self-evident model in ways Hitchcock's biographers, who all take it for granted, have not considered.

The first of these complications is that Hitchcock's life was not especially eventful. He was born into the family of an East End greengrocer and educated by Jesuits. He attended the Slade Art School, worked as a clerk at the W.T. Henley Telegraph Company, designed advertising copy, and wrote stories. When Paramount opened British operations under the name Famous Players–Lasky, he applied for a job with the studio, where his industry and mastery of several differ-ent technical aspects of filmmaking – scriptwriting, set design, intertitle design – advanced him to the rank of assistant director and then, under the auspices of Michael Balcon, director. The success of his third film, *The Lodger* (1926), was fol-lowed shortly by his marriage to Alma Reville, a continuity supervisor and editor, and the birth of their daughter in 1928. The rest of Hitchcock's story is largely a record of artistic achievement – *The Man Who Knew Too Much* (1934), *The 39 Steps* (1935), *The Lady Vanishes* (1938), *Rebecca, Shadow of a Doubt* (1943), *Notorious* (1946), *Strangers on a Train, Rear Window* (1954), *Vertigo* (1958), *North by Northwest* (1959), *Psycho, The Birds, Frenzy* – and expanding commercial success (the launch of *Alfred Hitchcock Presents* in 1955 and *Alfred Hitchcock's Mystery Magazine* in 1956, Hitchcock's decision to finance *Psycho* himself and to trade his rights in the film and his televi-sion ventures for a substantial block of shares in Universal Pictures), punctuated by the occasional commercial failure – *Waltzes from Vienna* (1933), *Lifeboat* (1944), *The Paradine Case* (1947), *Under Capricorn* (1949), *Topaz* (1969) – and the even more occasional personal milestone.

Even these milestones – his family's immigration to America in 1939, his pur-chase of a home on Bellagio Drive in Bel Air, his daughter's appearance, among her roles as an actress, in three films that he directed and ten segments of *Alfred Hitchcock Presents* that he did not, his reception toward the end of his life of numer-ous awards that evidently did not console him for his failure to win an Academy Award for Best Director despite five nominations – all turn out to be professional. Already during his lifetime Hitchcock was well-known for the extreme reserve of his private life, which posed such a contrast to his prodigious and well-advertised fondness for food and drink. On the set he was noted for his obsessive advance preparation – although Bill Krohn's *Hitchcock at Work* has gone far to dispel the belief that Hitchcock was "a control freak who pre-planned every shot" (9) – for the monosyllabic composure, very much at odds with his behavior with interview-ers, that made him unlikely to get into arguments with performers, and for his obligatory dark blue suits and neckties. He socialized exclusively with professional colleagues and had no close friends outside his family. He went home every night to the same wife, whose sixty-year relationship with him seems to have been less amatory than professional. As Taylor put it: "He did not go to parties, he did not have affairs with glamour stars, he did not really do anything but make pictures" (18). Or, as Spoto might add, Hitchcock's life apart from his work sounds thumpingly dull – nothing stands out at all.

In short, Hitchcock seems an unusually unpromising subject for biographers because his public life was so routine and his private life so private. An enterprising biographer might accept the opacity and apparent narrowness of Hitchcock's pri-vate life as a tonic challenge. Indeed, that is exactly what Spoto does in *The Dark Side of Genius*. But it is difficult, as Taylor acknowledges, to maintain the enabling assumption of all biographies of artists, that there are intimate and revealing con-nections between the artist's life and work, in the face of a public life that is so resolutely inexpressive and a private life that is so jealously guarded and perhaps so boring. Unlike so many other directors – Robert Siodmak, Nicholas Ray, Roman Polanski – whose more apparently eventful lives have failed to attract more biographical interest, Hitchcock's extreme personal reticence makes him something of a black box for biographers, who have fallen back to a great extent on either recycling and expanding the anecdotes with which the director had long regaled interviewers, especially in the case of Taylor, Chandler, and Falk, or plumbing the presumed depths beneath those anecdotes, as Spoto and McGilligan do.

A second complication for biographers pursuing a life-and-work approach to Hitchcock is the shape of filmmakers' careers as opposed to those of writers and artists. "Write what you know," aspiring novelists are repeatedly enjoined, and that is how authors from Jane Austen to F. Scott Fitzgerald have begun their careers, leaving a plainly marked trail of autobiographical concerns strewn throughout their early work for biographers to follow. But novice filmmakers who are assigned to projects willy-nilly rarely have the luxury of filming what they know. In this regard Hitchcock's early work, very typical of fledgling directors, is hard to rationalize under a life-and-work approach. Only four of his first sixteen films – *The Lodger, Blackmail* (1929), *Murder!* (1930), and *Number Seventeen* (1932) – could be called thrillers. The others include love stories (*The Pleasure Garden* [1925], *The Farmer's Wife* [1928], *The Manxman* [1929]), drawing-room dramas (*Easy Virtue* [1927] and *The Skin Game* [1931]), odysseys of variously beset adventurers of both sexes (*The Mountain Eagle* [1926], *Downhill* [1927], *Champagne* [1928], and *Rich and Strange* [1931]), a tale of the Irish troubles (*Juno and the Paycock* [1930]), the "musical without music" (Truffaut 85) *Waltzes from Vienna*, and *The Ring*, a boxing film that marked the only time in Hitchcock's career when he took screen credit for writing a script. Only with *The Man Who Knew Too Much* and *The 39 Steps*, it seems, did Hitchcock find a congenial métier, the serio-comic thriller, which he gradually developed and deepened, with occasional diversions like *Mr. and Mrs. Smith* (1941), for the rest of his career.

Biographers and analysts alike have pronounced the thriller not only the genre that brought Hitchcock his greatest commercial success but also the one that best expressed his abiding psychological preoccupations. The assumption of an autobiographical congruence between Hitchcock's life and the genre toward which he eventually gravitated has left them free to neglect his early non-thrillers except to the extent that they could be mined for supporting evidence of those concerns (the leavening of melodrama with farce in *The Farmer's Wife*, the stifling effects of family ties in *Downhill* and *The Skin Game*, the guilty pleasures of the male gaze in *The Pleasure Garden, Easy Virtue*, and *Champagne*). Commentators have retraced the steps Kenneth Burke once discerned in critics of T.S. Eliot:

In his early "Prufrock" days, when Mr. Eliot insisted that even quite personal lyrics were to be viewed not as in any sense self-portraits but as dramatic postures adopted professionally by the poet, the critics in the quarterlies generally abided by these rules. But later, when he began writing such poems of religious devotion as the *Quartets*, the rules somehow became altered; and the attitudes in these later poems were treated ... as a sincere personal interchange between Mr. Eliot and his God.

(30)

The assumption of a close autobiographical connection between Hitchcock's private obsessions and his chosen genre has led to a third complication. Because no director has been more closely identified with a given genre, the aptly named Hitchcock thriller, commentators mining Hitchcock's films for revelations about his life and vice versa have felt free to treat all his films, or at any rate all the thrillers they consider true Hitchcock films, as different versions of a single text. It is as if Hitchcock's greatest work were not *Rear Window* or *Vertigo* or *Psycho* but the grand narrative of his career. This tendency first blossomed in Eric Rohmer and Claude Chabrol's *Hitchcock: The First Forty-Four Films*, which found such unity in his films through *The Wrong Man* (1956) that the authors defined their method as "observ[ing] an order, a gradation, as in piano exercises," that "work[s] toward the depths slowly, hoping that our final insights will inevitably illuminate earlier commentary, just as Hitchcock's films throw mutual and instructive light on one another" (x). In other words, once Hitchcock's non-thrillers were discounted as apprentice work undertaken at the behest of others, the thrillers could be read as a single homogeneous master text for the purposes of both interpretation and biography.

This is an odd assumption because it draws such a sharp distinction between early projects that are presumably impersonal in their diversity and later, more consistently commercial projects that are held to be more expressive of their creator. In treating Hitchcock as his movies' only begetter, this autobiographical model overlooks, or at least downplays, the contributions of longtime collaborators like Eliot Stannard, Charles Bennett, Bernard Knowles, Jack Cox, Joan Harrison, Robert Boyle, Cary Grant, Ingrid Bergman, James Stewart, Grace Kelly, Robert Burks, George Tomasini, John Michael Hayes, and Bernard Herrmann. But perhaps the oddest implication of all is that Hitchcock's biography is valuable because it throws new interpretive light on a body of films that for a long time did not seem to require interpretation at all.

Although reviewers recognized from the beginning the paradoxical nature of Hitchcock's appeal, his consistent success in producing films that were brilliantly disturbing, Hitchcock was pigeonholed for many years as a successful entertainer largely because his films were so immediately accessible on a first viewing. Not until the early 1970s did the establishment of auteurism as "the dominant aesthetic discourse among journalistic and academic film critics" (Kapsis 70) change the image of Hitchcock – whom Universal had marketed as "the real star of *The Birds*" (Kapsis 83), the first Hitchcock film to pose interpretive problems for a mass audience – into that of a filmmaker whose work might actually have significant latent content beneath the darkly gleaming surface. Suddenly the obviousness that had made Hitchcock's films so successful with such a large audience became an invitation to plumb depths that were off-limits to all but the cognoscenti.

What is most notable about these potential obstacles to mapping Hitchcock's life and art onto each other is that they have all been resolved by recourse to the same authority: Hitchcock himself. The revelation of unsuspected depths in what might have seemed merely exceptionally proficient genre films was facilitated by the groundbreaking series of interviews Hitchcock gave François Truffaut at a crucial moment in his career. Although Hitchcock's responses to Truffaut's questions were as usual resolutely technical and anecdotal rather than interpretive, his emphasis on his obsessive pre-planning and storyboarding, his habit of glossing over the contributions of collaborators from Madeleine Carroll to John Michael Hayes, and his concomitant presentation of himself as the sole creative force behind his films provided compelling evidence in support of his position as the ultimate auteur. No one remembers the device Truffaut used to conclude his original series of interviews – Hitchcock's description of a dream project he hoped to complete someday – because Hitchcock never attempted the project, a film covering twenty-four hours in the life of a city. Indeed, if Hitchcock were defined by his deepest aspirations, he would be best remembered as the man who dreamed for years of directing an adaptation of J.M. Barrie's spectral 1920 drama *Mary Rose*, a property his Universal contract specifically forbade his adapting (Hitchcock, "Surviving" 62; McGilligan 652–53). But everyone remembers the device Truffaut used to begin his first interview – an invitation to Hitchcock to confirm the oft-told story about his father sending young Alfred down to the police station with a note that caused the police to lock him up for "five or ten minutes" with the admonition, "This is what we do to naughty boys" (25) – because it so economically establishes an autobiographical basis for the fear of the police and institutional authority that runs throughout his films. Despite his parsimony in revealing details of his private life, Hitchcock succeeded in establishing his biography as a key to uncovering a new dimension of films that had never seemed in need of higher criticism.

Contemporaneous commentators who identified Hitchcock with the thriller as both a vehicle of commercial success and the expression of his most personal fears and desires followed Truffaut in identifying *The Lodger* as "really the first Hitchcockian picture," echoing the director's own characterization of it: "[Y]ou might almost say that *The Lodger* was my first picture" (Truffaut 47, 44). The tendency to see Hitchcock's later films as more personal, more self-revealing, than his earlier films was fueled by Robin Wood, even though Wood's Leavisite perspective was moral rather than biographical. Inverting the preference of Lindsay Anderson and Penelope Houston for Hitchcock's British films, Wood argued so passionately in defense of the American thrillers that a generation of filmgoers, especially in America, agreed in marginalizing or dismissing his earlier films, which were a good deal harder to find. Although Maurice Yacowar devoted an entire volume to explicating the British films, it was not until Charles Barr's *English Hitchcock* (1999) that anyone took a life-and-work approach toward Hitchcock's first fifteen films. By emphasizing Hitchcock's national identity, his Englishness, and his dependence on his literary sources and his collaborators, especially "English literary figures" (8), Barr made available a much broader view of Hitchcock's biography even as he maintained the importance of Hitchcock's life to his work.

For over forty years, then, from the early 1960s to the present, Hitchcock's example provided the impetus to read his films biographically even as he kept his private life private. But Hitchcock's influence on later biographers and critics did not only extend beyond the grave; it extended nearly a generation back in time, to the earliest interviews the director gave. The director was as adept a storyteller with interviewers as with film audiences. Invited to discuss his forthcoming production of *Rich and Strange*, he summarizes the story of Dale Collins's novel at length before launching into a series of general rules for film production (Hitchcock, "Half" 7–9). Interviewed by Norah Baring, the female lead in *Murder!*, about the success of *The 39 Steps* and his plans to make *Secret Agent*, he begins by announcing that "Scrubby Carroll is in it again" and then proceeds to ground the outrageous epithet by telling the story of how he "made up [his] mind to present her to the public as her *natural* self" (Hitchcock, "Man Who Made" 11). In the 1936 series "My Screen Memories," he presents himself as a witty, relaxed, and voluble raconteur who praises performers like Peter Lorre, Robert Donat, Madeleine Carroll, and John Gielgud largely to the extent that they provide good material for anecdotes and who describes his ordeals directing *The Pleasure Garden* (8–12) with equal or greater relish. In the series "Life Among the Stars" the following year, he is not only equally generous in acknowledging the contributions of performers from Nita Naldi to Benita Hume to the success of his films but characteristically alert to the opportunity to repeat anecdotes about *The Pleasure Garden* from the earlier series (28–33) and to generalize from these anecdotes in a concluding quasi-narrative section titled "How I Make My Films."

Even before he left England for Hollywood, the publicity center of the universe, Hitchcock had mastered the art of self-promotion. His high-profile performers may have been the hooks that gave these recycled stories currency, but Hitchcock was indisputably the star who made an effortless transition from the comically beleaguered novice of *The Pleasure Garden* to the benevolent dictator who inspired Benita Hume and Norah Baring to new heights and released the force of Madeleine Carroll's natural personality. Though Hitchcock may not have had a particularly interesting life, he marketed himself from the beginning as an interesting person, a celebrity raconteur who excelled at treating and presenting stars like "Scrubby Carroll" as down-to-earth people. In the process of demythologizing such larger-than-life figures, Hitchcock succeeded in mythologizing himself as a giant-killer equally capable of launching the screen careers of Benita Hume, Ian Hunter, and Gordon Harker and of cutting stars like Donat and Carroll down to size.

By the time he arrived in America, Hitchcock had succeeded in establishing himself as the hero of the prophecy he had delivered in "Films We Could Make" in the 16 November 1927 edition of the *London Evening News*: "When moving pictures are really artistic they will be created entirely by one man" (quoted in Spoto, *Dark* 103). In *Spellbound by Beauty*, Spoto accurately identifies this pronouncement, and its apparent fulfillment in a series of films of which Hitchcock was "the sole creative force," as "the central element in his self-promotion and in the creation of the Hitchcock myth" (84, 86). It is, in other words, a hypothesis treated as a fact by agents and institutions (Universal Pictures, journalists conducting interviews, academic programs in film studies, Hitchcock himself) that have a vested interest in its factual truth.

Hitchcock's status as the sole creative force in his films is not the only product of the director's ceaseless self-mythologizing. Perhaps Hitchcock's most cherished myth about his career was that he longed to make personally satisfying movies but was forced to bow to commercial exigencies. "There's the constant pressure," he told Frank S. Nugent in 1946. "You know: people asking, 'Do you want to reach only the audiences at the Little Carnegie or to have your pictures play the Music Hall?' So you compromise. You can't avoid it. You do the commercial thing, but you try to do it without lowering your standards" (Hitchcock, "Mr. Hitchcock" 18). Indeed, he confided in Gerald Pratley, "[I]t is harder to make a film that has both integrity and wide commercial appeal than it is to make one that merely satisfies one's artistic conscience" (Hitchcock, "Credo" 37). At a stroke, this last remark not only places the desire to achieve both integrity and commercial appeal above mere integrity but assumes that Hitchcock has an artistic conscience, that his films express something deep and true about himself irrespective of their commercial appeal.

It is this last myth that Spoto, for all his latter-day revulsion against the myth of Hitchcock the sole creative force, remains most deeply invested in: that Hitchcock's films are personal in the specific sense of being autobiographical. In his discussion of *Vertigo* in *Spellbound by Beauty*, Spoto quotes Kim Novak, James Stewart, and screenwriter Samuel Taylor (226) in support of his earlier argument that *Vertigo* was Hitchcock's "ultimate disclosure of his romantic impulses and of the attraction-repulsion he felt about the object of those impulses: the idealized blond he thought he desired but really believed to be a fraud" (*Dark* 395). Spoto's more general assumption is that *Notorious, Vertigo, Marnie,* and *Frenzy* must be not merely personally expressive of Hitchcock's emotions, even though he is a supervising collaborator rather than a sole creator, but autobiographical, because they are about men who watch women, transform women, capture women, and consume women.

In support of this proposition Spoto contends that "the artist ... has no other raw material with which to work than his own inner life, however much it is to be treated and transmuted" (*Spellbound* 227). Despite Spoto's assurance, this romantic view of artistic creation is a heresy passing for the whole truth. Roberto Rossellini created his best-known films by drawing on his sociological observations of war-torn Italy, Jean Renoir his by drawing on his psychological observations of other people, Cecil B. DeMille his by shrewdly gauging the vagaries of the market, and countless filmmakers theirs by drawing inspiration from the novels and plays and stories they adapted. Theorizing that extroverted filmmakers like Rossellini and Renoir draw their inspiration from the world around them, introverted film-makers like Hitchcock and Fritz Lang from the world within them, Leo Braudy concludes that "Lang teaches us about ourselves; Renoir teaches us about the rest of the world" (50). Even to categorize a filmmaker as extroverted or introverted, of course, is already to speculate, and to argue that introverts create not only per-sonal but autobiographical cinema because they have no other choice is to mythol-ogize on a grand scale, a scale worthy of Hitchcock himself.

But Spoto's romantic myth of Hitchcock as involuntary autobiographer, which follows Hitchcock in its assumption that all films are and must be reflections of their director's personal views, is a response to an earlier myth that also takes its cue from Hitchcock. When Taylor emphasizes Hitchcock's "exemplarily conserva-tive, private private life" (18), he is simply expanding on Hitchcock's own reveal-ingly unrevealing remarks about his wife and himself:

> [F]or a thriller-movie-making ogre, I'm hopelessly plebeian and placid. ... [I]nstead of reading mysteries at home I'm usually designing a built-in cupboard for the house; ... I wear conservative clothes and solid-color ties; ... I share her tastes for modest living, but ... my tendency to utter terrible puns makes me a trial to live with.
>
> (Hitchcock, "Woman" 52)

Recast in the third person, this comically bland self-portrait would be familiar from countless television interviews with citizens whose neighbors have run violently amok: "He seemed like such a nice man ... quiet ... kept to himself." Both the myth that fuels Taylor's authorized biography – that although the director's pri-vate life may be a curious puzzle, it deserves to remain private because it is insu-lated from a body of work it neither explains nor is explained by – and the countermyth that inspires Spoto – that the director cannot help drawing on his most personal fears and fantasies to create autobiographical films – are fueled by Hitchcock himself, who remains, thirty years after his death, by far his most influ-ential biographer. McGilligan, unable to move beyond these enabling myths, has simply steered a middle course between them; Chandler and Falk have been con-tent to recycle them with the different emphases indicated by their titles. Falk's amusingly decorous *Mr. Hitchcock* implicitly promises to keep the director's private life private; Chandler's ruefully self-deprecating *It's Only a Movie* is yet another allu-sion to Hitchcock's mythology of the non-relation between life and art.

The iron control the posthumous Hitchcock exerts over his own biography has been costly in more ways than one. David Thomson, whose entry on Hitchcock in his *Biographical Dictionary of Film* is resolutely unbiographical, suggested in conver-sation that Hitchcock's penchant for self-mythologizing had consequences in his own life that paralleled Ernest Hemingway's. Both men were aggressively talented and aggressively self-promoting. Beginning with trademark stories they told about themselves and a public image they carefully crafted even before their publicists saw its commercial potential, they created personal mythologies that a vast audience found more potent than their work. Just as more American readers knew Hemingway as the virile, anti-literary writer who sought to purge his prose of humbug and insisted that writing about grace under pressure was a craft best rooted in intimate knowledge of the pressures of war, bullfighting, or big-game hunting than ever read *Men Without Women* (1927) or *A Farewell to Arms* (1929), more moviegoers were familiar with Hitchcock's ghoulishly cherubic profile, deadpan way with outrageous puns, and reputation for putting audiences through it than ever saw *Psycho* or *The Birds*. In the end, both men, like Citizen Kane, fell victim to self-created myths grown more powerful than them. The aging Hemingway, the strength and mental stamina he had mythologized fading under the onslaught of injuries he had sustained in the pursuit of authentic physical experience, killed himself with a shotgun when he was unable to live up to his own ideal. The aging Hitchcock, convinced by interviewers, acolytes, and his own insulation from the world that he was indeed the supreme ruler of his films, carried over his highly ambivalent fantasies of sexual domination – what Spoto calls "attraction and repulsion, the almost idolatrous gaze of his camera and the concomitant compulsion to tear [his heroines] apart" (*Spellbound* 59) – from the screen to the set with scarcely less disastrous results.

Hitchcock's tendency to mythologize himself eventually grew so powerful that it created a split between the idealized self he had created for the press, the fans, and his own gratification, and the self his collaborators, his commentators, and the world at large were willing to recognize. The personal myth he authorized of darkly unfettered imagination countered by all-consuming professional commitment, a puckish sense of humor, and a decorously veiled private life has been equally powerful and even more durable. Indeed it has offered a highly influential model for biographers of other filmmakers. Michael Curtiz was more prolific than Hitchcock. Howard Hawks directed a more varied body of work. And Victor Fleming's life was by any measure more interesting. But the directors who have received the most attention from biographers are those who supported a personal mythology the biographer could either record (Fritz Lang's determination to buck the Hollywood system, Stanley Kubrick's obsessive control over his projects) or create (Martin Scorsese's decision to leave religious life for a Hollywood career, Quentin Tarantino's life lived wholly through the movies). Filmmakers interest biographers to the extent that their lives can be mythologized in the Hitchcock mold.

It is possible that Hitchcock's biography is exhausted because there really is nothing new to add. What then are the possibilities for new lives of Hitchcock? When long-dead authors attract new biographers, there is usually a specific reason. Richard B. Sewall's *Life of Emily Dickinson* (1974) draws on a wealth of new material about Dickinson's family and her relationship with the men outside it. Richard Ellmann's *Oscar Wilde* (1987) rehabilitates a writer maligned during the final years of his life as a prophetic hero for a new generation. Fred Kaplan's *Henry James: The Imagination of Genius* (1992) sheds a new light on James's work by recasting the novelist's troubled sexuality as the wellspring of his fiction.

None of these scenarios seems likely for Hitchcock. Bill Krohn is surely correct in his assertion that "[b]ecause film-making generates an incredible amount of paperwork, it is a better documented creative activity than composing, painting, or even writing" (10). Yet the vast amount of production material on Hitchcock's films is not complemented by any significant private documents, letters to loved ones from whom he was separated or even a stack of memos like David O. Selznick's to collaborators he saw every day. And the professional acquaintances whose confidences to interviewers have driven all his biographies to date are passing away. As a filmmaker the value of whose work was subject to intense debate during his lifetime and whose personal habits have been debated with equal intensity since then, Hitchcock is not an obvious subject for radical revaluation precisely because the battles along these lines have already been fought for so long. Only a professional analog to Kaplan's private approach – not a reappraisal of Hitchcock's sexuality, but a new approach to his work in the context of production material concerning his collaborations, his relationships with particular studios, or the more general institutional powers of the British and American film industries – holds out anything like promise to future biographers. Whoever they are, their first task will be to exorcise the myth of Hitchcock, the leading force behind all his lives to date, and the most formidable obstacle to any new ones.

Works Cited

Barr, Charles. *English Hitchcock*. Moffat: Cameron and Hollis, 1999.

Braudy, Leo. *The World in a Frame: What We See in Films*. Garden City: Doubleday, 1976.

Burke, Kenneth. *Language as Symbolic Action: Essays on Life, Literature, and Method*. Berkeley: U of California P, 1966.

Chandler, Charlotte. *It's Only a Movie: Alfred Hitchcock: A Personal Biography*. New York: Simon and Schuster, 2005.

Falk, Quentin. *Mr. Hitchcock*. London: Haus, 2007.

Gottlieb, Sidney, ed. *Alfred Hitchcock: Interviews*. Jackson: UP of Mississippi, 2003.

Gottlieb, Sidney, ed. *Hitchcock on Hitchcock: Selected Writings and Interviews*. Berkeley: U of California P, 1995.

Hitchcock, Alfred. "Alfred Hitchcock's Working Credo." Interview with Gerald Pratley. *Films in Review* 3.10 (Dec. 1952): 500–03. Gottlieb, *Interviews* 34–37.

Hitchcock, Alfred, "Half the World in a Talkie." *[London] Evening News* 5 Mar. 1931. Gottlieb, *Interviews* 7–9.

Hitchcock, Alfred. "Life Among the Stars." *News Chronicle* 1–5 Mar. 1937. Gottlieb, *Writings* 27–50.

Hitchcock, Alfred. "The Man Who Made *The 39 Steps*: Pen Portrait of Alfred Hitchcock." Interview by Norah Baring. *Film Pictorial* 23 Nov. 1935. Gottlieb, *Interviews* 10–13.

Hitchcock, Alfred. "Mr. Hitchcock Discovers Love." Interview by Frank Nugent. *New York Times* 3 Nov. 1946. Gottlieb, *Interviews* 17–22.

Hitchcock, Alfred. "My Screen Memories." *Film Weekly* 2, 9, 16, 23, 30 May 1936: 16, 7, 28, 28, 27. Gottlieb, *Writings* 7–26.

Hitchcock, Alfred. "Surviving: An Interview with John Russell Taylor." *Sight and Sound* 46 (Summer 1977): 174–75. Gottlieb, *Writings* 59–63.

Hitchcock, Alfred. "The Woman Who Knows Too Much." *McCall's* Mar. 1956: 12. Gottlieb, *Writings* 51–53.

Kapsis, Robert E. *Hitchcock: The Making of a Reputation.* Chicago: U of Chicago P, 1992.

Krohn, Bill. *Hitchcock at Work.* London: Phaidon, 2000.

Leff, Leonard J. *Hitchcock and Selznick: The Rich and Strange Collaboration of Alfred Hitchcock and David O. Selznick in Hollywood.* New York: Weidenfeld and Nicholson, 1987.

McGilligan, Patrick. *Alfred Hitchcock: A Life in Darkness and Light.* New York: HarperCollins, 2003.

Rohmer, Eric, and Claude Chabrol. *Hitchcock: The First Forty-Four Films.* Trans. Stanley Hochman. New York: Ungar, 1979.

Spoto, Donald. *The Art of Alfred Hitchcock: Fifty Years of His Motion Pictures.* Second ed. New York: Doubleday, 1992.

Spoto, Donald. *The Dark Side of Genius: The Life of Alfred Hitchcock.* Boston: Little, Brown, 1983.

Spoto, Donald. *Spellbound by Beauty: Alfred Hitchcock and His Leading Ladies.* New York: Harmony, 2008.

Taylor, John Russell. *Hitch: The Life and Times of Alfred Hitchcock.* New York: Pantheon, 1978.

Truffaut, François, with the collaboration of Helen G. Scott. *Hitchcock.* Rev. ed. New York: Simon and Schuster, 1984.

Wilson, Edmund. *The Wound and the Bow: Seven Studies in Literature.* 1941. Rpt. in *Literary Essays and Reviews of the 1930s & 40s.* New York: Library of America, 2007. 271–473.

2

Hitchcock's Literary Sources

Ken Mogg

The bourgeois mind is really the inability to rise above the absolute reality of time and space [and attain] ... annihilation of the historical process.

Søren Kierkegaard (37)

Many of Hitchcock's most intriguing effects have antecedents in the novels of Charles Dickens (1812–70), which he read at school. In *Our Mutual Friend* (1865), the character John Harmon is thought to have drowned in the Thames, afterwards choosing for reasons of expediency to go incognito, and twice changing his name. He finds the sensation a peculiar one. "A spirit that was once a man," he says, "could hardly feel stranger or lonelier, going unrecognized among mankind, than I feel." However, he sees that "this is the fanciful side of the situation." His life has a "real side," which he determines to face. "I know I evade it, as many men – perhaps most men – do evade thinking their way through their greatest perplexity. I will try to pin myself to mine" (422).

Latent in the above passage is Dickens's fascination with ghosts, and especially a ghost's-eye view. Such a viewpoint also informs a trio of "ghost" films by Hitchcock comprising *The Wrong Man* (1956), *Vertigo* (1958), and *North by Northwest* (1959). Manny Balestrero (Henry Fonda), Scottie Ferguson (James Stewart), and Roger Thornhill (Cary Grant), the latter mistaken for the nonexistent George Kaplan, all undergo an experience like that of John Harmon. This needn't surprise us. For one thing, Dickens in his late novels consistently portrayed society as a literal death-in-life; related imagery occurs in Hitchcock's films from *Blackmail* (1929) onwards. For another thing, several of Dickens's precursors – the Bible, the painter and engraver William Hogarth, the artist and poet William Blake – influenced Hitchcock too. Thus his reading of Dickens served to underpin his awareness of a broad tradition. Another masterly Dickens novel in that tradition is *Bleak House*

A Companion to Alfred Hitchcock, First Edition. Edited by Thomas Leitch and Leland Poague.
© 2011 Thomas Leitch and Leland Poague. Published 2011 by Blackwell Publishing Ltd.

(1853), which Donald Spoto says "engraved itself on Hitchcock's memory" (*Dark 28*). The novel's ingredients – notably its interminable lawsuit but also its wintry setting and its several "ghost" references – show it to be an influence on *The Wrong Man*. That film gives one of Hitchcock's most beautiful but ambivalent portraits of his perennial subject, the bourgeois family. He inherited a critical view of the bourgeoisie from several pessimistic writers and playwrights born in the nineteenth century. But he also discovered the "anti-pessimistic" writings of G.K. Chesterton (1874–1936), which taught him how to transcend inevitable contradictions in his material and thereby to make what he chose to call "pure cinema" (Bogdanovich 476).

For a certain kind of imaginative artist, space and time are raw materials to be worked. Following the lead of Dickens, Hitchcock became such an artist. A shadowy figure at the start of *The Wrong Man*, he addresses us across the vastness of a deserted sound stage ("This is Alfred Hitchcock speaking"). While he appears distant and diminutive, his voice sounds close by, confiding. It's as if we were being given privileged interior information that transcends the space of its telling. Clearly this is more than a technical matter. The film will transcend space again when, like a ghost, the tracking camera penetrates Manny's closed front door and follows him down his hallway.

Time too will be transcended. After the Prologue, the film's credits are superimposed over a sequence set in New York's famous Stork Club, where Manny plays the double bass in a Latin band. But again matters aren't straightforward. Belying the festive connotations of couples dining lavishly and dancing under bunches of balloons, a series of near-invisible dissolves proceeds to spirit these people away. Technically, what we see is the evening's events condensed into a single moment of screen time: Hitchcock asserting the power of his medium. Yet the effect, as I have observed, is positively eerie (Mogg, *Story* 145). The moment foreshadows what Manny, after being mistaken for a holdup man and arrested, may become, namely, "[a] spirit that was once a man."

Seeing Manny as a typical bourgeois, Hitchcock wants to expose both his vulnerability and his shortcomings. Even when, after being released on bail, Manny describes his arrest as seeming like "a million years ago," he hasn't understood his experience. He hasn't begun to grasp – or has only incipiently begun to grasp – what philosophers mean by a time/space/causality nexus of workaday perception and so to transcend it. All Manny can do is cling to his religious faith and heed the homespun maxim that we hear him offer his two sons, aged eight and five, apropos learning to play the piano: "You mustn't let anything throw you off the beat." Of course, this isn't inconsiderable advice, and it might just have saved Richard Carstone, one of several victims in *Bleak House*.

Neither Dickens nor Hitchcock condescends. Both are concerned to explore the conceptual and expressive limits of their material and to simulate life. Significantly, *The Wrong Man* is full of coincidences, beginning with how Manny learns that he has a doppelgänger who has taken to robbing shops and offices in the Balestrero family's neighborhood of Jackson Heights in Queens, New York. In fact, the film contains several doubles of Manny and the actual criminal who resemble them in physical appearance and who wear similar overcoats. Manny brushes against one such person on the fateful afternoon he visits his insurance office to arrange a loan on his wife's policy. Coincidentally, too, the same building houses the office of Frank O'Connor (Anthony Quayle), who will be Manny's attorney at his trial. One readily thinks of Dickens, whose friend and biographer John Forster wrote:

> On the coincidences, resemblances and surprises of life Dickens liked especially to dwell. ... The world, he would say, was so much smaller than we thought it; we were all so connected by fate without knowing it; people supposed to be far apart were so constantly elbowing each other; and to-morrow bore so close a resemblance to nothing half so much as to yesterday.
>
> (112)

That's the stuff of both *Bleak House* and *The Wrong Man*. With heavy irony, both works emphasize the lumbering nature of time and human evolution, in effect Kierkegaard's "historical process." Sometimes visible spurts of movement do occur, but these only highlight a general lassitude. In *The Wrong Man*, Manny, seeking alibi witnesses for the robbery dates, visits an upstate resort where he and his family had spent a vacation the previous summer. Now he strides purposefully across the snow but achieves nothing definite. In Queens, people with pinched faces scurry across streets; caught in car headlights, they look like wraiths. Dickens in a famous passage pursues similar effects. The scene shifts for a time from dreary London to the estate of Chesney Wold in Lincolnshire, where rain seems forever to be falling. Lady Dedlock, who has her own connection to the oppressive Chancery lawsuit, is portrayed as suited to her name, caught in a state of suspended animation and unreality (fittingly, there's a paved terrace at Chesney Wold called "the Ghost's Walk"):

> My Lady Dedlock (who is childless), looking out in the early twilight from her boudoir at a keeper's lodge, and seeing the light of a fire upon the latticed panes ... and a child, chased by a woman, running out in the rain to meet the shining figure of a wrapped-up man coming through the gate, has been put quite out of temper.
>
> (56)

Chesney Wold is one of the novel's several "bleak houses"; by implication, another is England itself. The contrast in the passage above is with an otherwise unremarkable "happy family" represented by the child running to greet her father. There's a matching moment in *The Wrong Man*, and for a time the Balestreros too are almost happy. Then Manny's arrest and Rose's eventual breakdown change everything. Bleakness visibly sets in. Colin McArthur invoked the Cold War in summing up *The Wrong Man* as "the film which perhaps best conveys the underlying unease of 50s America" (quoted in Humphries 139).

That's a splendid point. However, what is missing from such a description of the film is the message that all is not lost. Hitchcock could be the most salutary of filmmakers, whose very act of creation overcomes, in Kierkegaard's words, "the uncertainty and chance which is found in the life of so many" and thereby annihilates "the historical process" (37). Hitchcock wanted audiences to feel more alive. Though *The Wrong Man*, in my view, doesn't quite come off, it makes a Dickensian-cum-Kafkaesque gesture that way. By contrast, *North by Northwest* draws on further literary sources to tell a version of the "wrong man" tale that is never less than exhilarating.

> The photoplay tells us the human story by overcoming the forms of the outer world, namely, space, time, and causality, and by adjusting the events to the forms of the inner world, namely, attention, memory, imagination, and emotion.
>
> Hugo Münsterberg (173)

North by Northwest opens with a ghostly green screen and crisscrossing lines that become a glass-fronted office block reflecting in distorted and even eerie fashion a street at rush hour. The immediate borrowing is from F.W. Murnau's *Sunrise* (1927), but we have only to remember that the screenwriter of that film, Carl Mayer, was a lover of Dickens's novels (Kracauer 256) to guess his own inspiration: the famous episode in *Our Mutual Friend* that satirizes the *nouveau riche* Veneering family by portraying their pretensions as in a vast drawing-room mirror (52–53). The episode is consistent with the same novel's other "ghostly onlooker" imagery. In turn, Dickens draws on the literary motif of the afflicted city, whose broad input includes William Blake's poem "London" (1794) and a famous passage in T.S. Eliot's *The Waste Land* (1922) evoking a fog-bound "Unreal City" inhabited by revenants. (The city is again London, yet Eliot takes particular inspiration from Baudelaire and Dante, in keeping with an English eclecticism.) Thornhill in *North by Northwest* flees such a city for its opposite condition. At Mount Rushmore he says, "I've never felt more alive," while his defeated foe Vandamm (James Mason) complains about the police's use of "real bullets." The unmistakably upbeat note is underlined by the celebrated phallic last shot. Nonetheless, Thornhill's return to New York City on the train with his bride Eve remains ambiguous.

The main reason Hitchcock portrays New York City as ghostly, the literary influences strongly suggest, is that every person needs to make his or her own meaningful reality. Unfortunately, many fail, staying other-directed. Such a lesson is driven home at Mount Rushmore, with its basilisk faces of the Presidents, another image with literary forebears. As for Blake's "London," its "mind-forged manacles" are evident in both *The Wrong Man* and *North by Northwest*, not least in the typically pinched or crabbed faces of their extras. Of course, both Manny and Roger start out habit-bound. Surreally, Manny is seen in literal manacles at one point. In Thornhill's case, we see him join his ageing business cronies at the Oak Bar of the Plaza Hotel, where a mural by Everett Shinn depicts a foggy New York of bygone days – another "Unreal City."

Journalist Otis Guernsey in 1951 gave Hitchcock the germ for *North by Northwest* by remembering a wartime incident and asking: Why not make a thriller about a man mistaken for a fake undercover agent (Krohn 202–04; McGilligan 464)? Immediately interested, Hitchcock would have recalled precedents. Falsely-imputed guilt had featured in his own work since his second film, *The Mountain Eagle* (1926), becoming ambiguous in his third, *The Lodger* (1926); its literary fore-bears included William Godwin's novel *Caleb Williams* (1794), which Dickens once commended to Poe. Mistaken guilt had been the basis of John Buchan's chase adventure, *The Thirty-Nine Steps* (1915), a Hitchcock favorite; related to it were stories in which a character chooses to go incognito or steals another man's iden-tity. The director had recently told Warner Bros. that he would like to film just such a work, David Duncan's *The Bramble Bush* (1948), set in San Francisco (McGilligan 456). Although the film was never made, there's an indebtedness to particular scenes from Duncan's novel in *The Wrong Man*, *Vertigo*, *North by Northwest*, and *Frenzy* (1972). For example, the incident in *North by Northwest* in which Vandamm's murderous henchmen set a semi-comatose Thornhill at the wheel of a car and launch it towards a cliff (see Duncan 130–31) was probably reworked from the *Bramble Bush* screenplay Hitchcock and his wife, Alma, started to write while holidaying at St. Moritz at the end of 1952.

In turn, Hitchcock may have been reminded of plays and stories in which the main protagonist is literally a nonentity. None of them, it's true, have a protagonist whose middle initial is said to stand for "nothing," but there are near-equivalents. The English satirical novel *The Diary of a Nobody*, by George and Weedon Grossmith, was originally serialized in *Punch* and published in book form in 1892. Its principal character, the suburban Mr. Pooter, is gently ridiculed; one of his neighbors, Mr. Padge, has a stock phrase, "That's right!," which Hitchcock would give to a meek juror in *Murder!* (1930). Likewise, Elmer Rice's famous Expressionist play *The Adding Machine* (1923), with its downtrodden clerk Mr. Zero, probably influenced the office sequence that begins Hitchcock's *Rich and Strange* (1931), later echoed at the start of *North by Northwest*.

Again, Otis Guernsey's idea may have reminded Hitchcock of stories about nonexistent persons, such as Buchan's idyllic *John Macnab* (1925), which is also about coming alive. Parodying a by-now conventional opening, no less than three public figures find themselves bored in London. To relieve the torpor, they accept Sir Archie Roylance's invitation to come to Scotland and pose collectively as "Macnab," in whose name they will engage in some harmless poaching and chal-lenge Roylance's unwitting landowner friends to unmask them. This is quintes-sential Buchan, with a sporty young woman interpolated for a spot of romance.

Hitchcock looked around for related material. In 1955, his former protégé Ronald Neame directed a lyrically told World War II thriller based on a true inci-dent, *The Man Who Never Was*. Later, Hitchcock sought the rights to Graham Greene's *Our Man in Havana* (1958), about a spy's phony reports from Cuba, but was turned down by Greene himself (Sinyard 108). One of the spy's supposed sightings, of a giant nuclear reactor hidden in the mountains, proves to be based on a new-model vacuum cleaner (Greene 78–79). Doubtless Hitchcock and screen-writer Ernest Lehman recalled this flight of fancy as they contrived *North by Northwest* figuratively out of nothing.

But in fact there was a great deal of material available to them, and *North by Northwest* borrows liberally. For the scene in the Chicago railway station men's room, where Thornhill disguises himself from the police by lathering his face and using a lady's razor, the filmmakers remembered an earlier Greene novel, *The Confidential Agent* (1939). The latter has structural resemblances to *North by Northwest*, though its dark, fatalistic prewar feel is very different. For two other likely borrowings with a rather lighter tone, the filmmakers would have gone back another decade. The episodic and immensely popular Bulldog Drummond adven-tures Cyril McNeile published as "Sapper" were a thick-ear equivalent of Buchan's Hannay tales. From the fourth of the novels, *The Final Count* (1926), two parallels with *North by Northwest* are striking. First, the novel has a scene in which spies take over the house of an absentee owner and install a phony lady owner to divert police suspicions ("Sapper," *Four Rounds*, Chapter 49 = Chapter 6 of the original novel). Later, the novel climaxes at the spies' remote hideaway on a Cornish cliff, where they wait for their dirigible to come and fly them to Russia (Chapter 51 = Chapter 8).

A high, rocky place was much favored for adventure climaxes. I'll discuss shortly the ways *North by Northwest* fits one of the above-mentioned literary traditions, which might be called "British picaresque," but first I need to note further Hitchcock connections to European culture generally.

> [Romantic Irony recognizes] that the world in its essence is paradoxical and that an ambivalent attitude alone can grasp its contradictory totality.
>
> René Wellek (14)

In *Albion: The Origins of the English Imagination*, Peter Ackroyd more than once mentions a "mongrel tendency" of English writers, dramatists, and architects to literally import into their work whatever was needful, especially new ideas or modes. The general idea was to please audiences. Yet Ackroyd can ask: "Is it a peculiar [English] disposition, also, to feel compelled to include no less than every-thing – just as Dickens filled his novels with crowds and Shakespeare filled the world with his characters – before concluding that all is vanity and empty striv-ing?" (59).

Some such paradox is built into Hitchcock's films, though it may be disguised. Spoto noted their "open-ended pessimism" (quoted in Hurley xiii). For all Hitchcock's willingness to borrow from many sources – whether from Antonioni or a sensation novel by Dickens's gifted friend Wilkie Collins – the overall tendency of the films is to affirm nothing except the life / death force itself, which is neutral. Hence Hitchcock's convenient emphasis on the visual, and his description of the films as "pure cinema." But the latter *isn't* nothing. Inevitably it opens itself to paradox and admits contraries. Blake's "London" comes from his *Songs of Innocence and Experience Shewing the Two Contrary States of the Human Mind* (1794). A poet's vision and the English tradition of which it forms a part give Hitchcock's films more than specific imagery. In this connection, I'm reminded that Dickens drew happily from stage melodrama. A striking passage in *Oliver Twist* (1838) refers to how its tragic and comic scenes alternate like "the layers of red and white in a side of streaky, well-cured bacon" (102). Far from criticizing melodrama, Dickens claimed that its sudden transitions approximate real life (102).

Still, Ackroyd's question above may need to be answered in the negative. Blake and Dickens were never just writers in an English tradition, and Romanticism was widespread. A Romantic outlook was by definition all-embracing (see Barzun 356). Not averse to puns, Goethe in Part One of *Faust* (1808) had invoked drama's mass appeal. A three-way discussion by The Director, The Poet, and The Clown had cited a play's need to "be exemplary in every fashion" (71), to offer something to everybody, for "The mass is overwhelmed only by masses" (73). It was an observation that both Dickens and Hitchcock, as popular entertainers, put into practice in their rich melodramas. Hitchcock might have been speaking for both of them when he told Spoto, "We try to tell a good story and develop a hefty plot" (*Spellbound* 85). He appears to have first encountered works by the German Romantic writers – Goethe, Hoffmann, the brothers Grimm, Heinrich Heine – in the early 1920s in Berlin (*Dark* 70–71). They too had often written in a pessimistic or grotesque vein, and Hitchcock clearly relished their work. In the 1940s he read Heine's melancholy verse-drama *Ratcliff* (1823) "several times" and wanted to film it (*Dark* 329). Its remote Scottish setting, a more extreme version of the Yorkshire hills and dales lately shown in William Wyler's *Wuthering Heights* (1939), would have appealed to him, for he had a penchant for things Scottish, perhaps because of his early fondness for tales by Scott, Stevenson, and Buchan and the plays of Barrie.

"By God!" he whispered, drawing his breath in sharply. "It is all pure Rider Haggard and Conan Doyle."

John Buchan, *The Thirty-Nine Steps* (Hannay 29)

Dickens's novels often employed the cross-country journey format of Bunyan's *Pilgrim's Progress* (1678, 1684) and of novels by Henry Fielding and the Scottish surgeon Tobias Smollett. Such a format, with its potential for colorful characters and sharp turns of events, would underpin much later British adventure and spy fiction – typical bourgeois reading-matter whose exponents included H. Rider Haggard, John Buchan, and Eric Ambler. But in Dickens's case it first showed itself in *The Posthumous Papers of the Pickwick Club* (1837). "Mr. Pickwick," writes Norrie Epstein, capturing the book's picaresque note, "is a modern pilgrim, or knight-errant" (58). At one point, this genial bachelor finds himself wrongfully incarcerated in the teeming Fleet Prison, which affords him a glimpse of human wretchedness. The "wrong man" motif probably came from Dickens's reading of *Caleb Williams*. It returns, of course, in both *The Wrong Man* and *North by Northwest*, where it can be positively Kafkaesque in its ambiences and implications.

The enduring quality of Hitchcock's work owes much to its general allusiveness. This bears on the films' Symbolist aspect, discussed later, but the following illustration is instructive. Hitchcock often told interviewers of his wish to film twenty-four hours in the life of a city, beginning with the arrival at market of produce fresh from the country. The theme would be defilement, how civilization reduces good things to waste matter. This could be an analogy of war, or a picture of the human condition generally. It, too, recalls Ackroyd's notion of an English disposition to be comprehensive but downbeat. Yet the picaresque format was often a salutary one, at least in its general tone. Dickens's intention for the most picaresque of his novels, *The Old Curiosity Shop* (1840), was always to preserve his heroine Little Nell from defilement as she makes her "progress" towards an (ambiguous) early death (42). Epstein sums up the novel:

> Reduced to its simplest form, *The Old Curiosity Shop* is a journey. ... Nell begins her odyssey as a healthy young girl and slowly moves westward, toward the symbolic realm of the dead. ... After suffering so long, Nell has reached a nirvana that is beyond struggle.
>
> (123)

Several Hitchcock films feature potential nirvanas. One is *North by Northwest*, whose Mount Rushmore climax includes a stunning moonlight shot of a plunging valley, seeming to invite Thornhill to "easeful death." Another is *Suspicion* (1941), whose glass-of-milk climax likewise echoes "Ode to a Nightingale" (by John Keats) and the poet's desire "To cease upon the midnight with no pain" (see Mogg, "Paradox"). In both cases, Hitchcock may have remembered Buchan's novel *Mr. Standfast* (1919), which cites Keats's poem (*Hannay* 594).

Buchan helped revivify the British picaresque. Besides Keats and Shakespeare, his favorite writers included Bunyan, Scott, Dickens, and Thackeray (*Memory* 32 and passim). In his own fiction, he drew on a variant genre of adventure stories that had emerged in late Victorian times and was associated by contemporary critics with the Highland novels Scott wrote between 1814 and 1831 (Bristow xii). Scholar Andrew Lang championed these new "romances" for their healthy values, attuned to a life-force that human beings shared with their primate ancestors (Bristow xii–xiii). Many of these stories described journeys or embraced notions of the White Man's Burden, as defined by Kipling's 1899 poem. Typically they described a journey northwards or westwards to a mountainous climax. Haggard's *King Solomon's Mines* (1885) is the archetype, containing this passage: "All that afternoon we travelled on along the magnificent roadway which headed steadily in a north-westerly direction" (101). At the end of the roadway lie the three "Silent

Ones," colossi carved into the steep mountainside, which narrator Alan Quatermain soon intuits represent "false divinities" – thus prefiguring the basilisk faces of the Presidents at Mount Rushmore in *North by Northwest*. Buchan wrote his own excellent variant of the Haggard tale, *Prester John* (1910), wherein young David Crawfurd goes *undefiled* by the pagan threat because he is careful always to remember his talismanic boyhood reading of *Pilgrim's Progress*. In turn, Sir Laurens van der Post, born in Africa in 1906, updated the idea in 1955 as *Flamingo Feather*, a novel Hitchcock wanted to film. But that project fell through, replaced by *Vertigo*.

Kipling's *Kim* (1901), whose plot mingles spies with holy men, thrilling adventures with ruminations on the soul along the Grand Trunk Road in North-West India, offers a masterly variant on Andrew Lang's idea of salutary adventure. It may be the least pessimistic of Kipling's Indian stories, several of which Hitchcock knew (Truffaut 138; Spoto, *Dark* 329). At the end, one of its two principal characters, the lama, has seen Nibban / Nirvana ("By this I knew the Soul had passed beyond the illusion of Time and Space and of Things. By this I knew that I was free" [288]). But like the Buddha before him, he prefers to linger in the world; he still wants to guide his protégé, the orphan Kim. For his part, Kim ambiguously wants to keep playing "the Great Game" into which the British Secret Service has inducted him. Mutatis mutandis, we may find much of *North by Northwest* (and *Vertigo*) here. The ever-worldly Thornhill's glimpse of nirvana isn't the real thing – it's only what tempts him from life – but in an important sense it might as well have been. *North by Northwest* is sufficiently surreal, and its parodic tone sufficiently pronounced, to imply a way of seeing different from, perhaps superior to, Thornhill's. Granted, this sumptuous film *is* about the real world and realpolitik. When a defeated Vandamm tells his American adversaries, "That wasn't very sporting … using real bullets," he is effectively acknowledging that times have changed since the era of the Great Game of Kipling and Buchan, with its old-fashioned, almost gentlemanly rules (see Williams 12, 16). Nonetheless, Hitchcock was never single-visioned; his films thrive on a poetic ambiguity.

Ironically, it was MGM's film *The Wizard of Oz* (Victor Fleming, 1939) that probably best summed up for Hitchcock and Lehman many of the picaresque elements I've been mentioning. (Its source, L. Frank Baum's 1900 children's story, is something of a confectionery *Pilgrim's Progress*.) The pair certainly had Fleming's film in mind. The giveaway is its scene at a crossroads adjoining a cornfield. Ernest Lehman has said that Hitchcock, for his film's crossroads scene, even thought of having Vandamm's men whip up a Kansas-style tornado to kill Thornhill (quoted in Baer 70). Both films invite the label "pure cinema." Critic Danny Peary, who contends that Fleming's film is finally, and reflexively, about Hollywood, explains that its story targets teenage girls who dream of running away from home to break into movies (474).

In truth, discontented Dorothy on her foster-parents' Kansas farm at the start of *The Wizard of Oz* looks forward to young Charlie (Teresa Wright) brooding about her bourgeois family at the start of *Shadow of a Doubt* (1943) even as she looks backward to another troubled young woman, Hitchcock's "favorite character in fiction," Emma Bovary (Spoto, *Dark* 42). Gustave Flaubert called *Madame Bovary* (1856) his "book about nothing" (xi) – that is, pure literature.

> They longed to live like a couple of Robinson Crusoes, for ever in this tiny spot which seemed to them, in their mood of bliss, to be the loveliest in all the world.
> Gustave Flaubert, *Madame Bovary* (248)

Hitchcock's affection for Emma Bovary, a vain yet touching character who epitomizes for countless readers romantic longing and at times almost the life / death force, is detectable in several of the films. The latter even incorporate some male Emmas. Four years before *The 39 Steps* (1935) with its crofter's wife pining for the lights of Edinburgh on a Saturday night, Fred Hill (Henry Kendall) in *Rich and Strange* had complained, "I want more life!" But Emma's influence on the films appears most clearly in the young women who so often find themselves imperiled or trapped, sometimes at least partly by their own imaginings or sexual dreaming. As young Charlie, feeling that she and her family are becoming moribund, summons Uncle Charlie (Joseph Cotten) to "save" them, her bespectacled younger sister, an Emma in training, devours Scott's *Ivanhoe* (1819). There is a bit of Emma in Eve Gill (Jane Wyman) in *Stage Fright* (1950), whom the screenplay describes as "apt to view everything in an overly-dramatic light" (quoted in Mogg, *Story* 113). And there's Marion Crane (Janet Leigh) in *Psycho* (1960). Marion and her boyfriend, Sam Loomis (John Gavin), share a dream of what in the screenplay Sam calls "a private island ... where we can run around without our ... shoes on." The director and his writer Joseph Stefano may have been remembering the famous episode of Emma and Léon in Rouen, in which the pair travel downstream to "their island," where they dream of living "like a couple of Robinson Crusoes." Marion's mad theft of $40 000 to try and implement Sam's fantasy, recalling Emma Bovary's running up of debt to sustain her extramarital affairs, further marks her as Emma's descendant.

These are just shadings. More crucial is what Terence Cave, in his Introduction to *Madame Bovary*, calls Flaubert's "dual vision" (see Flaubert xii), which almost certainly contributed to Hitchcock's own. Flaubert spoke of his need to *expose* the "half-witted, middle-class society" (55) that Emma daily moved in – which she herself supposed "an exception to some more glorious rule" (55) operating elsewhere – yet the very evenness of his writing might simultaneously let him present that middle-class world as a thing of beauty. He seems to have conceived such an effect purely ironically. But in *Marnie* (1964) there's surely more at stake when, for example, a slum street in Baltimore does look almost beautiful in the afternoon sun. We later hear Mark Rutland (Sean Connery) misquote a passage from Emerson's *Voluntaries* III. The full Emerson passage is famous for these lines: "So nigh is grandeur to our dust / So near is God to man" (Emerson 168). G.K. Chesterton would supply Hitchcock with similar thoughts.

Hitchcock appears to draw on at least two famous set pieces from *Madame Bovary*. Landowner Rodolphe's initial seduction of Emma takes place during an agricultural show. He leads her upstairs to an empty council chamber overlooking the public square. As banal official phrases waft through the window – "We must work together for good farming," "For the best use of oilseed cake," "Flemish manure – flax-growing – drainage" – the couple's hands meet and their fingers entwine. Understandably, Claude Chabrol (*Madame Bovary*, 1991) directed this scene as if it were the fireworks episode from *To Catch a Thief* (1955), deftly conflating it and an actual fireworks episode from Flaubert's novel that takes place the same evening (Flaubert 124–46).

A second set piece elaborately recounts Emma and husband Charles's excursion to the Donizetti opera *Lucia di Lammermoor* (1835) in Rouen, where they encounter Léon. From this chapter Hitchcock may have drawn inspiration for the "Storm Cloud Cantata" scene in both versions of *The Man Who Knew Too Much* (1934, 1956). The opera comes from the Walter Scott novel *The Bride of Lammermoor* (1819). Familiar with Scott's romances from her childhood, Emma readily enters into the tragic events onstage and identifies them with her own miseries. When the ill-fated hero enters, "Emma leaned forward, the better to see him, scraping the velvet of the box with her fingernails. Her heart drank its fill of his melodious lamentations which … resembled the cries of shipwrecked mariners in a storm" (215).

Flaubert's inclusion of incidents that occur elsewhere in the opera house – such as Charles's clumsy return at intermission from the buffet, carrying barley-water – would not have been lost on the "maximizing" Hitchcock. The chapter isn't suspenseful, exactly, but it reaches a definite climax when Léon arrives from out of the past. It's far from being what Hitchcock called one of those "no-scene scenes" (McGilligan 618), which advance the narrative or develop a character but don't build or take shape.

Suspense in Flaubert can well up from the broad conception of the work. Its author is renowned for the elaborate research, the meticulous writing, and the lengthy revision he expended in order to get the precise effect he wanted. For such artists, visible action isn't the *sine qua non*. In a letter of 15 January 1853 Flaubert wrote: "I now have fifty pages in a row without a single event" (Flaubert viii). Later he elaborated: "I think that this is rather characteristic of life itself. The sexual act may last only a minute, though it has been anticipated for months" (ix). Moreover, even a novel "about nothing" may in fact have a subject. Because it developed in time and space, Flaubert could imply his subject was "life itself." To that extent, and with his anti-bourgeois stance, he sometimes anticipated the subject matter of the literary Symbolists.

Somerset Maugham, in *The World's Ten Greatest Novels*, rebuked *Madame Bovary*'s author: "Flaubert was a pessimist. … The bourgeois, the commonplace, the ordinary filled him with exasperation. … He had no charity" (129). As I've begun to indicate, there was a vast strain of pessimism in nineteenth-century literature (see especially Binion *passim*), and Hitchcock absorbed much of it. Nonetheless, his films grew more tolerant in their general attitude. An anecdote about Flaubert can suggest the lucid way Hitchcock depicts the family in *The Wrong Man*. Flaubert's creative attunement to the French bourgeoisie at least kept him receptive to them. Then one day the almost willful anti-bourgeois outlook that had stopped him from marrying, for example, appears to have melted. He was out walking with his niece. Suddenly he saw, in the garden of a small house with a white picket fence, a representative middle-class family. The father was playing with his children, the mother was looking on happily. Whereupon Flaubert exclaimed, without irony, "Ils sont dans le vrai!" ("They are in the truth!": Commanville 90). This beautiful moment is an epiphany.

Hitchcock himself had to overcome both nineteenth-century and modernist prejudice against the masses. Imitating many British intellectuals of his period, some of whom he met at the Film Society, he would refer to "the moron masses" (Taylor 181). Here, obviously, were echoes of Flaubert's "half-witted" bourgeoisie. But in making *The Wrong Man* he was able both to valorize its bourgeois family and to mount a sophisticated critique of bourgeois failure to annihilate "the historical process." This did more than anticipate Scottie's attempt at self-overcoming in *Vertigo*. On Hitchcock's part, I think it showed conclusively that he had moved beyond what the philosopher Arthur Schopenhauer called the "interested," i.e., bourgeois, or workaday, consciousness to arrive at the flexible and compassionate insight of the poet-artist.

At the least, Hitchcock exemplified Keats's "poetic character." John Carey has noted how, depending on his purpose, Dickens might depict a given topic either sympathetically or with disapproval (*Effigy* 8–9). Carey adds that the poetic character was defined by Keats as essentially amoral and unprincipled (9), a description that suggests not only Dickens but Hitchcock, who claimed that no considerations of morality could have stopped him making *Rear Window* (1954), such was his love of cinema (Truffaut 319).

However, as they say in *Rebecca* (1940), there's a little more to it than that. It's true that the poetic character involves seeing a topic relatively disinterestedly, either one way or another (or first one way, then another). But sometimes artists may need to accept that contraries exist simultaneously.

> Within a context of humanistic response to Industrialization and to the constant rise of a complacent bourgeois class, … Symbolism was an all-encompassing phenomenon in the years from 1886 through 1905.
>
> Julia Tanski (148)

The fluid term "Symbolist" refers as much to a body of theory as to the work of certain writers and artists in France, Belgium, and elsewhere. Related or contributory movements were the Synthetist, Decadent, and Nabi movements (Doss-Davezac 250). Many Symbolist artists, notes Sharon L. Hirsh, "perceived themselves to be different from the crowd and … produced images imbued with the … vision of the hypersensitive outsider" (xviii). Their immediate aim was to penetrate work-aday appearances. In other words, they showed definite anti-bourgeois tendencies. When we note that Impressionism, though appreciated by the general public, was anathema to them (Doss-Davezac 255), we may sense something Hitchcock had later to take into account: two opposed ways of knowing life, the introvert and the extrovert. The validity of both ways required of him a complex dual vision. Although it was evidently the Symbolist painters whose work "immensely struck" Hitchcock (quoted in Chandler 19), it will be helpful to discuss some Symbolist writers and literary precursors. The director's arguably two most Symbolist films, *I Confess* (1953) and *Vertigo*, were both based on French literary originals – with significant input, in the case of the latter, from at least two Belgian novels.

Heinrich Heine, the expatriate German Romantic and author of *Ratcliff*, had referred to how "[t]ones, words, colors and forms … are merely symbols of the Idea" (Doss-Davezac 268), a passage Heine's fellow outsider Charles Baudelaire commended in his *Curiosités esthétiques,* republished in his *Oeuvres posthumes* in 1887 (Doss-Davezac 268). The timing of the latter was doubly apt. First, the Symbolist movement had recently begun to define its goals, putting emphasis on eternal meanings and Platonic ideas (Doss-Davezac 255–56). Second, the author of *The Flowers of Evil* was a major inspiration for the young Symbolist/Decadent writers (Doss-Davezac 258). Others were Edgar Allan Poe and the philosophers Plotinus and Schopenhauer. Their ideas were highly conducive to Symbolist pessimism. According to Shehira Doss-Davezac, Baudelaire's lines "I am the limbs and the wheel/the victim and the torturer" were part of a poem "which every schoolboy could recite in the 1880s" (251). Similar sentiments had been expressed by Schopenhauer when he wrote that "the world is hell, and men are divided into tortured souls and torturing devils" (251). Later those sentiments would be expressed visually by Hitchcock in what is sometimes called the "fire and ice" credits sequence of *Torn Curtain* (1966) but which I prefer to think of in Schopenhauer's terms, Will and Representation – anyway, a remarkable Symbolist passage in his films.

Doss-Davezac is at pains to show the positive side of a philosophy of pessimism. Had not both Schopenhauer and Baudelaire pointed the way? For one thing, had not Schopenhauer described the means to escape "a [workaday] world governed by space, time and causality" (Doss-Davezac 251–52)? Undoubtedly Baudelaire had sought "redemption through art. 'To blasphemy, I shall oppose heavenward yearnings; to obscenity, Platonic flowers'" (Doss-Davezac 259). Yet a quality simply of *Weltschmertz* may seem to characterize Georges Rodenbach's outstanding Symbolist novel, *Bruges-la-Morte* (1892), a clear precursor of *Vertigo*.

Though it may take inspiration from Poe's "Ligeia," *Bruges-la-Morte* is set in Bruges, the centuries-old Belgian town of canals and belfries and silent house-fronts. Symbolist artist Fernand Khnopff did a frontispiece for the first edition; decadent author Joris Huysmans would praise the novel for evoking a city "in every detail" (quoted in Rodenbach 5). After Hugh Viane has begun an affair with the chorus girl Jane, who bears an uncanny resemblance to his late wife, a passage refers to "the prying bourgeoises [who] exercised the most lynx-eyed surveillance over all the movements of Hugh" (45). Most of the houses had attached to their window ledges "the little mirrors known as *espions*" to reflect passersby and "furnish material for discussion" (45). Hitchcock may have remembered such mirrors when he included one in the opening sequence of *Topaz* (1969), showing a street outside the Russian Embassy in Copenhagen. These mirrors can symbolize various forms of voyeurism and surveillance – including the impulse that brings spectators to the cinema in the first place – but never freedom. *Vertigo* from the start has its own "surveillance" motif, inviting the audience to identify with Scottie's possible sadism, of which he is arguably never cured. Like Hugh Viane, he appears not to attain disinterestedness nor to access "the Idea" in itself. As for Hugh, he soon tires of the too-worldly Jane and perversely strangles her with tresses of his late wife's hair.

Much of *Bruges-la-Morte* ends up in Pierre Boileau and Thomas Narcejac's *D'entre les morts* (1954), though the tone has changed to accommodate the mystery-thriller genre. Narcejac was himself Belgian, had recently published a study of his fellow countryman, the brilliant Georges Simenon (*Le cas Simenon*, 1950), and now brought to *D'entre les morts* a rich Belgian heritage. *Bruges-la-Morte* underpins the later novel, even to a final strangulation scene. Nonetheless, there was probably an intermediary work, Simenon's *Lettre à mon juge* (1947). There, an unhappily married provincial doctor takes a mistress, Martine, who gives him for a time the happiness that had eluded them both, until he finally strangles her.

Yet the three endings are otherwise quite different. In the case of *Bruges-la-Morte*, which might be an allegory of Symbolism's own chimerical quest or soul-journey, by the time Hugh kills Jane we already know that he doesn't love her: "All that he [ever] desired was the conversion of his mirage into a reality" (41). After killing her, he is left with a feeling of "nothingness" (107). By contrast, *Lettre à mon juge* ends paradoxically, in a virtual love pact. Referring to his mistress's too-worldly side, which he had detested, the doctor explains, "I killed her that she might live" (215). For her part, Martine had seen her death coming and had not resisted. Simenon's triumph is to make us understand the doctor's explanation and recall such perverse authors as Poe, Huysmans, and Wilde while recognizing the self-deception born of love.

D'entre les Morts cleverly steers a path between these endings, concluding when its duped protagonist learns the truth and strangles the woman he had always supposed was "Madeleine." Finally, he bends and kisses her forehead, as if acknowledging that he has loved only a ghost. In truth, the novel wastes that last idea. *Vertigo*, by contrast, seizes it and renders it ambiguous. A nun speaks the film's epitaph – "I heard voices. God have mercy" – which I take to be both a reminder that we are all ghosts, voices in a San Francisco fog, and a fitting response to inevitable human delusion and suffering. Alternatively, such is her sinister apparition as she rises up through the belfry trapdoor that we may take the nun herself to represent whatever is ghostly and anti-life, whatever frowns on joy, whatever would forbid access by mortals to knowledge of higher mysteries which, for all we know, may themselves be ghosts, chimeras.

I Confess also takes after *Bruges-la-Morte*, seeking out what Terry Hale calls "the secret meaning of things" (Rodenbach 6). Historic Quebec City is another candidate for the title Rodenbach awarded Bruges: "the most Catholic of towns" (42). Father Michael Logan (Montgomery Clift) encounters the suspicion and hostility of Quebec's good burghers – represented by the judge and jury at his trial for murder – and must make his inner peace before God. The ending, however, lacks the ambiguity Hitchcock wanted, in which Logan would have gone to his death.

> The book ... called *The Man Who Was Thursday: A Nightmare* [1908] ... was intended to describe the world of wild doubt and despair which the pessimists were generally describing at that date; with just a gleam of hope in some double meaning of the doubt, which even the pessimists felt in some fitful fashion.
> G.K. Chesterton, *The Man Who Was Thursday* (144–45)

Bravo for GKC. I have noted how some of the most gifted writers of the nineteenth century, like Flaubert, managed to despise the masses and cast potentially harmful doubt on many of society's fundamental institutions, including the family. Chesterton would have none of this anti-populism. Wielding his characteristic paradoxes, he typically succeeded in both matching his opponents' brilliance and neutralizing their arguments. Neither side was necessarily right or wrong, of course. We might heed a Buddhist teaching, itself paradoxical, that all views are wrong views (Hanh 56). Reading the boisterous, anti-pessimistic Chesterton, who converted to Catholicism in 1922, helped liberate Hitchcock as a filmmaker. Spoto wisely notes: "It was Chesterton who defended popular literature, Chesterton who pointed out the archetypal fairy-tale structure of police stories, and Chesterton who defended exploration of criminal behavior [on the grounds, for example, that it could remind us of our values]" (*Dark* 40). And it was Chesterton who helped Hitchcock see the nineteenth-century literary scene cogently and comprehensively and then, in Chesterton's word, "transcend" it.

The Wrong Man has an upbeat end-title that many critics have seen as compromise. In fact, Hitchcock was happy to conclude his film that way, for it accorded with what he had taken from Chesterton: a belief that in the final analysis both "life" and hope should be propagated, because the world is ultimately "all right." By contrast, the arch-pessimist Schopenhauer roundly declared our condition "something that it were better should not be" (577). But Chestertonian paradox may encompass another wisdom that commands both these positions simultaneously. Indeed, Schopenhauer's own best insight, Oliver Sacks suggests, "is that the world presents itself to us under two aspects – as Will and [Representation] – and that these two aspects are always distinct and always conjoined. ... To speak in terms of either alone is to lay oneself open to a destructive duality, to the impossibility of constructing a meaningful world" (219). In other words, to adopt either position alone invites chaos.

A classic Chestertonian paradox informs "On the Alleged Optimism of Dickens" (1906), in which Chesterton praises Dickens for the *liveliness* of even his most humble or degraded characters. In Chesterton's view, invoking what he called "the central paradox of reform" (*Dickens* 270), such liveliness showed Dickens's superiority to naturalist writers like Zola and George Gissing. Dickens retained faith in the human race; his was a "transcendentalism" akin to "the religious conception of life" (270). Chesterton's argument allows neither optimism nor pessimism the upper hand: "We must insist with violence upon [the oppressed man's] degradation; we must insist with the same violence upon his dignity. For if we relax by one inch the one assertion, men will say he does not need saving. And if we relax by one inch the other assertion, men will say he is not worth saving" (270). Both assertions, says Chesterton, must be applied simultaneously: the oppressed man is both "a worm and a god" (270).

Such a paradox recalls Flaubert's epiphany about the "half-witted" bourgeoisie whom he suddenly saw as "dans le vrai!" We might call it a case of romantic irony. But Chesterton is talking more specifically about Dickens's style and tone, which both involve *counterpoint*. The result in the hands of a master is engaging, not least because there's a felt connection to life, as in Dickens's argument about the "streaky bacon" nature of melodrama and Hitchcock's response when Truffaut suggested that the essence of the films is fear, sex, and death: "Well, isn't the main thing that they be connected with life?" (Truffaut 319). Counterpoint, paradox, and sudden shifts of tone and perspective occur throughout Hitchcock's films, and they largely constitute those films' deep stylistic appeal, which can be riveting. Consider, for example, the way Manny and his family in *The Wrong Man* are both valorized and critiqued even as they are being thrust, seemingly without recourse, towards the chaos world, or the way Thornhill during the Mount Rushmore climax of *North by Northwest* appears puny but unstoppable, both a worm and a god.

A more purely tactical kind of paradox informs *The Man Who Was Thursday*. This remarkable phantasmagoria is literary-British in several respects, including an absurdist component worthy of Lewis Carroll and Edward Lear, and a picaresque set of incidents. It opens with a confrontation between the hero, Gabriel Syme, working for a secret arm of Scotland Yard, the "philosophical police," and the red-haired anarchist Lucian Gregory. Red hair in British fiction is usually a mark of villainy, and Gregory fits that bill. In representing "anarchy," he is made by Chesterton to stand for everything that the author most detested, not least a hundred years of Romantic and Symbolist/Decadent "pessimism" typified by Joseph Conrad's gloomy novel *The Secret Agent* (1907). Lucian is cocky: "'An artist is identical with an anarchist,' he cried. ... 'The man who throws a bomb is an artist because he prefers a great moment to everything'" (3). Opposing this Nietzschean-toned paradox, which anticipates the comparison of art and murder in Hitchcock's *Rope* (1948), Syme responds with several no less startling, but superior, paradoxes of his own, and the gist of them is this: to an open mind, the most poetic things are the Underground Railway and its timetable. He concludes: "Take your Byron, who commemorates the defeats of man; give me Bradshaw who commemorates his victories. Give me Bradshaw, I say!" (4).

We may be only moderately surprised by the postmodernism of such a sentiment. And we may suppose that it readily appealed to the engineering-trained Hitchcock, long an enthusiast of public transport and its timetables. In turn, we may recall how the pragmatic Thornhill in *North by Northwest* opposes "the art of survival" to the chilly, old-world aesthetics of Vandamm. Both Chesterton and Hitchcock were prepared to confront us with our fundamental values and to tell salutary tales that could make us better appreciate what Chesterton saw to be God's gift of life.

"Oh, we are all Catholics now," claims Syme (8). Comfortable in his faith from an early date, Chesterton was happy in his pages to celebrate "the variety of life" (quoted in Lambert 67). Commentators have reacted to this celebratory impulse in differing ways. Gavin Lambert concludes that the artistry of another Catholic, Graham Greene, excelled Chesterton's by always being "subtly unfaithful to his church," whereas Chesterton had substituted "one kind of bondage for another" (75). Probably some sophisticated aspects of Hitchcock's films, such as their open-endedness, were beyond the author of the Father Brown stories. Yet John Carey not only admires Chesterton but derides the myopic snobbery of numberless twentieth-century writers, including Greene. After noting how sympathetically Chesterton portrays suburbia in *The Man Who Was Thursday*, Carey contrasts him with H.H. Munro ("Saki"), whose story "The Mappined Life" likens suburban man to animals languishing in a zoo (*Intellectuals* 53–54). That story eschews the gentle satire of *Diary of a Nobody* and instead echoes Henrik Ibsen's *The Wild Duck* (1884), but without any saving poetry. So again tone seems the issue. Carey notes how Munro "specializes in wit which is glittering, hard and cruel, and which functions implicitly to elevate him above the vulgar humanity of the masses" (54). Such wit recalls both Wilde, whom Carey invokes, and another Hitchcock favorite, Max Beerbohm, of whom Chesterton observed that he "has every merit except democracy" (*Essays* 25). Yet Hitchcock, a veritable small "c" catholic, clearly was prepared to savor the work of *all* these authors – virtually necessitating his films' capacity for paradox and simultaneity. Chesterton, who so vigorously promoted such qualities in his writing, surely expanded Hitchcock's sensibility as no other English author could have done – not even Dickens, nor another favorite, H.G. Wells, whose intermittent populist sympathies barely overlaid a deep pessimism about humanity's ultimate fate (Carey, *Intellectuals* 118–51).

> You know your choice. You stay in prison, what your time calls duty, honor, self-respect, and you are comfortably safe. Or you are free and crucified. Your only companions, the stones, the thorns, the turning backs; the silence of cities and their hate.
>
> John Fowles, *The French Lieutenant's Woman* (362)

This chapter has been particularly about what Hitchcock took from nineteenth-century England. But equally it has been about how Hitchcock's imagination effectively annihilated "the historical process" in order to make "pure cinema" that was both gripping and meaningful. To speak of Hitchcock as a poet-artist risks forgetting him as an entertainer. Yet the more serious literary borrowings in his films didn't come there by accident, and often they have great resonance. The influence of *Bleak House* on *The Wrong Man* is palpable; the "symbolist" content of *Vertigo* can scarcely be denied; and *North by Northwest* is far from being about "nothing." In a recent article, Terry Teachout claimed that *North by Northwest* "is in truth 'about' excitement pure and simple" (Teachout). But he's mistaken. The film addresses at some level practically every word of the above epigraph from Fowles, drawing on both literary antecedents and Hitchcock's more overtly serious films, like *I Confess* and *The Wrong Man*, to inform it and stamp its authority and wit. Dickens's and Hitchcock's respective emphases on "ghostliness" imply a contrary state: the novelist's intuition that "we [are] all so connected ... without knowing it." Through his "central paradox of reform," Chesterton nurtured Hitchcock in that splendid vision as no other literary figure could have done, allowing the films a firm rhetorical basis.

The ambivalence of Hitchcock's films wasn't unique, even in Hollywood. On the contrary, it was Hollywood's genius to make films that appealed to a broad spectrum of viewers. Those films might simultaneously valorize and mock the universal subject matter they depicted, typically marriage and the family. The films of Billy Wilder leap to mind. Nonetheless, in various ways, Hitchcock's films *were* unique, notably in the "almost scientific clarity" (Houseman 235) with which their director sought to maximize each viewer's emotional involvement and to make that viewer feel alive. The films were on fertile ground whenever an identification figure intimated that he or she couldn't get enough of the heft and variety of life. In that respect, *Rear Window*, whose literary borrowings range from Hoffmann's "The Sandman" (1816) and "My Cousin's Corner Window" (1825) to H.G. Wells's "Through a Window" (1894), may be the quintessential Hitchcock film. It's pure, reflexive cinema, all right, about making and watching images, yet it carries a Symbolist (or perhaps Pirandellian) message. You can argue that the images belong to the photographer Jeff alone, and are purely subjective, that *no* particular message is implied. But isn't that fact simply another part of Hitchcock's grand design?

Works Cited

I am grateful to Richard Franklin (1948–2007), who loaned me his copies of studio screenplays for several Hitchcock films.

Ackroyd, Peter. *Albion: The Origins of the English Imagination*. London: Chatto and Windus, 2002.

Baer, William. *Classic American Films: Conversations with the Screenwriters*. Westport, CT: Praeger, 2008.

Barzun, Jacques. "Romanticism." *The Penguin Encyclopedia of Horror and the Supernatural.* Ed. Jack Sullivan. New York: Viking Penguin, 1986. 355–62.

Binion, Rudolph. "Fiction as Social Fantasy: Europe's Domestic Crisis of 1879–1914." *Journal of Social History*, Summer 1994. Web. 19 June 2008.

Bogdanovich, Peter. *Who the Devil Made It.* New York: Knopf, 1997.

Bristow, Joseph, ed. *The Oxford Book of Adventure Stories.* Oxford: Oxford UP, 1996.

Buchan, John. *The Complete Richard Hannay.* London: Penguin, 1992.

Buchan, John. *Memory Hold-the-Door.* London: Hodder and Stoughton, 1940.

Carey, John. *The Intellectuals and the Masses: Pride and Prejudice among the Literary Intelligentsia 1880–1939.* London: Faber and Faber, 1992.

Carey, John. *The Violent Effigy: A Study of Dickens' Imagination.* London: Faber and Faber, 1979.

Chandler, Charlotte. *It's Only a Movie: Alfred Hitchcock: A Personal Biography.* New York: Simon and Schuster, 2005.

Chesterton, G.K. *Essays by G.K. Chesterton.* Ed. John Guest. London: Collins, 1939.

Chesterton, G.K. "On the Alleged Optimism of Dickens." *Charles Dickens.* 1906. New York: Schocken, 1965. 263–87.

Chesterton, G.K. *The Man Who Was Thursday: A Nightmare.* 1908. Ware: Wordsworth, 1995.

Commanville, Caroline. *Souvenirs sur Gustave Flaubert.* Paris: Ferroud, 1895.

Dickens, Charles. *Bleak House.* 1852–53. London: Penguin, 1985.

Dickens, Charles. *The Old Curiosity Shop.* 1840. Harmondsworth: Penguin, 1972.

Dickens, Charles. *Oliver Twist.* 1837–38. Oxford: Oxford UP, 1982.

Dickens, Charles. *Our Mutual Friend.* 1864–65. London: Penguin, 1985.

Doss-Davezac, Shehira. "Schopenhauer According to the Symbolists: The Philosophical Roots of Late Nineteenth-Century French Aesthetic Theory." *Schopenhauer, Philosophy, and the Arts.* Ed. Dale Jacquette. Cambridge: Cambridge UP, 1996. 249–76.

Duncan, David. *Worse Than Murder.* New York: Pocket, 1954. Rpt. of *The Bramble Bush.* 1948.

Emerson, Ralph Waldo. *Collected Poems and Translations.* New York: Library of America, 1994.

Epstein, Norrie. *The Friendly Dickens.* New York: Viking Penguin, 1998.

Flaubert, Gustave. *Madame Bovary: Life in a Country Town.* 1856. Trans. Gerard Hopkins. Introduction by Terence Cave. Oxford: Oxford UP, 1981.

Forster, John. *The Life of Charles Dickens.* Vol. 1. Philadelphia: Lippincott, 1874.

Fowles, John. *The French Lieutenant's Woman.* 1969. Boston: Little, Brown, 1998.

Goethe, Johann Wolfgang von. *Goethe's Faust: The Original German and a New Translation and Introduction by Walter Kaufmann: Part One and Sections From Part Two.* Garden City, NY: Doubleday Anchor, 1962.

Greene, Graham. *Our Man In Havana.* 1958. Harmondsworth: Penguin, 1962.

Haggard, H. Rider. *King Solomon's Mines.* 1885. Paulton: Purnell, 1985.

Hanh, Thich Nhat. *The Heart of the Buddha's Teaching.* New York: Broadway, 1999.

Hirsh, Sharon L. *Symbolism and Modern Urban Society.* Cambridge: Cambridge UP, 2004.

Houseman, John. *Unfinished Business: A Memoir.* London: Columbus, 1988.

Humphries, Patrick. *The Films of Alfred Hitchcock.* London: Bison, 1986.

Hurley, Neil P. *Soul in Suspense: Hitchcock's Fright and Delight.* Metuchen, NJ: Scarecrow, 1993.

Kierkegaard, Søren. *The Living Thoughts of Kierkegaard.* Ed. W.H. Auden. Bloomington: Indiana UP, 1963.

Kipling, Rudyard. *Kim*. 1901. Oxford: Oxford UP, 1987.

Kracauer, Siegfried. *From Caligari to Hitler: A Psychological History of the German Film*. 1947. New York: Noonday, 1959.

Krohn, Bill. *Hitchcock at Work*. London: Phaidon, 2000.

Lambert, Gavin. *The Dangerous Edge*. London: Barrie and Jenkins, 1975.

Maugham, W. Somerset. *The World's Ten Greatest Novels*. Greenwich, CT: Fawcett, 1966.

McGilligan, Patrick. *Alfred Hitchcock: A Life in Darkness and Light*. New York: HarperCollins, 2003.

Mogg, Ken. *The Alfred Hitchcock Story*. London: Titan, 1999.

Mogg, Ken. "Alfred Hitchcock: Master of Paradox." *Senses of Cinema* May 2005: n. pag. Web. 22 Mar. 2010.

Münsterberg, Hugo. *The Photoplay: A Psychological Study*. New York: Appleton: 1916.

Peary, Danny. *Guide for the Film Fanatic*. New York: Simon and Schuster, 1986.

Rodenbach, Georges. *Bruges-la-Morte*. 1892. Trans. Thomas Duncan, revised and with an Introduction by Terry Hale. London: Atlas, 1993.

Sacks, Oliver. *Awakenings*. 1973. London: Pan, 1982.

"Sapper" (H.C. McNeile). *Bull-Dog Drummond: His Four Rounds with Carl Peterson as Described by Sapper*. London: Hodder and Stoughton, 1950.

Schopenhauer, Arthur. *The World as Will and Representation*. Vol. 2. Trans. E.F.J. Payne. 1959. New York: Dover, 1969.

Simenon, Georges. *Lettre à mon juge*. 1947. Trans. by Louise Varèse as *Act of Passion*. Harmondsworth: Penguin, 1965.

Sinyard, Neil. *Filming Literature: The Art of Screen Adaptation*. London: Croom Helm, 1986.

Spoto, Donald. *The Dark Side of Genius: The Life of Alfred Hitchcock*. Boston: Little, Brown, 1983.

Spoto, Donald. *Spellbound by Beauty: Alfred Hitchcock and His Leading Ladies*. New York: Harmony, 2008.

Stefano, Joseph. "Psycho." Screenplay. Revised 1 Dec. 1959. *Screenplays for You*. N.p. Web. 31 May 2010.

Tanski, Julia. "The Symbolist Woman in Alfred Hitchcock's Films." *Hitchcock and Art: Fatal Coincidences*. Ed. Dominique Païni and Guy Cogeval. Montreal: Montreal Museum of Fine Arts/Mazzotta, 2000.

Taylor, John Russell. *Hitch: The Life and Work of Alfred Hitchcock*. New York: Pantheon, 1978.

Teachout, Terry. "The Trouble With Alfred Hitchcock." *Commentary* Feb. 2009. Web. 9 Mar. 2009.

Truffaut, François, with the collaboration of Helen G. Scott. *Hitchcock*. Rev. ed. New York: Simon and Schuster, 1984.

Wellek, René. *A History of Modern Criticism: 1750–1950*. Vol. 2. New Haven: Yale UP, 1955.

Williams, Tony. "John Buchan and Alfred Hitchcock." *The John Buchan Journal* 33 (Autumn 2005): 10–22.

3

Hitchcock and Early Filmmakers

Charles Barr

A cinema-obsessive from youth, Alfred Hitchcock can be seen as a movie brat ahead of his time. Unlike those of the Lucas-Spielberg generation, he had no film school or film history classes to go to; like most filmmakers who began in the silent period, he did not go to university at all. But where others had studied at the University of Life, he constructed his own single-minded program of vocational study and training. As he told John Russell Taylor, looking back in old age: "I left school at the age of fourteen, went into engineering drawing and from there by a succession of logical steps into the cinema" ("Surviving" 60).

Others found their way into this young medium in unpredictable or indirect ways. Many came from theater, others had been "adventurers," traveling and doing a variety of jobs before drifting into films. Hitchcock's route was different. He spent a few years working for the Henley Telegraph and Cable Company, and went often to see plays in the West End of London, but these were, by his own account, two of the "logical steps" toward cinema, giving him design skills and insights into dramatic structure. Even his precocious knowledge of railway and shipping timetables led not to travel and exploration but to a *fantasy* control of time and space that would feed neatly into film construction. He told Taylor flatly, "I have no outside interests" ("Surviving" 60), and this seems to have been more or less true from the start. Theater and design and timetables, as well as his extensive reading, were subsidiary topics in Hitchcock's self-created film school.

But the central topic, naturally, was cinema itself. Alongside his assiduous filmgoing, he was a regular reader of the trade papers from his mid-teens, before judging, in 1920, that the time was right to join a production company; then he worked his way through a succession of subsidiary roles before becoming a director in 1925. The following year he married a colleague, Alma Reville,

A Companion to Alfred Hitchcock, First Edition. Edited by Thomas Leitch and Leland Poague.
© 2011 Thomas Leitch and Leland Poague. Published 2011 by Blackwell Publishing Ltd.

who was one day younger than him, but who had herself been working in the industry since the age of sixteen.

He was, then, to a remarkable extent, immersed in cinema, shaped by cinema, as he began his own fifty-year career as a director.

In the 1972 addendum to their original book-length interview, François Truffaut asked Hitchcock: "Are you in favor of the teaching of cinema in universities?" Hitchcock replied: "Only on condition that they teach cinema since the era of Méliès and that the students learn how to make silent films, because there is no better form of training. Talking pictures often served merely to introduce the theater into the studios" (Truffaut 334). He insists here on going back not simply to silent cinema, but to its very early stages, the time of Georges Méliès, whose short films are, like so many of their time, virtually devoid of editing. Hitchcock's professional interest in the medium is rooted in the pre-classical period. He dated his serious commitment as beginning soon after he left school in 1913, a year which in the now widely-accepted periodization of film history belongs to a transitional stage between early or primitive cinema and the emergence of the classical system – a system that is based, among other things, on consistent conventions for handling space and time through editing. The standard work *The Classical Hollywood Cinema* by David Bordwell, Janet Staiger, and Kristin Thompson convincingly suggests 1917 as the key year, if one has to be chosen, for the coming together of this system (231).

Hitchcock would become a vigorous proponent and exploiter of classical editing strategies, but he would also direct the two films made within mainstream cinema which most rigorously *renounce* editing: *Under Capricorn* (1949) and, even more so, its predecessor, *Rope* (1948), whose 79-minute narrative is made up of only eleven shots. He would later tell Truffaut that these experiments were misguided, but one doesn't have to accept this retraction, and the fact remains that he was, at the time, moved not only to conceive this idea of minimizing editing, but to follow it through with intense commitment and skill.

This may seem a paradox, but in the wider perspective it surely is not. Combined with his intelligence and staying power, Hitchcock's very distinctive formation makes him arguably the nearest we have to a universal representative of the medium of cinema, testing out an exceptionally wide range of its potentialities. He spans American and European cinema, commercial and experimental, silent and sound (not to mention cinema and television) – and montage and non-montage, or *pre*-montage: he reaches back toward the time of Méliès.

In describing Hitchcock, Jane Sloan astutely observes that "far from the lonely romantic artist, he appears to have been more of a sponge, eager to adopt the point of view that would sell, and open to any idea that seemed good, insistent only that it fit his design" (37). This process goes right back to his early years. He made himself as near as anyone could get to a *tabula rasa*, a blank page, ready to absorb and be imprinted with whatever was of potential use, from whatever source.

Four Currents

In his own acknowledgment of inspirations and collaborators, Hitchcock was selective, inconsistent, and often grudging. The more distant others were from him, the readier he was to give them a bit of credit; he was an expert in covering his tracks when he wanted to. In what follows, I draw especially on John Russell Taylor's authorized biography, the closest Hitchcock got to telling his own story, much more so than in the Truffaut interview; it is revealing both for what Hitchcock gives away and for what he conceals.

One person he did always give credit to was D.W. Griffith. For aspiring filmmakers in Britain as elsewhere, *Intolerance* (1916) was a major landmark. Michael Powell, when he caught up with it in his late teens, called it "the greatest experience I had had," and saw it twice in a week: "there has never been a film director like Griffith" (94). Herbert Wilcox, a decade older than Hitchcock, was preparing to enter the industry around the same time as him: "I would study *Intolerance*, see it several times and chart on paper the method Griffith used" (50). He must have analyzed both the editing of its individual stories and the way in which the four stories, set in different eras, were edited together to illustrate the theme of the film's title. Maybe Hitchcock did the same. In the words of Griffith himself, quoted in a playbill for the film's New York premiere: "The stories begin like four currents looked at from a hilltop. At first the four currents flow apart, slowly and quietly. But as they flow, they grow nearer and nearer together, and faster and faster, until in the end, in the last act, they mingle in one mighty river of expressed emotion" (quoted in Hansen 330).

I see this not just as an inspiration to the teenage Hitchcock, as to so many, but as a potent image for the way his own career would develop. There are four main currents, issuing from four different countries and cinemas: those of America, Germany, Russia, and his native Britain. They progressively flow together, creating the "one mighty river" of Hitchcock's cinema.

There may be smaller tributaries, from France or Sweden for instance, but these four are the dominant ones.[1] And "expressed emotion" is an apt term for the end product, anticipating one of Hitchcock's most consistent interview themes. In the early 1930s Hitchcock said to Stephen Watts that "[t]he basis of the cinema's appeal is emotional" (245). In the early 1960s, he phrased it this way to Truffaut: "Summing it up, one might say that the screen rectangle must be charged with emotion" (61).

It is tempting, in line with his own narrative of his career, to trace just three main currents, springing up successively: first, the influence of America, both through his early viewing of the work of Griffith and others, and through his first film job: working with Hollywood personnel for the short-lived British outpost of Famous Players–Lasky at Islington (1921–22). Soon after this comes the influence of Germany, again through both viewing and employment: as art director, and then director, on Anglo-German co-productions shot in German studios (1924–25). Finally comes the influence of Soviet cinema, starting in the later 1920s, when the films of Pudovkin and Eisenstein especially, supported by the writing and lecturing of both the filmmakers and sympathetic commentators, are making a big impact in the West.

That is the familiar framework, plausible as far as it goes, charting the formation of Hitchcock as a cosmopolitan filmmaker absorbing lessons about the medium from three pioneering schools: Hollywood narrative, German image-making, Soviet montage. He floats free, in this reading, of the British cinema which provides until 1939 his main base, but which can teach him little, leaving him all the freer to create his own "pick and mix" version of cinema, untethered to any distinct and positive national tradition. (Compare the wine trade. The established producing countries like France and Italy and Germany naturally favor their own wines, but Britain, with no production of its own to speak of, has historically constituted a more balanced and eclectic market. Hitchcock was like a wine connoisseur – indeed, he would become one himself – ready to use what came to him from a range of high-quality overseas producers.)

That framework, however, needs adjusting. The chronology is not as neat as the three-stage model makes it seem, partly because Hitchcock's British collaborators and contemporaries are by no means negligible. They constitute an important fourth current, a lot stronger than that of British winemaking, and they help to mediate and to anticipate elements of the other three.

Reville and Stannard

Two of his closest early associates start work in the British film industry in the mid-1910s, several years before he does, intensely caught up in it as it develops, in hesitant parallel with Hollywood, out of the transitional period. For a time, they are employed together at one of the more progressive production companies, London Films, but neither of them teams up with Hitchcock until the mid-1920s. They are Eliot Stannard, who in 1925 becomes the regular screenwriter on his block of nine silent films before *Blackmail* (1929), and Alma Reville, who in 1926 becomes his wife. Having worked as assistant director on his first three films, she remains a frequent collaborator on the script side, though not always receiving screen credit.[2]

Reville cannot be seen simply as an adjunct to her husband, duplicating his own journey. Like him, but more briefly, she works with the mainly American team at Famous Players–Lasky British (FLPB); that is where they first meet, in passing, in 1921; later, she goes with him to Germany. But, unlike him, she had served an initial apprenticeship at the heart of the British industry. If he himself was, as he liked to emphasize, American-trained, then she was British-trained. Recent research by

Nathalie Morris has laid out the extent of Reville's work at London Films and then Stoll in the five years before her move to FPLB in 1921. She worked on cutting and continuity for the prolific British director Maurice Elvey, even acting a role for him in *The Life Story of David Lloyd George* (1918).

Elvey's most consistent screenwriter at this time was Eliot Stannard. Morris plausibly suggests that their working relationship may have led Reville to recommend, or approve, this dynamic character as an appropriate writing collaborator for Hitchcock five years later (50).

But it is very possible that Hitchcock, as a systematic reader of film publications, would have had his eye on him already. In May–June 1918 Stannard wrote a high-profile series of five articles for the leading British trade paper *Kinematograph Weekly*, drawing on his extensive experience as a screenwriter since 1914. In addition, he gave lectures to professional bodies, which the paper reported, and contributed a booklet on "Writing Screen Plays" to a ten-part series on cinema published in 1920.

Even in the unlikely event that Hitchcock was unaware of all these items, they at least provide clear evidence of the strong *affinity* between the ideas of the two future collaborators. They contain unmistakable prophecies of some of the pronouncements about the medium that would later become familiar from Hitchcock's own discourse, dicta dealing with narrative construction, editing, and the economical use of telling detail. The 1920 booklet contains, for instance, a brilliantly lucid exercise based on this situation: "Let us suppose a child is suddenly taken ill and, while the distracted mother watches over the invalid, the father rushes off for the doctor" (16). The ponderousness of a representation tied to real time is contrasted with the manipulation of time and audience response made possible by judicious editing, laid out at the scenario stage. Key terms in the exposition are *cross-cutting*, *suspense*, and – a superb coinage – *time-anxiety*. The analysis clearly evokes Griffith, whose methods were, as we have seen, an inspiration to Hitchcock, as to so many others, including Eisenstein and Pudovkin – but this is years before any of these three were active as theorists or filmmakers.

Equally striking is the way Stannard anticipates some of the famous tropes of Soviet montage. In "The Use of Symbols in Scenarios," for example, he describes a scene he had scripted for Elvey's 1917 film *Justice*, whose leading character is imprisoned. "In order that you may more fully realise the horrors of solitary confinement I have shown a wild bird at liberty soaring upwards into the sky; the mental agony of the guilty is contrasted by the mental innocence of children playing in the sunshine." Compare the scene in *Mother* (1926), ten years later, where Pudovkin cuts from the imprisoned Pavel to the scenes of children and nature outside – a montage effect that he and others after him would make much use of in constructing their theories of film art. *Justice* has been lost, but the Elvey–Stannard collaboration of the following year, *Nelson*, survives. Before it goes into its main flashback narrative, it cuts between the German Kaiser and shots of a peacock, to convey his vanity. This too anticipates, by ten years, a celebrated instance of Soviet montage, the more elaborate cutting between Kerensky and peacock in an early scene of Eisenstein's *October* (1927). While it is unlikely that Eisenstein ever saw or heard about *Nelson*, the point is again the affinity. The current of British thinking about cinema, as represented by Eliot Stannard – very British, working at the heart of the native industry, but manifestly open to a wide range of ideas about the formal possibilities of the medium – is ready to impinge in a direct and fertile way upon Hitchcock some years later.

But before that, Hitchcock gets his own first involvement in the medium as a participant.

American Training

You have to remember that I was American-trained. When you entered the doors of that studio, you could have been in Hollywood. Everyone was an American. The writers were American, the directors were American.

Hitchcock, interviewed by Mike Scott for Granada TV, 1966

The studio at Islington in north London had been built by FPL to accommodate its British production arm. They pulled out after two years, and records of their presence are tantalizingly sparse. It seems that twelve features, all relatively modest, were produced, and that none of them survives. Hitchcock created title cards for some, perhaps all, of them, working first as an outside freelance and then leaving his day job at Henley's when offered full-time work around the studio.

The twelve films had, between them, five directors, all of whom otherwise worked entirely in Hollywood. Four were made by the Scottish-born Donald Crisp, and two each by Paul Powell, Hugh Ford, George Fitzmaurice, and John S. Robertson.

There was a similar continuity in the writing team, all women. According to Taylor's biography, "they ran a little factory whipping the material into shape, mostly from pre-existing plays or novels. ... There was little these ladies did not know about the technique of screen writing, and in Alfred Hitchcock they found an eager and attentive pupil" (*Hitch* 40). This rapid processing of source material sounds similar to the way Stannard had been operating for years elsewhere, and it is also interesting, prefiguring the Reville association, that two of the women worked with directors to whom they were married: Ouida Bergère on the two films directed by George Fitzmaurice, and Josephine Lovett on the two by John S. Robertson.

Fitzmaurice may have impressed Hitchcock with the pre-planned discipline of his working methods – Spoto (55–56) quotes a 1916 article by him, describing this approach – but Robertson must have impressed him as well, since in 1939 he named two of his films in a list of ten favorites that he was induced to provide for the New York press soon after moving from Britain (McGilligan 234). It's not clear how considered or serious the list was; surprisingly, it includes no film by Griffith or by

F.W. Murnau. All are silent films from the 1920s, apart from *I Am a Fugitive from a Chain Gang* (Mervyn Le Roy, 1932); all are American, apart from one German film, *Vaudeville* (aka *Variety*, E.A. Dupont, 1925). And it includes two by John S. Robertson, one made shortly before, and one shortly after, his brief time at Islington: *Sentimental Tommy* (1921) and *The Enchanted Cottage* (1924), based on plays by J.M. Barrie and Arthur Wing Pinero, authors who had made a strong early impression on Hitchcock. Robertson, who was two decades older than him and whose directing career ran from 1916 to 1935, is an obvious subject for more research.

One can speculate, too, about the contacts Hitchcock would have had with a third member of the FLPB directing team, Donald Crisp, whose association with Griffith went back at least as far as *Birth of Nation* (1915) and who had recently played Lillian Gish's sadistic father in *Broken Blossoms* (1919). Here is a direct link to the man who was incomparably the most influential filmmaker of Hitchcock's pre-Islington years, for him as for others.

Hitchcock routinely spoke of the impact of three of Griffith's major features, *Birth of a Nation*, *Intolerance*, and *Way Down East* (1922), and of the tension of their climactic chases. In his filmgoing youth he must also surely have seen some of the remarkable series of some 450 short films that Griffith directed between 1908 and 1913, without at the time necessarily knowing who made them, since they were publicized in the name of the company, Biograph, not the director. The modern story in *Intolerance*, the narrative strand that Hitchcock understandably dwelt on in his recollections, is a summation of two of the key strategies that Griffith had refined across those earlier films: the creation of suspense at the climax through crosscutting between different spaces and actions, and the heightening of both suspense and pathos through the selection of telling detail, such as the nervous hands of Mae Marsh as she awaits the courtroom verdict on her husband, and the set of knives waiting to activate the mechanism that will hang him if the rescuers fail to get there in time. These are precisely the strategies that Stannard's writings of 1918–20 picked up on and explicated, as later would the Russians.

Hitchcock himself reflected on the impact of American cinema, and of Griffith, in two early articles. In November 1927, in a London daily paper, he stressed the need to make the most of the rich opportunities for telling English stories by using the basic tools developed and tested by American film directors: "They have learnt, as it were, to put the nouns, verbs, and adjectives of the film language together" (quoted in Spoto 102). In February 1931, in *Film Weekly*, he wrote a vigorous encomium of Griffith under the title "A Columbus of the Screen," honoring him as the great pioneer of the medium, "the head of our profession." Some of it reads like undigested publicity material for Griffith's current film, *Abraham Lincoln* (1930), but we hear Hitchcock's voice clearly in some of the details, notably in his focus on a transitional film made in 1914, between the Biograph shorts and the epics: "Hardly any filmgoer of today has ever heard of 'The Avenging Conscience,' but that picture made in the first year of the War, was the forerunner and inspiration of most of the modern German films, to which we owe so much artistically" (81).

The Avenging Conscience (1914), a loose adaptation from Edgar Allan Poe, builds up to a long scene in which a murderer is questioned by a detective in the house where he has buried the body. A tense montage cuts back and forth between faces, tapping feet and fingers, nervous hands, and a clock face. One can see why the film appealed to Hitchcock in formal terms for this artful deployment of the "nouns, verbs, and adjectives" of the emerging film language, while his claim (whether historically correct or not) about the film's influence on Germany helps to blur the edges of the conventional narrative of his formation. Some of the key things that he would respond to in German cinema, when he got to know it a decade later, are indeed anticipated here by Griffith in a highly self-reflexive narrative, complete with distortions and superimpositions, of a young man who has rebelled against an oppressive father-figure and declines into nightmare and madness. Like *The Cabinet of Dr. Caligari* (Robert Wiene, 1920), it even has a teasing dream framework.

Nor was it just Griffith. Late in life, he told Charlotte Chandler that "I was thrilled by the movies of D.W. Griffith and the early French director Alice Guy" (Chandler 39). Guy's career ended in 1920; in 1913 she too had, in America, made a film of a Poe story, *The Pit and the Pendulum*. It does not survive, but one guesses that Hitchcock would have had this film in mind, since Poe was an author so important to him, as was Stevenson for "Strange Case of Dr. Jekyll and Mr. Hyde" (1886), a story he was still trying to film in the 1960s. Two versions of that tale were made almost simultaneously in 1920: in Germany (as *Der Januskopf*) by F.W. Murnau, and in Hollywood by none other than John S. Robertson. Hitchcock may have had no chance to see the former, which seems never to have been screened in England, and to have been quickly lost, but he would surely have seen the latter when it opened in London in July 1921, around the time that he was becoming a very junior colleague of its director at Islington.

So Hollywood was an important formative influence for Hitchcock not just for a whole range of formal and technical reasons – including its photography, which he perceived as being less flat than the British norm (Truffaut 31) – but because its narratives were already tapping into dark areas of guilt, the repressed, and the unconscious.

The Impact of Germany

My models were forever after the German filmmakers of 1924 and 1925. They were trying very hard to express ideas in purely visual terms.

(Quoted in Spoto 68)

The impact of German cinema on Hitchcock was all the stronger because it was delayed, and then came in a rush. Within the four years 1923–26 he worked in two

German studios, observed German production methods, saw new German films, and had a chance to start catching up on earlier ones.

German films had been excluded from the British market for nearly a decade. A five-year postwar ban was lifted a year early, and imports resumed from late 1922. Fritz Lang's films soon had prominent screenings in London: *Dr. Mabuse* (1922) in March 1923, *Der müde Tod* (1921) in February 1924, and *Siegfried* (1924) in May 1924. Hitchcock by then had made his first visit to Germany, as art director and scriptwriter for *The Blackguard* (1925), shot at UFA, where he admired the forest set created for *Siegfried* before dismantling it to make room for sets of his own.

He had stayed on at Islington after FPLB left, as one of the skeleton staff of what was briefly a "four-wall" facility. When the studio was bought by a team headed by Michael Balcon, Hitchcock became a member of the new, internationally-minded Gainsborough company. Balcon saw the value of using the superior technical resources of German studios. After *The Blackguard*, he set up a two-film co-production deal with Emelka in Munich, enabling Hitchcock to direct *The Pleasure Garden* (1925) and then *The Mountain Eagle* (1926).

Late in 1925, the Film Society was launched in London with the mission of showing films from outside the normal commercial repertoire: interesting new films and worthwhile revivals. Hitchcock was an early member; although nothing is on record, the consensus is that he attended a fair number of screenings in its early years. The Society's first few seasons were dominated by German films, old and new, including *Caligari* in its sixth program (February 1926) and *Dr. Mabuse* in its tenth (November 1926). But Hitchcock is specific in his focus on the years 1924 and 1925. The films from these dates that we know him to be referring to are Murnau's *The Last Laugh* (1924), Lang's two-part *Die Nibelungen* (*Siegfried* and *Kriemhild's Revenge*, 1924) and Dupont's *Vaudeville*. In addition, he may have seen Paul Leni's *Waxworks* from 1924 (the opening Film Society feature in October 1925); from other years, he certainly saw Lang's *Der müde Tod* (*Destiny*), and probably several others as well, including Murnau's *Nosferatu*, also from 1921, screened by the Society in December 1928.

Given the limits of this essay, I shall focus on Murnau, both because he seems the most solid influence and because the links with Lang, Dupont, and others have been extensively discussed elsewhere, notably in fine scholarly articles by Thomas Elsaesser and Sidney Gottlieb. The influence of *Vaudeville* is apparent in the fairground scene that begins *The Ring* in 1927, and the trapeze action at the circus that ends *Murder!* in 1930, a scene that has no equivalent in the source novel; it was Hitchcock himself, along with Reville, who adapted the novel, and *The Ring* was based on his own original script. The young Hitchcock must have been impressed by the architecture of Lang's sets and his framing, and by the intensity with which he orchestrated the often hypnotic acts of looking by his protagonists. Indeed two of the prime critical texts on Lang – the Jenkins and Gunning books respectively – are subtitled "The Image and the *Look*" and "Allegories of *Vision* and *Modernity*."

Along with Griffith, Murnau remains the only director to whom Hitchcock consistently gave unreserved credit. At UFA, he had been able to watch him at work on *The Last Laugh* and to talk to him. The film opened in London in March 1925 with much publicity, introduced in person by its star, Emil Jannings. Six elements in particular can be argued to have influenced Hitchcock's own practice. Some of them are found in other German films of the time, some of them he would have been exposed to elsewhere, but they are deployed and blended with a confidence that must have been even more impressive at the time than it is now:

(1)   There are no intertitles other than one which introduces the story's epilogue, plus the diegetic insert of the letter informing the hotel porter (Jannings) of his demotion. Narrative, relationships, and emotions are conveyed lucidly by visual means. Hitchcock would aim, not always with full success, to reduce the need for titles in his silent films, and, correspondingly, to reduce the reliance on dialogue in his sound films.

(2)   One means of conveying the porter's experience is by subjective camerawork, including unrealistically distorted images. From start to end of his directing career, Hitchcock would be ready to use such images: for Ivor Novello in *Downhill* (1927), Margaret Lockwood in *The Lady Vanishes* (1938), and Tippi Hedren in *Marnie* (1964), to name but three.

(3)   The impression of a bustling city is created by the skillful use of miniatures, not only of buildings but of vehicles and even of people. A wide-angle scene at the railway station – the porter goes there to deposit, and later to reclaim, his old uniform – is created by a blend of miniatures with real trains and people. Hitchcock witnessed this on set, and never forgot it. "What you can see on the set does not matter, explained Murnau – the only truth that counts is what you see on the screen" (Taylor, *Hitch* 57). In some of his 1930s films he would relish playing with comparable miniatures, as in the final chase of *Number Seventeen* (1932) and the initial establishing shot of *The Lady Vanishes*, and he was still, in shooting *Family Plot* (1976), his final film, paraphrasing Murnau's lesson about set construction: "Remember, all that matters, all that exists for the audience, is what is on the screen" (Taylor, *Hitch* 298).

(4)   Although those two station scenes are static, the film also deploys what became celebrated as German cinema's "unchained camera": freely moving, both for objective shots, as in the initial movement down in the hotel lift and then out from it, to establish the dramatic space, and for subjective ones. Hitchcock would initially be sparing in his movement of the camera, saving it up for special purposes, as for Novello's stagger through the streets of London on his way home at the end of *Downhill*, but some of his most memorable scenes, scattered through his work, involve Murnau's kind of unchained camera, including much of *Rope* and *Under Capricorn*.

(5)   *The Last Laugh* was thoroughly storyboarded in advance. The juxtaposition, in the DVD edition of the film in the Masters of Cinema series, of sketches with the corresponding film shots is similar to what has been done with a number of Hitchcock films. If Hitchcock was temperamentally predisposed to such a system, the encounter with Murnau reinforced this.

(6)   The porter's loss of his dignified job exactly coincides with the marriage of the young woman who is described on the credits as his niece, though one might

otherwise take her to be his daughter. This kind of oedipal intensity is already a common element in narrative cinema; a precisely comparable situation is found as early as Griffith's Biograph film *The Old Actor* (1912), with the young Mary Pickford in the daughter role. Unlike the early Griffith, Murnau underlines the tensions through eloquent shot/reverse-shot cutting between the old man and the young woman.

While the German influence has plausibly been seen operating in such earlier films as *The Lodger* (1926) and *The Ring*, both Hitchcock and Truffaut, at different points in their conversation (31 and 55), make connections, in passing, between Murnau and the apparently ultra-English rural comedy *The Farmer's Wife* (1928), adapted by Stannard from a successful play. This link is plausible too; indeed, as if in playful acknowledgment of *The Last Laugh*, the film showcases at some length a uniform very similar to that of the hotel porter, into which the farmer's servant resentfully struggles in order to greet guests arriving at a tea party. At a deeper level, the sadness of the widowed farmer as he watches his newly-married daughter prepare to depart with her husband is conveyed wordlessly, purely by the intercutting of looks. His musings about possible remarriage are expressed in subjective shots, imagining the respective candidates occupying a fireside chair. And in this his seventh film, Hitchcock is ready for the first time to make extensive use of the unchained camera. Its fluid movement around the house both counters the danger of staginess and beautifully communicates the active spirit of the woman with whom it generally moves, the housekeeper who is destined to become the farmer's wife.

The impact of *Nosferatu* appears later. I am assuming that Hitchcock saw it either during his time in Germany or when it was screened at the Film Society in 1928 (copyright problems stemming from the film's unlicensed use of Bram Stoker's novel made a commercial run impossible). As it happens, the film's screenwriter, Henrik Galeen, was in 1928 working at the same studio as Hitchcock, British International Pictures, one of a number of German personnel, Dupont included, who were brought over at this time. Galeen directed one film there, now lost, *After the Verdict* (1929), from a script by Alma Reville, and I like to think that this connection ensured that Hitchcock and Reville made a point of seeing the film on which Galeen and Murnau had collaborated. Two of Hitchcock's American films evoke it quite strongly. It has often been noted that Joseph Cotten's Uncle Charlie, who travels to Santa Rosa in *Shadow of a Doubt* (1943), is coded as vampire-like through a number of details, and in two structural ways: the ominous journey he takes from a corrupt East to bring infection to a house and a town, and the quasi-telepathic communication set up between him and young Charlie (Teresa Wright), recalling that between the young bride Ellen and the vampire Nosferatu. Moreover, when he arrives in town, Nosferatu takes up residence not in the same house as the vulnerable couple but in the large building behind it, which looms up oppressively across from their *rear window*. The last section of the film has the woman looking out obsessively at it, both dreading and inviting the vampire, who duly crosses over to her, like Thorwald in *Rear Window* (1954) crossing to confront Jefferies. The opposite space is, in both films, like a dream-screen, or nightmare-screen, where repressed forces dwell, or on to which they are projected. In both, the two spaces are rarely shown in the same shot, but are consistently linked by editing.

Soviet Theory

Hitchcock himself always related *Rear Window* to Pudovkin, montage, and the Kuleshov effect, comparing the way he manipulated close-ups of James Stewart, as Jefferies, with the way Lev Kuleshov (born, like Hitchcock, in 1899) had, in the famous exercise, manipulated close-ups of Ivan Moszhukin. Intercut Stewart with a cute dog, and his expression looks kindly. Intercut him with a scantily-clad young woman, and he becomes a dirty old man – even though the close-ups of him are exactly the same. This process is "the purest expression of a cinematic idea" (Truffaut 214).

Along with what he learned from Murnau about the design of the image, this is the big insight about the art of cinema that Hitchcock most consistently recycled. The Germans and the Russians have commonly been bracketed together as the two main influences on Hitchcock's mature cinema, but the German one is surely stronger. Essentially, Pudovkin and Kuleshov were telling him what he already knew.

The Soviet montage films were shown later, and less prominently, in London than those of Lang and Murnau. Their directors' careers began later, the British censors blocked any public screenings, and even Film Society screenings were delayed by a combination of censorship issues and Soviet bureaucracy. Eisenstein's *Potemkin* (1925) had been shown to great acclaim in Hollywood in September 1926 but was not presented by the Film Society until November 1929, the year in which the first English edition of Pudovkin's *Film Technique* appeared. Hitchcock's own directing career was by then well advanced.

It is true that he already had an indirect connection with these filmmakers through Ivor Montagu, translator of their works, a Communist, and co-founder of the Film Society. Montagu had worked with Hitchcock on the re-editing and titling of *The Lodger*, and then on his next two films, *Downhill* and *Easy Virtue* (1927); they would renew the association at Gaumont-British in the mid-1930s. But in later life, in a series of articles and interviews about Hitchcock, Montagu never suggested that he slipped him advance copies of Soviet films or texts; he stressed, rather, the German influence, and he himself had spent time investigating the German industry, as well as bringing over films from there for the Society.

Soviet theory owed much to the analysis of early American cinema, but its most celebrated document on the subject, Eisenstein's essay "Dickens, Griffith, and the

Film Today," was not written till the 1940s. Hitchcock had read Dickens and studied Griffith for himself. Then he worked with Stannard, who had done likewise, and who had indeed adapted two Dickens novels for the screen, *Dombey and Son* (Maurice Elvey, 1919) and *The Adventures of Mr. Pickwick* (Thomas Bentley, 1921). They had internalized the principles that Eisenstein would later theorize, just as they did not need to wait to read Pudovkin in order to grasp the constructional lessons of Griffith's *Way Down East* or Henry King's *Tol'able David* (1921).

As for the Kuleshov principle, Taylor traces Hitchcock's understanding of it as least as far back as his time at FPLB; as he would tell interviewers with relish, you could change the way audiences read an action or an expression by changing the intertitle (*Hitch* 40). Murnau too was already a skilled exponent of the kind of "creative geography" that would become associated with Kuleshov; André Bazin was quite wrong to suggest that his cinema owed little to editing. Take the first railway station scene in *The Last Laugh*, sometimes described as though it were a single shot, a complex image with a clock as a main focus (Spoto 68). In fact, the clock is shown only in a cutaway shot, cued by the porter's look, up and out of frame, very possibly shot in a different place at a different time. And the whole "rear window" set up in *Nosferatu*, as I have suggested, is pure Kuleshov, as well as being more in tune with the psychological coordinates of Hitchcock's cinema than anything found in the Soviet films, whose priorities were so different.

The main impact of the Soviet films and theories on Hitchcock comes in the sound period. In the turmoil surrounding the move to synchronized sound, he is likely to have been aware of the arguments put forward by Eisenstein, Pudovkin, and Alexandrov in their short manifesto "The Sound Film: A Statement from U.S.S.R.," published in *Close Up* in October 1928, a few months before he began shooting *Blackmail*. It argues that sound should not simply duplicate or reinforce the images but operate in *counterpoint*, a principle that Hitchcock would famously experiment with in *Blackmail* and incorporate into his own discourse about cinema. While he was well capable of going in this direction himself, the article may have helped to focus his ideas about sound, as, in the longer term, the Soviet films and writings assuredly did help him to focus and articulate his ideas about "pure cinema." In the Truffaut interview he spoke mainly in terms of the Kuleshov effect, but in 1934 he told Stephen Watts, "I think cutting has definite limitations. Its best use is in violent subjects. That is why the Russians made such effective use of it, because they were dealing with violence, and they could pile shock on shock by means of cutting" (Watts 245).

The one specific Soviet film that Hitchcock liked to refer to was *Potemkin*, and there is an unmistakable reference to it in the first sudden scene of violence in *Foreign Correspondent* (1940), set in Amsterdam on a broad flight of steps, like the Odessa massacre. The killing of the fake Van Meer (Samuel Adams) is shown in a brutal cut from the killer to a close-up of the victim, covered in blood, which lasts only a few frames, exactly – as a juxtaposition of stills would confirm – like the close-up of the protesting woman on the Odessa Steps, her face slashed by the soldier's sword. And compare other scenes where Hitchcock "piles shock on shock by means of cutting," ranging from the shower murder in *Psycho* (1960) back to the killing of Verloc by his wife in *Sabotage* (1936), whose fragmentary technique was evidently very confusing, at the time of shooting, to the American star Sylvia Sidney, playing Mrs. Verloc, though she changed her tune on seeing the film. This was the scene that Hitchcock used to exemplify his dictum, in his 1937 article "Direction," that "the screen should speak its own language, freshly coined" (256); the Soviet example had helped him by now to push this language beyond the standard "nouns, verbs, and adjectives" that he wrote of earlier, inspiring Sidney to remark, according to Taylor, that "Hollywood must hear of this!" (*Hitch* 140).

The British Base

So what has happened to the British current in Hitchcock's formation? When Balcon saw the first film directed by his protégé, *The Pleasure Garden*, his response was that it looked like an American picture. Shot in Germany, it opens with an elaborate staircase shot, a familiar German motif. In the front row of a theater, a man looks through opera glasses at a particular dancer, focusing on her legs; she notices, and returns the look aggressively. Point of view, shot/reverse shot – here is Hitchcock showing an immediate grasp of the sophisticated editing systems associated with Hollywood, and Germany too. But the exchange also echoes a short film made as early as 1900 by the British pioneer George Albert Smith, *As Seen Through a Telescope*. Man uses telescope to get a close-up view, which we share, of young woman's leg, and is knocked to the ground in punishment. This opening scene is emblematic of Hitchcock's work in its immediate mix of conventions from diverse sources.

In the two decades since those highly inventive early works by Smith and others like Williamson and the young Cecil Hepworth, British cinema had acquired a reputation for unambitious dullness. But Hitchcock in 1925 was working with an internationally-minded British producer in Balcon, and a screenwriter and an assistant director of high cinematic intelligence in Stannard and Reville, all three coming from the heart of the British industry. That reputation, so complacently invoked by Truffaut, could not be the whole story.

Compared with the films of Griffith, Murnau, and others I have referred to, those of Hitchcock's British predecessors remain hardly known and hardly seen. Christine Gledhill, however, has begun seriously to open up this field in *Reframing British Cinema 1918–1928*, based on a study of some 150 of the feature films that survive in the archives. She does not privilege Hitchcock's work, but instead comes at it indirectly, with challenging results. Of twenty references to him that are indexed, eight come under the heading "Hitchcock, Alfred: prefigured by earlier [British] directors." Among these directors are Maurice Elvey and Graham Cutts.

Both were in a sense rivals to the young Hitchcock, Elvey as the man who had been Alma's boss, and who had already gone to Hollywood to make five films in 1924–25, Cutts as the director on five of whose films Hitchcock worked in 1923–24. Cutts evidently resented him and turned against him, intriguing against him with the management, and Hitchcock certainly got his own back, not only eclipsing him spectacularly in career terms but, with Alma's help, belittling his reputation. The authorized biography dismisses both Cutts and Elvey as negligible, without feeling any need to investigate their work, as Gledhill does with great thoroughness.

Her account links both of them to a widespread "pictorial" approach, developed before 1920 in a considered attempt to mark out a clear and marketable path for a British national cinema, one formally distinct from the Hollywood model that was becoming established. However, "imagining film stories in terms of theatrical stages and pictures posed a challenge to a modernizing film industry seeking the capacity for narrative fiction now established by Hollywood" (93). Unlike such older directors as Hepworth, Cutts and Elvey met this challenge by incorporating elements of Hollywood-style analytic editing. Gledhill even refers to some of Hitchcock's editing as "Elveyesque" and takes a similar perspective on his relation to Cutts: "In terms of pictorialism, Cutts's particular contribution lay in an instinctive sense of the power of the look, not only as a means of controlling others but as generator of projected internalised visions. ... [He] anticipates and opens up the terrain Hitchcock would claim as his own" (114).

Hitchcock is thus seen not as in opposition to mainstream British cinema but as shaped by it, at least in part. *The Manxman* (1929) is "a product of the poetics of British cinema, demonstrating ... the rootedness of Hitchcock's techniques in its pictorial-theatrical practices" (122).

This classic triangle drama (two men, one woman) is his last silent film, and his last film based on a script by Stannard, who himself, in a career that started in 1914, had taken that journey from the relatively static pictorial style to a more flexible one. It demonstrates the way in which, to return to the four-stream *Intolerance* model, the British current has, during the silent period, merged with those from elsewhere. The presentation of the Manx fishermen is a good example of Eisensteinian "typage," and there is a strong Kuleshovian "creative geography" effect when two members of the triangle see, to their dismay, the boat bringing back the third member from abroad: faces and boat are shown repeatedly in alternate shots, never within the same space. As for Germany, one can link what Gledhill terms "the power of the look" – a particularly intense feature of the film, especially through the two oppressively dominant males, father and lawyer – with Lang as much as with Cutts, and there is a scene observed in sustained long-shot through a glass partition that seems to me an overt formal echo of the one in *The Last Laugh* where the porter learns of his demotion. And there are scenes of sophisticated analytic editing, making full use of shot/reverse shot and point of view, which we might want to associate primarily with Hollywood, like the melodramatic concentration of the story itself, filmed once before, in 1916, by the American George Loane Tucker.

But Gledhill's perspective is convincing as well: *The Manxman* has many scenes of frontal staging, tableau framing and – both indoors and outdoors – striking pictorial effects. We can note too how, in his first quartet of sound films, constrained by the limitations of the new technology, he makes a virtue of necessity by positively exploiting the strong theatrical moments and tableau framings in three stage adaptations – *Blackmail, Juno and the Paycock* (1930), *The Skin Game* (1931) – and one novel with a theatrical setting, *Enter Sir John* (filmed as *Murder!*). This is a mode to which he will periodically hark back, notably through the self-imposed discipline of long takes in *Rope* and *Under Capricorn*.

Hitchcock and Powell

The stills cameraman on *The Manxman*, as on its predecessor *Champagne* (1928), was Michael Powell. He collaborated on the script of *Blackmail*, and began his own directing career soon after. His career and Hitchcock's have a number of intersections and parallels, though the story has been told only from his side: "Like me, Hitch adored films and had great ambitions. Like me, Hitch was impatient with the men who financed the struggling British film industry, who looked inward instead of outward" (Powell 189).

Earlier, I quoted Powell's tribute to *Intolerance* alongside that of another aspiring British director, Herbert Wilcox. It is instructive, finally, to look at these three together, embodying as they do three kinds of ambitious career from a British starting point.

Wilcox too was, at least initially, outward-looking. He not only studied *Intolerance*, he went to Germany before Hitchcock did, directing his first film, *Chu-Chin-Chow*, at UFA in 1923, and it was he who imported Lang's *Die Nibelungen* for exhibition in London soon afterwards. He brought American stars to work in Britain and went to Hollywood in the same year as Hitchcock, in 1939, before returning home and continuing to direct into the 1960s. But despite these international contacts, he remained a relatively narrow British filmmaker known for two prolific strands of patriotic film, biopics and escapist society dramas, neither of which has worn well. He helps to illuminate by contrast the more productive internationalism of Powell and Hitchcock.

Powell's formation in the silent period was a cosmopolitan one, both as film enthusiast and then as film-studio apprentice: in his case, apprentice to Rex Ingram, which meant he was working for an Irishman with a Hollywood company (MGM) in a French studio, at Nice. For *Blackmail*, he claimed to have suggested the final chase and the climactic fall of the blackmailer through the glass roof of the British Museum, as detailed at some length in his autobiography (192–93). Powell's name does not appear among the minimal screen credits of the period, but his account is plausible for two reasons. One is that the death-fall would become a recurring climactic feature of his own later films, at the climax, including three spectacular postwar examples in quick succession: *Black Narcissus* (1947), *The Red Shoes* (1948), and *Gone to Earth* (1950). The other is that it would be typical of Hitchcock to be silent about such a debt, if he could get away with it – as he so easily could, at least during his lifetime, in the case of British collaborators.

As I have suggested elsewhere (*Vertigo* 14), Powell can be seen as "the Hitchcock who didn't go to Hollywood," though he had chances to do so; and he had extensive German connections, profiting, like Hitchcock, from working with German émigré craftsmen like art director Alfred Junge. His career stands as a definitive rebuke to Truffaut's remark about the incompatibility of Britain and cinema, as if Hitchcock's own career, with its strong British roots, did not render it dubious already: here is a figure of at least comparable stature to Hitchcock who not only emerges out of British cinema but stays committed to it. The most striking link between the two men comes through films made almost simultaneously and released in 1960. *Peeping Tom* is at one level an uncanny twin of *Psycho*, centered likewise on an attractive young man whose domination by a parent has led him to become a serial killer of women. It is also a profound self-reflexive essay on the medium of film within which its protagonist works. In the initial close-up of the woman screaming that follows *The Lodger's* credits and the climactic shot of the silent 16mm footage that Mark projects for himself under *Peeping Tom's* credits, re-running in black and white what we have already seen in color as he filmed it, the camera angle, like the woman's death-agony, is identical. Though Powell, as far as I know, did not make the link back to *The Lodger* explicit, he did note that his location had associations with Jack the Ripper. *Peeping Tom* explores some of the impulses that lead people to commit Ripper-type killings, filmmakers to make *Lodger*-type films of them, and audiences to want to watch them.

Powell also described his film as, among other things, a "history of cinema from 1906," and he might have taken it even further back than that, given that it repeatedly plays with the deconstruction of the film image into individual frames, evoking Eadward Muybridge. In an interview with Bertrand Tavernier in 1968, Powell goes as far as saying that he himself represents not simply one choice of paths within cinema: instead, *"I am the cinema"* (Lazar 29). The italics are there in the interview as printed, indicating the emphasis he must have given to those four words.

Powell had a full and energetic life outside cinema, but one can see what he means. All the strands of that life, and of that experience of cinema, fed into his own work. He contrasts himself, in fact, with Hitchcock, referring to him as a filmmaker who, like Renoir, carved out a distinguished but limited path. Here he is surely wrong. Hitchcock's filmmaking career starts earlier, ends later, and ranges more widely than Powell's; he too reaches back consciously toward the beginnings of the medium; and he became a public figure, an icon of cinema, as Powell never began to. To his "I am the cinema," Hitchcock could have replied, "What about me?" The very limitations of the film industry in Britain motivated him, like Powell, to seek out and absorb ideas from all over, and he did so with unequaled fullness and skill.

Notes

1. I particularly regret not having space to discuss the silent films made in Sweden and Hollywood by Victor Sjöström. Whether or not Hitchcock saw them in London, as he certainly had the chance to, they have an abundance of instructive parallels. Starting his career in 1912, Sjöström moved from a non-editing long-take style to the full classical system, exploiting both to their fullest extent, notably in, respectively, *Ingeborg Holm* (1913, shown in London 1914) and *The Scarlet Letter* (MGM, 1926). In effect, Hitchcock, in his late-1940s return to the long-take style, is going back over the ground that Sjöström had with supreme intelligence measured out.
2. Screen credits for Reville and Stannard on Hitchcock's British films are tabulated in Barr, *English Hitchcock* (16). Stannard's work is further discussed both there and in my chapter "Writing Screen Plays: Stannard and Hitchcock."

Works Cited

Barr, Charles. *English Hitchcock*. Moffat: Cameron and Hollis, 1999.

Barr, Charles. *Vertigo*. London: BFI, 2005.

Barr, Charles. "Writing Screen Plays: Stannard and Hitchcock." *Young and Innocent? Cinema in Britain 1896–1930*. Ed. Andrew Higson. Exeter: U of Exeter P, 2002. 227–41.

Bordwell, David, Janet Staiger, and Kristin Thompson. *Classical Hollywood Cinema: Film Style and Mode of Production to 1960*. New York: Columbia UP, 1985.

Chandler, Charlotte. *It's Only a Movie: Alfred Hitchcock: A Personal Biography*. New York: Simon and Schuster, 2005.

Eisenstein, Sergei. "Dickens, Griffith, and the Film Today." *Film Form: Essays in Film Theory*. Ed. and trans. Jay Leyda. New York: Harcourt, Brace, and World, 1949. 195–255.

Elsaesser, Thomas. "Too Big and Too Close: Alfred Hitchcock and Fritz Lang." Gottlieb and Allen 146–70.

Gledhill, Christine. *Reframing British Cinema 1918–1928: Between Restraint and Passion*. London: BFI, 2003.

Gottlieb, Sidney. "Early Hitchcock: The German Influence." *Framing Hitchcock: Selected Essays from the* Hitchcock Annual. Ed. Sidney Gottlieb and Christopher Brookhouse. Detroit: Wayne State UP, 2002. 35–58.

Gottlieb, Sidney, ed. *Hitchcock on Hitchcock: Selected Writings and Interviews*. Berkeley: U of California P, 1995.

Gottlieb, Sidney, and Richard Allen, eds. *The* Hitchcock Annual *Anthology: Selected Essays from Volumes 10–15*. London: Wallflower, 2009.

Gunning, Tom. *Fritz Lang: Images of Vision and Modernity*. London: BFI, 2000.

Hansen, Miriam. *Babel and Babylon: Spectatorship in American Silent Film*. Cambridge: Harvard UP, 1991.

Hitchcock, Alfred. "A Columbus of the Screen." 1931. Gottlieb and Allen 79–81.

Hitchcock, Alfred. "Direction." 1937. Gottlieb, *Hitchcock on Hitchcock* 253–61.

Jenkins, Stephens, ed. *Fritz Lang: The Image and the Look*. London: BFI, 1981.

Lazar, David, ed. *Michael Powell: Interviews*. Jackson: UP of Mississippi, 2003.

McGilligan, Patrick. *Alfred Hitchcock: A Life in Darkness and Light*. New York: Harper-Collins, 2003.

Morris, Nathalie. "The Early Career of Alma Reville." Gottlieb and Allen 41–64.

Powell, Michael. *A Life in Movies*. London: Heinemann, 1986.

Sloan, Jane E. *Alfred Hitchcock: A Guide to References and Resources*. New York: G.K. Hall, 1993.

Spoto, Donald. *The Dark Side of Genius: The Life of Alfred Hitchcock*. Boston: Little, Brown, 1983.

Stannard, Eliot. "The Use of Symbols in Scenarios." *Kinematograph and Lantern Weekly* 12 July 1917: 108.

Stannard, Eliot. "Writing Screen Plays." Lesson Six in the series *Cinema – in Ten Complete Lessons*. London: Standard Art Book Company, 1920.

Taylor, John Russell. *Hitch: The Life and Work of Alfred Hitchcock*. New York: Pantheon, 1978.

Taylor, John Russell. "Surviving." 1977. Gottlieb, *Hitchcock on Hitchcock* 59–63.

Truffaut, François, with the collaboration of Helen G. Scott. *Hitchcock*. Rev. ed. New York: Simon and Schuster, 1984.

Watts, Stephen. "On Music in Films: An Interview." 1933–34. Gottlieb, *Hitchcock on Hitchcock* 241–45.

Wilcox, Herbert. *Twenty-five Thousand Sunsets: The Autobiography of Herbert Wilcox*. London: Bodley Head, 1967.

4

Hitchcock's Narrative Modernism: Ironies of Fictional Time

Thomas Hemmeter

Death is the sanction of everything that the storyteller can tell.

Walter Benjamin (94)

Those who study Hitchcock have, over the years, associated his films with modernism, but this association is often grudging. It places his films on the margins of modernism; it relegates them to the category of self-reflexive experiments with cinematic form; and it suggests a diminution of his film narratives. Of the modernist arts, narration is the most vexed, given the emphasis of this artistic period and its movements on discovering or inventing radical aesthetic structures in response to broad social-industrial challenges to art and to civilization. For modernists, narrative seems paralyzed in its realistic representations of a world that needs radical, imaginative refashioning. The modernist novel, however, does engage with the modernist sense of cultural crisis through experiments with fictional form as a way to respond to a central concern of the period: time.

Modernist temporal concerns – the radical contingency of human time, the apocalyptic fear of the imminent end of human time, and an obsession with death – all figure strongly in Hitchcock's narratives, as they do in the modernist novel. In exploring the nature of Hitchcock's narrative modernism, I will examine the films' thriller stories (the MacGuffin plots) as legitimate sources of narrative power, a power evident in the parodic dualities that multiply the telling of stories and that open action stories simultaneously to death and to potential renewal. Hitchcock's films undercut the claim of the classical Hollywood narrative to control narrative time, disrupting this control by opening a perspective from the disorder of the narrative middle, by involving the narrator in the fictional world, and by denying narrative closure. Though Hitchcock's cinematic vision may seem to present a nihilistic perspective on narrative time as finished, on narrative action as

A Companion to Alfred Hitchcock, First Edition. Edited by Thomas Leitch and Leland Poague.
© 2011 Thomas Leitch and Leland Poague. Published 2011 by Blackwell Publishing Ltd.

futile, his narratives also suggest the hopeful possibility of narrative time experienced as a search for meaning. This search, defined by an urgent need to tell and retell stories, might best be approached as a modernist irony whose contradictory logic creates a path through meaninglessness to meaning.

The MacGuffin Plot: A Modernist Search for Meaning

Hitchcock's films exhibit a tense modernist ambiguity in energetic quest plots that are self-subverting. Hitchcock himself often mocked the notion that his film narratives might offer a logical development of events in conventional storytelling order. The director's MacGuffin anecdote, which presents a plotless dialogue in what appears to be an unfinished story, dramatically expresses the absurdity of grasping after logical or temporal meaning. As recounted to François Truffaut, the anecdote presents a conversation between strangers on a train in Scotland, the dialogue consisting of a series of questions and answers about a mysterious package. The conversation results only in a failed exchange. The person responding to the questions concludes by denying what he had first asserted, that the package contains a MacGuffin. Just as the tale leaves the questioner none the wiser, so Hitchcock's conclusion to the story places the MacGuffin-seeking film spectator in a similar position, because "a MacGuffin is actually nothing at all" (138).

Setting aside Hitchcock's disingenuous dismissal of narrative plausibility, we might consider the anecdote's rhetoric of questions – unanswered and unanswerable – as a modernist narrative device. For example, we can see Roger Thornhill (Cary Grant), the protagonist of *North by Northwest* (1959), as the questioner in the MacGuffin anecdote, interrogatively pursuing logic in a narrative discourse that disallows straightforward logic. The film's dominant "dialogue" pattern consists of questions called out by characters but left unanswered: the secretary in the opening scene to Thornhill, "Will you check in later?"; the deaf businessman at the Plaza Hotel as Thornhill is kidnapped, "Where is he going?"; Thornhill to his abductors, "Who is Townsend?"; Thornhill to Vandamm (James Mason), "Why was I brought here?"; Mrs. Thornhill (Jessie Royce Landis) in the Plaza elevator to the enemy agents, "You gentlemen aren't really trying to kill my son, are you?" None of these questions receives an answer. In a sense Thornhill and the other characters stand in for the film audience, asking for narrative meaning from plots featuring bewildering spy intrigues. When the film's narrative investment in these plots disappears like scaffolding – when the Professor (Leo G. Carroll) explains the spy plot to Thornhill by posing yet another question, as involving "government secrets, perhaps?" – the spectator is tempted to dismiss this MacGuffin plot entirely.

From a modernist perspective, however, the unanswered questions in this film's dialogue express the need to continue the search for meaning despite the ultimate impossibility of completing it. In his analysis of the mock-heroic narratives of James Joyce, Roger B. Salomon argues that Joyce mocks the very notion that a story might supply an explanation or a meaning; instead, his fictions present answers to questions only to mock these answers. Yet Joyce's characters, like their author and his readers, continue to seek answers to questions, so that a search for meaning is both affirmed and derided. In reflecting on the meaning of his day's (and life's) experiences near the end of *Ulysses* (1922), Leopold Bloom can only ask an absurdly trivial question about a mysterious mourner at a funeral he attended earlier that day. "Who was M'Intosh?" he asks about a character who, like Kaplan in *North by Northwest*, never meaningfully appears in the fiction (quoted in Salomon 127). There being no relevant answer to the character's question, the narrative leaves Bloom and the reader only with one more ironic interrogative. While such plots do reflect a nihilistic, Nietzschean perspective that strongly informs many modernist narratives, my analysis of Hitchcock's MacGuffin plots will explore a more common and less nihilistic modernist position that maintains a tension between the difficult search for and the outright rejection of narrative meaning.

Like the miraculous discovery of the double who releases Manny Balestrero (Henry Fonda) from a robbery rap in *The Wrong Man* (1956), the arbitrary and repeated rescues of Thornhill from certain death in *North by Northwest* reveal the power of chance events to intrude upon a Hitchcock narrative. Such random possibilities suggest a double, side-by-side quality of narrative meaning in which extremely unlikely events can seem both transcendental, motivated by narrative forces (fate, religious power, authorial gamesmanship) outside the operations of mere chance, and at the same time so absurdly arbitrary that their function in the film winds up both asserting and denying logical narrative order, so that we are left with yet more questions.

Some questions are raised by traditional approaches to Hitchcock's narratives. Is a film like *North by Northwest* asking us to accept its spy adventure armature as a meaningful foil to the romance story or as an allegory of human actions caught up in narrative whirlwinds of fate, chaos, or religious harrowing? Approached as a classical Hollywood narrative, the espionage plot in *North by Northwest* satisfies, however superficially, the structural needs of an orderly story. Thornhill's spy adventures within the thriller plot begin with a classical narrative loss – the character's identity – that produces a conflict, setting in motion a rapid series of connected events projecting a future goal that is eventually reached. The protagonist recovers his workaday identity, lost in the spy intrigue when he is mistaken for George Kaplan, and in the process recovers stolen espionage secrets and gains a wife after previous failures at marriage. This narrative logic appears in traditional approaches to Hitchcock's film stories, as in Lesley Brill's observation that the plots of films like *Young and Innocent* (1937), *Spellbound* (1945), and *Marnie* (1964) emphasize "the close relationship between moments of intense significance in life and the ways in which art reveals order in the chaotic-looking world" (244).

Although Brill's ascription of mimetic, archetypically romantic meaning operating in and through Hitchcock's narratives asserts an unusually traditional position, critics more commonly struggle to locate a classical narrative perspective in Hitchcock's films by uncovering meanings only loosely connected to the ostensible storyline. Interpreting *The 39 Steps* (1935), an earlier version of *North by Northwest*'s spy story, Tom Ryall concludes that the events of the MacGuffin plot are insignificant to the central concern of the film – the formation of the romantic couple – yet are functional for the way the plot launches a defined "narrative trajectory" by setting the characters "precise goals," which, "unimportant in themselves[,] nevertheless provide the central characters with a measure of control over events and with the means of restoring order" (134–35).

In dismissing the thriller stories as mere narrative instruments used to create thematic meanings, these denigrations of classical narrative order neglect the double-edged meanings conveyed precisely in and through the spy or murder stories. Though *North by Northwest* pushes the arbitrary, absurd logic of a MacGuffin plot to a more extreme level than *The 39 Steps*, both films develop a classical plot that functions simultaneously to reference narrative order and to undercut that order. Because classical narratives assume the loss and recovery of meaningful order, Hitchcock's MacGuffin plots undercut these assumptions doubly: through their absurdly arbitrary involvement of the protagonists in the espionage story, and through their revelation that no prior order existed to be lost.

In *North by Northwest*, Thornhill assumes Kaplan's role within the MacGuffin spy fiction by means of an extreme coincidence, a mistaken identity triggered by chance. He hails a telegraph boy at the same time as the boy calls for a Mr. Kaplan. Subsequently Thornhill exits the espionage plot twice, first by means of a faked shooting and later by a miraculous rescue from certain death atop Mount Rushmore. The accidental, fantastical nature of these entries and exits dramatizes violent breaks in temporal story order, assertions of narrative chance marking the character's loss and recovery of identity as radically contingent and provisional. Thornhill enacts the role of a bumbling spy named Kaplan whose decoy adventures make Thornhill a cartoon character of sorts. He becomes a roadrunner who cannot die although continually threatened with death, enjoying great agency and mobility in this marked-off, fictional time at the cost of losing his identity as a New York City advertising man, an identity he enjoyed in the time "before" the espionage adventure began.

However, the "before" time of Thornhill's life was equally unstable. The film's opening scenes show that Thornhill had lived his New York life in a state of temporal stasis, having retreated into an illusory time defined by his relationship with his mother, a woman who appears to be the same age as Roger, a woman who performs both as a sexless wife and a maternal refuge for this aging adolescent fearful of adult relationships. Retreating from aging and from time, Thornhill has already lost any meaningful identity before suffering a second loss in being mistaken for Kaplan. The adventures leading Thornhill through a nightmare loss of identity repeat on a narrative level his earlier loss of identity in living his empty New York life. This doubled loss undercuts the classical narrative structure built upon plot conflict, generating a single defined loss that leads eventually to a recovery – or at least an understanding – of what has been lost, hence to a restoration of order. In *North by Northwest* there is no defined order to lose. In temporal terms, Thornhill had already been stripped of ordered time before the spy adventures replicate this narrative state. Its opening scenes revealed to be more of the same and not a temporal rupture, its closing scenes imposing a contrived conclusion in a highly arbitrary rescue, the film eliminates the bookends of narrative structure, leaving the audience and characters in a prolonged adventure in the middle.

Violent Disruption of Narrative Point of View: The Perspective from the Middle

The MacGuffin plots' play with the possibility for narrative order and control – tentatively preserving while simultaneously mocking a coherent search for meaning – reveals a fundamental reordering of classical narrative time in Hitchcock's cinema. As H. Porter Abbott notes, *"narrative is the principal way in which our species organizes its understanding of time"* (3). Applying this understanding to modernist fiction, Peter Brooks maintains: "Narrative is one of the large categories or systems of understanding that we use in our negotiations with reality, specifically ... with the problem of temporality," i.e., with people's "time-boundedness," their "consciousness of existence within the limits of mortality" (xi). The limits of mortality recur obsessively in Hitchcock's films about violent death. Bradbury and MacFarlane explicitly connect the modernist obsession with a violent end of human time to an "apocalyptic ferment" in the narrative search "not only [for meaningful] form but also [for] significant time" (51). In this double search we might locate the critical nexus between Hitchcock's formalism and his approach to narrative, revealed in his films' modernist preoccupation with significant time.

As products of the British and Hollywood studio systems, Hitchcock's films reflect and play off the narrative standards of classical Hollywood stories explicated most completely by David Bordwell, Janet Staiger, and Kristin Thompson. According to Bordwell, narration controls fictional time as invisibly as possible. Story devices within the fictional world, as when characters must meet deadlines, make it appear that "the story action, not the narrator," decides "how long the action will take" and determines "the forward flow" of story events (45), thus evoking a future-oriented "arc of expectation" (47). "Classical editing strategies" create "durational continuity" (46) to smooth over time gaps in the story. Narrative closure "rewards the search for meaning and makes the time span we experience seem a complete unit" (47). Reliant on chains of cause and effect, classical Hollywood narration assumes a modest, almost invisible status as "character action and reaction convey the ongoing causal chain to us" (29). According to Bordwell, the classical narrative should not bring storytelling issues to the foreground because such issues create temporal dissonance; instead, "a discreet narration oversees time, making it subordinate to causality, while the spectator follows the causal thread" (47).

Hitchcock films often violate this orderly flow of temporal meaning, most dramatically in the death of Marion Crane (Janet Leigh) in *Psycho* (1960). In positioning Marion's murder so early in the film, Hitchcock strips the narrative of the structured coherence and continuity that might allow spectators to evade confronting the abrupt, arbitrary loss of her life. Though the sequence of events leading toward and beyond her murder creates a temporal duration experienced as radically contingent, Bordwell nonetheless declares *Psycho* a "limit-text" that may "dramatize some limits" of classical intelligibility but is still regulated by the "external norms" of the Hollywood system (81). Modernist storytelling is often obsessed, in the words of George Steiner, with the increasing uncertainty of "the relations between time and individual death" (quoted in Schleifer, *Rhetoric* 10); narratives increasingly abandon traditional approaches that offered consolation in the face of death and seek ways to connect storytelling to a new sense of time as a prolonged, suspenseful search for meaning without the support of a usable past or a meaningful future (Schleifer, *Rhetoric* 57). Because *Psycho* tells a story of death whose narrative causes lie less in Marion's actions than in the complex psyche of Norman Bates (Anthony Perkins) – if psyche he possesses – and whose narrative consequences, elaborated in the investigation of her disappearance, leave Marion's murder an event whose fictional meanings remain disturbingly open, *Psycho*'s subversive play with classical narrative control over time is occasion for investigating the film's modernism.

The place to begin this analysis is precisely in *Psycho*'s narration, particularly as revealed in the film's point of view and closure. In *Modernism and Time* Ronald Schleifer invokes Walter Benjamin to argue that traditional narrative can no longer console audiences for life's social disorder by fabricating a fictional order nor console them for the loss of mortal time by fashioning a fictional escape from time. In "The Storyteller," Benjamin asserts that narrative fictions must tell their stories from the perspective of death. The narrator must speak of, to, and from death as a concrete temporal event that marks the loss of time even as it energizes the telling, a telling that disrupts any idealized, transcendent conception of death (Schleifer, *Modernism* 98–99). Hitchcock's obsession with violent death exemplifies this urgent modernist perspective on storytelling.

Psycho's handling of cinematic point of view is one way that Hitchcock releases the disruptive power of mortal time. Before Marion Crane's death, spectators experience *Psycho*'s fictional time through their identification with Marion, sympathizing with her sense of temporal emptiness or decompression in the slow opening scenes that dramatize her social entrapment and sharing her anxious sense of time once she decides to steal the money and drive to Fairvale. These familiar understandings of dramatic time are overwhelmed in the montage rush of her death, a narrative cataclysm followed by a wandering time of sputtering investigations into her disappearance. Once Marion sinks from narrative sight, the film gains direction only through investigations into her whereabouts by characters of little interest to the audience. The narrated events in the final two-thirds of the film exhibit a drifting inquietude, suggestive of modernist narratives of futile wandering in novels like *Ulysses* and Virginia Woolf's *To the Lighthouse* (1927). Indeed, the latter features the abrupt death of Mrs. Ramsay, the chief identification figure, halfway through the story, after which the narrative wanders among various perspectives in an attempt to continue with and complete the story of the Ramsay family and their circle. *Psycho* presents something close to this modernist storytelling practice. Marion Crane's death does not open or close *Psycho*'s story but unveils time (in its loss) more directly, from the wandering and confused narrative middle.

A second temporal unveiling, less direct perhaps but ultimately more telling, shifts from the desultory film events to a different source of narrative energy: the entanglement of the film audience in storytelling time as they attempt to interpret the fragmented story. Though *Psycho*'s narrative produces the event of Marion's death and then continues to tell her story as it opens out into other stories – her murderer's story and the stories of those who investigate her disappearance – Marion's death story also emphatically opens out into a mental event occurring in the audience's mind. Hitchcock's explicit narrative goal in *Psycho* was to subject spectators to the violent murder of Marion Crane, the film's identification figure, and to transfer this violence into their minds so that their fearful expectations of further violence propel the story forward: "So, I was transferring [the violence from screen images to spectators' minds] by establishing the violence strong in the beginning and then got less and less violent as the film went on, thus letting their minds carry [the narrative]" (294). Not simply catalyzed by images Hitchcock creates and projects onto a screen, the fear of death requires spectators to advance the story in their minds through their engaged responses, responses completing the film story. This is Hitchcock's version of Benjamin's storytelling from the perspective of death.

Psycho's rupture of classical point of view is not unique in Hitchcock's films. *Sabotage* (1936), for example, presents a lengthy, half-humorous series of suspense scenes as a charming boy, Stevie (Desmond Tester) – the younger brother of the film's heroine, Mrs. Verloc (Sylvia Sidney) – carries a package containing a bomb across London until the bomb explodes, killing him and his fellow bus passengers. Occurring near the end of the film, this event provokes Stevie's sister to kill her husband (Oscar Homolka), the person most responsible for Stevie's fatal errand. Stevie's death fails either to resolve the plot conflicts or to move the story toward closure. Narrative causality is undermined because the domestic disorder of the Verloc family both precedes and follows the espionage disruptions of the MacGuffin plot; family disorder seems as responsible as international espionage for the film's violence. Paula Marantz Cohen finds *Sabotage* incoherent because it does not place the gratuitous death of Stevie under narrative control; in failing to serve a plot purpose, the boy's death releases a "wave of disorder" (44). Her difficulties integrating Stevie's death into the narrative are mirrored in Tom Ryall's struggles to identify the film's controlling point of view or its protagonist and his inability to reconcile the film's dark story with those of Hitchcock's more upbeat 1930s thrillers (130–35).

The modernist narrator too is often thrust into the temporal world of the fiction. This engaged position breaks from such earlier practices as realistic fiction's positioning of the narrator as a neutral observer existing apart from the fiction's temporal events, a "transcendental subject" able to comment on narrative proceedings from an imagined position outside time (Schleifer, *Modernism* 145, 180–81). Modernist narration, by contrast, refuses the order and control afforded by telling the story from a vantage point outside time. Modernist novels commonly entangle the first-person or subjective narrator in the temporal world of the fiction, doubling and multiplying the fictional perspective on time. Hitchcock's narrative doubling pulls film spectators into the fiction as co-narrators, their fears and anticipations and assumptions informing the film events even as the director's images do. Hitchcock's overt presence within the diegesis also entangles him richly in the narrative worlds his films create, marked particularly by his cameo appearances and his obtrusive cinematic style. Hitchcock's inveterate habit of writing and talking about his own filmmaking is also well known, as are his introductions to his television shows and his appearances in trailers for his films. In multiply announcing his authorial presence in so many ways, Hitchcock signifies his refusal to separate himself from the fictional time his films create.

Immersion in this disordered middle of a story logically leads modernist fictions to reject narrative closure. For Paul Ricoeur, modernist narrative time assumes a perspective of continuing crisis, an "endless transition"; modernist fictions reach conclusions only by converting "the imminent end into an immanent end" (24). Embedded in the ongoing unfolding of events, fictional time becomes a tense duration, a waiting for a future event that would end time at some undefined point, creating a conscious awareness of the future as protracted dread imagined from the temporal perspective of an anxious present – a "perspective from the middle" (Hollington 437). Despite the director's reputation for obsessively controlling every dimension of his filmmaking, many of Hitchcock's films, most notably *The Birds* (1963), conclude ambiguously, even multiply, indicating their refusal of classical narrative control over time. The last scene of *Strangers on a Train* (1951), which shows Guy Haines (Farley Granger) and Ann Morton (Ruth Roman) on a train where Guy once again encounters a stranger, as he had at the beginning of the film, can be read as reopening the film's story. With a wink, Hitchcock the narrator may be conveying the impossibility of closure for this odd couple, whose strained intimacy, far different from the behavior of the romantic couple in a classical plot who have achieved their desired goal, suggests that they remain strangers on this train, bumping through life on a vehicle provoking chance encounters and ever-shifting stories.

Psycho reflects a similar sense of temporal openness in its multiple endings, each of which adjusts the previous ending and none of which folds the fictional time of the film into a unified whole. The hermeneutic revelation of Norman as the killer dressed in his mother's clothing – when Sam (John Gavin) prevents Norman from attacking Lila (Vera Miles) in the fruit cellar – appears as a distinct temporal moment in the unfolding of events in narrative time. These events conclude the film's detective narrative, answering the question of who killed Marion Crane: Norman did. However, the psychiatrist's ensuing lengthy analysis of Norman's psychotic motives seems to stop narrative time and let the film end in exposition. Ultimately the psychiatrist's disquisition undercuts the detective narrative, concluding that Marion was killed by Mrs. Bates in possession of Norman's psyche, not Norman at all. A third ending occurs in the camera's disclosure of Norman in a cell, now inhabited by "Mother," who refutes the psychiatrist's account of her guilt in Marion's death, blaming her son instead. A camera dolly links this last scene to the psychiatrist scene spatially but not temporally, conjuring a psychic time of uncertain status and creating a causal ambiguity regarding Marion's murder that disturbs classical temporal continuity. The film's final image of the car holding Marion's corpse as it is winched from the swamp opens various temporal possibilities, one of which Laura Mulvey explores: the recovery of Marion's body "reiterat[es] death as the drive of narrative" (238). Her interpretation opens a psychoanalytic past as yet another narrative meaning – and another temporal ambiguity complicating closure – with Marion's body connected temporally to Norman's mother's body in an uncanny return of a repressed past. More chillingly, the slow emersion of Marion's casket-like car from the swamp ends the story with a modernist assertion of death as a mundanely concrete event, at once arbitrary and hopelessly poignant.

The Other Modernism: Does the Story of Death End Narrative or Begin Storytelling?

Like other contradictory features of modernism circa 1890–1940, its vaunted formalism reveals under close analysis a divided perspective: two opposed positions on the role of style and formal structure in artistic creation. Some saw modernist artists freed by the cultural crisis to create aesthetic systems and abstract realities transcending historical contingency through a "radical remaking of form"; others saw modernist artists "not simply … set free" but instead placed "under specific, apparently historical strain" by an "awareness of contingency as a disaster in the world of time." These "*two* Modernisms" are definable by the difference between Symbolism and Surrealism, the former marking out a private, aesthetic world of art whose ironic play with formal patterns refuses the "claims of time and history," the latter asserting the revolutionary power of art to create "social meaning" and "modern consciousness" through works reflective of the modern experience (Bradbury and MacFarlane 26–28). This divided perspective shows up in critical viewpoints on the meaning of narrative form in modernist fiction. One viewpoint, represented in Michael Hollington's synoptic account by Joseph Frank, asserts that "novels like *Ulysses* are designed as single, static images outside time, to be simultaneously apprehended" as "spatial form." An opposing viewpoint, represented for Hollington by Frank Kermode, argues for "something irremediably temporal" about storytelling form, its narrative "beginnings, middles, and ends" reflective "of ideas about time and history" that modernist narratives complicate by means of "liberating ironies about time" (432).

Although both strains of modernism show up in Hitchcock studies, most critics who explore the films' modernist qualities emphasize their aesthetic formalism at the expense of narrative, theorizing how their elaborate structures and technical displays insinuate abstract themes and meanings beneath the films' surface events. The auteurist Donald Spoto, writing in 1976, urged critics to delve more deeply into the meaning of his films "by passing *beyond* story and plot to theme and structure" (58). This critical perspective regularly locates narrative meaning in spatial patterns and structures, linking the modernist aesthetics of symbolism to the critical practices of another modernist body of thought, the structuralism of Ferdinand de Saussure. Saussure's structuralist thought, based on a picture of arbitrary signs operating within a closed system, carries forward on a linguistic plane the symbolist aesthetic emphasizing formal patterns. Both critical approaches neglect the temporal dimensions of narrative. Opposed to this formalist emphasis are the dynamic strains of narrative modernism that, refusing the hermetic aesthetic perspective, engage the social, historical world. The mystical Marxism of Walter Benjamin, the ironic vision of James Joyce, the phenomenology of Paul Ricoeur, the Freudian thought of Peter Brooks: all seek artistic passages to meaning in a temporal, historical world.

A sharply concise picture of Hitchcock as a symbolist or decadent artist appears in an essay by Thomas Elsaesser, whose analysis of Hitchcock's films reads narrative as a mask or MacGuffin hiding the films' semiotic meanings. He discovers in Hitchcock's playful devotion to "effects" or "tricks" evidence of "a will towards abstraction, and ... a modernist's conceptualisation of the artist's material" (7); formal designs draw "attention to a certain modernism in Hitchcock" revealed by places in the narrative where "the concrete quality of film appears as a disguise for the mechanical, the abstract" (6). This critical approach reflects the symbolist tradition of formalism, emphasizing abstract aesthetic structures and deemphasizing the concrete events of storytelling stressed by Benjamin as the essence of modernist narrative. Semiotic analysis discovers the meaning of Hitchcock's films in structural designs; story elements offer only a MacGuffin's play with meaning that, once offered, is canceled out. This aggressively formalist analysis reflects a modernist notion, picked up and reemphasized in postmodern analyses of Hitchcock like Tom Cohen's, of machine forces controlling the films' plots, a criticism consigning narrative to a secondary, even irrelevant position in the interpretation of Hitchcock's films.

In his *Readings and Writings* analyses of *North by Northwest* and *Psycho*, Peter Wollen directly confronts the formalist challenge to narrative meaning, attempting to analyze the structures of these films' stories without abandoning narrative altogether. In "The Hermeneutic Code" chapter he reconsiders his efforts and critiques the structuralist hermeneutics of Roland Barthes – because this approach prevents a film like *Psycho* "from becoming a fully modern text" and risks "dispensing with narrative altogether" (41) – and instead turns toward Freudian thought to unify the narrative strands of Hitchcock's modernist films. Likewise, in attempting to solve Wollen's formalist problem of unifying *Psycho*'s two stories (Marion's story and Norman's story), Laura Mulvey invokes Freud's *Beyond the Pleasure Principle*, itself a modernist text from 1920, to unify the narrative of *Psycho* by reading the film's uncanny story as a narrative death drive returning to a repressed past, the death of Norman's mother. Ultimately this analysis prevents Freudian thought from opening into narrative time by emphasizing the ways that "psychoanalysis draws liberally on spatial metaphor" (233). According to Mulvey, Hitchcock's films display "bold patterns that relate stories to the spaces in which they take place" (233). Narrative time gives way to narrative space: "the stasis of [Marion's] story's ending is inscribed into its spaces: the home brings stillness with it as the movement of the journey comes to its end" (237).

Using late Lacanian theory to advance psychoanalysis beyond Freud, Slavoj Žižek's interpretation of *Psycho*, like Mulvey's, accepts the structuralist premise that *Psycho* reveals "a kind of hybrid [plot structure] of two heterogeneous parts" (232). On Žižek's analysis, however, the event of Marion's death effectively ends the story of *Psycho*: "In terms of the inherent logic of the narrative, the story is already over, and saps the effect of closure; the final explanation of the mystery of the mother's identity changes into its opposite and undermines the very notion of personal identity …" (244; ellipsis in original). This radical Lacanian reading argues that, following Marion's death, the film story leaves behind its narrative world and conveys instead only the mechanical gaze of the camera. Like Elsaesser, Žižek traces narrative energy to a mechanistic source; like Mulvey, he moves from narrative time to structural space.

David Trotter adds an interesting wrinkle to this argument by noting that very early cinema trained the camera's neutral, mechanical gaze upon the material world and its chance events, whereas the intrusive artistry of narrative cinema, beginning with D.W. Griffith's systematic editing, imposed an artistic intelligibility and meaning upon the world so viewed. To recover this original machine gaze, cinematic fictions must remove the narrator and acknowledge "the founding absence of the human observer whose authority and compassion might have mediated" the "excess of presence" produced by the camera machine (79). Trotter argues for the modernism of this approach to narrative neutrality by exploring the strong experimental interest of High Modernist novelists and short story writers in the mechanical perspective of early cinema. In *Ulysses*, for example, events can occur without narrative design through the strategic elimination of a narrator as a "presiding consciousness"; the "story" in the "Wandering Rocks" chapter, for example, proceeds by a "new principle" that interrupts the story to "record, as a machine would," thus recovering "literature's original neutrality as a medium" (117).

Ultimately, however, Trotter's analysis repeats the avant-garde formalist rejection of narrative mediation in emphasizing the media of novel and cinema as neutral and timeless windows onto a world. Arguing that the camera eliminates the human distortion of narrative, he seeks a more direct, phenomenological access to the world. A different approach to cinematic form reworks narrative by emphasizing, not eliminating, the necessary mediation of non-human structures in efforts to capture a modernist hyper-consciousness of contingent time. One such structural mediation occurs through narrative itself, as in Paul Ricoeur's attempted synthesis of structuralist and dynamic models of narrative. Seeking a route around modernist storytelling blockage, Ricoeur interprets Marcel Proust's *Remembrance of Things Past* (1913–27) as connecting fictional time to readers' own experience of time through the medium of narrative. Grounded, like Hitchcock's narratives, in a death perspective, Ricoeur's conception places storytelling, with its dead, atemporal structures of art, between an understanding of the lived mortal time audiences bring to a narrative and a new understanding they take back to their lives. In other words, the cinematic narrative acts as a dynamic non-living medium lying between two lived understandings of time. Such narrative passages help viewers make temporal connections that might not be recognized without the extratemporal structures of narrative art (146–52).

This mediating power of fictional storytelling can be recognized in Hitchcock's ironic use of suspense. As commonly understood, formalist suspense operates merely as a narrative technique that empowers the auteurist director to manipulate fictional space, spectator knowledge, and aesthetic rhythms to control the responses of his passive audience. In the context of modernist apocalyptic understandings of time, however, suspense also provides temporal narrative mediation. In Hitchcock's films, narrative suspense works not only to provide thrills but to provoke audiences to experience narrative time as suspended in fictional activities, a time of mortal delay provoked by story events that variously neglect, avoid, confront, or simply wait for an unavoidable apocalyptic end, a "cool apocalypse" in John Orr's description (24–25). Hitchcock's modernist narrative suspense provides a passage between the audience's experience of lived time and their experience of film time as gaming with this dangling, contingent temporality.

In the last third of *Rope* (1948), for example, the film abandons its cat-and-mouse game with the viewer's uncertainty whether, when, and how David Kentley's corpse will be discovered in the chest, shifting the point of view more strongly to Rupert, the investigator, as he gradually moves toward discovering the body.

But far from providing closure to the film's narrative, the discovery leads to a different sort of suspense when Rupert (James Stewart), after delivering a self-righteous speech condemning the killers and exculpating himself, sits waiting for the outside world to ring down the curtain. After he fires several shots out the window to attract the police, the camera pulls back to a long shot to reveal a geometric composition placing Rupert at the apex of a triangle whose other points are Brandon (John Dall) and Phillip (Farley Granger). The mise-en-scène creates a modernist tableau, visually reinscribing Rupert into the story more as co-perpetrator of the crime than as amateur detective. The shot holds and holds across narrative time as an exhausted Rupert awaits a conclusion that does not and cannot come. In ironically repeating the triangular composition from the opening strangulation, with Rupert in the dying David Kentley's position between Brandon and Phillip, the film's narrative uses an inanimate design to mediate between two contrived fictional moments: that of Brandon and Phillip's hermetic story of revealing their murder and their victim and that of Rupert's contrived escape from time in rising above their story to a place of judgmental innocence. The suspense built through Rupert's detection and discovery becomes a suspense built upon his proclaimed innocence, a suspense whose burdensome waiting reopens the film's narrative as we recall that he provoked the killers' actions by advocating the rights of supermen to kill others. In effect, the film's narrative structure bridges the gap between the falsity of the detective-story suspense and a modernist confrontation with conflicted time that refuses Rupert's attempt to rise above involvement in the murder story. Doubled suspense reopens the temporal narrative world that Rupert's discovery of the body supposedly has closed.

Narrative Time as Passage: Liberating Ironies of Conflicting Desires

The very complexity of modernist stories – animated doubly by a desire for death and a desire to avoid death – creates difficulties of telling and interpreting these texts. Freud's psychoanalytic therapies are based on interpretations of complex stories. Similarly, modernist narratives create complexities demanding new methods of interpretation. One such complexity in modernist novels involves the problems of passing on a meaningful story. In analyzing the failure of William Faulkner's modernist novel *Absalom, Absalom!* (1936) to achieve narrative coherence, Peter Brooks notes that, despite its blocked transaction of meaning, the novel at least conveys the compulsive desire of its characters – and of its own fictional narrative – to speak and to be "recognized and heard." Though narrative speaking and hearing may yield no breakthrough understanding, the "desire [to tell] never will cease to activate the telling voices" (312). This Freudian emphasis on transmitting stories expands narrative meaning beyond the diegesis to what Brooks terms "the relation of telling and transmission," that is, the relation between narrator and audience (323). The doubled, contradictory drives within the fictional world are redoubled in the communication of this fiction to an audience, commonly resulting in radically open narratives that audiences are expected to complete.

Hitchcock's films dramatize the difficulty of confirming or passing on a story, as when the death of key witnesses prevents Manny Balestrero from proving his innocence in *The Wrong Man*. More positively, the coded messages passed on by dying characters in *The 39 Steps* and *The Man Who Knew Too Much* (1934 and 1956) paradoxically recreate narrative time. When the dying Annabella Smith (Lucie Mannheim), the espionage agent in *The 39 Steps*, passes on her secret mission to Richard Hannay (Robert Donat), he reluctantly inherits her role in the espionage plot, allowing the narrative to continue. More generally, struggling or failed communications in *The Lodger* (1926), *Blackmail* (1929), *Sabotage, I Confess* (1953), *Psycho*, *Marnie*, and both versions of *The Man Who Knew Too Much* express Hitchcock's modernist compulsion to tell and retell stories in a desperate effort to reach his audience. Beyond their obvious publicity function, the unflagging interviews and writings in which Hitchcock discusses his filmmaking strategies and recounts anecdotes about actors, writers, and plots suggest a modernist concern for passing on his narratives. In explaining his emphasis on telling a film project's "story in a very simple way, from beginning to end, in a fairly abbreviated version," Hitchcock imagines a young woman retelling the story of the film to her mother, narrating the film "just as clearly" as the director, completing "the whole cycle" (Truffaut 315). Hitchcock's emphasis on narrative retelling reflects a modernist storyteller's desire to create a narrative passage in time.

The story of young Charlie (Teresa Wright) in *Shadow of a Doubt* (1943), for example, is a palimpsest that overlies the story of her uncle (Joseph Cotten) and mother (Patricia Collinge), a deadly repetition of the Newton family tale of women's entrapment and men's patriarchal violence. In the film's final shot, the minister's eulogy overlaps with the dialogue between Charlie and her law-officer lover, Jack Graham (Macdonald Carey). In the former discourse, the minister's words frame Uncle Charlie's death as a narrative, projecting a future order built on a firm vision of the past: Uncle Charlie's gift to the community expresses familial love, as of a grateful son gained and lost. Speaking of such people, the minister intones, "The beauty of their souls, the sweetness of their character, live on with us forever." The minister's sentiment represents Charlie's idealized family narrative, a story she largely abandons after discovering her uncle's murderous past.

In her dialogue with Graham, Charlie suggests a very different story of Uncle Charlie's past by her comments on his hatred of people and the world. In response, Graham notes that the world, though not as bad as her uncle thought it was, "seems to go crazy every now and then, like your Uncle Charlie." In prefiguring Norman Bates's remark to Marion in *Psycho* over fifteen years later – "We all go a little mad sometimes. Haven't you?" – Graham's line, like the entire closing scene, opens a temporal future of flowing and uncontrollable disorder, of chance intrusions of violence in direct contradiction to the eulogy's orderly vision. Ironically, Charlie's efforts to preserve her family ideals, to protect the Newton family from her uncle, also preserve Uncle Charlie's role as part of an ideal family, allowing murderous family illusions to continue into the future. This disunified final scene undercuts the thriller plot resolution that Charlie, in killing her uncle, has brought about. Though the murder plot seems to have been brought to a definitive end, her family remains ignorant of what really has happened, and Charlie herself looks toward a future life likely to cast her in one of the roles – trapped wife, widow, or vulnerable single woman – that would once again repeat the film's narrative.

In layering two narratives built around death – characters like Uncle Charlie and Norman attempting to live outside mortal time as though outside the reach of life's accidents; characters like young Charlie and Marion Crane caught up in the powerful narrative grasp of chance events – Hitchcock's plots often present a failed or highly compromised narrative passage. What Peter Nicholls terms the "interactive temporalities" (253) of modernist irony, in which events of the past released in the present of the story offer possible release from repetition, do not always function therapeutically even in Hitchcock's ostensibly psychoanalytic plots like *Spellbound* and *Marnie*. However, one could argue that Charlie's position outside the church in *Shadow of a Doubt* suggests a narrative movement toward greater understanding. Despite the irony of her helping to maintain the very social structures that threaten her, she may have found a passage through narrative events toward a less confined position outside her family. When the same character plays both roles – Alicia Huberman (Ingrid Bergman) in *Notorious* (1946) or L.B. Jefferies (James Stewart) in *Rear Window* (1954) attempting to retreat from time while caught up in chance events – the films offer a tentative escape from the past by permitting characters to confront death in fantastical, transformative encounters or journeys. The success of this transformation requires recognition of the contingent, threatening loss of life as a loss necessary to life. As Peter Conrad summarizes this absurd logic in reflecting upon *Rich and Strange* (1931), a "sea-change can only happen if you die first" (273). Conrad concludes that Hitchcock's surviving characters learn to live on the run, citing the flight of the characters at the end of *The Birds* as an example of the need to respond to certain death by continually moving rather than turning to face it with Heidegger's existential stoicism (291).

But the ironic, qualified success of protagonists like Thornhill, Hannay, and Jefferies suggests that Hitchcock's modernist narratives allow possibilities beyond endless flight and the fatalistic acceptance of death, possibilities experienced and expressed precisely in fictional time. Hitchcock's MacGuffin plots produce ironic meaning through the fantasy of meaningful action. Such films display the "comic exuberance" (Behler 84) available in the frivolous disruption of play noted as a central quality of Friedrich Schlegel's vision of irony, which "must act" in its life energy (quoted in Behler 85). Hitchcock's narratives present such dynamic plots as desirable and entertaining while simultaneously depicting them as risibly implausible, an inclusive "Joycean irony" (Salomon 108) that mocks the heroic mode of espionage stories without dismissing their values. The earlier narrative values exist mainly as a lost reference. Yet these values, however qualified, absurdly continue to animate the modernist narrative.

The ironies of modernist parody can also disrupt structures of narrative control by deflating the progression of plot events whose logic depends on conventional understandings of aesthetic suspense. In "Hitchcock at the Margins of Noir," for example, James Naremore observes that *Strangers on a Train* violates its own suspenseful crosscutting between Guy's tennis match and Bruno's frantic efforts to recover from a sewer the incriminating lighter. Despite Hitchcock's careful management of "symmetrical design" in this montage sequence, the director slyly undercuts the suspense premise by revealing "that everything is in one sense pointless, founded on a formal technique or a trick" (270). When the murderous Bruno arrives first at the scene of the crime, he finds that he cannot plant Guy's lighter until the sun goes down. The film then leaves him to sit and wait for Guy to arrive at the fairgrounds while the spectator waits to discover whether Bruno will successfully incriminate Guy. The film's narrative deflates both the dramatic urgency of the characters' struggle to arrive first and the audience's anxiety over their race against time. This decompression of suspense time creates a temporal dissonance by opening up a fictional time beyond subjective or artistic motive, mocking narrative control over events. Modernist narratives often feature characters lingering or wandering about, waiting for something meaningful to happen, their anxiety built upon an understanding of time outside the contrived aesthetic anxieties produced by suspense. This sequence from *Strangers on a Train* encapsulates the temporal dissonance in films like *Rich and Strange, Rope, Rear Window*, and *Vertigo* (1958) as becalmed characters await a dramatic intrusion into their lives, even seeking to contrive suspense when their lives seem to deny it. Irony as a modernist doubling, however, asserts a qualified possibility of continuing on through narrative movement which, though it cannot escape human time, may provoke actions and create roles that at least keep characters from slipping into paralysis.

Though he does not pin down the narrative source of Hitchcock's irony, Peter Conrad comes close to locating the director's storytelling irony in surrealist suspense: not the "uneasy deferment of an inevitable end that makes time tick away so slowly" in *Sabotage*'s movement toward a climactic explosion, but the vertigo of mortal life's "anchorless uncertainty" (293). This radical contingency led André Breton to declare that Surrealism provides a "tiny footbridge over the abyss" (quoted in Conrad 293), opening a path whose ironic prospect evokes terror and absurd laughter alike. In their narratives, however, Hitchcock films create a more destabilizing, contradictory irony. Audiences want films to indulge, even prolong their fears through storytelling play so that loss of control operates within a structure of control. Yet they are self-consciously aware of the absurdity of the playing with time that life and modernist fiction both indulge and reject. This is why the bomb's explosion near the end of *Sabotage* is such a narrative surprise. It violates the controlled manipulation of fictional suspense time by letting the inevitable happen in the film. Is a sudden or eventual death in the audience's life any less a surprise, despite its certain occurrence in time? The complex laughter of Hitchcock's dark irony mixes with a terror born of certainty, not suspense. This is one reason why he could claim that *Psycho* was a comedy.

The incongruent juxtapositions of surrealist paintings, their side-by-side images producing an ironic disjunction like a train emerging from a domestic fireplace, appear differently in fiction films, as incongruent juxtapositions of narrative time. Here Breton's bridge sways between two moving, unstable temporal perspectives whose irony produces vertigo. Reading the confusion Scottie (James Stewart) experiences between his living present and an imagined past in *Vertigo* as an experience of desire, we might recognize the ironic gaps created by his seemingly endless, futile movements in narrative time, his search for a stable dream to order his waking life and his discovery of order in a mental breakdown that abruptly ends his search, only to have the narrative renew the story of that search in the last third of the film. The liberating irony of modernism exists not for this fictional character but for the film audience, in the ironic recognition that the pursuit of romantic ideals in life offers certain escape from time only in death. Fictional ruptures and deaths provide the only narrative bridge between the order of death and the disordered contingency of a living search for order. Surrealist narrative irony recognizes both the freedom of desire and the shadow of death in every medium and every language. This very mingling of potential with loss creates the narrative possibility for productive passage.

Modernist narratives also create mortal irony by positioning metaphorically dead people as actors and narrators in films as various as *Rich and Strange, The 39 Steps, Shadow of a Doubt, Rope, Strangers on a Train,* and *The Trouble with Harry* (1955) and in repositioning the withdrawn audience, classically removed from fictional time, as narrators subject to the temporal dislocations provoked by the very fictions whose telling they share but cannot control. "Dead" narrators include the non-living camera machine; the identification characters who die in the fiction, attempt to withdraw from the fiction's temporal world, or die to an earlier perspective when violently forced to adopt a new one; and the director Hitchcock himself, now dead for over thirty years. Yet another modernist irony is that narrative fiction allows Hitchcock's posthumous narration to continue. Indeed, through the mediation of telling, all the dead narrators in Hitchcock's film worlds assume living voices. Here fictional death provides a surrealist bridge, inviting living filmgoers to leave the fiction with a mortal understanding following their narrative sojourn outside time.

Hitchcock's narrative obsession with death has produced an ironic modernist liberation suggesting that even those who have left time through death may be able to return to living time through narrative. Modernist irony positions both characters and audience at once inside and outside the fiction, inducing a vertigo akin to telling a story from the chaotic middle of rushing events. Approached from the perspective of temporal irony, the ongoing, multiple delays of resolution in Hitchcock's narratives are both pleasing and frustrating for characters seeking escape from dreamlike adventures or family traps. Yet these characters, like the film audience, enjoy and even seek ways to prolong their sojourn within stolen time, experienced as desire or fantasy. Past and present mingle in ghostly telling, as the dead Rebecca in *Rebecca* (1940) speaks from the rooms of Manderley and through the voice of her trapped acolyte, Mrs. Danvers (Judith Anderson). Or, more benignly, as Madame Blanche (Barbara Harris) speaks to and from "the great beyond" in *Family Plot* (1976), where Hitchcock acknowledges the "great beyond" of his audience in the wink Blanche Tyler gives the camera in the film's concluding moments.

Works Cited

Abbott, H. Porter. *The Cambridge Introduction to Narrative*. Cambridge: Cambridge UP, 2002.

Allen, Richard, and S. Ishii-Gonzáles, eds. *Alfred Hitchcock: Centenary Essays*. London: BFI, 1999.

Allen, Richard, and Sam Ishii-Gonzáles, eds. *Hitchcock: Past and Future*. London: Routledge, 2004.

Behler, Ernst. *Irony and the Discourse of Modernity*. Seattle: U of Washington P, 1990.

Benjamin, Walter. "The Storyteller: Reflections on the Works of Nikolai Leskov." *Illuminations*. Ed. Hannah Arendt. Trans. Harry Zohn. New York: Schocken, 1969. 83–109.

Bordwell, David. "The Classical Hollywood Style, 1917–1960." David Bordwell, Janet Staiger, and Kristin Thompson. *The Classical Hollywood Cinema: Film Style and Mode of Production to 1960*. New York: Columbia UP, 1985. 1–84.

Bradbury, Malcolm, and James McFarlane, eds. *Modernism 1890-1930*. Sussex: Harvester, 1978.

Brill, Lesley. *The Hitchcock Romance: Love and Irony in Hitchcock's Films*. Princeton: Princeton UP, 1988.

Brooks, Peter. *Reading for the Plot: Design and Intention in Narrative*. Cambridge: Harvard UP, 1984.

Cohen, Paula Marantz. *Alfred Hitchcock: The Legacy of Victorianism*. Lexington: U of Kentucky P, 1995.

Cohen, Tom. *Hitchcock's Cryptonymies*. 2 Vols. Minneapolis: U of Minnesota P, 2005.

Conrad, Peter. *The Hitchcock Murders*. London: Faber and Faber, 2000.

Elsaesser, Thomas. "The Dandy in Hitchcock." Allen and Ishii-Gonzáles, *Alfred Hitchcock* 3–13.

Hitchcock, Alfred. "On Style: An Interview." 1963. *Hitchcock on Hitchcock: Selected Writings and Interviews*. Ed. Sidney Gottlieb. Berkeley: U of California P, 1995. 285–302.

Hollington, Michael. "Svevo, Joyce and Modernist Time." Bradbury and McFarlane 430–42.

Mulvey, Laura. "Death Drives." *Hitchcock: Past and Future*. Ed. Richard Allen and Sam Ishii-Gonzáles. London: Routledge, 2004. 231–42.

Naremore, James. "Hitchcock at the Margins of Noir." Allen and Ishii-Gonzáles, *Alfred Hitchcock* 263–77.

Nicholls, Peter. *Modernisms: A Literary Guide*. Berkeley: U of California P, 1995.

Orr, John. *Cinema and Modernity*. Cambridge, UK: Polity, 1993.

Ricoeur, Paul. *Time and Narrative*. Vol. 2. Trans. Kathleen McLaughlin and David Pellauer. Chicago: U of Chicago P, 1985.

Ryall, Tom. *Alfred Hitchcock and the British Cinema*. Urbana: U of Illinois P, 1986.

Salomon, Roger B. *Desperate Storytelling: Post-Romantic Elaborations of the Mock-Heroic Mode*. Athens: U of Georgia P, 1987.

Schleifer, Ronald. *Modernism and Time: The Logic of Abundance in Literature, Science, and Culture*. Cambridge: Cambridge UP, 2000.

Schleifer, Ronald. *Rhetoric and Death: The Language of Modernism and Postmodern Discourse Theory*. Urbana: U of Illinois P, 1990.

Spoto, Donald. *The Art of Alfred Hitchcock: Fifty Years of His Motion Pictures*. New York: Hopkinson and Blake, 1976.

Trotter, David. *Cinema and Modernism*. Malden, MA: Wiley-Blackwell, 2007.

Truffaut, François, with the collaboration of Helen G. Scott. *Hitchcock*. Rev. ed. New York: Simon and Schuster, 1984.

Wollen, Peter. *Readings and Writings: Semiotic Counter-Strategies*. London: Verso, 1982.

Žižek, Slavoj. "'In His Bold Gaze My Ruin Is Writ Large.'" *Everything You Always Wanted to Know about Lacan (But Were Afraid to Ask Hitchcock)*. Ed. Slavoj Žižek. London: Verso, 1992. 211–72.

PART II

Genre

5

Hitchcock and Romance

Lesley Brill

Introduction

Like most extraordinary storytellers, Hitchcock attains his distinctiveness not as a result of some mysterious, unique genius but from a profound understanding of the fundamentals of narrative art and an unsurpassed dexterity in applying them to his medium. In particular, much of his virtuosity derives from his ability to set the hopes and dreams of romance – in an expansive sense of that word – against the disappointments and nightmares of irony. The tension between the optimistic desire for romantic innocence and the fear of corruption and meaninglessness energizes all of his films, whether they finally gratify the former or grudgingly acknowledge the triumph of entropy and death.

The majority of Hitchcock's fifty-three feature films are either resolved in favor of romance or balanced between romance and irony, with the outcome of the plot usually favoring romance. Nonetheless, a significant number – including some that scholars are most devoted to analyzing – end ironically, with the defeat of aspirations, happiness, and sometimes life itself. Even the bleakest of Hitchcock's movies, however, hold out the hope of something better, usually until nearly the end of the story, and they acknowledge the defeat of romantic dreams with sorrow.

Across nearly fifty years of directing pictures, then, Hitchcock was predominantly a creator of romantic fictions. "Romantic," however, means more than a plot focused on love between a man and a woman, although that aspect is emphatically present in most of Hitchcock's films. But what is "romance" in general, and what in particular is Hitchcockian romance? As we consider these questions, we should keep in mind that "romantic" is a relative term: works of art are romantic in relation to other, less romantic works, as brightness is relative to darkness.

A Companion to Alfred Hitchcock, First Edition. Edited by Thomas Leitch and Leland Poague.
© 2011 Thomas Leitch and Leland Poague. Published 2011 by Blackwell Publishing Ltd.

The mode of romantic narratives is usually highly conventional – "Once upon a time ..." – and it is often intermittently unrealistic. In the films of Hitchcock and other creators of cinematic romance, familiar features of myth and folklore are modernized and naturalized in deference to the capacity of movies to create overwhelming presence. The outlines of conventional romance remain clearly visible, however, as does a traditional romantic fondness for astonishing plot complications and miraculous resolutions.

Plots of romantic fictions, including Hitchcock's, usually begin by establishing intriguing, often extraordinary assumptions and conditions, then proceed with a sort of "and then, and then" structure. The action develops much as improvisatory music does, as surprisingly as possible without losing track of the thematic ideas to which the opening commits the story. Suppose, for example, that a man happens to be in the wrong place at just the wrong time and is therefore mistaken for another man, as in *Saboteur* (1942) and *North by Northwest* (1959). Or he is all but convicted by unlucky circumstances of a crime he had nothing to do with, as in *The 39 Steps* (1935), *Young and Innocent* (1937), *I Confess* (1953), and *The Wrong Man* (1956). *The Trouble with Harry* (1955) opens with a kindly hunter mistakenly supposing that he has accidentally killed a passing stranger – whose corpse, moreover, circumstances require to be buried and dug up repeatedly. What if the birds of the world, or a part of it, inexplicably declared war upon humans, as in *The Birds* (1963)? Similar stories make up much of the core of the world's enduring narratives and are often called "romance." (The French and German word "roman," for what English speakers call "novels," underscores this tradition.) Romantic tales immediately raise our curiosity and, as they go from one excitement to the next, keep us turning pages, listening to the storyteller, or watching the movie and eagerly coming back for the next one.

The outlandish beginnings characteristic of romantic stories do not in themselves guarantee romantic continuations. That depends on the texture and shape of the narrative that follows and on its outcomes. Romantic plots typically take the form of a quest – often imposed on protagonists rather than chosen – that leads to a series of adventures. The killing, exposing, or imprisoning of an antagonist usually occurs as the penultimate action, while reaffirming the hero or heroine's innocence and rewarding him or her with a mate concludes the story. In fairy tales, those archetypal romances, the destruction of an evil king or witch, a ferocious dragon, or a troll leads to a wedding for a princess or prince.

In the less magical but still romantic world of the majority of Hitchcock's films, actions and social stratifications are analogous to those of fairytales and folklore but take on modern symbolic forms: the rescue of the wrongly convicted heroine of *Murder!* (1930) by the aristocratic hero; the saving of such breathtakingly beautiful heroines as Grace Kelly (who became a royal in real life) or Tippi Hedren, often at the conventional next-to-last moment. Frequently the sex roles are reversed, as in *Spellbound* (1945), where the psychologist played by Ingrid Bergman saves the handsome, enchanted (by amnesia and a "guilt complex") Gregory Peck.

Most often in Hitchcock's movies, the rescue is more or less mutual, a circumstance that is common in folklore and fairy tales as well. Princes, reawakened by peasant girls, in turn lift their rescuers from huts into castles. Similarly, in Hitchcock's romantic tales, lovers who save their counterparts usually find love and redemption themselves.

As to villains, Hitchcock's romantic movies replace evil wizards, wicked stepmothers, and corrupt royalty with similarly sublimated forms: traitors, parvenus, foreigners, or figures of equivocal sexuality. Especially common are a host of Hitchcock antagonists that Jung called "Terrible Mothers," an archetype that the director and his writers took over almost unchanged from the world of folklore. In addition to Norman's unnaturally persistent parent in *Psycho* (1960), we may count such powerful, destructive women as Mrs. Danvers (Judith Anderson) in *Rebecca* (1940), Mrs. Sebastian (Leopoldine Konstantin) in *Notorious* (1946), and Millie (Margaret Leighton) in *Under Capricorn* (1949).

Characterization in romantic stories is more complex than in melodrama, which it sometimes approaches; but the audience's sympathies nonetheless remain unequivocally attached to the protagonists, even figures marred by serious smudges. Examples include the high-handedness of Gilbert (Michael Redgrave) early in *The Lady Vanishes* (1938), the alcoholism of Lady Hattie (Ingrid Bergman) in *Under Capricorn*, the similar affliction and past promiscuousness of Alicia (Ingrid Bergman) in *Notorious*, and the initial insincerity and multiple ex-wives of Roger Thornhill (Cary Grant) in *North by Northwest*. Smudged or not, almost all romantic heroines or heroes share a quality of doggedness accompanied, usually, by a quick wit and an ingenuity parallel to that of the creators of their stories.

In the other corner, antagonists in cinematic romances are rarely handlebar-mustachioed villains. They may have some virtues and attract some pity. We may take Millie in *Under Capricorn*, Alex (Claude Rains) in *Notorious*, and Vandamm (James Mason) in *North by Northwest* as examples. Each is devoted to a master, wife, or girlfriend, respectively, and all cherish them with something they believe to be love. In every case, however, we are likely to conclude that their love is principally for themselves, and none of them would be easily mistaken for anything but villains. Consequently, the sympathy of most audience members will be overwhelmingly for the protagonists.

Besides the protagonists and the antagonists, a third kind of figure, which we may call the helpful stranger, recurs in many romances. In folklore, he or she may be human or not; elves, spirits, or other semi-divine creatures are common, as are talking animals and even plants. In the romances of Hitchcock and other directors, such figures take more ordinary forms as minor characters who pop up providentially to provide crucial assistance.

Time in romantic narratives cycles and recycles, typically ending the story with return and renewal. One of the archetypal romantic myths – the story of Proserpine's abduction, descent into Hades, and return to the world – is also a seasonal myth corresponding to fall-winter when she descends (which she must do annually) and spring-summer when she returns. In Hitchcock's movies, such descents and returns take somewhat more realistic forms, but the underlying structure remains. A frequent signal of that structure appears in his instinct to associate his heroines with flowers, which Proserpine was gathering when she was abducted and which bloom upon her return. Hitchcock's first film, *The Pleasure Garden* (1925), takes its heroine Patsy Brand (Virginia Valli) down desperate paths in "the East" where she loses love, her husband, and nearly her life. By the end of the movie, however, she has returned to a safe, civilized world, the embraces of her surrogate parents, and the clear implication that a new love may be just over the horizon.

Shadows of Proserpine's story are more visible in Hitchcock's third film, *The Lodger* (1926), with its heroine named Daisy (June Tripp), and a hero (Ivor Novello), deputized by his dying mother, who descends from his bright, geographically and socially elevated mansion into the fog of a working class London neighborhood. He ultimately reascends, carrying Daisy up with him. That he is nearly killed while down below has little to do with the Proserpine myth, but fits the shape of romance very well. Although Hitchcock did not use Daisy as the name of a heroine again, he did add an Iris and a pair of Roses. He set *Shadow of a Doubt* (1943) in Santa Rosa and connected flowers in that film with a young girl. More importantly, he persistently put his female protagonists in proximity to flowers.

As in the Proserpine legend, the plot in Hitchcock's romantic films often pivots upon something like a death and rebirth, or an approximation of such an action. In *The 39 Steps*, for example, the protagonist, Richard Hannay (Robert Donat), is shot at close range and slumps to the floor. Hitchcock immediately cuts away, leaving the impression that he has been seriously wounded or killed. This impression is quickly corrected, but the shape of a death and resurrection has been achieved by editing.

An enduring topic of discussion among Hitchcock scholars concerns the director's Catholic upbringing. The degree to which Hitchcock's religious education left a lasting imprint on his psyche or in his films will probably remain a subject for dispute. Beyond dispute, however, is the frequency of Christian settings and symbols in his movies. Churches provide settings for important scenes in both versions of *The Man Who Knew Too Much* (1934 and 1956), *Secret Agent* (1936), and backdrops for the conclusions of *Shadow of a Doubt* and *Vertigo* (1958). It is also common for Hitchcock's romantic heroes and heroines to carry Christian overtones in their characterization.

The situation of the unjustly accused innocent, of which Hitchcock was so fond, has a broad affiliation with Christ's earthly role. Neil Hurley, who has argued that Hitchcock was profoundly affected by his Catholic education, makes a similar point: "The 'wrong-person' motif is closely related to the secular transfigurations of the Christ" (76). That analogy is explicitly emphasized when the apparently insoluble dilemma faced by the hero (Henry Fonda) of *The Wrong Man* is miraculously resolved as he gazes at a portrait of Jesus. A little less pointedly, the hero of *The Lodger* undergoes a sort of near crucifixion by a mob convinced that he is

"The Avenger." At the end of *Vertigo*, Hitchcock puts Scottie (James Stewart) into a pose that recalls the same event. Similarly, when Blanche (Barbara Harris) slumps unconscious to the garage floor in *Family Plot* (1976), her arms are spread and her feet drawn up as in a horizontal crucifixion. Hurley maintains that Thornhill's "bleeding hand is a Christ-like sign" in *North by Northwest* and that Tippi Hedren undergoes "cruciform' suffering" when she is attacked near the end of *The Birds* (see Hurley's frame enlargements section). Father Logan (Montgomery Clift), the hero of *I Confess*, is explicitly likened to Christ. The female protagonists of *Stage Fright* (1950) and *North by Northwest* share the name Eve (Jane Wyman and Eva Marie Saint, respectively), and the latter is rescued from a devilish Vandamm by a man whose name evokes Christ's crown of thorns and crucifixion on a hill. Haunted by a painful past in *Notorious*, the protagonist (Cary Grant) has a name that he pronounces carefully at one point as "Devil-in." Earlier, Devlin and Alicia entered Rio de Janeiro via a shot of the statue of Christ overlooking the city.

How religious or irreligious Hitchcock may have been in his inmost soul we are unlikely ever to know; but we may guess with some confidence that the Christian romance – Dante called it *The Divine Comedy* – had substantial influence on the structures of his storytelling. Moreover, what is true theologically is true mythologically; variants of the Fall are widespread in such stories as Pandora's opening of the forbidden box, or a Golden Age preceding an Iron one. For Hitchcock, however, the shape of that idea seems to have been most accessible in Christian myth. His heroes and heroines, like everyone else according to Christian doctrine, possess hereditary faults. Symbolically if not literally, their quests may be seen as leading toward the remedying of those inherited injuries. From other theological and mythological perspectives, too, humans are inhabitants of a fallen world. All are inherently stained and injured and need to recover their innocence in order to regain health and wholeness.

For Hitchcock, innocence recovered has the superiority of something earned as opposed to something bestowed. It is conscious of itself in the way that life can be conscious of itself only through the knowledge of death. Like most makers of romantic narratives, therefore, Hitchcock paradoxically embraces human faults and misfortunes because they provide opportunities for overcoming them. From the Christian theological perspective, the Fall is ultimately a *felix culpa*, a fortunate fault that makes possible the glory of Christ's redemption of humankind.

Before leaving this general discussion of Hitchcock's relation to romance and focusing in more detail on particular movies, a final observation: Although in Hitchcock's oeuvre romance is often found with comedy, the two are not necessarily connected. A brief summary of what Northrop Frye called "pregeneric elements" or "*mythoi*" makes this clear (*Anatomy* 162). If we map these pregeneric elements onto Cartesian coordinates, the result is represented in Figure 5.1.

Romance opposes irony as comedy opposes tragedy. Thus romantic comedy and ironic comedy (often called satire) are equally possible, as are ironic tragedy or tragic romance. The last is rare outside grand opera, but Shakespeare's *Romeo and*

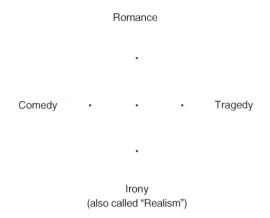

Figure 5.1

Juliet (1595) provides a well-known example, with its closing reconciliation of the Capulets and Montagues and its promise of golden statues to render the protagonists and their story immortal.

Deep suffering and irremediable destruction are incompatible with the happy universe of relatively pure comedy; such actions are not only compatible with romance, but indeed are part of the foundation on which it is erected. The endings of romances stress the cyclic rejuvenation of night to day, winter to summer, and death to life (a compensation that makes their inclusion in relatively comic fictional worlds possible). Thus romantic narratives need night, winter, and death. They also generally include the social integration that is a hallmark of comedy – typically signified by a concluding marriage or some other sequence of events that at once unites the protagonists and reunites them with their society.

Hitchcockian Love and Romance

For purposes of this discussion, let us divide Hitchcock's films into three categories: those in which romance is clearly dominant (but which nonetheless have some ironic elements), those in which romantic and ironic elements are relatively balanced, and those in which ironic elements dominate. In *The Hitchcock Romance*, I labeled these categories "Romances," "Mixed Romances," and "Irony." Although he starts from a different theoretical base, Richard Allen categorizes Hitchcock's films similarly as "romantic irony," "ironic ambivalence," and "narratives of ironic inversion" (12). Since this is an essay about Hitchcockian romance, I shall focus on the first category.

The solutions to most of the dilemmas that drive Hitchcock's narratives are embodied in the development of love between a woman and a man – at or near the center of at least forty-three of his surviving fifty-two features, by my count. Of course, not all of those films are romances; but all of the romances include love stories. To those movies we can apply what the director said in discussing the never-made film *The Short Night*, which he began before his health forced his retirement: "The main thing is the love story" (Hitchcock 61). Love between men and women, in Hitchcock's movies as in most folklore and fairy tales, is crucial to the struggle of innocence against the corruptions of experience. Through its grace, lovers can discover or find again in themselves the "unspoiled child whose heart is full of daisies and buttercups," as Alicia says in *Notorious* – a reawakening and nurturing of goodness and happiness that can flourish despite the experience of evil and misery. In most of Hitchcock's romances, a specific misfortune or infection from the past threatens present happiness. His heroes and heroines, as Saint Paul wrote, must "redeem the time, for the days are evil" (Ephesians 5:16). Love makes it possible for them to do so, as does a romantic fictional world.

Because it can never be fully deserved or earned, true love is always something of a miracle that injects a glorious abundance into a lean world of cause and effect, the world of experience. Nonetheless, Hitchcock, like Prospero in *The Tempest*, arranges things so that achieving love should be "uneasy … lest too light winning/ Make the prize light" (I. ii. 452–53).

Hitchcock called the excuse for the adventures that lead to rejuvenating love the "MacGuffin" – a device, as he explained, for catching something that doesn't exist (Truffaut 138–39). By the end of the picture, the MacGuffin is often largely replaced as the center of interest by the love story. Though Hitchcock gave it a new name, such an ostensible goal is a recurrent feature of adventure narratives from Odysseus's struggles to return home, through the grail-quests of medieval romances, to various adventures of modern cinema: The Little Tramp's seeking of Yukon gold in Chaplin's *The Gold Rush* (1925), expeditions seeking lost mines or other treasures in films like *King Solomon's Mines* (1937, 1950, 1985), and recent versions like *Star Wars* (1977) or the *Indiana Jones* quests. *The Lodger* supplies an early example of a MacGuffin, its pursuit of the Avenger all but disappearing in the successful conclusion of the love story. Similarly, the concern about the Nazi uranium in *Notorious* fades away near its conclusion.

By the end of most of Hitchcock's films – those that end happily – an energetic heroine has connected with a masculine counterpart. Before she achieves that connection, however, her circumstances usually cast her in the role of a young woman whose progress from the arms of a father or father-figure to those of a lover has been somehow retarded. She finds herself dwelling too long in the parental home; in or drifting toward a relationship with an inappropriate, usually older, man; or being aggressively courted or menaced by such a figure – one who should be a father or mentor rather than lover. Carol Fisher (Laraine Day) in *Foreign Correspondent* (1940) is acting as the companion and helpmate to her sinister father (Herbert Marshall). Young Charlie (Teresa Wright) in *Shadow of a Doubt*, Alicia in *Notorious*, and Eve in *North by Northwest* are all threatened or possessed by dangerous older men.

The selfless love between Hitchcock's heroines and heroes is pointedly opposed to the possessive libidinal egotism his antagonists feel for the objects of their desires. *Notorious* exemplifies this opposition. Alex feels "hunger" for Alicia and insists on possessing her as a proof of what he supposes to be love. By contrast, Devlin is able to love – and rescue – her when he forswears possession: "I couldn't see straight or think straight. ... It tore me up, not having you."

Love cures what ails us. Inevitably injured and deficient, people can be healed and made whole only by mutual love, the earthly analogue of heavenly grace. Hitchcock's love stories stress aspects that ally them to miracles and faith: plot improbabilities and unconditional commitment to the beloved, respectively. Their miracles usually occur when a woman and a man fall in love, often suddenly and almost always in unlikely circumstances.

In *Spellbound*, the bespectacled, somewhat prissy young psychoanalyst who dismisses love as a fiction created by poets (a traditional signal of what is about to happen to her) falls overwhelmingly for John Ballantine – who at the time is suffering from amnesia, the delusion that he is someone else, and an impending nervous breakdown. Nonetheless, he too falls. He describes the miracle that he and Constance are experiencing as "like lightning striking. It happens rarely." As her name promises, Constance's commitment to the man she loves remains unshakeable, even when all evidence seems to declare him insane and a probable murderer.

As is often the case, Hitchcock's cinematic technique during the lovers' first kiss corresponds to the miracle it is conveying. His long double exposure of the lovers' kiss with a series of yonic doors that open to a brilliant light is at once corny, exaggerated, implausible, comic, undeniable, and wonderful – like their love itself.

Love serves innocence. Both literally and metaphorically, the lovers' faith in the falsity of accusations against their counterparts is central to Hitchcock's romantic vision. Love discovers and nourishes the human goodness that survives in a corrupted world. Hitchcock's films urge the audience, like the lovers, to side with faith and love against appearance, prudence, and logic. As Constance says, "The heart can see deeper .... I couldn't feel this way toward a man who was bad."

In Hitchcock's ironic films, the longing for love is the same, but the world of the narrative does not accommodate it. Judy Barton (Kim Novak) falls to her death at the end of *Vertigo*; in the middle of *Psycho*, Marion Crane (Janet Leigh) is murdered, famously, in the shower; the most sympathetic female characters of *Frenzy* (1972) fall prey to the rapist-murderer Rusk (Barry Foster). Even within Hitchcock's romantic films, we find characters who are beyond love's redemption: Mrs. Danvers in *Rebecca*, Millie in *Under Capricorn*, and the suggestively named Adamson (William Devane) in *Family Plot*. All are what we might call faux lovers, and all apparently regard the world as a place unworthy of much moral concern. Another faux lover, Uncle Charlie (Joseph Cotten) in *Shadow of a Doubt*, declares it to be no more than "a foul sty."

For the most cheerful of Hitchcock's romantic films, *The Trouble with Harry*, even the past brings forth love and rebirth. In the person of Harry, it is repeatedly unburied and put to rest again with the happy results of the summery love of Sam

(John Forsythe) and Jennifer (Shirley MacLaine) and the autumnal flowering, as her name suggests, of Ivy Gravely (Mildred Natwick) and Captain Wiles (Edmund Gwenn). The innocence of all four lovers is finally confirmed, quite unconsciously, by a poetry-reading doctor with the vernal name of Greenbow (Dwight Marfield).

Hitchcock's Comic Romances

Hitchcock's comic romances define one of the poles of his oeuvre; the other is defined by such ironic and tragic works as *Vertigo* and *Topaz* (1969). Among the comic romances are *Young and Innocent, The Lady Vanishes, To Catch a Thief* (1955), *North by Northwest,* and *Family Plot.* Besides their happy endings and relatively scanty helpings of pain and destruction, all figure forth a world in which the romantic ideals of love and the recovery of innocence prevail. All bring lovers together and, in doing so, put some emphasis on the construction or reconstruction of family. Central characters are either freed from false accusations or, in the cases of *The Lady Vanishes* and *Family Plot,* otherwise validated. The restorations of romantic time blend with the caprices of a comic time that provides unexpected complications only to resolve them, usually with more surprises. The protagonists of Hitchcock's comic romances share with their creator a sense of humor and witty ingenuity that banish tragedy and assure us that everything will ultimately be all right.

Two somewhat neglected films, *Young and Innocent* and *To Catch a Thief,* exemplify the tendencies of Hitchcockian romantic comedy. Though *Young and Innocent* goes from one threatening adventure to the next and begins with a theatrically overcooked quarrel followed by a corpse, it keeps real pain at bay. The corpse produces a mistaken accusation against the hero of the film, Robert Tisdall (Derrick De Marney); but the hysterical silliness of his accusers, his sudden, incongruous infatuation with the chief constable's daughter, Erica (Nova Pilbeam), during his questioning, and the broad comedy of his escape from custody all confirm his foolish lawyer's apparently fatuous reassurance, "Mustn't be down-hearted on a morning like this, must we?"

In other contexts, Erica's flight from home and the charge of murder against Robert might hang heavy over the action; but except for few brief, energizing moments of anxiety or discouragement, the protagonists remain playfully cheerful as they pursue Robert's exoneration. *Young and Innocent* sets true love opposite its diseased inversion. The histrionic opening displays love-as-possession at its worst, while the dramatic cliché of thunder, lightning, and stormy breakers further the comic overstatement of the scene. "I'll shout if I want to!" rages the Drummer Man (George Curzon). "You're not going to get rid of me. ... You're my wife!" The love of Erica and Robert, on the other hand, is characterized by mutual protectiveness and admiration – including a measure of decorous erotic energy.

The "motto" that little Harold begins to read during the birthday party sequence reinforces the central theme: "Love calls but once, though passion oft …"

The development of love between Robert and Erica also tracks their maturation. Maurice Yacowar has pointed out that *Young and Innocent* is partly about Erica's growing up (218); William Rothman observes that "girls on the threshold of womanhood" recur throughout Hitchcock's movies (368); and Elsie B. Michie adduces Tania Modleski in observing that "one frequently finds in Hitchcock's films … the space for a narrative of female maturation" (42). The first indication of Erica's love comes when she brings bread and cheese for Robert to the old mill where he is hiding. To go there, she leaves her place at the family dinner table, an action suggesting that the beginning of love is also the beginning of her movement into independent adulthood.

Because *Young and Innocent* develops unequivocally as a comedy, the romantic theme of death and return is damped down. It remains, however, in the form of descents and ascents. Robert descends to the beach – as usual, the seaside is a dangerous place in a Hitchcock film – where he finds the body of the actress we saw in the opening scene. He also sees a flock of threatening seagulls, an image Hitchcock famously elaborated twenty-six years later. Searching for the raincoat that will exonerate him, he and Erica descend into the darkness of a sunken rail yard. When they flee the police by driving into an old mine, the floor collapses under the car. To save Erica, Robert reaches out for her hand in a close-up that Hitchcock will duplicate on the face of Mount Rushmore in *North by Northwest* and, ironically, near the end of *Saboteur*, on top of the Statue of Liberty.

Essential revelations take place on high, which Hitchcock manages both physically, by moving the action up, and optically, achieving a similar effect with the camera. Erica climbs a ladder to bring Robert his food; and Hitchcock is careful to photograph her as she ascends the stairs to her bedroom, into which Robert will clamber in magical, romantic moonlight. There, in a setting elevated and intimate, the crucial clue of a pack of matches from the Grand Hotel comes to light. In the hotel itself, Hitchcock lifts his camera for a celebrated 240-foot crane shot that ends on the incriminating twitching eyes of the actual murderer. The elevated shot, like a hand reaching out to save Robert from an abyss, frees him from suspicion just as he is being arrested.

The quest to clear the protagonist of an accusation, a plot device to which Hitchcock turned repeatedly, connects directly to the underlying theme of the recovery of innocence despite the assaults of experience. Structurally, the developing love of Erica and Robert, with its closing promise of a likely wedding, organizes the narrative as a refutation of the grim vision of marriage with which the film begins.

Like *Young and Innocent*, *To Catch a Thief* begins with a comically exaggerated sequence that simultaneously defines the foil against which the action will work and diminishes its threat. A travel poster tells us that we are in a land of pleasure, and the playful, witty verbal jousting of the central characters further holds real suffering at bay. Eventually the banter of the protagonists gives way to expressions of real feeling: declarations of love or moments when John Robie (Cary Grant) takes Francie Stevens (Grace Kelly) into his arms.

The conflict between true love and possessive passion reappears in *To Catch a Thief* in a surprising variation. The most obvious avatar of possessive, sexually greedy love is Danielle (Brigitte Auber), the real thief. The most formidable amorous antagonists, however, are the protagonists themselves. Their toying with each other initially appears as Francie's sexual attraction to an exotic (supposed) criminal and, on John's side, as rather idle play, which also serves to clear himself of suspicion and discover the real thief.

The love that overtakes the protagonists matures and completes them. Francie grows out of her identity as a self-centered, "pampered, insecure young woman"; John discovers that he is not the "lone wolf" he thought he was, that he needs the "help of a good woman." Pointedly, neither Francie nor John has a complete family before they meet. The promised inclusion of Francie's mother at the end wraps the story up in much the same way that Hitchcock closed *Young and Innocent*: a diminished family is enlarged and a new one begun. Love renews not only lovers but the people or societies whose lives they touch.

Like *Young and Innocent*, *To Catch a Thief* in its comic world diminishes the intensity of its gestures toward death and return – with the exception of an editing trick like that in *The 39 Steps*. John is apparently clubbed and dumped into the sea, following which Hitchcock cuts from the scene of the assault. A little later, however, he reappears alive and well. Nonetheless, *To Catch a Thief* has ascents in abundance and only a few harrowing descents or threatened ones. A high-speed chase along a twisting cliff-top road offers some chills, but it is resolved when Francie and John escape to enjoy a picnic overlooking the sea and embrace with real emotion for the first time. Other descents are even less alarming: John flops into a mass of flowers, is threatened by Danielle while swimming, and escapes the police by faking his suicide and driving away downhill.

Elevated settings proliferate, as one would expect from a movie about cat burglars. John's home is set high on a hill, and he often climbs to rooftops to escape pursuers or to pursue antagonists himself. Into this high-spirited, always inventive film, Hitchcock inserts an entertaining variation on another of his standard romantic motifs, ascents. Francie brings John up to her room to watch fireworks in a long, wonderfully silly, almost soft-core sequence. There the adolescent frivolity of Francie's and John's mutual seduction is fully matched by the adolescent frivolity of the filmmaker and his collaborators: obvious, suggestive double-entendre, an hysterical music track, and wildly speeded-up fireworks to symbolize the activity just off camera.

The MacGuffin of *To Catch a Thief*, the effort to clear John of suspicion by exposing the counterfeit "Cat," parallels the deeper concern of the film, the protagonists' maturing and achieving of adult love, their regaining of innocence. The collaboration of the insurance man Hughson (John Williams) and the presence of the police at the conclusion confirm the restoration of John's place in the larger society. The closing embrace into which he draws Francie is followed by her announcement of a future bliss that will include her mother and by a bell that ambiguously rings celebration, warning, and anticipation of a wedding – the last received with traditional ambivalence by the prospective bridegroom.

Other Hitchcockian Romances

Romantic narratives need not be comic. In Hitchcock's case, most are not, though the majority of his films, including some of his most ironic, contain considerable humor. Among the romances that few would call comedies, we may count *The Pleasure Garden*, *The Lodger*, *The 39 Steps*, *The Lady Vanishes*, *Saboteur*, *Spellbound*, *Under Capricorn*, the second *The Man Who Knew Too Much*, and *Marnie* (1964). *Saboteur*, *The 39 Steps*, and *The Lady Vanishes* often come close to comedy; *The Pleasure Garden* and *Marnie* approach tragedy. All contain the structures, themes, and imagery characteristic of the sort of romance upon which Hitchcock put his distinctive mark. Classifying them has little value in itself, but recognizing their genre is an essential step toward accurately understanding them and the place they have in Hitchcock's work as a whole.

Compared to comic romances like *Young and Innocent*, *To Catch a Thief*, and *The Trouble with Harry* – as well as to the ironic comedies *Rich and Strange* (1931) and *Mr. and Mrs. Smith* (1941) – the films listed above carry a heavier burden of pain, anxiety, and destruction. The husband of the heroine of *The Pleasure Garden* betrays her, drowns his lovely native paramour, and has to be killed when he goes mad and attempts to murder his wife. Marnie (Tippi Hedren) suffers debilitating anxiety, is forced to destroy her beloved horse when he breaks his leg, and attempts suicide. The McKennas' only son is kidnapped early in the second *The Man Who Knew Too Much*. Such threats and catastrophes in the other ambiguous romances could be easily enumerated. Even the most comic of them, *Saboteur*, begins with the onscreen incineration of the protagonist's best friend.

In a less benign world, the playfulness of the protagonists declines or disappears, but their romantic resourcefulness and doggedness remains. Knocked delirious by a heavy flowerpot, made to look foolish by a conspiracy whose motives she cannot guess, and ignored by the few fellow passengers who don't actively disbelieve her, Iris Henderson (Margaret Lockwood) in *The Lady Vanishes* continues to insist that Miss Froy (Dame May Whitty) has disappeared and refuses to abandon searching for her. For no initial reason beyond his sense that justice has miscarried, Sir John Menier (Herbert Marshall) devotes himself, in *Murder!*, to establishing the innocence of the young woman whose conviction he reluctantly agreed to as a jury member in her trial. The devotion of Mark Rutland (Sean Connery) to Marnie Edgar, as she points out, approaches the neurotic: "Look at yourself, Old Dear.

You've got a pathological fix on a woman who's not only an admitted criminal but who screams if you come near her." To which Mark can only reply, amusingly and amused, "I never said I was perfect."

The multiplication of adventures and intriguing locations also remains a feature of Hitchcock's uncomic romances. As in *North by Northwest* but in the opposite direction, the hero of *Saboteur* traverses much of the United States while attempting to prove his innocence. The protagonist of *The 39 Steps* follows a similar course across England and Scotland. *The Man Who Knew Too Much* begins in Morocco, *The Lady Vanishes* in an exotic Eastern European country; *The Pleasure Garden* removes its characters to a still more exotic "East," and *Under Capricorn* takes place, as its name promises, below the equator. The more domestic dramas of *Spellbound*, *The Lodger*, and *Marnie* manage to send their protagonists on trips to other cities, ski resorts, through London fog, on world cruises, and so on. Everywhere they go, adventure follows.

In accordance with the colloquial use of the word "romance," love between men and women remains at the center of Hitchcock's romantic adventures. It is worth repeating that Hitchcock – widely considered a cynical, playfully sadistic manipulator of audiences, plots, and actors – fills most of his films with love stories. In the romances we are considering now, the improbability of the love remains an important feature, as does the centrality of its role in establishing the innocence of one or both of the lovers, and in making possible the maturation and healing of both. The contrast between true selfless love and its demonic distortion as possessive passion remains emphatic. We also find explicit or suggested contrasts between good and bad families. Romances set forth narratives of rebirth and rejuvenation; and the family, generally speaking, is the site of human renewal.

The love between protagonists, if rarely of the "lightning striking" variety, remains improbable in its circumstances and, frequently, in the incongruous social status of its pairs. Antagonism marks the beginnings of the love stories of Hannay and Pamela (Madeleine Carroll) in *The 39 Steps*, Barry Kane (Robert Cummings) and Pat Martin (Priscilla Lane) in *Saboteur*, Iris and Gilbert in *The Lady Vanishes*, and Mark and Marnie. The famous Sir John in *Murder!* falls in love with an obscure commoner. Other unlikely class matchings characterize the lovers in *The Lodger*, *The Lady Vanishes*, *Under Capricorn*, and *Marnie*. Improbable circumstances and social mismatching infuse the love at the center of Hitchcock's romances with traces of the miraculous.

The contrast between true love and its egotistical inversion constitutes a theme that runs through most of Hitchcock's films, both romantic and ironic (where the latter sometimes prevails). *Under Capricorn* affords a complicated instance. The love of Lady Hattie and Sam (Joseph Cotten) is too selfless. Each is determined to sacrifice herself or himself for the other – which also means, unhappily, to sacrifice their love. Set against this too-mutually-devoted husband and wife are two other figures – ultimately of very different character – for whom love means possession. The first is Millie, the housekeeper, who strikingly resembles Mrs. Danvers in

Rebecca. The second is Charles Adare (Michael Wilding), the "youngest son of an Irish peer," who has come to Australia to seek a fortune he cannot inherit in Ireland. Like Hattie and Sam, Millie and Charles are victims of a class-based society.

Millie, in her desire to prize Sam from Hattie and possess him for herself, finds justification in "the Lord." As she perverts love, so she perverts religion. The analogy between romantic love and religious grace is clearly, if negatively, figured in Millie's demonic, death-infused distortion of both. Adare, on the other hand, finally renounces his desire to claim Hattie for himself. In doing so, he transforms himself from a false into a true lover, into something like an angel of salvation. When he makes possible the healing of Hattie's and Sam's marriage, he also heals himself.

The dynamics of true love and its ironic inversion have a similar complexity in *Marnie*. Mark's desire for Marnie begins with a desire for possession and control. As he comes to understand the degree of Marnie's psychological injuries, however, his love gradually turns into a desire to help her heal. At the same time, as in *Under Capricorn*, a clutch of true love's enemies oppresses or attacks Marnie. Sidney Strutt (Martin Gabel), who hired Marnie because of his attraction to her and whom she subsequently robbed, seeks to revenge his wounded vanity. Lil Mainwaring (Diane Baker), dwelling as a dependent in Mark's home (like Millie in Sam's in *Under Capricorn*), wants her sister's widower for herself. Marnie's mother, Bernice (Louise Latham), also like Millie, attaches a self-serving righteousness to a love that begins and persists as possession. Marnie was conceived because Bernice coveted "Billy's basketball sweater," which she obtained when she "let him." She concludes, "An' I got you, Marnie."

In less complicated ways, Hitchcock's other love stories set the true "love [that] calls but once" against grasping "passion." The faithful Patsy Brand and Hugh Fielding (John Stuart) in *The Pleasure Garden* balance the self-seeking, faithless Jill Cheyne (Carmelita Geraghty) and Levet (Miles Mander). The gentle Lodger approaches Daisy with a diffidence that contrasts with the aggressive possessiveness of Joe (Malcolm Keen), who handcuffs her at one point, declaring, "After I put a rope around the Avenger's neck, I'll put a ring on Daisy's finger." Early in *Spellbound*, a man-hating, nymphomaniac patient explicitly opposes Constance, calling her "Miss Frozen Puss."

In *Spellbound* we also see the way in which the opposition between supportive and self-centered lovers blends into a similar opposition between loving and self-seeking families or family members. Dr. Murchison (Leo G. Carroll) serves as a sort of "terrible father" to Constance, willing to sacrifice her happiness for his. His opposite, Dr. Brulov (Michael Chekhov), Constance's mentor and professional father, risks arrest on Constance's behalf. A more obvious opposition of families arises in the second *The Man Who Knew Too Much* between the McKennas – retired singer Jo (Doris Day), her physician husband Ben (James Stewart), and their son Hank (Christopher Olsen) – and the subversive Draytons. In *The Farmer's Wife* (1928) and *Under Capricorn*, contrasting actual or potential families duplicate pairings in love: respectively, Samuel Sweetland (Jameson Thomas)/Minta Dench (Lilian Hall-Davis) versus Samuel and the numerous unsuitable women he courts, and Sam/Hattie versus Sam/Millie.

Actions approaching death and return become less sublimated as Hitchcock's romantic stories become less comic. *Murder!* provides an extended example, with its heroine imprisoned literally in the shadow of the gallows to which she is sentenced. The Lodger is snatched from the brink of death and taken to a heavenly white hospital ward. Miss Froy disappears to be recovered, eventually, from mummy-like bandages. Mark finds Marnie nearly drowned and revives her with artificial respiration. Like Diana (Norah Baring) in *Murder!*, John Ballantine in *Spellbound* is convicted of murder and imprisoned.

The strong causal connection of past sins or mistakes to present woes is empha-sized by descents to regions evocative of Hades. The importance of ascents in uncovering or confronting the sickness originating in the past and of love in curing it connects Hitchcock's romantic movies with mythic, religious, and folkloric fore-bears. Indeed, descents or threatened falls toward demonic regions and contrast-ing ascents to love and illumination remain characteristic of Hitchcockian romance, comic or not. Mark discovers Marnie in the pool below him when she attempts suicide. Later, he drags her up the steps into her mother's home where, sitting on another flight of stairs, she recovers the memory that promises to return her to health. The Lodger descends both physically and socially, then reascends with Daisy to his brilliant mansion overlooking the city. The hero of *Saboteur* ends his quest at the summit of the Statue of Liberty, in the arms of the woman he won while striving to prove his innocence.

The final, liberating ascent in the second *The Man Who Knew Too Much* is under-taken not by a person but by the voice of Hank's mother. Attempting to contact her son in the embassy where she believes him imprisoned, Jo loudly sings her signature song, "Que Sera, Sera." A pan and a series of eight still shots trace her voice as it ascends a staircase, then goes down a hall to a close-up of a door and doorknob, behind which Hank awakens to respond with shrill whistles to his mother's voice, now faint on the soundtrack. This acoustic ascent, traced with conspicuous virtuosity, will restore the broken family.

Remembering that ascents, actions suggesting rebirth, and the miracle of love all serve the restoration of innocence – literally and metaphorically – we understand why Hitchcock's favorite MacGuffins set the protagonist the task of refuting spuri-ous accusations. In *Under Capricorn*, Sam is cleared of the charge of assault; equally important, Hattie's addiction to drugs and alcohol is revealed to have been largely the result of Millie's machinations. The restoration in *The Lady Vanishes*, similarly, has not to do with a criminal accusation but with the revelation of the truth of the heroine's perceptions. The criminal accusations against Marnie are true enough, but the disclosure of her childhood traumas nonetheless restores her essential innocence. "Will I go to jail?' she asks. Mark replies, "Not after they [her victims] hear what I have to tell them."

The importance of exposing and detoxifying a poisonous past, explicit in *Marnie*, implicitly underlies most of Hitchcock's romances of false accusation. In some, the theme is subtle: Jo's gradual recovery of a position of equality in her marriage and the reassertion of the professional status she sacrificed to her husband's medical career, or Iris's rejection of the expedient, apparently loveless marriage to which she consigns herself at the beginning of *The Lady Vanishes*. The redemption of the past is direct and explicit in *The Lodger* and *Under Capricorn*, both of which ultimately cure the infections that past killings have carried into the present.

As in comedies, evaporating the miasma of the past restores and elevates the social standing of the protagonists. Authority figures are often on hand to certify such social rehabilitation. The police take Mr. Memory's revelations at the end of *The 39 Steps*, while Pamela and Richard take each other's hand. The regained innocence of protagonists also ripples outward into their relations with other people in reconstituted or newly constituted families. The father-figure Brulov is joined by a puzzled ticket-taker, who adds a touch of social authority at the end of *Spellbound*. The presence of Foreign Office authorities does the same thing more emphatically at the end of *The Lady Vanishes*. Offstage, offscreen applause at the end of *Murder!* adds social approbation for Diana and Sir John. Mildly and with some irony, the sign that flashes "TONIGHT GOLDEN CURLS" evokes a social authorization of the alliance of Daisy and the Lodger as their story ends.

The high degree of overt conventionality and self-reflexivity of Hitchcockian (and other) romantic stories reinforces the social authority of the tales themselves. At the same time, their conspicuous artifice and often astonishing plots support their emphasis on the miraculous – especially, for Hitchcock, the miraculous power of love.

All the movies I've been discussing emphasize what Sir John, in the backstage romance / thriller *Murder!*, called the mingling of "the techniques of art" and "the technique of life." *The Pleasure Garden*, also a backstage story, was another such blend, both of genre and "technique." The second *The Man Who Knew Too Much* similarly melds art / life and backstage romance / thriller. *The Lady Vanishes*, *The 39 Steps*, and *Under Capricorn* are rich with images and actions of art and pretense. Besides the stratagems required to conceal the kidnapping of Miss Froy, *The Lady Vanishes* also emphasizes performance by its inclusion of the magician Signor Doppo (Philip Leaver) and his equipage. *The 39 Steps* begins and ends in a music hall, and it features along the way numerous impromptu performances by Hannay and his antagonists. *Under Capricorn* opens with a welcoming ceremony for a new governor and sets a crucial sequence in a formal dress ball.

That film also includes in its opening the conspicuous artifice of a dramatic music track, a portentous voice-over announcing "And now our story begins," and a setting of obviously painted backdrops, which will be more or less repeated at the end. *Spellbound* begins with similarly dramatic music, and a written narrative that starts with a quotation from *Hamlet*; the story that follows includes the conspicuously arty dreamscapes of Salvador Dali. The shedding tree and leaves that scuttle in the wind as *Spellbound* commences are recycled from the opening of an earlier Hitchcock film, *Number Seventeen* (1932), an ambitious experimental blend of Russian montage, Dada, and a Shakespearean wise fool that could hardly be more emphatically artificial and that has the conventional romantic conclusion including a man and woman coming together, a comic helper, the exposure of villains, and the social authorization of the police.

The opening credits for *Marnie* are inscribed on what may be Hollywood's most venerable cliché for such things, turning book pages. Given that Hitchcock's film-making mantra was to wonder "how one might do this otherwise," we can assume that his use of such a worn-out device had a purpose beyond economy.

And so it did. Like the artificiality of *Under Capricorn* and *Spellbound*, and like the self-reflexivity of all of Hitchcock's romances, that of *Marnie* – including its much criticized obvious rear-projection and its painted backdrops – declares not the falsehood of fable but a fabulous concentration of truth. Like the other romances, it is a parable, not a slice of life. All the romances are dramatic in the way that Hitchcock famously defined drama: "life with the dull bits cut out" (Truffaut 103). Hitchcock's movies in general, and his romances in particular, represent not the realistic, mostly random noise of daily life, but what such noise conceals, the underlying meaning that the compression and stylization of art reveals.

Ambiguous Romances and Hitchcockian Irony

Whatever their outcomes and dominant tone, all Hitchcock films are structured by the tension between romantic and ironic modalities. From this tension comes much of the suspense of which Hitchcock was famously the master. In what I have elsewhere called "mixed romances" (Brill 70 ff.), the modalities of romance and irony are more or less balanced and the tension between romantic and ironic elements and outcomes remains at least partly unresolved. Such ambiguous romances constitute a large plurality of Hitchcock's films.

Although their romance is to varying degrees tempered by the reversals and disappointments of irony, the themes, images, and narrative conflicts of Hitchcock's ambiguous romances duplicate those of his less open-ended films: innocence / corruption, ascents / descents, true love / passionate egotism, the need to form or reconstitute families, and so on.

One film that is resolved mostly but not quite definitively in favor of romance, *Rear Window* (1954), contains an image that illustrates the way in which romance and irony are simultaneously opposed and mutually implicated. In a photographer's lightbox, we see a negative of a female model. Hitchcock then pans to the positive image, on a magazine cover, of the same photograph. At once opposite and duplicate, reflecting the same reality, these images define each other. The ideas "negative" and "positive" can arise only from contrast. The same is true of romance and irony.

In the conclusions of virtually all of Hitchcock's ambiguous romances, love prevails. But it is compromised, complicated, or diminished. The proper couples are together at the end of Hitchcock's last silent film, *The Manxman* (1929), and his first talkie, *Blackmail* (1929); but they have been disgraced and exiled in *The Manxman*, and in *Blackmail* they share a terrible secret: the woman's stabbing of her assailant and the couple's responsibility for the death of another man, a scoundrel indeed but nonetheless innocent of the killing. The female protagonist is with a sympathetic detective and likely lover at the conclusion of *Sabotage* (1936); but that couple also shares a secret: her murder of her husband, however extenuating the circumstances. Their relationship began, moreover, while the woman was married, like the relationship between Guy Haines (Farley Granger) and Anne Morton (Ruth Roman) in *Strangers on a Train* (1951) – again with extenuating circumstances, and again entwined with the killing of a spouse. So too in *Dial M for Murder* (1954). In *Suspicion* (1941), the threat of a murderous husband is raised to be largely but perhaps not quite entirely disarmed at the end. Husband and wife are together at the end of *The Paradine Case* (1947), but only after the husband's catastrophic infatuation with a gorgeous murderess has all but ruined his career and his marriage. And so forth; in the ambiguous romances love triumphs, but … At the end of *Shadow of a Doubt* the proper couple – which includes, again, a detective – also share a secret, the appalling career of young Charlie's uncle as "the Merry Widow Murderer." They hear his virtues being extolled at his memorial service within the church while they stand on the steps, significantly outside.

If the lovers in Hitchcock's ambiguous romances cannot entirely recover innocence, neither can the protagonists who suffer false accusations. At the end of *The Wrong Man*, Manny Balestrero (Henry Fonda) is exonerated, but his wife remains emotionally ill and beyond his reach. (An attached coda, however, assures us that she eventually recovers.) The couple – again, the man is a detective – at the end of *Stage Fright* departs another scene of death by walking through alternating pools of light and deep shadow that reflect the mixture of the heroine's innocence and involvement. At the end of *Frenzy*, Richard Blaney (Jon Finch) is cleared of the crimes for which he has been imprisoned, but his ex-wife and his lover are dead, and as yet another detective points out, "there's no real way to compensate in cases like these."

Least common among Hitchcock's movies are those in which irony wholly dominates. They include *Easy Virtue* (1927), *The Skin Game* (1931), three of the director's most admired pictures – *Rope* (1948), *Vertigo*, and *Psycho* – as well as one of his least loved, *Topaz* (1969). The issues, images, and actions repeat those of the romances, but as parodies and ironic inversions. Love fails and miracles go missing. If Hitchcock's romantic heroines and heroes descend in order to rise, his ironic protagonists rise only to fall. The romantic movies are full of ascents to truth and salvation; in the ironic ones ascents lead to deception and death. Innocence cannot be recovered, for it is finally absent from radically ironic films. Yet even in these pictures, the hope for love, innocence, and family are pervasive. When those dreams are frustrated or reversed, the tone is not so much resignation or an acknowledgment of the inevitable as shock and grief at a world so uncongenial to romantic desires.

Conclusion

To what extent was Hitchcock personally committed to the happy endings of his romantic films, or indeed to the romantic aspirations that inform all his movies, whether romantic, ambiguous, or ironic? Ultimately, this question is no more answerable than the question of his religious feelings. Despite the morbidly cynical public persona that he cultivated, Hitchcock's career-long attraction to romantic narratives – or, in the case of ironic ones, to stories that raise the same hopes – may well indicate a sentimental predilection. Or it may simply tell us what we already know: that he was a master storyteller who knew what would excite, energize, and satisfy his audience. Most likely, both.

Frye maintains that "critics are either *Iliad* critics or *Odyssey* critics" (*A Natural Perspective* 1). There are also *Iliad* and *Odyssey* directors. Hitchcock, although a master of ironic narrative, remained across his long career as a film director on balance an *Odyssey* auteur, consistently attracted to romantic and semi-romantic stories. (If we include the TV shows he directed and to some extent oversaw, the balance between romance and irony is perhaps more delicately poised.)

Hitchcock's romantic films affirm that we can redeem time and regain innocence. They supply a benevolent fictional deity, the filmmaker, who at once creates a universe and imitates one that exists beyond his fictions. The wanderings, descents, and deaths of Hitchcock's ironic films are not less Hitchcockian than the purposeful quests, ascents, and rebirths of the romantic ones, but they are less frequent. Like many in his audience, Hitchcock may have fervently hoped for saving, rejuvenating love. And, like many, he may have feared that such a thing might not be possible, or might not happen to him. All his films reflect that hope and fear. Individually, and as a total body of work, they mostly favor hope.

Works Cited

Allen, Richard. *Hitchcock's Romantic Irony*. New York: Columbia UP, 2007.

Brill, Lesley. *The Hitchcock Romance: Love and Irony in Hitchcock's Films*. Princeton: Princeton UP, 1988.

Frye, Northrop. *Anatomy of Criticism: Four Essays*. 1957. New York: Atheneum, 1967.

Frye, Northrop. *A Natural Perspective: The Development of Shakespearean Comedy and Romance*. New York: Columbia UP, 1965.

Hitchcock, Alfred. "Surviving: An Interview with John Russell Taylor." *Sight and Sound* 46 (Summer 1977): 174–75. *Hitchcock on Hitchcock: Selected Essays and Interviews*. Ed. Sidney Gottlieb. Berkeley: U of California P, 1995. 59–63.

Hurley, Neil. *Soul in Suspense: Hitchcock's Fright and Delight.* Metuchen, NJ: Scarecrow, 1993.

Michie, Elsie B. "Unveiling Maternal Desires: Hitchcock and American Domesticity." *Hitchcock's America.* Ed. Jonathan Freedman and Richard Millington. New York: Oxford UP, 1999. 29–54.

Rothman, William. *Hitchcock – The Murderous Gaze.* Cambridge: Harvard UP, 1982.

Truffaut, François, with the collaboration of Helen G. Scott. *Hitchcock.* Rev. ed. New York: Simon and Schuster, 1984.

Yacowar, Maurice. *Hitchcock's British Films.* Hamden, CT: Archon, 1977.

6

Family Plots: Hitchcock and Melodrama

Richard R. Ness

In his autobiography, actor Esmond Knight describes Hitchcock's exasperation, midway through the filming of *Waltzes from Vienna* (1933): "After an exhausting day in a stuffy studio in which an enormous crowd of extras were assembled, he announced, 'I hate this sort of stuff. Melodrama is the only thing I can do'" (78). Despite Hitchcock's own revealing assessment of the nature of his work, the relationship of the director's films to melodrama has received little consideration from Hitchcock scholars. The concept of melodrama is addressed only marginally, if at all, in the major critical surveys, and those who have discussed the form in relation to Hitchcock have tended to focus on individual films rather than his work as a whole. Similarly, although a great deal of attention has been given, particularly by feminist critics, to the subject of melodrama in film, the key texts in this field usually mention Hitchcock in passing, preferring instead to canonize as auteurs of melodrama such directors as Douglas Sirk, Vincente Minnelli, Frank Borzage, and King Vidor.

A number of factors may account for this neglect. Encouraged by Hitchcock, scholars may have taken the melodramatic quality of his films as a given. As Michael Pressler observes, Hitchcock's "currency as a director of 'ideas' has perhaps led us to neglect his skill as a melodramatist, even though he always preferred speaking of his films in those terms" (6). An even more likely reason to avoid the term "melodrama" in reference to Hitchcock is that the word is still often used disparagingly. In "Dickens and Hitchcock," Edward Buscombe suggests that this may be due to the perception of melodrama as "popular, and therefore crude," and as appealing to the lower classes (107). Indeed, "It was partly its association with melodrama," writes Christine Gledhill, "that inhibited the acceptance of cinema as a serious object of study" (5), though one might equally argue that it was its association with early cinema that kept melodrama from being considered as a serious object of study.

A Companion to Alfred Hitchcock, First Edition. Edited by Thomas Leitch and Leland Poague.
© 2011 Thomas Leitch and Leland Poague. Published 2011 by Blackwell Publishing Ltd.

Another factor that may account for the failure to consider melodrama in relation to Hitchcock is that, despite the vast amount of scholarly work on the subject, there appears to be no consensual definition of the term. Pam Cook acknowledges that "[i]t is notoriously difficult to define melodrama" (14), while Russell Merritt contends: "Melodrama has joined the long list of once precise words hopelessly blurred and debased by popular misuse" (25). Merritt adds that even Thomas Elsaesser's "Tales of Sound and Fury" deploys such a broad definition and range of references that it is hard to determine what (if anything) could be excluded. Certainly the term has long since outgrown its original, literal meaning of drama with music, though this definition retains its relevance to Hitchcock's work.

Contemporary scholars tend to accept the more general definition, summarized by Jackie Byars in *All That Hollywood Allows*, that "melodrama exploits excessive uses of representational conventions to express that which cannot (yet) be said, that which language is incapable of expressing" (13). In cinema these "representational conventions" involve not just music but a range of aesthetic elements, including editing, camerawork, and expressive uses of other types of sound. Hitchcock's films abound in excessive uses of these conventions: the blurring of the background conversation during the breakfast table scene in *Blackmail* (1929), the elaborate crane shot from the top of the stairs down to the key in Alicia's hand in *Notorious* (1946), the editing of the shower scene in *Psycho* (1960). To appreciate how Hitchcock incorporates such melodramatic gestures as integral aspects of the narrative within a single film, one need only consider *Young and Innocent* (1937), which opens with a deliberately over-dramatic argument punctuated by thunderstorm effects – a device Hitchcock will employ in later films, most notably *Under Capricorn* (1949) and *Marnie* (1964) – and climaxes with the famous elaborate crane shot into the twitching eyes of the murderer.

The self-conscious nature of these gestures in Hitchcock's films demonstrates his willingness to acknowledge and employ the conventions of melodrama while at the same time making the audience aware of them. The technical aspects and innovations of Hitchcock's work have been much analyzed, but mainly in relation to his best-known films. Yet such self-conscious gestures are evident even in works that do not readily seem to adhere to the Hitchcock formula, indicating the importance of this tradition in Hitchcock's worldview. An examination of Hitchcock's employment of melodrama in works that have been ignored or dismissed as uncharacteristic not only reveals significant connections to his more highly regarded films and offers valuable insight into his primary concerns, but also demonstrates the range of melodramatic forms he inherits and explores, from silent melodrama (*The Pleasure Garden* [1925]) and literal drama with music (*Waltzes from Vienna*) to women's melodrama (*Under Capricorn*) and Douglas Sirk–style domestic melodrama (the 1960 TV production "Incident at a Corner").

Hitchcock's ability to incorporate and interrogate melodramatic conventions is already evident in his first solo directorial effort, *The Pleasure Garden*.[1] The early scenes seem to be setting up a typical silent-era example of what Gledhill calls "scenarios of persecuted innocence" (32), often modeled on the work of D.W. Griffith, one of the few filmmakers Hitchcock gratefully acknowledged as an influence. Although the plot is founded on seemingly one-dimensional character types and established dichotomies – rural vs. urban, civilization vs. savagery, innocence vs. corruption, tradition vs. modernity – throughout the film Hitchcock relies on audience awareness of the conventions of melodrama to subvert expectations and, as Donald Spoto observes, "punctuates the melodrama with satirical touches" (5). Maurice Yacowar notes that the film provides "a basic reversal of the traditional worldly city mouse and the naïve country mouse" (20), the latter seemingly in the person of Jill Cheyne (Carmelita Geraghty), who arrives at the Pleasure Garden Theatre seeking employment as a dancer and becomes roommates with the allegedly more experienced Patsy Brand (Virginia Valli). Rather than the virtuous rural heroine of silent melodrama, however, Jill proves to be an ambitious social climber and rejects her boyfriend Hugh Fielding (John Stuart) in favor of the wealthy Prince Ivan (C. Falkenburg), who can improve her social and financial status. By contrast, the flirtatious Patsy enters into a serious relationship with and soon marries Hugh's friend Levet (Miles Mander), although his darker side begins to emerge during their honeymoon, eventually leading to madness and murder in the film's final act.

Hitchcock's undermining of expectations is evident in his introduction of the principal characters. Patsy's blonde hair and flirtatious attitude establish her as a worldly and independent type, but Hitchcock immediately warns viewers that first appearances can be deceptive, as Patsy reveals to a lecherous client at the dance club that the golden curl he admires so much is a fake and hands it to him as a keepsake. Hitchcock also plays games with one of the most familiar character signifiers in the silent era, the use of a moustache to signal the villain. (In the Truffaut interview, Hitchcock describes the scene in *Blackmail* where he uses the shadow from a chandelier to create a moustache for the lecherous artist Crewe as "a sort of farewell to silent pictures" [69]). The Pleasure Garden's manager, Hamilton (George Snell), is first presented in the manner of the classic villain of melodrama; he sports not only a moustache but a top hat (a signifier of wealth, always suspect in melodramas) and is wreathed in cigar smoke as he stands in front of a "Smoking Prohibited" sign. This initial image positions him as the potential serpent in this theatrical Eden, but instead he proves to be rather benign, and his greatest sin is seeking to pay his dancers as little as possible. By contrast, Hitchcock also employs the moustache with Levet, but this time more legitimately as a warning to the audience that his affection for Patsy is potentially deadly.

By contrast, Jill seems reminiscent of Griffith's innocent heroines. She is first seen in a medium close-up with the dark background creating a Griffith-like masking effect around her. The characterization of Jill as naïve victim continues as she discovers her money has been stolen and Patsy agrees to take her in, although the flirtatious smile Jill gives to the men hanging around backstage as she leaves the theater with Patsy provides the first hint that she is not as innocent as she appears.

Hitchcock continues to undermine melodramatic conventions as Jill and Patsy spend their first night together. Jill immediately contradicts the image of the self-sacrificing rural heroine when she tells Patsy, "I wasn't going to spend my life being companion to a sick old lady in the country," and Patsy acknowledges the stereotype when she jokingly responds, "It's lucky for you, O Village Maiden, that you fell into the poor but honest hands of Patsy Brand." As Yacowar notes, "The line is true but in its playfulness it detaches Patsy and Hitchcock from the serious tones of romantic melodrama" (25).

Hitchcock follows this exchange with a scene in which Jill restores her virtuous image by kneeling to pray, only to be disrupted by Patsy's dog licking her feet, a Hitchcock touch that, as Kirk Bond notes, combines "Griffith and Bunuel in the same scene!" (32). While Patsy seems to regard Jill's innocent gesture with detached amusement, it is Patsy who ultimately will prove to have the more sincere religious convictions, as she prays before a statue of the Sacred Heart on her honeymoon and tells Levet she has been "praying for our happiness." Patsy's adoption of the traditional female role in silent melodrama becomes even more apparent a short time later when she helps a group of urchins in the village where she is honeymooning in a scene that could have come directly out of a Mary Pickford film. Just as Hitchcock uses the moustache on Hamilton to parody a melodramatic cliché and on Levet to reinforce it, he employs Jill to undermine the stereotype of the virtuous heroine and Patsy to redeem it.

The introduction of religious elements into the film suggests a potential morality play, a concept reinforced through the Biblical implications of the film's title. Befitting its classic three-act structure, the film has three separate gardens, each with increasing levels of corruption. The first of these is the location that provides the film's title. Although the voyeuristic opening shots suggest an Eden where young female dancers are paraded for the pleasure of the male customers, the women prove to be the ones in control, as Patsy rebuffs the advance of an older patron and Jill successfully holds out for more money when auditioning for Hamilton. Lake Como serves as the second garden, a seemingly idyllic retreat for Patsy and Levet's honeymoon.[2] But Hitchcock subtly foreshadows the disintegration of their relationship in a shot of a wilted flower dropping from Patsy's hand, which Levet caresses while they sit at an outdoor table. Later Levet chastises Patsy when he sees her with the local children, calling them "filthy brats" and thoughtlessly tossing away the rose she gave him in a sentimental moment.

The last of the film's gardens is the primitive outpost where Hugh and Levet are to be stationed for two years. Although Sidney Gottlieb, in his extensive comparison of the film to the 1923 Oliver Sandys novel on which it was based, notes that in the book the location is established as India, in the film the setting is referred to only as "the East" and seems to be a kind of exotic Neverland of the type that only exists in movies, mixing elements of the Far East and tropical South Sea island locales (perhaps reflecting Hitchcock's own lack of worldliness at the time). Whereas Gottlieb suggests that in the book the setting becomes a signifier of otherness that reinforces cultural differences between East and West, in the film it serves to emphasize Levet's regression to the primitive.

It is the final section of the film that critics have found most problematic and to which has been applied, in a derogatory way, the term melodramatic. Bond, for example, claims that in the final scenes "something went radically wrong" (32). Yet these scenes provide the first indications of elements of melodrama on which Hitchcock would later build his reputation, including issues of obsession, passion, murder and guilt, and also demonstrate the director's other acknowledged influence besides Griffith, the German expressionist filmmakers and particularly F.W. Murnau. (In fact, the setting and sense of brooding passion anticipate Murnau's collaboration with Robert Flaherty on *Tabu* [1931].) Levet's brutal murder of his native mistress appears in retrospect to be the most characteristically Hitchcockian moment in the film, and the expressionist influence is especially evident in the lighting of the subsequent scene of Levet's haunting by her spirit. The influence of Griffith returns in the climax, which echoes the finale of *Broken Blossoms* (1919) as the now crazed Levet attacks Patsy with a sword while she cowers behind a door, Hitchcock alternating low angle shots of her assailant with high angle shots of Patsy and using the framing of the latticework to place particular emphasis on her terrified eyes. In keeping with the melodramatic tradition, the villain is dispatched by the timely arrival of a gun-wielding guide, leaving Patsy to find happiness in domesticity as she nurses the ailing Hugh.

While critics have tended to regard Hitchcock's directorial debut as uneven, they at least have found in it evidence of motifs and preoccupations that would find greater development in his later work. By contrast, *Waltzes from Vienna* has been dismissed as the least characteristic example of the director's work, especially compared to his next film, *The Man Who Knew Too Much* (1934), which is widely regarded as firmly establishing the Hitchcock style. But in *English Hitchcock* Charles Barr makes a direct link between *The Pleasure Garden* and *Waltzes from Vienna* by comparing a scene in the former, in which Hitchcock holds on a shot of two chairs onto which Patsy and Jill throw their clothes as they undress offscreen, to the elaborate two-minute-and-fifty-second take in the latter that shows two servants carrying on a flirtation while simultaneously taking orders from their superiors who are bathing offscreen in opposite rooms. Barr notes that the two scenes demonstrate the refinement of Hitchcock's techniques during the seven years and sixteen films that separate them, from the relative simplicity of the earlier scene to the formal complexity of the later one.[3]

Barr also challenges Hitchcock's dismissal of the film in the anecdote Esmond Knight recounts by asking, "And yet what is *Waltzes from Vienna* itself but a melodrama?" (127). As Barr notes, the film fits the original definition of the term, as drama with music, perhaps better than any other film Hitchcock made. Certainly *Waltzes from Vienna* foregrounds music as an integral element of the drama. And it might even be argued that the subsequent musical set pieces that formed a significant aspect of later Hitchcock films – including the celebrated Albert Hall scene in both versions (1934 and 1956) of *The Man Who Knew Too Much*, the "Drummer Man" sequence in

Young and Innocent, and the ballet performance in *Torn Curtain* (1966) – might never have been possible without the experimentation in *Waltzes from Vienna*, particularly the treatment of the triumphant public performance of the "Blue Danube Waltz."

Although in his few discussions of the film Hitchcock referred to it as a musical without music, he presumably was referring to the lack of traditional song interludes, since much of the film is constructed around musical elements. Hitchcock establishes the privileged position of music in the film's discourse in the opening close-up of a horn being blown by a member of the Vienna Fire Brigade, which effectively drowns out the exchange between the fire chief and a baker, Leopold (Hindle Edgar), who is trying to tell him the location of the fire. As the brigade nears its destination, it finds the street blocked by a marching band performing Johann Strauss Senior's "Radetzky March." The music of Strauss continues to weave in and out during much of this opening section, moving effortlessly between diegetic and non-diegetic functions.

In an upstairs room of the café where the fire has occurred the heroine, Rasi (Jessie Matthews), is rehearsing a song, accompanied by the junior Strauss, Schani (Esmond Knight), both of them apparently oblivious to the fire. Hitchcock immediately undercuts melodramatic convention when Leopold climbs into the upper window and dramatically announces that he has come to rescue Rasi, only to have her respond, "What do you want me to do? Swoon?" The two men begin to argue about which of them will rescue Rasi, all the time comically tossing her around like a prop, employing a favorite Hitchcock composition of the female lead framed by two sparring males. The parody of damsel-in-distress plots continues as Leopold clumsily attempts to carry Rasi down a ladder, catching her skirts in the process so that she ends up on the street in her underwear.

Though this opening scene sets up a potential romantic comedy situation in the rivalry of the two men over Rasi, the main plot is built on two sources of conflict common to the melodramatic tradition, class and age differences. Both of these concepts are effectively introduced through the character of the Countess (Fay Compton). The issue of class is first raised when Rasi races into a dress shop in her underwear and is rebuked by the dress shop owner for entering in such a state, especially in front of her distinguished customer, the Countess. When Rasi offers an insincere apology, the Countess responds, "Don't you speak disrespectfully of your betters, my dear." A short time later, when the Countess meets Schani and asks if he is a composer, he responds, "I'm a son of a – composer." Schani notes that his father does not believe he has compositional talents, and his observation that in his father's orchestra he plays second fiddle is clearly meant both literally and figuratively. The Countess suggests that his father is in fear of "hearing youth knocking at the door," setting up a conflict between past and present both in familial relationships and in artistic developments.

The generational conflict surfaces again a short time later when father and son clash during a rehearsal session, with Schani arguing that every art must march forward and the elder Strauss (Edmund Gwenn) objecting to the insinuation that he and his music are at a standstill. As Yacowar notes, this conflict "replays roughly the same tension we found in *The Skin Game*, the passage of power and social authority from the stiff traditional old way to the flexible and cunning new" (162). In *Waltzes from Vienna*, however, it plays out in a series of musical challenges. Schani's father momentarily gains the upper hand by forcing Schani to perform one of his own compositions, then ridiculing it in front of the entire orchestra. Strauss Senior's authority will be challenged later by Rasi, who disrupts another of his rehearsals and tosses his sheet music in the air when he calls Schani's music absolute rubbish. Ultimately, youth and artistic progress prevail in the successful public performance of Schani's "Blue Danube Waltz" during an outdoor festival.

The conflict between father and son musicians is paralleled by Rasi's defiance of her own father, who wants her to marry someone who will go into the pastry business and continue a generations-old family tradition. Rasi's challenge to her father's authority also has a class dimension, since the success of the elder Strauss has given his family a certain status in society and Rasi's father clearly wants her to marry someone more suited to his lower social standing. Ironically, it is in the working-class environment of the bakery, which Schani has agreed to tour in an attempt to conform to the wishes of Rasi's father, that the younger Strauss finds his inspiration for what will become the "Blue Danube Waltz," just as it is a comment by a maidservant about the Countess's blue dress that inspires the work's title. Music becomes the great reconciler of class differences, with Schani's eventual success establishing a more populist form of performance, as demonstrated by his presentation of the waltz at a large public festival, in contrast to his father's performances in isolated indoor venues to entertain the aristocracy.

The class conflict becomes most pronounced in the triangle involving Rasi, Schani, and the married Countess, who has asked the younger Strauss to set some of her verses to music (a plot element that also reinforces the generational conflict, since the elder Strauss has refused a similar request on her behalf by the Countess's husband). As with the other major developments in the film, Hitchcock musically establishes the triangle by intercutting between Schani and the Countess singing a duet and Rasi alone in a garden providing a solo for the second verse. Later, Hitchcock employs a series of dissolves to create a sense of continuous action as he parallels scenes of Schani dedicating separate copies of his waltz to the Countess and to Rasi, and providing each with a manuscript bearing her dedication, drawing particular attention to the contrast between the large diamond ring on the Countess's hand and Rasi's ringless finger. In a reversal of the earlier scene showing Rasi framed between two arguing male characters, Hitchcock frames Schani between the two women when they find out about the dual dedications and he tries to explain himself. As a distraught Rasi rushes out of the room, Schani follows, telling the Countess, "There are some things that are more important than success." Schani tries half-heartedly to conform to Rasi's class expectations by going to work at the bakery, but again angers Rasi when he accepts the invitation of the Countess to perform at the festival.

As with the establishment of the romantic triangle in musical terms, throughout the film Hitchcock incorporates a number of deliberately self-conscious musical gestures, ranging from the comedic use of a descending piano line as a servant tumbles down a flight of stairs to the highly (melo)dramatic moment when Rasi, after arguing with Schani's father, rushes out of the rehearsal hall toward the camera to the accompaniment of a drum roll from the orchestra as it begins its practice, her slamming of the door accented by a cymbal crash. Hitchcock conceived of the creation of the "Blue Danube" itself as something that would develop gradually during the course of the film (an idea he would attempt with less success in *Rear Window* [1954]), inspired by events that were part of the ordinary progression of the plot, most notably the activities in the bakery that provide the rhythms for the various passages.

All of these musical gestures lead up to the film's major musical set piece, the public performance of the "Blue Danube" at the festival, which provides the blueprint for the much better known Albert Hall sequence in *The Man Who Knew Too Much* the following year. In the article "On Music in Films" written around the time *Waltzes from Vienna* was released, Hitchcock elaborates on his intention for the scene: "I arranged the cutting to match the rhythm of the music. It is difficult to describe in words. You must visualize the film moving in time with the music. In the slow passages the cutting is slow, when the music quickens the mood of the melody is followed by the quick cutting" (244). In fact, the construction of the scene is even more elaborate than Hitchcock suggests, since it is designed not just to reinforce the rhythm of the music but also to increase tension as the major conflicts reach a climax. As the performance begins, Hitchcock employs an elaborate tracking shot around the orchestra, but then builds in a series of cuts as the piece develops, not only providing an appropriate visual corollary for the changes in the music but also allowing for alternating close-ups of Rasi and the Countess, culminating in a shot of Rasi crying with her head on a table because she believes Schani's success means that she has lost him. The generational conflict is also incorporated into the performance with the entrance of Schani's visibly angry father, who has arrived late at the festival where he was to have performed after being deliberately detained.

Although the "Blue Danube" performance provides the climax of the film both visually and musically, it remains for the romantic triangle to be resolved. For this final segment Hitchcock again employs melodramatic conventions. The Countess's jealous husband, sporting both moustache and monocle, arrives at the festival and discovers that his wife has gone to Schani's apartment. A rare instance of melodramatic non-diegetic underscoring accompanies shots of the Countess arriving at Schani's house and Rasi racing through the streets to warn them that the Count is on his way. When the Countess's husband arrives, he finds an incriminating scarf belonging to his wife, who is hiding in another room. While this signifier of her potential infidelity has echoes of *Othello*, Hitchcock employs it mainly for a bit of comic business. The situation is resolved when Rasi emerges from the other room, having allowed the Countess to escape through a window and climb down a ladder, essentially reducing the aristocratic Countess to the same position in which Rasi had found herself at the beginning of the film. Yacowar notes that in the original stage production Rasi ends up with Leopold, but Hitchcock's decision to reconcile Rasi and Schani, while subverting and overcoming class barriers, is more in keeping with the traditions of romantic comedy than melodrama. As Yacowar observes, "This romantic conclusion brings the film into the archetypal form of comedy, lovers' dissension dissolving into marriage" (166).

If the 1934 *The Man Who Knew Too Much* can be seen as the beginning of a new phase in Hitchcock's career, then *Waltzes from Vienna* must be regarded as the summation of a previous period. Certainly it marks the culmination of a period of increasing exploration of the potential of the camera, resulting in the elaborate long takes in *Waltzes*. It also marks one of the last times Hitchcock would explore father–son conflicts, a theme previously addressed most prominently in *Downhill* (1927) and *The Skin Game* (1931). Hereafter, Hitchcock would focus on father-daughter interactions (an understandable shift given the birth of his daughter a few years earlier) and later on relationships between mothers and children of both genders. Class issues also would be dealt with less overtly in Hitchcock's later films, although they would continue to be an important element throughout his career. Perhaps most significantly, Schani's insinuation that his father is standing still, and his statement on the need for every art to move forward and be open to new ideas, can be seen as Hitchcock's own comment on the static nature of the British film industry in the early sound era and his defense of his attempts to experiment with the potential of cinema. Ironically, it was in a film usually considered his least characteristic that Hitchcock made his most explicitly personal declaration of his artistic credo.

One other important contribution made by *Waltzes from Vienna* to Hitchcock's later work is summed up by Yacowar, who observes that

> in this film for perhaps the first time Hitchcock gives the women the power of will and mind. ... There were wise, strong women in Hitchcock's earlier films but this is the first one in which the women are so clearly superior to the men, in strength of will, character and virtue.
>
> (165)

Although these strong-willed female characters would continue to be a feature of Hitchcock's work, the remainder of his British films would focus on heterosexual couples who attempt to achieve a kind of gendered equilibrium. Hitchcock's first American film, however, would signal a move toward greater emphasis on women's issues and female psychology.

Much feminist work on melodrama has emphasized "women's pictures." Here Hitchcock's connection to the form has been acknowledged, although this attention has focused largely on the first of his two 1940 Hollywood films, *Rebecca* (see Doane and Gallafent), a film many Hitchcock scholars consider problematic. Despite Tania Modleski's defense of *Rebecca* as "a milestone in Hitchcock's work" in relation to issues of gender identification (55), many critics have been content to accept Hitchcock's claim in his interviews with Truffaut that the film is not really a Hitchcock picture because its emphasis on the feminine is more characteristic of producer David O. Selznick than of its director. Yet nearly all of Hitchcock's films of the 1940s – with the exception of *Rope* (1948) and, to a lesser extent, *Saboteur* (1942) – can be regarded as women's films. Most of these works have at their center a female character who undergoes a life-altering change as a result of some significant realization. Some of these heroines must confront shattered illusions about an idolized male, as in *Foreign Correspondent* (1940), *Shadow of a Doubt* (1943) and *Spellbound* (1945), others their own troubled past, as in *Notorious* (1946) and *The Paradine Case* (1947).

Providing an appropriate bookend to *Rebecca* for this period of Hitchcock's work is *Under Capricorn*, another film often dismissed as uncharacteristic of the director. Although it is a much more personal example of the women's film than the Selznick-produced *Rebecca*, the film has received surprisingly little attention from feminist critics. Yet *Under Capricorn* serves as a pivotal work in summarizing the women's melodramas that preceded it, while introducing concepts that will find greater, and darker, expression in *Vertigo* (1958). In *Under Capricorn* Hitchcock again incorporates the melodramatic structure while also critiquing it, as Mark Rappaport avows in his analysis of the film. "[W]hat makes Hitchcock unique," he writes, "is that when he puts the female character and her perilous journey at the center of the action, it is not in the soggy tradition of women-in-jeopardy. ... [T]he women in Hitchcock's American films neither expect nor get any special dispensation because they're women" (52). *Under Capricorn* might even be seen as an attempt to correct the problematic third act of *The Pleasure Garden*, with its account of lovers whose conflicts surface after they have fled to an exotic setting. Rather than presenting the husband as the traditional villain of melodrama and allowing the heroine to find love with another, however, Hitchcock emphasizes the need of *Under Capricorn*'s couple to work through the complications in their relationship.

In addition to its connections to other Hitchcock films, *Under Capricorn* contains echoes of key works in the sub-genre of women's melodramas. The dinner party that the wives of several prominent society leaders make excuses for not attending recalls the scene in *Stella Dallas* (King Vidor, 1937) where no one comes to Laurel's birthday party because of gossip involving her mother, while the heroine's reference to sitting on the heather when she recalls her courtship with her husband in Ireland evokes memories of that most influential of women's melodramas, *Wuthering Heights* (William Wyler, 1939). Even more direct are the connections to *Gaslight* (George Cukor, 1944), evident not only in the casting of Ingrid Bergman and Joseph Cotten in the lead roles, but also in the attempts to convince the heroine that she is losing her sanity and in the scenes of her humiliation in front of the servants and at a public event.

The casting of Bergman and Cotten also, of course, provides direct links to earlier Hitchcock films. Like Uncle Charlie, whom he played in *Shadow of a Doubt*, Cotten's Sam Flusky, who allegedly murdered his wife's brother and still has "a reputation for violence," expresses contempt for the superficiality and hypocrisy of the upper classes. At one point Hitchcock dissolves from a medium close-up of Sam to the dancers at a society party, directly recalling the dissolves to shots of dancers that signal Uncle Charlie's murderous impulses in the earlier film. Bergman's role as Lady Henrietta Flusky parallels her role in *Notorious* as a woman who must redeem herself from a scandal in her past, and the connection to the earlier film is most evident in the climax in which Bergman's Lady Hattie is drugged by the housekeeper Millie (Margaret Leighton), the other dominant female in the household.

Millie is an obvious counterpart to Mrs. Danvers (Judith Anderson) in *Rebecca*, a film that is also evoked by the pattern of a couple haunted by a death from the past and more directly in the humiliation of Hattie in front of her servants when she attempts to seize control of the household from Millie. Yet if Hattie recalls the heroines of earlier women's melodramas, she also intriguingly anticipates the challenge to patriarchal authority by the female characters in *Vertigo*. Hattie's initial appearance, barefoot and intoxicated, at the dinner party attended by prominent men who represent the various patriarchal institutions of society (the law, the clergy, the medical profession), anticipates the story of the mad Carlotta Valdes told by the bookstore owner in *Vertigo*. The character of Hattie also offers some insight into the real (and unknown) Madeleine Elster (Kim Novak), who comes from a "mad line" of female ancestors and, like Hattie, is more socially and financially prominent than her husband. Although Sam does not go to the extremes of Gavin Elster (Tom Helmore), he nevertheless can be accused of killing his wife symbolically if not literally through his refusal to forget the past and let "bygones be bygones." Fittingly, when old family friend Charles Adare (Michael Wilding) tries to help Hattie by buying her a mirror to show her how beautiful she really is, he refers to it as "a successful reincarnation," ironically anticipating the more equivocal and largely duplicitous identities (Madeleine/Carlotta/Judy) projected onto the heroine of *Vertigo*.

The arrival of Charles not only provides a potential romantic triangle, but also brings to the forefront the class issues that are the main source of melodramatic tension in the film. Despite the attempt of Australia to position itself as a classless society, where "a man's past is his own business," a hierarchal order still clearly exists, and early in the film Charles is warned by his cousin, the newly appointed Governor of New South Wales (Cecil Parker), not to get involved with Sam because of his reputation. Sam himself is caught between classes, having risen to a position of prominence in Australia after having served time in prison but still unable to escape his past as the stable groom who married into society. Thus he can shift from the rather arrogant position of examining a potential secretary as though he were buying a horse to an expression of vulnerability when he reveals his belief that he is not good enough for Hattie and that the tension between them arises from her desire to be among "her own sort." Sam's inferiority complex is fueled by Millie, who constantly reminds him that the gentry operate by different rules. She also plants seeds of suspicion that Charles's relationship with Hattie may be motivated by more than mere friendship and provides another potential romantic triangle by seeking to eliminate Hattie so she can have Sam to herself.

Millie's own sense of class inferiority makes the film's domestic sphere the site for class struggle as she and Hattie fight for control of the household. Millie's displacement of Hattie's authority is brilliantly evoked when the camera cranes from Sam and Charles talking outside Sam's house to Hattie in an upstairs window, then back down, and a short time later repeats the movement, this time to reveal Millie, now visible through the window, preparing to administer medicine to the reclining Hattie. Hattie's first attempts to take control of the household are met with humiliation as Millie arranges for the empty liquor bottles hidden in Hattie's room to be displayed in front of the servants, but with Charles's help she eventually does assert her authority as mistress of Minyago Yugilla. Sam, too, eventually reasserts his position as master over Millie, and as she leaves for the last time she tells him, "I'm not good enough for you, I know that. I'm only good enough to work for you and slave for you."

Along with issues of class that hark back to Hitchcock's early British period, *Under Capricorn* both incorporates and challenges the religious undercurrents that were evident in *The Pleasure Garden*. Hattie's first entrance occurs just as the gentlemen assembled at dinner have completed a benediction (which seems as much an acknowledgment of their own status as of God's grace), linking her disruption of the patriarchal order to liturgical concerns. Sam's recollections of his life with Hattie back in Ireland are filled with religious allusions, claiming that she jumped fences on her horse as though "the Kingdom of Heaven were on the other side" and describing her as an angel while admitting that he had a bit of the devil in him. Sam later quotes the Biblical concept of "the great gulf fixed" to explain the distance that formed between them after being banished to Australia from their idyllic Irish Eden. But the most overt, and negative, religious references involve Millie's fanaticism, especially in her attempt to destroy Hattie while asserting that she knows "the Lord's way." This also provides the most dramatic gesture in the film: as thunderclaps rage outside, the camera dollies in to the shrunken head Millie has planted in Hattie's bed.

Hitchcock reaffirms the melodramatic tradition in the finale as Hattie, having been freed from Millie's evil influence, goes to the Governor to plead for the release of her husband, who has been accused of attempting to kill Charles during an altercation. In *deus ex machina* fashion Charles, having recovered from his wounds, arrives to clear Sam and facilitate the reconciliation of the couple. Yet as Gallafent observes, "the pleasures of melodrama are not mainly constituted around the reconstruction of the couple" (103), and if Millie's ouster and Charles's sacrifice seem to reaffirm the power of the hierarchal structure, the film's value – like melodrama's generally – comes in having exposed and challenged the ideological deficiencies of the social order. While Hitchcock may have been able to dismiss *Waltzes from Vienna* and *Rebecca* as uncharacteristic of his work, as films he had been forced to make at the behest of their producers, he could make no such claim about *Under Capricorn*, which he chose to make after forming his own independent production company. It is telling that Hitchcock would choose to return both to the aesthetic considerations (most notably a more extreme use of the long takes with which he had begun to experiment in *Waltzes from Vienna*) and, more significantly, to the thematic preoccupations – with class and gender imbalances especially – found in these earlier works, indicating that these are very much Hitchcockian concerns.

In his analysis of *Under Capricorn*, Rappaport describes it as "the movie no one wants to write about" (42). Extending the term "movie" to include Hitchcock's television productions, that dubious honor more accurately belongs to "Incident at a Corner," which Hitchcock directed for *Ford Startime* in 1960. What little has been written about the production consists mainly of brief and variously accurate reference-work plot synopses (see McCarthy and Kelleher or Grams and Wikstrom). Though regarded as a minor effort, the program is actually an acute indictment of the potential for corruption beneath the genteel surface of civilized society. It also comes the closest of any of Hitchcock's works to the Sirkian style of melodrama, which employs saturated colors, emphasizes how conflict arises within the nucleus of family and community, and focuses on female characters who dare to challenge these social structures. These elements recall Sirk's productions of the 1950s while also anticipating Hitchcock's more psychologically disturbing films of the 1960s, *The Birds* (1963) and *Marnie*.

If Hitchcock's forties films emphasized identification with female characters, in the fifties he returned to a preoccupation with the couple – although, as *Strangers on a Train* (1951) indicates, not always in a traditional heterosexual configuration – often placing the pair within the larger context of communal interactions, most notably in *Rear Window* and *The Trouble with Harry* (1955). This focus on community in the fifties films can of course be seen as a post–Red Scare response to a climate of fear and mistrust, in which the community can be a source of unity but also an environment in which the individual can be destroyed by lies and innuendo. As in *Rear Window* and *The Trouble with Harry*, a search for truth in "Incident at a Corner" leads to escalating complications exposing the potentially ugly realities in a seemingly orderly community, while ironically also bringing disparate elements of the community together.

In the casting of actress Vera Miles, the structural device of a couple joining forces to expose a community's corruption and, perhaps most interestingly, the use of the surname Crane for a character who sets the events in motion, "Incident at a Corner" inevitably invites comparison to *Psycho*, released the same year. Yet in many ways the television production can be seen as the flip side of *Psycho*, employing bright Sirkian color schemes instead of stark black and white, and emphasizing verbal domestic exchanges over visual violence and horror. In *Psycho* the couple is working to uncover the truth of Norman's dark family secret, while in the television production they are trying to expose the falsity of the charges made against a family member. One might even extend these comparisons to the different mediums employed for each production and the spectator's relationship to them. *Psycho*'s exploration of evil within a family is designed for a communal viewing experience, whereas "Incident at a Corner" presents a study of community corruption intended to be viewed in a more familial environment.[4]

The reviews of "Incident at a Corner" quoted in Grams and Wikstrom tend to focus on the opening, which repeats from three different angles the incident of the title, involving elderly crossing guard James Medwick (Paul Hartman) getting into a confrontation with prominent community member Mrs. Tawley (Leora Dana) over her failure to slow down at an intersection. This description suggests a *Rashomon*-like approach to the material. But whereas in *Rashomon* (1950) each version of the central incident is different, based on the selfish motivations of the teller, in Hitchcock's production the views of the incident are objective and remain exactly the same in terms of action and dialogue, with only the perspective changing. Thus where Akira Kurosawa uses his structure to question the nature of truth in *Rashomon*, Hitchcock reaffirms the concept of an absolute truth and instead examines how a community can be destroyed through indifference to it and a willingness to embrace lies and innuendo, a concept established even before the three views of the incident, as Hitchcock presents the opening credits over extreme close-ups of mouths whispering into ears.

As he did with the establishment of a rural–urban dichotomy in *The Pleasure Garden* and the romantic comedy genre cues in *Waltzes from Vienna*, which in neither case turned out to be the film's main focus, Hitchcock plays with audience expectations at the outset of "Incident at a Corner." Following the confrontation between James and Mrs. Tawley, Hitchcock seems to be setting up the kind of murder plot often used in teleplays for his own series. Georgia Crane (Eve McVeagh), who lives across from the school, recognizes the crossing guard and, afraid he will expose her past, suggests to her husband, Harry (Jack Albertson), that something needs to be done. Hitchcock again employs melodramatic convention by having music enter dramatically as Harry asks, "What if I get rid of the old man?"

Instead of the expected murder story, however, Hitchcock explores the complex dynamics that play out within family and community as James is accused, by way of an anonymous note, of being "a little too fond of the kids ... of the girls." Hitchcock first undermines the security of the family unit by having the news of the accusation against James revealed while members of his family have gathered at his home to celebrate his birthday (in a particularly effective moment, as James goes back into the house after talking to the sheriff, we hear the family singing "Happy Birthday" offscreen, their voices tapering off as they apparently see his troubled face).

Jane Medwick (Vera Miles) is the granddaughter of the crossing guard and, appropriately for a film about perspectives, has been tutoring Mrs. Tawley's son, Ron (Warren Berlinger), in how to measure angles. When Jane and her fiancé, Pat (George Peppard), decide to challenge the accusation, they face opposition from other family members, particularly her Uncle Jeffrey (Bob Sweeney), who is less concerned with exposing the truth than with avoiding further possible scandal for the family. Once Jane and Pat decide to find out who was behind the anonymous note, they face further opposition from various members of the community, especially when their suspicions turn to Mrs. Tawley, whose husband is a prominent banker. When the school principal defends Mrs. Tawley's character, Pat responds, "Her husband owns a bank. Does that give her character?" Pat also accuses the principal, like Uncle Jeffrey, of being less concerned with revealing the truth than with keeping up the appearances of the community. Later, when Pat talks to a lawyer about possibly filing a slander suit against Mrs. Tawley, the lawyer responds that Pat is on the wrong side of public opinion and admits that he is concerned about the possible repercussions if he takes the case. Although they have no direct evidence, Jane and Pat confront Mrs. Tawley at her home and accuse her of writing the note. The scene, presenting her in a red dress that sets her off against the elegant white décor, provides the most visually Sirkian moment in the film.

Throughout Jane and Pat's meetings with various community members, Hitchcock makes use of slight high angles. This stylistic device sets up the most self-conscious gesture in the episode. As Pat begins to make a speech to the members of Jane's family about how anyone can be destroyed by a lie, Hitchcock cuts to an extreme high angle, then to a series of increasingly closer shots while Pat points to the various family members and claims, "I can cast you all beyond the social pale with a pencil and a piece of paper."

Jane is injured when she confronts Ron Tawley after finding him lurking outside James's house. In a scene disturbingly reminiscent of *Lifeboat* (1944), the family circles around Ron, threatening to turn him over to the police unless Mrs. Tawley admits to writing the note and retracts the accusation. Eventually Jane acts as the voice of reason, saying she will not testify against Ron, for she realizes the accusations they are making against Mrs. Tawley have no more foundation than the ones made against her grandfather. In keeping with the melodramatic tradition, the suspicions against Mrs. Tawley prove to have been the result of a coincidence over two similar sounding words, and once she is cleared, her husband joins forces with Jane, Pat, and James to restore the communal order and uncover the truth, which finally leads back to Georgia and Harry. While James's assertion to Georgia that he never would have spread stories about an incident that happened to her when she was only sixteen provides the obligatory happy ending, it only comes after Hitchcock has demonstrated how easily the fragile fabric of seemingly secure social institutions such as family and community can be destroyed, a theme he would continue to explore in his later films.

The paradox of melodrama has always been that it seeks to expose through disguise, by revealing truths about our social condition through forms of popular entertainment. It is fitting, therefore, that it is when Hitchcock is least characteristic in his uses of melodramatic conventions that he is most revelatory, exposing his deepest personal preoccupations, which extend far beyond the intricacies of plot construction or manipulation of the audience. Whether demonstrating his own ambivalence toward the melodramatic tradition (*The Pleasure Garden*), defending his more experimental and deliberately self-conscious approach to cinema (*Waltzes from Vienna*), exploring his fascination with female psychology and expressing his disdain for an oppressive class system (*Under Capricorn*), or demonstrating how the fragile fabric of our seemingly civilized society can be ripped asunder as easily by human weakness and mistrust as by more violent means ("Incident at a Corner"), Hitchcock employs the conventions of popular entertainment to expose the realities and repressions of dominant ideology.

Notes

1. As other scholars have noted, there appear to be at least two different versions of *The Pleasure Garden* in circulation, the so-called Rohauer edition and a longer version attributed to the National Film and Television Archive, which was shown on European television. Although the Rohauer version is shorter, it contains a number of different scenes and actually extends some parts of the film, particularly the wedding scene and a number of incidents involving Patsy's landlords. Both prints were examined for this essay.
2. Spoto claims that in the honeymoon scene "the appearance of a snake on a tree arouses our suspicion that evil inhabits this apparent Eden" (5–6), but this image was not evident in either of the two versions of the film viewed for this essay.
3. As with *The Pleasure Garden*, there are at least two cuts of *Waltzes from Vienna*. For many years the only available version of the film was taken from a French dubbed print that ran less than an hour. In addition to eliminating nearly half an hour from the film, including the climactic scene at Schani's house, the French version rearranges the order of some scenes.
4. Although *Psycho* has usually been discussed in relation to the horror genre, Bosley Crowther in his review of the film for the *New York Times* at the time of its release noted the film's connection to the melodramatic tradition: "That's the way it is with Mr. Hitchcock's picture – slow buildups to sudden shocks that are old-fashioned melodramatics. … It may be a matter of question whether Mr. Hitchcock's points of psychology, the sort highly favored by Krafft-Ebing, are as reliable as his melodramatic stunts."

Works Cited

Barr, Charles. *English Hitchcock*. Moffat: Cameron and Hollis, 1999.
Bond, Kirk. "The Other Alfred Hitchcock." *Film Culture* 41 (1966): 30–35.
Buscombe, Edward. "Dickens and Hitchcock." *Screen* 11.4–5 (1970): 97–114.

Byars, Jackie. *All That Hollywood Allows: Re-Reading Gender in 1950s Melodrama*. Chapel Hill: U of North Carolina P, 1991.

Cook, Pam. "Melodrama and the Women's Picture." *Gainsborough Melodrama*. Ed. Sue Aspinall and Robert Murphy. London: BFI, 1983. 14–28.

Crowther, Bosley. Rev. of *Psycho*. *New York Times* 17 June 1960: n. pag. Web. NYTimes.com. 15 July 2010.

Doane, Mary Ann. *The Desire to Desire: The Woman's Film of the 1940s*. Bloomington: Indiana UP, 1987.

Elsaesser, Thomas. "Tales of Sound and Fury: Observations on the Family Melodrama." 1972.Gledhill 43–69.

Gallafent, Ed. "Black Satin: Fantasy, Murder and the Couple in 'Gaslight' and 'Rebecca.'" *Screen* 29.3 (1988): 84–103.

Gledhill, Christine, ed. *Home Is Where the Heart Is: Studies in Melodrama and the Woman's Film*. London: BFI, 1987.

Gottlieb, Sidney. "Hitchcock and the Three Pleasure Gardens." *Hitchcock at the Source: The Auteur as Adapter*. Ed. David Boyd and R. Barton Palmer. Albany: SUNY P, forthcoming.

Grams, Martin, Jr. and Patrik Wikstrom. *The Alfred Hitchcock Presents Companion*. Arlington: OTR, 2001.

Hitchcock, Alfred. "On Music in Films." Interview by Stephen Watts. 1933–34. *Hitchcock on Hitchcock: Selected Writings and Interviews*. Ed. Sidney Gottlieb. Berkeley: U of California P, 1995. 241–45.

Knight, Esmond. *Seeking the Bubble*. London: Hutchinson, 1943.

McCarthy, John, and Brian Kelleher. *Alfred Hitchcock Presents: An Illustrated Guide to the Ten-Year Television Career of the Master of Suspense*. New York: St. Martin's, 1985.

Merritt, Russell. "Melodrama: Postmortem for a Phantom Genre." *Wide Angle* 5.3 (1983): 24–31.

Modleski, Tania. *The Women Who Knew Too Much: Hitchcock and Feminist Theory*. New York: Methuen, 1988.

Pressler, Michael. "Hitchcock and the Melodramatic Pattern." *Chicago Review* 35.3 (1986): 4–16.

Rappaport, Mark. "*Under Capricorn* Revisited." *Hitchcock Annual* 12 (2003–04): 42–66.

Spoto, Donald. *The Art of Alfred Hitchcock: Fifty Years of His Motion Pictures*. New York: Hopkinson and Blake, 1976.

Truffaut, François, with the collaboration of Helen G. Scott. *Hitchcock*. Rev. ed. New York: Simon and Schuster, 1984.

Yacowar, Maurice. *Hitchcock's British Films*. Hamden, CT: Archon, 1977.

7

Conceptual Suspense in Hitchcock's Films

Paula Marantz Cohen

A question that has been a subject of debate in recent years is whether a film can be suspenseful on subsequent viewings. When arguing that it can, theorists invoke ideas like "the paradox of suspense" or "the expectation of uniqueness" to explain what the viewer brings to bear in order to simulate the original experience (see Carroll, "Paradox"; see also Gerrig). What they have not considered, however, is that the suspense experienced in a subsequent viewing may be of a different kind than the suspense experienced on first viewing – that it may activate fears and anxieties that come into play only when there is some degree of familiarity with the narrative in question.

Hitchcock laid the groundwork for such distinctions when he explained the difference between *surprise* and *suspense*. Surprise involves the occurrence of something shocking or disturbingly unexpected: it is what we feel in *Strangers on a Train* (1951), for example, as Guy (Farley Granger) creeps up the stairs to Bruno's father's bedroom and encounters the dog on the landing and then Bruno (Robert Walker) in his father's bed. Both of these events are jolts to the characters' and the viewers' expectations.

Suspense, by contrast, which Hitchcock saw as more central to his films, involves concern for how a character will respond to a threat about which the audience is already informed (Truffaut 73). Here, viewers feel suspense *for* the character rather than fright or shock *with* the character. This is what we feel when Miriam (Laura Elliott) is stalked by Bruno at the fairground in the same film. We may not like Miriam, but we nonetheless feel empathy for her in her situation: a sense of anxiety and distress on her behalf, knowing she is under threat.[1]

But doesn't surprise become more like suspense when we see the film a second time? When we watch a film again, we know what will happen, but since we are familiar with the characters, we still feel suspense on their behalf. We may even

A Companion to Alfred Hitchcock, First Edition. Edited by Thomas Leitch and Leland Poague.

feel *more* suspense in knowing more about them and thus caring about them more. A good example occurs in *Psycho* (1960). When the film first opened in theaters, audiences experienced the surprise of Marion's stabbing (both the shock of the sudden violence and the deviation from convention with the killing of marquee star Janet Leigh midway through). Hitchcock famously decreed that the theater doors be closed to latecomers so as to guarantee this effect. However, once the scene became known – and it is now known even to those who haven't seen the film – the surprise disappears. We now expect that Marion will be killed in the shower, yet we still feel anxiety as we watch her move toward this fateful end. Indeed, knowing what will happen increases this feeling as we watch something that we now understand better – and that finds resonance in our own private anxieties. Stripping away surprise can produce suspense of a more profound sort.[2]

Yet the ability of suspense to continue, albeit changed, from first viewing to subsequent viewings may have a limit. A film's ability to sustain suspense seems based on the viewer's investment in its world. When the characters no longer look and behave like us, when the story line appears hackneyed and the cinematic techniques primitive, suspense diminishes. I know that many film instructors have experienced, as I have, the disappointment of seeing a class lose interest in a film that we think is enormously suspenseful. For whatever reason (e.g., our age or our position as teachers), we remain connected to the world of the particular film and are moved by it; students who don't have that connection feel little.

This leads me to postulate a second kind of suspense, one that extends the suspense situation into a larger social/historical arena. I will call this sort of suspense *conceptual suspense* because it relies on our concern about the fate of an idea rather than an individual character. Conceptual suspense makes it possible for certain films to continue to be suspenseful not only when the outcome is known but also when supposedly realistic elements in the film no longer reflect the contemporary world and when production values and techniques no longer reflect contemporary practice. This sort of suspense seems particularly relevant to Hitchcock, and especially to his American films made between 1940 and 1960, judged to be his masterpieces. These films, outmoded though they are in many ways, seem to grow more, not less, powerful with the passage of time.

A pivotal film with regard to Hitchcock's use of conceptual suspense is the 1943 *Shadow of a Doubt*. This film, which falls almost exactly midway in Hitchcock's career, is shot in black and white, has no overt sex, little explicit violence, and a setting and style of discourse very much of its time. Yet it nonetheless sustains suspense not only with film scholars but also with more cinematically naive audiences. I have shown it to undergraduates who find it intensely suspenseful even though their usual movie diet consists of contemporary action and horror films.

To understand why this is, I want to begin by considering *Shadow of a Doubt* in light of Noël Carroll's classic 1984 definition of suspense. "Suspense occurs," argues Carroll, "when a moral outcome is improbable and, conversely ... suspense does not occur when an immoral outcome is improbable" ("Theory" 82). In other words, we feel suspense on behalf of what we feel *should* happen in the face of a serious threat designed to forward what we think *shouldn't*.

This seems like a logical enough bare-bones formula, yet when we apply it to *Shadow of a Doubt* it doesn't apply, at least not in an obvious way. One problem lies with the issue of "moral outcome." There is no denying that the film has a moral element, though what that element consists of deserves some thought. At first, it may seem that the two central characters divide the moral landscape between them. Uncle Charlie (Joseph Cotten) is a serial murderer. His namesake and niece, young Charlie (Teresa Wright), seems his opposite, as wholesome and idealistic as he is jaded and degenerate. Still, the dichotomy presented by the two characters is complicated by young Charlie's feeling of kinship with her uncle, and by her uncle's sense that his murders are morally justified. As Hitchcock explained to François Truffaut: "he's a killer with an ideal; he's one of those murderers who feel that they have a mission to destroy" (153). The scene in which Uncle Charlie gives young Charlie a ring and pronounces them to be "like twins" never fails to produce discomfort in audiences because it muddies the moral distinction we want to assume exists between them. In the end, moreover, young Charlie is compelled to kill her uncle and enter murderous territory herself.

Another problem with Carroll's definition of suspense is the issue of probability. Carroll maintains that for suspense to exist the moral outcome must be improbable and the immoral one probable. Early in *Shadow of a Doubt* it seems that Uncle Charlie (about whom, at this point, we know nothing) is soon going to be arrested by the two detectives who are following him. Making Uncle Charlie's apprehension *probable* tends, by Carroll's formula, to suggest that his escape is the moral outcome, the probability of his arrest working to imply that he is innocent. Indeed, part of the early situational suspense of the film is the impression produced by the first scene (though admittedly not presented without ambiguity) that he is someone like Robert Donat in *The 39 Steps* (1935), being pursued for mistaken reasons, and that we need to root for him to elude his pursuers and emerge triumphant. Once we know more about Uncle Charlie, we can no longer root for him, especially as he begins to threaten the life of young Charlie. Yet the initial presentation of his role in the family and the fact that his sister, Charlie's mother (Patricia Collinge), is enamored of him still make it difficult for us to want him apprehended.

This leads to the question of where the moral outcome lies in the film. Is there some concept, connected to the characters but not identical with them, that we feel is threatened and that we feel needs to be rescued?

I would argue that there is, and that this is the concept of the *family*.[3] This family idea is attached to both young Charlie and Uncle Charlie. Their mutual connection to it connects them to each other. We want the survival of this family idea in the face of complex and powerful efforts to destroy and discredit it by Uncle Charlie and, in some sense, by young Charlie as well. The fact that both of these characters are so strongly attached to the mother figure (Uncle Charlie's sister and young Charlie's mother) drives this point home. The detectives who are after Uncle Charlie pose as researchers studying the typical American family and make the mother the central object of their "study." Though their research is a ruse, it ironically reflects what the film itself is after – the delineation of a family idea – which it shows to be threatened on a variety of fronts: by Uncle Charlie's murderous behavior and young Charlie's restless discontent as well as by her mother's distractedness, her father's ineffectuality, and the behavior of the "merry widows" whose loneliness draws them to Uncle Charlie. This threatened family idea activates, I would suggest, a deep-seated anxiety in viewers that continues to be felt and indeed intensifies as time goes by. For it is not only that our own families have necessarily undergone change since we first viewed the film, but the family as an institution has, since the film's release, been increasingly subject to disruption and disintegration. In other words, we have moved away *in practice* from the ideology of the intact nuclear family that the film delineates, while still holding to it *in imagination*.[4]

Shadow of a Doubt is, therefore, a film about the fate of an institution as much if not more than it is about the fate of individual characters. I would argue further that it is a pivotal film in this respect. The institution of the family that it delineates is the template for a family idea that informs Hitchcock's subsequent films and that is present in varying degrees and with varying force in the entire corpus of Hollywood film from the 1940s onwards.

Shadow of a Doubt was not Hitchcock's first attempt to use the family as a structure in his films. He had done so, some two years before coming to America, in *Sabotage* (1936), based on Joseph Conrad's gloomy 1907 masterpiece *The Secret Agent*. Hitchcock would later tell Truffaut that he didn't think a great novel was a useful source for a film. We see why when we look at his film based on Conrad's novel, then compare it to *Shadow of a Doubt*, which was free from such influence.

The Secret Agent contains a witheringly cynical view of the family. The central female character, Winnie, marries for purely self-interested reasons: she needs a home for herself and for her mentally handicapped brother, Stevie. Her husband, Verloc, has motives for marriage that are more flagrantly self-centered: he needs someone to take care of his household and provide him with the comforts that support his essential laziness. When unforeseen circumstances draw him into an anarchist plot, he indulges his laziness once again and uses his wife's brother to transport a bomb that explodes accidentally, with fatal results. Winnie, deranged by grief, proceeds to kill her husband in retaliation for her brother's death.

In adapting the novel to the screen, Hitchcock tried to use the plot line without completely succumbing to Conrad's cynicism. In the novel, all the adult characters are selfish and exploitative, and no one retains a moral position. In Hitchcock's film, only Verloc and his anarchist friends are debased and corrupt. Mrs. Verloc's motives for marrying her husband are left unexplored so that she appears to be a simple victim, and a detective in pursuit of Verloc, much like the detective in

Shadow of a Doubt, is introduced as a wholesome love interest. Although the boy (Desmond Tester) dies in the film as a result of Verloc's cowardice and carelessness, and although Mrs. Verloc (Sylvia Sidney) kills her husband (Oscar Homolka) in retaliation for that death, the film diverges from the novel (whose heroine commits suicide) by having her rescued following the murder by the detective (John Loder), who shields her from arrest. They run off together, disappearing into the crowd in a makeshift happy ending.

The film was a box office failure, and its lack of success seems to turn on its inability to sustain conceptual suspense. To be sure, there is empathetic suspense enough: we know that the boy is carrying a ticking bomb and are made to sit through the painful interval as the time set for the explosion approaches. But by not allowing the boy to escape, Hitchcock leaves audiences with no reason to care about the escaping couple at the end. The idea of the family, which the boy embodied, has been destroyed and cannot be resurrected. The death here stands for more than itself; it is the death of an idea as well as a boy. No death in a Hitchcock film, before or after, is as conceptually damaging to its core values.

In *Shadow of a Doubt* Hitchcock no longer makes use of an antecedent text by a great European author. Instead, he controls the film's script more completely, drawing for assistance on the well-known American playwright Thornton Wilder, who had made his reputation with *Our Town*, his 1938 play lauding the values of small-town family life. Indeed, Hitchcock told Truffaut that this play was the reason he wanted Wilder on the film (152). In *Sabotage*, Stevie's death left an empty space at the family dinner table which so disturbed his sister that she was prompted to kill her husband. In *Shadow of a Doubt*, Uncle Charlie also disrupts a scene at a dinner table, blithely usurping the paternal place. Here, however, the usurpation is temporary and purged at the end of the film so that the family is allowed to resume where it left off. Thus, if Hitchcock shatters the family irrevocably in *Sabotage*, he threatens but saves it in *Shadow of a Doubt*. One structural change is irreparable; the other is temporary and remediable.

Richard Allen sheds light on the dynamic involved here when he notes a dual drive at work in many Hitchcock films. On the one hand, he says, there is the drive "to find out the content of a mystery because we need to allay our fears about the secret." At the same time, he also notes that we are inspired "to find out the secret on account of the fear it causes. As in a taboo situation, we are drawn to the secret like a moth to a flame" (59). Suspense coheres, in other words, in the desire both to dispel fear and to experience fear or, to translate this duality into other terms, to *maintain* order and to *disrupt* order. This dual drive is precisely what is at issue in the representation of the family in *Shadow of a Doubt*, which must at once be transgressed and maintained, broken apart in order to be strengthened and reproduced.

The disruptive impulse in *Shadow of a Doubt* is visible at the outset. The fact that young Charlie is restless and discontented, that her mother is overworked, and that her father (Henry Travers) seems like a foolish figurehead all feed into the idea that the film is critiquing the nuclear family. Based on the history given by his sister, Uncle Charlie is the product of just such a family himself (his injury as a child kept him tied to the home with such intensity that he could not psychologically leave it), and his crimes reflect this attachment. They are morally motivated, as Hitchcock explained to Truffaut: he punishes widows for being independent. One could say that through his death he manages to punish young Charlie for her desire to break away from the family at the beginning of the film – ironically, by leading her back to that family at the end.

Yet to suggest that *Shadow of a Doubt* is a serious attack on the family would be wrongheaded, since in so many ways it extols the virtues of small-town family life. The cheerful home, the humorous squabbling siblings, the flighty but lovable mother, the warm-hearted, ineffectual father all capture our sympathy and arouse our protective impulses. Thus the film, though it may critique the family in some respects, supports it in countervailing ones, and this tension between critique and support, transgression and maintenance, is precisely the source of its ability to sustain interest and generate suspense. One could argue that *Sabotage* was a box office failure precisely because it failed to maintain this balance: the death of Stevie transgressed the family idea so radically that it became impossible to maintain, thereby losing the investment of the audience. *Shadow of a Doubt* is masterful in supporting that investment. It pits the fresh and lovely young Charlie against the jaded, amoral Uncle Charlie. She wins, but only by reinforcing a kinship between them that cannot be fully erased.

In this context, Uncle Charlie serves as both a genuine threat to young Charlie's family and a necessary disruption of it – the "miracle" needed to shake things up. His disruptive presence not only serves the suspense plot but also serves the practical, long-term end of bringing young Charlie together with the detective whom she will likely marry – allowing her to make an orderly transition from her family of origin into a new family that extends the original one in space and time. This is a successful "moral outcome," in Noël Carroll's terms, insofar as it is a *bildungsroman* for the family itself.

Shadow of a Doubt was Hitchcock's sixth American film, made at a point when he had definitively settled into his adopted home and into his own life as husband and father. He had been married for seventeen years and had a fourteen-year-old daughter – young enough to be securely tied to her family of origin but old enough to have opinions and desires of her own. The film was made when American society was in the midst of turbulent times. The 1940s American family was an ostensibly conventionalized structure that was experiencing the dislocating effects of World War II and, with them, economic and cultural shifts that would both rigidify its structure in the short term and erode it in the coming decades (Mintz and Kellogg).

The family model that Hitchcock presents in *Shadow of a Doubt* was a stylized version of his own family and of that of the culture in which he worked. It was also a template that would have powerful, enduring importance for his subsequent films and arguably for all films that generate a certain kind of ideological investment from their audiences. For even as we have moved away from the assumption that a conventionalized nuclear family is the norm, we still hold to it as an ideal – or at least as that against which existing families are measured and understood. Viewers may describe the family in *Shadow of a Doubt* as dated, small town, sugar-coated, sexist, or by any number of dismissive terms. But the model it presents remains recognizable and, I would argue, subliminally comforting, so that its disruption becomes a source of anxiety and the possibility of its restitution a source of desire for viewers even today. To put the family back in order – to save not just young Charlie but the idea of the family that Uncle Charlie threatens (but also yearns for himself) – creates a concern that links the contemporary viewer's empathy with a more systemic idea. The family and the film, in other words, are analogous structures, and Hitchcock constructs the film so that it makes the fate of the family correspond to its own drive for satisfying closure. It does so even as it hints at the idea that Uncle Charlie is a metaphorical expression of young Charlie and of the threat that the family must experience when those who have been bred inside of it must break with it, if only to reproduce it.

Hitchcock found an important trope on which to elaborate a personal and social vision when he made *Sabotage*, where he revised Conrad's use of the family to fasten the individual into a context of meaning parallel to the suspense plot. But he realized the idea fully only in *Shadow of a Doubt*, where "saving the threatened family" became the moral outcome and thus the source of conceptual suspense. This film was a moment of balance and integration. After it, Hitchcock replayed the idea in various truncated guises. In subsequent films, experiments in form were made to parallel changes, breakdowns, shifts and rifts in the structure of the family. These experiments allowed him to lift the suspense genre out of the realm of mere entertainment into that of social and existential critique. The films built on this template are classics of conceptual suspense. That is, they continue to generate suspense not only on second and third viewing, but in different historical contexts where their plots are well-known and their technical effects seem conventional or outmoded. This is because the narrative of family life that underlies them remains a source of investment and anxiety for viewers.

We can see this structural use of family by considering the difference between Hitchcock's 1934 *The Man Who Knew Too Much* and its 1956 remake. In the earlier version, the family is a loose structure, with gender roles in disarray and a young girl of indeterminate age as the object of the kidnapping plot. In the later version, the family has become conventionalized in keeping with 1950s American culture. We now have an authoritarian physician father, a domesticated wife (a once-famous singer who has retired from the stage to care for her family), and a child, now a young boy rather than an older girl (a change in gender that may be intended to remedy the loss of the boy in *Sabotage*). As in *Shadow of the Doubt*, the family is anatomized and critiqued, but in the end "saved." The "moral outcome," in Noël Carroll's terms, is achieved against the odds.

Yet for all their structural similarity, the difference between *Shadow of a Doubt* and the 1956 *Man Who Knew Too Much* is also noteworthy. The former, despite its darker undercurrents, has an essential lightness and optimism. The latter is a strained effort at return, a derivative film in more ways than one. One has only to compare the family conversation at the beginning of *Shadow of a Doubt* with the stilted banter on the bus at the beginning of *The Man Who Knew Too Much* to see the difference. And the last scene, when Jo, Ben, and son Hank (Doris Day, James Stewart, and Christopher Olsen) appear in the hotel room to face their rather debauched group of friends, spells this out. The family has become a performance of itself: not a dynamic entity, but a preserved specimen, like something in the taxidermy shop visited earlier in the film. This staged representation of family points forward to the mummified mother figure in *Psycho*.

In films like *Stage Fright* (1950), *Strangers on a Train*, *Psycho*, *The Birds* (1963), and *Marnie* (1964), Hitchcock goes further afield for his material. Solving a mystery and repairing a damaged or disrupted family remain mutually reinforcing goals, but fear of the disruptive energies the family generates now begins to grow over-whelming. Hitchcock never sacrifices a literal child again as he did in *Sabotage*, but he increasingly presents us with central characters who, as adults, are cases of arrested development – psychologically destroyed by the excesses or inadequacies of the families that bred them. This is the case for Uncle Charlie, as well as for Bruno, Norman Bates, and Marnie.

It is possible to view Hitchcock's more disturbing films of the 1950s and 1960s as mirroring a crisis in his own family and in the cultural institution of the fam-ily in which he was working. His daughter's role in *Psycho* seems to reflect a paternal anger and disappointment, the seeds of which can be traced back to *Strangers on a Train*. But this hardly prevents these films from positing the pres-ervation of the family as the desirable, if not the achievable, goal. Despite the complications and horrors the films portray, they still encourage us to imagine compensatory measures for the restitution of the family, more so perhaps in repeated viewings than in initial ones. The best example of this pattern is *Vertigo* (1958). Arguably Hitchcock's most nihilistic film, it can be made to fit a different agenda. The film's final image seems at first to be one of unmitigated existential horror: Scottie (James Stewart) leaning over the abyss where his "true love" has fallen for the second time. But my students generally refuse to accept the nihil-istic ending. I take their reaction as somehow conditioned by the film itself, or at least by the film as it becomes associated with a receding ideology of the fam-ily. For my students voice what I must acknowledge to be my own powerful wish, a wish that has grown more powerful the more times I see the film: that Scottie turn to the discarded option of the long-suffering Midge (Barbara Bel Geddes). "He'll realize that he should be with her," my students insist. They want Scottie to settle down with a nice, practical-minded woman, much as young Charlie settles down with a nice, practical-minded man at the end of *Shadow of a Doubt*.

Vertigo may not seem to be a family film, but underlying its strangeness and sense of alienation exists the shadow of the couple as the template for the family. Like *Shadow of a Doubt*, the film generates conceptual suspense by placing this idea under threat and making its rescue seem improbable. As a result, the woman who had initially seemed like an overly conventional, rather boring companion for the hero now seems intensely desirable, precisely what is needed to salvage the threatened family idea.

In his last film, *Family Plot* (1976), Hitchcock can be said to have definitively discarded the family idea that had been a source of conceptual suspense for so many of his greatest films. The movie begins by appearing to support its title – making the reconstitution of a parent-child bond the seeming focus of the suspense plot. The attempt of Julia Rainbird (Cathleen Nesbitt) to bestow her money on the illegitimate son of her estranged sister suggests that a crime against family will be assuaged and a wounded family healed. With this idea in place, we are initially presented with a paradox regarding the moral outcome: the restitution of the family is now at odds with the apparent criminality of the character who would receive restitution. It is a version of the situation in *Shadow of a Doubt*. But instead of using conceptual suspense in the service of this paradox as in the earlier film – finding a way of maintaining the family idea in the face of disruption – this film drops the family idea altogether. Julia Rainbird and her story disappear early in the movie, and the focus shifts to a cat-and-mouse game among unrelated individuals. The result is to deprive the film of the emotional nexus that would allow us to care about its characters, which is akin to what Fredric Jameson calls the "waning of affect" characteristic of postmodern expression (15). In *Sabotage*, Hitchcock noted that he had made a mistake, betraying his audience's emotional investment when he killed the boy and destroyed the family idea he had carefully put in place. In *Family Plot*, he does the reverse, raising the possibility of saving a once-abandoned boy, now a degenerate adult, but refusing to let this plot run its course. The result is one of the least satisfying, least enduring of Hitchcock's films.

I have concentrated on Hitchcock's use of the family idea as the basis for conceptual suspense because I believe that the films that fall in this category represent his greatest contribution to cinematic art. However, in closing I want to acknowledge another idea that he employed in the service of conceptual suspense and that is central to his oeuvre – that of social justice. One of the anecdotes Hitchcock liked to tell involved being sent by his father to the police station to be locked up for some childhood misdemeanor. The story is suggestive on a number of fronts and can be commandeered to explain various facets of Hitchcock's filmmaking. But taken in the most literal and obvious sense, it is a simple cautionary tale: if the police can lock up a child at the behest of a father, what might they do at the behest of higher, more powerful figures in government or society? This question is explored in early films like *The Lodger* (1926), *The 39 Steps*, and *Young and Innocent* (1937), and threads its way through to the end, most notably in *North by Northwest* (1959) and *Frenzy* (1972). As Hitchcock's family films activate our investment in the family as a place of nurture and love for its members, these other films activate our investment in the government as a source of justice and protection for its citizens. And just as the family idea is threatened in the former films, so is the social ideal threatened in the latter, as officials of government are shown to pursue or even scapegoat innocent men. Yet while some of these "mistaken identity" films – *The 39 Steps* and *North by Northwest* in particular—have an enduring charm, they do not have the same power as films like *Shadow of a Doubt*, either *The Man Who Knew Too Much*, or *Vertigo*. One reason for this difference may be that error and duplicity on the part of government have become less surprising in a contemporary world. Vietnam and Watergate changed our relationship to authority, and Carroll's formula for suspense—"a moral outcome is improbable"—no longer works against the grain of normal expectations. The effect is the reverse of what I discussed in *Shadow of a Doubt*, where the moral outcome seems probable in its detail (we rather expect Uncle Charlie to be caught) but the threat to the family idea, which we still hold sacred, becomes the basis for conceptual suspense. Films involving government conspiracy or wrongdoing may still be suspenseful in the details of their plots, but they are no longer suspenseful in conceptual terms because our idea of social justice has been so profoundly compromised.

An exception is *The Wrong Man*. This 1956 film is the most unsettling of all Hitchcock's films that turn on the idea of social justice because it is the one film that links the idea of justice to the idea of the family. When the protagonist (Henry Fonda) is accused of a crime that he did not commit, the mistake shatters his family. The range and pathos of this result make for a different effect than in other mistaken identity films, where individuals alone are shown to suffer. *The Wrong Man* is again reminiscent of *Sabotage*, where the sacrifice of a family member (in this case, the protagonist's wife, played by Vera Miles) becomes more than the emotional fabric of the film can bear. It is a hard film to watch. That said, it continues to exert enormous power if one has the fortitude to sit through it.[5]

It is beyond the scope of this chapter to consider at length the legacy of conceptual suspense that Hitchcock pioneered. One could argue that the heirs of his mistaken identity films include subsequent political and corporate conspiracy films, from *All the President's Men* (Alan J. Pakula, 1976) to *Michael Clayton* (Tony Gilroy, 2007), as well as fantasy projections of social manipulation like *The Matrix* (Andy and Larry Wachowski, 1999). The legacy of the family idea is more complicated. Although films involving family trauma certainly continue to be made, few link the family to a suspense plot while grappling with the complexity of the family idea in the way Hitchcock did.[6] This difference seems a function both of his unique genius and of changes in the family in our current society, making a generic family harder to represent on screen. While we can still be drawn into a film like *Shadow of a Doubt* as it evokes a nostalgic desire for an intact nuclear family, we are less able to accept this representation as realistic in a contemporary setting. Instead, the idea of the family as the locus of conceptual suspense seems to have been replaced by the idea of the home. The vulnerability of the home is a suspense motif in cinema from its beginnings. We see it in the terrorized mother and children in *The Lonely Villa* (D.W. Griffith, 1909), for example, and it is present in 1950s films like *The Desperate Hours* (William Wyler, 1955) and *The Night of the Hunter* (Charles Laughton, 1955) and 1970s films like *A Clockwork Orange* (Stanley Kubrick, 1971) and *Straw Dogs* (Sam Peckinpah, 1971). More recently, however, the "home invasion movie" has become something of a genre. *Funny Games* (Michael Haneke, 1997 and 2007), *Panic Room* (David Fincher, 2002), *The Dark Hours* (Paul Fox, 2005), *Them* (David Moreau and Xavier Palud, 2006), *Inside* (Alexandre Bustillo and Julien Maury, 2007), and *The Strangers* (Bryan Bertino, 2008) are among a string of recent films in which the violation of the home is at issue. Such films reflect an increased fear of the erosion of distinctions between private and public space, already present in Hitchcock's mistaken identity films. These films also reflect a sense that the outside world is more dangerous and unpredictable than ever before. Finally, the home in these films can be seen as a practical substitute for the family: a static, physical symbol of what is, in our current society, fractured and changeable. Of course, replacing an organic idea like the family with a static, material one like the home limits the depth and variety of what can be expressed.

A film like *Shadow of a Doubt* sustains suspense because it manipulates with great mastery and delicacy a uniquely useful and enduring idea – the idea that the family, while being oppressive and crippling in some respects, is also a site of comfort, refuge, and hope. This idea, in all its complexity and subtlety, has not lost its power and seems likely to hold viewers in thrall for a very long time.

Notes

1. Smith refers to "direct" versus "shared" or "vicarious" suspense, focusing, in her discussion of the latter, on the element of identification of the viewer with the character. Allen uses the term "subjective suspense" (41). See also Beecher, who differentiates between emotional suspense and a more probability-driven, mathematical sort of suspense.

2. Relevant to this notion is C.S. Lewis's observation: "We do not enjoy a story fully at the first reading. Not till the curiosity, the sheer narrative lust, has been given its sop and laid asleep, are we at leisure to savour the real beauties" (103). See Prieto-Pablos for a provocative if sketchy treatment of the role of ideological investment in suspense narratives.

3. I have discussed the family dynamic in general in *The Daughter's Dilemma* and in Hitchcock's films, including *Shadow of a Doubt*, in *Alfred Hitchcock: The Legacy of Victorianism* (70–74). Indeed, *Shadow of a Doubt* has been the subject of numerous readings that take into account the importance of the family (examples include Wood, McLaughlin, and Michie). However, these readings do not see the family idea as the engine for the film's suspense.

4. Some might argue that instead of *conceptual suspense* I should use the phrase *ideological suspense*, in line with Robin Wood's assertion about *Shadow of a Doubt*: "What is in jeopardy is above all the Family—but, given the Family's central ideological significance, once that is in jeopardy, everything is" (292). I prefer, however, a more neutral, less politically charged phrase. Readers can draw their own conclusions as to what kind of idea the family is.

5. In Chapter 7 of *Alfred Hitchcock: The Legacy of Victorianism*, I discuss *The Wrong Man* as the harbinger to a paradigm shift in Hitchcock's later work, seeing it, with *Vertigo*, as the last of his films still tethered to a family idea.

6. A number of provocative family films come to mind: *Interiors* (Woody Allen, 1978), *Ordinary People* (Robert Redford, 1980), *The Ice Storm* (Ang Lee, 1997), *American Beauty* (Sam Mendes, 1999), *The Squid and the Whale* (Noah Baumbach, 2005), and *Revolutionary Road* (Sam Mendes, 2008), for example. Yet in all of these, the family idea is the central focus rather than the conceptual underpinning for a suspense plot, as in Hitchcock's films. Exceptions that do have some degree of suspense, like *In the Bedroom* (Todd Field, 2001) and *Before the Devil Knows You're Dead* (Sidney Lumet, 2007), depict such profound family dysfunction as to render the family idea irrecuperable.

Works Cited

Allen, Richard. *Hitchcock's Romantic Irony*. New York: Columbia UP, 2007.

Beecher, Donald. "Suspense." *Philosophy and Literature* 31.2 (2007): 255–79.

Brewer, William F. "The Nature of Narrative Suspense and the Problem of Rereading." Vorderer, Wulff, and Friedrichsen 107–27.

Carroll, Noël. "The Paradox of Suspense." Vorderer, Wulff, and Friedrichsen 71–91.

Carroll, Noël. "Toward a Theory of Film Suspense." *Persistence of Vision* 1 (Summer 1984): 65–89.

Cohen, Paula Marantz. *Alfred Hitchcock and the Legacy of Victorianism*. U of Kentucky P, 1995.

Cohen, Paula Marantz. *The Daughter's Dilemma: Family Process and the Nineteenth-Century Domestic Novel*. Ann Arbor: U of Michigan P, 1991.

Conrad, Joseph. *The Secret Agent: A Simple Tale*. 1907. Garden City, NY: Doubleday Anchor, 1953.

Gerrig, Richard J. "The Resiliency of Suspense." Vorderer, Wulff, and Friedrichsen 93–105.

Jameson, Fredric. "Postmodernism and Consumer Society." *Postmodernism and its Discontents: Theories, Practices*. Ed. E. Ann Kaplan. London: Verso, 1988.

Lewis, C.S. *On Stories: And Other Essays on Literature*. New York: Harvest, 1982.

McLaughlin, James. "All in the Family: Alfred Hitchcock's *Shadow of a Doubt*." *A Hitchcock Reader*. Second ed. Ed. Marshall Deutelbaum and Leland Poague. Chichester, UK: Wiley-Blackwell, 2009. 145–55.

Michie, Elsie B. "Unveiling Maternal Desires: Hitchcock and American Domesticity." *Hitchcock's America*. Ed. Jonathan Freedman and Richard Millington. New York: Oxford UP, 1999. 29–53.

Mintz, Steven and Susan Kellogg. *Domestic Revolutions: A Social History of American Family Life*. New York: Free Press, 1989.

Prieto-Pablos, Juan. "The Paradox of Suspense." *Poetics* 26.2 (1998): 99–113.

Smith, Susan. *Hitchcock: Suspense, Humour and Tone*. London: BFI, 2000.

Truffaut, François, with the collaboration of Helen G. Scott. *Hitchcock*. Rev. ed. New York: Simon and Schuster, 1984.

Vorderer, Peter, Hans J. Wulff, and Mike Friedrichsen, eds. *Suspense: Conceptualizations, Theoretical Analyses, and Empirical Explorations*. Mahwah, NJ: Lawrence Erlbaum, 1996.

Wood, Robin. *Hitchcock's Films Revisited*. Rev. ed. New York: Columbia UP, 2002.

PART III

Collaboration

8

"Tell Me the Story So Far": Hitchcock and His Writers

Leland Poague

[W]hen a script is completed, whether I write it or somebody else writes it, it's mine, in the sense that I have to absorb it and like it in order to interpret it on the screen.

Frank Capra (Friedman 50)

[T]he themes and style that have come to be known as "Capraesque" can just as well be called "Riskinesque."

Joseph McBride (193)

Frank Capra and Alfred Hitchcock are often discussed together. Both were eager to be "a name above the title" (Leff 16), even if that put their relationships with key collaborators at risk, most famously Capra's with screenwriter Robert Riskin and Hitchcock's with screenwriter John Michael Hayes. Robert Kapsis has compared Capra's *It's a Wonderful Life* (1946) to Hitchcock's *Vertigo* (1958) by way of elaborating how "the art world of film" (2) appropriates art works and apportions aesthetic distinction. Though initially box-office disappointments, both films eventually benefited from the post–World War II auteurist category shift whereby at least some Hollywood films were approached via reading strategies that had typically been reserved for "art films."

Though I have professed a director-centered *politique des auteurs*, for which the Capra claim of incorporation and interpretation in my first epigraph is axiomatic, I do not doubt the truth of McBride's subsequent rejoinder in defense of Riskin and of screenwriters generally.[1] In *English Hitchcock*, Charles Barr organizes his study by reference to Hitchcock's sources and collaborators, paying special attention to novelists Marie Belloc Lowndes (*The Lodger* [1913]) and John Buchan (*The Thirty-Nine Steps* [1915]) and to the ways their influence subsequently plays out in the screenplays authored or co-authored by Eliot Stannard and Charles Bennett

A Companion to Alfred Hitchcock, First Edition. Edited by Thomas Leitch and Leland Poague.

respectively.[2] My current remarks extend Barr's approach to Hitchcock's Hollywood period by considering how movies often discussed as "Hitchcock films" can just as well be understood as John Michael Hayes films or Ernest Lehman films.

Though many inhabitants of the art world of film reside in university English departments, academic film criticism evinces a striking neglect of Hollywood writers, which some attribute to laziness. Ernest Lehman does, in the following passage, where he speaks in the voice of a deadline-harried auteur critic:

> A Robert Aldrich film is a Robert Aldrich film, and please don't confuse me. I wouldn't know how to *write* this review if I had to take into account what I don't know: namely, what was written in the screenplay and what was put in by the director, the producer, even the star. So let me write the review as if Aldrich, the director, created the picture.
>
> (Boeth 170)

Lehman brings his own sense of artistic hierarchy to bear here. He does not urge that we track casting directors or special effects technicians. He conflates criticism with reviewing, and assumes that reviewers are chiefly tasked with doing historical justice, of giving credit where credit is due – no easy task in a world where "[s]creen credits mask almost as much as they reveal" (Leff 281). Though the following analyses involve questions of evaluation, they are mainly interpretive in orientation, as seeking to specify what Hayes and Lehman likely contributed to the films they wrote by way of a shaping vision, an underlying perspective. I take this approach as the most aesthetically appropriate and practicable way of gaining the knowledge Lehman assumes most critics lack.

My chapter title derives from Evan Hunter's account of his collaboration with Hitchcock on *The Birds* (1963) and *Marnie* (1964). "Tell me the story so far" (16) was Hitchcock's way of prompting Hunter to summarize progress to date on the developing treatment of *The Birds*, the extended elaboration of which preceded the screenplay proper. As numerous accounts suggest, these tale-telling sessions were a source of intense pleasure to Hitchcock, his "raison d'être" in Lehman's estimation (Spoto 407), and they were also a means by which "he edited the script before any of it was actually written" (Hunter 23).

Hitchcock's similarly close collaborations with so many writers over the years is prima facie evidence that Hitchcock was not a writer-director like Preston Sturges, Billy Wilder, or Woody Allen. Thomas Leitch is closer to the mark in claiming that "[a]ll of Hitchcock's films were adaptations – if not of somebody else's novel or play, then of somebody else's original screenplay" ("Hitchcock," 75). But "original" screenplays were (in fact) few in number – most of those, like the scripts for *North by Northwest* (1959) or *Torn Curtain* (1966), had origins in Hitchcock's past conversations or readings or his earlier films – so it is fair to say that Hitchcock's writers were also adaptor/collaborators who incorporated Hitchcock's sources and ideas in the same process whereby he incorporated theirs. When Hitchcock, echoing Capra, says, "[f]or better or worse, I must do the whole thing myself" (Truffaut 329), then, he is obviously not saying he *did* everything so much as he is expressing his commitment to the material, that he *means* it, all of it. Similarly, assertions by John Michael Hayes or Ernest Lehman to the effect that he "wrote" the screenplay of (respectively) *Rear Window* (1954) or *North by Northwest* can be taken literally – both have remarked upon the care Hitchcock took to film the screenplay as written (Marshall 222; Baer 69) – but should also be taken metaphorically, as a measure of the effort and commitment each devoted to the task, even if neither ever worked entirely alone, at least not when writing for Hitchcock.

Considerations of space and history dictate somewhat different treatments of Hayes and Lehman. In lieu of biography, I provide historical framework via filmographic entries for each, though I have excluded made-for-television projects. (Hayes or Lehman received solo script credit unless otherwise noted.) Hayes did four films for Hitchcock, and I approach his body of work inductively, paying equal attention to all periods and genres. By contrast, Lehman wrote only two scripts that eventually became Hitchcock films, though he spent over twenty years trying to write "the Hitchcock picture to end all Hitchcock pictures" (Engel 47). In Lehman's case, I proceed more deductively, focusing chiefly on *North by Northwest* and *Family Plot* (1976), with the goal of specifying how they are "Lehman" films, though a crucial intertext turns out, not surprisingly, to be *Sweet Smell of Success* (1957).

John Michael Hayes

Red Ball Express (d. Budd Boetticher, 1952), *Thunder Bay* (d. Anthony Mann, 1953; story, co-script), *Torch Song* (d. Walter Lang, 1953; co-script), *War Arrow* (d. George Sherman, 1953; story, script), *Rear Window* (d. Alfred Hitchcock, 1954), *To Catch a Thief* (d. Alfred Hitchcock, 1955), *The Trouble with Harry* (d. Alfred Hitchcock, 1955), *It's A Dog's Life* (d. Herman Hoffman, 1955), *The Man Who Knew Too Much* (d. Alfred Hitchcock, 1956), *Peyton Place* (d. Mark Robson, 1957), *The Matchmaker* (d. Joseph Anthony, 1958), *But Not for Me* (d. Walter Lang, 1959), *Butterfield 8* (d. Daniel Mann, 1960; co-script), *The Children's Hour* (d. William Wyler, 1961), *The Carpetbaggers* (d. Edward Dmytryk, 1964), *The Chalk Garden* (d. Ronald Neame, 1964), *Where Love Has Gone* (d. Edward Dmytryk, 1964), *Harlow* (d. Gordon Douglas, 1965), *Judith* (d. Daniel Mann, 1966; co-script), *Nevada Smith* (d. Henry Hathaway, 1966; story, script), *Iron Will* (d. Charles Haid, 1994; story, co-script).

Hayes wrote four films for Hitchcock: *Rear Window, To Catch a Thief, The Trouble with Harry*, and the remake of *The Man Who Knew Too Much*. Critics are generally agreed that they represent a break in Hitchcock's development, a shift from the desperate and relatively humorless romanticism of films like *Notorious* (1946) and *I Confess* (1953) in the direction of "rounded characters" and "an optimistic viewpoint" that yielded, via sparkling dialogue and VistaVision colors, "a high degree of excitement, wit, and sophistication" (DeRosa 203–04). Since three of the four Hayes/Hitchcock movies were properties that Hitchcock had purchased or developed well before Hayes was brought on board, however, it is just as likely that the collaboration prospered because Hitchcock's mood had brightened and found its match in the youthful enthusiasm that Hayes brought to their joint efforts as that Hayes had turned Hitchcock's noir-tinged postwar gloom somehow sunny.

More to the point, describing the four Hayes/Hitchcock films as exceptions to the Hitchcock rule begs the question of how well they embody a Hayesean thematic. In *Writing with Hitchcock*, Steven DeRosa is more attuned to the Hitchcockness of the films than to their Hayesean features, and he depends openly on Thomas Leitch's discussion of Hitchcock in *Find the Director* – where Leitch emphasizes the comedy of "paranoia" overcome in the Hayes pictures (166) – to substantiate his claims about the "affirmative" and "sympathetic" qualities that distinguish the Hayes Hitchcock from other Hitchcocks. Thus "[v]oyeurism, fear of intimacy, fear of death, and the loss of a loved one" – Hitchcock themes all, and serially of the four films he did with Hayes – are more "palatable" and "accessible" than usual because the Paramount films, exceptionally for Hitchcock, emphasize "the individual becoming one with his community" (DeRosa xii–xiii). DeRosa's "isolated" individuals are mostly male – L.B. Jefferies (James Stewart) in *Rear Window*, John Robie (Cary Grant) in *To Catch a Thief*, Ben McKenna (James Stewart) in *The Man Who Knew Too Much* – while the community they are saved by and for is implicitly feminine and is troped in all of the Hayes/Hitchcock films by the estate of marriage, which the men initially see as a threat or as a situation requiring domination. Indeed, DeRosa's most emphatic addition to the Leitch-derived picture of the Hayes/Hitchcock films is his discussion of Stella (Thelma Ritter) in *Rear Window*, a version of the "worldly wise, rough-around-the-edges mother" figure who appears repeatedly in Hayes, often as a kind of comic chorus, like Mrs. Stevens (Jessie Royce Landis) in *To Catch a Thief* (81; see also 23–24, 132).

A less Hitchcock-centered picture of Hayes would see both the "isolated" male protagonist and the role of women in Hayes in less optimistic terms, though Hayes does employ a species of dramatic redemption that is strikingly akin to what Robin Wood has called Hitchcock's "therapeutic" theme. A figure of special interest is what I will call, after a late instance, the "Nevada Smith" character, someone wounded or traumatized whose anger or thirst for vengeance is all-consuming. Of course, "Nevada Smith" is a nom de guerre, the alias of Max Sand, played by Alan Ladd in *The Carpetbaggers* and by Steve McQueen in *Nevada Smith*. In the latter film, which takes place largely in the Old West, Max Sand's parents are killed – his father is white, his mother is Kiowa, and much is made of Max's half-breed status, especially via the inclusion of an idyllic interlude with members of a Kiowa band who nurse him back to health after a vicious knife fight – and Max spends the remainder of the film hunting down his parents' killers, with some tutorial assistance from a gunsmith named Jason Cord. In *The Carpetbaggers*, which takes place from the mid-1920s through the late 1930s, Smith works for Cord Senior until the latter's sudden death, functions as surrogate father to Jason Cord Junior (George Peppard), and eventually becomes a Cord employee again when the younger Jason takes over a movie studio where cowboy-star Nevada Smith ("the Robin Hood of the Rio Grande") makes kid-friendly westerns.

A curious feature of both films is the role played by writing. Nevada survives that knife fight by virtue of a *McGuffey's Primer* tucked in his shirt, and Junior apparently spent his adolescence researching and writing a history of Max Sand. Indeed, the movie that provides Cord's entrée into motion pictures is *The Renegade's Coat* – from a story by Nevada Smith, about a cowboy named "Max Sand," obviously based on Cord's own manuscript. Moreover, among his first acts as producer is to call for rewrites, expressly for the purpose of putting more women into the story ("It's time somebody gave the West back to the grownups"). The lead female role eventually goes to Rina Marlowe (Carroll Baker), Jason Cord's widowed stepmother and, before long, Mrs. Nevada Smith. Hence the transferential Freudian logic whereby the younger Jason becomes the "angry man" in *The Carpetbaggers*, anger that is literally knocked out of him by Nevada Smith in a bare-knuckles confrontation in the film's penultimate scene. Jason's fear that he would go insane, like his long-deceased and never-mentioned twin brother, is replaced by the sobering realization that he has become "Jason Cord," an embittered and compulsive drunk.

This "angry man" figure is neither the only Hayesean male nor a late development. *Red Ball Express*, Hayes's first film, has two subplots beyond its war-movie "keep the gas and ammo coming" main story, parts of which are narrated in voiceover by a character who frequently carries the manuscript of his war-novel–in-progress on his person. In one subplot, a former boxer and sports journalist (Sidney Poitier) seeks to transfer from the transport unit and then changes his mind after his commanding officer, Lt. Campbell (Jeff Chandler), holds an impromptu funeral service, against orders, for another black soldier in their anomalously integrated unit. In the other, a sergeant whose brother had driven big rigs with Campbell in civilian life and been killed in a wreck, burned alive in a truck fire from which Campbell could not extract him, spends most of the film badmouthing his immediate commander – until one night the unit's novelist deliberately runs his truck, loaded with gas cans, into a German tank. The resulting flames are so hot that neither the sergeant nor Lt. Campbell can approach the wrecked vehicle when they try to rescue Private Partridge, who had jumped at the last minute and been knocked cold.

Likewise, *It's A Dog's Life* features multiple male characters, among them the Bull Terrier named "Wildfire" (aka Prince Galahad of Wyndham Estates) who narrates the film in a witty combination of canine puns (e.g., the film's title) and what we might call Bowery Latin, and Dean Jagger's bereaved widower character, "The Terrible Tempered Mr. Wyndham." The latter too has a secret, known only to old time stable hand Jeremiah Noland (Edmund Gwenn): Wyndham's numerous business trips were really medical in nature, the result of repeated heart attacks implicitly connected to the death of his wife. Though he seems mostly concerned with breeding show-dog St. Bernards, his propensity for competition is also expressed through betting. Indeed, when he threatens to fire Noland if the latter doesn't get rid of Wildfire, whom Noland has lately rescued from the high-stakes dog-fighting culture at Corbin's Saloon, Wyndham's daughter challenges him with a wager of her own. If Wildfire wins a local dog show, both the dog and master can stay. The other angry male is Wildfire himself, whose announced goal in life is to kill his father for abandoning his mother. As it happens, Wildfire's father is Champion Regent Royal, and by film's end Wildfire does confront and defeat his sire in the Grand National Championships held at Madison Square Garden. But Wildfire is so impressed by his father's dignity in defeat that he jumps to Regent Royal's defense when the latter is threatened by a pack of larger dogs. The resulting chaos sends dogs and owners and judges scrambling helter-skelter into the city streets, where Wildfire is reunited at last with his mother (and with Miss Ladyship the second, who will soon give birth to a litter of little Bull Terriers). The "redemption" motif adduced earlier is thus clear in both *Red Ball Express* and *It's A Dog's Life*. As Robin Wood elaborates this *"therapeutic* theme" in reference to Hitchcock, we see a character "cured of some weakness or obsession by indulging it and living through the consequences" (71). Exactly this happens repeatedly in Hayes, and not only in his Hitchcock scripts. ("Fire," I might add, is a repeated token of fixation in Hayes. It plays an especially resonant role in *The Chalk Garden*, as we will see, and is evident as well in the "fireworks" sequence in *To Catch a Thief.*)

Another recurrent feature is what I will call "the gambler" character in Hayes. A crucial instance is the theatrical producer Russell Ward (Clark Gable) in *But Not For Me*, the remarriage plot of which is another instance of the redemption theme. The film's chief feature is its unremitting reflexivity. The play Ward finally produces (on money anonymously provided by his former and future wife) is inspired by, and stars, his twenty-something secretary (Carroll Baker), whose frustrated passion for him he sees primarily as a dramatic resource. But Ward's bookkeeper finds his initial script a "worn out piece of tripe written by a has-been" and observes that, among Ward's numerous extravagances, his gambling is getting out of hand ("The money you've spent on gambling this year would support all the women in Schenectady for a week"), though the implication is clear that all of Ward's show-biz activities amount to gambles.

As it happens, Ward is not the "angry man" character in this film, a role assigned instead to Jeremiah MacDonald (Lee J. Cobb), the hard-drinking has-been writer Ward has engaged. (Most of MacDonald's ire is reserved for a rotund émigré film producer who has, in the producer's own words, "sold out" to television.) While Jason Junior in *The Carpetbaggers* proves that the angry man can be a gambler (and a film producer) in Hayes, there are also numerous instances where the gambler appears apart from, sometimes in opposition to, the angry man. If we see Bertani (Charles Vanel) as the angry man in *To Catch a Thief*, for instance, then it makes Hayesean sense to see John Robie and Francie Stevens (Grace Kelly) as gamblers, though their casino meet-cute is stage managed by H.H. Hughson of Lloyd's of London (John Williams), whom Robie implicitly nominates a gambler when proposing a "long shot" scheme to recover the jewels Robie is supposed to have stolen. The gambling motif also makes an early appearance in the Hayes script for the second *Man Who Knew Too Much*, where Hank McKenna's bus-window association of North Africa with Las Vegas prompts recollection of the bad luck Ben McKenna had experienced shooting craps on an earlier family vacation. Ben's appetite for risk will be sorely tried by film's end, with both his marriage and Hank's life at hazard.

An extraordinary instance of the Hayesean "gambler" figure – a dealer in Chinese securities when she's not tracing runaway husbands or arranging things "primarily matrimonial" – is Dolly Levi (Shirley Booth) in *The Matchmaker*. She may also be the strongest and most successful embodiment of the "worldly wise, rough-around-the-edges mother" figure in Hayes. She not only plays fairy godmother to the Anthony Perkins/Shirley MacLaine couple, against the senex iratus threats of Paul Ford's Mr. Vandergelder, but does so wisely enough to win the human heart that "Old Wolf Trap" Vandergelder had kept "locked up" in his office safe since the death of his first wife. Yet Dolly is not literally a mother, any more than Stella (to the best of our knowledge) is in *Rear Window*. And real mothers in Hayes, especially in the early 1960s films, often prove less than skillful at helping others, especially their daughters, negotiate the complexities of (gendered) existence.

The most extreme of Hayes's ineffectual or distressed mothers is the widowed Ann Wandrous in *Butterfield 8* – played by Mildred Dunnock, who also plays Mrs. Wiggs in *The Trouble with Harry* and Miss Thornton in *Peyton Place* – who is depicted as both deceived and self-deceiving regarding the sexual escapades of her photo-model daughter, Gloria (Elizabeth Taylor). The anxiety she displays whenever Gloria fails to return home for the night is implicitly sexual in its motivation – at one point she wonders how Gloria would be different "if only she had a father who was wise enough and strong enough to keep her on the right path" – but she recoils when Gloria describes herself as the "slut of all time" as prologue to revealing the "miracle" of her adulterous relationship with Weston Liggett (Laurence Harvey). What her mother never hears about, however, is the sexual abuse Gloria suffered at the hands of her mother's "friend," Major Hartley, her only serious suitor after her husband's early death. He taught Gloria "more about evil than any thirteen-year-old girl in the world knew," Gloria tells her musician friend Steve (Eddie Fisher), and she "loved it, every awful moment of it." Though Gloria wants desperately to acquire the kind of inner beauty "that comes from self-respect," even her relationship with Liggett (another "angry man" and military veteran) smacks of masochism, the self-doubt that brought them together literally driving Gloria to her death as a frantic Liggett chases her towards Boston and her car goes off the road.

Other Hayes scripts that feature variously dysfunctional mother/daughter relationships include *The Chalk Garden*, *Harlow*, and *Where Love Has Gone*. In these last two films sexual abuse is also at issue. The underage Jean Harlow (Carroll Baker) threatens to accuse her stepfather of sexual predation when he attempts to prevent Mama Jean (Angela Lansbury) from signing her daughter's first studio contract – though Marino Bello (Raf Vallone) eventually denies the charge, accusing a now more mature and sexually willing Jean of misreading him. And *Where Love Has Gone* – often discussed in connection with the lurid Cheryl Crane murder case in which Lana Turner's daughter killed Turner's mob-connected lover – uses flashback narration to delay our discovery that a daughter's killing of her mother's lover was motivated by the daughter's sexual relationship with her soon-to-be step-father, was indeed her response to the announcement of the engagement. Though her divorced father – Luke Miller (Michael Connors), a Medal of Honor–winning bomber pilot – tries to convince a juvenile court that his ex-wife killed Rick Lazich and is letting their underage daughter, Danielle (Joey Heatherton), take the rap because she will get off easy, her mother, Valerie Hayden (Susan Hayward), eventu-ally reveals that the sculpture chisel that killed Lazich was actually meant for her, then roars away in her car and kills herself in her sculpture studio before her pursuing ex-husband can stop her. The variously lethal car chases in *Butterfield 8*, *The Carpetbaggers*, and *Where Love Has Gone* thus provide tragic counterpoint to the more comically depicted car chases in *To Catch a Thief.*

In *The Chalk Garden*, by contrast, the child abuse is more psychological than physical. Here Deborah Kerr plays Miss Madrigal, an ex-felon who takes on the task of governess to the mentally disturbed teenager Laurel (Hayley Mills). Laurel has become a "Pathological Imaginer" and pyromaniac in response to her mother's adultery and her father's early death. But a primary source of Laurel's fictionaliz-ing is her grandmother's apparently baseless insistence that Laurel, in the hope of disrupting her mother's remarriage, had fled the wedding hotel into Hyde Park, where she had been "attacked," implicitly sexually, though Mrs. St. Maugham (Edith Evans) had refused to allow a doctor to examine Laurel or the police to question her. As it happens, Laurel is really a pawn in the dispute between her mother and her grandmother. The grandmother's disapproval of her daughter's sexuality turns out to be envy, as if caring for Laurel were Mrs. St. Maugham's way of knocking a generation off her own age.

The Children's Hour addresses similar psychological themes – of lies becoming truths unless and until something more true, and more loving, intervenes – though here the grandmother's responsibility for her granddaughter's sexual accusations (apart from the fact that she repeats them) is left unclear, along with the where-abouts of the parents of young Mary Tilford (Karen Balkin). Clear enough in *The Children's Hour*, however, is the implication that Mary's unfounded belief that her teachers hate her expresses an underlying conviction that she is unloved and unlov-able, and clear also is the literally deathly consequence of her accusations: Martha Dobie (Shirley MacLaine) commits suicide upon deciding that her newly acknowl-edged lesbian affection for Karen Wright (Audrey Hepburn) is hopeless. That Miss Madrigal in *The Chalk Garden* was perhaps wrongly convicted of murdering her stepsister – as if she had once been a young Mary Tilford and were seeking to save Laurel from a similar fate – thus makes a kind of desperate Hayesean sense. It also confirms the importance of *The Man Who Knew Too Much* in the Hayesean canon as being the first Hayes film where saving a child – whether from disputatious parents or international kidnappers – is a primary issue. Because Hayes once said *Rear Window* and *Peyton Place* were his favorite films (Green 185), I will conclude this brief sketch of Hayes/Hitchcock by discussing each in turn, *Rear Window* with reference to *Thunder Bay*, and *Peyton Place* with reference to *The Trouble with Harry*.

The Leitch/DeRosa description of Hayes as authoring parables of paranoia comically overcome by reaffirmations of community and sexuality certainly applies to both *Thunder Bay* and *Rear Window*. What they most obviously have in common is an A-list cast headed by James Stewart. In both, Stewart depicts a World War II veteran whose postwar métier amounts to a continuation of his masculine war-era lifestyle. Though his passion for wildcat oil exploration has taken Steve Martin (Stewart) to Mexico, Guatemala, and Venezuela, his "dream" project in *Thunder Bay* – upon which he has wagered his mustering out pay and that of his partner, Johnny Gambi (Dan Duryea) – is to be the first to find oil in the Gulf of Mexico. Doing so requires not only the design of a feasible, hurricane-proof drilling platform, but the numerous vessels, including a war-surplus LST, necessary to map the oil field and erect the oil derrick, as if Martin and Gambi had never left the Navy. Likewise, when Lisa Fremont (Grace Kelly) suggests that globetrotting photojournalist L.B. Jefferies could open his own photography studio in New York City and do fashion shoots, he responds: "Can you see me driving down to the fashion salon in a jeep, wearing combat boots and a three-day beard?" And though Lisa's courageous search of the Thorwald apartment ultimately proves that she will "go anywhere and do anything and love it," the implication is strong that Jeff's anxiety over the fate of Mrs. Thorwald (Irene Winston) is as much a matter of renewing his wartime relationship with detective Tom Doyle (Wendell Corey) as it is of proving that marriage is potentially deadly. Given that Jeff's wartime work was photo reconnaissance, his spying on Lars Thorwald (Raymond Burr) is simply more of the same. Jeff even uses flashbulbs as weaponry, when Thorwald invades his apartment, just as Steve Martin uses dynamite in *Thunder Bay* to run geophonic tests of the sea bed, though the test runs look and sound like depth charge attacks.

Both films include a major female character named Stella. In *Thunder Bay*, Stella (a blonde Joanne Dru, looking very much like Grace Kelly in Technicolor) is effectively the "angry man" opposite Steve Martin's "gambler" figure, and she is the first and most vehemently "paranoid" of the Port Felicity, Louisiana residents when Martin and Gambi arrive to begin exploration, though her distress is less environmental than sexual and emotional; she became worldly wise in Chicago, where she spent three years learning about "filthy men" and their "filthy money" before returning home, as if from the sex wars. She is especially distressed when her younger sister takes a liking to Johnny Gambi, and Martin responds by promising to keep Gambi away from Francesca (Marcia Henderson), as if he were taking on Stella's burden of anger. Comically enough, Johnny's love of Francesca is true; Martin *et al.* strike oil; even the "Golden Shrimp" come back, attracted by the drilling platform; and Stella, her idealism renewed by Martin's example, accepts Martin's closing promise that "better" is possible and agrees to return with him to Port Felicity.

By contrast, the worldly-wise Stella in *Rear Window*, far from being antagonistic in matters sexual, openly lobbies on behalf of the marriageability of Lisa Fremont. The film's most obviously "angry man" is Lars Thorwald, though most discussions of the film's voyeurism motif see Thorwald's murder and dismemberment of his wife as enacting Jeff's fears and desires – what Tania Modleski has called Jeff's "retaliatory aggression" (74) – in which respect Jeff is the film's most obvious instance of an isolated paranoiac who values masculine autonomy over community. Indeed, Modleski adduces Hitchcock's description of *Rear Window* in the Truffaut interview to affirm that "gender reversal" (72) is at the heart of the film, as if Jeff's hostility to Lisa were partly a consequence of Jeff's distressing similarity, as a housebound invalid, to *Mrs.* Thorwald, a reversal that is subsequently confirmed in the education Jeff receives, via the intuitions of Lisa and Stella, in "the victimization of women by men" (78). Perhaps writing the story of Steve Martin, who takes on the burden of a woman's anger and is repeatedly threatened by angry men himself, provided Hayes with an education in empathy and vulnerability that served him well when he turned Cornell Woolrich's 1942 short story "It Had to Be Murder" into Alfred Hitchcock's *Rear Window*.

"I asked my agent to find me a story about a small town," recalled Hayes when talking about the genesis of his *Peyton Place* screenplay (DeRosa 206). In light of the odd circumstance that outtakes from *The Trouble with Harry* were eventually used as part of the scene-setting montage sequences that establish the temporal and social environs of the later film (Green 186), it is tempting to read the "small town" New England element of *Peyton Place* as a "sanitized" retreat into nostalgia or pastoral, especially by contrast with the gender and class brutality on view in the 1956 Grace Metalious novel Hayes was adapting (Hendler 190). That Hayes was often at his most reflexive when his films were set in the past complicates the nostalgia charge considerably, as does the fact that "pastoral" itself is often a sophisticated urban genre, as the New York reception of *The Trouble with Harry* confirms (Sikov 152–53). But the past on view in both *The Trouble with Harry* and *Peyton Place* is far from sanitary – as the sequence of cleaning up Harry's corpse and clothes in preparation for his examination by Dr. Greenbow (Dwight Marfield) comically, mythically indicates – and the Hayesean therapy on offer requires a confrontation, in both cases, with an impromptu grave and a premature burial.

According to Ed Sikov, the "trouble" with Harry is that the film's principal characters – Miss Gravely (Mildred Natwick) and Captain Wiles (Edmund Gwenn), the widowed Jennifer Rogers (Shirley MacLaine) and the artist Sam Marlowe (John Forsythe) – "have invested his lifeless body with a frightening degree of their own repressed sexuality" (151). There is a literalness to this repression that Sikov somewhat elides. Harry Warp, clearly the film's "angry man," arrives at Highwater expressly for the purpose of claiming the sexual favors of his estranged wife, who objects by clunking him with a milk bottle; he subsequently mistakes Miss Gravely for Jennifer, dragging her into the bushes and seeking to have his way with her, making "horrible, masculine sounds" until she clocks him with her metal-cleated shoe heel. Moreover, a primary motive for burying Harry the third time is to protect the sexual privacy of Jennifer Rogers (this film's "secret," involving the death of Jennifer's first husband and her subsequent unconsummated marriage to her superstitious brother-in-law), though Jennifer's acceptance of Sam's proposal requires public recognition that Harry is deceased, hence that she is free to (re)marry. Fortunately, Jennifer's son, Arnie (Jerry Mathers), is literal-minded about time in ways that make credible the plan to disinter Harry yet again so Arnie can (re)find him and Jennifer can report his demise to Calvin Wiggs (Royal Dano) without further ado once it is clear that Harry died of natural causes.

A death by apparently natural causes – though the cause is never specified – is also at the heart of *Peyton Place*, also connected to a mother who fears revealing her sexual past and raises a child alone in an insular New England village. The woman is Constance MacKenzie (Lana Turner), who runs the local dress shop. Her illegitimate daughter, Allison (Diane Varsi), an aspiring writer who is also the film's narrative voice, finds her mother too "perfect" in matters of sexual propriety, unaware that the deceased father whose photo she worships was married to another woman when she was born. Like the "perfect" Lisa in *Rear Window*, Connie is another Hayesean heroine associated with fashion, though the explicit link between clothing and voyeurism – "men can see much better than they can think" so a "low-cut neckline does more for a girl's future than the entire Britannica encyclopedia" – is one she finds threatening as an influence on her daughter and a reminder of her own past. Connie is thus an angry woman like the worldly-wise Stella Rigaud in *Thunder Bay*.

Her "angry man" counterpart is Lucas Cross (Arthur Kennedy), a ne'er-do-well drunk whose family, a wife and three stepchildren, live in a tarpaper shack the older stepson leaves in the opening scene. One night, in the absence of his wife, who works as Connie MacKenzie's housekeeper, Cross rapes his teenage stepdaughter, Selena (Hope Lange). The town doctor (Lloyd Nolan) refuses her plea for an abortion, though he forces Lucas to sign a confession and leave town. When Selena miscarries, Doc Swain reports the incident as an appendectomy. Lucas eventually returns, on leave from the World War II Navy and in the wake of his distraught wife's suicide, to claim Selena. She kills him with a fire log as they struggle and then buries his body in the sheep pen. She eventually confesses her crime to Connie MacKenzie, though not her reason for killing Lucas, which she implores Doc Swain to keep secret. Though Selena's claim of self-defense at her subsequent trial is supported by testimony from Allison MacKenzie, who had once seen Lucas strike Selena, the most incriminating element of the prosecution case is Selena's unreported burial of Lucas, as if she were covering up a crime rather than her sexual victimization, which she fears will jeopardize the legal career her fiancé hopes for. As it happens, the prosecution calls Connie MacKenzie to the stand and Connie's confession of maternal inadequacy, directed more at her estranged daughter than the jury, prompts Doc Swain to come forward and testify to the brutality of Lucas Cross, though the real target of his scorn is the small-mindedness that has made everyone "prisoners of each other's gossip" and made Selena fear their scorn more than prison.

Early in *The Trouble with Harry* Sam Marlowe observes that "the authorities like to know when people die" and advises the anxious Captain Wiles: "If you're not careful, you will get a murder charge lined up." What seems an instance of comic paranoia in the earlier film becomes literally the case in *Peyton Place*, which rewrites *The Trouble with Harry* in a more realistic register. Both films are examples of Hayesean therapy in which secrets are shared and traumas overcome through experience. Jennifer Rogers finally brings Harry home and his deadness to her becomes real in a way that sets her free. Connie MacKenzie comes to realize that her efforts to protect her daughter risk driving her away, as if accusations of promiscuity were effectively imperatives. In both cases the opportunity of a second chance at love – Jennifer's with Sam, Connie's with high school principal Mike Rossi (Lee Philips) – depends crucially on the example or agency of children. Arnie is vital to the sequence of events that brings Captain Wiles and Miss Gravely together, by retrieving the rabbit that Wiles shot and supplying time-bending circumlocutions that make the film's hopeful conclusion possible. Similarly, Allison's sexually honest and healthy relationship with Norman Page (Russ Tamblyn) not only occasions her mother's angry revelation of Allison's illegitimacy but her subsequent Christmas Eve confession of desire to Mike Rossi. Of course, there is nothing in *The Trouble with Harry* as brutally sad as the rape of Selena Cross by her stepfather or the subsequent suicide of Selena's mother. Yet the public rejoicing at Selena's acquittal – not to mention the subsequent reconciliation of Allison and Connie – strikes a utopian social note that is arguably more forceful, for being more earned, than the happily artificial conclusion of *The Trouble with Harry* with its community of four smiling co-conspirators and the last-moment reminder of the millionaire art patron who grants their wishes.

Ernest Lehman

The Inside Story (d. Allen Dwan, 1948; co-story), *Executive Suite* (d. Robert Wise, 1954), *Sabrina* (d. Billy Wilder, 1954; co-script), *The King and I* (d. Walter Lang, 1956), *Somebody Up There Likes Me* (d. Robert Wise, 1956), *Sweet Smell of Success* (d. Alexander Mackendrick, 1957; story, co-script), *North by Northwest* (d. Alfred Hitchcock, 1959), *From the Terrace* (d. Mark Robson, 1960), *West Side Story* (d. Robert Wise, Jerome

Robbins, 1961), *The Prize* (d. Mark Robson, 1963), *The Sound of Music* (d. Robert Wise, 1965), *Who's Afraid of Virginia Woolf?* (d. Mike Nichols, 1966; prod., script), *Hello, Dolly!* (d. Gene Kelly, 1969; prod., script), *Portnoy's Complaint* (d. Ernest Lehman, 1972; prod., script), *Family Plot* (d. Alfred Hitchcock, 1976), *Black Sunday* (d. John Frankenheimer, 1977; co-script), *Sabrina* (d. Sydney Pollack, 1995; earlier co-script).

Though the "Lehman" qualities of *North by Northwest* and *Family Plot* are hardly exhausted by describing their commonalities, we can certainly start there. The tradition of criticism on each film emphasizes metafictionality, in both cases a matter of construction (via the "double chase") as well as dialogue (where "theater" becomes an overt motif, often wittily linked to sexuality). Cary Grant's Roger Thornhill, mistakenly identified as the nonexistent George Kaplan and subsequently as a murderer, is thus doubly associated with a MacGuffin-like nothingness. The Pirandellian roundelay of chase and counter-chase – the cops and the "errand boys" chasing Thornhill while he chases Kaplan – becomes more complicated when Roger falls for the double agent Eve Kendall (Eva Maria Saint), the beloved accomplice of the villainous Philip Vandamm (James Mason), who goes by her own name in both contexts, and for whom Thornhill subsequently plays the "Kaplan" role in agreeing to be "shot" in the cafeteria at Mount Rushmore so her espionage bona fides can be confirmed just as Vandamm prepares to flee the country. A hint of the film's sustained rumination on the performative follows close upon Kaplan's apparent misfortune, when Eve and Roger meet in an MGM forest and she asks if he was hurt. He responds by reference to his emotional life, as being hurt in love, though she had meant to invoke his extempore stunt work in the cafeteria: "You did it rather well, I thought. ... Considering it's not really your kind of work."

The metafictionality of *Family Plot* is implicit in its title, which refers not only to the Shoebridge family plot in the Barlow Creek, California cemetery but also to various sexually-related designs or schemes: the backstory intrigue wherein Julia Rainbird (Cathleen Nesbitt) forces her sister Harriet to give up her illegitimate son for adoption rather than disgrace the family name; the plan whereby the spirit medium "Madame Blanche" Tyler (Barbara Harris) and her cab-driving actor boyfriend, George Lumley (Bruce Dern), accept the guilt-ridden Julia's reward-sweetened mandate to find her foundling nephew by "psychic" means in the apparent absence of any living memory of his present name or whereabouts; and the scheme whereby the otherwise reputable jeweler Arthur Adamson (William Devane) and his live-in paramour, Fran (Karen Black), lead secret lives as kidnappers whose payoffs include exotic gemstones and risk-enhanced erotic thrills.

Again there are multiple chases, as the cops and Blanche and George alike are on the trail of Adamson, who turns out to be the missing Rainbird heir; as Joe Maloney (Ed Lauter) and subsequently Adamson and Fran start trailing George and Blanche out of fear that they are after the kidnappers or, though Fran does not originally realize this, out of fear that they have pegged Maloney and Arthur – childhood friends when Arthur was known as Eddie Shoebridge, the adopted son of the otherwise childless Harry and Sadie – as having started the fire that supposedly killed the entire Shoebridge family, though Eddie's body was never found, his tombstone in the family plot notwithstanding. All of the major characters except Joe Maloney, moreover, employ multiple names or identities: Blanche as the deep-voiced "Henry," her connection in "the great beyond" who intercedes between Julia and "Harriet"; George as "Frank McBride," a lawyer seeking information about Eddie Shoebridge; Adamson as Adamson, though Maloney still calls him Eddie and Blanche is eager to call him Mr. Rainbird; and the shape-shifting Fran, who repeatedly sports elaborate costumes and makeup – wigs, high-heeled boots, prosthetic jowls – to disguise an identity that seems the most ephemeral of the bunch (she tells Arthur that she fell in love with him because she needed "stability in [her] life"). So it is not surprising that *Family Plot* too employs the language of theater as a way of referencing performance, both professional (George is an actor when not driving a cab or posing as a lawyer) and sexual ("On this very evening you're gonna see a standing ovation"). Only slightly more surprising is the film's playful evocation of Plato's famous cave in the safe room whose occupants are told to sit with their backs to the entrance whenever Fran and Arthur enter.

One scene especially recalls *North by Northwest*, though it condenses several scenes from the earlier movie: the episode in which Blanche and Lumley ride her white Ford Mustang down a mountain road after Joe Maloney sabotages the brakes. Of course it evokes the scene in *North by Northwest* when Vandamm's henchmen, having liquored Roger to the gills, put him in a Mercedes and try to run him off a cliff, then follow when he seizes control and leads them on a merry chase en route to the Glen Cove police station. But it also evokes the Prairie Stop sequence in *North by Northwest*, especially in the shot of Blanche and George running away from Maloney's car after having survived the crash of Blanche's; indeed, the subsequent down-the-mountain plunge of Maloney's out-of-control vehicle, especially in its ironically fiery coda, evokes the moment when the crop duster plows into the tank truck and explodes. Also of interest is what Stanley Cavell would call a "death and revival" moment (261). In *North by Northwest* this involves Roger's exit from the Park Service station wagon that evacuated him from the Mount Rushmore cafeteria, as he rises like Lazarus from his stretcher and offers Eve apologies for his harsh words in the auction scene. The like moment in *Family Plot* occurs when George and Blanche emerge from her wrecked Mustang, Blanche out the top, through the passenger side window, and George out the bottom, through the driver's side. His "rebirth" (Sterritt 317) seems the more difficult passage, especially with her foot on his cheek, as if his pliant face were that of an infant squeezing out of a birth canal. (Contrast all of these exits with Marion Crane's entombment in the trunk of her newly-acquired Ford in *Psycho* [1960].) Finally, rather like Roger and Eve in her Pullman berth aboard the Twentieth Century as described by Richard Millington, George and Blanche, in their ride down the mountain, play out a scene of bodily intimacy that emphasizes their physical weights and entanglements; in *Family Plot*, at least, this moment effectively "marries" them. Blanche's post-reward matrimonial hopes are most clearly confirmed in Lumley's gesture of picking her up in his arms and carrying her away from the vehicle, as if across some honeymoon threshold.

Describing *North by Northwest* and *Family Plot* in these terms gets us only so far in the direction of assessing their "Lehmanesque" qualities, if for no other reason than that metafictionality and sexually loaded dialogue are equally typical of John Michael Hayes, as *Rear Window* alone demonstrates. In fact, there is a Lehman story that can look very similar to Hayes's fables of angry men and worldly-wise women: *From the Terrace*, for example, uncannily anticipates *The Carpetbaggers*. But the "Lehman story" is unique in tone and in crucial details, though telling it requires a brief excurses on Lehman's fiction, particularly the writings culminating in the movie version of *Sweet Smell of Success*.

Lehman spent nearly a lifetime retelling and refining the story of J.J. Hunsecker and Sidney Falco. The earliest publication in the sequence, a short story entitled "Hunsecker Fights the World," appeared in *Collier's* in April 1948, its final iteration on Broadway in 2002 as a Marvin Hamlisch/Craig Carnelia musical with Lehman as one of several producers. The three magazine stories elaborating the relationship between Broadway columnist Harvey (later J.J.) Hunsecker and his press-agent flunky Sidney Wallace (later Falco) are all set forth in the first person and the past tense. Each one shows Sidney encountering and, like Lehman, endlessly repeating a reason for self-disgust, always related to his entanglement in the viciously destructive world of Broadway scandal-mongering. The most notorious of these, of course, is the smear campaign in the novella "Sweet Smell of Success" and the movie *Sweet Smell of Success* against crooner/jazz guitarist Steve Dallas, whose offense is not that he is a dope-smoking commie, though Sidney plants that rumor and the necessary evidence in both cases, but rather that he is beloved of Hunsecker's sister, Susan, whom he hopes to marry.[3]

Doubtless the most Hitchcock-resonant moment in these stories occurs in "Hunsecker Fights the World," where Sidney accompanies Hunsecker to his sister's graduation from an exclusive women's college. There Hunsecker delivers a pre–*Feminine Mystique* commencement address, which he concludes in the story's opening moments: "… And Reno will have to fold its roulette tables and steal away into the night, if each one of you will remember" that "Home … is where you hang … your heart" (183; ellipses in original). When Hunsecker and Sidney return to New York on the train, however, Hunsecker reveals his political ambitions for the US Senate – "what's left for me after the Pulitzer Prize?" (187) – and the two of them encounter a sophisticated young woman in the dining car, a "melancholy beauty" in a "well-tailored suit" (188) who obviously anticipates the Eve Kendall character in *North by Northwest*. Though Hunsecker offers to promote her acting career in his column, Lorna Hale pointedly asks Sidney not to take her name down after Hunsecker tells him to. When Hunsecker reclaims the spotlight by boasting of the money he won from Sidney at gin rummy, Lorna gets up, says, "It's going to be a long night. I could go for some gin rummy myself," and tells Sidney, more or less as Eve tells Roger, that she's "in the third car back, Compartment C" (190).

After dinner, Sidney surreptitiously visits Lorna, who confesses that her invitation was meant as a slap at Hunsecker motivated mostly by her conviction that she and Sidney are two of a kind, because she had "stayed married to a man I didn't love, because he gave me power and luxury and more money than I could use" (192). She is on her way back from Reno, though she wishes she had "found out sooner" that the prostitution of a loveless marriage "wasn't worth it" (192–93). The implication that Sidney should divorce Hunsecker as Lorna had divorced her former spouse is unmistakable. That he agrees is also clear, especially after he retrieves a deck of cards from Hunsecker's compartment, risking the latter's ire, and races back to Lorna: "I was hurrying desperately because I knew I was too late ... a couple of years too late ... but just for tonight I didn't want to be too late, for either of us" (194).

The desperately guilty first-person intimacy so often on view in Lehman's short fiction is hard to transfer to the screen, though the voiceover subjectivity of Lehman's only self-directed script, *Portnoy's Complaint*, takes on new resonance in the context of Lehman's "Sweet Smell of Success" stories. More to the point, sexuality is often what Lehman characters feel most guilty about, as Lehman's adaptation of the Philip Roth novel amply confirms. Similarly, Hunsecker's motive for sideswiping his sister's relationship with Steve Dallas in the novella "Sweet Smell of Success" is clearly incestuous, given her description of him as a pathologically possessive guardian who nearly beat to death a teenage boy who had dared to kiss his then fifteen-year-old sister. In the movie, Hunsecker's motives are murkier, though they clearly involve the erotics of power, especially as Burt Lancaster portrays him, pretending brotherly concern while coldly pulling strings behind the scenes. Partly because the film eschews first-person voiceover, Tony Curtis's Sidney Falco seems to enjoy his con-artistry as much as bemoan it. The bigger the lie, the better, he apparently believes, literally following Hunsecker, whose McCarthyesque moral outrage escalates as he sinks deeper into self-righteousness nastiness. The closest the film Falco comes to a moral crossroads is his momentary refusal to unleash the ham-fisted Lt. Kello on Steve Dallas (Marty Milner). But his protest becomes a counter-epiphany when he realizes, even in his refusal, what the price of his cooperation would be: "If you gave me your column I wouldn't do a thing like that." J.J. promptly obliges, offering Falco three months as guest columnist so that he can spirit Susan away on a cruise.

Apart from the smeared and cop-battered Dallas, however, at least in the film version, the two primary victims of the frame-up are Rita (Barbara Nichols), the single-mother cigarette girl whom Falco pimps to columnist Otis Elwell (David White) so that Elwell will print the Dallas smear in his column, and Susan Hunsecker (Susan Harrison), who responds to the news that Dallas was hospitalized after resisting arrest by planning to commit suicide for the express purpose, she tells Sidney, of severing his ties to her brother. Although Sidney prevents her from leaping from the balcony of her brother's downtown apartment, a late-arriving J.J. takes him to have sexually assaulted his sister, an inference she pointedly refuses to deny even though she stops Hunsecker from beating Falco senseless. (In the novella, Susan literally "smears" Sidney with her lipstick to make the rape story stick, and the tale concludes with him pleading for mercy while Hunsecker threatens assault.) Rita is one of numerous Lehman women – put-upon secretaries, aspiring actresses, unloved wives, unlovable daughters, even the occasional teacher or governess, as in *The King and I* and *The Sound of Music* – who are treated as tools of male power, often at the hands of what I would call Lehman's "bad father" figure, like the Hunsecker of the novella. And Susan Hunsecker is exemplary of Lehman's "woman on the verge," a female so fed up with male neglect or indifference that death – often from a great height, like the balcony-prone Julia Treadway (Barbara Stanwyck) in *Executive Suite* or Mary Jane "The Monkey" Reid (Karen Black) in *Portnoy's Complaint* – seems her only recourse, though none ever actually jumps. So it is easy enough to see Roger's secretary in the opening scene of *North by Northwest* as a Rita figure, especially as she takes dictation regarding her boss's sexual itinerary. More to the point, Eve Kendall is another instance of a woman pimped for the sake of male interests – what the born-again Roger describes in the forest scene as "this dirty business," picking up a phrase that resonates throughout *Sweet Smell of Success* – who is rescued from a similar demise by the loving reach of the reborn Roger and a fortuitously unsportsmanlike sharpshooter.

Another "woman on the verge" in Lehman – also associated with danger and heights via her helicopter transit from police station to golf course – is Fran in *Family Plot*. Adamson explicitly describes danger as leading from sickness to eros; Fran's love for him, traversing the space between her desire for "stability" and his for sexual "torture," binds her to him in ways she finds increasingly distressing, especially when it becomes clear that killing Blanche and Lumley is next on the agenda. Fran thus recalls Portnoy's "Monkey," also played by Black and similarly torn between sexual gamesmanship and the imperative of marriage. Casting may also be a reason for seeing Adamson as recalling an earlier Lehman character. Though he does her no harm, Adamson also employs a female underling, Mrs. Clay, played by Edith Atwater, who played Hunsecker's worldly-wise secretary in *Sweet Smell of Success*. This apparently over-subtle hint is confirmed by dialogue from the 13 January 1975 version of Lehman's script, where Adamson, in response to Fran's "we *could* stop here," spoken in the wake of the first kidnapping episode, replies: "I couldn't if I tried, sweetheart. I'm hooked on the thrills, drunk with success and freaked out with visions of *unlimited* purchasing power" (33–34). Although those lines sound more like Falco than Hunsecker, and their explicitness is out of keeping with the cool hauteur of Devane's Arthur Adamson, the idea that Lehman imagined Adamson as Hunsecker-like in his willingness to play God (or Satan) with the lives of others is repeatedly confirmed in *Family Plot*.

Describing *North by Northwest* and *Family Plot* as evocative of *Sweet Smell of Success* and *Portnoy's Complaint* risks leaving their sunnier aspects unaccounted for. In the latter two films, whatever hope remains attaches to the two young women – Susan Hunsecker and Mary Jane Reid – each of whom is last seen walking down a New York City street in more or less near proximity to a wounded or desperate man whose influence she is fortunate to survive. This is not the kind of "therapeutic" ending that we get in *North by Northwest* or in most of the Hitchcock/Hayes films. If anything, Adamson in *Family Plot* is even more the psychopath than J.J. Hunsecker. He is closer to the Uncle Charlie of *Shadow of a Doubt* (1943) than to the improvisatory, self-renewing theatrics of Roger Thornhill and Eve Kendall, especially given Eve's kinship to Lorna Hale, whose dining car invitation to Sidney Falco openly expresses an ethic of feminist authenticity only latent in Eve's self-disgust and willingness to "bed down" with Vandamm on behalf of a Kafkaesque "alphabet soup" intelligence agency. The more negative implications of *Family Plot* are largely relegated to a distant past, surfacing mostly in Fran's increasing if silent distress at Adamson's refusal to quit the kidnapping racket, as if she too wished for a Lorna Hale–style divorce, and they are framed or contained by the Blanche/Lumley plot, for which there is little precedent in earlier Hitchcock or Lehman films.

Chasing or finding someone, often paired with romance, is common enough. Think of *The 39 Steps* (1935) and *Shadow of a Doubt*. (*Family Plot* takes up the telepathy motif from the latter, in a far more comic register.) Or think of *North by Northwest* and *The Prize*. Then again, only a few Hitchcock films – *Number Seventeen* (1932), *Jamaica Inn* (1939), *Marnie* – focus on working-class grifters. Though Lehman's Sidney Falco is a grifter, he travels in ritzy Broadway circles. And there is slim precedent in either canon for the straightforward private-eye proposition that links Blanche and George with Julia Rainbird. If Blanche and George are guilty of something, it's poverty and showmanship, and those are balanced against an enthusiastic sexual candor – all the talk about "crystal balls" and "standing ovations" – owing much to Lehman's path-breaking sexual explicitness in his adaptations of *Who's Afraid of Virginia Woolf?* and *Portnoy's Complaint*. The closest we come to the Blanche/Lumley dynamic in either auteur's earlier films would seem to be the relationship between Robert (Derrick De Marney) and Erica (Nova Pilbeam) in Hitchcock's *Young and Innocent* (1937), which anticipates the showbiz backdrop of *Family Plot* (Robert is a screenwriter suspected of strangling an actress), and the relationship between Rocky (Paul Newman) and Norma (Pier Angeli) in Lehman's *Somebody Up There Likes Me*, where the couple's romantic and marital loyalties are charted over an extended period of time. Though we get few temporal cues, the screwball "bile and banter" relationship (Corliss 191) between Blanche and Lumley always seems tinged with affection and endearment, as if they are a couple of long standing. Indeed, on the basis of Barbara Harris's resemblance to Alma Reville (McGilligan 723), I am inclined to see Blanche as Hitchcock's homage to his wife, his most loyal of collaborators, and Blanche's closing wink to the camera as Hitchcock's valedictory acknowledgment of his audience and of the artfulness of the bond that his camera establishes between his stories and his viewers.

I credit this last cinematic gesture to Hitchcock because Hitchcock wrote it and filmed it over Lehman's objection (McGilligan 728). Ironically, it was a conviction that *Family Plot* was not sufficiently or successfully Hitchcockian enough that induced Lehman to work on the script of *The Short Night* (Spoto 538). That Lehman saw the film as returning Hitchcock to Hitchcock's origins is evident in a small detail clearly attributed to Lehman in the published script, a close-up of a weathercock "with its swaying arrow pointing northeast" (Freeman 103) as the Concorde carrying Joe Bailey departs JFK for London where Joe hopes to pick up the trail of Gavin Brand by tracking Brand's wife and sons. David Freeman sees "northeast" here as evoking "northwest" (239), thus linking the romance of Joe Bailey and Carla Brand to that of Roger and Eve in Lehman's first Hitchcock script. In each case, an amateur intelligence agent romances a woman whose assistance he needs in order to meet his Cold-War nemesis face to face. Gavin Brand is explicitly identified as a murderous or "bad" Lehman father, akin to both the Professor (Leo G. Carroll) and Vandamm in *North by Northwest*, though his last-second hesitancy to shoot Bailey, lest he show himself a killer in the presence of his sons, is vaguely to his credit. And Carla Brand is another Lehman "woman on the verge," trapped in a loveless marriage, though her doubts about Brand are brought to focus by her impassioned response to Joe, whose victimization at Gavin's hands – Joe's CIA brother was one of Brand's forty-three victims – mirrors her own and her fears for her children.

But Joe Bailey is also one of the most "Hayesean" of Lehman's heroes. Bailey backhandedly acknowledges as much by confirming to the "professorial" CIA agent who contacts him after Brand's escape from prison that his anger at Brand is unabated: "I can't be the only one still angry" (100). Moreover, it is hard not to see the script's conclusion, in which Carla and Joe chase down the train carrying Brand and his sons toward the Soviet Union, as evoking the Hayes/Hitchcock *The Man Who Knew Too Much*, especially when Joe, echoing Mrs. Drayton in the latter film, urges Roy and Neal Brand to call to their mother: "She'll hear you" (215). Not having read Lehman's version of *The Short Night*, I cannot confirm how many of these details appear there. But it speaks to the complexity of film authorship that the published script – especially to the extent that it represents the last of Lehman's attempts to write "the Hitchcock picture to end all Hitchcock pictures" – should evoke both Hayes and Lehman so thoroughly.

Notes

Research for this chapter was undertaken with the support of the Iowa State University Department of English and the university's Center for Excellence in the Arts and Humanities. I am also grateful to my Iowa State colleagues Matthew Sivils and Geoffrey Sauer, whose assistance and advice were essential to my work.

1. During his lifetime, Frank Capra shared screen credit with Robert Riskin on thirteen films, though I mistakenly report the total as twelve in the Chronology of *Frank Capra: Interviews*. (*Mea culpa*.) The definitive account of Riskin's career is Ian Scott's aptly titled *In Capra's Shadow*.

2. On the career of Charles Bennett, see John Belton's "Charles Bennett and the Typical Hitchcock Scenario" and Chapter 9 by Tania Modleski in this volume.

3. The publishing history of Lehman's "Hunsecker" stories is most complex. Only "Hunsecker Fights the World" kept the same title in all of its versions; Hunsecker didn't become J.J. and Sidney didn't become Falco until the 1957 film, and not in print until the 1998 publication of the Odets/Lehman screenplay. "The Nicest Thing to Do" became "It's the Little Things That Count" in the 1957 collection *The Comedian and Other Stories* (114–28), though only then does the original's Lester Michel become Sidney Wallace, and Hunsecker's name is added, appearing once in a quick aside. The main tie between "Nicest Thing" and the rest of the saga is the Rita plot, which first appears here and was subsequently brought into the screenplay. "Sweet Smell of Success" first saw print as "Tell Me about It Tomorrow" and didn't regain Lehman's preferred title until the 1957 collection *Sweet Smell of Success and Other Stories* (7–64). Only in the Overlook edition of 2000, which reprints the earlier two collections in a single volume, are all previously published versions of the three stories brought into alignment with the screenplay and each other as regards character names, though other details remain incongruous. All direct quotations are to the most recent text, and I have used "Falco" as Sidney's last name except where I am clearly referring to the earliest version of "Hunsecker Fights the World." For an intriguingly scandalous account of the making of *Sweet Smell of Success* see Kashner. Though James Naremore's *Sweet Smell of Success* monograph appeared after this chapter was completed, his account of the screenplay's revision by Clifford Odets is variously illuminating.

Works Cited

Baer, William. *Classic American Films: Conversations with Screenwriters.* Westport: Praeger, 2008.

Barr, Charles. *English Hitchcock.* Moffat: Cameron and Hollis, 1999.

Belton, John. "Charles Bennett and the Typical Hitchcock Scenario." *Film History* 9 (1997): 320–32.

Boeth, Richard. "Screen-Writers of the 70's." *Cosmopolitan* July 1975, 168+.

Cavell, Stanley. "*North by Northwest.*" *A Hitchcock Reader.* Second ed. Ed. Marshall Deutelbaum and Leland Poague. Chichester, UK: Wiley-Blackwell, 2009. 250–63.

Corliss, Richard. "Ernest Lehman." *Talking Pictures: Screenwriters in the American Cinema 1927–1973.* New York: Overlook, 1974. 188–95.

DeRosa, Steven. *Writing with Hitchcock: The Collaboration of Alfred Hitchcock and John Michael Hayes.* New York: Faber and Faber, 2001.

Engel, Joel. *Screen Writers on Screen Writing: The Best in the Business Discuss Their Craft.* New York: Hyperion, 1995.

Freeman, David. *The Last Days of Alfred Hitchcock: A Memoir Featuring the Screenplay of "Alfred Hitchcock's The Short Night."* Woodstock, NY: Overlook, 1984.

Friedman, Arthur B. "Popular Art: Frank Capra." *Frank Capra: Interviews.* Ed. Leland Poague. Jackson: UP of Mississippi, 2004. 34–69.

Green, Susan. "John Michael Hayes: Qué Sera, Sera." *Backstory 3: Interviews with Screenwriters of the 1960s.* Ed. Patrick McGilligan. Berkeley: U of California P, 1997. 174–92.

Hendler, June. *Best Sellers and Their Film Adaptations in Postwar America: From Here to Eternity, Sayonara, Giant, Auntie Mame, Peyton Place.* New York: Peter Lang, 2001.

Hunter, Evan. *Me and Hitch.* London: Faber and Faber, 1997.

Kapsis, Robert E. *Hitchcock: The Making of a Reputation*. Chicago: U of Chicago P, 1992.

Kashner, Sam. "*Sweet Smell of Success*: A Movie Marked by Danger." Vanity Fair *Tales of Hollywood: Rebels, Reds, and Graduates and the Wild Stories behind the Making of 13 Iconic Films*. Ed. Graydon Carter. New York: Penguin, 2008. 79–104.

Leff, Leonard J. *Hitchcock and Selznick: The Rich and Strange Collaboration of Alfred Hitchcock and David O. Selznick in Hollywood*. New York: Weidenfeld and Nicolson, 1987.

Lehman, Ernest. "Alfred Hitchcock's Family Plot." 13 Jan. 1975. Typescript. PDF accessed via Script City. 29 June 2009.

Lehman, Ernest. *The Comedian and Other Stories*. New York: Signet/NAL, 1957.

Lehman, Ernest. "Hunsecker Fights the World." *Collier's* 17 Apr. 1948: 16+.

Lehman, Ernest. "The Nicest Thing to Do." *Cosmopolitan* May 1949: 36+.

Lehman, Ernest. *Sweet Smell of Success and Other Stories*. New York: Signet/NAL, 1957.

Lehman, Ernest. *Sweet Smell of Success: The Short Fiction of Ernest Lehman*. Woodstock, NY: Overlook, 2000.

Lehman, Ernest. "Tell Me about It Tomorrow." *Cosmopolitan* Apr. 1950: 32+.

Leitch, Thomas. *Find the Director and Other Hitchcock Games*. Athens: U of Georgia P, 1991.

Leitch, Thomas. "Hitchcock and His Writers: Authorship and Authority in Adaptation." *Authorship in Film Adaptation*. Ed. Jack Boozer. Austin: U of Texas P, 2008. 63–84.

Marshall, J. D. "'You Go and Talk with Cary—Delay, Delay, Till It's Too Late'—John Michael Hayes." *Blueprint in Babylon*. [Los Angeles:] Phoenix House, 1978. 213–33.

McBride, Joseph. "Riskinesque: How Robert Riskin Spoke Through Frank Capra and Vice Versa." *Written By* (Dec.–Jan. 1999): 46–53. *The Best American Movie Writing 1999*. Ed. Peter Bogdanovich. New York: St. Martin's Griffin, 1999. 190–202.

McGilligan, Patrick. *Alfred Hitchcock: A Life in Darkness and Light*. New York: Harper-Collins, 2003.

Millington, Richard H. "Hitchcock and American Character: The Comedy of Self-Construction in *North by Northwest*." *Hitchcock's America*. Ed. Jonathan Freedman and Richard Millington. New York: Oxford UP, 1999. 135–54.

Modleski, Tania. *The Women Who Knew Too Much: Hitchcock and Feminist Theory*. Second ed. New York: Routledge, 2005.

Naremore, James. *Sweet Smell of Success*. Basingstoke, UK: Palgrave Macmillan; London: BFI, 2010.

Odets, Clifford, and Ernest Lehman. *Sweet Smell of Success*. London: Faber and Faber, 1998.

Scott, Ian. *In Capra's Shadow: The Life and Career of Screenwriter Robert Riskin*. Lexington: UP of Kentucky, 2006.

Sikov, Ed. "Unrest in Peace: Hitchcock's Fifties Humor." *Laughing Hysterically: American Screen Comedy of the 1950s*. New York: Columbia UP, 1994. 150–78.

Spoto, Donald. *The Dark Side of Genius: The Life of Alfred Hitchcock*. Boston: Little, Brown, 1983.

Sterritt, David. "Alfred Hitchcock: Registrar of Births and Deaths." *Hitchcock Annual* 1997–98: 3–18. *Framing Hitchcock: Selected Essays from the* Hitchcock Annual. Eds Sidney Gottlieb and Christopher Brookhouse. Detroit: Wayne State UP, 2002. 310–22.

Truffaut, François, with the collaboration of Helen G. Scott. *Hitchcock*. Rev. ed. New York: Simon and Schuster, 1984.

Wood, Robin. *Hitchcock's Films Revisited*. Rev. ed. New York: Columbia UP, 2002.

9

Suspicion: Collusion and Resistance in the Work of Hitchcock's Female Collaborators

Tania Modleski

Collaborate: 1. To work together especially in a joint intellectual effort. 2. To cooperate treasonably as with an enemy occupation force.

American Heritage Dictionary

To begin, let us take as a parable Daphne du Maurier's 1938 novel *Rebecca*, on which Hitchcock based his 1940 film of the same name. The story's protagonist, never named, suspects her husband, Maxim de Winter, of having been in love with his first wife, Rebecca, a beautiful, adventurous, high-spirited woman of impeccable breeding whom everyone purportedly adored. A dowdy ex-companion to a vulgar American woman, the protagonist possesses none of the traits abundantly possessed by Rebecca and is in agony throughout the novel because she assumes that everyone, including her husband, is comparing her unfavorably to the former Mrs. de Winter. When she learns that her husband in fact hated Rebecca for her infidelities and possible lesbianism and that he has actually killed her, she reports,

> I had listened to his story and part of me went with him like a shadow in his tracks. I too had killed Rebecca, I too had sunk the boat there in the bay. I had listened beside him to the wind and water. I had waited for Mrs. Danvers' knocking on the door. All this I had suffered with him, all this and more besides.

(289)

In the film, by contrast, Hitchcock captures the "collaboration" between the protagonist (Joan Fontaine) and her husband by having the camera track the

A Companion to Alfred Hitchcock, First Edition. Edited by Thomas Leitch and Leland Poague.
© 2011 Thomas Leitch and Leland Poague. Published 2011 by Blackwell Publishing Ltd.

movements of Rebecca on the night she died. As Max (Laurence Olivier) tells the story of his wife's death, the camera follows Rebecca's movements on the night she died as she walked toward her husband to confront him. The character herself, Rebecca, does not appear in the shot as she would in a proper flashback, however. While we are to understand that Max is seeing in his mind's eye the events of the night in question, we also sense that the protagonist is imaginatively sharing his vision, for in fact the shots are from neither character's point of view.

Significantly, up until this point in the novel and the film, the character has identified herself with Rebecca, or tried to, as when she dresses up in a sophisticated outfit and styles her hair. In other moments she is forced to "become" Rebecca unwittingly, for example when Mrs. Danvers (Judith Anderson), housekeeper and personal maid to Rebecca, tricks her into dressing up in the outfit Rebecca once wore to a costume ball. We might say that the character begins as a sometimes unwilling collaborator with Mrs. Danvers and the ghost of Rebecca in keeping the defiant Rebecca "alive," and subsequently collaborates with her Rebecca-haunted husband, identifying so strongly with him that she envisions herself as a participant in the actions the evening Maxim buries Rebecca's body at sea.

The scenario I have outlined here suggests the two poles of female collaboration in the films and in the authorship of the films I examine here. Just as the protagonist of *Rebecca* becomes a collaborationist by repudiating the powerful, spellbinding woman at the story's core and participating in the cover-up of the truth of her death, the female collaborator may entirely join forces with a misogynist director rather than, as a feminist might wish, insert a discourse that collides to some degree with the masculinist one. To the extent that du Maurier would have us identify wholly with the protagonist, whose story is told in the first person, the author herself could be considered a collaborationist from a feminist point of view.

Yet while a cursory reading of the novel might lead us to believe that it unequivocally sides with its protagonist, and therefore with Maxim, it is important to note that the influence of Rebecca does not entirely wane even after the protagonist learns of Maxim's hatred for his former wife. Not only does Rebecca's faithful servant and earthly emissary, Mrs. Danvers, set fire to Manderley to insure that the couple will never enjoy the de Winter family estate, but Rebecca's death itself is construed as a win for Rebecca. Even after Maxim is cleared of the crime of murder, he recalls Rebecca standing there laughing the night she died. "It was her last practical joke. ... I'm not sure if she hasn't won, even now," says the novel's Maxim (380). In the film, too, although Maxim is not technically guilty of his wife's murder, he says to his agent, Frank Crawley (Reginald Denny), "Rebecca always wins," and he recalls her standing and laughing before him, trying to provoke him to kill her. Thus, while the protagonist ends by collaborating with her husband in the cover-up of Rebecca's death, Rebecca herself – she who mocks and defies patriarchal laws and the norms of feminine propriety – has the last laugh.

Producer David O. Selznick, with whom Hitchcock notoriously became a most unwilling collaborator, insisted that Hitchcock remain faithful to du Maurier's novel, that he, in a sense, collaborate closely with the source text – a task Hitchcock detested. (He would later repudiate the film, telling François Truffaut that *Rebecca* is "not a Hitchcock picture," a view from which Truffaut dissented [127]). Selznick believed that readers of the novel thoroughly identified with the protagonist – from which it would presumably follow that he believed the novel's readers and the film's spectators would entirely assent to the protagonist's embrace of patriarchy and would repudiate the evil matriarchal world represented by Rebecca and Mrs. Danvers. Yet recent research has shown that female spectators' more equivocal identification made their collaboration with the text more complicated. Ironically, the film's marketers believed the audience would identify with Rebecca or, perhaps more accurately, would identify with the protagonist insofar as she identified with Rebecca. The marketers staged Rebecca look-alike contests and created tie-ins like a Rebecca Luxury Wardrobe and Rebecca Make-up Kits so female viewers could resemble "the famous little lady who wasn't there" (Edwards 29). Even in real life, then, Rebecca perhaps won, to paraphrase Max – the female practical joker matching wits with the notorious prankster, Hitchcock himself.

Up until now I have, for heuristic purposes, set up too rigid an opposition between collaborator and collaborationist. The reality is more complicated. On the one hand, all of us are obviously under the sway of the dominant ideology. Claire Johnston long ago observed that women involved in filmmaking inevitably employ the codes and conventions of patriarchal ideologies and genres. It is impossible for women working within a male-dominated cinema to effect a radical break with it, even were they inclined to do so. But there are moments when their texts reveal the tensions and contradictions that are the result of their marginal positions. One may perhaps speculate that du Maurier, a product of her time, was ambivalent about her characters and, while depicting Rebecca as evil, nevertheless subverted the conventional love story at the heart of the female Gothic – for example, devising a decidedly unromantic, even gloomy, afterlife for Max and his wife. To the extent that the love plot is undermined, du Maurier may be said to be in league with Rebecca, if only unconsciously.

On the other hand, no one is *entirely* under the sway of the dominant ideology. And this of course includes Hitchcock. Robert Boyle and other Hitchcock collaborators have noted how much Hitchcock liked women and surrounded himself with them, how he relied implicitly on the judgment of Alma Reville, his wife, whose influence on the films is incalculable. Nevertheless, given the hostility toward women that infuses many of his films and that sometimes characterized his attitude toward his lead actresses, I am compelled to examine the extent to which women who worked with the director colluded in this hostility and the extent to which they worked against it. How much of the ambivalence toward women seen in Hitchcock's films is owing to the input of ambivalent women living in a male-dominated society and working with a dominating male director? In what ways might women have complicated his vision – or even helped to establish it? How much of what we call a Hitchcock movie drew on the contributions of women who were so often either uncredited or subordinated in the credits?

A number of other Hitchcock films thematize women's collaboration with men's stories, whether or not these stories prove to be true. Such films include, in addition to *Rebecca*, *The 39 Steps* (1935), *Young and Innocent* (1937), and *Spellbound* (1945), in each of which the woman must work with the hero to establish his innocence of a crime he is suspected of committing. Many of the later films are more complicated variations of the theme of male/female collaboration. In *Notorious* (1946), Alicia (Ingrid Bergman), partly through her love of the hero, Devlin (Cary Grant), becomes an agent for the US government and marries a German man in order to spy on him. She and Devlin are supposedly collaborating, but his jealousy and suspicion of the relationship she has with her husband nearly causes her death. In *Shadow of a Doubt* (1943), young Charlie (Teresa Wright) at first refuses to believe that her Uncle Charlie (Joseph Cotten) is the Merry Widow murderer; when she does acknowledge the truth she collaborates with him to keep it from coming out because it would, as she says, kill her mother. In *Rear Window* (1954), Lisa (Grace Kelly) is drawn into a collaboration with Jefferies's story about the man across the courtyard, who, Jeff (James Stewart) insists, has killed his wife (critics have often seen this murder story as expressing Jeff's fantasy). In *Vertigo* (1958) another kind of collaboration involves Judy (Kim Novak) very reluctantly allowing herself to be made over by Scottie (James Stewart) into Madeleine, the woman with whom Scottie fell in love but who was made up first by another man, Gavin Elster (Tom Helmore), who uses Judy in his successful plot to kill his wife. In *North by Northwest* (1959), Eve (Eva Marie Saint) appears to be collaborating with Roger (Cary Grant) in his escape from the police, who suspect him of murder, only to have the story turned round upon Roger's discovery that she is the villain's paramour; when her innocence is established (she is an agent for the US government), the two collaborate to bring the villain down.

We might call the difficult interactions of women with men depicted in Hitchcock films "suspicious collaborations," a theme most pronounced in the films scripted by Charles Bennett. An illuminating instance of this theme can be seen in Bennett's adaptation of mystery writer Josephine Tey's *A Shilling for Candles* (1936), the film of which was titled *Young and Innocent*. It involves a man who is suspected of murdering a famous actress and is on the run from the police. Most commentators agree that the novel is one of Tey's lesser efforts, but the novel contains one terrific chapter in which Erica, the constable's daughter, sets out to find the suspect, Robert Tisdall; she is utterly convinced of his innocence and with grit and courage takes charge of investigating for clues, which she does in fact uncover. One episode involves her going into an inn frequented by men and countering their suspicion of her presence by joining in with their ribaldry and winning them over with her wit and humor. The film largely preserves this scene, but it occurs after Erica's uncertainty about Robert's guilt has turned into a conviction of his innocence. In the early part of the film, Erica (Nova Pilbeam) is unsure whether or not to believe his protestations of innocence; this ambivalence is vividly portrayed when the two of them are in her car at a fork in the road and point-of-view shots emphasize her uncertainty about whether to take the left fork, to help Robert (Derrick De Marney) escape, or the right fork, which leads back to the police. The right fork is closed for roadwork, a fact that, irrationally enough, puts to rest Erica's doubts.

It might seem that the novel, though written by a woman, is less feminist than the film since the novel's Erica never doubts the hero for an instant and is in fact dedicated to helping him from the first. Yet her take-charge attitude, her fortitude, and her independent actions on the man's behalf make her a strong and admirable character. Tisdall takes no amatory interest in the very young heroine. The film's Erica is older than the girl in the novel and must be won over by the charming hero with whom she falls in love. While I do not wish to overstate the case, Laura Mulvey's famous statement that "Sadism demands a story" (22) applies here to a degree. The overcoming of suspicion through "love" may elicit in the viewer a certain smugness at seeing the woman become convinced of what we know already. Yet in contrast to the novel, in which Erica appears only intermittently apart from the one crucial chapter, the film gives her much more prominence, and the collaboration between her and Robert to thwart the police and find the killer is humorous and endearing.

The one exception to the suspicious collaborations thematized in the early films is *The Lady Vanishes* (1938), based on a novel titled *The Wheel Spins* (1936) by crime writer Ethel Lina White. Here the suspicion involves not a "wrong man" being pursued by police and/or crooks, but a woman named Iris (Margaret Lockwood) who is convinced that someone she meets on the train – a Miss Froy (Dame May Whitty) – appears to have vanished into thin air. Various characters doubt Iris or, for selfish reasons of their own, pretend to doubt her because they don't want to get involved. Her sanity is called into question, and at one moment Iris even suspects herself of having hallucinated her encounter with Miss Froy. In the novel Iris feels virtually alone in her belief in the existence of this person. There is a male character, only vaguely hinted at as a possible love interest, who hits upon the solution to the case by, amusingly enough, imagining how he would write up a fictional account of the disappearance of Miss Froy (who has been seized and wrapped from head to toe in bandages and whose captors claim to be taking this very ill patient to a hospital). Iris seizes on this explanation as the true one, but even its inventor doesn't believe his own story! Eventually, under the influence of drugs, she approaches the patient and rips off the patient's bandages, revealing Miss Froy.

The film adds a more involved love interest, Gilbert (Michael Redgrave), and a whole new introductory section. Iris is depicted as a callow and high-spirited young woman who on her last night at the inn bribes the innkeeper to end the noise she hears above her bedroom by kicking out its occupant – a man named Gilbert who studies folk music and who has brought peasants to dance in his room so he can observe them. Gilbert goes into Iris's room and threatens to undress and sleep in

Iris's bed. Of course she backs down, but not without insulting him, whereupon he says, "I think you're a bit of a stinker too." The ensuing ordeal Iris undergoes is shadowed by a sensation that she is being given a comeuppance for her early, somewhat shrewish behavior.

In the film Gilbert has a central role in the investigation of Miss Froy's disappearance. He goes along with Iris's story until another woman claims to be Miss Froy. At this point Iris doubts her own story until Gilbert sees proof of Miss Froy's existence – a label from Miss Froy's special brand of tea. Gilbert hits on the solution to the crime and the two collaborate to expose the plot and find Miss Froy. Thus, while *The Lady Vanishes*, like *Young and Innocent*, reverses the power relations between hero and heroine, making the latter more subordinate than in the novel, both films, taking their cues from the novels, offer depictions of two plucky and on the whole likable female characters and preserve many of their more admirable traits. All the same, the eroticization of the detective plot in many of the early films is most intriguing. The films appear to betray an awareness of the need to secure women's consent to male rule, suggesting that love and the promise of marriage will override any suspicions women harbor about the men with whom they throw in their lot.

Critics often remark that Hitchcock was obsessed with the exploits of Jack the Ripper, a fact that would appear to lend credence to his reputation as a misogynist. Therefore, it is fascinating to me that the text he chose to adapt when he made what he would come to regard as "the first true 'Hitchcock movie'" (Truffaut 43) was originally written by a woman, Marie Belloc Lowndes, author of *The Lodger* (1913). Before Lifetime Television, before *Rebecca*, women were interested in investigating crimes committed against women and actively telling stories about such crimes. This activity speaks, it seems to me, not of women embracing their victimhood but of their desire to gain some control over it. Indeed, the story Lowndes writes, far from regaling the reader with the gruesome details of the Ripper's crimes, is in fact a *dissection* of a female collaborationist, a woman whose dreadful suspicions that she is harboring a killer give way to her knowingly sheltering and protecting the ultimate misogynist, who in novel and film calls himself "The Avenger."

The novel opens on a scene in which Mr. and Mrs. Bunting, former servants to upper-class families, are revealed to be in destitute straits as a consequence of a string of economic misfortunes. They are residing in a lodging house they have bought in a sketchy London neighborhood, but the rooms they hoped to let out have gone unrented for a long while. The novel portrays their suffering – their hunger and self-sacrifices – very vividly. Poor Mr. Bunting has given up so many of his small pleasures that he cannot even afford a ha'penny paper to indulge his avid curiosity about the gruesome killings that have all of London in a state of delectable fright. Throughout the novel, Lowndes, like Hitchcock after her in so many of his works, foregrounds the kinds of voyeuristic pleasure that stories of hideous crimes against women afford the public. The irony that the Buntings will soon be sheltering the perpetrator of these crimes, who will enable Mr. Bunting to indulge once again in his guilty pleasures, is not unlike the kind of irony we have come to associate with Hitchcock.

Thus when a lodger (*the* Lodger), clearly a gentleman if somewhat odd in his demeanor, knocks on the Buntings' door and enters into an agreement to rent rooms at a generous price, the landlady is understandably overjoyed. Her happiness, however, is short lived. The novel deftly portrays Mrs. Bunting's growing suspicion that she is actually harboring the serial killer, and it does so for the most part indirectly: that is, we are not explicitly told for quite some time that Mrs. Bunting suspects her lodger, Mr. Sleuth; rather the novel details her fearful wakefulness as he quietly goes out in the middle of the nights on which victims are killed, or it gives a sense of her immense relief when the morning paper does not announce a new murder to have been committed during the course of one of the lodger's nocturnal sojourns. Even more morally comprising is Mrs. Bunting's joy when she discovers a murder *has* been committed on a night the lodger has apparently remained indoors.

As time goes on, it is clear that Mrs. Bunting cannot but be aware of her lodger's guilt. The transference of guilt from the lodger to Mrs. Bunting so deftly and subtly conveyed by Lowndes is motivated at first by dire necessity, but as the novel proceeds we see how both class and gender come into play in explaining Mrs. Bunting's need to protect her lodger. In economic terms, the lodger's departure would mean certain ruin for the Buntings, while his continued presence means "respectability" as well as "security" (115). Mrs. Bunting also seems to be operating true to the norms of her gender as understood by Lowndes, who presents the reader with something like a feminist analysis of female collaborators with male outlaws:

> In the long history of crime it has very, very seldom happened that a woman has betrayed one who has taken refuge with her. … In fact, it may also be said that such betrayal has never taken place unless the betrayer has been actuated by love of gain, or by a longing for revenge. So far, perhaps because she is subject rather than citizen, her duty as a component part of civilized society weighs but lightly on woman's shoulders.
>
> (109)

In addition to casting an analytical gaze on Mrs. Bunting's behavior, Lowndes, it might be argued, transfers guilt onto and implicates the reader insofar as we are drawn at first to pity the Buntings' circumstances and then to rejoice when the couple is snatched from the fate of those who "struggle rudderless till they die in workhouse, hospital, or prison" (7).

In his film *The Lodger* (1926), Hitchcock relegates the landlady (Marie Ault) to a relatively minor part and promotes the novel's ingénue, Daisy (June Tripp) – child of the landlady and her husband in the film; daughter of Mr. Bunting by his first wife in the novel – to a major role. There is, to be sure, a chilling scene showing us the landlady's dread as she begins to suspect the Lodger (Ivor Novello) and wakes up at night to the sounds of the Lodger leaving his room, descending the stairs, and going out of the house. Powerless at this point, her fears are discredited since, in the Hitchcock version of the story, the Lodger is innocent, is in fact himself searching for the Avenger, whose first victim happens to have been his sister. While Hitchcock chose to forego working out the transference of guilt theme through the interplay of the characters, it is tempting to speculate, given his acknowledged long-term indebtedness to the novel, that Lowndes's stunning treatment of this theme stayed with him when he chose to take it up in many of his later films, like *Shadow of a Doubt* and *Strangers on a Train* (1951).

Although the film's landlady is not guilty of complicity with the Lodger, Hitchcock certainly makes viewers aware of *their* complicity with the throngs avidly seeking details about the Avenger's latest crimes. From the opening shot, in which we see a close-up of a woman screaming, to the scenes of newspapers rolling off the presses and being hawked by newsboys to the scene in which the Lodger is playing chess with Daisy, and reaches for a poker, saying, "Be careful, I'll get you yet" (we think he might be going to bludgeon her, but he is really intending to stoke the fire), we wait for the scene in which we get to see the Ripper begin ripping. Critics have not sufficiently recognized, moreover, that Hitchcock's Daisy (utterly wholesome in the novel, in which she is a companion and servant to an elderly relation) makes her living as a model, putting herself on display, and is a flirtatious character whose sexuality could easily make the viewer feel subliminally complicit with the Avenger, whose brand of justice lies in meting out the harshest punishment to seductive women.

As in many of Hitchcock's early films, the hero – in this case, the Lodger – is a suspicious but innocent character whom the heroine trusts while the other characters and the film's audience believe in his guilt. She finds herself involved in a triangular relationship, caught between the Lodger and the policeman Joe (Malcolm Keen), a repellent fellow who playfully handcuffs her at one point and actually compares himself to the Avenger, noting that both are fond of "golden curls." In a particularly ghastly turn of phrase Joe promises to put a ring on Daisy's finger as soon as he puts a noose around the Avenger's neck. I have noted elsewhere Hitchcock's tendency to place the heroine between criminals and figures of the law, suggesting that *both* are menacing to women, who are presumed guilty – sexually speaking – until proven or rendered innocent. While the novel does not go to the same lengths as the film in suggesting affinities between the figure of the law and the criminal, it certainly does play with similar ironies. In the novel, the policeman who is friend to the Buntings and would-be wooer of Daisy is a more likable fellow than the one in the film, but he hasn't a clue that, all the while he regales the Buntings with the latest news of the police investigation of the Avenger, the latter is residing within his friends' cozy domestic space.

Furthermore, in the novel the courtship of Joe and Daisy begins when Joe invites Daisy into the world of gruesome crime. Seizing on what he believes is a chance to get her on a date and away from her parents, he offers to take her to the Black Museum at Scotland Yard, "a regular Chamber of 'Orrors" where knives, poisons, and life-like casts of the heads of hanged men are all displayed for the voyeuristic pleasure of those permitted to view them. "'And can you go there whenever you like?' asked Daisy wonderingly. She had not realized before what extraordinary and agreeable privileges are attached to the position of a detective member of the London Police Force" (69). But the course of true love does not run smoothly through the Chamber of 'Orrors, for Mr. Bunting excitedly horns his way into the invitation, while for her part Mrs. Bunting sarcastically thanks Joe for giving Daisy "such a rare treat" – sarcasm that is lost on her listeners (70).

Turning now from collaboration between men and women as a theme in the films to women who collaborated with the director in the making of the films, one must begin with Alma Reville, Hitchcock's wife. Although Reville received much less credit in later years for her work than in the British films made by the pair, there is strong agreement among those who worked with Hitchcock that she was crucially involved in the making of his pictures, at every stage of their development throughout his entire career. (See Barr for an account of Reville's work with Hitchcock in the British period.) In addition to her working on scripts and continuity for many of his films, Hitchcock was vitally dependent on her opinion of his work. According to his long-time assistant, Peggy Robertson, Reville's contributions amounted to co-authorship. Hitchcock would be in agonies of despair, she observed, if his wife noticed a problem with a single scene or shot. For instance, when Hitchcock and Reville were viewing *Vertigo* for the first time, Robertson tells us, Alma turned to her husband and said that the film would be marvelous – as long as he got rid of a particular shot of Kim Novak. "I don't know which shot you mean, Alma," said the puzzled director. "The one where [she runs across the square and] her legs look awful." According to Robertson, Hitchcock replied, "Well, I'm sorry you hate the film, Alma," and for a while he was inconsolable (quoted in McGilligan 561–62). He ordered the offending footage eliminated.

The words used by Hitchcock's long-time art designer Robert Boyle to characterize Hitchcock's relations with his wife strike me as particularly revealing, in light of the director's demonstrable ambivalence about women evidenced in both his films and his occasional on-set behavior. "It was partly *reliance*, partly *fear*," Boyle observed. "She was the fulcrum [of] his life, no matter what his fantasies were" (quoted in Moral 131). (Undoubtedly when Boyle speaks of the director's fantasies he is referring to the director's much discussed obsessions with young actresses like Grace Kelly and Tippi Hedren.) But, psychoanalytically speaking, fear and fantasies are not opposing terms: fears inhabit the site of unconscious fantasy just as much as desire. As I argue in *The Women Who Knew Too Much*, Hitchcock films show both sympathy with women and fear of them, to the point where in the films women often undergo extreme punishment, as in *Notorious*, *Psycho* (1960), *The Birds* (1963), and *Frenzy* (1972). In addition, as critics have long noted, Hitchcock's films frequently revolve around rivalries between a younger woman and an unpleasant or even monstrous older woman who seeks to keep the young woman away from the hero (usually, her son). In the films it is generally the older woman who is the resentful person, whereas in life it was Hitchcock himself who, like Norman Bates, may have unconsciously resented his reliance on the woman who so confidently exercised the power of the cut. Speaking in an interview with Richard Allen of a triangle that involved Hitchcock, Reville, and herself, *Marnie* screenwriter Jay Presson Allen remarks, "We were always together. Hitch was jealous. He liked to get me alone because he likes to be the only one. I don't say that he didn't have some resentment at this stage of the game in Alma's input but he was mistaken." Richard Allen responds, "He had some resentment?" "Not conscious," the screenwriter replies. "Not conscious at all because it was a very happy marriage. It was a very good marriage. Unconsciously he wanted to be 'it'! Most artists do" (15).

I am especially intrigued by the work Reville undertook during the early part of Hitchcock's American period. While some of these works drew on a favorite Hitchcock theme – suspicion-haunted relations between the sexes – a new darkness enters the tone of these works, which depart greatly from what Leonard Leff calls "the frisky tone" of the British pictures (43). The period I want to consider, beginning with the film *Rebecca*, overlaps with the script writing of Joan Harrison. Harrison was hired by Hitchcock in 1935; she was to stay with him for seven years, first as secretary, and then assistant. Her first screenwriting assignment was the adaptation of Daphne du Maurier's *Jamaica Inn* (1936) for Hitchcock. She subsequently left Hitchcock to strike out on her own and became one of the first women producers in Hollywood. She returned to Hitchcock years later to produce the TV shows *Alfred Hitchcock Presents* and *The Alfred Hitchcock Hour*. As producer (and occasional writer) she not only worked with some of Hitchcock's prize crew members, like Robert Boyle, but also such noteworthy directors as Robert Siodmak and Jacques Tourneur.

As with Reville, frustration greets the scholar and archivist who wishes to learn more about Harrison and about the extent of her collaboration with Hitchcock. It is clear that Hitchcock depended on her greatly during the years she worked with him; that he had a marked respect for her; and that she produced several film treatments and also worked and reworked most of his scripts at this time, all of which also bore the name of at least one man. These include *Rebecca*, *Foreign Correspondent* (1940), *Suspicion* (1941), *Saboteur* (1942), and, according to some sources, *Shadow of a Doubt*. Happily, thanks to a splendid, well-researched essay by Christina Lane, we know something about Harrison's years as a film producer, knowledge that helps shed retroactive light on her work with Hitchcock. According to Lane, several films produced by Harrison focus on the "pathological and often violent underside of marriage and family" and constituted "rigorous investigations of happy endings and normative family institutions" (113).

Reville and Harrison worked on many drafts of *Rebecca*, for which Harrison received a film credit (Reville did not) and earned an Academy Award nomination, along with co-writers Robert Sherwood and Charles Bennett. In between *Rebecca* and *Suspicion*, films in the tradition of the female Gothic, Reville and Harrison worked on the screenplay for *Foreign Correspondent*, along with Charles Bennett. This underrated film contains some of Bennett's usual plot devices, in particular the story of a man of whom the heroine is suspicious but then comes to love.

When a news reporter, John Jones (Joel McCrea), is sent abroad to cover events in Europe, he stumbles across a plot to assassinate a Dutch diplomat; he soon falls in love with Carol (Laraine Day), the daughter of a British pacifist, Stephen Fisher (Herbert Marshall). Jones is unable to convince Carol or anyone else of the existence of such a scheme, but soon she changes her mind and falls in with his attempt to uncover the plot. Yet a new, darker element enters the picture, complicating the easy capitulation with which heroines in Hitchcock films fall into men's arms after suspecting them of criminal behavior. For it turns out that, unbeknownst to his daughter, Stephen Fisher is not working for peace at all but is a traitor in league with the enemy.

In this film the love plot and the spy plot intersect as they did so often in Hitchcock's films in the British period, but the stakes have been upped, in that the daughter alternates between suspecting her lover (first of fabricating or imagining the whole business related to treason and then of attempting to seduce her) and suspecting her own father of treason. Beginning with *Rebecca*, familial ties are imperiled as they have not been before, but will be again in increasingly perverse ways throughout the rest of Hitchcock's career. In *Foreign Correspondent*, the father is redeemed when he swims away from the wreckage to which the other survivors of a plane crash cling, sacrificing himself so that the overburdened section of wing will carry the others to safety. Such redemption of male characters will become increasingly rare in Hitchcock films.

Of course, in *Suspicion*, authored by Alma Reville, Joan Harrison, and Samson Raphaelson, the hero, Johnnie (Cary Grant), does promise to redeem himself at the end, to face up to his various crimes, which include embezzlement, and to accept the consequences – prison time – for his misdeeds. Notoriously, however, critics have viewed these avowals with a great deal of skepticism. The ending of this film, in which the wife's suspicions of her husband – that he is a murderer and is plotting *her* murder – are revealed to be unfounded, is for most critics too sudden and too pat to be believed. Hitchcock himself spoke of his dissatisfaction with the film's ending, telling Truffaut that he wanted the male protagonist to be guilty of murdering his wife. Critics from Donald Spoto to Mark Crispin Miller have argued that there is no evidence Hitchcock ever really intended to depict Grant as a killer. In fact, both Miller and Spoto point to memos in which the director "stated emphatically that he wanted to make a film about a woman's fantasy life" (Spoto 244).

For Miller, who draws on Truffaut's remark that *Suspicion* may be viewed as a critique of *Rebecca*, Lina (Joan Fontaine) is a ridiculous character whose fantasy life has been formed by romances and Gothics like *Rebecca*, and whose suspicions about her husband are unfounded. Oblivious to the fact that he is in a long line of critics who represent mass culture as feminine and oblivious as well to the dark ambiguities evident in both the novel *Rebecca* and the adaptation, Miller sees women's novels and women's films as genres of fantasy *par excellence*. As regards Gothic novels in the tradition of *Rebecca* and *Suspicion*, feminists have long shown how they provide an outlet for women's suspicions about their husbands and the fears women may experience in a world where male violence against women is common. The title of Joanna Russ's groundbreaking article on Gothics, written years ago, says it all: "Somebody is Trying to Kill Me and I Think It's My Husband." Given that Hitchcock's films explore this theme quite openly, as in *Dial M for Murder* (1954), *Rear Window*, and *Vertigo* (in the case of *Shadow of a Doubt*, the title might read, "Somebody is Trying to Kill Me Because My Husband is Dead"), the premise per se was hardly anathema to Hitchcock.

That said, it is certainly true that the script contains moments in which Lina's romantic pleasure, at the beginning of the movie, and her fears, as the film progresses, are mocked. When she and Johnnie declare their love for one another, for example, Lina faces away from him as they embrace, exclaiming, "Here we are alone in my home. The house that I was born in!" – as if the entire drama of the love scene were hers alone. Sometimes the music swells excessively to ridicule Lina, as when she finally receives a telegram from Johnnie ten days after their first romantic encounter.

In this initial love scene, which takes place on a windy hill, Johnnie arranges Lina's hair in a ridiculous manner that makes both him and the audience smile. However, Lina's remark that she always feels that men like him are laughing at women like her might indeed hit its mark with some of the film's female spectators. And there are plenty of reasons as the tone of the film darkens, and Lina's suspicions deepen, to identify with the woman's deepest fears. Johnnie is given certain moments in which he appears frightening – most notably, when he and Lina are dining with the mystery writer Isobel Sedbusk (Auriol Lee) and are told about a poison that is undetectable in a corpse. At the end of the discussion, Isobel pronounces Johnnie, among others, to be incapable of murder, but as he agrees with her, a close-up shows his smiling face transform into an ominous look before the fadeout.

Another moment when Johnnie's sinister side is emphasized occurs when he discovers that Lina is trying to talk Beaky Thwaite (Nigel Bruce) out of handing all his money over to Johnnie to advance a get-rich-quick real estate scheme. Suddenly, a door opens wider to reveal Johnnie behind it; he has overheard her conversation and is very angry. Climbing the stairs with Lina, he chastises her darkly for interfering in his affairs. The mise-en-scène of the stairs, with the spidery shadows on the wall, gives Johnnie's warning to his wife a very sinister feel. In the next scene, Lina is shown cutting hedges with her face to the camera. Miller's reading of the scene – meant to further his argument that Lina is a self-obsessed, foolish woman and that Hitchcock mocks not only her but an audience gullible enough to identify with her, at least initially – merits lengthy quotation:

> On the morning after Johnny [sic] has so angrily chastised Lina for her prying, she appears, unkempt and gloomy, and wielding an enormous pair of shears, which she uses to trim back a hedge, her emphatic strokes and absent, bitter look suggesting that, in her imagination, it is not actually the hedge which she is punishing. Just then, her husband appears towering in front of her, on our side of the hedge, his back toward the camera, so that his upright head repeats the figuration of the twigs before her. Violently startled at his greeting, she immediately shifts out of her sullenness and into a devoted, pleading attitude: "Are you still angry about last night?" she asks. ... "I was afraid that you'd stopped loving me!"

To Miller, Lina's words appear "self-serving" and "affecting"; they imply, he contends, that Lina feels Johnnie "has turned on her" and "she would like to kill him for it or alter him" (268–69).

Though Miller claims to be speaking for all film viewers, the gender-suspicion of his own reading emphasizes Lina's supposed desire to castrate her husband, even to kill him. While Miller reads her expression as "sullen" and "bitter," it is equally possible to see her as simply tense and upset. Johnnie's sudden appearance, combined with the many sudden appearances he makes in the film, rather like Mrs. Danvers in *Rebecca*, feels ominous. Moreover, in the scene in question, when Johnnie reassures Lina that he loves her "very much," his avowal is delivered in a perfunctory manner at best, and rather than stay for a moment to reinforce his words, he simply wanders off. My point it that neither the words nor the images in this scene (and others) yield themselves to a singular definitive reading.

That *Suspicion* is susceptible of at least two, often opposed, interpretations that are influenced by gender may be due to the evolution of the film script. Reville and Harrison's early work on the script adhered to the Gothic theme of the villainous husband out to kill his wife. In Francis Iles's *Before the Fact*, the 1932 novel from which the film was adapted, Johnnie really is a murderer and really does kill his wife. Sam Raphaelson was hired to develop the script, and he and Hitchcock set out to make Johnnie a more likable character than he appears in the novel and the Harrison/Reville versions. For example, they cut a scene in which Johnnie appears to have stolen a rich lady's brooch. In the end, however, Hitchcock's efforts to clean up Johnnie met with partial success at best: Once the film was completed, one of the film's producers confiscated the footage and, according to biographer Patrick McGilligan, spliced together "a condensed version ... that erased *all* suspicion of Johnny's [sic] crimes" (289). The result was a film of about 55 minutes. When Hitchcock protested furiously, the offending scenes were restored. The notion that Raphaelson and Hitchcock were successful in portraying a less menacing Johnnie than appeared in the early versions of the script is contradicted by this account, even allowing for the paranoia implicit in the Production Code. It is, moreover, certainly not the case, *pace* Donald Spoto, that Johnnie turns out to be "innocent of everything except foolishness and fiscal irresponsibility": he can be cruel, as when he pawns his wife's most prized possession to make a wager on a horse, and he embezzles money from his employer – an act for which the term "fiscal irre-sponsibility" seems woefully inadequate (246). Lina may overreact to Johnnie's behavior, but her reactions are not entirely without foundation.

In the early Harrison / Reville versions, the film was to have started with Lina looking at a picture of a dashing Johnnie in the *Illustrated London News*, and then glancing up to "confirm that the rather boorish individual across from her is the same man" (Krohn 78). A romance is thus signaled from the very beginning. In the film the scene worked on by Raphaelson and Hitchcock begins comically with Johnnie, after entering the compartment, looking up and down the dowdy figure of Joan Fontaine in a point-of-view shot and appearing somewhat disconcerted by what he sees. Subsequently he is confronted by the conductor and tries to talk his way out of being booted into third class, for which he holds a ticket. Out of money, Johnnie reaches over into Lina's purse and picks out a stamp – "legal tender, legal tender," he says, comically waving away the disgruntled conductor. It is *after* this incident that the shot of Lina comparing Johnnie as he appears in the magazine to Johnnie as he appears sitting across from her occurs; the promised romance is thus partly undercut by initially making Lina into exactly "the kind of woman men always laugh at," to recall Lina's words.

We might say, then, that we have a case of dueling genres (comedy vs. romance / Gothic), each markedly gendered. It is certainly not clear, as I have argued, that the comedy, generally achieved at Lina's expense, wins out over the Gothic. According to Donald Spoto, as the script was being written by Raphaelson, Harrison and Reville were adding scenes "according to Hitchcock's specifications." Raphaelson found the resulting scenario to be "hopelessly tangled, a mixture of mood and style and motivation that could never sort itself out on film" (quoted in Spoto 244). I prefer, however, not to regard the film as a failed one, the product of an unhar-monious, not to say suspicious, collaboration. Rather, the clash of moods and styles along with the notorious impossibility of ending the film plausibly are evi-dence of a stalemate, a standoff between the sexes who often cannot "sort them-selves out" in art or in life. We are each of us caught up in our own genres, our own fantasies or compulsions: Gothic fantasies in Lina's case, gambling in Johnnie's.

Shadow of a Doubt is about how a young woman's suspicions of her beloved uncle are confirmed when she learns he is the "Merry Widow murderer" sought by police nationwide. Although many think of the film as a masculine project, the product of a collaboration between Hitchcock and playwright Thornton Wilder, it was heavily influenced by women and represents an extension of the themes present in *Rebecca*, *Foreign Correspondent*, and *Suspicion*, films that deal with violence that erupts from within the couple or the family rather than intruding from without.

Alma Reville worked on the script, along with, according to some sources, Joan Harrison. Once Wilder departed, other women made improvements to the script, including Patricia Collinge, the actress who plays Emma, the mother in *Shadow of a Doubt*. Collinge gave the character more dignity than she possessed in the original script, and most importantly, she wrote the moving words her character speaks upon learning that her beloved brother Charlie is leaving the next day. Emma ends the speech, which begins by talking about what Charlie meant to her growing up, by saying of marriage, "You know how it is, you sort of forget you're you. You're your husband's wife." (One can't help but wonder how these words struck Reville, a former director in her own right.) Whereas the mother has previously seemed content with her self-effacing role in the family her voice at this moment rings clear and true as she mourns her vanished self. Collinge also rewrote the scene between young Charlie and the detective (Macdonald Carey) in the garage. Initially it was to have been a love scene with Charlie accepting his proposal. In the rewritten scene Charlie does not accept the proposal. Given the discontent she has expressed regarding family life, and in particular her disapproval of her hard-working mother's subordinate role in the family at the beginning of the film, and given the appalling reprisal (in the person of Uncle Charlie) that this discontent elicits, it certainly seems fitting that she would not want to rush into marriage.

In laying out his ideas for the film, Hitchcock had said that he wanted the film to be a comedy of small town manners and felt that the comedy should be got from "those characters who were 'not in the know'" (McGilligan 308). The person who supplied much of this comedy was Sally Benson.

Benson wrote the novel *Meet Me in St. Louis* (1942) and also worked on the screenplay for that film. Her lightly satiric and humorous stories were popular and critically acclaimed. She wrote much of the dialogue for the younger children, Ann and Roger (Edna May Wonacott and Charles Bates), who add greatly to the film's comedy as well as to its darker undertones. For example, younger daughter Ann, who is an avid reader, upbraids her father for reading murder mysteries: "Here I am only ten years old and I wouldn't be seen reading the things you read." Now, in *Meet Me in St. Louis*, the 1944 Vincente Minnelli version of which Robin Wood puts on a continuum with Tobe Hooper's *The Texas Chainsaw Massacre* (1974) in the film genre he dubs the "American family comedy," the father is sidelined, rather like the father in *Shadow of a Doubt* whose place is usurped by Uncle Charlie. (In effect Charlie figuratively makes his sister a widow.) In the novel, the many females in the household easily overturn the father's decision to move to New York, where he dreams of having his own business. The mother and the girls go on a successful hunger strike at the dinner table, led by Tootie, the youngest child, who remarks that "father isn't the only one in this family. There are eight, not counting father" (260). Tootie, a rather ghoulish child, is reminiscent of Ann, who at one point proudly proclaims, apropos of the game "Step on a Crack," "I broke my mother's back *three times*." Further, Benson's work, which tends to view with amusement the preening of young girls obsessed with boys and boyfriends, is the likely source of Ann's wonderful lines, spoken when young Charlie refuses the ring offered by her uncle, "She's just pretending, like girls in books. The ones who say they don't want anything always get more in the end."

Taking into account the various contributions of women to the final screenplay of the film – Hitchcock's favorite, he claimed on more than one occasion – we can see how the film spoke to the anxieties of women at that period in history. That it takes place, aside from a couple of key scenes, within domestic space and fills that space with horror reveals sensibilities resistant to the Happy Homemaker ideal that was to emerge in the years following World War II.

Finally, I come to one of Hitchcock's most controversial films, *Marnie* (1964), for which the screenwriting credit goes exclusively to one woman, Jay Presson Allen. For once, no man's name is attached to the script, and no man can claim to have done most of the work or complain that his work was messed up by women's interference, as Raphaelson had done in the case of *Suspicion*. Unfortunately for the feminist critic, however, *Marnie*, a film in which the central couple are, with reason, deeply suspicious of one another, might appear to be the work of an unregenerate collaborationist.

Drafts of *Marnie* were in fact written by men, first Joseph Stefano, who wrote *Psycho*'s screenplay, and then Evan Hunter, the screenwriter of *The Birds*; nevertheless Allen, who has protested her ignorance at the time of the existence of previous screenplays, took the story in a different direction. Hunter has maintained that Hitchcock fired him because of Hunter's reluctance to write one particular scene – the scene where Mark (Sean Connery) rapes his wife Marnie (Tippi Hedren) during their shipboard honeymoon. Hunter wrote a passionate plea for Hitchcock to delete the scene, which was taken from the novel. He wrote, "Mark is *not* that kind of a person. Marnie is obviously troubled, and he realizes it. Stanley Kowalski might rape her, but not Mark Rutland. Mark would do exactly what we see him do later – he would seek the help of a psychiatrist" (quoted in Moral 39). Such are the paradoxes of feminist criticism that many feminists (myself included) believe the rape was dramatically necessary because (per Richard Allen) it creates more sympathy for Marnie and makes for a stronger indictment of patriarchy as well. Out with compassionate sensitive men! In with the rapists, fetishists, and sadists among them!

In any case, Hunter's script is not without problems. His paternalism comes through quite clearly in a letter to Tippi Hedren about the heroine's motives. In Hunter's script, Marnie has a real father, a seafaring man who dies at sea around the same time that her mother is "entertaining" a sailor. As in the film, Marnie's traumatic encounter with the sailor leads to his death. Hunter diagnoses Marnie's behavior as part of an "Oedipal" or "psychological complex" centered on her father (quoted in Moral 32–34). Having confused the death of the sailor with the death of her father and blamed her mother for her father's death, Marnie steals money from men and brings it to her mother as a symbolic act of restoring the father. Thus in Hunter's version Marnie only *seems* to care about her mother, whereas for many feminists the mother–daughter bond depicted in the movie is one of its redeeming and most moving features.

Jay Presson Allen had no qualms about putting in the rape scene; she even maintained, according to Hunter at least, that the rape was the sole reason Hitchcock wanted to make the movie. At a conference held at NYU in 1999 that brought together Hitchcock critics and collaborators to commemorate the centennial of Hitchcock's birth, Allen was pressed about the rape. She answered with apparent equanimity that many women fantasize being raped and cited the scene from *Gone with the Wind* (Victor Fleming, 1939) in which Clark Gable carries Vivien Leigh up the stairs to rape her (10). Susan White responded that one difference between the two films was that Scarlett O'Hara enjoyed the experience while Marnie did not (11). A look at the first draft screenplay suggests that Allen did in fact envision the scene to play more like a love encounter from a female romance than an assault. Here is some of the language she used in the initial script to describe what is supposed to happen during the act:

> Gently, but compulsively, he pulls her to him, softly, coaxingly covers her face with kisses … it is not just his desire that has finally overflowed, but his very real love for her. And it is love that dictates the manner in which he takes her … not simply using her, but courting, caressing, desperately urging her response.
>
>   (Quoted in Moral 45; ellipses in original)

By contrast, Hitchcock's own language could not be more brutal. He reportedly said to Evan Hunter, when Hunter tried to resist including the scene, "Evan, when he sticks it in her, I want that camera right on her face!" (Hunter 89).

In the end we have a scene that has confused many critics – Mark rips Marnie's clothes, apologizes, gently covers her with his robe, then pushes the petrified woman back on the bed. The confusion among critics mirrors a larger social confusion that persists to this day about when to call something rape. At the centennial conference, Robin Wood said to Allen that in his view what is going on in the scene cannot simply be described as rape. It is more ambiguous, he argued:

> What happens is Mark bursts into Marnie's room. He is obviously drunk [this is not at all obvious to me] and desperate. He grabs her night-dress and tears it down so she's standing there in front of him naked and she looks appalled. He is ashamed. He seems to sober up immediately. He's very gentle with her. He takes off his dressing gown, his bathrobe, and puts it around her shoulders. She becomes completely passive. Now, the way I read it, Marnie knows she is being raped but Mark does not know he is raping her.

Allen, clearly relieved at the "out" Wood provided her after having been pestered by the audience about the rape, said, "You're absolutely right" (20).

Given how often, in real life, men think they are not raping women when they clearly *are* raping them, it is hard to see how this "failure of communication" mitigates the act of rape. While Allen soft-pedals and romanticizes the inevitable rape and thus contributes to the misunderstandings that surround the issue of rape, Hitchcock, whether motivated by lascivious desires or not, focuses on the reaction of the woman, Marnie – a woman who, after all, screams out "No" and nowhere indicates that she changes her mind. In doing so, he makes it just a little bit harder for the audience to feel that the man's desire takes precedence over or is equivalent to the woman's pain. Here is certainly a case where "the woman's discourse" used by Allen – the discourse of women's romances – has a conservative effect. Of course, I mean conservative in a political sense. But perhaps we can also detect in Allen's language both as it appears *in* the script and in her discussions *of* the script a desire to conserve the female body and protect it from outright assault (Mark is not merely having his way with Marnie; he is "desperate" for her response). What appears to have been a very willing collaboration between scriptwriter and director may, on an unconscious level, suggest suspicion of male desires and designs.

Reader-response criticism has long recognized that reading or viewing a text involves the collaboration of the critic. We bring to the texts our own preoccupations, beliefs, feelings, and desires. As a feminist critic looking for marks of female authorship in male texts, I bring a set of politics quite different from that of many Hitchcock viewers and critics, and believe myself to have entered into collaboration with the female contributors to the films. I have found meanings that many of them might repudiate, in turn viewing my reading as an act of collaborationism with a feminist movement from which they wish to distance themselves. With respect to these women I have exercised a hermeneutics of suspicion: I have delved beneath the surface of certain films, sometimes disregarding what may have been the collaborators' intentions, to find meanings lying beneath the surface. In the past, such has been my method in dealing with Hitchcock's films, which have usually been considered products of a single auteur. Certainly, if one rejects the notion that Hitchcock as auteur was in conscious control of all aspects of his texts, then one must in good faith extend this suspicion of the auteur to his collaborators.

Paul Ricoeur, who is most closely associated with the term "hermeneutics of suspicion," frequently pointed to Karl Marx, Friedrich Nietzsche, and Sigmund Freud as the theorists whose work exemplified a "suspicious" approach to interpretation (see Ricoeur 32). For Freud, of course, the unconscious revealed meanings beyond the understanding of the conscious mind. In this chapter I have followed Freud and feminist psychoanalytic critics who show how women's unconscious in a patriarchal society is shaped in myriad ways that are different from men's, and at times I have been at pains to reveal the imprint of women's unconscious on the films. Ricoeur, however, stressed the importance of not simply restricting oneself to the wholly negative activity of denunciation (of, say, exposing Hitchcock as a misogynist) but of suspending disbelief and remaining open to what the text might have to say to (and about) us collaborators. This openness required me to acknowledge the force and rightness of some of Hitchcock's choices. To take *Marnie* as my example: however crude Hitchcock's intentions might have been in describing what he wanted to be shown in the rape scene, the end result is to make us question the authority of the film's supposed hero and to elicit the feminist interpreter's sympathy for its trapped and caged heroine.

Thus do I find myself at the end of this chapter in a position not unlike that of Hitchcock's early female protagonists whose suspicions of the men with whom they are linked give way to trust – in my case, certainly, a qualified trust. Such trust is warranted in part because Hitchcock himself seemed to have been open to his female collaborators, most notably his wife (although not, we recall, without some resentment of his dependence on her). Finally, though, I am left with a question that involves a kind of hermeneutic spiral. When did the women take their cue from Hitchcock's expressed (or unconscious) desires and when did they lead him along paths he might otherwise not have taken? Often there must have been a mutuality of influence that renders the matter ultimately undecidable. Just as the figure of the spiral in *Vertigo* suggests the impossibility of attaining a final truth about woman – and hence about man – the feminist critic's search for definitive answers about the nature and extent of the female collaborator's *contributions* is inevitably thwarted, and the enterprise must in the final analysis remain speculative.

Works Cited

Allen, Jay Presson. "An Interview with Jay Presson Allen." By Richard Allen. *Hitchcock Annual* (2000–01): 3–22.

Barr, Charles. *English Hitchcock*. Moffat: Cameron and Hollis, 1999.

Benson, Sally. *Meet Me in St. Louis*. 1942. St. Louis: Virginia Publishing, 2004.

du Maurier, Daphne. *Rebecca*. 1938. New York: Avon, 1997.

Edwards, Kyle Dawson. "Brand Name Literature: Film Adaptation and Selznick International Pictures' *Rebecca*." *Cinema Journal* 45.3 (Spring 2006): 32–58.

Hunter, Evan. *Me and Hitch*. London: Faber and Faber, 1997.

Iles, Francis. *Before the Fact*. New York: Harper and Row, 1932.

Krohn, Bill. "Ambivalence (*Suspicion*)." *Hitchcock Annual* (2002–03): 67–116.

Lane, Christina. "Stepping Out from Behind the Grand Silhouette: Joan Harrison's Films of the 1940s." *Authorship and Film*. Ed. David A. Gerstner and Janet Staiger. New York: Routledge, 2003.

Leff, Leonard J. *Hitchcock and Selznick: The Rich and Strange Collaboration of Alfred Hitchcock and David O. Selznick in Hollywood*. New York: Weidenfeld and Nicolson, 1987.

Lowndes, Marie Belloc. *The Lodger*. 1913. Chicago: Academy Chicago, 1988.

McGilligan, Patrick. *Alfred Hitchcock: A Life in Darkness and Light*. New York: HarperCollins, 2003.

Miller, Mark Crispin. *Boxed In: The Culture of TV*. Evanston: Northwestern UP, 1988.

Modleski, Tania. *The Women Who Knew Too Much*. Second ed. New York: Routledge, 2005.

Moral, Tony Lee. *Hitchcock and the Making of Marnie*. Lanham, MD: Scarecrow, 2005.

Mulvey, Laura. *Visual and Other Pleasures*. Bloomington: Indiana UP, 1989.

Ricoeur, Paul. *Freud and Philosophy: An Essay on Interpretation*. New Haven: Yale UP, 1970.

Russ, Joanna. "Somebody is Trying to Kill Me and I Think It's My Husband: The Modern Gothic." *Journal of Popular Culture* 6.4 (1973): 666–91.

Spoto, Donald. *The Dark Side of Genius: The Life of Alfred Hitchcock*. Boston: Little, Brown, 1983.

Tey, Josephine. *A Shilling for Candles*. 1936. New York: Pocket, 1980.

Truffaut, François, with the collaboration of Helen G. Scott. *Hitchcock*. Rev. ed. New York: Simon and Schuster, 1984.

White, Ethel Lina. *The Wheel Spins*. New York: Harper, 1936.

Wood, Robin. "The American Family Comedy: From *Meet Me in St. Louis* to *The Texas Chainsaw Massacre*." *Wide Angle* 3.2 (1979): 5–11.

10

A Surface Collaboration: Hitchcock and Performance

Susan White

In his careful cultivation of his directorial reputation, Alfred Hitchcock was not averse to a bit of ironic drama. His most often-repeated comment on actors, that they are "cattle," playfully invokes the image of his whip-wielding brethren, Josef von Sternberg and Erich von Stroheim. Critics have debated this comment ever since. For every actor who complained of Hitchcock's abuses, others have come forward to describe their relationship with the director as warm and supportive. A more nuanced representation of Hitchcock's attitude toward acting may be found in a less lurid remark he made to Peter Bogdanovich: "Relying on actors is borrowing from the stage. I think that montage is the essential thing in a motion picture" (476).

Any consideration of acting in a director's works must recognize how performances are manipulated by visual and sound style. This is particularly the case with Hitchcock's cinema. The distinctive qualities of the director's mise-en-scène, camera movement, editing, and sound recording produce uniquely inflected spectatorial relationships to the characters embodied by actors on the screen. The films illustrate cognitive processes and emotional states of characters with extraordinary subtlety and with little to no emphasis on a "mimetic" approach requiring actors to feel the emotions being projected. Often, the films construct character and propel plot by means of complex external cues that draw upon or expand the existing range of expression an actor brings to a film. Hitchcock habitually uses an actor's brand name and experience as raw material to construct "a meticulously designed and functional" performance (Pomerance 127), requiring intensive preparation and foresight, first by writers, then by storyboard artists, and finally by the actors themselves.

Hitchcock's reputed torment – or micromanagement, to say the least – of performers like Kim Novak and Tippi Hedren, and the performances that torment

A Companion to Alfred Hitchcock, First Edition. Edited by Thomas Leitch and Leland Poague.
© 2011 Thomas Leitch and Leland Poague. Published 2011 by Blackwell Publishing Ltd.

helped to elicit, influenced his films as much as his camaraderie with Cary Grant, Grace Kelly, and Anthony Perkins. The carefully crafted dialectic of humor and fear, irony and suspense characterizing Hitchcock's films and self-presentation was forged in the conflicts he seems to have felt about acting, and was crucial in shaping the performances in his films.

In what follows, I delve into the complexities of Hitchcock's relationship to actors in order to show how the striking performances of the films are inseparable from their vivid technical and narrative effects and, further, how the work depends not upon the lone determination of a brilliant auteur, nor the tortured production of a Method actor, but rather upon a collaboration – albeit one that is cruel as well as collegial – between actor and director. For reasons of space I consider only Hitchcock's sound films, and for the most part actors who appeared in his American works. I examine the form of Hitchcock's collaborative impulse that drew him to work with, upon, and in reaction to the surface of the actor in order to produce paradigmatic Hitchcockian performances. This "collaborative impulse" is also, of course, strongly inflected by the framework of gender roles and relationships that characterized the industrial and personal context within which Hitchcock worked. The films situate actors in a complex and changing system of gender construction in which questions of identity are conflated with the problems of role-playing and the difficulties of acting in a Hitchcock film.

Hitchcock's most interesting films undermine traditional theatricality – sometimes through exaggeration – with intensely self-reflexive narratives and techniques. These techniques include character typing, a device heavily relied upon in the silent and early sound films. Again and again we find the cop, the man on the street, the frightened young woman, the dowager – and the important recurrent type of the sexually ambiguous male or female, such as Esme Percy's Handel Fane in *Murder!* (1930) or Judith Anderson's Mrs. Danvers in *Rebecca* (1940). There are countless examples of Hitchcock's reliance on silent film techniques in his sound films, many dependent upon montage for their power. One of the best-known instances of a characteristic early montage effect is found in a later Hitchcock film, in the Eisenstein-like sequence of close shots (or "big heads," as Hitchcock called them) of the long-suffering Tippi Hedren's face as she watches the eponymous birds carry out a savage attack on a gas station. Hitchcock's emphasis on the "external" is also documented in Laurent Bouzereau's interview with Diane Baker, who plays Lil Mainwaring in *Marnie* (1964):

> He didn't talk about motivation. He expected all that to be there, and you'd work that out. I remember him coming up to me in the window shot, when I'm looking out the window down into the front of the house, and he wanted a certain look. And just simply made … fixed my face with his hands exactly how he wanted me to look. He put his hands there, and he simply shaped my face. He didn't want to tell me what to be thinking. He didn't really want any thinking, but I understood, we're making a movie. And if he can get what he wants exactly as he wants it by moving

my face in a certain way, or placing it in the light in a certain way, then that's it. No one knows when they see the movie how it came about. Except that it was right for the moment.

Doug Tomlinson notes that "Hitchcock generally disapproved of his performers indulging in a theatrically based psychological construct" (107). His problems with Method actor Montgomery Clift on *I Confess* (1953) only reinforced this disapproval. Tony Perkins, certainly influenced by the Method, was another matter, as I'll consider later in this chapter.

His usefulness in a montage sequence was one of the many virtues of an important Hitchcock collaborator, Cary Grant. Carey Martin has detailed this collaboration, noting that Hitchcock wished to place Grant in starring roles in at least ten films in addition to the four they did make together. Grant was well suited to incarnate the acting effects that Hitchcock wanted, in which images of the actor are characterized by some combination of *recognizability, typage, graphic impact, clarity of gesture,* and *distinctive facial expression* – even in the cases where that expression conveys ambiguous or conflicting emotions or a manipulated "blankness." Hitchcock's films also exploit the unique timbre and inflection of actors' voices, whether they are stars or supporting players.

As a trained acrobat, Grant exercised an unusual degree of control over his body, and in collaboration with Hitchcock produced an extraordinary range of balletic movements, both dramatic and comical. The screwball comedies of the 1930s had exploited the unsurpassed elegance and just plain goofiness made possible by Grant's rangy physique and willingness to take a pratfall. Because of the discipline of his body, his experience in pantomime, the distinctive form of his physique, and the graceful drape of his clothing, Grant was a particularly apt subject for the kind of graphic representations that the films deploy to such powerful effect.

Grant's celebrity, already nearing its sustained height by 1940, served a number of functions in the collaborations between director and actor. Hitchcock often described Grant's ability to make the audience "identify" with him as his major virtue as an actor:

> One doesn't direct Cary Grant, one simply puts him in front of a camera. And, you see, he enables the audience to identify with the main character. Cary Grant represents a man we know. He's not a stranger.
>
> (Bogdanovich 476)

Grant's recognizability – the fact that he can be identified instantly as well as identified *with* in a psychological sense – remains one of the most important elements in his usefulness for Hitchcock. Despite what Hitchcock says, however, "Cary Grant" is clearly a construction – and a problematic one at the beginning of his career. He was rejected after his first Paramount screen test because of "bow legs and a thick neck," in addition to "an unplaceable voice," and sloping shoulders that had to be built up by padding in his suit (Smith 31). The actor's status as the oxymoronic idealized everyman with a hint of darkness was both exploited and developed in the Hitchcock films.

Hitchcock's extended play on Grant's star image in *North by Northwest* (1959), as described by James Naremore, works to complicate some of Hitchcock's most prevalent themes – the theatricality of everyday life, the necessity of role playing, the precariousness of identity (216). In both *Suspicion* (1941) and *North by Northwest* women respond with sexual arousal to the "recognizable" Cary Grant character, as when Lina (Joan Fontaine) spots Johnnie (Grant) in a magazine photo in *Suspicion,* or when Eve Kendall (Eva Marie Saint) recognizes Thornhill from the newspaper photo of the UN murder. Tokens of notoriety seem to sharpen female desire for the feckless charmer, a plot point used to lesser effect in Leo McCarey's *An Affair to Remember* (1957).

One finds vivid examples of both Grant's recognizability and his powerful graphic potential in the early use that Hitchcock made of Grant's silhouette – also an important device in the manipulation of James Stewart's screen presence, and in Hitchcock's own iconic self-presentations. Hitchcock's purposeful deployment of the silhouette, like that of the cast shadow, was a sustained homage to the expressionist masters who were his strongest early influences. The silhouette and the recognition factor come together as a crucial effect at the beginning of *Notorious* (1946), where Grant is first shown from behind and in deep shadow – a seemingly anonymous silhouette, but already putting the stamp of his stardom on the film. Grant's silhouette was used to similar effect in the famous staircase scene in *Suspicion,* where his physical elegance and the glow of the possibly fatal glass of milk, along with the disturbing quality of Grant's studiously blank face, enhance the sinister effect of the dark outline of his body.[1]

Grant's effectiveness in montage sequences is demonstrated time and again. As Carey Martin has written, in the very first scene of *Suspicion,* as Johnnie Aysgarth and Lina McLaidlaw meet for the first time, montage is used both to reveal and to mask characters' emotions. Martin notes how the "technique of montage" keeps the audience from "fully understanding [Johnnie's] thoughts," contributing significantly to the richness of the film's often-critiqued ambiguous ending. Under the broad rubric of the "impassive" expression, Grant produces an enormous variety of nuanced quick gazes, small movements, tilts of the head, and so on. As Naremore puts it:

> Perhaps the secret lay in Grant's posture and behavior, which implied both an unpretentious casualness and a lack of vanity. There was a touch of diffidence in some of his reactions and a generous, almost stagy, cheerfulness in his smile. Unlike most theatrically trained actors, he frequently played scenes with both hands stuffed in his pockets, gesturing with his elbows or with slightly hunched shoulders – an unassuming, boyish stance that made him seem shy and unaffected.
>
> (217)

Throughout *Suspicion* Grant's face acts as a continually changing landscape of emotions that demand audience interpretation. He is both more transparent (that is, he telegraphs emotion more directly) and more opaque than Laurence Olivier in *Rebecca*; though Olivier also plays a man who may be a wife-killer, his range of expression is much more limited than Grant's. While both of these films, as well as *Notorious* (1946), follow the conventions of the female gothic, in which we watch the woman watching the male object of her desire, more time is spent in *Suspicion* focusing on the expressive clues dropped by this man than in either of the two other films.

Grant is less "impassive" in *Suspicion* than he is contradictory, his facial expressions more often minimalistic than truly blank. They sometimes flit rapidly across the screen as clear and distinct but incompatible mental states. The sinister look and low-key lighting in the scene where Johnnie announces Lina's father's death, for example, shifts rapidly (in the same shot, as Grant walks toward Lina and the camera) to a somber and (perhaps) tender facial expression as he tries to comfort her. The effect is so subtle that it's difficult to distinguish where it occurs – or even if it is a Kuleshovian illusion. As Beaky Thwaite (Nigel Bruce) points out, Johnnie is a formidable liar: his smile is often as open and genuine as any in Grant's screwball comedies; and as often as he self-consciously darts his eyes at Lina, gauging her responses to what may or may not be his lie, he engages us with warmth and frankness. The process of looking at Grant in *Suspicion* is thus especially intense, and is very different from our pleasure in looking at the actor in, say, *North by Northwest*.

Grant's sleekness and ease of motion are fully celebrated in *North by Northwest*. Despite his character's identity crisis, his status as object of veneration is as stable as that of the towering monument in the film. Rather than searching for the meaning implied by his facial expressions, as in *Suspicion* and *Notorious*, we witness the actor's confrontation with spaces and landscapes heavily freighted with symbolic meaning, and strongly dependent for their meaning upon the powerful visual effect of Grant's placement against them. By the time *North by Northwest* was filmed, Hitchcock's play with what might be termed Grant's "surfaces" is in full force. No detail is too small to figure in Grant's visual impact.

Whereas Marlon Brando's self-declared habit of "acting with his makeup" indicated his distaste for an unchallenging role, Grant's acting with this "surface" – including his clothing – constitutes a serious work of art. For both Naremore and Ulrich Lehmann, the suit Grant wears in *North by Northwest* is a durable fetish object. In contrasting Grant to his Oak Room Bar drinking buddies,

[Hitchcock asked] nothing more than variations on his habitual superficial charm and ironic superiority [which are] established by clothing Thornhill in a bespoke suit by Savile Row tailors Kilgour, French & Stanbury – an establishment frequented by Grant as well. The supporting cast in [the Oak Room Bar] scene offers off-the peg backgrounds, providing the common sartorial language … of the 1950s, so paradigmatically embodied by Gregory Peck's *Man in the Gray Flannel* suit in the eponymous film of 1956.

(Lehmann 470)

The suit is a costume for all occasions, fully adapted by Grant's physical genius to the many parts Thornhill must play in the film. In *North by Northwest's* many plays-within-the-play, characters are both actors and critics. Thornhill plays his roles to greater and greater acclaim as the film advances.

In attending to the Shakespearean theatricality of *North by Northwest*, we are inevitably engaged in what Erving Goffman calls "frame analysis," which concerns how meaning and performance shift with context and vice versa. Hence it comes as no surprise that James Naremore invokes (and quotes) Lev Kuleshov in discussing Grant's screen persona. Like Chaplin, Fairbanks, and Pickford, whom Kuleshov admired because their behavior was "exceptionally succinct, quickly and clearly comprehended by the viewer," Grant, in Naremore's words, "possessed a quality of efficient vivacity" that enabled him to fit his actions to "the precise needs of a given sequence" (225).

Nowhere are Grant's "Kuleshovian" properties more evident than in *Notorious*. The sustained impassivity he shows amounts to emotional ungangliness. As a "fatheaded guy full of pain," his usual lightness has a leaden core. The film puts Hitchcock's familiar trope of the spy-as-actor through its paces. As soon as they are on assignment, T.R. Devlin (Grant) and Alicia Huberman (Ingrid Bergman) are always acting – unlike Richard Hannay (Robert Donat) in *The 39 Steps* (1935) and Roger Thornhill (at least at first) – *deliberately* and for a specific audience, using silent film technique to telegraph false gaiety in long shot across a chessboard-patterned ballroom, or in a tight shot at the racetrack, so that Alex Sebastian (Claude Rains) may read it. An ability to signal theatricality without overplaying might well be added to the list of traits Hitchcock preferred in his actors.

Opposite Grant in *Notorious*, as in his other Hitchcock films, is the iconic blonde, probably the most familiar "type" Hitchcock used. The director often said that the Hitchcock blonde was the type of woman, particularly the type of Englishwoman, who combined what François Truffaut described as "a cool surface" and "an inner fire" (224). Though not English, the Ingrid Bergman character in *Spellbound* (1945) certainly qualifies as Hitchcockian in exhibiting a contrast between outer demeanor and inner desire. But although Bergman was one of Hitchcock's favorite collaborators, she is not the quintessential "graphic type" of the Hitchcock blonde. She represents, instead, one of the "resistant" blondes, those whose struggles with the transformation the director wanted to perform upon them can be read in the films as well as in biographical accounts.

Certainly the creative collaboration between Hitchcock and his actresses stands in stark contrast to most of his collaborations with male actors. From the sound test for *Blackmail* (1929), in which he asks Anny Ondra if she has "slept with men," through the violence reportedly visited upon Tippi Hedren as he sought to invent her star persona, Hitchcock "shaped" his female stars more intrusively and aggressively than he did the male ones. Like Vera Miles and Kim Novak, Bergman resisted being made over in appearance and manner and having her career hijacked. Although Bergman is "transformed" during the course of both *Spellbound* and

Notorious – moving between what Robin Wood has called the "good" and "bad," the "natural" and "unnatural" Bergmans (313–14) – she never quite conformed to what Hitchcock wanted. As Alicia in *Notorious* she is a vision in icy white, suitable to the image of the cool blonde, preparing to go to the Sebastians' dinner party. But even as the ice queen, her body language is fluid and radiates vulnerability, as when Captain Prescott (Louis Calhern) hangs the rented jewels around her neck, or when Devlin pulls her into a kiss under Alex's jealous eyes. Bergman exudes malleability onscreen, even when she briefly plays the role of a spectacle-wearing scientist in *Spellbound*, but she is also, as Wood notes, "defiant" and not entirely within the norms of femininity (too tall, too strong, too athletic). Offscreen, Bergman was not willing to be manufactured in accordance with the desiring machine that was Hitchcock, and left him for her spell of notoriety with Roberto Rossellini.

Among the actresses who underwent the Hitchcock transformation without evident trauma and seem to have enjoyed mutual respect in their relationships with the director, Grace Kelly occupies a privileged place. Kelly had a few important roles before she began working for Hitchcock, notably in *High Noon* (Fred Zinnemann, 1952) and *Mogambo* (John Ford, 1953), both of which depicted her character as a reserved woman who is nevertheless passionately in love. Kelly's patrician accent and her ability to move from subdued to exquisite in appearance are qualities fully appreciated and finely honed in her Hitchcock films. Her "graphic impact" is powerful, linked both to her beauty and to her impeccable carriage. In *Dial M for Murder* (1954), Hitchcock's first film with Kelly, her Margot Wendice is independently wealthy and apparently desires the full-time care of her husband, Tony (Ray Milland). Both of these facts contribute to Tony's murderous hatred of his wife, who in her loneliness had turned to a lover, Mark Halliday (Robert Cummings).

That both dependency and independence in women inspire hatred – not only in this film but in *Strangers on a Train* (1951), *Rear Window* (1954), and numerous other Hitchcock movies – places the woman in a double bind from which she often is unable to extricate herself. For Kelly's characters, the double bind always involves a latent hostility to the very graphic qualities Hitchcock prizes in the actress. As Tania Modleski has pointed out, Kelly's "perfection" in *Rear Window*, as in *Dial M for Murder* and *To Catch a Thief* (1955), is in itself enough to visit male anger upon her (76).

In *Rear Window*, Kelly's Lisa Fremont develops her ability to "act," in both senses of the word, which is crucial both to plot and to subtext. Lisa's challenge is to demonstrate that her iconic beauty can coexist with brilliant acting abilities (her persuasive pleading with Thorwald and explanations to the police, shown in broad gestures readable across the courtyard) and with the derring-do that L.B. Jefferies (James Stewart) requires in a partner.[2] Lisa is a double threat, her athletic limbs unhampered by the couture clothes she is wearing, much as Bergman's athleticism troubled the femininity of her sometimes languid acting in her films with Hitchcock.

Margot's perfect beauty is on display early in *Dial M for Murder*, whose events will render her by the last scene exquisitely drab. She makes an appearance early in the film in a closely fitted red gown with long, peek-a-boo lace sleeves. This is the film's only costume designed specifically for Kelly (by Moss Mabry) – as for Janet Leigh in *Psycho* (1960), the rest are off the rack. In this scene Margot realizes fully the visual power first wielded by another Hitchcock model, Daisy (June Tripp) in *The Lodger* (1926). While Daisy's diegetic profession is modeling, Margot is without profession – but is played by an accomplished fashion model whose profession deploys an obvious theatricality that often destabilizes conventional gender roles (Butte 115). What's extraordinary about Kelly in *Dial M for Murder* is precisely her ability to model without modeling, achieving, like Cary Grant, perfect photogeneity through posture and line. Milland as her husband perfectly matches Kelly's patrician quality, playing Hitchcock's typically smooth villain, reminiscent of Brandon (John Dall) in *Rope* (1948) or Vandamm (James Mason) in *North by Northwest*, but also reeking faintly of the sleazy *arrivisme* of Jack Favell (George Sanders) in *Rebecca*. Kelly's star image of vulnerability and toughness (*High Noon*'s Quaker capable of killing a man) reaches its apogee in the scene where she stabs Swann – future Bond villain Anthony Dawson – in self-defense.

In *To Catch a Thief*, jewels work metonymically to reinforce Kelly's status as a fetish object. Frances Stevens's chastity is at first figured by the fact that she does not wear jewelry, but this chastity is belied by the passionate kiss she initiates with near-stranger Grant in her first sequence in the film. Kelly's posing is much more static in this film than in her previous films with Hitchcock, the full force of her potential as a fiery jewelry model saved for the costume-ball climax of the film. Jewelry tells a sadder tale in *Vertigo* (1958). Here Madeleine Elster (Kim Novak) is the icy blonde, distant to the point of pathology, whose passion, when finally fully revealed, is generated by the brunette Judy Barton (also played by Novak) who lies beneath the construct called "Madeleine." Significantly, jewelry plays a crucial role in the deception of Scottie (Elster tells him that the jewelry Madeleine wears once belonged to Carlotta Valdes, the mad great-grandmother who ostensibly "possesses" her) and also in his disillusionment (when Judy asks Scottie to help her put on the necklace she had, for love of Scottie, sentimentally retained).

Kim Novak was a top box office star when Harry Cohn loaned her out to Hitchcock to make *Vertigo*. She was already ill at ease in her sex kitten roles, and this malaise was a part of the star image she projected, exemplified by her role in Joshua Logan's *Picnic* (1956), where her character suffers under the lecherous scrutiny of the townspeople. Virginia Wright Wexman has described in penetrating detail the machinations of the studio system in the creation of Novak as star, with its obvious parallels to her role as Judy, a young woman "transformed into a celestial beauty by a controlling man." Though Cohn "arranged to have her constantly watched, forced her to live in her studio dressing room and eat only food prepared by the chef, and called her 'the fat Polack,'" Novak did assert a modicum of independence by such gestures as "keep[ing] her surname despite its ethnic overtones" (80).

Wexman is right to question the auteurist perspective that would place Hitchcock as the singular power controlling performances in the films. Hitchcock's casting of his films was constrained by the systems in which he worked, and, further, he was always part of a team (whose most important member was Alma Reville) that weighed in on casting decisions. But Hitchcock's contribution to the cultivation of the star was certainly as important as Cohn's – and the film would be less interesting if it did not resonate with Hitchcock's often obsessive efforts to mold his performers.

Novak's two characters in *Vertigo* are convincingly crafted. They move differently, wear clothes differently (Judy is braless, for example, whereas Madeleine seems to be wearing a "cantilever" bra in her near-drowning scene), speak and smile differently, and are, of course, filmed differently. In constructing her as an ideal, Hitchcock sought a mysterious stillness in Madeleine's expressions and gestures, which stands in contrast to the vivid expressiveness of the ill-fated Midge (Barbara Bel Geddes) and Judy. Indeed, Novak's attempts to discuss her character's "inner motivation," according to Patrick McGilligan, were met "with a stone face." Hitchcock also told Novak that she was too communicative: "If you put in a lot of redundant expressions on your face, it's like taking a sheet of paper and scribbling all over it. ... Much easier to read if the piece of paper is blank" (554–55).

Some of the most powerful scenes in *Vertigo* do involve Novak's "blankness" of expression – and these moments hold clues to the nature of Hitchcock's subversiveness in constructing character through acting, as I will discuss below. Like those of Grant in *Suspicion*, Novak's "blank" expressions are more accurately described as minimalistic. But what lies beneath these impassive looks is more complex than Johnnie's (or Maxim's) potential murderousness. Novak's trancelike state among the sequoias, for example, speaks of the invasion of the present by the past, of Madeleine as an immutable object of desire. So too do those moments when Novak (as Madeleine) poses in profile for Scottie's benefit (or detriment). Even Judy, who is much more animated, sometimes conveys emotion through a Kuleshovian blankness, as in the controversial scene where the flashback conveys her recollections while Judy looks with understated distress toward the camera.

James Stewart, like Grant, brought a pantomime's repertory of gesture and facial expression to Hitchcock's films, thrown especially into relief by Hitchcock's careful use of "the big head" and the body's silhouette. Even Stewart's "impassive" looks are much more readable than those of some of Hitchcock's other actors, and he often grimaces or twists his face in a way that Grant or Farley Granger seldom do. Stewart said of his own work in films that he didn't "act," he "reacted." His openness as an actor contributes to this reactive quality, especially useful to Hitchcock in *Rear Window*. In her work on the "male gaze," Laura Mulvey treats the film as something of a blueprint for male visual aggression. Jefferies, after all, names his female courtyard neighbors after their salient body parts and wields an absurdly phallic camera lens with which to do his most penetrating looking. But as Modleski and others have noted, the passivity and suffering of Jefferies are just as important to the film as his aggressively masculine gaze.

In *Rear Window*, as Modleski astutely observes (72), Jefferies more closely resembles the invalid Mrs. Thorwald than her murderous husband: he lies helplessly in his pajamas as a member of the opposite sex plots against him. His features register fear, amusement, irony, and desire – all in *reaction* to what he is seeing. Stewart's peculiar aptness for embracing the polarities of male behavior – aggression and masochistic suffering – both renders him the most memorable consumer and victim of blondes in Hitchcock's films and makes him a threatening figure within the order of patriarchy. Stewart's emotive face and the lines of Kelly's elegantly clad body – as well as the acidic matronliness of Thelma Ritter – are the real stars of the film.

In *Vertigo*, his fourth film with Hitchcock, Stewart has become a super-sensitive instrument. McGilligan notes that Stewart was a "full business and creative partner on *Vertigo*, as on all his films with Hitchcock" (546). Perhaps this sense of control contributed to Stewart's ability to take acting risks in *Vertigo*, a film that "would elicit Stewart's darkest high-wire act of vulnerability, passion, and rage" (554).

Dennis Bingham, in *Acting Male*, notes that the boyish prewar Stewart, "with his gentle manner and unathletic body" (28), had an open, receptive look, the ability to faint gracefully, and a rising hysteria in his voice when frustrated, all of which contributed to the quality that critics have often described as "feminine." Stewart's postwar films, especially those with Anthony Mann, retooled the star's image, focusing on his whip-lean body and his expertise with subtle facial expressions, including the ability to project a jarring grimness with a mask-like and sometimes contorted face.

Despite Stewart's gender ambiguity, Bingham dismisses *Rope* as a miscasting of the actor. Arthur Laurents, who wrote the script and was having an affair with one of the film's stars, Farley Granger, at the time of shooting, wondered if Stewart even understood the homosexual overtones of the film (Granger would have preferred James Mason in the part). It is curious that Hitchcock explored the fluid nature of the actor's gender identity in the films where Stewart – who seems, according to the accounts I've read, to have been heterosexual – is for plot purposes a heterosexual bachelor. His character's verbal aggression toward his two former students in *Rope* does have a dangerously homosexual edge to it – but Stewart "contains" the danger by turning to one of his familiar acting personae: the blustering, indignant representative of true morality, later caricatured in John Ford's *The Man Who Shot Liberty Valance* (1962).

It is rather counterintuitive that such play with gender ambiguity is less well explored with Grant, who was widely rumored to have been bisexual and who certainly toyed with "coming out" in some of the films he made with Howard Hawks (e.g., the famous "Because I just went gay all of a sudden!" in *Bringing up Baby* [1938], the cross-dressing in *I Was a Male War Bride* [1949]). In his autobiography Laurents states in no uncertain terms that both Grant and Montgomery Clift were approached to play homosexual characters in *Rope* – and in Laurents's opinion both refused because they were afraid that the film would result in outing them as gay or bisexual themselves (131). I'll venture to say that Hitchcock entertained the idea that *Rope* should be a "coming out" film for Grant – that he wished to explore Grant's physiognomy and bodily movements in a queer context, as he would with Perkins in *Psycho*. *Rope* with Grant cast as a gay character would comprise a kind of missing link in Hitchcock's films. Instead, despite (or because of) his physical beauty, and the fact that his star image was certainly open to readings of his persona as "feminine," the trajectories Grant's characters followed in the 1950s films were adamantly heterosexual/Oedipal (Bellour 77ff.).

As in *Rear Window*, if not in *Rope*, Stewart's performance in *Vertigo* projects gender ambiguity played to its extreme. In his development of this contradictory character, Stewart alternates between sustained affect and scenes where that affect shifts wildly, between minimalist expression and the agonized grimaces refined over the course of a career. In the early scene in Midge's apartment, for example, Scottie strikes a callow, relaxed, and playful attitude until he tests his phobia by climbing onto a stepladder. The scene ends with his spectacular collapse onto Midge as he falls from the ladder under the spell of another "vertigo shot." Any masculine superciliousness is wiped from his expression.

The scene in Gavin Elster's office, when Scottie is recruited to tail Madeleine, has multiple layers of theatricality. Elster (Tom Helmore) is not only offering a master class in acting (as Vandamm says of Thornhill in *North by Northwest*, though in this case Elster is "really" acting) but is simultaneously, *sotto voce*, interrogating Scottie ("Do you want a drink now?") to determine his fitness as a victim. Stewart deploys, with tremendous naturalism, his "professional" demeanor in the scene, posing direct questions in an authoritative voice. He is a veteran detective suspicious of Elster's motives, but terribly lacking in perception. The straightforward professionalism with just an edge of masculine contempt that Scottie conveys during this meeting with Elster blends Stewart's postwar flintiness with the almost pathological vulnerability of some of his prewar characters.

Scottie first falls under Madeleine's spell at Ernie's restaurant in San Francisco. The restaurant's interior is shot in sumptuous colors. Novak in emerald green is set against a deep red background, her back to the camera, white skin and blonde hair glowing like the luminous glass of milk in *Suspicion*. We are deeply inside Scottie's range of knowledge via eyeline matches and point-of-view shots. As Madeleine floats by, her affect supremely understated, she pauses for a moment, allowing Scottie to take in the face and body that he later wishes to recreate. He turns his head away from Madeleine, with a stricken expression, seeming more to intuit than to see her. Madeleine, in silhouette, turns away from Scottie in a kind of graphic match or false continuity shot, their eyes never meeting. It's as if the turning of their heads, though differently motivated (Madeleine is looking toward Gavin Elster), is one and the same motion, deriving from a deeply emotional source.

Neill Potts reads this scene as an example of the way Hitchcock uses space, point of view, and performance to signal to the audience the existence and concerns of the characters' minds. In that moment in the scene where Scottie and Madeleine seem to see one another without looking, Potts finds a kind of "stretching" of the point-of-view shot: "Despite the supposed break from depicting his optical POV, the camera captures a key image in that part of the scene which Scottie later recalls in his mind" (94). This technique, in combination with the film's performances, renders its work on identification and point of view complex, even confounding.

The film continues with what are often silent takes in which Scottie maintains a relatively unchanging expression, as when he pursues Madeleine in his car, brow wrinkled, lips slightly pursed, thinking almost audibly and occasionally interjecting slight gestures of frustration. In a brilliant scene in *Psycho*, Janet Leigh also has an internal dialogue while driving, but the film resorts to voiceover to express those thoughts. The voiceover is appropriate and inspired, but also throws into relief Stewart's acting abilities – his way of conveying so much without words.

Scottie undergoes a metamorphosis during the course of the film. From the close-lipped detective he becomes a pleading suitor, leaning earnestly toward Madeleine, or exhorting her in his commonsensical Jimmy Stewart tones in an attempt to dispel her psychological troubles. As he attempts to follow Madeleine up the bell tower stairs and witnesses her fall, he again resorts to a gesture theatrically indicating terror: the back of his hand brought up to his face as his eyes bulge with horror and sweat pours from his face (another familiar Stewart acting tic). Scottie also sustains his expression when Midge visits him in the hospital and, suffering from melancholia, he vaguely follows her voice, never quite knowing that she is there.

The blankness or unreadability of Madeleine's face has often been interpreted as an index of her absorption in her fictional ancestor, Carlotta Valdes. Modleski points to the way that *Vertigo* also positions Scottie as deeply absorbed in Carlotta, to the extent that her madness overwhelms him, leaving him catatonic. For Modleski, Scottie's identification with the sad Carlotta, the mad Carlotta, through the agency of Madeleine, reminds him (his character) of his own bisexual nature – insofar as Madeleine's supposed absorption in and by Carlotta represents women's bisexual attachments to their mothers (51). To return to an earlier moment in this essay, it may be no coincidence that Lil Mainwaring (Baker) may be experiencing a bout of bisexual jealousy when she delivers her studiously blank expression, so carefully shaped by Hitchcock (see Knapp 302 and 306). While *Strangers on a Train*'s Bruno (Robert Walker in the performance of a lifetime) expertly rolls his eyes and even faints in the service of his performance of homosexuality, Guy (Farley Granger) keeps his own expressions under control – pushing away the current of homosexual attraction to Bruno that moves like a riptide under the film.[3] Interestingly, another exemplar of Hitchcock's work with the silhouette creates a kind of "stain" in the narrative, as Slavoj Žižek might say (66), a moment when Guy's sexual confusion and sense of guilt come to the surface. Guy is talking blithely of his future with one of the police agents who have been casually keeping tabs on him since the murder of his wife. Suddenly, Bruno's distinctive outline surges up in long shot on the steps of the Jefferson Memorial, only slightly inflecting Guy's facial expression as he encounters the return of the repressed. In this case, a long shot has the impact of a close-up.

The last image in *Vertigo* is a capstone of Hitchcock's work with the silhouette, and anticipates the much more Gothic work with shadows in *Psycho*. Scottie leans forward from the bell tower's ledge, his outline taking on the familiar shape of James Stewart, actor, performing despair. His body outlined in black appears elsewhere in the film, notably in the dream sequence, and figures prominently on the posters advertising *Vertigo*. It is with a certain wistfulness that one looks back at the exhausted junior senator in *Mr. Smith Goes to Washington* (1939), when Smith strikes an identical pose, arms slightly extended, hands limp, legs apart, head bowed: an icon of defeat tempered only by Frank Capra's problematic optimism.

Like *Vertigo*, *Psycho* features an actor whose early film career was built around an image of wholesomeness and mild sex appeal. Anthony Perkins was a bobby-soxer idol and minor singing sensation in the late 1950s. Trained as a stage actor in summer stock and college theatricals, Perkins broke into film with the underwhelming Spencer Tracy vehicle *The Actress* (George Cukor, 1953). For his subsequent 1954 appearance on Broadway, replacing John Kerr in Elia Kazan's production of *Tea and Sympathy*, Perkins was coached by Karl Malden in the tenets of Method acting. With its focus on repressed homosexuality, the play echoed some aspects of Perkins's life and anticipated – albeit in rather different terms – his role as sexually confused young man in *Psycho*. Like Stewart's, Perkins's star persona projected an endearing awkwardness, that of an all-American boy who has not yet adjusted to his adult body. The deepest pleasure of *Psycho* results from twisting that face toward monstrosity.

The character Norman Bates was tailored to fit the Perkins persona, albeit weirdly. Once MCA quietly secured screen rights to Robert Bloch's horror novel without mention of Hitchcock, the director worked first with writer James Cavanaugh and then with Joseph Stefano, who had never before written a screenplay. (Trading horses, or writers, in midstream was a typical Hitchcock modus operandi.) Stefano, who received sole credit for the screenplay, found the project fascinating, but felt he couldn't create an effective protagonist from the fat, middle-aged character described in Bloch's novel. When Hitchcock mentioned that he was thinking of casting Perkins as the lead, Stefano immediately envisioned a character with the warmth and sensitivity, as well as the underlying instability, that Perkins had already brought to his roles (Rebello 39). Perkins's strong rapport with Hitchcock, and the director's consequent willingness to take his suggestions, are evidence that Hitchcock meant what he said – that he didn't care how actors got where they needed to be, as long as they could achieve the look he wanted. Many of Perkins's ideas for Norman Bates's character were integrated into the script, most famously the tic of eating candy corn, which serves a number of narrative functions. Because of this unusual synchronicity among the creative forces at work in *Psycho*, the film's portrait of Norman Bates has become an eerie emblem stamped upon the consciousness of post-1960 filmgoers. Seldom has a film redrawn the landmarks of a human face as drastically as *Psycho* did Perkins's. The stark simplicity of the film's lighting and the character's facial expressions boil down to their essence earlier depictions of Hitchcock's killers. Thus, the baroque shadows on the face of Crewe (Cyril Ritchard) in *Blackmail* as he contemplates raping Alice (Anny Ondra) have become a universe of chiaroscuro lighting whose slight shifts reveal new depths of Norman's mind. It is now impossible to look at pre-1960 images of Perkins as a young romantic lead without seeing the sinister potential of his closely set eyes and dark brows, which tend toward meeting in the center of his forehead.

Each viewing of *Psycho* reveals new subtleties in Perkins's changing physiognomy, making the film as much a sculptural as a cinematic project. In the parlor scene, for example, Norman does not move from his chair, but minor changes in his position and in the angle of the camera hint at his unstable identity. While the shots of Leigh remain relatively fixed, her acting controlled and minimalistic in a way that offers an ironic contrast with the deformity of her famously screaming face in the shower, shots of Perkins vary from a straight-on to a low angle, emphasizing his working Adam's apple, his earnestness, and his resemblance to the stuffed birds of prey hovering over him. The camera moves to a close-up as Norman leans forward in his chair to deliver a speech that seems to derive from Mother's consciousness. Stefano's script includes the suggestions for the actors' movements:

NORMAN
(High fury now)
Well? You meant well? People always mean well, they cluck their thick tongues and shake their heads and suggest so very delicately that …
The fury suddenly dies, abruptly and completely, and he sinks back into his chair. There is a brief silence.
Mary watches the troubled man, is almost physically pained by his anguish.
("Screenplays for You")

Pin lights emphasize the darkness of Perkins's eyes during this speech. But when he leans back and relaxes, his smile seems effortless and wipes away the moment of savagery. One of the most extraordinary instances in which light and darkness work to make visible Norman's internal life occurs when the murderer is sinking Arbogast's car into the swamp. Hearing the offscreen voice of Sam (John Gavin), he turns his head toward the camera, his face briefly opening up to show what lies beneath. As in the parlor scene, Norman is framed in a full shot, emphasizing his angular body, with its swift, twitchy movements, which sometimes border on gay stereotypes. But these are not the only stereotypes he invokes. The moment when he stands in the doorway of the bathroom in Cabin 1, contemplating the bloody crime scene, Norman hunches his already high shoulders, projecting an apparently contradictory pose: the stiff stoicism of the couple depicted in Grant Wood's painting *American Gothic*. Hitchcock's use of the silhouette and angle is so refined in this film that he can make obvious effects seem subtle, as when Norman stands in darkness at the top of the stairs leading up to the old house, a figure still recognizable almost fifty years after the film was made – another "long-shot close-up."

The end of *Psycho* works in counterpoint to the remarkable expressiveness of Perkins's face during the rest of the film. As "Mother" he deliberately creates an impassive and unreadable face, sitting in stillness like the corpse s/he has become. The only movement here is the dissolve to a grinning skull and another that takes us back into the swamp of Norman's sexual confusion, violence, and necrophilia.

The apotheosis of Hitchcock's work with the blonde revolves around the creation of Tippi Hedren as a star. Hedren was "discovered" by one or both Hitchcocks (accounts vary), who saw her in a television commercial in which she smiled appreciatively at a boy's wolf whistle – a gesture Hitchcock liked. With her broad forehead and high hairline (not unlike those of women in medieval portraits), very light blonde hair, large eyes with curled eyelashes, long legs, classical nose, and refined manner, Hedren was made-to-order Hitchcock heroine. Indeed, the "recognizability" factor in her films with Hitchcock resided not in her own celebrity but in the fact that she was a new "Hitchcock blonde."

Another former model, Hedren is poised, restrained, aloof. Her aura is not only cool but brittle. Despite the scenes of soul-baring enacted by her characters in *The Birds* (1963) and *Marnie*, Hedren comes across as all surface. The director went through his usual routine of restyling Hedren's hair and wardrobe, sending her masses of flowers, and lunching with her daily, as he had with many of his actresses. He coached Hedren extensively, especially on *Marnie*, in which he went through every scene with her, as she recalled, "feeling by feeling, reaction by reaction" (McGilligan 643). But this one-sided relationship with his leading lady seems to have been much more intense than in Hitchcock's earlier courtships of stars. During the filming of *Marnie*, a pet project of Hitchcock's for which he had tried unsuccessfully to bring Grace Kelly out of retirement, the director "watched closely over her scene, hovered and stared, adopting the same inhibiting attitude toward her that Mark Rutland [Sean Connery] assumes toward Marnie in the film" (McGilligan 645). For *The Birds*, both on film and on the set, Hitchcock amped up the violence wrought upon the blonde, to the point of literal torture. And when Hedren's flinty surface is cracked, out comes the piercing timbre of a frightened child, a contrast that Hitchcock played up in both of his films with the actress. Her performances in *The Birds* and *Marnie* are effective, even astonishing, for so inexperienced a performer. She's often subtle and ironic, as when her character in *The Birds* dismisses her small emotional breakdown by saying, "Perhaps I should join the other children," an impeccably delivered line. Both films work to reduce her to a bedraggled, inarticulate child – a role Hedren also played well, but, as she later testified, to her psychological detriment (McGilligan 645).

In her two films with Hitchcock, Hedren is able to make transitions in emotion both "believable" and strangely heightened, as when she deploys Marnie's inchoate personalities. The repugnance Marnie feels at the touch of men obviously reinforces the argument that the film addresses lesbian desire. Both because and in spite of her acting talent, Hedren was the perfect blank screen for Hitchcock. The turmoil of sexual identity is contained by a green suit or discreet manners or carefully arranged hair. I think that Hitchcock got what he wanted from Hedren, if not in life, then in the film. Marnie is a skillfully crafted and memorable character, played for kitsch but also deeply serious.[4]

This essay has focused, for the most part, on Hitchcock's leading players in his American sound films. Much of its analysis, however, could readily be applied to performers in smaller roles – for example, the best-known bit player in Hitchcock's oeuvre: Hitchcock himself. The theatricality of Hitchcock's cameos, like his silhouette in the titles of *Alfred Hitchcock Presents*, points to the enacting of a role as pure artifice, in which a graphic effect, a familiar voice, and an expressively inexpressive face created an endearing and iconic brand name. Of the many interpretations of Hitchcock's cameo appearances in his films, Thomas Leitch's is most congruent with my view of how Hitchcock uses actors: "The sole purpose of such apparitions – they cannot truly be called characters, for Hitchcock makes no pretense of playing a role shaped by the requirements of the diegesis – is to be recognized" (3). Whether this recognition is of a familiar screen idol's face, or of a horror emerging from the deepest recesses of the mind, spectators continue to see themselves and their unnerving others in Hitchcock's films.

Notes

1. The transition from Grant's silhouetted back to his well-lit and handsome face is an instance of a pervasive Hitchcock device, in which the turning of a head creates suspense or terror. The opening of *Notorious* partially exploits this device – but the most shocking instance is when "Mother" is turned on her chair toward Lila Crane (Vera Miles) in *Psycho*, revealing the skull face. There is something primally threatening about a face we cannot see or read, whose intentions we cannot gauge.

2. Naremore identifies three kinds of theatricality that mark the performances in *Rear Window*: the "vividly presentational" gestures and expressions of the actors playing the "rear window" characters, shot in distant long takes that require melodramatic pantomime to signal their thoughts and behaviors; the intimate, naturalistic technique used by Stewart as he watches his neighbors; and the more conventionally theatrical business of the supporting players, including Kelly (243, 245).

3. Throughout *Hitchcock's Bi-Textuality*, Robert Samuels proposes that Hitchcock's films can be read as constructing their characters as fundamentally bisexual, hence effectively deconstructing the heterosexuality-homosexuality dyad.

4. Donald Spoto has commented extensively on the Hitchcock–Hedren relationship in *The Dark Side of Genius*. Also worth noting is Camille Paglia's precise if hagiographic description of Hedren's acting accomplishments in *The Birds* (e.g., at 27).

Works Cited

Bellour, Raymond. "Symbolic Blockage (on *North by Northwest*)." Bellour, *The Analysis of Film*. Ed. Constance Penley. Bloomington: Indiana UP, 2001. 77–192.

Bingham, Dennis. *Acting Male: Masculinities in the Films of James Stewart, Jack Nicholson, and Clint Eastwood*. New Brunswick: Rutgers UP, 1988.

Bogdanovich, Peter. *Who the Devil Made It*. New York: Knopf, 1997.

Bouzereau, Laurent, dir. and prod. "The Trouble With *Marnie*." 1999. Universal Studio Home Video. Special feature included with Marnie. Universal, 2000. DVD.

Butte, George. "Theatricality and the Comedy of the Mutual Gaze in Hitchcock's Cary Grant Films." *Hitchcock Annual* (1997–98): 114–136.

Knapp, Lucretia. "The Queer Voice in Marnie." *A Hitchcock Reader*. Ed. Marshall Deutelbaum and Leland Poague. Second ed. Chichester, UK: Wiley-Blackwell, 2009. 295–311.

Laurents, Arthur. *Original Story By: A Memoir of Broadway and Hollywood*. New York: Knopf, 2000.

Lehmann, Ulrich. "Language of the PurSuit: Cary Grant's Clothes in Alfred Hitchcock's *North by Northwest*." *Fashion Theory* 4.4 (Jan. 2000): 467–85.

Leitch, Thomas. *Find the Director and Other Hitchcock Games*. Athens: U of Georgia P, 1991.

Martin, Carey. "The Master of Suspense and the Acrobat of the Drawing Room: How the Relationship of Cary Grant and Alfred Hitchcock Shaped Their Collaboration in *Suspicion, Notorious, To Catch a Thief* and *North by Northwest*." *Film Journal* 12. N.p. April 2005. Web. 31 May 2010.

McGilligan, Patrick. *Alfred Hitchcock: A Life in Darkness and Light*. New York: HarperCollins, 2003.

Modleski, Tania. *The Women Who Knew Too Much*. Second ed. New York: Routledge, 2005.

Naremore, James. *Acting in the Cinema*. Berkeley: U of California P, 1988.

Paglia, Camille. *The Birds*. London: BFI, 1998.

Pomerance, Murray. "Two Bits for Hitch: Small Performances and Gross Structure in *The Man Who Knew Too Much* (1956)." *Hitchcock Annual* 9 (2000–01): 127–145.

Potts, Neill. "Character Interiority: Space, Point of View and Performance in Hitchcock's *Vertigo*." *Style and Meaning: Studies in the Detailed Analysis of Film*. Ed. John Gibbs and Douglas Pye. Manchester: Manchester UP, 2005. 85–97.

Rebello, Stephen. *Alfred Hitchcock and the Making of* Psycho. New York: Dembner, 1991.

Samuels, Robert. *Hitchcock's Bi-Textuality: Lacan, Feminisms, and Queer Theory*. Albany: SUNY P, 1998.

Smith, Ian. "'My Name's Not Chaplin': *North by Northwest* and the Screen Persona of Cary Grant." *Film Studies* 2 (Spring 2000): 29–43.

Spoto, Donald. *The Dark Side of Genius: The Life of Alfred Hitchcock*. Boston: Little, Brown, 1983.

Stefano, Joseph. "Psycho." Screenplay. Revised 1 December 1959. *Screenplays for You*. N.p. Web. 31 May 2010.

Tomlinson, Doug. "'They Should Be Treated Like Cattle': Hitchcock and the Question of Performance." *Hitchcock's Rereleased Films: From* Rope *to* Vertigo. Ed. Walter Raubicheck and Walter Srebnick. Detroit: Wayne State UP, 1991. 95–108.

Truffaut, François, with the collaboration of Helen G. Scott. *Hitchcock*. Rev. ed. New York: Simon and Schuster, 1984.

Wexman, Virginia Wright. "The Critic as Consumer: Film Study in the University, *Vertigo*, and the Film Canon." *Film Quarterly: Forty Years—A Selection*. Ed. Brian Henderson and Ann Martin. Berkeley: U of California P, 1999. 76–91.

Wood, Robin. *Hitchcock's Films Revisited*. Rev. ed. New York: Columbia UP, 2002.

Žižek, Slavoj. *Tarrying with the Negative: Kant, Hegel, and the Critique of Ideology*. Durham: Duke UP, 1993.

PART IV

Style

11

Aesthetic Space in Hitchcock

Brigitte Peucker

Films, Stephen Heath famously reminds us, "take place" – they establish scenographic space, and their spectator "*completes* the image as its subject" (53). Situated at the center of the perspectival system that underpins narrative film, the spectator is "placed" in relation to its images. With Hitchcock's *Suspicion* (1941) as his example, Heath notes that the portrait that anchors the film's narrative – the portrait of Cedric Hardwicke's General McLaidlaw (a speaking name if ever there was one) – establishes the scenographic space of Hitchcock's film as perspectival, the Quattrocento view. But at the fringes of this film's discourse, Heath suggests, is another kind of space. It is intimated when a look cast by a character offers a glimpse of a different visual organization. As it happens, this character is Benson (Vernon Downing), a detective, and the object of his look is astonishing, perhaps even shocking, to him. It is a still life in the Cubist manner – a copy of Pablo Picasso's *Pitcher and Bowl of Fruit* (1931) – and its notion of space is in marked contradistinction to that of the McLaidlaw portrait.[1] If the still life's transgression against the portrait's perspectival system is a joke in this film, writes Heath, then it is a telling one. While the detective's glance at the painting is irrelevant to the film's narrative, Heath argues, it nevertheless serves "to demonstrate the rectitude of the portrait, the true painting at the centre of the scene, utterly in frame in the film's action" (23).

But the scene in question takes place in the home of McLaidlaw's daughter, Lina (Joan Fontaine), and her husband, Johnnie Aysgarth (Cary Grant), and the general's portrait is *not* at its center, even figuratively. It doesn't grace the mantle, as it had in the McLaidlaw residence: indeed, it's on the floor, propped up against a wall, askew, dethroned. A modern landscape painting hangs over the Aysgarth fireplace in its stead, while the copy of the Picasso hangs in the foyer. True, this landscape doesn't

A Companion to Alfred Hitchcock, First Edition. Edited by Thomas Leitch and Leland Poague.
© 2011 Thomas Leitch and Leland Poague. Published 2011 by Blackwell Publishing Ltd.

flaunt the rules of perspective, but neither is McLaidlaw's paternal gaze centrally positioned in this space. After the detectives leave, Lina returns to address her father's portrait, denying that anything untoward has happened. But at this moment, two dark lines of shadow – at a diagonal – are visible across the paternal portrait, undermining its unity, its coherence.

My question, therefore, is this: What if the joke here were of another kind – one whose point were not to confirm the "proper" rendering of the McLaidlaw portrait but rather to affirm the *tear* that the Picasso-esque still life promotes in the sceno-graphic space of classical cinema? What if the multiple perspectives that coexist in Cubist space – the painting's rupture of the film's aesthetic illusion, in other words – were the point instead? Or what if the spectator's (here Benson's) puzzlement at a painting that forecloses continuity between his diegetic world and the work of art were the issue? To put it differently: When in their different ways *Rear Window* (1954) and *Vertigo* (1958) figure transactions between a spectator and the world of art, what is at stake? Why is it that in Hitchcock's *Torn Curtain* (1966) pivotal scenes take place in aesthetic spaces – in an art museum and in a theater in which a ballet is being performed? How are artifice and illusion related to diegetic reality? *Murder!* (1930) traps the villain when the "techniques of art" are brought to bear upon life; in *Stage Fright* (1950) a theater curtain opens onto the "real" city of London, while the theater's safety curtain kills the murderer at the film's end. Scenes of nature in Hitchcock's films are often heavily aestheticized, as even a passing glance at *North by Northwest* (1959) makes clear. Why is the painted backdrop of the harbor scene in *Marnie* (1964) allowed to "show"? When aesthetic space so frequently spills over into the real world of the characters – and even into the space of the audience – is something other than modernist self-reflexivity at play? These are some of the questions this essay takes up. In undertaking to elaborate on the confusion of Benson and other Hitchcock characters, it hopes to dispel some measure of our own.

Hitchcock's interest in the theater is well documented and needs no reiteration here. Many of his films take plays as their source, and performance spaces punctuate his films from the beginning. The chorus girls of *The Lodger* (1926) are likely targets for a murderer whose penchant is for "golden curls," and when its blonde heroine Daisy (June Tripp) displays herself as a model in a fashion salon, we sense that we should fear for her life as well. It's been quipped that in Hitchcock the theater is the "perfect place to die" (Zupančič 73), and in fact death and the theater often go hand in hand. The reason for this isn't anti-theatrical sentiment, I suggest, but rather a profound enjoyment of the complexity introduced by juxtaposing the registers of theater and diegetic reality, coupled with the shock of the real that disrupts illusion as only death can. The spatial and ontological manipulation to which Hitchcock subjects the spectator is one source of our pleasure in viewing his films.

Call it spectatorial manipulation, or call it aesthetic play: in *Murder!* the theater curtain goes up, it would seem, on the actress Diana Baring (Norah Baring), but then a cut reveals that she is not on stage but in jail, hearing in voiceover (in memory, we wonder?) what seems to be a theatrical dialogue on stage – until a second cut reveals in its turn that the conversation is taking place "in the real" of the narrative, between her stage manager and a policeman. Early on in the film, then, classical continuity editing is disrupted in order to introduce the idea of continuity between life and art. Indeed, this is the metaphor that shapes the narrative of this film. If the playwright protagonist Sir John Menier (Herbert Marshall) habitually applies "the technique of life to the problems of my art," as he puts it, he determines to do the opposite as he seeks to exonerate Baring from the crime of murder. An interior monologue over images of Sir John shaving indicates that the interest he has in clearing Baring's name is partly libidinal – "very attractive, I thought." Deliberately invoking *Hamlet*, Act III, scene ii, Sir John employs the technique of the play-within-a-play to bring the real murderer to light, inviting the villain to make suggestions about how "the plot" of Sir John's play should go.

Reinforcing the fluidity with which *Murder!* treats the binaries of art and life, theater and film, the film uses references to hybridity to figure its ontological complexity. The real murderer, Handel Fane (Esme Percy), is called a "half-caste," a phrase that suggests a mixed-race heritage, though he will turn out to have been a transvestite actor instead. Further, Fane is in costume at the moment of committing the murder for which Diana Baring is convicted, and it's typical of Hitchcock's dark humor that Fane masquerades as a policeman. The murderer as actor in the role of policeman calls to mind the voiceover dialogue between stage manager and policeman near the beginning of the film, the voiceover heard by Baring, a dialogue that oscillates between fictive and real in the spectator's understanding. The confusion of categories that the actor/policeman-as-murderer generates contributes to our uncertainty about the status of persons and events. Toward the end of the film, the murderer's suicide will take place as part of another performance, a circus act in which he's dressed as a diva in feathers. Fane's death is the culmination of his performance, but his costume of feathers turns the tragedy into ugly farce, and the real is reinstalled within performance as Fane commits suicide. In a macabre moment Sir John tells Baring to reserve her real tears over Fane's death for Sir John's new play, where they will be "useful." In the film's final scene Sir John and Diana Baring kiss – and then a theater curtain falls. If the film's spectator is briefly led to believe that the witnessed kiss occurs in the film's diegetic reality, this illusion is quickly dispelled. Instead, this scene takes place on stage as part of a performance of Sir John's new play – based on the "real-life" story of Baring. But perhaps the play will in fact foreshadow life's events. Although applying the "techniques of art" to life – entrapping the murderer by way of the play – results in a death that resolves some ambiguities, it doesn't fix the film's oscillation between the registers of art and diegetic reality. Aesthetic play is privileged. The assumption is that spectators will relish uncertainty to the end.

Ontological complexity in Hitchcock's films is often tied to the theater. We see this emphatically in *Stage Fright*, a film premised upon a "lying image" (Casetti 106). At issue in this film is more than "the superimposition of appearance and reality common to all representation," Francesco Casetti writes (107); rather, it is the fact that the flashback shortly after the film opens – narrated by the murderer, as it turns out – is a lie. Hence "the images," Casetti concludes, "are false" (110). What makes them particularly deceitful and trying for the spectator is that Jonathan Cooper (Richard Todd) – narrator, liar, and murderer – occupies the same position as the film's Hitchcockian enunciator insofar as the film images that illustrate the liar's tale appear to be authorially sanctioned images, unmarked, no different from those that illustrate the narrative as a whole. The narrator, who "should have been the mirror and conscience of representation" (Casetti 110), proves to be in every way unreliable. I certainly agree. This is what many readers of Agatha Christie's *The Murder of Roger Ackroyd* – published in 1926, and no doubt known to Hitchcock – found so objectionable about Christie's novel. When its narrator turns out to be the killer, a central convention of the detective genre is undermined. What is at stake is the *grounding* of representation. If in *Suspicion* it's the perspectival system that is undermined from within by a modernist work of art that has jettisoned that system, here it's the "truth" of narration that's called into question. This modernist strategy may be found in high as well as in popular culture, as André Gide's novel *The Counterfeiters* (1926) makes clear.

But Hitchcock's film doesn't open with Jonathan and his friend Eve Gill (Jane Wyman) riding in a convertible through the streets of London, with Jonathan's flashback narration illustrated in seemingly present-tense images. Rather, it opens on a theatrical safety curtain, adorned with a rococo pattern of images over which the opening credits appear. Slowly, the curtain lifts to reveal the city of London – represented not by stage scenery, but by a filmic image. Here, too, a curtain is torn – or rather lifted – to reveal a different ontological register, an effect easily created by filmic means, by back projection and editing. In *Stage Fright*'s opening, the safety curtain functions as the hypothetical fourth wall of theater, lifted to allow the spectator passage into a space figured as the "real," a non-theatrical world. The film's opening invites the spectator into the scene of its drama; it doesn't leave us in the space of the movie theater.

The camera is at pains to undermine theatrical space by displaying to our view scenes that are clearly "offstage," uncontainable by theater. But although we spectators may appear to leave the realm of the theater as we figuratively enter the filmic space of London, it is the point of the film that we decidedly do not. *Stage Fright* is rife with sequences that model the continuity of artifice and the diegetic real with one another; *Murder!*'s play-within-a-play conceit is omnipresent, if more diffuse, in this later film. There is the sequence, for instance, in which Jonathan the murderer intrudes upon a stage performance in order to speak with Eve, merging easily with actors who are rehearsing on stage, his "real drama" hidden as his face is hidden under a hat or by an embrace. When artfulness and honesty are not always reliably discernible from one another, their confusion is sometimes played to comic effect, as when Eve's mother (Sybil Thorndike) refuses to believe the truth about both Jonathan and the detective, saying, "Now you're going too far."

Eve's various efforts at role-playing are often clumsy. Those who count – her mother, even without her glasses, and the detective with whom she falls in love – never think that she is anyone other than herself, although later the detective will worry that she's deceiving him just when she is most truly herself, at the moment of their kiss. Lest an anti-theatrical impulse be imputed to moments such as these, we should note that Eve's efforts at *acting* – always on behalf of detection – are at the heart of *Stage Fright*'s ethical impulse.

In discussion with Eve, her father (Alastair Sim) speaks of the folly of "transmuting melodrama into real life," but in fact it is artifice – acting and staged scenes – that allows "the truth" to come out. If Eve's role as Doris the maid is clumsily played, it nevertheless leads to revelations. Moreover, her father's ruse of painting a doll's dress with his own blood as a spectacle for Marlene Dietrich's Charlotte leads to the actress's breakdown.[2] Dressed to represent Charlotte, the doll in a white frock with a real bloodstain brings the scene of the murder vividly to Charlotte's mind, disrupting her garden-party performance of "La vie en rose." The real in the form of blood functions prominently in the display of the doll and invades Charlotte's performance by the affect that it produces. Indeed, it necessitates the act's termination.

The safety curtain – lifted at the film's opening to invite us into *Stage Fright*'s filmic world – eventually comes crashing down again at its end. The truth begins to emerge when Eve in her role as Doris engages Charlotte in an incriminating conversation broadcast in the theater via a hidden mike and loudspeakers. At the conclusion of Eve's performance, there is applause from her father, her audience in an otherwise empty theater. But the impression that order has been reinstated is only temporary. Shortly thereafter, we find Eve sequestered with Jonathan among theatrical props. Seated next to a deranged murderer in a painted cardboard coach with rococo designs, Eve discovers that she's in genuine danger. In what will be her most convincing performance, she gently catches the hands that are about to strangle her and tells Jonathan that she will help him to escape. By means of Eve's convincing lie, she traps Jonathan on the proscenium stage, where he's quickly surrounded. When someone yells, "Drop the iron curtain and cut him off," we understand that Jonathan will be both cut off and cut up. The safety curtain lives up to its name for the film's heroine, but for Jonathan, prevaricating narrator and murderer, it's the instrument of poetic justice. At the heart of representation, truth comes in the form of death.

If the film's play with reality and illusion is overt in sequences such as those described above, it could be argued that in retrospect they make the deceptive flashback narration of its opening all the more convincing. For Casetti, the film's duplicity – its manner of imaging a lie – is counteracted by Eve's function as the film's internal spectator, who sees and listens attentively, just as the audience does, and guides us to the truth. But Eve arrives at the truth not by being a spectator but by acting. Or call it lying. At the film's end she clearly has no intention of helping Jonathan escape, and the distinction between performance and lie is deliberately blurred.[3] And while Jonathan, the lying narrator, proves to be a criminal, Hitchcock as enunciator implicates himself in the deception that is fictioning, as well. After repeated viewings, I'm still convinced that the film has both a "fake" Hitchcock cameo and a real one. The Hitchcock impersonator (Robert Adair) of the faked cameo appears in the pub scene. Interestingly, the pub's doors are etched glass with a rococo-style pattern similar to those that adorn both the theater's safety curtain and the interior doors of Charlotte's house. Their artifice, in other words, implicates the pub as one of the spaces that is both aesthetic and deceptive. Small wonder, then, that this is the place where the Hitchcock look-alike diverts our attention. The real Hitchcock is in evidence later, briefly, as a passerby on a city street. The film's deliberately stagy doubling of the author is yet another play on truth and illusion, but it also sets off a bad fake from a "real" author. Whether self-consciousness in representation has a redemptive function is another matter, of course, but its presence confirms the central importance that the spectator's aesthetic experience holds for Hitchcock.

Death in Hitchcock's films often occurs on stage, but it takes place in museum spaces too, as when the villain of *Blackmail* (1929) falls through the glass cupola of the British Museum. Presenting in another register the imbrication of art and death that informs the earlier portion of the film's narrative, the introduction of this space is not arbitrary. A shot of the building's neoclassical façade at a slight angle is followed by one of Tracy (Donald Calthrop) ascending the stairs of the imposing structure. A cut to the space of the colonnade has no function other than to stress the columns' cold, imposing symmetry. With the police in hot pursuit, the blackmailer enters a hall whose space is centered on a large curtained portal in the background, in what one could call deep space. The spectator's attention is drawn to the centrally positioned door where two human figures gesticulate while the blackmailer makes his way to the middle of the hall at an angle. He then enters the Egyptian galleries, where a subsequent shot reveals receding doors – the perspectival corridor – leading from one display space to another. In these spaces the dead body and the work of art are coterminous, death and preservation go hand in hand, and time is embalmed.

Evading the police, the blackmailer ducks behind a glass case. A medium close-up reveals him in a complex, multi-layered composition: he stands in front of the glass case, which reflects his image over the objects on display there, while – on the right side of the display-glass – we see the reflection of running policemen. Already identified with the display, in some sense already a relic, the blackmailer is figuratively contained in the space of art. His only escape is the passage through the perspectival corridor – which offers no escape at all. There follows the shot that features the most memorable image of the film: the blackmailer shimmying down a rope at the left hand side of the film frame, alongside an Egyptian colossus. A subsequent cut to the reading room, shot from above, reveals the space as a pattern of concentric circles of tables from which other tables radiate outward. The blackmailer chooses not to enter its geometric layout and heads instead for the museum roof.

Focusing on the spatial arrangement of this museum sequence, we notice an alternation between spaces shot frontally, stressing central perspective (spaces of pursuit) and those in which the pursued traverses a space obliquely, at an angle, temporarily evading the symmetrical arrangement of the space. But the black-mailer meets his death when he falls through the glass dome and into the rotunda that houses the reading room. In other words, he arrives at the center of the British Museum after all: he is contained by its symmetries in a theatrical moment not presented to the spectator's view.

Unlike the blackmailer, Michael Armstrong (Paul Newman) escapes pursuit by an East German security agent in *Torn Curtain* when he makes a detour through Berlin's Old National Gallery, which we first see as a photograph in a tourist bro-chure. A shot of the photo is followed immediately by a shot of the same image as a full-size building "in the real." But this image is more painting than photograph; as Steven Jacobs tells us, only the doorway and front pillars were constructions (58). The impossibility of shooting in East Germany during the Cold War gave Hitchcock free rein to shoot the film in the controlled atmosphere of the studio. Not surprisingly, the museum sequence is the height of artifice. *Blackmail's* con-cern with the constraint imposed by central perspective, for example, resurfaces here. Armstrong enters the museum through the center of the portico-enclosed courtyard along a walkway toward a door at the center of the neoclassical structure, his path leading directly to the vanishing point of the perspectival corridor. But the path he takes, indicated in the tourist brochure, did not exist in the courtyard of the actual building: it was added both for the film's version of the brochure and for the museum sequence.

As Frieda Grafe points out, moreover, the film's museum sequence employs matte shots alternating with shots of Armstrong walking on a painted studio floor: the paintings we see on the museum walls are paintings of paintings – not the real thing at all (5). The claustrophobia promoted by the setting is intense; the painted spaces contain the three-dimensionality of the actor's body. Hurrying through the deserted galleries, Armstrong is enclosed in the space of representation. In an overhead shot he stands on an octagonal mosaic floor pattern, halted at the center of several concentric circles from which vectors emanate – a centric pattern, as Rudolf Arnheim calls it, such as the one in which the blackmailer dies (4). In *Torn Curtain*, too, our awareness of symmetry is intensified by neoclassical architecture. Armstrong repeatedly passes through the perspectival corridor. On the stairs, shot from behind, he's a figure that sutures us into the image.

The museum is empty. While it's the setting of a chase sequence, Armstrong is the only person we see on screen. Armstrong's pursuer is reduced to the sound of his footsteps and his once-seen shadow. Several times the camera alternates an omniscient view of Armstrong with a shot of the same space again – now empty, just vacated by Armstrong – the empty shot evoking the point of view of the visu-ally absent but sonically present East German agent. (Surely this drama of vision speaks to the surveillance procedures of the German Democratic Republic, over which the invisible eye of the State presided.) Aside from Armstrong himself, the human figure is present only in the form of nineteenth-century statuary. A white marble Cupid and Psyche (both winged figures) dramatizes the subject of pursuit in an erotic register, a clue perhaps to the evasion of heterosexuality of which critics sometimes accuse Armstrong. Further, a deeply black sculpture – perhaps a Leda and the swan, perhaps a coupling even more violent – is placed aggressively in the foreground of one sequence, much of which it blocks out. A Hitchcockian blot par excellence, the sculpture paradoxically marks the entry of the real, of death, into the space of artifice. Standing in place of the invisible spy who represents the violence of the State, the sculpture denies Kant's mandate that the aesthetic object be detached from life.[4]

It's clear that the oppressiveness of central perspective here emblematizes the rigidity – not the rectitude – of the State, whose unilateral vision extends to the control of all aspects of life and art. But it is also the ideological implication of central perspective itself – as control over the visual field – that is at issue. While no Cubist paintings with multiple points of view offer escape, Armstrong and the film camera generally traverse this space obliquely, at an angle, as if in opposition to the frontality of central perspective. When Armstrong finally leaves by a simple back door (of a museum, we wonder?), he is released from its symmetrical arrangements, and we heave a sigh of relief.

In some sense it is the museum itself – a series of paintings, after all – that's the curtain that must be torn to reveal the theatrical space that is East Germany. And there's little doubt that the film's title also refers to the "tear" in scenographic space that occurs when the film figures the passage from one ontological register to another. And while it refers to the Iron Curtain as having been penetrated by an American spy, doesn't it also suggest Pliny's famous story of Zeuxis and Parrhasios, two artists engaged in a painting contest? Zeuxis was able to fool a flock of birds with his rendering of grapes, but Parrhasios, the painter who fooled the human eye, won the contest with his painting of a curtain so real that Zeuxis requested he open it in order to display his painting. And if the illusionistic space of the museum opens out into the space of a simulated, theatrical East Germany, it's no wonder that Armstrong must escape from it by way of a theatrical stage, through the simulated hellfire of a ballet performance. This is imaged on the stage of a ballet performance to Tchaikovsky's *Francesca da Rimini: Symphonic Fantasy after Dante* (1876) – a composition noted for the swirling musical chromaticism by which it suggests the flames of hell to the ear.[5]

In *North by Northwest* aesthetic spaces are also natural spaces. Mount Rushmore features the most obvious convergence of nature and art, with the presidential heads carved into its surface. Like the portrait of McLaidlaw, they are symbolic of a patriarchal order to be undermined by art and play. In *North by Northwest*, release from the perspectival system occurs in the aestheticized spaces of nature. In his analysis of this film's "scenotopes," spaces organized as a language, Fredric Jameson suggests that those most clearly imbued with "a sense of the 'aesthetic' as such" are the cornfield and the pine woods (50). For Jameson, the latter evokes a "distinctive Cézanne landscape" (60). More specifically, as I've argued elsewhere (100), in the pinewoods setting, as in Cézanne, we find an oscillation between a Cubist three-dimensionality suggested by depth of field and the flattening of space produced by an emphasis on line. (The fact that the pine forest was created on a set with trees imported from South Dakota confirms that this arrangement is intentional.) And the earlier cornfield sequence contains frames which have a nearly abstract feel, despite the presence of Cary Grant as Roger Thornhill incongruously in their midst. Here it's the lack of horizon line and the drab colors of the desiccated fields that flatten space. This is the space of death not only because nature is dried up, a maze of dried stalks and leaves, but because it's a space in which Thornhill, like Armstrong caught in the symmetries of the mosaic floor, is the target of the evil agents who control it. For in this space, too, a geometrical, perspectival space is created by the intersecting lines of two highways and a truck emerges out of its vanishing point to run over Thornhill, threatening to enter spectatorial space.

If the different types of space in *North by Northwest* create a sense of heterogeneity in this film, the aestheticizing metaphor of theater connects them all. *North by Northwest* is saturated by role-playing – whether it's on the part of foreign agents or US agents, on behalf of the bad guys or the good guys. When Thornhill dresses in the ill-fitting uniform of a Red Cap in order to escape capture at a railroad station, a shot of the station suggests that Thornhill has been eerily reproduced and the red caps dot the frame with color. In a moment of tongue-in-cheek self-reflexivity, a surprised hospital patient (Patricia Cutts) dons her glasses and seems to recognize Grant as the actor he is – as himself. Even death is theatrically feigned when Eve Kendall (Eve Marie Saint) "shoots" Thornhill in the visitor center's cafeteria in order to escape suspicions of disloyalty to her putative lover or his cause. And throughout the film, the foreign agent Vandamm (James Mason) accuses Thornhill of acting. Even an elevator ride contains a staged "scene." But the tour de force gesture toward theater lies in "George Kaplan," a character invented by the "United States Intelligence Service" whose clothes and personal effects the agency moves from hotel room to hotel room in order to simulate Kaplan's existence. When Vandamm and his henchmen take Thornhill for Kaplan, they are merely finding a body to inhabit – to play – his character.

Vandamm's accusation against Thornhill, whom he takes for Kaplan – that he is always acting – both does and doesn't miss the point. Theater as artifice and play unites the film's disparate spaces, inflecting them alike with the aura of the aesthetic. The theatrical metaphor promotes a spectator who is engaged in its pleasurable game playing. Thornhill, on the other hand, trapped in these structures, complains to the Intelligence Agency's Professor (Leo G. Carroll): "I don't like the games you play." (On the evening the games began, Thornhill missed a theater date with his mother.) Sometimes a film's games with illusion and reality expand to contain its spectator. *North by Northwest* features a number of objects that threaten to break through the theatrical fourth wall: a speeding truck, a swinging fist, a gun aimed directly into the camera and at the viewer. These moments of danger for the film's characters suture the film's audience into the action to such a degree that we may find ourselves pulling back to avoid an impending blow. Thus we briefly experience the same confusion of registers – is it art? is it life? – that so often confounds Hitchcock's characters. In moments when diegetic space spills over into the space of the movie theater, we experience the merger of ontological registers – of the figured with the real – that may be one of the central reasons that art attracts us at all.

In *Rear Window* the intrusion of filmic space into the space of the spectator is brilliantly figured. This film connects the cinematic to the theatrical when the blinds that are opened at the film's beginning reveal a series of picture windows that position James Stewart's L.B. Jefferies as the spectator of both. It is Jefferies's aestheticized experience of reality, in any case, that is at issue. Eyes trained on the narratives that unfold before him, he is separate from the space in which they occur, divided from them by a courtyard which functions as a moat. As critics have often noted, it's at the moment when Lisa Fremont (Grace Kelly) crosses over into one of them and involves herself in the murder story Jefferies believes he's been watching that she finally succeeds in capturing his interest. For Jefferies, reality in the form of Lisa enters a space that for him has been both "real" and aesthetic, a merger of the murder story genre with the New York everyday. Lisa, a participant in his life, now becomes an actor in another's When another actor in the drama across the courtyard – the murderer, in fact – crosses that courtyard and enters Jefferies's apartment through the door usually positioned behind Jefferies, it is as though the murderer were entering the film from the space of the movie theater.

At this point in the film, the (figurative) merger of aesthetic space and reality takes a frightening form. This moment complements and reverses the intrusion of diegetic reality (Lisa) into what is perceived as an aestheticized space by Jefferies – at once the space of fiction and "real life." Now *Rear Window* suggests that the murderer enters the frame from the position of the film's spectator. As spectators, then, we again experience a collapse of registers. This collapse is expressed at the level of the narrative when Jefferies falls out of his window and into the courtyard that was the scene of his aestheticized experience. Jefferies's literal fall is also the "Fall" from Paradise, since the film implies that thereafter he will now acknowledge his love for Lisa. But in a minor key this sequence figures the collapse of spectatorial space into the space of spectacle that occurs when the murderer enters from our place. Twice over the space of the movie theater figuratively collapses with the space of the screen.

But can't we see the spatial relations I have just described from another vantage point as well? Throughout the film, Jefferies has most often been found in the position of the Albertian spectator, the spectator from whose place the perspectival system is drawn. His eye has been in a position of control over space, has seen through the pane of glass – the "window on the world" the perspectival system creates – and gazed at the scene laid out for his viewing eye. When, however, a figure in that scene leaves it to appear from what for Jefferies (who so often has his back to us) is the space behind him, Jefferies must turn around to face him. Read in terms of central perspective, I would argue, this scene in *Rear Window* emblematizes the multiple perspectives that define the Picasso-style still life in *Suspicion*. By suggesting spaces of such ontological complexity, Hitchcock's film simulates Cubist spatial simultaneity and disrupts the unitary point of view of the perspectival system. In doing so, it points toward that "other" space that detective Benson of *Suspicion* regards with puzzled fascination. When Doyle (Wendell Corey), also a detective, looks with similar puzzlement at a painting in *Rear Window*, it should be noted that this too is a modernist still life.

Of course *Vertigo* is the film in which the confusion of ontological registers – between reality and illusion – most poignantly takes center stage. Indeed, it's a case study of someone for whom this confusion is nearly pathological. The James Stewart character, Scottie, is the dupe of role-playing with criminal intent, and it's his peculiar fate to fall for the character Madeleine, played by Judy (and in the real by Kim Novak). Around this "false" Madeleine a narrative is created designed to ensnare Scottie. It concerns a mysterious case of "possession" – a staged fascination with death – played out in a repetitive series of silent tableaux, each of which aestheticizes and eroticizes the Madeleine figure for Scottie. A graveyard scene, for instance, poses Madeleine in a gray suit among graveyard statuary, a sculptural figure herself. In this sequence of tableaux the museum space of the Palace of the Legion of Honor in San Francisco is of particular significance, and entrapment is again the issue. Scottie, who's been pursuing "Madeleine," discovers her seated before a portrait of the "mad Carlotta," her supposed ancestress. Within the aestheticized space of the gallery, Scottie as spectator regards the motionless figure of the seated "Madeleine." In a series of point-of-view shots, the camera traces the path of his vision as it makes connections choreographed in advance by Judy as actress and her "director," Elster (Tom Helmore), husband of the real Madeleine, who is the victim of the plot. Scottie's gaze moves back and forth between objects in the portrait and their copy in the supposed reality of the diegesis, which is actually a simulated one. This museum is also a theater.

The camera establishes connections between the bouquet of flowers held by the painted woman and those held by the "real" woman seated before her, and it acknowledges the similarity between the real and the represented whorl of hair. "Madeleine," in the meantime, stares fixedly at the portrait as though in a trance of identification. In each scenario – in Madeleine's acted one and in Scottie's – lines of force connect viewer and viewed. For Scottie, this scene rehearses the connection of a material body – Novak as Madeleine – with a painted one, once more anchoring erotic attraction in an art effect.[6] During these transactions between art and reality, "Madeleine" is seated across from the portrait, her eyes raised to encounter its painted eyes. It is a posed meeting of gazes. Scottie, on the other hand, looks at this scene from an oblique angle; his position is not the centered position of the Albertian spectator. Here Scottie's angle of vision suggests that the "off center" nature of his look, a look that collapses reality and fantasy, is that of madness. What is acted by Madeline is enacted in the diegetic real by Scottie.

Small wonder, then, that when Scottie's ex-fiancée, Midge (Barbara Bel Geddes), shows Scottie her copy of the portrait with her own face – glasses and all – replacing Carlotta's, Scottie flees in horror. This scene takes place in Midge's studio apartment, also represented as the space of art. Its walls are covered with modernist works and Midge, an illustrator, is first seen sketching a brassiere that is displayed on a wire frame attached to a corner of her drafting table, resembling a modernist mobile. The shock at the unnaturalness of Midge's portrait is experienced not only by Scottie but also by the film's spectator, for whom the incongruous conjunction of Midge's head with the body of Carlotta is also startling and uncanny. Such disjunctive, anti-illusionist effects are modernist effects. After Scottie's point-of-view scan of the portrait, he looks offscreen at Midge, shaking his head in dismay. The subsequent point-of-view reverse shot of Midge shows her seated on a coffee table at screen left, looking up at Scottie, with the Midge-as-Carlotta portrait to screen right. If Midge now resembles Madeleine on her museum bench, then Scottie is in the position of the portrait that is the object of her look. The triangulated relation of the first scene of looking, in the museum, is repeated, but with a difference.

What we the spectators see from Scottie's perspective is almost a split-screen effect, except that the line formed by the canvas bisects the film frame at a diagonal. In this second scene of looking at a woman and a portrait, now placed side by side, Scottie's look is again at a diagonal, askew. In a sense, this is how his look has been represented from the start. Before Scottie's first glance of Madeleine at Ernie's Restaurant, it's the emphatically mobile camera that reveals her sculptural neck and back. Scottie does not see her this way: craning his neck, he sees her at an angle. In this film, it isn't just the vertigo effect that distorts Scottie's vision. While the vertigo shot as visual paradigm may stand in for the duplicity around which *Vertigo*'s plot is constructed, it is Scottie's angled vision, deviating from central perspective, that sets him apart. How? As a kind of modernist, yes, but also as someone who displays a "bordering subjectivity" (Saito 208), someone who transgresses the boundary between fantasy and reality, art and life. But like the detective peering at the Picasso-like still life, he's also the means to another angle of vision, another kind of space.

Scottie doesn't fall in love with the "real" Madeleine, Elster's wife, whom we never see except as a falling corpse. He falls in love with a role played by a woman who possesses a certain face and body, no matter how she is made up or dressed, no matter what her manner. The real Judy becomes the unreal Madeleine under the direction of Elster, then returns to being the real Judy, whom Scottie feels compelled to turn into Madeleine. If the physical substratum of the image, the body of the actress, always grounds her image, conferring a sense of reality on it, this decidedly doesn't hold for the locations in which Hitchcock's films are set. Of course the city of San Francisco is recognizably the backdrop of *Vertigo*, as is London in *Blackmail* and *Frenzy* (1972), for example, or New York in the opening scenes of

North by Northwest. But since Hitchcock usually shot in the studio, he resorted repeatedly to back projections, matte shots, miniatures, and painted sets. *North by Northwest* uses a photographic image of Mies van der Rohe's Seagram building for its credit sequence, but promptly turns it into a film screen of sorts. The UN building is in evidence, as well, but an overhead view is the height of artifice and abstraction, a modernist painting. A model was used for the scene in the Frank Lloyd Wright–style cantilevered house where Vandamm and his henchmen hide out. And the presidential heads on Mount Rushmore were reconstructed in the studio, enabling the actors to scramble across their cheeks and noses in greater safety and without governmental protest. If the metaphor of the body as the material support of acting is literalized by this space, its artifice is likewise amply in evidence.[7]

The meditation on the actor's body in its relation to acting and artifice that we find in *Vertigo* is also central to *Marnie*. The film begins with a close-up on an overtly sexualized yellow purse held by a woman in a suit, shot from behind, which expands to contain her entire body as she walks along the platform of a railroad station. It is a tracking shot, the camera a stalker pursuing the woman closely, then halting its motion as she continues to move. The sequence takes place in an unreal space. The station is empty, there are two stationary trains, but there are no other people: there's no motion in the frame save the motion of the woman. It is a perspectival space, complete with receding lines and a vanishing point, and it has a nearly abstract feel. The two trains are at diagonals that would meet at the vanishing point if they could be extended far enough, and the woman's head is located just under the place where the platform's roof, shot at an angle, meets the vanishing point as well. Interestingly, the woman walks along a red line that leads directly to this point in the film frame; only in the final second of the shot does she swerve a bit to frame left and put down her suitcase. Her long black hair stands in contrast to her yellow purse; the grays and browns of the station are accentuated by the red stripe that constitutes her path into the depths of the frame. There is something unreal about the hair; the woman appears to be wearing a wig. Minutes into the film we still haven't seen her face. We will not see it until we first see long black hair in a basin, its color washing away to uncover the yellow beneath. Visually, the blonde hair recalls the unnaturally bright purse, both avatars of the feminine. This modern-day birth of Venus from the water anchors this film's sexuality in fetishism.

It soon becomes clear that the body in the opening sequence is not Tippi Hedren's – it is a heavier, fleshier body. One reason for this act of substitution is to emphasize this procedure as central to the film. Acts of substitution extend back in time to Marnie's conception, when her mother traded her virginity for a basketball sweater. Marnie herself plays one role after another, her hair at times black, brown, red, and blonde (her "true" hair color). She has purchased and discarded one set of tasteful clothes after another, clothes that are different yet interchangeable, a disguise that isn't one. After the first sequence, Tippi Hedren's body is a constant, as is her face – once we see it – and that face makes her easily recognizable. No one is fooled. But both body and face are presented as belonging to an actress, made up and in costume. The camouflaging coloration of Marnie's clothes – their under-stated, pale colors, along with the blacks and whites that spell elegance in the Hitchcock heroine – admit her to Mark Rutland's sophisticated, upper-class world. As Sean Connery's Mark points out, so do her diction and her understated man-ners. Marnie has no need of a Pygmalion to transform her; she has created this image on her own. But beneath her controlled exterior is a turbulent, traumatized interior.[8] While the film asserts that Marnie is in every sense contained within representation, her acting in the service of theft has its origins in trauma and deprivation.

It's not in Marnie's image that her psyche is fully reflected; her illness is signaled by her disturbed vision. Again red is the color of intense affect, and warning chords provide recurrent aural accompaniment to Marnie's reaction to it. Red gladiolas in her mother's house trigger her first "attack." Her response is the same during the first dream sequence at her mother's house, and red ink spilled on her white blouse at work has a similar effect. At the races, a jockey's silks with red polka dots on a white background trigger it again. A second dream in the Rutland house connects the color with the traumatic event expressed in her fear of red: "No, Mama, don't cry. Don't hurt my Mama!" During the association game with Mark playing ama-teur psychoanalyst, the cue "red" provokes her to shout, "White! White!" Finally, a red riding habit will set off the chain of events that leads to Marnie's mercy killing of her horse. Red is the color of affect, but it is also the color of blood, the substance for which the red color in this film so obviously substitutes. The code would seem to be a simple one, the associations the film provides readily decipher-able. Interestingly, however, Marnie "sees red" only metaphorically: while some-thing red is the object of her look, it's her image that's suffused with that color in virtually each instance, with red flashing light extending to fill the film frame (McElhaney 89). If the suffusion of the film frame suggests a permeability between the image and its material support, does it signal their artifice – the color red as paint – or a "reality" they have in common – the color red as blood? In some sense, the red film frame disturbs the spectator's vision, transferring the character's symptom to us. Like a wash over realist images, it cloaks representation in pure color.

The thunderstorm experienced in Mark's office is the exception to the rule that Marnie's image and the film frame turn red during her "attacks." In this sequence red light flashes in the window, not on Marnie, although the light immobilizes her against the door as she begs someone, in a child's voice, to "stop the colors!" In a film whose system of metaphors is so carefully contrived, why is Marnie's image not suffused with red during her experience of the storm, as is the case in all other instances? Mark's effort to "stop the colors" leads to an embrace, and the camera moves in to a tight close-up of their mouths, hers wearing surprisingly red lipstick. Here Marnie's very red mouth seems to substitute for the omitted suffusion. As we discover, the origin of Marnie's trauma lies in the murder she committed as a five-year-old, when she killed a sailor with a poker both in defense of her mother and – it's suggested – in disgust at his kiss. Mark's kiss both taps into and covers over the repressed memory, and the fleshiness of the couple's features in extreme close-up seems to stand in for a more private encounter – or the body's interior spaces. At the end of the film, there is an alternation between Marnie's dreamlike reliving of the killing and the diegetic present, in which Marnie and Mark confront her mother (Louise Latham). Marnie's dreamlike memory sequences are set off from the "present" by means of color. They have the sepia tones of old photographs until crimson blood covers the white of the sailor's shirt, and, filling the frame, covers the screen itself. As Marnie and Mark leave her mother's house at the film's conclusion, its red brick walls are prominent in the frame. They are covered with raindrops from yet another thunderstorm, which look for all the world like drops of blood. Thus the mother's house is rendered as her body – another representation of a female interior, bleeding.

In *Vertigo*, the nature of Scottie's subjectivity requires that transactions with his object of desire be aestheticized. In *Marnie,* the neurotic and the aestheticized woman are collapsed into the film's title character, and Mark Rutland, her husband and would-be lover, is an amateur zoologist who reads Freud. Mark implicitly likens Marnie to a jaguarundi he had once trained to trust him, and there's another phenomenon in nature he tells Marnie about as well. Found in Kenya, in appearance it's a beautiful, coral-colored "flower." But when one reaches out to touch it, the flower is discovered to consist of hundreds of small insects. Reading this natural phenomenon as camouflage by means of which bugs escape the eyes of hungry birds, Mark also alludes to the gap between appearance and reality in *Marnie*, a thief in disguise as a "decent" woman, and to her neurotic avoidance of male touch. Jacques Lacan's discussion of mimicry within the context of the gaze sheds further light on Mark's anecdote.

Lacan refers to the work of Roger Caillois, who argues that insects do not take the shape or coloration of other insects or plants in order to defend themselves from their predators, who are in any case not deceived. In making his argument, Caillois refers to the behavior of a crustacean called a caprella which, when it settles among "quasi plant-animals" known as brizoaires, resembles their stain-like intestinal loop. It isn't adaptation, argues Caillois, that motivates the caprella's behavior. Rather, the caprella's tendency to imitate is located in a "depersonalization by assimilation to space" (28). "Stain," of course, is the operative Lacanian term, and the caprella, by imitating the stain, "becomes a picture," is "inscribed in the picture" (Lacan 99). This is the origin of mimicry, Lacan claims with Caillois: the activity of the caprella is *not* Darwinian, it does not exemplify adaptive behavior, but rather, as Kaja Silverman writes, it is a matter of "visual articulation" (149). Contrary to Caillois, however, for whom mimicry in lower creatures is akin to art in human beings, Lacan asserts that, beyond this simpler form of mimicry, there are mimetic activities in which only human beings can participate: "travesty, camouflage and intimidation" (99). In offering the image of the Kenyan insect "flower" to Marnie as an image for herself, Mark also refers to the way in which Marnie – with her disguises that don't actually function as disguises – positions herself within representation. For the subject, claims Lacan, the aim of imitation is ultimately "to be inserted in a function whose exercise grasps it" (100).

Let me return now to the opening scene with its stunningly abstract rendering of the perspective system, with a woman moving toward the vanishing point, and then swerving from it. What purpose does it serve in the film? Interestingly, it finds its visual correlative in the artifice of the film's harbor scene, I would suggest, a scene for which *Marnie* was repeatedly criticized. With its obvious recourse to a painted backdrop and its open use of a set, it is unnatural in the extreme. But it's precisely this constructed, aestheticized space, like so many in Hitchcock, that is so utterly in keeping with *Marnie's* meditation on the relation of illusion and reality. The moment when we see the space of the harbor most clearly is the one in which Mark and Marnie drive away from her mother's house at the end of the film. Shot from above – always a sign of authorial intervention in Hitchcock – the rowhouses on either side of the street echo the diagonal lines formed by the trains in the film's opening. The road functions as the red line – red thread or red herring? – between them, leading to the huge ship that more than one critic describes as "looming." The ship is located where the vanishing point of the frame would be, but its painted quality renders it an image on a theater flat, a flat that obscures non-diegetic space, a barrier between representation and some suggested other, "real" space, perhaps the space behind the movie screen.[9] In this sequence the moving car that substitutes for the moving woman also swerves from the perspectival center-line, moving diagonally across the space of the road from right to left in anticipation of the right turn that takes it out of the frame. In *Marnie*, too, then, as in other films that I've discussed, deviation from the perspectival system is represented – here not only once, but thrice, if we include Marnie's first visit to her mother's – and precisely within aestheticized spaces, spaces notable for their artifice. These are the spaces in which the tension between representation and abstraction is at its most intense.

To be seized by representation, to be taken into it. Sometimes this is the determining impulse for characters in Hitchcock's films. The movement between aesthetic space and diegetic reality is often suggested in formal terms, as we have seen. The oscillation between illusion and "reality" is in evidence as well in the spatial and ontological manipulation to which his films subject their spectator. This kind of oscillation is the stuff of theater, where real bodies underpin the roles imposed upon them, and feigned emotions can produce real tears. But the oscillation between illusion and abstraction is equally determinative for painting, where, Clement Greenberg writes, "the painter's first task had been to hollow out an illusion of three-dimensional space" through which one looked "as through a proscenium on a stage" (136). With the coming of modernism, however, Greenberg argues, this stage became shallower and shallower, "until now its backdrop has become the same as its curtain" (136). While the painter may still inscribe recognizable images upon this "curtain," the illusionistic space surrounding those images disappears.

In Hitchcock's films we repeatedly find moments when film collapses into painting, or realistic spaces provide modernist views. Despite the presence of the tiny human figure within it, the overhead view of the UN Building in *North by Northwest* is surprisingly flat, exposing a space that oscillates between the representational and the abstract. Deflating the feigned three-dimensionality of film, it emphasizes the film frame, its support. And consider moments when the color red in the Hitchcock film figures blood, or remains unimaged, mere paint. Or when, filling the frame, it signals the distorted vision of the spectator or cloaks the representational image in a color wash. Toward the end of *Spellbound* (1945), when a gun seems to shoot straight out at the camera and into our space, the film frame is briefly suffused with red. While this flash of color signals an afterimage – a real effect of vision – it points equally to its own artifice, a flash of red amidst the black and white of the rest of the film.

Consider, too, the moments when the theater curtain, theater's hypothetical fourth wall, is metaphorically torn, permitting movement both into and out of aestheticized spaces, from theatrical to cinematic to spectatorial space and back again. Interestingly, the baroque ornamentation of the theater curtain in *Stage Fright* links representation to a period in the history of art when trompe l'oeil effects flourished, when games with illusion and reality took center stage. While modernism in the radical form of abstract expressionism wholly rejects representation, in its earlier period – in the work of Magritte, for example – aesthetic game playing and illusion flourish. In *I Confess* (1953), set in Quebec, the murderer attempts to evade capture by hiding in a famous hotel, the Château de Frontenac, a recognizable place in a real city. But suddenly he finds himself on a stage, a theatrical space from which he shoots his gun into the camera and at us. In so doing, he figuratively tears a hole in the scenographic space of cinema. Indeed, this is what occurs whenever a shot, a fist, or a truck seems to burst out of the screen and at the spectator – violent irruptions all. But Hitchcock's ultimate *va banque* game is with death. In *Stage Fright*, we recall, the filigreed design on the curtain isn't painted on soft toile. It decorates an iron surface: a safety curtain that spells death when it falls to good effect on a murderer. Invading representation from within, the real in the form of death is the linchpin of Hitchcock's art. It's the real that prompts the rigorous artifice of his films.

Notes

1. In the text of his essay, Stephen Heath merely refers to the painting as "Picasso-like," but in his first footnote, Heath identifies this subtly different copy as based on the Picasso still-life.
2. Dietrich traveled with a doll collection, and her dolls often appeared in her films.
3. Casetti thinks otherwise: "The young man's effort works precisely through deception, whereas that of the young woman revolves around hidden facts. It is exactly this polarity between a lie and a secret that gives the different trajectories their significance" (111).
4. These black and white winged statues figure among the multiple references to *The Birds* (1963) that occur in *Torn Curtain*.
5. This *Torn Curtain* sequence echoes an episode in *The 39 Steps* (1935) where a stage performance is similarly interrupted. In the earlier film, the stage is a place to hide in plain sight. It is also the space of performance and political intrigue, and the place of death.

6. According to the production notes on the Collector's Edition DVD of *Vertigo*, the portrait was by John Ferren, who also painted the film's dream scenes.
7. Visually, the space is ludicrous. It's only the desire for a happy end that makes the spectator overlook its artifice and, given the characters' position on a precipice, overlook the cut to a space even more unbelievable, the berth of a sleeping car. Since Thornhill and Eve cannot realistically survive their cliffhanger, a literal fall metamorphoses into a figurative one.
8. As Joe McElhaney argues, in *Marnie* an "enormous investment in surface intensity" deriving from European modernist cinema remains connected to paradigms of classical cinema and character psychology (89).
9. Slavoj Žižek reads the looming ship differently, and multiply, as "a stain which blurs the field of vision," a "fantasy element which patches up the hole (the blank) in reality," and "the massive presence of some Real which fills out and blocks the perspective openness constitutive of 'reality'" ("Why" 119).

Works Cited

Casetti, Francesco. *Inside the Gaze: The Fiction Film and its Spectator*. Trans. Nell Andrew with Charles O'Brien. Bloomington: Indiana UP, 1998.

Caillois, Roger. "Mimicry and Legendary Psychasthenia." Trans. John Shepley. *October* 31 (1984): 16–32.

Grafe, Frieda. "Verblichen, die Farben der DDR: Hitchcock's Palette und Rohmer als Vermittler." *Filmfarben, Schriften*. Vol. 1. Berlin: Brinkman & Bose, 2002. 85–97.

Greenberg, Clement. "Abstract, Representational, and So Forth." *Art and Culture: Critical Essays*. Boston: Beacon, 1961. 133–38.

Heath, Stephen. "Narrative Space." *Questions of Cinema*. Bloomington: Indiana UP, 1981. 19–75.

Jacobs, Steven. *The Wrong House: The Architecture of Alfred Hitchcock*. Rotterdam: 010 Publishers, 2007.

Jameson, Fredric. "Spatial Systems in *North by Northwest*." Žižek, *Everything* 47–72.

Lacan, Jacques. *Four Fundamental Concepts of Psychoanalysis*. Ed. Jacques-Alain Miller. Trans. Alan Sheridan. New York: Norton, 1981.

McElhaney, Joe. "Touching the Surface: *Marnie*, Melodrama, Modernism." *Alfred Hitchcock: Centenary Essays*. Ed. Richard Allen and S. Ishii-Gonzáles. London: BFI, 1999. 87–105.

Peucker, Brigitte. "The Scene of Art in Hitchcock II." *The Material Image: Art and the Real in Film*. Stanford: Stanford UP, 2007. 87–103.

Saito, Ayko. "Hitchcock's Trilogy: A Logic of Mise-en-Scène." *Endless Night: Cinema and Psychoanalysis, Parallel Histories*. Ed. Janet Bergstrom. Berkeley: U of California P, 1999. 200–47.

Silverman, Kaja. *Male Subjectivity at the Margins*. New York: Routledge, 1992.

Žižek, Slavoj, ed. *Everything You Always Wanted to Know About Lacan (But Were Afraid to Ask Hitchcock)*. London: Verso, 1992.

Žižek, Slavoj. "Why Does the *Phallus* Appear?" *Enjoy Your Symptom! Jacques Lacan in Hollywood and Out*. Second ed. New York: Routledge, 2001. 113–48.

Zupančič, Alenka. "A Perfect Place to Die: Theatre in Hitchcock's Films." Žižek, *Everything* 73–105.

12

Hitchcock and Music

Jack Sullivan

Alfred Hitchcock conjured more kinds of musical spells than any other movie director in history. From the insidious charm of "Miss Up to Date" in *Blackmail* (1929) through the rocketing fandango in *North by Northwest* (1959) to the mock-mystical chorus in *Family Plot* (1976), Hitchcock experimented with musical genres and effects of very kind, including complex symphonic scores, pop songs, Viennese waltzes, jazz, cabaret, Cagian noise effects, and electronic sound. He entrusted music to bring to life ideas and submerged passions that could not be captured by dialogue or the camera – even his own. Music does more than provide tension and excitement for "the master of suspense," though it certainly does that. In its most ambitious moments, it becomes an interior narrator, cueing not straightforward good or evil, happiness or sadness, but complex psychological and moral states.

With the exception of his iconic collaboration with Bernard Herrmann, Hitchcock's music has received scant critical attention. Yet the music mattered, not only when it was an integral part of a successful film, but when all else was in disarray. "I didn't give you a great picture," he told Maurice Jarre after the disastrous *Topaz* (1969), "but you gave me a great score." He collaborated with, fought with, and fired some of Hollywood's most prominent composers. One of the latter, Henry Mancini, maintained that collaborating with Hitchcock was the quintessential composer-director dynamic, every minute a life-and-death engagement. The director's droll cameo in *Rear Window* (1954), apprehensively fiddling with a clock as he looms over his composer, expresses his intense personal involvement in the musical process.

Hitchcock envisioned moviemaking musically, comparing himself to composer, maestro, and orchestrator, making numerous analogies between scoring and moviemaking. Storyboards, he said, were like musical notation, close-ups like trumpet

A Companion to Alfred Hitchcock, First Edition. Edited by Thomas Leitch and Leland Poague.
© 2011 Thomas Leitch and Leland Poague. Published 2011 by Blackwell Publishing Ltd.

solos, long shots "an entire orchestra performing a muted accompaniment" (Truffaut 335). He orchestrated scenes in his head before his composer wrote the sounds, though the actual orchestration might turn out very differently: the Arbogast murder in *Psycho* (1960) was "like music, you see, the high shot with the violins, and suddenly the big head with the brass instruments clashing" (276). At least twice, he commented that his relationship with his audience was that of an organist playing his instrument.

Hitchcock thrusts music directly into the narrative, depicting singers and songs, mysteries and codes, musicians and orchestras, stages and dressing rooms. He resisted the Hollywood cliché that music should be accompaniment or imitation, imagining it rather as a preternatural force, abstract yet peculiarly alive, an idea implied in the sound notes for *The Wrong Man* (1956), where the music should "sneak in" Manny Balestrero's cell like a "very soft" invader. As John Williams puts it, music was not only Hitchcock's "signature," but "a character" – an unmistakable presence, sometimes aggressively physical, as in *Psycho*, sometimes evanescent, as in the distant song keening through *I Confess* (1953).

Hitchcock's musical explorations fall basically into three stages: the low-budget British films, full of songs, marching bands, and other types of diegetic sound; the great symphonic period from *Rebecca* (1940) to *Psycho*, where Hollywood money and Golden Age composers allowed him to experiment lavishly with complex scores; and the final period of decline where musical distinction was more sporadic. These categories are neither neat nor mutually exclusive: *Waltzes from Vienna* (1933) and the original *Man Who Knew Too Much* (1934) have major symphonic moments, though they are diegetic; a few American films are deliberately bereft of symphonic music, notably *Rope* (1948), the tiny cue sheet for which lists only seven items, and *The Birds* (1963), which relies on electronic effects and awestruck silence. The all-diegetic *Rear Window*, Hitchcock's most dazzling fantasia on popular song, is actually a complex series of American riffs on British Hitchcock. In a class by itself is *The Man Who Knew Too Much* remake (1956). With its lonely Herrmann underscore, its huge onscreen symphony orchestra and chorus, and its finale featuring Doris Day singing Livingston-Evans songs, it is not only a revisiting of the original British version but an apotheosis of Hitchcockian methods.

Hitchcock established a musical style early. As with many of his obsessive themes and visual designs, he established signature motifs at the beginning, then spent the rest of his career creating endlessly inventive variations. His 1925 debut, *The Pleasure Garden*, opens with a frenetic shot of a spinning chorus girl; other silent movies like *Downhill* (1927) and *The Ring* (1927) depict dancers, dance halls, and stages as exuberant backdrops to disaster, a counterpoint Hitchcock would continue to weave throughout his career. The moment sound became available in 1929, he seized upon the new medium with a series of elaborate experiments. In *Blackmail*, the first British sound film, Cyril Ritchard sings "Miss Up to Date" to Anny Ondra in a charming aria that ends with the singer stabbed to death by the heroine as he assaults her, linking music to a drama of disturbing psychological and moral ambiguity. "Miss Up to Date" continues to haunt the film as the heroine's tragic leitmotif, moving with startling fluidity from source music to symphonic underscore, unveiling a music of the subconscious that establishes an interior point of view and fuzzing the distinction between "diegetic" and "nondiegetic" music long before those terms were codified.

Blackmail also experiments with noise music, especially in the audacious breakfast knife montage, an excruciating crescendo of guilt grounded in what Hitchcock called a vocal drone. It even has early samples of Hitchcock's aural transferences, as when Alice's scream is transformed into that of the concierge. All this in 1929, and several score details – sinister harp and organ, lonely timpani solos, sudden silence following dramatic crescendos, spinning arpeggios linked to circular visuals – became signatures as well.

Once he had access to sound, Hitchcock confidently established other aural trademarks. In *Murder!* (1930) he used orchestral sound as a doorway to love and truth. Shaving at his mirror, Herbert Marshall hears the Prelude and Liebestod to Wagner's *Tristan and Isolde* (1865) on the radio, its yearning suspensions evoking the realization that he is attracted to the woman he has doomed to the gallows, and that she is probably innocent. Moviemakers had already begun to use Wagnerian leitmotifs as character markers, but Hitchcock's Wagnerian stream of consciousness was new, inaugurating his vision of music as an active, mysterious force that soars over the action, influencing it for good or ill.

Waltzes from Vienna, from three years later, was a flop but a significant one, pushing musical experimentation in several directions at once. A behind-the-scenes look at the musical and sexual conquests of the Strauss family, this intricate oedipal drama depicts Johann Strauss Junior's overthrow of his father as the Waltz King through the composition and premiere of the "Blue Danube" waltz, his muse inspired by both his younger and older lovers. This cinematic operetta anticipates *The 39 Steps* (1935) and *The Man Who Knew Too Much* in its depiction of onstage orchestras from multiple points of view. It also foreshadows *Rear Window* in its dreamlike blend of songs and street music floating in and out of windows; its depiction of how a song is conceived, composed, and performed; and its revelation of how dramatically music can shape lives. Even its notes are important. The film opens with Johann Strauss Senior's "Radetzky March" being played in the streets, signifying that the elder Waltz King rules. This is the first of many ingenious Hitchcock marches, from the Salvation Army escape in *The 39 Steps* to the steely Soviet marches in *Topaz*. The penultimate *Waltzes from Vienna* scene presents a breathless chase cue, one of Hitchcock's first, and a stream of waltzes full of ambivalence and longing as the young Strauss (Edmond Knight) takes the forbidden Countess (Fay Compton) in his arms once more. Out the window a crowd sings a wordless chorus of the "Blue Danube," an homage to the new Waltz King and an early sample of Hitchcock's fascination with offstage choruses, for him a kind of Holy Grail. During *Rebecca* and *Vertigo* (1958) he undertook lengthy, fruitless searches for the wordless chorus in J.M. Barrie's theatrical 1920 ghost story, *Mary Rose*, which had haunted him since childhood, and for *Torn Curtain* (1966) he tried unsuccessfully to acquire the rights to Ravel's *Daphnis and Chloe* (1912). (Peggy Robertson reported that the "finicky French" wouldn't permit excerpts.) In the coda of *Waltzes From Vienna*, the defeated father (Edmund Gwenn) wanders inconsolably among empty chairs in the near-deserted bandstand following his son's triumph. When a young girl requests his autograph, he obliges, then hesitates, and with a wistful look takes her program back and adds "Senior" under his name, proud of his son in spite of himself. As the lights go down on the bandstand, he moves off-camera in silhouette on a final, bittersweet "Blue Danube" cadence, ending the film with exquisite ambiguity, the kind Hitchcock would strive for in many later films.

Alas, Hitchcock was as grumpy about *Waltzes From Vienna* as the critics, but it was clearly a valuable laboratory for musical thought and practice, as revealed by a prescient, surprisingly comprehensive interview he did for Stephen Watts of *Cinema Quarterly* in 1933 as he was editing the film. Lamenting that movie music "as an artistic asset of the film is still sadly neglected," he establishes a fundamental link between music and cinema, asserting that editing and scoring conspire to create "the *tempo* and mood of the scene." From here on, he wrote this concept directly into his music notes and into his films. In the finale of *Waltzes*, for example, he does not need to cut to the frantic approach of the Countess's enraged husband (Frank Vosper) because the score can do it: the "feeling of approaching climax can be suggested by the music." Music can mark a character and "heighten intensity," but it also has a deeper "psychological use," establishing an emotional subtext, an "underlying idea" that often contradicts the looks and words of characters onscreen rather than imitating them (Hitchcock 242–45). Following this principle throughout his career, Hitchcock used upbeat vernacular music as counterpoint to scenes of menace, creating a mysterious tension that intensifies suspense more than any conventional suspense cue could. In *Sabotage* (1936), "Who Killed Cock Robin?" is the catalyst for a lethal epiphany; in *Notorious* (1946), Cary Grant's investigation of Claude Rains's deadly wine cellar is spiked by swinging Brazilian dance music; in *Rear Window*, a romantic song by Franz Waxman plays from a window of partiers as the villain assaults Grace Kelly; in *The Trouble with Harry* (1955), a little boy discovers a corpse to the swells of Herrmann's most pastoral music; in *The Birds*, surely the most unforgettable example, schoolchildren sing "Risseldy Rosseldy" as murderous crows mass behind Tippi Hedren. "Hitchcock wanted counterpoint," the late Maurice Jarre told me in an interview, "not icing on a cake like most Hollywood directors."

Hitchcock ticks off a surprising number of significant principles and analogies in seemingly casual interviews. Anticipating Erich Korngold, he ties cinema to opera, something he had hinted at in *Murder!* "It may sound far-fetched to compare a dramatic talkie with opera, but there is something in common": the techniques of opera allow music that "echoes" dialogue and "subtly comment[s]" upon action (Hitchcock 244, 245). From here on, Hitchcock referenced opera even when he didn't use singers. In *Vertigo's* dressing scene, Bernard Herrmann's aching suspensions deliver another homage to *Tristan and Isolde*; in *Under Capricorn* (1949), Ingrid Bergman's revelatory soliloquy intoned against Richard Addinsell's ravishing score is so like grand opera that the cue sheet calls it "Henrietta's Aria." During Hitchcock's Hollywood years, his basic sound was operatic. Indeed, his orchestra often sounds like something that could erupt from the pit at the Met. John Williams notes that "many directors would be afraid to have music that loud, that emphatic – they might think it's too operatic." Joseph Stefano told me that after hearing Herrmann's music for *Psycho*, he realized that Bernard Herrmann had "taken the picture and turned it into an opera."

Singers are everywhere in Hitchcock, and even non-singers have a way of suddenly bursting into song or banging a significant motif on the piano. For Hitchcock, music is an inextricable part of human identity, and he didn't mind violating the strictures of realism to make the point. *The Trouble with Harry* begins with Sam Marlowe (John Forsythe) singing "Flagging the Train to Tuscaloosa" over a pristine Vermont landscape, a vocal encore to Herrmann's orchestral main title and a commentary on the film's drama of disappearing love mates. In the carnival scene in *Strangers on a Train* (1951), Robert Walker, Hitchcock's most charismatic killer, briefly joins his victim and her two boyfriends in a carousel quartet singing "The Band Played On" before stalking her in the Tunnel of Love. Like many of Hitchcock's musical decisions, this one was carefully planned, as indicated in the final script in the Warner Brothers archive:

> Miriam and her friends begin to sing the song being played on the Calliope
> Close up Miriam
> As she starts to sing, she glances back
> Close-up Bruno
> He is starting to join in the singing
>
> (32)

Hitchcock makes his characters own their songs by performing them, creating a free-floating music drama that obliterates distinctions between underscore and source music. *The Paradine Case* (1947) opens with Alida Valli, the doomed heroine, playing Franz Waxman's haunting title melody on the piano in the opening scene as she waits for the police to come arrest her, a tune the audience has just heard, and one that exactly fits her coolly seductive beauty; "Ordinary" Smith (Michael Wilding), the detective in *Stage Fright* (1950), plays Leighton Lucas's sinuous piano tune for the heroine, establishing his leitmotif and planting a musical memory. Even in such striking set pieces, the techniques of opera still "subtly comment" on action.

Often, songs comment on musical space and the mysterious properties of sound, on how a melody soars, crumbles, and finally reveals truth. In the second *Man Who Knew Too Much*, the *Storm Cloud Cantata* – composed for the original film by Arthur Benjamin – provides spectacular stage music linked with Hitchcock's most elaborate suspense montage. In the sound notes, Hitchcock explains that he has taken "dramatic license to preserve the same volume of sound whether we are in the hall, the lobby or the corridor, and this should remain so in order not to disturb the musical unity of the cantata." Eschewing realism, he opts for the big operatic gesture. The music exists in its own abstract realm, not as accompaniment; musical unity must be preserved. But in the pop music section of the picture, where Doris Day saves her abducted son by singing "Que Sera, Sera," the drama depends on how the music would actually travel and recede up a staircase, so Hitchcock specifies finicky crescendos and decrescendos. By hiring a popular singer for a lead part, as he had done in *Blackmail*, *Waltzes From Vienna*, and *Stage Fright*, he again mimics the position of opera director.

As Elisabeth Weis points out in her pioneering *The Silent Scream*, the performance is as crucial as the music in establishing truth, especially guilt or innocence. Farley Granger botches his Poulenc playing in *Rope*, raising James Stewart's suspicions; the distracted timpanist (George Curzon) in *Young and Innocent* (1937) throws off the singer of "No One Can Like the Drummer Man," his mangled playing leading to his unmasking as the villain. And Marlene Dietrich blows her performance of Edith Piaf's "La vie en rose" in *Stage Fright* as the camera tracks a boy scout approaching the stage with a bloodstained doll, a clue to her guilt in a murder conspiracy. ("The only murderer is the orchestra leader," she insists.)

As Hitchcock matured, his innovations with songs took on increasing confidence and complexity. The most vibrant experiment is the pop surrealism of *Rear Window*, featuring some 39 songs, ballets, "improvisations," boogies, and "jukeboxes" by Waxman, Leonard Bernstein, Richard Rodgers, Jay Livingston, Johnny Burke, Schubert, Mendelssohn, and others; many play through the protagonist's window, many simultaneously, in a haunting Ivesian mosaic. Neither Jeff (James Stewart) nor Lisa (Kelly) sings, plays, dances, or turns on radios, but everyone around them does, enacting or mocking their fantasies. The relationship between music and meaning in a given scene is intriguingly unpredictable: sometimes direct, sometimes deviously ironic, sometimes random. In *Rear Window* as in *Waltzes*, Hitchcock shows the composition of a song, in this case Franz Waxman's "Lisa," from conception through noodlings and rehearsals to full performance and recording. That a song saves a life is nothing unusual for Hitchcock, but the subtle way he transfers its meaning from the leitmotif of one character, Lisa, to the redemption of another, Miss Lonely Hearts, is uniquely satisfying.

Another genre besides song that resonates through Hitchcock is the waltz, an ostensibly staid form he invested with near-mystical properties. Again, *Waltzes From Vienna* is the template. The "Blue Danube" is a spiritual bond between Strauss Junior and his younger lover, Rasi, especially during its composition; at the piano, they sing the same enchanted motif of the "Blue Danube" with mounting ecstasy as it erupts in their imaginations. Anticipating Teresa Wright's memorable phrase, the waltz "jumps from head to head." A waltz can also hypnotize crowds: at the "Blue Danube" premiere, mesmerized audience members, as if moved by unseen powers, suddenly find themselves moving onto the dance floor as the scene glides into ballet. Hitchcock presented music as a bringer of chaos as well as restoration, and the waltz is no exception. The "Blue Danube" dazzles the crowd as Schani's father and younger lover, both betrayed by its triumph, erupt into despair and tears, the father toppled from his musical throne by the son, the younger lover outmaneuvered by the older.

On a broader level, waltzes signify the treachery of nostalgia, an important Hitchcock theme. Viennese waltzes were ideal: sooner than anyone thought, they became an emblem for a fading grandeur, an Old World past vanishing in the onslaught of modernism and two world wars. Hitchcock joined composers from Ravel to Berg in associating Viennese waltzes with crumbling worlds. "Wiener Blut," linked with the glamorous allure of Cary Grant's Johnnie, a spendthrift and womanizer who may also be a murderer, dances through *Suspicion* (1941) with elegant imperturbability, immune to the growing anxieties of Johnnie's wife and the deterioration of their marriage. In the famous scene where Grant glides up a shadowy staircase with a possibly poisoned glass of milk, the waltz suddenly darkens with subtle harmonic distortions and a doleful gong.

Hitchcock used many other waltzes besides those by Strauss, including Franz Waxman's for the excruciating Manderley Ball scene in *Rebecca*, Lyn Murray's "Big Waltz" for the intricate maneuverings in the costume ball in *To Catch a Thief* (1955), and Dimitri Tiomkin's "Dial M" and "Martini" waltzes fizzing with insolent insouciance through double kisses and double crosses in *Dial M for Murder* (1954). The most chilling example is from *Shadow of a Doubt* (1943), where Franz Lehar's "Merry Widow" waltz becomes a mystical bond between young Charlie and her charismatic uncle. The "Merry Widow" plays in the main title with whirling dancers from long ago, a ghostlike montage that reappears, teasingly unexplained, in surreal dissolves. Uncle Charlie, who clearly yearns for a return of the "Merry Widow" era, praises the good old days, the "wonderful world" of the past, and denounces the "foul sty" of the present. Like other nostalgia-obsessed villains, he radiates the darkness he ascribes to others.

Hitchcock's fascination with dance was not to limited to waltzes. Diverse forms of ballet became a central design in his kinetic double and triple chases, including the race along the stage in the finale of *The 39 Steps*, the umbrella-assassination in *Foreign Correspondent* (1940), the ballet mecanique workplace montage in *Rich and Strange* (1931), the dancelike sequence that takes the two main characters though the train station in *Strangers on a Train*, the complex fandangos in *North by Northwest*, and Juanita's murder in *Topaz*, Hitchcock's most formal dance of death. Ballet was not just metaphor. In *Rear Window*, Miss Torso dances under Jeff's happily voyeuristic gaze to Waxman's "Rhumba" and "New Ballet," Bernstein's "Fancy Free," and Schubert's *Rosamunde*; in *Torn Curtain*, Paul Newman and Julie Andrews escape from the Soviets during a ballet of Tchaikovsky's *Francesca da Rimini* (1876), a thrilling music-suspense sequence that brings this pallid film to sudden life. Unlike the irony and duplicity that characterize so much of Hitchcock's vernacular music, the thrill of ballet provides a straightforward energy for action and suspense.

Jazz, however, is layered with double meanings. According to Patricia Hitchcock O'Connell, her father was not an avid jazz fan, but he clearly appreciated the genre. Jazz is a cheerful surface masking dread, but that façade, unlike the case with waltzes, is one of suave modernity rather than retro elegance. Like Weill, Milhaud, and other jazz-obsessed European émigrés, Hitchcock used the form as an emblem of modern reality signifying risk and danger. One of the most original examples occurs in the underrated comedy *Rich and Strange*, which depicts a young middle-class couple struggling to revitalize their stale marriage. "I want life, life I tell you!" shouts Fred (Henry Kendall), the repressed hero, who takes his wife (Joan Barry) to a Paris dance hall, where "life" exuberantly splashes across the screen in the form of New Orleans jazz mingled with burlesque. In a dynamic deep-focus shot, jazz players lean aggressively up to the front of the frame, as if wishing to smash through it. Hitchcock captures both the excitement and underlying anxiety of the Paris jazz scene between the world wars, a desperate gaiety masking impending collapse.

Hitchcock's most sustained jazz riff is *The Wrong Man*, based on the true story of Christopher Emmanuel Balestro, played by Henry Fonda. In the regimented, segregated society depicted by Hitchcock, the police use Manny's career as a jazz bass player in their case against him. Jazz was still viewed by much of American society as a cause and reflection of deviant behavior: all those "women, drinks, a pretty high old time there," as a police officer puts it. Bernard Herrmann's Prelude, which Manny's band performs at the Stork Club, is a Latin jazz number with a corrosive undertone – champagne poured over acid. Dismissed for years by critics who claimed it was too dour for a proper jazz number, it subtly embodies Manny's ostensibly upbeat but vulnerable existence as a working musician struggling to support his family. Music is a cathartic force that keeps Manny going when he's out on bail and keeps his two boys sane during their father's imprisonment. Manny tells his children to never "let anything throw you off the beat." Assuring them that they both have talent, he promises to give them music lessons, a pledge that becomes an emblem of hope. "He'll give us music lessons as soon as he can," one of his sons says, consoling his depressed brother. Staying on the beat becomes a mantra, a key to survival echoing the history of jazz itself as an emblem of resistance in the face of injustice.

Hitchcock's work with big symphonic scores began in 1939 with *Rebecca*. The dense cue sheet has seventy-one items, most by Franz Waxman, but two by Johann Strauss and six by Max Steiner. The scope is striking, especially given the skimpy cues in British Hitchcock. With few exceptions, the haunted tapestry of mood and character sketches – spiced with an electronic instrument called the novochord – envelops the film from beginning to end, as Herrmann's *Vertigo* score would eighteen years later in another movie about a struggle to rebury a dark past. Several long scenes, most notably the hypnotic tracking shot as the second Mrs de Winter approaches Manderley's West Wing, delete all dialogue and nonmusical sounds, creating a huge space for Waxman's mesmerizing pedal point. A consummate craftsman, Waxman used a chamber "ghost orchestra" to invoke a character no longer among the living, one never shown in photograph or flashback; only during the confession scene, when the real Rebecca is revealed, does a full orchestra play her theme in all its seductive malevolence.

Rebecca marked the beginning of delicate, sometimes explosive negotiations between Hitchcock, his composer, and (in this case) his micromanaging producer. While Victor Fleming was shooting *Gone with the Wind* (1939) across the street, David Selznick hired Max Steiner to do *Rebecca* as well, then switched to Waxman for the latter. He also asked Waxman "to help with a few things on GWTW while Steiner is finishing up" and planted several of his favorite Steiner cues into *Rebecca*, all the time denouncing both composers for slowness. Though commentators assumed that Hitchcock had little to do with *Rebecca*'s music since Selznick exercised such stern control, the archives reveal a decisive December conference between Hitchcock and Waxman that yielded voluminous music notes. In the end, Waxman's score was so triumphantly successful that he was asked by the Standard Symphony Hour to compose a symphonic suite immediately after *Rebecca*'s 1940 premiere, an early instance of movie music becoming classical.

Miklos Rozsa's score for *Spellbound* (1945), Hollywood's first psychiatric thriller, went a step further. It was programmed as a concert suite by Leopold Stokowski and broadcast on the radio before the film's release, helping to sell the movie in advance. *Spellbound* is also an example of what Hitchcock called the "psychological use" of music, a revelation of the subconscious rather than just a mood setter or character marker. Full of suppressed longing, the score tells us that Ingrid Bergman's psychiatrist-detective is in love with her possibly murderous patient long before she knows it herself. Ambivalence is built into the music's structure. The love theme and the "paranoia" theme, as Selznick called them in his notes, are variants of each other, revealing the thin line between love and terror, one of Hitchcock's favorite ideas. As with *Rebecca*, the music propels the movie rather than supporting it. The long razor blade and "awakening" scenes have no sounds or dialogue, only Rozsa's alternately eerie and soaring harmonies. Hitchcock also asked Rozsa to "score [the] entire sequence" of the patient's famous dream, a defense against Selznick's didactic insistence that Gregory Peck's voiceover explain it rather than allowing Hitchcock's editing and Salvador Dali's images to speak for themselves. For Hitchcock, music was a far more reliable narrator of the subconscious than words.

Despite Selznick's interference, Rozsa produced en enormously popular work. He won an Academy Award and went on the road to promote both the music and movie. After *Spellbound*'s initial surge of popularity, however, the score, like the film itself, suddenly became controversial. Hitchcock complained to Truffaut that the music was overwrought, and ever since, academics have piled on. (In the latest *Hitchcock Reader*, for example, Thomas Hyde brusquely dismisses "Miklos Rozsa's grotesquely overdramatic score" [156]). The public, perhaps a better judge, has always embraced it, as have many prominent critics outside the academy. *Musical America*'s Shirley Fleming regarded it as a supreme example of Golden Age film music; Michael Dirda, the Pulitzer Prize–winning editor at the *Washington Post,* believes it cuts deeper than any other Hitchcock score. The most surprising turn in the music's fortunes came in the twenty-first century, as a new wave of enthusiasm for the theremin, which Rozsa had introduced in *Spellbound,* gave the film and its music an unexpected boost.

How much Hitchcock influenced scores is a subject of debate. He was not a musician himself and, as Tiomkin, Jarre, and Herrmann attest, had no interest in trying to micromanage a composer's work. According to Joseph Stefano, his non-musician status was an advantage; he respected composers because they spoke a language that he did not. Yet Stefano says that Hitchcock had an uncanny ability to anticipate what a score should sound like: "He almost heard it before it was written, and it was also true with scripts." There was a downside: if he did not like the final product, if it did not jibe with what was in his imagination, "out [went] the score," and the composer with it, as happened with *Torn Curtain* and *Frenzy* (1972). Similarly, John Waxman attests that what his father wrote in *Rebecca, Suspicion,* and *The Paradine Case,* all hauntingly beautiful scores, was "established by Hitchcock's vision. He knew what he wanted." The paradox is summed up by Maurice Jarre, who like others was given wide freedom and latitude: "He said 'do what you want' – but he knew what *he* wanted."

To make his intentions clear, Hitchcock supplied his own music notes. These became increasingly detailed and imaginative as he worked with composers through four decades. Just how acutely he imagined sounds is suggested by his manipulation of the fateful cymbal crash at the end of Herrmann's imperious main title in *The Man Who Knew Too Much* remake, a sound montage that subconsciously prepares the audience for what is to come: "At the very outset, the ring of the cymbals should carry over into the whine of the tires on the roadway." Because Herrmann had Hitchcock's trust, the notes for this film have a relaxed, witty tone, as illustrated by his jovial directive for the final scene: "After Jimmy Stewart's line about picking up Hank, Mr. Herrmann will take over … a few ladylike snores might be permitted." Some of Hitchcock's most precise notes are for *Frenzy,* where he was determined to make a comeback after three successive flops. In the hotel scene, he instructs Ron Goodwin (who replaced the fired Henry Mancini) to "continue the music into a very unusual agitato (if at all possible) – right through until the police throw open the door, and we see the empty room – in silence." In the hospital escape, he calls for music that is "furtive, but humorous. 'Dear Mr. Musician – Please do not make the mistake that this is a heavy dramatic scene of escape.'" Typically, Hitchcock cues tempos, moods, spotting, and sudden silence, one of his most powerful signatures; he is also clear on what the music should *not* do.

His intentions were most fully realized in his work with Bernard Herrmann. Indeed, a surprising consensus holds that Hitchcock–Herrmann is the greatest director–composer team in film history. Selznick had considered hiring Herrmann as early as *Spellbound,* an indication that his musical taste was better than is often supposed. By the time Hitchcock landed him in 1955, the lush nineteenth-century style of Steiner and Korngold had peaked, making Herrmann's brooding asperity all the more refreshing. (On Broadway, a similar pattern would soon emerge as the sumptuous idiom of Rodgers and Hammerstein gave way to the sardonic attenuations of Stephen Sondheim, whose *Sweeney Todd* [1979] is an homage to Hitchcock–Herrmann.) Herrmann's gripping intensity and harmonic ambiguity are indelibly associated with Hitchcock's mature work. Herrmann was Hitchcock's secret sharer, a harbinger of energies darker and more dangerous than Hitchcock's cool sensibility easily permitted. Herrmann pushed Hitchcock's cinema deeper than ever into a world of anxiety and obsession. Even the delectable *North by Northwest* has wrenching moments one does not associate with comedy cues. Before their deplorable breakup over the score for *Torn Curtain*, their partnership was the most fruitful in Hollywood history, yielding one masterpiece after another. Only Fellini–Rota in Italy had an equally epic run, and only the seemingly inexhaustible team of Steven Spielberg and John Williams has achieved anything comparable since.

Their personalities were dramatically opposite – Hitchcock imperious and controlling, Herrmann notoriously explosive and prone to tantrums. Yet the two had much in common: an uncompromising professionalism, a hatred of mediocrity, a mordant sense of humor, and a contempt for the Hollywood establishment matched by a longing for its approval. Besides their strong artistic connection, the two had luck on their side. When Lyn Murray got them together for lunch following his work for *To Catch a Thief*, they immediately hit it off, as he thought they would, and Hitchcock had the power to bring Herrmann aboard. As Donald Spoto reminded me, Herrmann became available at the moment when Hitchcock became his own producer: "Remember that Hitchcock had no choice of composer until he also produced his films – and even then he had to use mostly studio personnel. His clout enabled him to have Herrmann, who was not attached to a studio in any case."

An important example of this clout is their most important collaboration, *Vertigo*. An early studio memo states that the music was to be furnished by Paramount staff, but Hitchcock hired Herrmann, kicking out several pop cues in the process. *Vertigo* was their fourth project, and by now the two had a productive give and take that transcended each man's implacable independence. Hitchcock invited Herrmann onto the set before scenes were shot to discuss ideas, timing, and spotting, an aural storyboarding paralleling the visual. He expressed strong ideas about the musical design and emotion, then got out of the way, yet he also provided incisive music notes, down to the doleful clang of a bell in the graveyard scene.

In some instances, Herrmann coaxed Hitchcock into more music. The notes for the restaurant scene state a preference for a "moment of silence, when Scottie feels the proximity of Madeleine." Hitchcock wanted to banish music and also "take all the sounds of the restaurant away," leaving us with "Scottie's sole impression of her." But he left the final decision to Herrmann, who wrote "Madeleine's Theme" for the scene, a piece of melancholy sensuality that haunts the remainder of the movie, re-invoking Scottie's psychological "impression" even after Madeleine's death. The removal of all sound other than the score, a Hitchcock signature, allows the music to have an overwhelming presence and eroticism. In other instances, Hitchcock called for more music. For Judy's daring dressing scene, he again took out all other sounds because "Mr. Herrmann may have something to say here," finally telling him, "We'll just have the camera and you." He allowed Herrmann three minutes of trembling lyricism, a crescendo of yearning unlike anything in cinema, the culmination of the "psychological use" of music. As Hitchcock told Herrmann, "music will do better than words there" (quoted in Smith 360).

Like many of Hitchcock's riskier scores, *Vertigo* almost failed to materialize. Herrmann had only ten weeks to complete a work that has enough ideas for three or four symphonies. Then a series of musicians' strikes and walkouts sent Hitchcock's production people in a chaotic scramble from Los Angeles to London to Vienna to record the music with three different orchestras, knocking Herrmann off the podium in the process. Yet it was the music, captured on a vivid Mercury LP, that kept *Vertigo* alive after the film flopped at the box office and vanished until the 1980s. The score's stock is now breathtakingly high, and not just among Hitchcock specialists: the *New Yorker*'s Alex Ross regards it as the cinema's finest score, Joseph Horowitz as greater than any American symphony. (These generalizations seem like hyperbole until one tries to think of exceptions.) *Vertigo* became a popular symphonic suite as well as the basis of Herrmann's achingly beautiful Clarinet Quintet. Herrmann invoked the score once again in a series of ghostly variations for Brian De Palma's *Obsession* (1975), itself an homage to *Vertigo*. Pastiches continue to proliferate, including an "installation" by Douglas Gordon, who calls *Vertigo* "the sound of cinema music for an entire generation" (quoted in Sullivan 234).

Herrmann's *Psycho* is even more iconic, and certainly more notorious. If *Vertigo* is the cinema's sound of obsession, *Psycho* is its sound of terror, its primal scream. It too is a masterpiece that almost didn't happen, though for very different reasons. "The Murder" is probably the most immediately recognizable and widely referenced of all film cues, yet Hitchcock's music notes reveal that he originally wanted the shower scene to proceed without music, and for the picture as a whole to have scant music. This was not really new: Hitchcock had used silence to powerful effect in the knife killings in *Blackmail* and *Sabotage*. But halfway through production, he fretted that this experiment in silence was falling flat, that something wasn't working, and contemplated cutting *Psycho* up for television. Herrmann passionately believed in the project and was convinced his music could make a crucial improvement. He wrote the shower cue in secret, against Hitchcock's explicit directive – something that simply wasn't done – and boldly played it for him after Hitchcock returned to the set from a Christmas break. This breach of authority may well have been the first indication of an eventual Hitchcock–Herrmann meltdown, but its immediate effect was to jump-start a faltering project. Abruptly reversing himself, Hitchcock suddenly became energized about *Psycho*, praised Herrmann openly (something he rarely did with any collaborator), and gradually assented to other cues as well. Beginning with the least music, *Psycho* ended up with more than any Hitchcock film except *Vertigo*.

No one had ever heard Hollywood music so ostentatiously astringent. Scary-movie scores with mild dissonance and eventual closure were one thing, but the uncompromising modernity of *Psycho* was new. That Herrmann used only strings, normally a Hollywood marker for schmaltzy romance, was even more startling. Joseph Stefano, who was treated to the score in a private screening by Hitchcock, was stunned: "When I heard it, I nearly fell out of my chair. Hitchcock said the music raised *Psycho*'s impact by 33%. It raised it for me by another 30." Hitchcock wanted Stefano's reaction because the latter was a composer and a straight shooter, someone Hitchcock trusted. Stefano was particularly impressed by the sultry chord progression in the opening scene when the lovers rise from the hotel bed and begin talking: "It was as if Bernie was lying on the floor at the feet of John [Gavin] and Janet [Leigh]. And as they talked, he sent a geyser of music that came up right between them. It was so breathtaking that I gasped. You should go back and listen to it!" This vision of a score as a force of nature is a testament to the strange palpability of Hitchcock's music. It is also a reminder that the slashing glissandos in "The Murder" and "The Knife" are not the only remarkable cues in *Psycho*. From the ominous Prelude to the final wrenching discord, the music projects its characters' restless despair even as it establishes its own space as a symphony of dread. Like *Vertigo*, it continues to flourish as a concert piece in the twenty-first century, even with audiences normally hostile to "modern music."

Herrmann worried that Hitchcock resented his pivotal role in films like *Psycho* and *Vertigo*. This was not necessarily paranoia: according to John Williams, "Hitchcock may have felt that his style was too dependent on Herrmann's music, and that may have wounded his pride." In *The Birds*, Hitchcock made sure Herrmann was no longer the star but one part of an intricate sound team; because of the unique nature of the soundtrack, Hitchcock himself was able to exercise an unusual amount of control, something he relished. This time he was resolute about having no music – at least not the traditional kind. Truffaut pointed out the great paradox of *The Birds*: "There's no music, of course, but the bird sounds are worked out like a real musical score" (294). Using the New York City Ballet's electronic keyboard, the Trautonium, Hitchcock "scored" *The Birds* in his lengthiest notes, delineating an astonishing variety of bird sounds, from those that "assail the ears of the audience to perhaps an almost unbearable degree" to "the equivalent of a brooding silence." Reading these reveals a master of sound at the height of his power. After Annie (Suzanne Pleshette) dies, for example, Hitchcock specifies that the bird sound should be "quite subdued so that it does not detract from the silence of death which should surround the cottage of Annie. We might even consider, although we shouldn't be definite about it, an odd croak or two from the murderers on the porch roof as though they are satisfied with their handiwork." Here again is Hitchcock's emphasis on the power of silence as a force that can "surround" an environment; the "odd croak" suggests he imagined the birds as formidable characters with their own script, indeed the principal ones since the entire movie shows them gradually displacing the human players until, as the final note chillingly puts it, "We are left alone with the birds. All we hear is this brooding, massing murmur which should continue as the picture fades out."

Eschewing the symphonic tradition he had pioneered for over thirty years, Hitchcock took a daring leap into the electronic avant-garde, fusing natural "found" sounds with electronic ones in the manner of Varese and Cage. During the sixties, he was fascinated by modern music, ordering up recordings of Stockhausen, Bartók, Boulez, and Shostakovich – the last of whom he tried unsuccessfully to hire for *Topaz*. He had experimented with electronic sound as early as *Rebecca* and *Spellbound*, but here electronic timbres and textures – with the exception of a Debussy Arabesque and the school song, "Risseldy Rosseldy" – carry the entire soundtrack. Electronic sounds create the unique austerity of *The Birds*, just as Herrmann's "black and white" strings evoke the gray modernity of *Psycho*.

The bracing triumph of *The Birds*, featuring Hollywood's most successful avant-garde film score, was followed by a long fall off a big cliff. Herrmann boasted to colleagues that he co-directed *The Birds*, a statement that cannot have sat well with Hitchcock, especially since he was under pressure from Lou Wasserman and MCA to terminate Herrmann, in their eyes a grumpy dinosaur. The box office failure of *Marnie* (1964) made matters worse, plunging Hitchcock into a dark, vulnerable mood. During the production of *Torn Curtain*, an even greater flop, longstanding issues involving authorship and envy came to a boil. In November 1965, Hitchcock sent Herrmann a lengthy, cranky memo commissioning *Torn Curtain* and also accusing him of plagiarizing his own score from *Joy in the Morning* (Alex Segal, 1965) for *Marnie*. One wonders how much of this is projection. Hitchcock, after all, often plagiarized himself, playing fresh variations on basic shots and motifs, sustaining the same idiosyncratic style even as he made movies of great variety – very much as Herrmann did with his scores. This time, he insisted that Herrmann write something new, a sixties beat for an audience that was "young, vigorous, and demanding"; it was "extremely essential" that Herrmann jettison "the old pattern." When Herrmann responded that he appreciated Hitchcock's "suggestions," a Hitchcock surrogate fired back that these were no such thing, but "requirements."

Stubbornly independent as ever, and eager to help a film that looked increasingly like another bomb, Herrmann ignored all the warnings, writing a dense, dissonant score, exactly what Hitchcock forbade. As he had done with *Psycho*, he also created a dramatic cue for the big murder scene even though Hitchcock specified no music. Upon hearing the Prelude at Goldwyn Studio – nothing else – Hitchcock angrily fired Herrmann in front of the orchestra, a bruising public humiliation. The finest director–composer team in Hollywood history was suddenly, shockingly over. John Addison, Herrmann's hastily hired replacement, produced the one mediocre score in Hitchcock's cinema, one literally phoned in, and one that, ironically, does not remotely carry a sixties beat.

Claude Chabrol, David Raksin, and others blame Hitchcock for this debacle, but the firing involved complicated emotions concerning authorship and authority on both sides. We should remember that Hitchcock stuck his neck out to defend

Herrmann to his corporate superiors and felt betrayed when Herrmann defied his directives, especially since his warnings were so clear. His relationship with his composer was a barometer of his independence and self-confidence, both of which were at an all-time low during this period. Had he felt stronger, he might have given Herrmann another chance, though it is by no means clear Herrmann could have given Lew Wasserman and company what they demanded. Stefano says the issue was simple – Hitchcock "didn't like the score" – but on the set of *Topaz*, Hitchcock told Maurice Jarre that Herrmann's ego was the problem: "His head started to be too big." John Williams also believes clashing egos were an issue. He remembers Peggy Robertson saying that Hitchcock thought "Benny was repeating himself and quoting himself," a memory backed up by the archives. But Williams believes that the breakup was ultimately about personal issues that "had nothing to do with music or film. ... [T]hey ended up being two matadors opposing one another." Given their dramatically different personalities and the work-for-hire nature of the business, it is remarkable that their collaboration lasted so long and yielded so much sublime music.

In his finale, *Family Plot*, Hitchcock's confidence apparently returned. John Williams describes him as "very professional and strong" in his musical direction, but also "very easy and congenial," despite his visibly failing health. Williams was surprised at Hitchcock's knowledge of classical music, his unusual "breadth of interest and intimacy in the concert repertory," and the two spent a great deal of pleasurable time discussing Vaughan Williams, Walton, and other mutual favorites. Hitchcock's hiring of Williams showed that his musical instincts were deft to the end. Though his sweeping, melodic style is very different from Herrmann's floating modal harmonies and slashing motifs, Williams was the heir to the Herrmann aesthetic. (He actually asked Herrmann's permission before accepting Hitchcock's invitation for *Family Plot*, afraid that an unvetted acceptance might cause bitter feelings from a friend and mentor.) Like Herrmann, Williams has an unmistakable sound made further distinctive by orchestrating everything himself. His rocket to fame took off as Herrmann's was coming down. Indeed, the latter's death in 1975 – right after adding the traumatic "Madhouse" cue from *Psycho* to the final notes of *Taxi Driver* (Martin Scorsese, 1976) – was regarded by many in the industry as the last nail in the coffin for expensive orchestral scores, which were falling victim to synthesizers and pop tracks – the dreaded sixties beat that Hitchcock wanted from Herrmann. But the triple hits of *Jaws* (Steven Spielberg, 1975), *Close Encounters of the Third Kind* (Steven Spielberg, 1977), and especially *Star Wars* (George Lucas, 1977), all tied directly to their scores, dramatically changed the game.

After he heard the score for *Jaws*, Hitchcock decided that Williams was the composer he wanted. Despite his bad ending with Herrmann, he never abandoned symphonic sound, as demonstrated by *Topaz* and *Frenzy*. Overshadowed by blockbusters like *Jaws* and *Close Encounters*, *Family Plot* is often overlooked by film music buffs, yet it provided Hitchcock with an elegant swan song. Among other pleasures, it offers a summation of Hitchcock's musical signatures: whirling ostinatos, aggressive pizzicatos, sinister harp passages, thematic crisscrossing, sudden silence after crescendos, and fusions of orchestral and "real" sounds, especially chimes. Its lonely timpani solos, a longtime Hitchcock trademark, are played by Williams's father, who had performed under Herrmann during the Hitchcock era. There is also a reprise of Hitchcock's fondness for offstage choruses. He ordered a recording of Debussy's choral nocturne, *Sirens*, then directed Williams to compose the ethereal chorus for the séance scenes that open and close the film.

Looking back at Hitchcock's epic and complicated career with music, a few things are clear. Early Hollywood scores like *Rebecca* and *Spellbound* helped change the way movie music was received, marketed, performed, and recorded. These are material matters that can be verified. Hitchcock also significantly raised the importance of diegetic and found music in the narratives of non-musicals. In addition to vernacular tunes, snatches of Beethoven, Mendelssohn, Schubert, Schumann, Wagner, Tchaikovsky, Delius, Poulenc, Cole Porter, and others play through the films, creating diverse meanings and atmospheres. This musical saturation began early in his British years, continued in Hollywood, and has been picked up by directors like Kubrick, Spielberg, and others who engage in lavish use of symphonic pastiche.

The Hitchcock–Herrmann phenomenon is a trickier matter. Though it certainly raised the bar, it is questionable whether it left an identifiable legacy. Alex Ross believes it showed audiences what music could accomplish in a Hollywood movie. Occasionally a film features a score, like *Vertigo*'s and *Psycho*'s, that creates its own powerful space, but Ross believes this is rare in contemporary film scoring. (Danny Elfman's work for Tim Burton's films and Jonny Greenwood's score for *There Will Be Blood* [Paul Thomas Anderson, 2007] are, I believe, among the rarities.) Steven Smith, Herrmann's biographer, takes a similarly cautious view:

> It didn't really change anything in Hollywood; not until the '70s did makers of thrillers like De Palma begin to have Herrmann-esque scores, and it wasn't until the '80s that major Herrmann plagiarism really kicked in on movie soundtracks. I think it's fair to say that in recent years, those BH-AH scores have been recognized by non-film music buffs as memorable in their own right, and they're certainly masterpieces; but outside of composers studying (or stealing) the way those scores work, I don't think they were game-changers – just exceptional examples of a composer-director partnership.
>
> (Personal communication, 11 Aug. 2009)

On the other hand, *Musical America*'s editor, Sedgwick Clark, believes the legacy continues strongly in the team of Spielberg–Williams. As we have seen, a great deal can be said for this linkage. Williams himself sees important similarities in how Hitchcock and Spielberg treated music and how he worked with them: "Both were very comfortable with music, very happy to have the orchestra playing a lot, both interested in intimate details like tempo and spotting. Much of their filmmaking style has to do with their use of music – music that has an idiosyncratic stamp. Steven is a different personality, sunnier, more optimistic, less skeptical – a very different view of life. But where music is concerned and its function, they are very similar."

Despite the clarity and persistence of Hitchcock's musical signatures over a long career, the music itself offers no single, fixed meaning: it can be lifesaving, as in *Murder!* and *Rear Window*, malevolent, as in *Shadow of a Doubt* and *Strangers on a Train*, or both, as in *The Lady Vanishes* (1938) and the remake of *The Man who Knew Too Much*. It is stereotypically associated with mayhem, with traumatic cues like "The Murder" from *Psycho*, "Alicia Collapses" from *Notorious*, and "Mood" from *Rope*, but it also graces scenes of surpassing delicacy: the exquisite vocalise in *I Confess*, the soprano-piano warm-up during Grace Kelly's dreamlike entrance into *Rear Window*, the Ravelian habanera in *Vertigo*'s museum scenes. Hitchcock's music is sublimely unfixed, filled with ambivalence and longing, anxiety and ambiguity, cuing its flawed characters' troubled psyches. It often conveys contradictory moods – drollery and dread, for example, in the comedies – or acts against what we see on the screen, setting up a restless counterpoint.

Yet occasionally it breaks free from this maelstrom to shine a clear light on the story and sound a resolution that words cannot, as when Doris Day sings "Que Sera, Sera" and saves her son, when Robert Donat remembers Mr. Memory's ditty and saves his country, and when the composer inspires Miss Lonely Hearts to live instead of die. The blind pianist in *Saboteur* (1942) articulates the redemptive power of music when he tells the hero on the run that he believes in his innocence because musical sound helps him see "intangible things." For Hitchcock too, music was a way into the intangible, offering momentary connectedness in a fractured world. Miss Lonely Hearts's statement at the end of *Rear Window* could well be Hitchcock's own: "You have no idea what this music means to me."

Works Cited

Film archives

All quotations are from the following film archives unless otherwise indicated:

British Film Institute, Library and Information Services, London, UK.
Margaret Herrick Library, The Alfred Hitchcock Collection, Academy of Motion Picture Arts and Sciences, Beverly Hills, California.
Museum of Modern Art, Film Study Center, New York, New York.
RKO Studio Collection, Arts Library Special Collections, Young Research Library, University of California, Los Angeles, California.
David Selznick Collection, Harry Ransom Humanities Research Center, University of Texas, Austin, Texas.
Syracuse University Library, Department of Special Collections, Syracuse, New York.
Warner Brothers Archive, School of Cinema-Television, University of Southern California, Los Angeles, California.

Print sources

Hitchcock, Alfred. "On Music in Films." Interview by Stephen Watts. 1933–34. *Hitchcock on Hitchcock: Selected Writings and Interviews.* Ed. Sidney Gottlieb. Berkeley: U of California P, 1995. 241–45.

Hyde, Thomas. "The Moral Universe of Hitchcock's *Spellbound*." *A Hitchcock Reader.* Ed. Marshall Deutelbaum and Leland Poague. Second ed. Chichester, UK: Wiley-Blackwell, 2009. 156–63.

Smith, Steven. *A Heart At Fire's Center: The Life and Music of Bernard Herrmann.* Berkeley: U of California P, 1991.

Sullivan, Jack. *Hitchcock's Music.* New Haven: Yale UP, 2006.

Truffaut, François, with the collaboration of Helen G. Scott. *Hitchcock.* Rev. ed. New York: Simon and Schuster, 1984.

Correspondence with the author

Steven Smith, 11 Aug. 2009.
Donald Spoto, 4 Jan. 2005.

Interviews with the author

Maurice Jarre, 8 June 2005.
Joseph Stefano, series of interviews, 1999–2005.
John Waxman, series of interviews, 1999–2005.
John Williams, 29 Jan. 2003, 21 Apr. 2006.

13

Some Hitchcockian Shots

Murray Pomerance

In studying or making reference to the works of Alfred Hitchcock, it has become a virtual fetish to focus on characters, scenes, plots, and outcomes. Few are the viewers, professional or lay, who neglect the centrality or importance of the "Hitchcock blonde," the moment of "Hitchcockian suspense," or the typical (read, dark and gruesome) "Hitchcock story." To argue the case – as François Truffaut, Ken Mogg, Bill Krohn, William Rothman, and I have done – that Hitchcock was more interested in cinema itself than in the stories his films contained seems to many a digression from what is truly essential, namely, appreciation of a certain kind of thriller unfolded with a certain chain of surprises as experienced by characters personified by especially glamorous movie folk: James Stewart, Cary Grant, Ingrid Bergman, Eva Marie Saint, Kim Novak, Janet Leigh, and the rest of the famous crowd. I take the case here to be somewhat more pointed, however. The most profound and delicate of Hitchcockian meanings are to be found at the cellular level, in the structure of his imagery, indeed in the Hitchcockian shot, where we find time and again, from his earliest works onward, evidence of an intensely philosophical mind hard at work upon profound problems of perception, social arrangement, and knowledge. For example, that in *Psycho* (1960) a serial killer is finally curbed by police and psychiatric authorities is one of a number of diegetic facts owing to the skeleton of the Robert Bloch novel that was Hitchcock's source. But the moment when Lila Crane (Vera Miles), opening the door to the Bates mansion with her left hand, trails her right hand behind her, pointing sweetly and in balletic gesture to the past (the past before motels existed), offers considerations on another order from the plot of the film, allowing us to reconsider all of the film's action in terms related to poise, modernity, bi-directionality, progress, and unfolding.

I intend here to study a number of forms of the Hitchcockian shot, delving into his work at will and focusing far less on the thrust of plot than on specific moments

A Companion to Alfred Hitchcock, First Edition. Edited by Thomas Leitch and Leland Poague.
© 2011 Thomas Leitch and Leland Poague. Published 2011 by Blackwell Publishing Ltd.

as configured on the screen. An exhaustive treatment of Hitchcock's more than fifty brilliant films is beyond the scope of this essay, whose true purpose is to inspire a certain creative reflection on the part of those who would wish to see more in Hitchcock than they have seen before, and this with a deeper love. Because I will forego compositional effects involving editing and shot arrangement, I will have little to say of the beautiful and captivating shot/countershot effects Hitchcock achieved; or about transitional effects such as the pictorial dissolve, a cross-fade in which Hitchcock matches pictorial elements; or, in general, about the extensive significance-for-plot of any particular image I've chosen. I take the shots as quotations, much as a devoted reader of written text might abstract as an epigraph some powerful and reverberating sentence or line of poetry. The shots I adumbrate constitute efflorescences or gestures much repeated over the course of a long career. This is what makes them biographical and auteurist, since evidently Hitchcock had a recurring need to see the world, and show it, a particular way.

Although it has been said before, it can be said again: Hitchcock was a master of the frame, and every nuance of his image is vital, no aspect decorative. In Hollywood, he was one of relatively few filmmakers who cared, and knew, about special effects, and his sense of camera position is cunning and impeccable.

A final caveat is an observation. Scholars and fans discuss Hitchcock's plots more often than his images for a number of reasons, but the most salient of these is that it is far easier to speak of stories, causations, and events than of composed images. When we say that a picture is worth a thousand words we mean in part that words struggle in trying to reach the objective and present factuality of light, form, balance, distance, and shape. Finding language to match an image presents a challenge.

Here are nine types of shots we find in Hitchcock over and over again:

1.   The Object Reverie

Marc Augé reflects that "[i]n Western societies, at least, the individual wants to be a world in himself; he intends to interpret the information delivered to him by himself and for himself" (30). One regards objects through a distance that separates and individualizes both the observer and what she sees, and one takes them to be for oneself: meaningful, that is, in private, esoteric terms. The Hitchcockian "object reverie" never ceases to struggle with this imperative, since it works to position an object as part of a social constellation. Hitchcock, we must always remember, was a sociological observer. Take for example a pair of opera glasses. They are being held by a man in a tuxedo, well positioned to get a good view of the stage of the Royal Albert Hall in *The Man Who Knew Too Much* (1956) yet also of the audience, specifically of a man sitting in a box opposite, soon to become the target of a bullet. While the glasses are instrumental for the assassin's gaze, to magnify it, to isolate it from the distractions of the scene, they also work to organize and punctuate our own way of looking, since they replace the front part of what is otherwise a rather hideous face (the performer, Reginald Nalder, had suffered chemical burns) in a kind of prosthetic projection outward into interpersonal space. They signal an intensification of ocularity, ocularity that becomes focus, focus that becomes aim, aim that is attached to a pistol, a pistol that is the agency of a revolution, a revolution that is the mechanism whereby power will be shifted in a country so distant we cannot even know its name. The shot itself shows the man gazing offscreen at the contralto Barbara Howitt as she intones with orchestral accompaniment under the baton of Bernard Herrmann, but then he swivels toward us, nothing less than an organic camera mount upon which the double lenses, attached to the head (a sign of the multiform Technicolor apparatus), now come into alignment with the corpus of the viewer, who must therefore stand in for the President this killer intends to shoot. In the glasses we can see nothing but shiny blankness, a hint of the power of looking and the relative powerlessness of what the looker turns his gaze upon.

In *Strangers on a Train* (1951) the evil killer Bruno (Robert Walker) is on his merry way to place a cigarette lighter belonging to his dupe, Guy (Farley Granger), at the whistle-stop scene of a murder. Jostled at curbside, his hand opens in reflex and the lighter drops through a sewer grating. He struggles to retrieve it within the limited moments available to him. The camera cuts to a view beneath the street and shows us the catch basin, all dark and putrid, with the gleaming lighter resting upon a thin ledge and Bruno's desperate fingers probing for it, yet not finding it. This object is at once trivial – quintessentially nondescript, even though it has a telltale insignia that will do the identification work Bruno desires – and richly indicative. On the one hand, everybody who smokes (and in the early 1950s almost everybody did) has a cheap lighter, a kind of personal prop; on the other, the lighter is a mechanization of allumation, not an inert thing but a working device, thus evidence of a technologizing process. This process, whereby the world becomes complex, signal, and rationalized, is the one that turns swatting a ball into the formality of a tennis match, or the primitive thrill of riding a boat through a dark tunnel into a ritualized mating game. The film will conclude with an adventure in and upon a far greater device, the carousel, an elaborate mechanism for producing intoxicating spins (like the painting technique of Bruno's rather dotty mother).

Similarly trivial is the matchbook in *North by Northwest* (1959) – also for smoking, but artfully monogrammed and thus sophisticated. First seen in the dining car, when Roger Thornhill (Cary Grant) elucidates his "trademark" initials for Eve Kendall (Eva Marie Saint), it returns in the South Dakota aerie of her villainous lover Vandamm (James Mason); having scribbled inside it, Roger tosses it down to the Persian carpet beneath her feet, where it becomes visible in macro close-up as Eve flips it open to read the lifesaving warning inside: "They're onto you. I'm in your room." The shot features not only text as object but orthography as object – a penmanship that must be perfectly open to reading on quick glance – as well as the thing itself, a matchbook that can be beneath desire, yet beyond trash. The henchman

Leonard (Martin Landau) sees it, too, bends down, picks it up, but then, instead of studying the too-simple little thing, drops it on the coffee table from which Eve can easily retrieve it when he isn't looking. Though Roger never smokes in this film, he apparently always carries one of his monogrammed matchbooks.

A central object may be chemical or biological, like the dark waters swilling in a sink early in *Marnie* (1964) as black dye is being rinsed out of someone's hair. Soon, very soon, we will discover that it is Marnie, and that she is blonde, the black liquid showing not only darkness in motion but also duplicity, masquerade, and imposition. In *Vertigo* (1958) we have a shot of Madeleine (Kim Novak) at Ernie's when she stops in front of the camera and we see her central feature, an ear. I have written at some length elsewhere about the importance of this ear, and others, in the structure of this film (*Eye* 255 ff.). An object might be a space, like the distance between the hand of Mrs. Verloc (Sylvia Sidney) and a kitchen knife in *Sabotage* (1936). An object shot can be unobtrusive, the very antithesis of all the ones I've described so far: the bass fiddle Manny Balestrero (Henry Fonda) is fingering in the opening shots of *The Wrong Man* (1956), a very old and traditional wooden instrument directing us back to the European history of Manny's heritage and also to the foundational, deeply establishing notes it plays: he is the common man, he is one of those who have what Paul Goodman called "the power of when the bottom drops out," and so it is that, in his trial and tribulations to come, Manny by virtue of his double bass becomes our most elemental moral principles put to the test.

Also with Hitchcock, the object shot can be spectacular: the blossoming indigo dress in *Topaz* (1969) that opens itself vulnerably and tantalizingly at the moment when Juanita de Cordoba (Karin Dor) falls dead upon a cold marble floor, all this spelled out with an overhead shot that emphasizes the graphic order of human frailty; or the blatant gigantism of objects when they invoke mortality, hopelessness, the end of the line: the coffee cup in *Notorious* (1946), from which Alicia Huberman (Ingrid Bergman) has slowly been sipping the lethal poison administered by Mrs. Sebastian (Leopoldine Konstantin), now gleaming directly in front of the lens while its user shrinks in the background, or the gun Dr. Murchison (Leo G. Carroll) points at Constance Peterson (Ingrid Bergman) in the finale of *Spellbound* (1945), a lethal thing that is also a lethal principle now swollen to overtake all other principles – of rationality, of discourse, of illumination, of transcendence – invoked in the film.

2.   The Topographic Shot: Setting as Map

As much as cinema is flux it is also orientational array, and Hitchcock, obsessed since his adolescence with trains, schedules, and the organization of movement in great cities (Spoto 20), knew this implicitly. Annette Michelson's comment that cinema offers "not merely a general, panoramic view of the landscape but … a machine for the generation of infinite compositional variations" (Michelson 57, quoted in Conley

26) – written in reference to René Clair's photograph of the Eiffel Tower but readily generalized – suggests a basis for what might be called the Hitchcockian "topographic shot," one which centers on the arrangement or design of space as an explicit, self-avowed feature. One finds these shots all through the Hitchcockian oeuvre: the snowy village created with miniatures in the opening of *The Lady Vanishes* (1938); the shadowy, receding moors by early light as Richard Hannay flees police capture in *The 39 Steps* (1935); Phoenix at 2:43 in the afternoon, surveyed meticulously like a map of itself in a series of overlapping pans and then zeroed in on, as the camera finds a single hotel room and enters to watch Sam Loomis (John Gavin) and Marion Crane (Janet Leigh) finishing their lunchtime tryst in *Psycho*; the long shot of Marrakech's Place Djemaa el Fna in hot, contrasty noontime light in *The Man Who Knew Too Much* (1956), juxtaposing tourism, commercial hubbub, traditional landmarks, and frenzied populations. In the same film, a camera mounted near the topmost balcony in the Albert Hall shows the array of performing and listening forces arranged for a summer evening concert: not only the musicians ready to play and the audience ready to hear but also the vast spherical void in which the sound will reverberate and take form, this mapped space an acoustic basin or sacred font that will house sanctified and petrified emotion.

We can think of the lengthy panning commencement of *Rear Window* (1954), configuring the apartment complex as a map of narrative possibilities; the establishing shot of Mount Rushmore in *North by Northwest* as a map of potential action lines (Ernest Lehman actually did map lines on a postcard-style variation of this view before writing the finale); the vast cornfield intersection seen from a high crane in the same film, where the quadrants of space visible in a single shot locate in advance the marking points of an elaborate, suspenseful choreography between man and aircraft soon to come; the picture postcard shots of the tiny Vermont village that is the setting of *The Trouble With Harry* (1955), its pristine buildings flooded by the vast dry ocean of dying, morbidly spectacular autumnal vegetation appropriate to a film about the mystery of death; the elevations of the Statue of Liberty in *Saboteur* (1942), premonitions of verticality and danger; and the long shot showing the configuration of the auditorium space in *Stage Fright* (1950), with special emphasis on the dividing line between stage and audience where the curtain falls to rest, fit emblem of an essay on theatricality as dualism and schism, mask and performance. A similarly splitting treatment is given the Leipzig *Lekturverein* for *Torn Curtain* (1966), another film about performance as related to intelligence. Viewing the pronounced vertical slope of the seats there, Hitchcock's camera establishes a power differential between Lindt (Ludwig Donath) and Armstrong (Paul Newman) that pervades the entire story. *Strangers on a Train* has an explicit map shot, as Bruno shows Guy which room in the Anthony mansion his hated father will be sleeping in (though the map does not show where the family dog will be waiting). And if we consider Tracy (Donald Calthrop) escaping from police at the end of *Blackmail* (1929), we find it hard not to see the meticulous and overt manner in which shots of the British Museum are arranged to give a view of their relation to display space.

Nor must we forget the celebrated gull's-eye-view shot of Bodega Bay on fire in *The Birds* (1963), a picture of the world as seen by those who can transcend it, and also a blunt invocation of being gulled, since it is created by mattes.

In each of these shots, some synopsis or condensation of narrative action is implied by a detailed rendering of the space in which that action will occur. Rather than using settings casually or arbitrarily, Hitchcock gives them full consideration as active agents in the recounting, and shows them openly in their agency.

3. Apotheoses of Affect

In 1959, Michel Mourlet published in *Cahiers du cinéma* what the journal called an "extreme opinion" about film: "[A]rt has always been a representation of the world, which is to say a chance offered to contingent and incomplete reality to finish itself definitely, according to our desires." In that world and in that finishing, primary is the affective body, agency of the drama and simulacrum of the viewer's self (the now-vanished viewer's self, since the body of the viewer is suspended in favor of the body onscreen). Further, writes Mourlet, "The most acute proximity of the actor's body conveys both the obsessive fear of, and the wish for, seduction" (24, 30, translations mine). One of Hitchcock's trademarks is the situational climax, the moment when a character's realization is so powerful and overwhelming that her body must be understood as an internal locus of feeling, memory, and sense. But his motto was the principle of touching his audience: "You deliberately … control their thoughts" (Truffaut 269). The audience had to feel what the character felt. "Someday," he told Ernest Lehman, "we won't even have to make a movie – there'll be electrodes implanted in their brains, and we'll just press different buttons and they'll go 'ooooh' and 'aaaah' and we'll frighten them, and make them laugh. Won't that be wonderful?" (Spoto 406). We may think of the "affective apotheosis" as a shot in which the narrative world, extended to its limit of possibility in a moment of heightened probability and power, is made subjectively apprehensible to the viewer through a construction, positioning of character, or implicating movement.

In *The Birds*, for example, trouble first descends from the air as Melanie Daniels (Tippi Hedren) crosses Bodega Bay in a rowboat. When the offending gull suddenly flies into the shot, exactly as it enters Melanie's consciousness, we are nearly as surprised as she is. In *The Lodger* (1926), Mrs. Bunting (Marie Ault) worries about the identity and purposes of the young man she has just taken in as a lodger (Ivor Novello) – is he the Avenger? – and her fear and excitement are given over to us by virtue of a shot looking upward from her parlor as she gazes at him pacing in his room: the floor is constructed of glass so that the camera can see his feet stepping back and forth. As the actor Handel Fane (Esme Percy), brought in for a delicate interrogation in *Murder!* (1930), sits at the desk of Sir John Menier (Herbert Marshall), he keeps reaching for an ashtray in a shot that links his fingers, whose genius is touch (the loving touch, the performing touch, the killing touch), with ashes, the end of everything (Wilson 112). Or consider an acoustic embedding, as when a woman's scream conveys the discovery of a murder in *Blackmail* or *The 39 Steps*, or when a dog's whine conveys the murder of his master in *Secret Agent* (1936) – a shrill, persistent, animal cry that collapses the distance between the killing on a mountaintop nearby (as seen through a telescope) and the victim's gemütlich home environment, where people artfully converse. In *I Confess* (1953), the murderous sacristan Keller (O.E. Hasse) stands at the foot of a stepladder looking up in desperation to the invisible face of his priest, who, turned to us but away from him, is painting the walls of the rectory "antique white." Keller is white with fear, but we, positioned in the wall that is being whitewashed, are white with purity.

Several nights into the honeymoon of Marnie (Tippi Hedren), after its overwhelming culmination – when she has been tamed by the zoologist/publisher/lover Mark Rutland (Sean Connery) in the lush cabin of a cruise ship – the camera stares out a porthole at the blue, blue sea, which seems to have changed direction during a fade-out and fade-in on the same shot. When Michael Armstrong in *Torn Curtain* has prised the secret of Gamma-5 from the obsessive genius Lindt in Room 29, the camera jumps to a close shot of the old German's face as he registers first shock, then realization, and in a stunning use of the crane, we swoop up into the air as we hear Lindt bellow, "I forbid you to leave this room!" We must add to the list the last moments of Brenda Blaney (Barbara Leigh-Hunt) in *Frenzy* (1972). Strangled by Bob Rusk (Barry Foster), her eyes and tongue popping out, her blouse undone, her creamy skin fills the screen as we occupy the murderer's satiated point of view. And the desperate carousel shot in *Strangers on a Train*, with a little man crawling under a carousel speeding out of control to reach the lever that can make it stop (shot live, with a real operator risking his life). And the worst nightmare of Scottie (James Stewart) in *Vertigo*, when he stares down and the world both falls away and springs forward at once (a shot made with a $19 000 wooden model photographed on its side after the studio estimated a special effects job that would cost more than twice as much). Or a shot in *Psycho* rarely mentioned as such: Marion is in the shower; a dark female form is reaching to draw back the shower curtain, knife in hand; but *Marion is oblivious*, even and exactly to the degree that we, showering with her, are aware. What is being carved in the famous shower scene, then? Not Marion, for she doesn't really exist, but our perception and understanding.

4. Explicit Designs

Hitchcock's career had begun in design, and even a casual glance at his films reveals again what was present earlier in the numerous pencil sketches he made for sharing his visual ideas with cinematographers and designers, that he organized his dramatic ideas using principles of graphic composition, balance, depth, shading, angularity, proximity-distance, shape, and, from 1948 onwards, color. For emphasis, punctuation, or caesura, however, Hitchcock sometimes included shots in which the design is *explicit as such*, shots that seem to cry, "All this by design," or perhaps to imply that it is by Design that we exist. However one interprets such shots, they are usually timed for shock and achieved with the greatest elegance, not to say an ironic simplicity that becomes palpable when we consider the directness of the idea being conveyed. I am thinking of the street crowd in the rainstorm in *Foreign Correspondent* (1940), filmed in black and white from above, with hundreds of milling strangers each hiding under a slick black umbrella. Equally powerful is the confession shot in *I Confess*, as we see light streaming over the face of Father Logan (Montgomery Clift) as he sits in the booth with Keller, the intense shadows of the grille falling over Keller as he tries through language to escape his fate.

A remarkable shot early in *Notorious* has Alicia at her soirée talking to a seated gentleman (Cary Grant). He is positioned with his back to the camera, his torso and tidily cropped hair all dark and mysterious. She faces him and us in a garish black-and-white striped garment that shrieks duplicity, indecisiveness, moral agony (her father has just been sent to prison for Nazi collaboration, and she is alone, lost, at sea). The general store run by Mrs. Wiggs (Mildred Dunnock) in *The Trouble With Harry* is an abstract expressionist delirium, reflecting the wildly colored expressionist canvases of Sam Marlowe (John Forsythe) that line its walls, by virtue of the array of gaily colored and haphazardly placed products all round. The United Nations exterior in *North by Northwest*, shot (we are to believe) from the top of the Secretariat looking down as Roger flees – the array of pathways and implantations is a pure design, out of Malevich; this reminds us that Roger's fate is designed by his Creator. There is a similarly modernist bent for line and colored space in the exterior shots around Scottie's house in *Vertigo*, as he meets Madeleine (Kim Novak) there the day after rescuing her from the bay. And in *Strangers on a Train*, the theme of crossed pathways and crossed fates integral to the plot is signaled by a dissolve to a shot of crisscrossed railway tracks. In *Frenzy*, once she is quite dead on her comfortable chair, Brenda Blaney is shot from above, frozen, eyes agape, and becomes something of a cubist masterpiece.

5.   Hitchcockian Auras

Garry Winogrand once said that he photographed in order to see what things looked like photographed, and one often has the sense that Hitchcock operated in the same way. There are numerous occasions in which some galvanizing little pressure, some locking twist is given a shot, usually through application of an effect of some kind, so that regardless of the diegetic moment the vision is sent home as pure effect. In *Vertigo*, Scottie has found a shopgirl named Judy Barton (Kim Novak) and has transformed her so that she will resemble Madeleine Elster, whom he passionately and hopelessly loved. Now, for the final touch, she has gone into her bathroom and fixed her hair, and as the music swells and he gazes (through our eyes), she emerges. Suffusing the space through which she floats ever closer to Scottie is a kind of sea-green mist that softens her features and makes her seem stellar. In *The Birds*, Lydia Brenner (Jessica Tandy) goes to visit her neighbor after a bird attack and discovers him on the floor of his bedroom, quite dead. But Hitchcock uses a much imitated triple jump cut to give three rapid, increasingly proximate visions of his face, from which the eyes have been entirely pecked out. Or, in *Strangers on a Train*, Bruno, having come uninvited to a fancy soirée, takes a moment to show a society matron how he would go about strangling someone to death. The aura here depends on the delicious Norma Varden's facial expressions rather than any cinematographic effect. We see by her eyes, slowly tightening, then expanding, then going into freeze, that he has been carried away and is strangling her for real.

There is the fall of the nefarious Fry (Norman Lloyd) from the Statue of Liberty in *Saboteur,* extended through slight slow motion; and its match, the tumble of Valerian (Adam Williams) from Mount Rushmore in *North by Northwest*. In both cases we peer down to see the body recede, as in the policeman's fall from the rooftop that opens *Vertigo*. There is the sudden jump of the camera in *North by Northwest* to a balcony position looking down on Vandamm as he confides to Leonard that he plans to dispatch Eve "from a great height"; this matches a shot in *The Man Who Knew Too Much* (1956) when it is from distinctly above that we see the terrified Ben and Jo McKenna (James Stewart and Doris Day) hearing their kidnapped son on a telephone.

Two "Hitchcockian auras" are worth special note, amid the dozens of others I have not space to mention, even if special effects are not involved: *Torn Curtain's* close shot on the fingers of Gromek (Wolfgang Kieling) as he is gassed in a cooking stove and passes into a state of uncontrollable twitching just before his end: they are on his killer Armstrong's neck, beautifully suggesting an embrace and supporting François Truffaut's claim to Hitch that he filmed his love scenes like murders and his murders like love scenes (345). And the look on the face of L.B. Jefferies (James Stewart) when his girlfriend Lisa (Grace Kelly) is trapped by the butcher Lars Thorwald (Raymond Burr) in his apartment across the way, Jeff wheelchair-bound and able to do nothing, not even turn away or cease to see the horror before him. This optical paralysis was established in *Spellbound* when John Ballantine (Gregory Peck) suddenly recalled his own vision as a boy of something equally horrifying that he couldn't stop seeing and couldn't stop.

6.   Effects Distancing

As much as it was necessary for Hitchcock to draw his audience into the action, it was sometimes more vitally useful to keep them out, to block our access or, more powerfully, to suspend us – much as Jeff and Ballantine are suspended in the two examples just above. In a particular type of shot, special effects are invoked to create an impossible moment – that is, a vision that is raptly engaging and thoroughly believable even though irrational or non-existent in everyday life. In *Vertigo*, Scottie hangs from a bent gutter and looks down into the street below – a very clear transition from a studio shot to an artist's rendering, yet aesthetically credible because of the inbred fear of heights Hitchcock's audience could be counted on to harbor. The *Psycho* shower scene terrifies in part because of the rapid succession of very brief shots, edited so that one has a sense of slashing space and form in every direction; any single more conventional shot, extended in duration, would ruin the sequence. A certain magical effect is achieved in *The Man Who Knew Too Much* (1956) when the villains rehearse the moment of the killing, which is timed to a bar in the *Storm Cloud Cantata*. They play the piece over and over, each time putting the needle of their phonograph down at the precise spot in the score that they need to hear. With a real recording one could never be so precise. In *The Birds*, Mitch (Rod Taylor) walks Melanie up into the dunes behind his house, and there in the tranquility and remove she tells him the story of her life. The glorious perspective in the distance, shining with green and purple and invoking coasts, liminality, natural undulation but also a horizon beyond which any danger might be mobilizing, is a painted backdrop, not a real scene. Mitch and Melanie are not only set off in a delicious privacy but also enclosed in a vast but limited space in which illusion, trickery, and deceit are subtly invoked to at least the same degree as honesty, confidence, and feeling.

One particular shot in *Marnie* has received considerable attention as a failure on the filmmaker's part. This is the final moment, in which Mark and Marnie drive away from her mother's house in Baltimore. The little street lined with brick row houses and culminating in the harbor itself – Hitchcock was creating a street in London's East End (Krohn *et al.* 41, in an English translation Bill Krohn kindly provided me) – with the prow of a huge docked ship jutting right against the end of the road, is filmed on a sound stage using a painted drop. There is a certain storybook feel to the shot, and by implication to the entire tale, an overt pictorialism that suggests the fabricator's hand. Other shots in this film set us up for this split feeling of being at once inside and outside the tale, at once distanced and diagnostic; sympathetic toward Marnie and her problems yet suspicious, even paranoid, in the face of everything she "reveals." Hitchcock knew very well what he was doing here and exasperated even some of his technical staff, who knew too, yet didn't exactly approve:

WHITLOCK: Robert, you've got to admit it's one of the most talked of scenes in any movie. Notorious though it might be.
MICHELSON: But he is the final arbiter on these things. You know, you can scream all you want, but if he likes it, that is *it*.
BOYLE: But he's also willing to put up with technical flaws if he feels it does the trick for him.

(Krohn et al. 42–43)

The effect of the painted drop was to engender a certain kind of diegetic space, both prettified and gritty, both overwhelming and distancing. Marnie herself is cut off from social relations and social space in exactly this way.

7.   The Character Capture

Any filmmaker might need to use a shot to define, position, and highlight a principal or subordinate character in order to structure a cinematic narrative by accurately framing an important narrative moment. Benjamin recollected that Baudelaire had credited the portraitist with a "quick grasp" (41). However, Hitchcock frequently snatches summative character shots, in which the full expression of a character's attitude, feeling, knowledge, position, history, and understanding is given in a single brilliant coup. These shots stand out as iconic in his work.

In *The 39 Steps*, the crofter's wife (Peggy Ashcroft) stands inside the open doorway of her husband's cold little cottage in the middle of the night, her new friend Hannay (Robert Donat) having crept off and left her now bereft of hopes that he will magically lift her away to "the City." Dropping back down, unsalvageably, to the hard truth of her painful life, she waits. In *Saboteur*, the blind Phillip Martin (Vaughan Glaser) stands at his door in a kind of echo of this shot, "looking out" into the night as Barry Kane (Robert Cummings) flees. Martin's heartfelt belief in the true principles of American liberty – that men are essentially innocent and good – is shining from his face, even though his eyelids are gently closed. At the finale of *Vertigo*, Scottie Ferguson perches in the tower of the mission church of San Juan Bautista, his arms outstretched against the stark beclouded sky to signal that now, with Madeleine / Judy truly lost to him forever, he has neither world nor agency nor hope. In *The Man Who Knew Too Much* (1956), as young Hank McKenna (Christopher Olsen) lingers captive upstairs at the embassy, he hears his mother's voice wafting on the air (she is downstairs, crooning "Que Sera, Sera" to a bored audience of diplomats and their wives), and Lucy Drayton (Brenda De Banzie) approaches him at the locked door of the chamber, gazes into his face with the fulsome love of a woman who has always wanted, but never had, a child, and says, "Whistle, Hank! Whistle as loud as you can!" In *Strangers on a Train*, the warped Bruno Anthony is gazing at his mother's (rather abstract expressionist, indeed hideous) portrait of her husband, and with an icy, painted mirth smeared across his face, explodes, "Oh, Mother – that's Father!" By comparison with the falsity of his face, its desperation, its frighteningly boundless expressiveness, the painted "monster" is genteel. In the same film, after Bruno tests out his strangling skills on the society matron at the party, Babs (Patricia Hitchcock), the younger sister of Guy's girlfriend Anne (Ruth Roman), is seen in close-up, her eyes round as saucers behind her saucer-sized eyeglasses, as she whispers, "He was looking at *me!*" In *Rope* (1948), having realized that his former students are a pair of cold-blooded murderers, Rupert

Cadell (James Stewart) lectures them on moral philosophy and tells them he intends to turn them in to a justice system that will bring mortal punishment. As he points angrily, rage spreading over his face and into his posture, his eyes suddenly open in a rictus of pain and realization, as though all the world has only now become apparent, and behind him, outside a window, a neon sign flashes on and off, red as blood.

A tiny, delicate butterfly of a moment in *Shadow of a Doubt* (1943): Emma Newton (Patricia Collinge) is about to learn that her beloved brother Charles (Joseph Cotten), who has been visiting the family and bringing back to her fond, entrancing memories of a sweet, distant childhood, is now suddenly leaving town. (A serial murderer, he realizes he is on point of being caught.) She is entertaining company in her parlor, offering deviled eggs with all the kindness and simplicity that can be summoned by a woman who has given up her whole true self, who has lost the person she once was; as someone's wife, "you sort of forget you're you." Graceful and innocent, she says, "It's the paprika makes it pink," a statement at once about her diligent, caring labors in the kitchen (which are oft invoked in the film), about her desire to be a good hostess (for her husband's sake), and about the color pink, which is the only explicit reference to color anywhere in this black-and-white film. Emma is pink with happiness, at least now; she is flushed pink with gentility and generosity; she is pink in the memories of her childhood; and, because she is pink, she is grippingly alive.

A powerful character capture can focus not on a face or posture but on an appendage. At the finale of *North by Northwest*, Leonard has his foot above the whitening hand of Roger Thornhill, who, hanging by one arm from Mount Rushmore, is gripping the suspended Eve Kendall with his other. In an excruciating forward dolly into a macro-close shot, and over a sostenuto note in Herrmann's score, slowly, methodically, sadistically, Leonard's foot comes down, a foot in a shabby shoe, a foot that says everything about the man.

8.   Pictured Pictures

"The setting of actors and objects," writes Mourlet, "their positioning inside the frame should express everything" (27). It is fair to say that Hitchcock is not only meticulous about this but takes care to position his camera outside the frame: my eye watching his work is one of the objects he chooses to place. While many film-makers make this positioning of the camera "theatrically" invisible, Hitchcock tends to make us aware not only of what we are seeing but, at the same time, of the fact that thanks to his camera we are seeing it. What can we say when his shot contains not an explicit world to which one may give attention but a two-dimensional rendition, a recursion? The shot of a painting is a frequent Hitchcockian device, self-reflexive as such because of the filmmaker's notable art collection (see Gunning) and because the canvas-within-the-frame is usually a short-form commentary on characters and their situation. It is not art in general that characters live with – that catches our gaze – but a very particular work, something especially and pointedly indicative: the portrait of mysterious Carlotta Valdes hanging near de Largillière's proud *Gentleman* and van Loo's *Architecture* in *Vertigo*; the expressivist "masterpiece" rendering Bruno's father; dour General MacLaidlaw (Cedric Hardwicke) in *Suspicion* (1941), looking down from his perch on the wall to register disapproval of his daughter and her romance; deceased Mr. Brenner hanging near a piano at which Melanie plays a Debussy "Arabesque," always reminding Lydia of the man her son didn't manage to be; or the chubby, rubicund Prime Minister hanging in a gilded frame over the head of the Ambassador (Mogens Wieth) in *The Man Who Knew Too Much* (1956) – a figure of dominance, of excessive stability perhaps, and, as we can see when we look at the two men together in a single shot, of paternity.

In *Blackmail* there is a pair of art works, one by the professional Crewe (Cyril Ritchard), of a joker grimacing into the viewer's face and pointing an accusing finger – but at whom? the painter who made him? – and one by the utterly amateurish Alice (Anny Ondra), who has tried to draw a flapper, Crewe guiding her hand, and peremptorily signed her name.

Sometimes the pictured picture indicates class and attitude, as with the abstract painting in the foyer of the new Aysgarth residence in *Suspicion* – an attitude that the visiting policemen, denizens of the working class, cannot quite fathom. There are the prints of clipper ships and early San Francisco, betokening bourgeois taste, in the plush ruby-red office of Gavin Elster (Tom Helmore) in *Vertigo*. There are the bucolic landscapes, symbols of the remove of the leisure class, lining the library of the estate of Lester Townsend (Philip Ober) in *North by Northwest*. Part of what makes Vandamm seem at home here, even though he is a squatter, is the match between the class these paintings invoke and the class his suave and restrained manner display.

Hitchcock uses pictures as clues. The self-portrait Midge (Barbara Bel Geddes) paints "à la Valdes" (actually painted by Henry Bumstead) in *Vertigo* is a direct indication of self-condemnation and withdrawal on the part of a character who has every reason for commanding our interest but no continuing purpose in the plot. The photograph of a racing car crash taken from the side of the race track shown at the beginning of *Rear Window* signals Jefferies's recent history, accounts for his leg cast, and points to the sort of adventurousness that might shrink from the lobster and chiffon of the world of Lisa Fremont. In *Stage Fright* there is a remarkable photograph, examined briefly but intensively by Jonathan (Richard Todd) when he goes to the house of his lover Charlotte (Marlene Dietrich) to retrieve her blood-stained dress: the expressions of the persons shown here, Charlotte and her platoon of dancing boys, say everything about his deep relation to her and about the real focus of her attentions (see Pomerance, *Horse* 126 ff.). A close look at Jonathan's own face in this photograph is a stunning clue to his future in the film as well. Nor are clues missing when Hitchcock frames a poster of *The Enforcer* (Bretaigne Windust, 1951) in the vitrine of a Québec theater in *I Confess*, as Logan marches through the city attempting to forestall his arrest for a murder he did not commit.

In *Marnie*, for a very brief moment, the screen is filled with a framed photograph that Mark treasures upon his desk: of Sophie, the jaguarundi he had captured and tamed as part of his general study of arboreal predators of the rain forest. Her stunning green eyes, her ferocity, her perfectly equivocal feral intensity and disinterest are, of course, a match for Marnie's, and when Marnie is looking at her, she is explicitly seeing herself.

A summative moment is ironically to be found in Hitchcock's very early *The Lodger*, when the strange and unidentified young man who comes to rent a room in Mrs. Bunting's house is first shown the space he will occupy. The walls are covered with cheap reproductions of portraits, most in the Pre-Raphaelite style. All of the subjects are women, women gazing out without seeing, women offering the slightly unfocused and disconnected eye that indicates they do not see us seeing them but only themselves being seen (Berger). The Lodger is offended sharply by these pictures, and one by one turns them to the wall, then has them removed. What is left are pallid rectangles upon the wallpaper, traces where faces had been – or traces of where traces of faces had been (see Pomerance, "Light"). If pictures on the wall are meaningful, how much more meaningful is their absence.

9.   The Dancing Camera

Discussing a number of ballet films, including *Shall We Dance* (Mark Sandrich, 1937), *The Unfinished Dance* (Henry Koster, 1947), and *The Red Shoes* (Michael Powell and Emeric Pressburger, 1948), Adrienne McLean makes a fascinating comment: "No really burning questions, even aesthetic ones, are ever asked" (159). Hitchcock did not make ballet films. There is a ballet sequence set to Tchaikovsky's *Francesca da Rimini* (1876) climaxing *Torn Curtain*, a social dance central to *The Lodger* and *Saboteur*, a cotillion used as setting in *Suspicion*, a dancer warming up to "Fancy Free" in *Rear Window*, a repetitive motif of waltzing widows in *Shadow of a Doubt*, but no devotion to the ballet. Yet often, quite as though it were as obsessed with dancing as Vicky in *The Red Shoes* –

LERMONTOV: Why do you want to dance?
VICKY: Why do you want to live?

– Hitchcock's camera moves choreographically, "asking burning questions," describing in a single shot or a matched pair of shots what can only be apprehended as a feeling and expressive gesture of its whole machine-like body and sensibility. This includes moments when the camera is in action and moments when a character, suddenly repositioned before the lens, gives the feeling that the camera has moved around him. It is camera motion as gesture, not surveillance.

In *North by Northwest,* when Vandamm has met Thornhill, they circle around the library like two gladiators about to contend. The camera begins by watching Vandamm describe a semicircle, his eyes thrust forward. Then Hitchcock cuts to a perfectly matching shot, the second half of the circle, with Thornhill picking up the same speed of movement, his eyes the same height off the floor. The camera also inscribes a circle that evokes Manny Balestrero's perception of his jail cell in *The Wrong Man.* There is a rotating dance in *Murder!,* too, as the camera circles around the jury room to show every juror but one, the one who will turn out to count.

Four dancing moves of the Hitchcockian camera are so entrancing, so deeply imbricating and engaging, that I wish to conclude by stepping through them one by one. In *Rebecca* (1940), the new Mrs. de Winter (Joan Fontaine), a stranger to Manderley upon whom the giant mansion sits like a grossly oversized garment, and a young woman who has married above her class and simply does not understand much of the code that is being whispered around her, has taken the bold step of arranging a masquerade party. The housekeeper, Mrs. Danvers (Judith Anderson), by no means her friend, has recommended a costume based on a huge portrait hanging on the wall (another pictured picture, to be sure, in which the face of the long-dead de Winter relation somehow fades into obscurity by comparison with the marvelous frilly dress she is wearing). We see the girl fixed into her garment, the last stitches pulled. She walks out of her bedroom and finds the central staircase. Her new husband, Maxim (Laurence Olivier), is down below, his back turned, wrapped in conversation. She steps down, step step step, down down down, as the camera gently drops with her, its tight focus on her face as strict as her smile. Her head cants a little, vulnerably, and the lips part in a smile that is emphasized – made acute – by our dropping movement as she makes it. "O, love me!" she means to say, and soon, far too soon, we have reached the floor.

In *Notorious,* and then later in *Marnie,* we have matching shots, with a complex and elegant soirée in progress in a fancy house. Starting from a position near a balcony overlooking the business, the camera slowly descends, dancing its way to earth like an aircraft sniffing for the runway, with the same purposeful, exact, unrelenting trajectory. In the first, we have our eye on a key being clutched in a woman's hand, and we descend directly, slowly, evenly, tactically into a close-up of the thing itself. In the second, we must travel to the front door, *ding-dong!,* as it opens and we see the last face on earth we wish to see.

In *The Man Who Knew Too Much,* we are at the embassy, where Hank is somewhere stowed away. Jo must sing out so that her invisible voice can find him. And find him it does, in its invisibility and its prescience. The voice hunts as we hunt, occupying our eyes, haunting these stairways and corridors, regarding these closed doors, door after door, then only a particular door … It is the camera dancing silently, borne aloft on Jo's voice, dancing yet now stopping, breath held, at the one door which is the future and the end of feeling. Childhood found.

Works Cited

Augé, Marc. *Non-Places: An Introduction to Supermodernity*. Trans. John Howe. London: Verso, 2008.

Benjamin, Walter. *Charles Baudelaire: A Lyric Poet in the Era of High Capitalism*. Trans. Harry Zohn. London: Verso, 1997.

Berger, John. *Ways of Seeing*. London: BBC, 1972.

Conley, Tom. *Cartographic Cinema*. Minneapolis: U of Minnesota P, 2007.

Gunning, Tom. "In and Out of the Frame: Paintings in Hitchcock." *Casting a Shadow: Creating the Alfred Hitchcock Film*. Ed. Will Schmenner and Corinne Granof. Evanston: Mary and Leigh Block Museum of Art and Northwestern UP, 2008. 29–47.

Krohn, Bill. *Hitchcock at Work*. London: Phaidon, 2000.

Krohn, Bill, with Don Shay, Bob Swarthe, Serge Le Peron, and Olivier Assayas. "Ils Ont Fabriqué 'Les Oiseaux.'" Roundtable on *The Birds* with Albert Whitlock, Robert Boyle, Harold Michelson, and Richard Edlund. *Cahiers du cinéma* 337 (June 1982): 36–48.

McLean, Adrienne L. *Dying Swans and Madmen: Ballet, the Body, and Narrative Cinema*. New Brunswick: Rutgers UP, 2008.

Michelson, Annette. "Dr. Crase and Mr. Clair," *October* 11 (Winter 1979): 30–53.

Mogg, Ken. *The Alfred Hitchcock Story*. Rev. ed. London: Titan, 2008.

Mourlet, Michel. "Sur un art ignoré," *Cahiers du cinéma* 98 (Aug. 1959): 23–37.

Pomerance, Murray. *An Eye for Hitchcock*. New Brunswick: Rutgers UP, 2004.

Pomerance, Murray. *The Horse Who Drank the Sky: Film Experience Beyond Narrative and Theory*. New Brunswick: Rutgers UP, 2008.

Pomerance, Murray. "Light, Looks, and *The Lodger*." *Quarterly Review of Film and Video* 26.5 (2009): 425–33.

Rothman, William. *Hitchcock—The Murderous Gaze*. Cambridge: Harvard UP, 1982.

Spoto, Donald. *The Dark Side of Genius: The Life of Alfred Hitchcock*. Boston: Little, Brown, 1983.

Truffaut, François, with the collaboration of Helen G. Scott. *Hitchcock*. Rev. ed. New York: Simon and Schuster, 1984.

Wilson, Frank R. *The Hand: How Its Use Shapes the Brain, Language, and Human Culture*. New York: Pantheon, 1998.

PART V

Development

14

Hitchcock's Silent Cinema

Sidney Gottlieb

When we think of Alfred Hitchcock, we normally gravitate to the films of his middle to later years. *Shadow of a Doubt* (1943), *Notorious* (1946), *Rear Window* (1954), *Vertigo* (1958), *Psycho* (1960), and *The Birds* (1963) are among the titles with which audiences are most familiar and on which his reputation usually rests. And even for those with a somewhat more comprehensive view, the term "early Hitchcock" usually goes back no farther than to his justly praised thrillers of the 1930s, from *The Man Who Knew Too Much* (1934) to *The Lady Vanishes* (1938). This view of Hitchcock is far too limited. It not only overlooks the critical earliest part of his work, the ten films he directed before the introduction of talking pictures, but also downplays a key fact about his entire career that is perhaps best conveyed by what may seem to be a tendentious overstatement: Hitchcock was in fundamental ways a silent filmmaker from beginning to end, purposefully, determinedly, and self-consciously so.

There is, of course, much more to Hitchcock's films than images and editing, and we should not underestimate his mastery of sound, including dialogue, music, and sound effects, all expertly integrated into his visual design. But silent films, filmmaking theories, and techniques provided Hitchcock with influences that he never outgrew and a template for his art that he modified and expanded but never abandoned. Hitchcock's experiences in making films before the advent of synchronized sound were not merely an apprenticeship in an evolving art form, and his first films were far more than occasionally interesting but generally forgettable rough drafts on the way to his memorable masterpieces. His silent films are a bedrock of experimentation and achievement, and we should begin – although not end – our examination of Hitchcock as a silent filmmaker with an overview of the films he made in the 1920s.

A Companion to Alfred Hitchcock, First Edition. Edited by Thomas Leitch and Leland Poague.
© 2011 Thomas Leitch and Leland Poague. Published 2011 by Blackwell Publishing Ltd.

It is worth going back to even before the beginning. Before he directed on his own, he assisted in a variety of ways on at least nineteen films (see the filmography in McGilligan 751–56). Of these, *Woman to Woman* (1923) is the most intriguing – Hitchcock himself refers to this well-received melodrama with great pride and affection – but no copy of it is known to exist. Copies do exist, though, of the German release version of *The Blackguard* (1925), a film directed by Graham Cutts (with whom Hitchcock worked on five projects) but "built" by Hitchcock: he is credited for "Bauten," and we know from a variety of sources that this likely included adapting the source novel to a screenplay, composing the intertitles, art and set design, and the actual direction of some sequences. It is difficult to know exactly what Hitchcock may have been responsible for in the finished film, but there are numerous Hitchcockian elements that anticipate the early films he directed. Although framed as a historical epic, *The Blackguard* is basically a melodrama, the story less of Adrian Lewinski (Bernhard Goetzke), who gives up his career as a world-famous violinist to lead a world-altering revolution, than of Michael Caviol (Walter Rilla), struggling to escape an abusive home, navigate the perils of the exceptionally affectionate care of his patron, an artist whose erotic longing is unmistakably displayed in his famous painting of Michael unclothed, and reconcile the demands of his own art (he is Lewinski's prize student) with his love for Maria (Jane Novak), the much-abused wife of a selfish grand duke. Love vs. duty, which Hitchcock often cited as his fundamental theme, is central, perhaps less as an ethical dilemma than as a mechanism of pain. The film focuses repeatedly on images of a suffering man and a beleaguered woman, and the pressures that torment and wear them down are powerfully conveyed by constant reminders that they are objects of visual scrutiny (within the drama itself, not just by the eye of the camera). *The Blackguard* is a study of the power of the gaze, and for Michael even more than Maria, both of them relentlessly seen and overseen, it is a sign of his vulnerability, not his strength.

Filmed in Germany, like the first two films he directed, *The Blackguard* gives us useful insight into the complexity of the German influence on Hitchcock. We tend to associate this first and foremost with expressionism, and this film certainly has such elements: non-naturalistic special effects, an interest in hypnagogic and oneiric consciousness, a shadowy and monumental mise-en-scène that dwarfs the characters and reinforces a sense of the *unheimlich*, and a sense of the fundamental eccentricity, if not perversity, of the self and human relationships. But at the heart of *The Blackguard* is an aspect of early German cinema often overlooked: the Lubitsch touch, and not just the Lubitsch of grand historical romance, but especially the Lubitsch specializing in social observation, the foibles of the well-to-do, and the comedy of manners. The most recognizable aspects of the Hitchcock touch in *The Blackguard* evoke Ernst Lubitsch, perhaps mediated by D.W. Griffith: *Broken Blossoms* (1919) and *Orphans of the Storm* (1921) are key models as well as Lubitsch's *Passion* (1919) and social satires. There is evidence that Hitchcock directed a dream sequence, inserted twice, showing Michael walking heavenward on a long staircase to accept the painful responsibility of dedicating himself to his art (see Taylor 40), and the visual style here echoes Fritz Lang and F.W. Murnau more than Lubitsch. But if I had to guess which other parts Hitchcock directed or substantially shaped, I would call attention to the sequence in the dance hall, which shows the socially disguised and accepted cruelty of the Grand Duke Paul (Robert Scholz) to Maria and foreshadows similar scenes that will appear in *The Pleasure Garden* (1925), *Downhill* (1927), and *Champagne* (1928); several kissing sequences, always a center of attention for Hitchcock, that dramatically reveal the developing relationship between Michael and Maria (including one with a cut to a dog indicating approval – both the dog's and the director's – of their intimacy); and a tour de force sequence focusing on just their hands, subtly telling us all we need to know about the tension in their situation and the plangency of their love. These scenes in particular alert us to how training in the Lubitsch touch prepared Hitchcock for the films he turned to next.

The multiple talents Hitchcock displayed in *The Blackguard* and the other films he assisted on were recognized and rewarded. Producer Michael Balcon sent him back to Germany, this time as director – and, as we know from his own entertaining reminiscences, as bursar, talent coordinator, diplomat, counselor, and overall worrier (see Hitchcock, "Memories" 8–12). It is important to avoid the common auteurist tendency to confuse DNA with a fully-developed organism, but even with this caution in mind there is much to admire in Hitchcock's first completed film, *The Pleasure Garden*, as an accomplishment and not just a preview and promise of what's to come. From the very beginning, Hitchcock boldly proclaims this a signature film, not only by literally signing his name in the credit sequence – "Alfred J. Hitchcock" is handwritten on one of the cards – but by opening with a distinctive and dazzling sequence that is both an overture and a show-stopper. After a dizzying and exhilarating descent down a circular staircase, dancers perform onstage for a row of spectators, whose rapt attention is reflexively scrutinized by a camera panning across them. But the gaiety is complicated by sinister undertones: the gaze of the mostly male audience, typified by one older gentleman in particular, is insistent, intrusive, and not just appreciative but lecherous. Patsy Brand (Virginia Valli), the woman he focuses on, first laughingly accepts his gaze – she is well aware that being looked at in such a way is built into her profession and her fate as a woman – but soon feels the need to defend herself, returning the gaze with remarkable determination. What begins as light farce soon threatens to turn into tragedy, and the rest of the film expands outward from this memorable Hitchcock moment to explore the dynamics of the gaze, the perversity of desire, the instability of identity, and the particular vulnerabilities of women – although, to be fair (or cynical), in depicting the battle of the sexes Hitchcock shows that both men and women are capable of emotional and physical assaults.

The Pleasure Garden is an effectively and intricately structured whole, not just an assemblage of moments and special effects. As Maurice Yacowar points out (20), Hitchcock moves the film carefully through four settings that emblematize his main themes. The film opens in a theater literally called the Pleasure Garden, which is, like the rest of the world, primarily a stage for perennially reenacting the fall. The setting changes to the home that Patsy stays in, presided over by Mr. and Mrs. Sidey (Ferdinand Martini and Florence Helminger), beneficent and sometimes sternly protective parent figures. But it is a beleaguered and vulnerable home, a recurrent theme in Hitchcock, invaded first by Jill Cheyne (Carmelita Geraghty), Patsy's foil, who turns out to be more vamp than victim – and she is a vamp to Patsy as well as to the men she seduces, leaving her distraught – and then by Levet (Miles Mander), who takes Patsy away to an unhappy marriage. He first takes her on a honeymoon to Lake Como, but this setting, like the others, is used ironically: the picturesque backdrop is counterpointed by frequent shots showing the couple's distance and incompatibility, underscoring what Charles Barr identifies as one of the major themes of the film, "the danger of romantic self-delusion" (28). The film ends in another garden turned wilderness, the Far East, where Levet loses all self-control and must be killed before he kills Patsy, and where even the best of men, Hugh Fielding (John Stuart), Patsy's kindred spirit and presumably future partner, barely survives a prolonged hallucinatory illness, the roots of which go deeper than any literal jungle fever.

There is a deep structure to the film beneath its precisely modulated sense of place. Barr praises what he calls the sophisticated "systematic editing" (29) evident in several key sequences, where patterns of repetition and alternation develop the story but also establish rhythms and associative links, reveal psychological depths of characters, and help Hitchcock assert strong rhetorical control over the audience. And the individual sequences are part of a broader design of contrast and parallel editing whereby each action or character in effect comments on another. For example, intercut shots of Patsy and Jill each handling the advances of a lover convey the shared plight of women as they run a gauntlet of threatening men, but also contrast one woman, detached and resourceful, mastering the game of love, with another, sincere and sympathetic, overmatched by it. And intercut shots of Levet and Hugh show the difference between a snake and an innocent as well as the common fate each one faces in his own way, overwhelmed by the vertigo at the heart of eros. Some of these contrasts are akin to the often simplistic Manichean pattern of contrast and alternation in many Griffith films, but there is also the glimmering of something far more complex: the constant recalibration of perspective and judgment and the intricate interconnection of scenes that Hitchcock constructs out of the pairings and doublings in such films as *Shadow of a Doubt* and *Strangers on a Train* (1951), not-too-distant relatives of *The Pleasure Garden*.

Hitchcock returned to Germany for his next film, *The Mountain Eagle* (1926), described by contemporary reviewers as a stylistically interesting but slow moving and "not too convincing" tale of jealousy, anger, tangled and intensely oedipal family relations, and miraculous and improbable reconciliations set in a small village (see the synopsis and reviews reprinted in Barr 216–17). It may well be that these motifs reflect yet another sign of Hitchcock's deep debt to Griffith, in this case his many backwoods/rural melodramas, culminating in *Way Down East* (1920), but confirming any such critical speculations will have to wait until a print of this eagerly sought but to date lost film surfaces.

While even his earliest works are recognizably and foundationally Hitchcockian, the director's third film is a considerably more fully realized and extensive *summa* of a "Hitchcock movie," as he told Truffaut (43), and not just because it is the first in his long line of suspense thrillers involving murders. It is convenient to refer to it simply as *The Lodger* (1926), but we should not overlook the significance of the full title, *The Lodger: A Story of the London Fog*, which conveys that his subject is not only a character but a condition, that mood and atmosphere are as important as plot (his artistic guides are the school of Turner as well as the school of Dickens), and that this is a city film, an entry in a genre he often expressed interest in, that examines social as well as individual pathology.

The Lodger is a remarkably mature and assured film, establishing a full ensemble of expressive and thematic formulas as well as the presiding principle that these are not be used formulaically. Nearly all the major components of what would soon be labeled the Hitchcock touch are present in this film, handled with impressive subtlety and complexity. For example, the main character here is Hitchcock's archetypal "wrong man," but one who illustrates that this category has numerous built-in twists. The lodger (Ivor Novello) is suspected of and punished for the Jack the Ripper–type murders that, as it turns out, he did not commit, and there is a literal apotheosis of victimization near the end of the film as he is crucified – although not killed, unlike Christ, the original wrong man according to Hitchcock. But though he is not guilty of what he is accused of, the Lodger is far from innocent: his ambiguous and inscrutable behavior justifies the suspicions of those around him; his presence is both threatening and disruptive to all he meets; and the evidence confirming that he is not the Avenger who murders a fair-haired woman every Tuesday also reveals that he is nonetheless an avenger on his own tortured quest. As is well known, the lodger in Marie Belloc Lowndes's 1913 source novel is incontrovertibly the murderer, and Hitchcock often expressed regret that he was not able to end his story with this revelation. But the film is arguably better, and certainly more Hitchcockian, because he contrives to have it both ways: the lingering impression of the Lodger – which is also Hitchcock's comment on the human character in general – is that he is Janus-faced, both wrongly and rightly suspected of being monstrous.

Also prominent in *The Lodger* is the Hitchcock blonde. His subsequent films focus more on exploring her consciousness, but here she is primarily and effectively used as an icon of power and stimulation as well as victimization, qualities that may well be interrelated. We are never told anything directly about why the Avenger kills, but Daisy (June Tripp) is a test case allowing us to study the complex dynamics set in motion by attractive fair-haired women and understand why they are treated as they are by the men in their lives. Daisy is a figure of desire that is both humanizing – the Lodger, otherwise morose, quite literally comes to life in

Daisy's presence – and torturing, prompting obsessive attention, worry, and even physical distress. The antinomies of desire – pleasure and pain, approach and avoidance – are particularly well-captured in a carefully choreographed kissing sequence between Daisy and the Lodger late in the film, where special effects, disorienting cuts, and histrionic gestures and expressions dramatize a man's inextricably linked romantic agony and ecstasy, with Novello skillfully playing a Hitchcock part that will later be trademarked by James Stewart.

Daisy is not only an object of desire and vulnerability – in one scene she sits naked in a bathtub while the always potentially menacing Lodger hovers just outside the door – but a figure of self-assurance and bravado, both implicitly and explicitly a challenge (and thereby an insult) as well as an attraction. Her independence is a provocation to her boyfriend, Joe (Malcolm Keen), who not entirely jokingly puts handcuffs on her. And her characteristic laughter, first shown early on when her father (Arthur Chesney) ineptly falls to the floor and is unable to get up just as the mysterious Lodger enters the house, resonates throughout and is linked to the film's repeated insistence on the precariousness of male authority, presumably a main cause of the male hysteria that is everywhere present. Tania Modleski persuasively demonstrates (17–30) how the punning portmanteau word "mans/laughter" is central in Hitchcock's later film, *Blackmail* (1929). Significantly counterpointing this pattern is the recurrence of womans/laughter in nearly all the films that precede *Blackmail*, and Daisy is a particularly good example of the risks faced by the Hitchcockian woman who laughs too much.

The Lodger is a compendium of key Hitchcock themes and tones, particularly his most unsettling ones. Epistemic and moral uncertainty prevail, with devastating consequences. Appearance and reality are extremely difficult to distinguish, and throughout the film one cannot confidently know who is who or what is what. Truth is elusive and rarely comforting, and without reliable knowledge of the world, other people, and even ourselves, trust and confidence wither. Accordingly, *The Lodger* is less a murder mystery than a study of the corrosive power of suspicion, an early example of the Blakean wisdom from "Auguries of Innocence" (1803) at the core of two of Hitchcock's later masterpieces, *Suspicion* (1941) and *Shadow of a Doubt*, that "If the sun and moon should doubt, they'd immediately go out." The sun and the moon do go out in *The Lodger*, obscured by the enveloping fog of the chaos world, a world of violence and perhaps even more debilitating confusion.

Perhaps the most sophisticated Hitchcockian element of *The Lodger* has to do with the surprising way the director answers the question posed by the title of H.A. Vachell's 1916 stage version of the source novel, *Who Is He?* He, it turns out, is us. Contagion is an overriding metaphor throughout the film, one of many elements Hitchcock may have borrowed from Murnau's *Nosferatu* (1922), and the Avenger not only kills women but works his way into the public mind and body. Incessant media reports, conversations, fantasies, and even impersonations of the Avenger reveal the public fascination with the horrific, and the menacing figure who is never shown in the film soon becomes everywhere present. The Hitchcockian exchange of guilt, whereby the shadowy qualities of one person mirror or otherwise flow into another, is writ large here, and it is not just Joe and the Lodger who are linked with the Avenger. Ironically, the most extended and shocking sequence of violence in the film shows not the Avenger but the good people of London on a murderous rampage. The lynch mob pursuing, catching, and nearly killing the Lodger includes not only the easily incited public and perhaps even the director himself – a large round-faced man prominent in the front row of the mob is either, as some, including Hitchcock himself, claim, his second cameo appearance in the film or an extra with an uncanny resemblance to him – but, more important, the film audience as well. We are shocked by but also secret sharers in the disturbing things we see on screen, a dynamic that Hitchcock spent a career elaborating. The message at the end of *The Lodger* is, as Barr says, that "We all have violent and vengeful potential within us" (41), and Hitchcock insists that his audiences take the "we" in that statement personally and include ourselves in the chilling indictment and the experience of that complicity. *The Lodger* confirms that early in his career Hitchcock knew that he was making more than entertainments and finely constructed works of art: from the very beginning his films are, as Yacowar shrewdly notes, "moral tests for his audiences – and often traps" (41).

While in retrospect *The Lodger* is often seen as establishing the model of the Hitchcock film as a thriller, none of his next six films follows that path, but each is deeply Hitchcockian and helps expand our understanding of that term beyond the limits of the thriller. Each deserves careful attention, although there is only space here for brief notes on some key points of interest.

Downhill is, as Yacowar notes, Hitchcock's "first full confrontation with the chaos that hovers round a complacent existence" (45), and it contains his most extensive depiction of the subjective experience of delirium, disillusionment, and disintegration caused by sternly oppressive father figures, a variety of horrifying women, and the realization that the clear light of day – that is, an accurate perception of the world – engenders rather than banishes nightmares. It is perhaps Hitchcock's most resolutely anti-romantic film – heterosexual love is alternately a joke, a disappointment, and a disorienting and potentially fatal illness – and is an early but quite fully developed examination of one of his most fundamental subjects, the disenchantment born of coming of age and coming to knowledge. Roddy Berwick (Ivor Novello) ends as not a man but an "old boy," a harrowing phrase if we understand it as Hitchcock intends.

Easy Virtue (1927) turns Noel Coward's 1924 satire featuring a woman triumphantly slipping the noose of a closed-minded society into a more far-reaching existential analysis of a less resourceful "woman under the influence," suffering under inescapable life pressures symbolized by constant scrutiny. Larita Filton (Isabel Jeans) is above all a spectacle, vulnerable to visual dissection by an artist who freezes her image on a canvas, the upper-class family and friends of John Whittaker (Robin Irvine), her second husband, who turn dinners and parties into opportunities for contemptuous stares, and the legal apparatus, established as a mechanism for painful inquisition and display. Cameras are everywhere – even sketched into the background of many intertitles – and this leitmotif prepares us for the grand finale, which as Hitchcock admitted is perhaps a bit clumsy but tellingly operatic: after her second trial and divorce, Larita invokes suicide and sacrifice – "Shoot," she bids the photographers who surround her, armed with cameras – as a weary capitulation to and a stinging indictment of what throughout the film has been a process of perpetual murder.

Looking at his silent films as a group, it is interesting to see how Hitchcock alternates between films focusing on crises in masculinity and crises in femininity, occasionally in the best of these works looking at both of these subjects as intrinsically connected. The main female figure in *The Ring* (1927) is primarily a catalyst, a center of attention but not a center of consciousness, although there are some shots that attempt to give the audience an awareness of her inner drama as the object in the more central conflict between men that happens over but somewhat apart from her. The boxing ring is a particularly good stage for this conflict, partly because it allows for a not entirely sublimated expression of the real violence that underlies human relationships and partly because it subtly reminds us that a woman isn't necessary to provoke violence but is an inevitable accelerant. Jack Sander (Carl Brisson) and Bob Corby (Ian Hunter) would fight each other anyway (masculinity is their profession, and fighting is what men do), but the presence of Mabel (Lilian Hall-Davis) – Jack's wife, then Bob's lover, then Jack's helpmate again, in effect remarrying him – intensifies and prolongs their battle and places their violence in the context of one of Hitchcock's favorite plots, constructing the couple out of the triangle. The fairground setting of much of the film adds a carnivalesque dimension that serves less as a reminder of liberating human energies than of irrepressibly disturbing impulses, evident in the actions of the characters and in the eruptions of stylistic excess that rightly make this, as Thomas Leitch notes, "the most expressionistic of all [Hitchcock's] films" (280).

While *The Ring*, like so many of Hitchcock's films, examines intimate relationships in terms of sexual desire, possessiveness, and power, *The Farmer's Wife* (1928) studies marriage in the light of the pathos of loneliness. The death of Farmer Sweetland's beloved wife in the opening scene establishes the presiding absence dominating the remainder of the story, and to say that here silliness fills the role played by vertigo in Hitchcock's later films on loss and attempts at reparation alerts us not to any failure of intelligence or sensitivity in this early film but to its deep reserve of comic wisdom and magic. The occasionally ridiculous and off-putting bravado of Samuel Sweetland (Jameson Thomas) as he attempts to fill the chair of his departed wife is less a deep-seated character flaw and indication of patriarchal misogyny – he is for the most part a truly benign and admirable father figure – than wit's-end defensiveness. He is corrected by woman's laughter, as each person on his list gleefully asserts her independence and his folly while turning down his proposal, readying him for an epiphany that saves him from despair. Minta Dench (Lilian Hall-Davis), the household maid, slowly moves to an epiphany of her own, and the complexity and delicacy of her feeling as she becomes aware of her own desire, her suitability as the farmer's wife, and Sweetland's acknowledgment of her as his "last woman" – the film repeatedly echoes even as it parodies Murnau's *The Last Laugh* (1924), stylistically as well as thematically, with its frequently moving camera and shots visualizing subjectivity – are memorably conveyed by Hall-Davis's understated expressions, body language, and micro-gestures, and Hitchcock's patient and charming choreography of the transformation of the new couple. The film ends with a vision of sustaining intimacy that requires no kiss to certify it, perhaps because it satisfies needs and desires that are even deeper than sexual ones.

Champagne in many respects remakes *Downhill*, but in a markedly different key. While it too is about an expulsion from a home dominated by a strict father, the precipitating cause is not suspicion of a moral indiscretion by a young man but a young woman's playful and willful attempt to assert independence. And while there is, as Barr notes, a serious undercurrent in recurrent images of "somewhat sinister masculine power" (64), class-based inequities and abuses, and real threats to a vulnerable fair-haired female, the adventures on a slippery slope are played mostly for laughs – of a particularly meaningful kind. *Champagne* is Hitchcock's most extensive representation of one of Hitchcock's key motifs, especially in his early films, woman's laughter, here a sign of an indomitable female buoyancy that, far more than any alcoholic bubbles, allows one to see the world "through a glass sparkly," as one of my students, Leo Goldsmith, perceptively remarked in a class-room discussion of the film.

Betty Balfour, the most popular British female star of the day, plays The Girl with her usual energy and pluck, and our response to the film rests largely on how much weight we give to these qualities, and accordingly, how we interpret one key sequence in which they are displayed. Seeing these traits as eccentricities born of privilege, Yacowar considers the film an utter failure, largely because it mounts only a partial and inconsistent critique of an obnoxious upper-class society and places a "spoiled rich girl" (79), undeserving of our sympathy, interest, or moral admiration, at the center of some temporary inconveniences from which the men in her life will rescue her. When at the low point in her life she sits across the table from her boyfriend, who is on such a rescue mission, and suddenly starts to dance in her seat, Yacowar calls this "false hilarity, a lonely attempt to expel or to conceal one's glum isolation" (79) and embarrassment. Another way to see this moment, though, following clues Hitchcock leaves throughout the film, is as a thoroughly engaging and instructive affirmation of high spirits – a laugh in the face of her dour boyfriend (Jean Braden) and her oppressive but vital surroundings – and a sign of identification and solidarity with another woman in the cabaret where she works whose gestures she mimics at this important moment of decision: they are not floozies or spoiled rich girls but resolutely wild women, and their hilarity is the "moral alternative" Yacowar says that the film lacks (80). I don't want to overstate the achievement of *Champagne*, an undeniably flawed and uneven film. But Hitchcock's own judgment of it as "probably the lowest ebb in my output"

(Truffaut 57) should be challenged by a fresh appreciation of the physical and corresponding philosophical vibrancy of its main character, a Hitchcock blonde who laughs away both privilege and victimization.

Such laughter is much harder to come by in Hitchcock's next film, *The Manxman* (1929), which examines the serious consequences of a triangular relationship that is far more complicated than this simple geometric image usually suggests. The legs in a triangle, connecting what we can call points A, B, and C, are bidirectional, running AB, AC, BA, BC, CA, and CB, a potentially Escher-like schema that Hitchcock turns into a richly realized drama of love and friendship with multiple centers of consciousness and shifting attention to the six relationships that emerge when three people interact. The entire film, like the very popular 1894 Hall Caine novel it was based on, is set under the shadow of a stern biblical warning: "What shall it profit a man if he gain the whole world and lose his own soul?" This question applies to each of the main characters and foreshadows a story about missteps but also the possibility of redemption. Kate Cregeen (Anny Ondra), a lively and attractive blonde pub maid, seems naturally drawn to Pete Quilliam (Carl Brisson), a good-hearted and jovial fisherman with no prospects, but pursues his friend, Philip Christian (Malcolm Keen), an ambitious lawyer from a distinguished family. Philip is an active advocate for the local fishermen and willing go-between for shy Pete in his courtship of Kate, but his status as a rising figure of established authority pulls him away from both Kate and Pete. Even simple Pete is drawn into the pursuit of material things, and when he leaves to make enough money to allow him to marry Kate, his absence and falsely reported death create the circumstances by which he loses his beloved. Impersonal fate and chance loom throughout, but these large grindstones (pictured literally in several scenes in the film) are set in motion by irresistible human desire that is both fulfilling and disturbing.

The Manxman is deeply cinematic, but as Christine Gledhill notes (119–22), its visual design relies less on editing than on pictorial effects. The setting effectively depicts a natural world of rocks and water that dwarf and "enisle" tiny human beings and a domestic architecture of windows, doors, tables, and narrow hallways that separate and confine the characters. And Hitchcock shows the inner life of the main characters, the subtleties and particularities of their emotions and thoughts, not by complex cutting and point-of-view shots but by carefully composed tableaux, many of which revolve around a highly articulated variation on his characteristic emphasis on the gaze. Although he typically portrays the gaze as a mechanism of power and punishment and features it as a key element in his analysis of the dynamics of engagement and spectatorship, here Hitchcock repeatedly foregrounds the averted gaze, moments when characters avoid each other's eyes and look away from each other. Looking downward, upward, and away from another character are all, of course, time-honored theatrical conventions and a key part of the visual vocabulary of early cinema, especially in melodrama. But far beyond a cliché, the averted gaze is at the expressive, thematic, and structural core of this film, signifying guilt, shame, vulnerability, a complex refusal of intimacy, and a correspondingly painful isolation and interiority. The many instances of this motif culminate in a final tableau where Kate, Philip, and Pete stand separately, heads akimbo, at this moment representing an irreparably fractured triangle (the price of forming a couple) as Kate and Philip prepare to take their baby and leave Pete behind. Much, though not all, has been lost, and perhaps something has been found: there is some hope that the new pair will no longer avoid each other's gaze, and the final image of the film shows Pete smiling and gazing out into the open possibilities of the sea. But the film is haunted by the repeated experience of what Kate states simply in one of many moments of extreme tension: "I can't face him." This fundamental impediment to human relationships is felt and enacted by many characters throughout Hitchcock's films, and it would be well worth examining in detail how the averted gaze in such films as *Notorious*, for example, is one of Hitchcock's key signifiers of distress and disrupted, if not impossible, intimacy.

In discussing his films with Truffaut, Hitchcock called *The Manxman* "my last silent one" (61), but this is a misleading statement in several respects. He did release one more picture without sound, but under complicated circumstances. *Blackmail* began as a silent film, was partially reshot and reworked with sound, then released first in a version billed as "Britain's first talking picture" and shortly after in a different version without sound – although containing some material reshot for the sound version, as Barr notes (81) – to make it available in the many movie houses not yet equipped with the latest technology. Modern critics generally agree on the importance of *Blackmail* as, in the words of Robin Wood, an "early major work [of Hitchcock's] in which all the tensions and contradictions that structure the later films are clearly articulated" (243), but base their judgments and focus their commentary almost exclusively on the sound version, with special attention to Hitchcock's strikingly innovative and effective use of sound and music. Much of what they say applies to the silent version as well, but the films often work differently, and in some key places their meaning diverges. Wood's deservedly high praise of *Blackmail* can be pointedly illustrated by a brief analysis of the silent version.

The film is structured as a thriller wrapped around a melodrama, a compound form that allows Hitchcock to raise questions about the operation and even the legitimacy of the law while he focuses extensively on a young woman overmatched by the force of circumstances that squeeze and shape her. Alice White (Anny Ondra) is in most ways neither heroic nor exceptional: alas, she is typical and for the most part easy to identify with in that her life is marked by multiple traps and limited horizons. She dreams of escape, but has limited resources. The settings she moves among underscore her predicament: a drab home in which the price of comfort outweighs its minimal advantages; an artist's flat, envisioned as a site of escape, excitement, and fulfillment but in reality, perhaps like art itself, a place of disappointment and danger; the city streets, which embody society's indifference and evoke nightmares; and a police station, a house of exposure and humiliation, not protection.

The constricting relationships and spaces of her life are conveyed by Hitchcock's complex use of what we have seen is one of his favorite images and structural patterns. Alice lives in not just one but three triangles. Unlike those in *The Manxman*, where a triangle sketched multiple options and possibilities (as well as tensions) of love and friendship, the triangles in *Blackmail* schematize limited choices, dead ends, and sources of pain. Alice, her mother (Sara Allgood), and her father (Charles Paton) form one triangle. While her parents are not the self-satisfied and censorious monsters they are in the play on which the film was based, here their bland domesticity and weary ordinariness represent exactly what we have in mind when we say, with a tremor in our voice, that there must be more to life than this. The second triangle in Alice's life seems more promising, and the allure and attentions of the artist Crewe (Cyril Ritchard) allow Alice to imagine at least a momentary alternative to the prospects and the defects of Frank Webber (John Longden), her fiancé. But these two men turn out to represent not so much alternatives as variations on abuse and control, death by fire and death by ice. The third triangle links Alice, Frank, and Tracy (Donald Calthrop), the blackmailer who tries to profit from his knowledge of Alice's secret. Hitchcock's presentation of this last triangle is particularly complex and skillful. A pivotal sequence just before the climactic chase conveys the shifting relationship of the trio by adjustments in their position in the frame, and by the end of the sequence we see that the real alignment is not Frank and Alice vs. Tracy but Alice and Tracy, both of them knowing and sympathetic victims, vs. Frank, obtuse, stern, and manipulative. In an early example of the Hitchcockian exchange of guilt, Tracy becomes not only allied with Alice but a stand-in for her and, ironically, her greatest benefactor: when he bursts through the window to escape, he does what Alice is too paralyzed to do, and his accidental death as he is chased by the police closes the case as far as they are concerned and frees her from them, although not from a higher standard of morality which is, to her credit, her primary concern.

Blackmail is a tour de force of cinematic style even before the addition of sound and music. It is an encyclopedia of editing techniques, all used skillfully and for a wide range of functions: to move the narrative along smoothly and economically, as in the Hollywood pictures Hitchcock admired, and build to a Griffith-like climax based on crosscutting; to create Eisensteinian shocks and also associative and intellectual montages, linking Alice and Tracy, for example, and creating not just images (that is, direct representations) but visual metaphors of far-reaching entrapment, powerlessness, unreliable and failed authority, victimization, and distress; and to establish rhythmic and structural patterns by carefully placed repetitions that create constant echoing effects. These echoes amplify the effect of many moments in the film – for example, when Tracy extends just his arm into the frame while pleading with Frank near the end, recalling the artist's dying gesture, we know he is doomed – and also reveal the larger plan of the film as one in which, as Wood notes, "the end answers the beginning" (249). The first part of the documentary police procedural that opens the film is replayed at the end, but as the saying goes, this time it's personal, no longer bearing down on an anonymous suspect. Throughout the film special effects are carefully integrated into a strategy of visualizing the instability and indifference of the world and showing from within Alice's "tranced" (Barr 173) and traumatized sensibility. Dissolves reinforce the unsettling fluidity of the surroundings; repeated dolly-ins heighten the invasive mood of the film and underscore the key theme of the intrusive and fixating gaze; and frequent tableau shots, as mentioned above, allow Hitchcock to visualize the relative power, powerlessness, and changing alliances of the characters, with Alice often receding from the center.

Hitchcock's cinematic ingenuity is no mere formalist exercise but a means to strengthen *Blackmail* as a provocative critique of the forces of order and authority in society, a disapproving dramatization of how men silence women and attempt to shape them to suit their interests, and a case study in guilt. Much of our response to the film and interpretation of it depends on our sense of Alice's character, particularly the motivation behind her attraction to the artist and her reaction to the consequences. If her walk on the wild side seems to be a foolish flirtation of an impetuous young girl, then we are liable to have in the very least mixed sympathy during her ensuing difficulties. But if we see Alice as perhaps naïve, irresponsible in deceiving Frank and not protecting herself more carefully, but prompted by a restless and in many respects admirable urge to break from her restrictions, escape from a relationship that promises nothing but dull routine, and for once experience the liveliness of life, we can judge her, like Marion Crane (Janet Leigh) many films later, as complicit in her fate but still see her as far more sinned against than sinning. Similarly, if we see Alice as traumatized into submission, *Blackmail* becomes a bleak fable portraying a woman living a life of unremitting oppression and entrapment, the butt of continual male laughter, especially at the joke that her survival depends on the fact that some other poor soul has even worse luck than her. But the film is somewhat less bleak if we give Alice credit for a more complex response to catastrophe, whereby she is shocked not into submission but into a full reckoning with her actions, culminating in a confession that is not a capitulation to legal authority but an exemplary acknowledgment of responsibility to a higher conception of morality and human conduct. Hitchcock himself may have been unsure about where this leaves her, and us, and it is interesting to note that he filmed two different versions of her final confession to Frank. In the sound version, Frank says that he already knows her secret, but her response is that he doesn't truly "know" it, that he cannot know fully what happened nor the consequences for her, a bitter commentary on the limits of even the most intimate of relationships. In the silent version, though, when Alice confesses, "I did it," Frank mouths, "What?" Here Hitchcock relies not on suspense, the prolonged revelation of the known, but shock and surprise, the unexpected revelation of the unknown. Alice's confession stuns Frank, and he turns away from her, but then holds her to his side with both hands. When they walk out the door, they are expressionless, and there is very little sense that they have escaped and triumphed in any way. But they begin the serious business of the rest of their lives together on a foundation of honesty and sympathy, without the sobering reminder at the end of the sound version that these may not add up to much.

While Hitchcock was working on the first version of *Blackmail*, he was already preparing for the inevitable: "I was using talkie techniques, but without sound," he recalled ("Memories" 14). The reverse of this statement, though, is equally true, and alerts us to a key way in which Hitchcock's creativity looked backward as well as forward: he spent the rest of his career using silent film techniques but with sound. As he headed into the era of the talkies, Hitchcock was determined to avoid making films that were, as he frequently complained, "photographs of peo-ple talking" (Truffaut 61). In defining and practicing what he called "pure cinema" (Bogdanovich 476) he rested everything on a simple principle: "[I]t must be pictures first and last" ("Close" 249). If he carefully prepared himself for the new technol-ogy, he also cleverly anticipated its malfunctioning and limitations:

> I try to tell my story so much so in pictures that if by any chance the sound apparatus broke down in the cinema, the audience would not fret and get restless because the pictorial action would still hold them! Sound is all right in its place, but it is a silent picture training which counts today.
>
> ("Close" 247)

If we look closely, Hitchcock's silent picture training is everywhere present, even in his sound films, especially in their reliance on visual narrative, constant experimentation with montage as the foundation of cinematic meaning and emo-tion, and inventive use of camera movements, variations in image size, and spe-cial effects. And while Hitchcock was famously shy in his interviews and writings about identifying influences, his films are filled with homages to a wide range of silent films, a strategy that allows him to acknowledge, incorporate, and surpass his forbears.

Blackmail is thus Hitchcock's last film without sound, but not the end of his silent cinema. While it is often studied as a transition to a new style of filmmaking, it is even more fittingly an example, a synecdochic embodiment, of the continuity between early and later Hitchcock, one aspect of which is perfectly expressed by the fact that it is both a sound and a silent film. So are the films that followed it.

Works Cited

Barr, Charles. *English Hitchcock*. Moffat: Cameron and Hollis, 1999.

Bogdanovich, Peter. *Who the Devil Made It*. New York: Knopf, 1997.

Gledhill, Christine. *Reframing British Cinema 1918–1928: Between Restraint and Passion*. London: BFI, 2003.

Gottlieb, Sidney, ed. *Hitchcock on Hitchcock: Selected Writings and Interviews*. Berkeley: U of California P, 1995.

Hitchcock, Alfred. "My Screen Memories." *Film Weekly* 2, 9, 16, 23, 30 May 1936: 16+, 7, 28+, 28+, 27. Gottlieb 7–26.

Hitchcock, Alfred. "Close Your Eyes and Visualize!" *Stage* (July 1936): 52–53. Gottlieb 246–49.

Leitch, Thomas. *The Encyclopedia of Alfred Hitchcock*. New York: Facts on File, 2002.

McGilligan, Patrick. *Alfred Hitchcock: A Life in Darkness and Light*. New York: HarperCollins, 2003.

Modleski, Tania. *The Women Who Knew Too Much: Hitchcock and Feminist Theory*. Second ed. New York: Routledge, 2005.

Taylor, John Russell. *Hitch: The Life and Times of Alfred Hitchcock*. New York: Pantheon, 1978.

Truffaut, François, with the collaboration of Helen G. Scott. *Hitchcock*. Rev. ed. New York: Simon and Schuster, 1984.

Wood, Robin. *Hitchcock's Films Revisited*. Rev. ed. New York: Columbia UP, 2002.

Yacowar, Maurice. *Hitchcock's British Films*. Hamden, CT: Archon, 1977.

15

Gaumont Hitchcock

Tom Ryall

[H]e finally discovered himself as an artist with the series of thrillers beginning with The Man Who Knew Too Much.

(Lovell 71)

[H]e had perfected his form, and had made an unbroken series of triumphs from The Man Who Knew Too Much *on.*

(Taylor 147)

Before The Man Who Knew Too Much, *spy-saboteur pictures weren't really Hitchcock's specialty. Now, suddenly, he discovered that they fit him like a second skin.*

(McGilligan 169)

The profile of Alfred Hitchcock's English or British film career is well known. Following his early films for Gainsborough in the mid-1920s, he was hailed as the bright young talent in the British cinema and, in the words of studio publicity director Cedric Belfrage in *Picturegoer*, as "the youngest director in the world" (60). He had previously worked for the American company, Paramount, at Islington Studios, and he remained there as a studio employee when producer Michael Balcon acquired the facility in the early 1920s. He directed five films for Gainsborough, including *The Lodger* (1926), which established his early reputation, but then signed a lucrative contract with British International Pictures (B.I.P.), one of the large combines formed in the late 1920s. Hitchcock moved from the small Gainsborough studio with its limited facilities and joined a company that had studios at the newly-built Hollywood-style Elstree complex and an impressive roster

A Companion to Alfred Hitchcock, First Edition. Edited by Thomas Leitch and Leland Poague.
© 2011 Thomas Leitch and Leland Poague. Published 2011 by Blackwell Publishing Ltd.

of foreign directors and stars. His career, however, went into decline in the early 1930s, and his final film at B.I.P., *Lord Camber's Ladies* (1932), was a quota picture Hitchcock produced, leaving the direction to another. In 1933 Hitchcock left the studio with a reputation that had slipped somewhat from the "Alfred the Great" label bestowed upon him in the mid-1920s.

At Gaumont British he embarked upon "the classic thriller sextet," to use Raymond Durgnat's formulation (20), the cycle of thrillers made between 1934 and 1938 that established or, one might claim, re-established him as Britain's leading film director. The six Gaumont films define "English Hitchcock" for many critics and commentators, and Hitchcock himself confirmed their significance in a resigned acknowledgement of his image as a director of thrillers during a 1950 interview for the *New York Times Magazine*: "If I seem doomed to make only one type of picture, the movie audience is responsible. People go to one of my films expecting a thriller, and aren't satisfied until the thrill turns up" (quoted in Brady 131–32).

Accordingly, Gaumont Hitchcock tends to dominate discussion of British or English Hitchcock. This is understandable, as the homogeneity of the sextet – five of whose six titles are concerned with espionage – gives them both a consistent and settled distinctiveness and a clear generic relationship to subsequent Hollywood titles such as *Foreign Correspondent* (1940), *Saboteur* (1942), *Notorious* (1946), *The Man Who Knew Too Much* (1956), *North by Northwest* (1959), *Torn Curtain* (1966), and *Topaz* (1969).

In addition, they are the films from which Hitchcock's popular reputation as "master of suspense" derive and are easier at first glance to absorb into that conception of the director's artistic identity than, for example, pre-Gaumont films such as *The Farmer's Wife* (1928), a bucolic comedy about a widower's courtship attempts from the 1920s, or *Rich and Strange* (1931), a study of suburban ennui from the early 1930s. As Charles Barr has noted, the years from the mid-1920s until Hitchcock's departure for Hollywood in 1939 can be regarded as "the gradual and uneven process of his *becoming* (or anyway starting to become) the Hitchcock we think we all know" (*English* 11). While the years before 1934 had established Hitchcock as a very important British filmmaker, as Robert Kapsis has noted, his "reputation as a thriller director evolved more slowly than his reputation as England's finest director" (21).

This chapter considers the Gaumont British films from a number of perspectives. How do they relate to the sixteen feature films that Hitchcock directed prior to joining Gaumont British? Do they mark a key development in the formation of "Hitchcock" and the "Hitchcockian"? Do they consolidate elements present in the previous films? What influence did the studio context have on the films? How does the cycle relate to the structures and conventions of the British cinema of the time and, in particular, to the generic traditions of the crime/thriller in both its literary and cinematic manifestations? How does Hitchcock's work relate to the films of his contemporaries, both successful and significant filmmakers such as Alexander Korda, Anthony Asquith, and Victor Saville, as well as the ordinary craftsmen whose work dominated the crime/thriller genre?

Studio Contrasts

The studios that Hitchcock worked at during his British career were very different entities both in terms of scale and ethos. Gainsborough was a small-scale operation in the 1920s, though, with the ambitious Michael Balcon as its head, it was merged with Gaumont British towards the end of the 1920s to form a large, vertically integrated combine. B.I.P. was set up as a large-scale, internationally-oriented company that recruited an impressive roster of directors and stars from the leading filmmaking nations of the world as well as indigenous talent such as Hitchcock. By the early 1930s, however, the studio had abandoned its international production policy in favor of modestly budgeted films designed to meet the needs of the company's growing cinema circuit. Film budgets were relatively large in the early days of B.I.P., but by the early 1930s, "the average expenditure on a film was only £10 000 – less than double that of the standard quickie" (Chibnall 12). Hitchcock's period of "decline" was also the period in which B.I.P. was retrenching and scaling back its earlier ambitions.

It was at this point that Hitchcock moved to a company that was repositioning itself as an internationally-oriented studio with an ambitious program of relatively high-budget films. In 1934, in contrast to the parsimony at B.I.P., Gaumont British was about to embark on a program of films budgeted mainly at £50–60 000, with a few titles at the £100 000 mark (Sedgwick 334–36). It was also a studio with a markedly different cultural ethos than that prevailing at B.I.P. The conventional distinction has been formulated by Rachael Low: "the B.I.P. management saw themselves as being engaged in big business, not as nourishing and building up a team of creative artists in the way that Balcon, Bruce Woolfe and others had tried to do" (189). Such a distinction does square with the notion of Hitchcock flourishing initially in the creative and supportive environment of Balcon's studio and then becoming somewhat lost in the larger B.I.P. studio, where he was still a relative newcomer among a number of experienced directors and stars from Hollywood and Germany. It should be noted, however, that Hitchcock did have problems at Gainsborough when Balcon's distribution head, C.M. Woolf, shelved *The Lodger* on the grounds that it was too artistic, "too highbrow" (Montagu 76), and *Blackmail* (1929), one of Hitchcock's most successful British films, was made at B.I.P. *The Man Who Knew Too Much* (1934), Hitchcock's first picture for Gaumont British, also fell foul of Woolf's skepticism about the director when he ordered the film's release as the lower half of a double bill.

Pre-Gaumont Hitchcock Films

Although four of Hitchcock's pre-Gaumont films – *The Lodger, Blackmail, Murder!* (1930), and *Number Seventeen* (1932) – were crime-based pictures, they did not really resemble the classic thrillers in an obvious way and none were espionage films. The others were adaptations of middlebrow plays and novels, including works by

Noël Coward, Hall Caine, Clemence Dane, John Galsworthy, and Sean O'Casey. Their subject matter was various: the tribulations of a disgraced public schoolboy (*Downhill,* 1927), a fraught romantic triangle (*The Manxman,* 1929), the Irish civil war of the early 1920s (*Juno and the Paycock,* 1930), and the life of the composer Johann Strauss Junior (*Waltzes from Vienna,* 1933). Indeed, perhaps in the absence of a coherent thematic authorial identity, critical definitions of Hitchcock during this period tended to focus upon the bravura and virtuoso qualities of camerawork and editing in the silent pictures and the innovative qualities of the sound in the early "talkies," *Blackmail* and *Murder!* In the 1930s John Grierson referred to such stylistic distinctiveness as "the Hitchcock touch" (76). In a later commentary, Tom Leitch has suggested that the first decade of Hitchcock's career is best characterized in terms of narrative form rather than in the familiar specificities of genre: "The hallmark of Hitchcock's early films is not suspense but narrative wit, a way of establishing sequence, causality, or thematic connection which plays on the audience's narrativity, their ability to follow and enjoy a story" (43).

Though there are no obvious predecessors for the thriller cycle, the crime-based films do contain salient elements – such as police and criminal activity, murder, suspense, mystery, theft, guilt – that can be related to the films of the sextet. The early films also contain a range of stylistic and thematic elements later to be developed and explored both in the thriller sextet and in Hitchcock's subsequent Hollywood pictures. Indeed, Michael Walker's exhaustive inventory of Hitchcock's motifs contains many references to the pre-Gaumont films, including five entries for the costume biopic, *Waltzes from Vienna,* on the face of it the least Hitchcockian film in his entire oeuvre (470).

A major Hitchcockian motif – the gaze – appears at the very beginning of his first directorial assignment, *The Pleasure Garden* (1925). The film opens in a theater, and within a handful of shots there is a voyeuristic point-of-view sequence, a man gazing at one of the dancers on stage. It is a complex sequence in which, as Walker has noted, the man's voyeuristic gaze is somewhat undercut by the dancer who "returns his gaze with a look that is challenging rather than flirtatious" (164). *Downhill* and *Champagne* (1928) both incorporate complex hallucinatory and fantasy sequences which anticipate the variety of ways in which subsequent Hitchcock films, British and American, display an interest in the representation of dreams, memories, fantasies, hallucinatory experiences – phenomenological concerns central to cinema in general as well as Hitchcock's cinema in particular.

In terms of the broader subject matter, a number of the pre-Gaumont titles are concerned with the familiar Hitchcockian "wrong man" figure and its thematic corollary, the transference of guilt. Such a figure appears in Hitchcock's second feature, *The Mountain Eagle* (1926), in *The Lodger* and *Downhill* and, most notably, in *Blackmail.* In addition, there is a wrongly accused woman at the center of *Murder!,* and the related figure of the vulnerable woman, familiar from many Hollywood titles, also crops up in pre-Gaumont Hitchcock. Charles Barr has noted of *Rich and Strange,* "As so often with Hitchcock, the vulnerable woman becomes and remains the film's emotional centre" (*English* 121), but the figure is also at the center of *The Manxman, Murder!,* and *Blackmail* as well. Some of the classic themes adumbrated by Peter Wollen – the notion of "common guilt and exchanged guilt," "the theme of chaos narrowly underlying order," "the theme of temptation, obsession, fascination and vertigo," and that of "uncertain, shifting identity and the search for secure identity" (*Signs and Meaning* 140) – can also be identified, though again intermittently and arguably concentrated in specific films. *Blackmail*, for example, embodies the descent into chaos, the circulation of guilt among the leading characters, and the temptation that leads the central female character into trouble. The film also incorporates the notorious Hitchcock blonde in the character of Alice (Anny Ondra), a figure that was to assume an especial importance to Hitchcock's 1950s films, though one which can be traced back to Hitchcock's earliest films, such as *The Lodger, Downhill,* and *Easy Virtue* (1927). In short, it is not a difficult task to pinpoint a number of Hitchcockian themes and motifs, figures of narrative structure and style, in the films of the 1920s and early 1930s.

The main difference between pre-Gaumont Hitchcock and Gaumont Hitchcock is the generic specialization involved in the latter. However, discussion of the generic context of Hitchcock's films has been somewhat overwhelmed by his massive authorial reputation, by the force of his "biographical legend," the construction of which effectively began in the 1920s with the Cedric Belfrage article in *Picturegoer.* "Hitchcockian" has taken its place as a term in the world of cultural criticism alongside "Shakespearean," "Byronic," and "Wagnerian," terms which indicate the ways in which reference to a specific artist's name means not only a body of work occupying a prestigious cultural position but also a powerful and influential artistic template constructed partly by plays, poems, operas, and films and partly by the discursive world occasioned by them. Like the other artists mentioned, and like Carl-Theodor Dreyer in David Bordwell's account (9–10), Hitchcock possesses a biographical legend constructed partly by the films, partly by his own comments on his career, and partly by the world of film criticism and analysis. Central to that legend is the thriller genre, so much so that the term "a Hitchcock thriller" has a hint of tautology. Ironically, Hitchcock's critical rehabilitation in the 1930s was based on films that derived clearly from well-established literary and cinematic generic traditions. He was rehabilitated as a genre director rather than as the auteur who was to dominate Hitchcock criticism from the 1950s onwards.

The Sextet: Gaumont British

Hitchcock's move to the Gaumont British studio enabled the renewal of his previously fruitful professional collaborations with individuals such as Ivor Montagu, who had prepared *The Lodger* for its successful release in the mid-1920s, and with screenwriter Charles Bennett, whose play had been the basis for the highly acclaimed *Blackmail*, one of Hitchcock's most successful B.I.P. films. In addition, the move reunited Hitchcock with producer Michael Balcon, who had presided over his early career at Gainsborough. Once the cycle was under way, such continuities were strengthened, and Hitchcock's creative team became more consistent. Ivor Montagu acted as Associate Producer on three films, Bennett worked on the scripts of five of the six films, and the cinematographer Bernard Knowles worked on four of the films. In addition, of course, Alma Reville, Hitchcock's wife, had formal credits for continuity on five of the six films as well as continuing the informal role she had played in his career since the 1920s. Thus, as Balcon suggests in his autobiography, Hitchcock became an effective production category at Gaumont British (62–63), a stable unit producing a specific type of film.

"The classic thriller sextet" did not represent a complete break with the past but rather united two impulses from earlier Hitchcock films, as Rohmer and Chabrol were the first to observe (38): the somewhat austere moral universe of *Murder!* and the action, adventure, and suspense from *Number Seventeen,* a blend of the serious and the popular that could provide high-quality entertainment accessible on a variety of levels. The elements figure in different ways across the cycle and are blended in different ways, in different proportions, producing a varied series of inflections of the thriller/espionage genre, and a run of films which can be distinguished from Hitchcock's previous work in terms of their precise generic identity. As has been noted, murder, mystery, and suspense were present in a small number of Hitchcock's pre-Gaumont films, but in the classic cycle they are foregrounded consistently and, with a single exception, contextualized in the espionage/thriller genre. The following sections examine several aspects of the cycle in order to gauge the extent to which the films represent significantly fresh departures for Hitchcock and the extent to which they refer back to the body of work produced at Gainsborough and B.I.P.

The Sextet: Narrative Structures

For many, *The 39 Steps* (1935), Hitchcock's adaptation of John Buchan's novel, is the emblematic thriller embodying English Hitchcock in general, and, more specifically, defining the Hitchcock thriller. This is partly because of its great success at the time of release but also because it stands as a template for such subsequent Hitchcock films as *Young and Innocent* (1937) from the sextet and such American titles as *Foreign Correspondent, Saboteur, North by Northwest,* and *Torn Curtain.* Its qualities – a fast-paced narrative, swiftly moving from situation to situation, turning on coincidence and involving the flight and pursuit structure – derived from Buchan's novel, indeed from Buchan's work as a whole; they indicate the influence of the writer on the genre as well as on its most prestigious cinematic practitioner. Buchan's *The Thirty-Nine Steps* (1915) is divided into episodic chapters united and paced by the flight and pursuit or chase theme, which Hitchcock regards as central to his own cinema. In a 1950 interview he explained that

> the chase seems to me the final expression of the motion picture medium. Where but on screen can automobiles be shown careening around corners after each other? Then, too, the movie is the natural vessel for the chase story because the basic film shape is continuous. Once a movie starts it goes right on. You don't stop it for scene changes, or go out and have a cigarette.
>
> (Hitchcock 125)

In the same interview Hitchcock also speaks of Griffith as an influence and, in particular, emphasizes "the suspense of the chase" as embodied in the climactic sequences of *The Birth of a Nation* (1915), *Intolerance* (1916), and *Way Down East* (1920). The key ingredient Hitchcock added to the Griffith influence was the "psychology and character" that he derived from a number of writers:

> I have derived more from novelists like John Buchan, J.B. Priestley, John Galsworthy, and Mrs. Belloc Lowndes than from the movies. I like them because they use multiple chases and a lot of psychology. My chases are the result of using all the resources of modern film techniques to combine what I got from those novelists with what I got from Griffith.
>
> (131)

To an extent, a flight/pursuit/chase structure can be detected in such pre-Gaumont films as *The Lodger, Blackmail,* and especially *Number Seventeen*. Many of the Gainsborough and B.I.P. films, however, are less frantic and action-orientated, more focused on character and psychology. Though they have their share of other Hitchcockian qualities, films such as *Easy Virtue, Downhill, The Ring* (1927), *The Farmer's Wife, The Manxman, The Skin Game* (1931), and *Waltzes from Vienna* have little of the tension and suspense associated with the director.

Young and Innocent and to a lesser extent *The Man Who Knew Too Much* share the fast-paced, scene-shifting narrative form of *The 39 Steps*. But what of the remaining films of the sextet? *Sabotage* (1936) is located entirely in London, mainly in and around Verloc's cinema, with limited excursions for key events such as the death of Stevie (Desmond Tester) near Piccadilly Circus and lunch at Simpson's. It is not structured around a chase; suspected saboteur Verloc (Oscar Homolka) is identified at an early stage in the proceedings and the film, like, for example, *Rear Window* (1954), concentrates on the confirmation of villainy – Verloc's involvement in sabotage. *Secret Agent* (1936) has a different narrative structure, again involving a red herring, a false MacGuffin – Caypor (Percy Marmont), the misidentified foreign agent and assassination target – which takes up the first two-thirds or so of the film. It is only in the final half-hour, when the true identity of the agent is discovered, that the film adopts a flight and pursuit structure. The remaining film, *The Lady Vanishes* (1938), is mainly a trainboard drama confined to a single albeit mobile location – from which Miss Froy (Dame May Whitty) apparently disappears – but its singularity provides something of a contrast to the multiplicity of locations that Hannay visits in his pursuit of the man with the missing finger joint in *The 39 Steps*.

The Sextet: Visual Style

Hitchcock critics like John Grierson writing in the early 1930s identified the director's frequent usage of the stylistic flourish – elements of film technique which display the potential of the medium and which have the capacity to draw attention to the artifice involved in a narrative film. Examples of virtuoso filmmaking – what Grierson called "the Hitchcock touch" (76) – are frequent in Hitchcock's pre-Gaumont films. They include the overhead staircase shots and the celebrated shot through the glass floor in *The Lodger*; the clever transition from the trial sequence to the past by way of an image of a wine decanter in the early part of *Easy Virtue*; the dissolve from the inky blackness of the water into which the suicidal Kate (Anny Ondra) throws herself to the Deemster's inkwell at the beginning of her trial in *The Manxman*; the extended subjective sequence in *Downhill* representing the delirium of Roddy (Ivor Novello) during his journey home; and the sound bridge between Alice's scream at the sight of the vagrant's outstretched hand and the landlady discovering the body in *Blackmail* together with the film's more celebrated "knife" sequence, with its distorted soundtrack.

Similar examples of the Hitchcock touch found in the sextet include the shot of the fingers pointing to the bullet hole in the window through which Louis Bernard (Pierre Fresnay), the French agent, is shot in *The Man Who Knew Too Much*; the famous sound bridge from the scream of the landlady discovering the body of Annabella Smith (Lucie Mannheim) to the screech of the train whistle in *The 39 Steps*; the stylized montage sequence of the killing of Verloc in *Sabotage*; the overhead shot from the bell tower in the church where the organist is murdered in *Secret Agent*; the virtuoso camera movement from extreme long shot to the close shot of the killer's twitching eyes in *Young and Innocent*; and the shots containing the deliberately-oversized wine glasses in *The Lady Vanishes*.

These are mainly isolated images, and although they have a tendency to stand out from the narrational flow – hence "touches" – they are brief moments in what are usually fast-paced narratives moving rapidly from sequence to sequence. Another aspect of Hitchcock's work deriving from his pre-Gaumont days was a tendency to build the narrative around a series of setpieces, memorable sequences based on striking dramatic contexts. In some cases this involved well-known landmarks like London's Albert Hall for the assassination attempt in *The Man Who Knew Too Much* and the London Palladium, where the enemy agent is caught in *The 39 Steps*. In others, the setting was a crowded public place, such as the election meeting in *The 39 Steps*, or an unusual setting such as the chocolate factory in *Secret*

Agent, where the true identity of the foreign agent is revealed to Ashenden (John Gielgud) and the General (Peter Lorre). As with the Hitchcock touch, the building of the narrative around visually striking set pieces predates the Gaumont pictures, most notably in the chase through the British Museum in the climax of *Blackmail.*

Although the films of the sextet are fast-moving narratives with goal-orientated heroes and heroines and with enigma and resolution structures, the films do contain examples of shots, scenes, and sequences whose function and motivation is artistic as well as narrative or generic. Yet their goal-oriented narration may be regarded as a brake on the set piece or the stylistic flourish, a disciplining of spectacle by the relentlessly forward-moving narrative with its set of simple goals – rescuing a kidnapped daughter, finding a foreign agent, tracing a lost raincoat, finding Miss Froy.

The Sextet: Heroes and Couples

The classic spy novels from the early twentieth century revolved around the adventures of a range of masculine heroes. One key definition of the espionage hero is from Erskine Childers's novel *The Riddle of the Sands* (1903), whose protagonist is defined as "the amateur agent or accidental spy, the sleepy young Englishman whose lassitude and political complacency are shattered when he stumbles across some fiendish plot" (Trotter 40). It is an important definition and one that fits the Hitchcockian world. Yet the heroes of early spy literature were a little more varied than that. Some were amateurs inadvertently caught up in events. Indeed, Buchan's Richard Hannay started this way but became a professional agent in the course of his career on the page. However, some were professionals like William Le Queux's Hugh Morrice or W. Somerset Maugham's Ashenden, the latter drawn from Maugham's own experiences during World War I.

The Hitchcock spy films drew on the range of heroes available from the literary genre, notably Hannay and Ashenden in *The 39 Steps* and *Secret Agent* respectively. However, the first of the spy films drew, loosely, from another classic hero. *The Man Who Knew Too Much,* in Hitchcock's own words to Truffaut, was "based on an original Bulldog Drummond story by 'Sapper'" (109). The Drummond character had been featured in a number of films previously, most famously played by Ronald Colman in *Bulldog Drummond* (Richard Jones, 1929), a Hollywood "Sapper" adaptation. However, Colman's suave Drummond was transformed, perhaps lost completely, in the Hitchcock picture. The male lead in Hitchcock's film, Bob Lawrence, is played by Leslie Banks, a bluff, stodgy Englishman, somewhat upstaged initially by a professional agent, a Frenchman who flirts outrageously with Lawrence's wife (Edna Best). She then upstages Lawrence himself by preventing the assassination at the Albert Hall and then by displaying her prowess with a rifle and rescuing Betty (Nova Pilbeam), their kidnapped daughter. In a telling adaptation of the hero figure, the film divides the character in two, locating the traditional ingenuity and skill of the hero in the central female character.

It is the more masculine and purposive Richard Hannay, Buchan's emblematic hero, that draws more precisely in *The 39 Steps*, the second film of the sextet, on the conventional image of the spy-adventurer, although there are still key differences between the Hitchcock Hannay (Robert Donat) and the Buchan version. In the film, as in the novel, Hannay is an accidental spy inadvertently embroiled in the world of espionage, but through an encounter with a female agent rather than with Scudder, the male spy in the novel. Indeed, the key difference between the film and the novel, between the worlds of Hitchcock and Buchan, is the introduction of a number of female characters and the provision of a romantic dimension nowhere present in the original novel. It is, as Toby Miller has pointed out, a key change: "The change in gender of the dying spy from novel to film is crucial, part of Hitchcock's adaptation of Buchan's homosociality into a story world where female characters are powerful figures on whom men must rely for direction, ideas and succour" (324).

Hannay's chance encounters with Annabella Smith, with the crofter's wife Margaret (Peggy Ashcroft), and most clearly with Pamela (Madeleine Carroll), his eventual partner, all have sexual overtones and indicate the romantic themes that Hitchcock would pursue rigorously in his American career, sometimes in the context of the espionage tale, sometimes not. *Secret Agent*, based on two of Maugham's Ashenden stories, also grafts a romantic theme onto the espionage concerns, a dimension absent from the source stories. Ashenden, the central character, is provided with a "wife" (Madeleine Carroll), a fellow spy, as a cover for his activities, and the film is as much about their developing relationship as it is about espionage and adventure. *Young and Innocent* and *The Lady Vanishes* also interweave romance and adventure, love and crime, with the adventure strand a comment on the romantic strand, a testing of the relationship just as much as a testing of the ingenuity, courage, and daring of the espionage hero.

Romantic concerns are, of course, central to popular narrative cinema. As a key study of the classical Hollywood film suggests, the "classical film has at least two lines of action, both causally linking the same group of characters. Almost invariably, one of these lines of action involves heterosexual romantic love" (Bordwell, Staiger, and Thompson 16). Each film in the sextet has a distinctive line of action revolving around the staples of the espionage genre – mystery, suspense, the chase, the MacGuffin, and so on – but the ways in which romantic concerns are presented differ across the films. Romance is barely present in *The Man Who Knew Too Much* and only an embryonic presence in *Sabotage*, films which feature married couples and family concerns and subordinate the second line of action to generic themes. *The 39 Steps*, *Secret Agent*, *Young and Innocent,* and *The Lady Vanishes*, however, interweave their generic concerns more closely with romance, embedding the couple theme securely within the flight and pursuit structure, which becomes a test of relationships as well as an end in itself. It is this dimension that can be linked as closely to the pre-Gaumont films as the generic elements of murder, mystery, and suspense. Hitchcock's first film, *The Pleasure Garden*, has strong romantic elements – marriage, infidelity, a romantic triangle – while *The Farmer's Wife* is about a middle-aged widower's courtship attempts; both *The Ring* and *The Manxman* focus on romantic triangles, and *Rich and Strange* is about the testing of a marriage. Even the major crime titles, *The Lodger*, *Blackmail* and *Murder!*, interweave the investigation of crime with romances between the central characters.

Beyond tying up the loose ends of the espionage or crime narrative strands, the endings of the sextet provide a final image that ties up the romantic narrative line. The sole exception is *The Man Who Knew Too Much,* with its final image of the reunited family. The others focus upon the romantic couple, though not uniformly. *The 39 Steps* ends on a close shot from behind Hannay and Pamela focused upon their joining hands, complete with the handcuffs; *Sabotage* ends with Ted (John Loder) and Mrs. Verloc (Sylvia Sidney) making their way through a crowd after the bomb blast effectively masks her responsibility for killing her husband while indicating the promise of a new relationship; *Secret Agent* ends with a close-up of the now legitimately married Ashenden and Elsa; *Young and Innocent's* final image is a close shot of Erica (Nova Pilbeam) gazing first at her father, then at Robert (Derrick De Marney), her romantic partner; and *The Lady Vanishes* ends on a close shot of Miss Froy from behind Gilbert (Michael Redgrave) and Iris (Margaret Lockwood), now together as couple. All of these endings constitute in their different ways examples of "that favorite culmination of classical cinema, the construction of the heterosexual couple" (Wood 282–83) and confirm that "one of the underlying purposes of the conventional film is to manufacture the couple, to dramatize with however many variations, the archetypal bourgeois and patriarchal romance" (Gottlieb, "Art" 133).

It might be suggested, however, that Hitchcock does not always or simply offer the conventional romantic couple resolution but injects a degree of ambiguity into some of the endings. *Secret Agent's* postcard image of the couple could be regarded as ironic; *Sabotage* ends with the newly formed couple moving into the future with the secret of Mrs Verloc's guilt, an echo of the ending of *Blackmail* without an equivalent of that film's mocking jester image to reinforce the ambiguities of its ending; the final image of *The 39 Steps* – hands and handcuffs – is "unresolvably ambiguous," according to Robin Wood (283); and the closing image in *Young and Innocent* – Erica gazing from father to prospective lover in a shot with very clear Freudian undertones – moves the ambiguity in directions more fully explored in Hitchcock's subsequent American films.

Generic Contexts: Literature and Cinema

In addition to harkening back to Hitchcock's earlier films, the sextet can also be positioned in relation to the crime/thriller/espionage genre in both literature and film. An espionage genre in a broad cross-media sense was well-established prior to the 1930s. Indeed, it was a generic current that had established itself rapidly in Edwardian Britain as a key component of popular culture:

> Between 1908 and 1918 Britain was invaded by an army of fictional spies. They landed in their thousands on bookstalls and in bookshops. They used the short story to establish themselves in hundreds of newspapers and magazines, successfully infiltrated dozens of popular stage plays, and were even spotted in cinemas and on the pages of children's comics.
>
> (Hiley 55)

The Hitchcock thriller cycle is quite precisely rooted in this broad genre. As Ina Rae Hark has pointed out, the sextet was "derived from the major strains of the British espionage novel of the early twentieth century" (9). Popular writers such as Herman Cyril McNeile ("Sapper"), John Buchan, and Edgar Wallace had established the contours of the genre with international conspiracies, flights and pursuits, disguises and duplicities, and an array of heroic figures ranging from the "four just men" to Bulldog Drummond and Richard Hannay. Spies also figured in more elevated literary practices like Somerset Maugham's *Ashenden* (1928) and, most notably, two Joseph Conrad novels, *The Secret Agent* (1907) and *Under Western Eyes* (1911).

The sextet appears in the cinematic context of the crime/thriller, a significant genre constituting, on one estimate, around one in five of British films made in the 1930s (Shafer 26). Indeed, James Chapman has suggested that "the 1930s in particular have an excellent claim to be regarded as the golden age of the British film thriller" (75), though its powerful presence in the cinema of the time prompted some negative responses. For example, Russell Ferguson, writing in the documentarists' journal, *World Film News*, commented critically on the preponderance of criminal images in popular cinema, suggesting with icy irony that the "national life, as reflected in British films, is full of interesting features. We are a nation of ... detectives ... secret servicemen, crooks, smugglers, and international jewel thieves" (quoted in Chapman 81). In a more positive and celebratory fashion, Peter John Dyer has argued the cultural importance of the genre for British cinema in general:

> The Thirties' British cinema had always been at home with melodrama; unsubtle, somehow innocent melodrama at that, of an oddly national variety, reflecting the carving up of chorus girls by blonde and blue-eyed ex-officers in seaside hotels, the doping of racehorses, and coffee growing cold over the *News of the World*. This was the world that the British cinema understood best: which produced in Alfred Hitchcock, its one true "critics' director", and in Walter Forde, Carol Reed, George King, Arthur Woods and David MacDonald some half-dozen adept disciples.
>
> (80)

The Hitchcock sextet relates to various titles from the genre defined by Dyer. A number of non-espionage films, such as *Rynox* (Michael Powell, 1932), *Rome Express* (Walter Forde, 1932), *The Ghost Camera* (Bernard Vorhaus, 1933), *The Clairvoyant*

(Maurice Elvey, 1934), *The Man Without a Face* (George King, 1935), *The Passing of the Third Floor Back* (Berthold Viertel, 1935), *Seven Sinners* (Albert de Couville, 1936), *They Drive By Night* (Arthur B. Woods, 1938), *This Man Is News* (David MacDonald, 1938), *A Window in London* (Herbert Mason, 1939), *Girl in the News* (Carol Reed, 1940), and *Night Train to Munich* (Carol Reed, 1940), contain familiar thriller elements, perhaps even Hitchcockian elements, such as murder, mystery and suspense, wrongly accused men and women, flight and pursuit, trainboard action including crashes, and screwball romantic comedy, with its combative depiction of sexual relationships. Espionage found its way into the 1930s British cinema as a sub-genre of the crime film, most notably in Hitchcock's sextet, but also in other ways, including a number of historical films including *Me and Marlborough* (Victor Saville, 1935) and *Spy of Napoleon* (Maurice Elvey, 1936), and comedy vehicles such as *Bulldog Jack* (Walter Forde, 1935), a Bulldog Drummond spoof featuring Jack Hulbert, *Old Mother Riley in Paris* (Oswald Mitchell, 1938), and *Strange Boarders* (Herbert Mason, 1938), based on an E. Philips Oppenheim novel. There were also espionage films set in the First World War, such as *I Was a Spy* (Victor Saville, 1933), *Moscow Nights* (Anthony Asquith, 1935), *Knight Without Armour* (Jacques Feyder, 1937), and *Dark Journey* (Victor Saville, 1937).

Hitchcock benefited from the rich cultural context depicted by Dyer, the bedrock of themes and conventions constituted by the broad thriller genre from which the sextet emerged. The cycle was made in the years 1934 to 1938, a period which saw some two hundred thrillers produced, of which around fifty were espionage films of various kinds (these and subsequent statistics are drawn from Gifford). Although many of the spy films were cheaply produced "quota quickies," some were big budget productions from major studios like Gaumont British and Korda's London Films. The Gaumont British studio production schedules also provided a more proximate creative context within which the Hitchcock cycle could flourish. Two films in particular prepared the ground for the sextet. The first was *Rome Express*, whose trainboard narrative and array of varied characters marks it as an obvious predecessor of *The Lady Vanishes* and prefigures the trainboard action in *The 39 Steps* and *Secret Agent*. The second, *I Was a Spy*, as the title indicates, featured the espionage subject matter of the cycle as well as Madeleine Carroll in the leading role.

I Was a Spy, a biographical film based on the exploits of a real-life female agent from World War I, traced the way in which a Belgian nurse (Carroll) is drawn into the world of espionage through her family; she is an accidental spy, the female counterpart of Childers's heroes and Richard Hannay. She falls in love with the German counter-agent (Herbert Marshall) and they work together. The film celebrates her as an ordinary woman caught up in the momentous events of the period. Although it does have suspenseful moments, such as the blowing up of the German gas cylinders, its dominant concern is the courage and sacrifice displayed by her and her romantic partner. *Rome Express* is partly a crime thriller about the theft of a valuable painting and partly a portmanteau film along the lines of Hollywood's *Grand Hotel* (Edmund Goulding, 1932) in which the stories of a number of characters are interwoven with a common setting linking them together. Apart from the opening and a brief sequence at the end, the film is set on board a train traveling from Paris to Rome. It knits together the stories of a jaded Hollywood film star, a suburban golf club bore, an adulterous couple, a Poirot-like French policeman, and a philanthropic though miserly millionaire, together with an assortment of villains with interests in the art of theft.

I Was a Spy looks forward to Hitchcock's spy films, though Saville himself referred to the film as "a spy story with a difference – it was a true one" (Moseley 66). Its factual basis in the memoirs of Martha Knockhaert, the Belgian nurse at the center of the film, separates it from the more overtly entertaining and fanciful Hitchcock films. The difference is most evident in the somber, downbeat ending in which the heroine's partner is executed. These factors give *I Was a Spy* a tone very different from that of most of the Hitchcock films, although *Secret Agent*, based on Maugham's war experiences, does share its sobriety as well as its World War I setting, and *Sabotage* has a dark and somber quality unredeemed by the romantic resolution of the ending. Although Madeleine Carroll plays Martha Knockhaert, her glamour and sexual allure, capitalized on in her Hitchcock films, is absent from the austere portrayal of courage in the Saville film. In contrast, *Rome Express*, though not an espionage film, has closer affinities with the sextet both in theme and tone. Indeed it looks like a blueprint for *The Lady Vanishes*. The key common factor between the two films is Sidney Gilliat, who adapted the short story on which *Rome Express* was based and provided some of the dialogue. Gilliat, who had worked with Hitchcock at B.I.P. in a minor capacity, had written the screenplay for *The Lady Vanishes* with his collaborator, Frank Launder, for another director. When production delays brought the project to a halt, Hitchcock acquired the screenplay and chose it for the final film of his contract with Gaumont British (Brown 89).

I Was a Spy, set in German-occupied Belgium, was part of a significant strand of the espionage genre that focused on World War I. Some eleven of the fifty or so espionage films made in Britain between 1934 and 1938, including, of course, Hitchcock's *Secret Agent*, had a World War I setting. While many of these were low-budget quota pictures, three of them – *Moscow Nights, Knight Without Armour*, and *Dark Journey* – were high-profile British films. All were made by Alexander Korda's London Films, which boasted an international orientation, lavish production expenditure, and a cosmopolitan array of creative talent and major international stars, such as Marlene Dietrich, Conrad Veidt, Robert Donat, and Madeleine Carroll.

The similarities to Hitchcock's espionage films, however, are limited. Asquith's *Moscow Nights* follows the pattern of interweaving romance with espionage in pre-revolutionary Russia. The romantic strand is a love triangle involving Captain Ignatoff (Laurence Olivier), a young officer recuperating after a battle injury; Natasha (Penelope Dudley-Ward), the young nurse who looks after him while he is in hospital; and Brioukow (Harry Baur), a wealthy, middle-aged grain merchant and war profiteer whose marriage to Natasha has been arranged by her mother. The second strand – announced in the opening title, "Espionage" – involves a spy ring organized by Madame Sabline (Athene Seyler), a fictional predecessor of Hitchcock's Miss Froy in *The Lady Vanishes. Knight Without Armour*, a film that cost £300 000, around six times the costs of the individual Hitchcock pictures (Drazin 168–69), also blends espionage and romance, again in Russia during World War I and in the early years of the revolution. A.J. Fothergill (Robert Donat) is an English journalist based in Russia who gets drawn into the British secret service and is soon caught up in the politics of the period, rescuing and falling in love with an aristocrat, the Countess Alexandra (Marlene Dietrich). The film mixes the chaotic early days of the revolution with flight and pursuit when Fothergill helps the Countess to escape her imprisonment. The spectacle of Donat and Dietrich fleeing through the countryside provides an echo of Donat and Carroll's handcuffed flight across the Scottish moors in *The 39 Steps*.

Dark Journey was directed by Victor Saville, an old associate of Hitchcock and something of a specialist in espionage subjects. Like some of Saville's earlier titles, the film focuses on a female spy, a French fashion entrepreneur based in Sweden and operating as a double agent. As in the Asquith and Feyder films, there is a strong romantic dimension, with the female spy falling for one of her German opponents, a reprise of the situation in the factually-based *I Was a Spy*. However, in the earlier film, the couple are split apart when the male protagonist is executed at the end of the film, whereas *Dark Journey* ends with a promise of a future for the couple. As with *I Was a Spy*, the war setting provides the films with a dramatic backdrop to the potential adventure and romance of the genre. Indeed, both *Moscow Nights* and *Knight Without Armour* pay considerable attention to that background, providing thereby a stronger sense of historical issues but perhaps a weaker sense of the drama and intrigue of espionage. *Knight Without Armour* does, it is true, have the "couple in flight" quality of *The 39 Steps* but not the sense of adventure, daring, and risqué sexuality of the Hitchcock film.

Trainboard settings like that in *Rome Express* were popular with both novelists and filmmakers during the 1930s. Graham Greene's *Stamboul Train* (1932), Agatha Christie's *Murder on the Orient Express* (1933), and Ethel Lina White's *The Wheel Spins* (1936), the novel on which *The Lady Vanishes* was based, were published during the decade, and films as diverse as *Seven Sinners* (Albert de Courville, 1936), *Oh Mr. Porter!* (Marcel Varnel, 1937), and *Night Train to Munich* used the railway as a framework for their drama or comedy. Before joining Gaumont British, Hitchcock had used an extended train sequence for *Number Seventeen*, his final film for B.I.P., and there are important trainboard passages in both *The 39 Steps* and *Secret Agent*. However, *The Lady Vanishes* is, for many, the paradigmatic train film, overshadowing *Rome Express*, its studio predecessor, and establishing Hitchcock as the master of the trainboard melodrama. The train motif itself, of course, is utilized in a number of Hitchcock's American titles, including *Suspicion* (1941), *Shadow of a Doubt* (1943), *Strangers on a Train* (1951), and *North by Northwest* (Walker 374–77).

Yet a cursory analysis of another train film from 1930s British cinema indicates the extent to which the motif, together with a number of others associated with

Hitchcock, had a strong generic basis. *Seven Sinners* was based on a script by Frank Launder and Sidney Gilliat, working in collaboration for the first time. Gilliat, of course, had scripted *Rome Express*, and *Seven Sinners* incorporates three train sequences and three train crashes. The train sequences punctuate a story about a private detective who discovers a dead body in his hotel room and falls under suspicion for the murder. He takes it upon himself to probe the mystery and follows a tortuous and extensive trail of investigation from France back to England, accompanied by a woman who eventually becomes his romantic partner. Finally, the culprit is tracked down and apprehended in a cinema showing a newsreel of the final train crash. *Seven Sinners* was released at the end of 1936, after *The Man Who Knew Too Much* and *The 39 Steps* but in the same year as *Secret Agent* and *Sabotage*. In addition to the train motif, it has other resemblances to the Hitchcock films. For example, the film follows the flight and pursuit pattern characteristic of Hitchcock; the central characters are a combative romantic couple along the lines of Hannay and Pamela (*The 39 Steps*), Ashenden and Elsa (*Secret Agent*), and Gilbert and Iris (*The Lady Vanishes*), couples formed in the course of pursuits; it has a "respectable villain," a French police inspector, eventually unmasked as the murderer, an equivalent of Professor Jordan in *The 39 Steps*; and the finale – a shootout in a cinema during the screening of a newsreel about the various train crashes – both echoes the cinema setting in *Sabotage* and prefigures a similar sequence in *Saboteur*, one of Hitchcock's early Hollywood films.

"Gaumont Hitchcock" and Hitchcock

"Gaumont Hitchcock," the thriller sextet, is clearly a very important phase in the director's career, the most important period in his British career for many. The cycle has been characterized in terms of artistic self-discovery by Taylor, McGilligan, and Lovell (Taylor 147; McGilligan 169; Lovell 71). With films such as *The 39 Steps* and *The Lady Vanishes*, Hitchcock "perfected his form" and hit upon a cinematic genre which fitted him "like a second skin," and "discovered himself as an artist." The thrillers rescued Hitchcock's career, re-established his "creative prestige," and restored his position as Britain's leading film director. In addition, the films attracted American attention. For example, Hitchcock was voted the best director of 1938 for *The Lady Vanishes* in the recently established New York Film Critics Awards (Kapsis 23). The success of the films paved the way for his eventual Hollywood career. Their qualities – in Peter Wollen's words, "the mix of spy film and screwball comedy" ("Hitch" 16) – embodied his strengths as a filmmaker and created Hitchcock as "the master of suspense," one of the strongest dimensions of the Hitchcockian legend.

Apart from a few titles – *The Lodger* and *Blackmail* in particular – the success of the cycle overshadowed that of the previous films, most of which offered little to support Hitchcock's popular image as a thriller director. Hitchcock's own comments on the pre-Gaumont period have contributed to this opinion. He remarked to Truffaut that *Champagne* was "the lowest ebb in my output," opined that *The Manxman* was "a very banal picture," and spoke about the "creative decline" in the period just before he rejoined Balcon at Gaumont British (Truffaut 67, 69, 109). The Gaumont sextet, on the other hand, has been represented as a release of Hitchcock's creative energies hitherto largely untapped in the constricted production conditions at B.I.P. in particular. Peter John Dyer wrote of Hitchcock being "condemned for eight years following *The Lodger* to filming Galsworthy, Philpotts, O'Casey, Coward, Clemence Dane and Ivor Novello" (80). For Dyer, the sextet signaled "Hitchcock's declaration of independence" (80) from the middlebrow adaptations and the artistic stylistic touches aimed at highbrow critics. At Gaumont, Hitchcock lowered his intellectual sights, picked up generic threads intermittently present in his pre-Gaumont career, and embarked on the sextet. Thereafter, as Dyer suggests, Hitchcock "went in for making thrillers for the unsophisticated. *The Man Who Knew Too Much* … was outright melodrama, deficient in structure and flawed in its logic. But its very recklessness gave it an excitement hitherto unknown in the British cinema" (81). Where Rohmer and Chabrol had identified a "skillful dosage" (38) of pre-Gaumont elements feeding into the cycle, Dyer saw a sharper divide, a breaking free from some of the inhibiting elements associated with the middlebrow entertainment projects favored by B.I.P.

However, it could be argued that the sextet represents a kind of Hitchcockian settlement for a strong generic context within which to work. Many of the narrative patterns and themes in the six thrillers are present in other examples of the thriller/espionage genre. Murder, flight and pursuit, the "wrong man," trains, secret agents and spies, and the formation of the couple: all can be found in the work of Asquith and Saville, Walter Forde, David MacDonald, George King, and Carol Reed, amongst others, though they derived as well from the literary traditions of the early twentieth-century thriller. For one of English Hitchcock's most acute and supportive critics, the turn to genre was not wholly without cost. Despite the excellence of the Gaumont films, Charles Barr has suggested that they "represent a narrowing down and in some ways even an impoverishment" (*English* 132) of the body of work completed in the early Gainsborough and B.I.P. periods. Indeed, it is the pre-Gaumont films that relate more strongly to the great American pictures: "Some of his profoundest Hollywood works will seem to reach back to the early English films, and to rework both formal and thematic elements from them that are not present in the thrillers" (*English* 132).

Dreams, fantasies, nightmares, the gaze, and "powerful Oedipal stories" (Barr, *Yesterdays* 20), can be found in pre-Gaumont films such as *The Lodger*, *Downhill*, *Champagne*, *The Manxman*, and *Blackmail*, and it is these titles with their dark discourse of fantasy and sexuality that look forward to the major Hollywood films. Such themes can be found intermittently in the sextet, but the generic constraints of the comedy thriller tend to iron out the bleaker implications of the Hitchcockian world as embodied in *The Manxman* and *Blackmail* in particular. *Sabotage* with its "guilty secret" ending, *Secret Agent* with the assassination of "the wrong man," the "crofter's wife" sequence in *The 39 Steps*, and *Young and Innocent* with its explicitly Freudian ending perhaps hint most explicitly at the dark dimensions more fully explored in the later films. Gaumont Hitchcock is a specific phase in the career of a remarkably versatile filmmaker that has acquired an emblematic force in Hitchcock criticism. The sextet, a series of films that enabled critics to pinpoint with ease a quite specific Hitchcock, constitutes only one of the many Hitchcocks that criticism has produced over the longer term – one whose generic optimism and conventional sexuality is a long way from such acknowledged American masterpieces as *Vertigo* (1958) and *Psycho* (1960).

Works Cited

Balcon, Michael. *Michael Balcon Presents ... A Lifetime in Films*. London: Hutchinson, 1969.

Barr, Charles, ed. *All Our Yesterdays: 90 Years of British Cinema*. London: BFI, 1986.

Barr, Charles. *English Hitchcock*. Moffat: Cameron and Hollis, 1999.

Belfrage, Cedric. "Alfred the Great." *Picturegoer* Mar. 1926: 60.

Bordwell, David. *The Films of Carl-Theodor Dreyer*. California: U of California P, 1981.

Bordwell, David, Janet Staiger, and Kristin Thompson. *The Classical Hollywood Cinema: Film Style and Mode of Production to 1960*. New York: Columbia UP, 1985.

Brown, Geoff. *Launder and Gilliat*. London: BFI, 1977.

Chapman, James. "Celluloid Shockers." *The Unknown 1930s: An Alternative History of the British Cinema, 1929–1939*. Ed. Jeffrey Richards. London: Tauris, 1998. 75–97.

Chibnall, Steve. *Quota Quickies: The Birth of the British 'B' Film*. London: BFI, 2007.

Drazin, Charles. *Korda: Britain's Only Movie Mogul*. London: Sidgwick and Jackson, 2002.

Durgnat, Raymond. *The Strange Case of Alfred Hitchcock, or The Plain Man's Hitchcock*. Cambridge: MIT P, 1974.

Dyer, Peter John. "Young and Innocent." *Sight and Sound* 30.2 (1961): 80–84.

Gifford, Denis. *The British Film Catalogue 1895–1985: A Reference Guide*. Newton Abbot: David and Charles, 1986.

Gottlieb, Sidney. "Hitchcock and the Art of the Kiss." *Framing Hitchcock: Selected Essays from the* Hitchcock Annual. Ed. Sidney Gottlieb and Christopher Brookhouse. Detroit: Wayne State UP, 2002. 132–46.

Gottlieb, Sidney, ed. *Hitchcock on Hitchcock: Selected Writings and Interviews*. Berkeley: U of California P, 1995.

Grierson, John. *Grierson on Documentary*. Ed. Forsyth Hardy. Rev. ed. London: Faber and Faber, 1966.

Hark, Ina Rae. "Keeping Your Amateur Standing: Audience Participation and Good Citizenship in Hitchcock's Political Films." *Cinema Journal* 29.2 (1990): 8–22.

Hiley, Nicholas. "Decoding German Spies: British Spy Fiction 1908–1918." *Intelligence and National Security* 5.4 (1990): 55–79.

Hitchcock, Alfred. "Core of the Movie—The Chase." Interview by David Brady. *New York Times Magazine* 29 Oct. 1950: 22+. Gottlieb, *Hitchcock on* Hitchcock 125–32.

Kapsis, Robert E. *Hitchcock: The Making of a Reputation*. Chicago: U of Chicago P, 1992.

Leitch, Thomas. *Find the Director and Other Hitchcock Games*. Athens: U of Georgia P, 1991.

Lovell, Alan. "Introduction (to interview with Ivor Montagu)." *Screen* 13.3 (1972): 71.

Low, Rachael. *The History of the British Film, 1918–1929*. London: Allen and Unwin, 1971.

Miller, Toby. "39 Steps to 'The Borders of the Possible': Alfred Hitchcock, Amateur Observer and the New Cultural History." *Alfred Hitchcock: Centenary Essays*. Ed. Richard Allen and S. Ishii-Gonzáles. London: BFI, 1999. 317–31.

Montagu, Ivor. "Interview: Ivor Montagu." *Screen* 13.3 (1972): 72–113.

Moseley, Roy, ed. *Evergreen: Victor Saville in His Own Words*. Carbondale: Southern Illinois UP, 2000.

Rohmer, Eric, and Claude Chabrol. *Hitchcock: The First Forty-Four Films*. Trans. Stanley Hochman. New York: Ungar, 1979.

Sedgwick, John. "Michael Balcon's Close Encounter with the American Market, 1934–1936." *Historical Journal of Film, Radio and Television* 16.3 (1996): 333–48.

Shafer, Stephen C. *British Popular Films 1929–1939: The Cinema of Reassurance*. London: Routledge, 1997.

Taylor, John Russell. *Hitch: The Life and Times of Alfred Hitchcock*. New York: Pantheon, 1978.

Trotter, David. "The Politics of Adventure in the Early British Spy Novel." *Intelligence and National Security* 5.4 (1990): 30–54.

Walker, Michael. *Hitchcock's Motifs*. Amsterdam: Amsterdam UP, 2005.

Wollen, Peter. "Hitch: A Tale of Two Cities (London and Los Angeles)." *Hitchcock: Past and Future*. Ed. Richard Allen and Sam Ishii-Gonzáles. London: Routledge, 2004. 15–21.

Wollen, Peter. *Signs and Meaning in the Cinema*. Expanded ed. London: BFI, 1998.

Wood, Robin. *Hitchcock's Films Revisited*. Revised ed. New York: Columbia UP, 2002.

16

Hitchcock Discovers America: The Selznick-Era Films

Ina Rae Hark

The first act of *Rebecca* (1940), Alfred Hitchcock's debut American film under his contract with David O. Selznick, plays out at Monte Carlo among the brooding Cornish aristocrat Maxim de Winter (Laurence Olivier), the shy young Englishwoman who will become his second wife (Joan Fontaine), and her employer, the wealthy and vulgar Mrs. Edythe Van Hopper (Florence Bates) of New York and Palm Springs. A monstrous embodiment of everything an Englishman might find off-putting in Americans, Mrs. Van Hopper talks too loudly and too much, is over-familiar with acquaintances, pretends to be all-knowing when she is anything but, has a *nouveau-riche* sense of entitlement, and demonstrates a basic coarseness beneath her affected mid-Atlantic accent and expensive jewelry – epitomized by the close-up of her stubbing out a cigarette in a jar of cold cream.

While apparently long familiar with people trying to avoid her, Van Hopper has a rationalization for every snub. After de Winter abruptly walks out on their hotel lobby conversation even before the coffee he has ordered for the three of them arrives, she recounts the story of a "well-known writer who used to dart down the back way whenever he saw me coming. I suppose he was in love with me," she adds, "and wasn't quite sure of himself." Unable to imagine people motivated by anything other than her own social-climbing acquisitiveness, she accuses her paid companion of being a gold-digger who entrapped de Winter, possibly even by sleeping with him, and exits the film with a sarcastic valedictory: "Good luck!"

It's tempting in retrospect to read this part of the film as an allegory for Hitchcock's decision to sign a contract with an American producer and his confrontation with the parvenu power brokers in Hollywood. Though he doubtless wished to mock them with aristocratic wit, he was nonetheless dependent on them for financial survival and just as insecure as *Rebecca*'s heroine. He would of course make a different

A Companion to Alfred Hitchcock, First Edition. Edited by Thomas Leitch and Leland Poague.
© 2011 Thomas Leitch and Leland Poague. Published 2011 by Blackwell Publishing Ltd.

choice than the second Mrs. de Winter. Pressed to decide between New York and coming "home to Manderley," she opts for the latter. Perhaps her encounters with Mrs. Danvers would eventually make her consider her poor opinion of Mrs. Van Hopper in a different light. Hitch went to the US and never returned full-time to England, including those difficult years in the 1940s when it too burned like Manderley, not from internal rot but from external totalitarian threat.

According to Patrick McGilligan, the move to America was inevitable for Hitchcock. "In England, already in his youth, Hitchcock began to nurture his own composite nationality. 'I would say,' he once explained, 'that I was – if it is a word – Americophile'" (1). Thus, in dealing with American subjects and American characters, the director is both skeptic and enthusiast. In the introduction to their collection of essays on Hitchcock's America, Jonathan Freedman and Richard Millington observe how "at the center of Hitchcock's Hollywood films stands a sustained, specific, and extraordinarily acute exploration of American culture" (5). But that exploration took nearly the entire decade to complete as Hitchcock labored to find his bearings. The events depicted in *Rebecca, Foreign Correspondent* (1940), *Suspicion* (1941), *Lifeboat* (1944), and *The Paradine Case* (1947) take place primarily or entirely in Europe. *Saboteur* (1942) and *Notorious* (1946) deal with the threat of Nazism. *Spellbound* (1945) views Americans through the lens of European-born psychoanalytic theory. Only *Mr. and Mrs. Smith* (1941) and *Shadow of a Doubt* (1943) qualify as purely American in subject matter, characters, and location. Although Hitchcock fussed about the ersatz quality of being encouraged to make "English" pictures in California, he hardly campaigned for the chance to plant his storylines firmly in the United States.

As several scholars have observed, Hitchcock would always cultivate an image of Britishness and "never hesitated to cast his films – even those set primarily in America – with British actors" (Deutelbaum and Poague 137). His films of the 1930s had often immersed Britons in webs of Central European intrigue. With a world war in progress for most of the years of his association with Selznick, he had only to add Americans to this mix, allowing him both to work from familiar paradigms and to craft a sense of American identity from the contrasts with the European pro- and anti-fascist forces at play.

Another factor in giving Hitchcock a gradual transition into the conventions of Hollywood cinema was Selznick's bias toward "women's pictures." While we don't usually think of the master of suspense as an analogue to George Cukor or John Stahl, a great majority of his most successful British films either have female protagonists or feature women as equal or dominant partners in a leading couple: *The Lodger* (1926), *Blackmail* (1929), *The Man Who Knew Too Much* (1934), *Sabotage* (1936), *Young and Innocent* (1937), *The Lady Vanishes* (1938). In explaining why Hitchcock during the forties remained on "the margins of film *noir*," that very masculine genre, James Naremore notes that "[a]gain and again, Hitchcock invited his audience to identify with the point of view of women" (272) either as "a product of his personal inclination or his commercial calculations" (273). The only model of male subjectivity Hitchcock had so far developed to focalize the narrative and drive the plot appeared first in *The 39 Steps* (1935): the famous "wrong man" hero whose greatest skill is running for his life and eluding capture. The contract with Selznick, the initial success with the "female gothic" *Rebecca*, and the shortage of dynamic male stars because of the war provided all the excuses Hitchcock needed to continue to film his female-propelled narratives as he worked out a type of American masculinity that could supplement the genial cipher on the run for which Robert Donat's Richard Hannay, himself a colonial, was the original.

If we examine the female protagonists in Hitchcockian cinema, a consistent trope emerges: a woman becomes romantically involved with a man who may be a murderer. It plays out in a number of different ways. He may indeed be a murderer or at least intend murder either to a third party or to the woman herself. On the other hand, suspicions about him held by others, if not always by the female protagonist, usually prove groundless. The audience may either possess a certainty the characters lack (that Hannay is innocent of Annabella Smith's murder, say) or remain completely in the dark, guided often by identification with the woman's own perceptions, although those can be mistaken, like the second Mrs. de Winter's in *Rebecca*. Once Hitchcock gets to America, his use of this trope takes on features that permit him, as he moves into the 1950s, to use it in films that feature a male protagonist. The result is an American masculinity defined by psychological imbalance.

As befits a transitional period, the Selznick-era Hitchcock films are comparatively contingent and relational. America and Americans gain definition through the differences that mark them off from the English and Continental characters of the 1920s and 1930s. At the same time, Hitchcock perfects his paradigm of male villainy but has not yet worked through to the male heroes of the American period for whom these villains – usually psychopathic – served as dark doubles. He left Selznick to produce films for his own company, Transatlantic Pictures, and at the end of the decade he still occupied that middle ground as a "Hollywood" director always with one eye on his British homeland.

Innocents Abroad: *Foreign Correspondent* and *Lifeboat*

The American protagonists of Hitchcock's two films that take place during the war in Europe find themselves in the middle of the Atlantic. Flying back to the US on the trail of an undercover German agent pretending to be a British peace activist, reporter Johnny Jones (Joel McCrea) has his plane shot down over the ocean in *Foreign Correspondent*. An American ship rescues him and a few other survivors clinging to the plane's wing in minutes, but all the action in *Lifeboat* takes place in that craft in which American and British survivors of a torpedoed freighter and the Nazi captain of the ship that sank them drift for weeks.

In both films, the American characters are "innocents" compared to the European ones. By this term I do not refer to their moral state but to their relative simplicity and narrowness of both reference and vision, especially as it concerns the nature of the fascist threat. With five American characters, *Lifeboat* can delve into the permutations and combinations of this blinkered colonial mindset, but *Foreign Correspondent* sketches it out in broad strokes by putting a quintessentially American character into the tried and true plot of the director's British thrillers.

Like the first, this second film of Hitchcock's in America, on loan out to Walter Wanger for a long-deferred adaptation of Vincent Sheehan's memoirs, has a naïve protagonist dropped headlong into a world of intrigue and threat where everyone else is seemingly in the know. Just as the second Mrs. de Winter stands outside the society of Manderley because of her different social class, Johnny Jones sticks out like a sore thumb at the peace conference. Yet these outsiders soon discover the truth that all the *cognoscenti* have missed: the admired centers of these social and political networks, Rebecca and Stephen Fisher (Herbert Marshall), are not what they seem to be. They are evil at the core.

While this character positioning might suggest the director working through his own status as a stranger in a strange land, we should note the transposition. The strange land is Europe and England, not the United States. Americans abroad occasionally crop up in Hitchcock's films throughout the rest of his career, but he never made a film about a Briton mystified by life and customs across the pond. In the entirely British films of the Selznick years, *Rebecca*, *Suspicion,* and *The Paradine Case*, the casting of American actors Joan Fontaine and Gregory Peck in the lead roles replicates the pattern on a meta-level, especially as both project nothing so much as feeling woefully inadequate and out of place. Leonard Leff notes that Hitchcock wanted an American for the second Mrs. de Winter "to stress her isolation at Manderley" (51) and also pushed for Peck to star in *Paradine*, although that's not what Hitchcock told Truffaut concerning the latter. Given how seamlessly British actors fit into the director's American-set films, he may intend by the role reversal a cultural statement about British adaptability versus American inflexibility rather than a configuration of his own personal situation.

Foreign Correspondent defines Europe as a place to which cadres of elites apply various complex theories and analyses, masking with assorted conferences, position papers, and secret treaty negotiations the truth that it is a "bedeviled continent" upon which the crime of fascism goes undetected and unpunished. The solution *New York Globe* editor Powers (Harry Davenport) fashions is to assign a dogged, none-too-bright crime reporter to the European beat. Johnny Jones is a goal-oriented and slightly mercenary pragmatist who will do anything to get a story – especially if the assignment comes with a substantial expense account. Although Joel McCrea is more than adequate in the role, Hitchcock badly wanted Gary Cooper for that "simple, almost dopey, American quality that Cooper specialized in" (Rossi 28).

What Jones's "fresh, unused mind" lacks in intellectual sophistication it makes up in on-target intuition. He speaks of being able to "feel" and "smell" that things are amiss. The Europeans regard such gut motivations skeptically, often condescending to Johnny's naiveté. "Your childish mind is as out of place in Europe as you are in my bedroom," sniffs Carol Fisher (Laraine Day), who also accuses him of talking through his hat. Losing hats is a recurrent problem for Johnny, adding to the pattern of references to his deficient brainpower. Of course, Carol also ends up falling in love with him, and he exposes the Nazi conspiracy with the same dogged earnestness that wins her over.

Nevertheless, Johnny's tunnel vision and lack of perspective also hint at an American tendency to achieve limited, personally advantageous goals without regard for the consequences to others. American isolationism at the time of the film's production supposedly motivated the addition of the final stirring call to arms Johnny broadcasts from London during the Blitz, but this speech in fact denominates America as the last place that the light of freedom shines and urges American self-defense more than the entry of the United States into a war in defense of Europe. In his zeal to get his scoop, Johnny shows himself initially unconcerned with the danger to Van Meer (Albert Bassermann) his investigations might produce, and the only reason he considers killing the story later is because it might cause shame and distress to his fiancée, Carol, when her father's treason comes to light. He even engages in some self-deprecating humor when his unwonted consideration of big-picture issues causes to Carol to remark, "You've turned European on me overnight." He quickly assures her that he is still as big a jackass (read Yankee) as ever.

If Johnny alone discovered the treason of Stephen Fisher, *Foreign Correspondent* would seem to endorse his straightforward pragmatism as preferable to European nuance and complexity. Late in the film, however, we learn that British journalist Scott ffolliott (George Sanders) has suspected Fisher for over a year, and the two men together free Van Meer and bring down the German spy operation. Scott's demeanor contrasts completely with Johnny's. He peppers his speech with "old boys" and "old girls," a stereotype of the Hollywood Englishman, and his habitual mode is irony. Whereas Johnny is all dogged earnestness, Scott never seems quite serious, no matter how urgent the situation. Even though Stephen Fisher's Britishness is merely a thin veneer, he and Scott always seem far more in tune with each other than either does with Johnny, who provokes the same wry putdowns that Mrs. Van Hopper elicits from Maxim de Winter.

Deception and fascism go hand in hand, here and in most of Hitchcock's anti-Nazi films. The head of the Universal Peace Party actually works to facilitate the German war effort, Johnny's bodyguard has actually been hired to kill him, a supposed tramp has to dirty his hands to play his part, the spies substitute an imposter for Van Meer and then assassinate him, windmills turn against the wind to signal a plane to land. Yet the film implies that convoluted indirection is also a European trait and not just a fascist one. What's needed is a stalwart American who can cut the Gordian knot because he's not afraid to take on figures of authority to get at the truth, whether these figures be a police officer, a rigidly neutral American ship captain, or even Hitler, whom Johnny identifies as a prime source for information.

Within the adventure narratives of the typical 1930s thrillers that Charles Bennett, who worked on the *Foreign Correspondent* screenplay as well, wrote for Hitchcock, such naïve idealism appeared harmless. However, as this film got closer and closer to completion, the realities of actual warfare rather than spy-novel hijinks provoked producer Walter Wanger to add the epilogue of Johnny broadcasting during an air raid. *Lifeboat* also reflects this change of tone. Its Allied survivors of a Nazi attack eventually cede authority over their course to the German U-boat captain, Willy (Walter Slezak). He's competent, efficient, a forward planner and utterly ruthless while they flounder, take votes in the name of democracy, and bicker about every decision. Only when they revolt at his calm recitation of all he's done in the name of their survival do they unite in order to murder him savagely. Even though Hitchcock described this mob as "like a pack of dogs," he also meant their action to be necessary:

> So here was a statement telling the democracies to put their differences aside temporarily and to gather their forces to concentrate on the common enemy, whose strength was precisely derived from a spirit of unity and of determination.
>
> (Truffaut 156, 155)

Britain is represented among the survivors by crewman Stanley "Sparks" Garrett (Hume Cronyn), an unassuming and humane fellow who steers the boat and successfully woos American nurse Alice MacKenzie (Mary Anderson) during the ordeal. One other British survivor, the shell-shocked Mrs. Higley (Heather Angel), throws herself overboard on the first night in the boat in grief over her baby's death. But differences between Americans and Britons receive much less attention than in *Foreign Correspondent*. The film focuses instead on the conflict between all the others and Willy, and even more pointedly on the conflicts among the Americans.

John Steinbeck, the good leftist who wrote the original treatment for the film, stressed the political strife between the capitalist Rittenhouse (Henry Hull) and the communist Kovac (John Hodiak), with the story focalized through the latter in the treatment. Although Steinbeck doubted that Hitchcock shared his political beliefs (Leff 112), *Lifeboat* does view American social distinctions in a different way than the other Hitchcock films of the Selznick era. Hitchcock often divided US residents along the axes of small town vs. big city, provincial vs. sophisticated, west coast vs. east coast. Here, though, class warfare predominates. On the one side we have the blue-collar able seamen of the freighter: Stanley, Kovac, Gus Smith (William Bendix), and George "Joe" Spencer (Canada Lee). The others range from middle-class nurse Alice to famed photojournalist Constance Porter (Tallulah Bankhead) and millionaire industrialist Rittenhouse.

Willy, an officer and a surgeon in civilian life, wins the backing of the upper-class survivors, since they are more comfortable around people like him than they are around the less educated crew members. The Nazi movement did not begin with the upper classes, to be sure, and the film leaves it open whether it is this particular Nazi's background or fascism in general that has a greater appeal to the well-to-do citizens of the democracies. Throughout Hitchcock's career, it should be noted, espionage masterminds tend to disguise themselves as citizens of the countries they seek to undermine and often resemble no one so much as cultivated English gentlemen like Professor Jordan (Godfrey Tearle) in *The 39 Steps*, Stephen Fisher in *Foreign Correspondent*, Alex Sebastian (Claude Rains) in *Notorious*, and Philip Vandamm (James Mason) in *North by Northwest* (1959).

Among the proletarians on the lifeboat, ethnic differences stand out, as they do not among the others. Kovac and Gus personalize their antipathy toward the Germans because of their backgrounds. As a Czech-American, the former identifies with the invasion of his ancestral homeland by the Germans. Gus, on the other hand, wishes to distance himself from any family he might have left in Germany because of what the Nazis have done, even changing his name from Schmidt to Smith. Although Kovac is an angry leftist intellectual, Gus is good-hearted but none too bright, speaking in slang and obsessing about his dancing partner Rosie, the girl he fears may be cheating on him. Yet neither ever trusts Willy, Kovac through knowledge of previous German behavior, Gus through pure instinct. And it is Gus who exposes the Nazi's treachery, although it costs him his life to do so.

The final working-class character, African American steward "Joe," occupies a liminal position between progressive and stereotyped portrayal. He's skeptical when Connie offers him full voting rights in choosing their captain, no doubt because she often calls him "Charcoal." (Then again, she calls Kovac "Commissar" and "Tovarich" – and she's in love with *him*.) Ultimately he stays above the fray, trusting God and abstaining from the survivors' democratic deliberations. But this includes the fact that he elects not to participate in Willy's murder and tries (without success) to keep Alice from staining her soul with the German's blood. He's the one who first saves Mrs. Higley and takes care of practical matters with quiet competence. Yet his religiosity, flute-playing, and status as a reformed pickpocket threaten to make him a cliché. "*Lifeboat* partially escapes racial stereotypes by understandably showing people forging a united front in the teeth of extraordinary, life-threatening conditions," observe Clayton Koppes and Gregory Black (402). Noting that Joe's declining to vote may be a way that the film pronounces him unfit to do so, they still acknowledge that he is important in the history of Blacks onscreen simply by being present on the boat.

Despite this more diverse cross-section of Americans Steinbeck's initial treatment provides, Hitchcock departs from Steinbeck in focalizing the film through Constance Porter, who with a change in gender could feasibly represent Johnny Jones at a further stage of his career, after becoming a renowned foreign correspondent through his Huntley Haverstock reportage. Connie came from the same neighborhood near the Chicago slaughterhouses that Kovac did, but she has parlayed her drive and luck (and, as played by Tallulah Bankhead, her sexuality) into an upper-class cover much like that provided by Johnny's *nom de plume*. Like Johnny, she will do anything for a story, and it's been her only priority for much longer than it has been his. But as the days in the lifeboat strip her of everything, including the diamond bracelet that took her out of the South Side, a prized possession she willingly sacrifices to try to feed the survivors, what remains is good old American pluck. She is the one who rouses the despondent passengers after they fear that killing Willy has doomed them all. She reminds Rittenhouse, who for all his wealth and power turns out to be a feckless paper tiger, that he too is a "self-made man." Thus class differences are rendered more apparent than real, and the common denominator for the Americans turns out to be the same pragmatism and self-reinvention we see in *Foreign Correspondent*.

But *Lifeboat*, like its predecessor, also shows that America has no theoretical understanding of what gives rise to fascism and powers its success. As I've written elsewhere about the film:

> [W]hen the young Nazi sailor they pull into the boat asks, 'Aren't you going to kill me?' the passengers are still stymied as to how to offer a convincing counter-argument when confronted by the Fascist mentality ('What are you going to do with people like that?'). The best they can do is refer the question to Gus and Mrs. Higley, dead at Nazi hands, whose heavenly perspective may perhaps provide insight unattainable by those still among the living.
>
> (344)

Some contemporary reviewers, led by Bosley Crowther and Dorothy Thompson, accused Hitchcock of siding with the Nazis, because those representing Britain and the United States look so incompetent and gullible compared to Willy. Of course, deploring Allied weaknesses is not tantamount to siding with the fascists, but the luck and instincts that enabled the triumph of Johnny Jones (and also, to be fair, the protagonists in the English spy thrillers) start to look inadequate to the task of victory in a real war rather than a Boys' Own Adventure.

Blurred Nazionalities: *Saboteur* and *Notorious*

As a counter-balance to the two films in which Americans encounter Nazis on their European battlegrounds, Hitchcock produced two films in which Nazis operate from enclaves in the Americas. *Saboteur* simply transferred the plot of *The 39 Steps* to the United States, with the foreign agents framing an innocent man for one of their acts of violence, sending him on a cross-country journey to clear his name by foiling the even bigger plot they are pursuing, while at the same time coupling with a young woman initially bent on turning him in. As in that English thriller and *Foreign Correspondent*, the head of the fascist conspiracy appears to be a prominent citizen and native but has in fact insinuated himself into respectable society in order to operate a sleeper cell.

Much more than its predecessors, however, *Saboteur* ponders the nature of the populace that nurtures such betrayers. Partly because it was made in wartime, the film uses quite a bit of dialogue and action to define what is best about America and show why those strengths will defeat fascism. *Saboteur* also highlights the diverse landscapes of the United States, contrasting the vast open spaces of the west with the skyscrapers of Manhattan, just as it juxtaposes the ranch of fascist conspirator Charles Tobin (Otto Kruger), complete with horses and cowboys, to the New York mansion of his ally Mrs. Sutton (Alma Kruger), with its large staff of liveried servants. The film also begins the director's fascination with America's monumentalism, a trip to Boulder Dam balanced by the famous climax in which hero and antagonist dangle from the torch of the Statue of Liberty. As David Lehman observes, "Hitchcock's America is vast and dwarfs the individual" (32).

Although several of the characters are as garrulous and fatuously all-knowing as Mrs. Van Hopper, *Saboteur*, in keeping with the reliance on instinct and intuition that characterizes Americans in the other anti-Nazi films, stresses first and foremost that Americans can sense innocence and are loath to betray someone who claims to be falsely accused to the police. The mother of Ken Mason (Virgil Summers), the friend of protagonist Barry Kane (Robert Cummings) who dies in an inferno caused by sabotage at the aircraft plant where they both work, admits to confusion when the police tell her that Barry is guilty of the crime, but Mrs. Mason (Dorothy Peterson) does not alert them to his presence in her house. A truck driver who gives Barry a lift later cheers on his escape from the police who have apprehended him, going so far as to actively misdirect them. Of course, this trust may appear to be mere gullibility. Barry easily infiltrates Tobin's gang by putting up a good bluff, while he and his girlfriend Pat (Priscilla Lane) can persuade none of the guests at Mrs. Sutton's party that the place is a nest of enemy saboteurs.

The film reserves a more accurate moral compass, however, for those on the margins. The microcosm of democracy that *Lifeboat* would later present appears here among a group of circus sideshow performers, who perceive Barry's innocence while also noting that "the normal are normally unkind." And the central spokesperson for true American virtue is Pat's Uncle Phillip (Vaughan Glaser), a blind musician who lives in a simple, if well appointed, rustic home with his dog. He's the sort of wise elder extolling the worth of ordinary folks that we see also in Van Meer. His populist platitudes include avowals that hitchhiking is "the purest test of the American heart," that America's being "easy to get lost in" is "one of its charms," that it is his "duty as an American citizen to believe a man innocent until he's been proved guilty," that sometimes duty requires breaking the law, and that his blindness enables him to see "intangible things, like innocence."

What would lead a US citizen to turn traitor, then? Pat finds "that hard to believe about any American." As much as *Saboteur* provides an answer, it again points to the lack of ideology in motivating such a decision, Phillip Martin's pronouncements to the contrary. Fry (Norman Lloyd), the actual saboteur, "doesn't mind killing Americans for money"; Tobin cites wealth and power as his goals and admires totalitarian regimes simply for their efficiency in getting things done. Like *Foreign Correspondent*, *Saboteur* portrays Americans as self-interested pragmatists who are still susceptible to the claims of love, loyalty, and the plight of the underdog. This and their instinctive distrust of authority keep most of them from succumbing to the lures of fascism.

Notorious, Hitchcock's final anti-fascist film, is the only one to stand as a major work. All the others suffer first and foremost from their B-list casts; here we have luminous major stars Ingrid Bergman and Cary Grant as the leads. *Notorious* also has the advantage of combining the best aspects of his films made for Selznick and those made on loanout. On the one hand, it benefits from being packaged by Selznick, who gave especially useful input during the screenwriting process. But his sale of the package to RKO for production and distribution gave Hitchcock firm authority over shooting and editing. According to Leff, "Post-production control at RKO gave Hitchcock the power to make the first American picture he could call his own" (218). Another of Leff's claims gets to the heart of *Notorious*'s greatness among both the English and American spy thrillers: "Forced by [Ben] Hecht and Selznick to address characterization, Hitchcock opened himself to people, not things. The sound and fury of *The 39 Steps*, *The Lady Vanishes*, *Foreign Correspondent* and *Saboteur* – those dynamically edited action sequences – signified nothing compared to the emergent psychological intensity of *Notorious*" (181).

Notorious starts off as a sort of sequel to Carol Fisher's story, only through a view of Nazism much darkened by the revelations that the end of the war in Europe brought. Despite the ruthlessness with which he and his associates carry out their intrigue, Stephen Fisher is portrayed primarily as a German patriot whose country's interests run counter to those of the United States and Great Britain, not a genocidal monster. Carol never repudiates him and he dies by an honorable, sacrificial gesture. The father of Alicia Huberman (Ingrid Bergman), on the other hand, is clearly an unrepentant traitor, turning his back on the country that welcomed him and his daughter and gave them citizenship, shouting threats at his trial as to what dire fate awaits the US "next time." His suicide in prison reads more as cowardice than sacrifice. The wiretaps agent Devlin (Cary Grant) plays back to Alicia reveal her complete disdain for his politics. "I love this country," she declares, and refers to his fellow Nazi subversives as "murderous swine."

While Alicia's mother, like Carol's, was born in the country where their fathers operate as sleeper agents, Carol blends into English life far more seamlessly than Alicia, with her heavily accented English, into American (although Laraine Day's nonexistent British accent strains the comparison a bit). Alicia adopts a renegade pose, drinking too much, becoming sexually promiscuous, and telling Dev that she has no truck with patriotism or "coppers." The film implies that she believes her failure to turn her father in to the authorities, despite her private repudiation of him, makes her just as much a traitor; she degrades herself out of guilt, compounded by self-loathing because of the degradation. The terrible double bind she steps into when Dev and his bosses recruit her to spy on Alex Sebastian and his cronies is that she can redeem herself as an American patriot only by prostituting herself as a woman.

Johnny Jones reluctantly allowed Scott to make Carol an unwitting pawn in the scheme to bluff Van Meer's location out of her father with her fake kidnapping, but Dev violates Alicia's trust in far more damaging ways. They fall in love during the short period in which they get settled in Rio before Sebastian returns (and the film suggests that Alicia falls for Dev much earlier, that she agrees to work for American intelligence only because he will be her handler). Yet Dev knows too much about Alicia's "notorious" sexual past to commit to her fully by articulating his love. Furthermore, he would fail in his job if she refused to sleep with Alex in order to gain entry into the group of former Nazi scientists he heads. Devlin both trusts Alicia to be fundamentally decent and redeemable, despite her sordid reputation, and fears that his trust is misplaced. Thus he defends her honor twice to his superiors, who consider her simply a slattern, yet compels her to accept the assignment without knowing that he did defend her, refusing her pleas for some hint that he thinks her better than the mission requires. Hitchcock several times shoots him from behind, and he often reads as the man who turns his back on the woman who so abjectly craves his approval.

Their relationship for most of the film is a masochistic tangle in which Alicia's self-loathing prevents her from asserting her worth without Devlin's unconditional commitment and his lack of certainty makes him treat her with cold contempt because she cannot bring herself to reclaim her virtue in isolation from her particular feelings about him. Dev's excuse that he was "a fat-headed guy, full of pain" hardly covers the perverse trajectory his love takes over the course of the narrative.

Alex Sebastian serves to triangulate Alicia's guilt and desires concerning her father and Dev. With Alex she plays the loyal Nazi daughter, while the undercover efforts that lead to the exposure of the uranium refining plans of his cell compensate for her failure to inform on her father. Like Devlin and his superiors, Alex does not doubt Alicia's political loyalties, despite evidence that might give him pause, but becomes obsessed with the prospect of her infidelity. Whereas the Americans ascribe Alicia's promiscuity to a defect of her nature – she's simply "that type of woman" – the European Alex merely doubts his ability to hold the affections of such an attractive younger woman, particularly when the competition is the suave and handsome Devlin. Ironically, Alex cements his claim by making "an honest woman" of Alicia when he proposes marriage, a development none of the Americans had anticipated.

The creepily incestuous attachment of Madame Sebastian (Leopoldine Konstantin) to her middle-aged son makes Alicia's willingness to go through with the wedding even more disturbing than it is on the surface. Given Sebastian's parallels to her own father, it is almost as if Devlin's boss Prescott (Louis Calhern) would gladly authorize her incestuous union with him. The spy agency seems to assume that the pragmatism inherent in the American character throughout these '40s films here knows no limit. Indeed, although the Nazis are working to manufacture an atomic weapon, the Americans had already dropped one by the time *Notorious* was released. "For the Western soul," John Beebe notes, apropos of Alicia as a representative of postwar American guilt, "the most conspicuous part of the departed fathers' dark undigested legacy was the nuclear bomb, the deployment of which suddenly linked Roosevelt and Truman to the ruthlessness of Hitler and Stalin" (32).

Mental Cases at Home: *Shadow of a Doubt, Mr. and Mrs. Smith,* and *Spellbound*

If *Notorious* finally allows Hitchcock an undisputed artistic success with his favored plot about Americans, to show them fighting Nazis, it obviously does not point toward a successful formula for portraying the nation and its citizens in the absence of this foe. With its three major characters played by European performers and its perspective firmly anchored in a woman's psychology, it also doesn't show how Hitchcock was going to fashion narratives around the American males who, as Richard Allen observes, usurped female agency in typical Hollywood cinema:

> [S]omething is lost in Hitchcock's American films by the insistent sexualization of the female persona demanded by the star system where feminine agency is reduced to an expression either of sexuality or of motherhood. ... But women in Hitchcock's English thrillers are defined more by their agency than by their sexual identity, and this idea is carried over into some of the "transitional" films of the 1940s and the 1950s such as *Lifeboat* and *Stage Fright* [1950], until Hitchcock's portrayal of femininity, in the context of his overall approach to storytelling and style, is completely Americanized.
>
> (*Romantic* 86)

However, if Hitchcock's narrativization of femininity becomes more Americanized as he moves through the Selznick era, his corresponding deployment of masculinity never does. One would be hard-pressed to name a single male protagonist of the director's American films who approaches the norm of the Hollywood leading man.

Although he did discover that Cary Grant's native Britishness was sufficient to allow him to carry the leading role in English-style thrillers like *To Catch a Thief* (1955) and *North by Northwest,* the in-control masculinity of traditional American protagonists never appeared. Even though all its characters are supposed to be British or European, the plight of American star Gregory Peck in *The Paradine Case* is emblematic. Cast in a role similar to that of one Hitchcock's few confident male puppet-masters in his English films, Sir John Menier (Herbert Marshall) of *Murder!*

(1930), Peck's barrister Anthony Keane does not free the innocent woman accused of murder and win her love for himself, though he does drive a "wrong 'un," to use William Rothman's term, to confess guilt and commit suicide. Unlike Diana Baring in *Murder!*, Mrs. Paradine (Alida Valli) is guilty as sin and contemptuous of Keane and his infatuation.

Except for the success of David Smith (Robert Montgomery) in wooing back his wife in *Mr. and Mrs. Smith*, the Selznick-era films limit the triumphs of the American male protagonist to fighting Nazis. In the two women-centered films set in the United States, however, Hitchcock began to work through Hollywood conventions of masculinity to discover two types of men and two basic scenarios that would lead to the greatest triumphs of his career in subsequent decades.

According to Leonard Leff, *Shadow of a Doubt*, the third Hitchcock film set in America, was the first on which he was deeply involved with the scripting process (105). The director wanted a balance of mundane small-town domesticity and the suspense brought about by the invasion of the sinister Uncle Charlie (Joseph Cotten). On the one hand, he went for realistic typicality, going on location to Santa Rosa, California, casting some of the townspeople, and collaborating on the script with Thornton Wilder, author of the classic American drama *Our Town* (1938). On the other hand, Hitchcock did not want to go with the Hollywood convention of a bucolic backwater, its denizens out of touch with modernity – "[L]ife in a small town lit by neon signs," was how he described the film's Santa Rosa (quoted in Leff 105).

Yet for all Hitchcock's care in making this an American story, its narrative premise was one that he had used in slightly different forms in his British pictures. It's a premise rooted in three character types that form a romantic triangle. At the apex is the naïve young woman torn between an alluring but dangerous man and a trustworthy but boring police officer. In *The Lodger*, the dangerous man's danger appears to be a case of mistaken identity; though his actions suggest that he is the serial killer of blonde women, the killer is in fact an object of his extra-legal pursuit, in revenge for his sister, one of the killer's blonde victims. The heroine ends up in a relationship with him, casting aside the policeman suitor. In *Blackmail*, the danger from the man is real, an attempted rape. The woman kills him and ends up (although not particularly happily) with the policeman, who conceals her crime, making her blackmailer the scapegoat. The same resolution occurs when the heroine of *Sabotage*, after one of his bombs explodes in her young brother's possession, kills the anarchist she has unwittingly married; the undercover policeman spying on her husband agrees to keep her secret and a romance seems to be in the offing.

Although in *Shadow of a Doubt* the relationship involves an uncle and a niece, the incestuous overtones of the infatuation Charlie Newton (Teresa Wright) has with Charles Oakley (Cotten) have long been noted by scholars. Young Charlie also kills this dangerous man when he reveals his true colors and becomes attached, perhaps engaged, to another boring policeman (Macdonald Carey), who will keep her secret from the world. Discussions of Hitchcockian masculinity have often taken off from the concept of the "dandy" as described by Thomas Elsaesser. Elsaesser is careful to point out that the category of the dandy includes many Hitchcockian villains but is not limited to them: "From Ivor Novello in *The Lodger* (1926), Peter Lorre in *The Man who Knew Too Much* (1934), Robert Walker in *Strangers on a Train*, down to James Mason in *North by Northwest*, Hitchcock's villains are often either sharp dressers or aristocratic aesthetes made 'sinister' by stereotypically homosexual traits or hints of sexual perversion" (10).

Interestingly, he describes Novello's character as a villain, even though he turns out not to be the serial killer, while he includes Cary Grant in *Suspicion* as a dandy who is among the director's *"heroes"* (10). In fact, as Richard Allen's essay on Hitchcockian "metaskepticism" makes clear, both Novello's and Grant's characters are extremely ambiguous. In the sources their respective films are adapted from, each is in fact a killer. In the films, each is exonerated at the last minute and not in a totally ironclad way. Even more apropos of Uncle Charlie's characterization, the men they appear to be are respectively a sexual psychopath and a sociopath.

Shadow of a Doubt, for the first time, positions the dandy-as-crazed-serial-killer in the lead male role. As in *The Lodger*, there is another suspect; his death while fleeing the police appears to exonerate Uncle Charlie, but young Charlie knows the truth and kills him while defending her own life. While she allows everyone but her boring policeman/future husband to read him as audiences are asked to read the troubling Lodger and Johnnie Aysgarth, we do share the secret. Moreover, Hitchcock has found a way to fashion a type of masculinity that will dominate his later American films, and it is his immersion in the Hollywood discourses about the subject that helps him discover it. The two most prominent are the general fascination with Freudian psychology by American culture in the 1940s and the related association between male over-attachment to the mother and deficient virility.

The first film set in America that Hitchcock directed might have pointed him in this direction. When *Mr. and Mrs. Smith* came to him as a ready-made package at RKO, he agreed to direct this screwball comedy, a genre far from his comfort zone, because of his friendship with one of its stars, Carole Lombard. He had not worked in the pre-production phase and did not have his usual input into script development and casting. Indeed, he admitted to Truffaut that the material was completely foreign to him: "Since I really didn't understand the type of people who were portrayed in the film, all I did was to photograph the scenes as written" (Truffaut 139). Among the people in this "comedy of remarriage," to use Stanley Cavell's term, is Jefferson Davis Custer (Gene Raymond), who courts Ann Smith (Lombard) when it turns out her passionate but volatile marriage to husband David has been nullified by a jurisdictional technicality. The "other man" in such comedies often is either an effete and excitable foreigner or a naïve, puritanical denizen of the American South or West. Ann herself hails from the Idaho-Nevada line but has thoroughly assimilated to Manhattan sophistication; Jeff, although David's New York–resident law partner, is much closer to his Confederate roots and Southern gentility. He is also more deeply invested in retaining his parents' approval then either of the Smiths. Such characters in fact often have mother issues, like the two played by Ralph Bellamy in *The Awful Truth* (Leo McCarey, 1937) and *His Girl Friday* (Howard Hawks, 1940).

Ann breaks off her engagement to Jeff and returns to David because the former's gentlemanliness eventually makes him a virtual eunuch in her eyes. Jeff never displays physical affection and refuses to become jealous of David's frantic attempts to win her back. Indeed, should Ann prefer her ex over him, he will withdraw his claim with no hard feelings. His polite refusal to become irrational – as David often appears to be in stalking Ann – and fight for her love in the end makes Ann view Jeff as neither a man nor a mouse, or even a monkey, as she adds in exasperation. Moreover, a scene in which David pretends to be delirious and mistake Jeff for Ann, complete with hand-holding and caresses, renders him positively effeminate.

Though Leff calls Alex Sebastian "the first of the director's 'mama's boys' " (181), that is the case mostly in the sense that the domineering mother who appears as early as *Easy Virtue* (1927) is represented onscreen so vividly here. Jeff's mother can be seen as a more recent precursor. The member of Tobin's group of saboteurs who escorts Barry east speaks of his mother keeping his curly hair long for an unusually long time, and in a background conversation in *Spellbound* one of the detectives complains that, when he declined a promotion that would take him out of the town where his dependent mother lived, his superior accused him of being a mama's boy.

Certainly the connection between mothers, emasculation, and murder had occurred unequivocally by the time *Shadow of a Doubt* premiered, perhaps not coincidentally the year after Philip Wylie's screed *Generation of Vipers* (1942) excoriated "mom" and "momism" for much that was wrong with the United States. The Newtons of Santa Rosa have no trouble believing the ruse of police detectives who gain entrance to their home posing as pollsters for a study on the "representative American family." The mother, Emma (Patricia Collinge), is hardly a monstrous harridan. Except for being overly obsessive about home décor and the proper procedures for folding eggs into cake batter, she is a lovely woman and nurturing parent. Rather, it is the whole system of bourgeois domesticity that has produced a household of emotionally stunted individuals (see Michie and McLaughlin). Even Emma avows that after marriage "you sort of forget you're you." Her daughter Ann (Edna May Wonacott) lives only in novels; her son, Roger (Charles Bates), immerses himself in scientific trivia; her husband, Joe (Henry Travers), is an anxious bank clerk concerned only about his latest pay raise. To relax, Joe reads mystery novels and debates his friend Herb (Hume Cronyn), a milquetoast bachelor who lives with an always "just middling" mother, over the most efficient ways they might kill each other and get away with it.

Only the older daughter, Charlie, sunk into depressive ennui, connects their discontents to the nature of family life. She is not quite as explicit as McLaughlin, who observes that the Hitchcockian family, "in the course of its normal and natural existence, produces the most oppressive of tensions and the calm matter-of-factness with which it does so is what makes it so frightening" (153). Nevertheless, her concerns about her mother's diminished possibilities – as if seeing in them a map of her own future – and her father's desire to "talk about money when I'm talking about souls" indicate her recognition that the housewife/breadwinner dynamic is unbearable. In this realization Charlie connects, apparently telepathically, with the one member of her family who has never been domesticated, her mother's spoiled youngest sibling, Charles. She believes that he will shake up their dull routine but has to learn in the course of the film that, in his violent rejection of domesticity, he is its strongest guarantor.

A man who romances, swindles, and then strangles rich widows, Charles has money to burn without ever having to become a wage slave. His contempt for those men who have to bow and scrape to provide for their families is apparent when he visits Joe's bank to deposit $40 000. Yet wealth means nothing to Uncle Charlie except apparently to provide a nice wardrobe – part of the merry widow bait – and his ever-present compensatory cigars. He tosses wads of cash carelessly on the floor of his shabby Philadelphia rooming house and declares himself "not interested in money." Indeed he seems to acquire it only to keep it out of the hands of the dangerously independent wealthy widows it empowers and whom he stalks and loathes for their idleness, foolishness, and vanity, as well as a repulsive physicality that causes him to dub them "fat, wheezing animals."

Uncle Charlie's psychosis has its symbolic origins in a collision with modernity, the moment when he crashed his new bicycle into a streetcar, fracturing his skull and nearly dying. When he recovered, the quiet, studious boy he had been was transformed into a restless hellion. Perhaps occurring just before World War I, the accident demarcates a shift away from the Victorian power relations within the family represented by the photographs of the Oakley parents he keeps in a safe deposit box, unlike the money with which he is so careless. Now he sees families as sites where women exceed their allotted place, or at least fail to temper desires to go beyond it. And the men who head them are far too weak to contain these desires. As Michie notes, the film shows "the idealized images of mother, home, and family not to be based on absolute, permanent, or fixed values but to be articulated as part of a system of fears and desires that work to counter one another" (49). Thus, to Charles, the whole modern world, even small town Santa Rosa, is a paper-thin façade covering up a "foul sty" populated by swine.

This façade conceals not just the desires the misogynistic Merry Widow killer punishes, but the tendency of American life and its repressions to nurture insanity. No one else in the Newton family besides young Charlie ever learns Charles's true nature, and the town gives him a hero's funeral. Indeed, everything rests on their ignorance of what he represents. In his apt comparison of *Shadow of a Doubt* to another "small-town movie," Frank Capra's *It's a Wonderful Life* (1946), Robin Wood writes, "What is in jeopardy is above all the family – but, given the family's central ideological significance, once that is in jeopardy, everything is. ... [T]he ideological project is to acknowledge the existence of sickness and evil but preserve the family from their contamination" (292, 297). But Jack Graham, stepping in as a voice of both the law and patriarchy, is only mildly reassuring in telling her that Charles's dim view of the world is not a correct one: "It's not as bad as that. Sometimes it needs a lot of watching. It seems to go crazy now and then, like your Uncle Charlie." While psychopathic serial killers are the extreme case, Graham's words, and *Shadow of a Doubt* as a whole, stress that there is something intrinsic to American society that produces mental instability, particularly among its male members.

Charles Oakley proved the model for the Hitchcockian male psychopath who becomes the focus of the narrative, eclipsing the nominal protagonist. In this film, as in so many made for Selznick or previously in England, that protagonist is a woman. That Hitchcock made the psychopathic Bruno Anthony (Robert Walker) the film's dominating presence in *Strangers on a Train* (1951) and transformed the naïve woman and her boring policeman boyfriend into the naïve man and his boring, well-connected girlfriend revealed that the formula was not anchored in specific gender configurations. (*Rope* [1948] was an excellent dress rehearsal. *Strangers on a Train* simply had the Brandon-type character murdering for Farley Granger, not with him.) As the director's career progressed this pattern remained, although the woman of the couple usually was the chief adversary and potential victim, as in *Dial M for Murder* (1954) and *Psycho* (1960). But he did round out his career in *Frenzy* (1972) by going back to the territory of *The Lodger*, filming in London the story of a British psychopathic serial killer of women, this time showing us not just the wrongly accused, but the actual perpetrator, who, thanks to Hitchcock's three decades in Hollywood, is especially fond of his mum.

Not every American film apart from the espionage thrillers created a compelling psycho to eclipse the normative male lead. However, these men also often seemed in need of some psychiatric help, albeit for neuroses rather than psychoses. Their template emerged in *Spellbound*, Hitchcock's second film to be produced and released by Selznick International Pictures. Leff claims that Hitchcock was perhaps at odds with Selznick over the subject matter, since this was "a picture about psychotherapy, not psychopaths" (117), only the latter and not the former appealing to the director. John Ballantine (Gregory Peck), an American doctor suffering from a guilt complex because of a childhood accident in which his brother died, develops hysterical amnesia when he witnesses the murder of a psychiatrist he had consulted, a murder whose circumstances evoke those of the original trauma. Representing himself to be the dead man, Dr. Anthony Edwardes, he travels to the sanitarium of which Edwardes was scheduled to resume directorship. The film traces his gradual recovery under the guidance of Constance Petersen (Ingrid Bergman), the female psychiatrist who falls in love with him, even as he is arrested and wrongly convicted of the murder, and succeeds in freeing him when she deduces that the actual culprit is Dr. Murchison (Leo G. Carroll), the current head of Green Manors whom Edwardes was coming to replace.

Jonathan Freedman points out that even as Hitchcock deployed psychoanalysis in *Spellbound* and several later films because of its usefulness in structuring a detective narrative, he undercut all notions of its actual therapeutic efficacy. Nevertheless, the Freudian vocabulary did provide him a shorthand through which to demarcate those protagonists who hadn't been made into psychopaths by their culture but still occupied a continuum that led to Charles Oakley, Bruno Anthony, and Norman Bates. This in turn enabled him to craft American male protagonists who were complex neurotics instead of two-dimensional sane ciphers, although the film that most faithfully replicates *Spellbound*'s narrative use of Freudian psychology, *Marnie* (1964), switches the genders of hysteric and amateur therapist.

Hitchcock had pursued the idea of the man wrongly accused of a crime several times in his British films, but the link between that man and the true killer was rather arbitrary. The idea of the two being bound by the "transference of guilt" famously described by Rohmer and Chabrol, of the murderer somehow acting upon a subconscious desire the protagonist's superego prevents him from acting upon, really emerges only here. Granted, John Ballantine doesn't have any vested interest in the death of Dr. Edwardes, as Guy Haines (Farley Granger) does in the murder of his troublesome wife, Miriam (Laura Elliott); nor is there even a metaphorical connection, as when L.B. Jefferies (James Stewart) finds his own reservations about marriage mapped onto the neighbors across the courtyard, including Lars Thorwald (Raymond Burr). Here the link is metonymic. The behavior that his amnesia and guilt complex trigger – supplanting the murdered Edwardes as head of Green Manors, demonstrating homicidal tendencies as a result of his nervous collapse – mimics that of Dr. Murchison, who resented being replaced after a bout of nervous exhaustion and killed his successor in order to hang on to his post.

This link becomes clear with Ballantine's symbolic dream about the murder, rendered for the audience in a Salvador Dali–designed sequence. For him, it represents his meeting with Edwardes in a club and the subsequent murder on the ski slopes by Murchison. On the other hand, Murchison, upon hearing Dr. Petersen describe it, says that the club sounds like a version of the sanitarium. It is particularly relevant in the waking world as well that the two patients the film concentrates upon are a man with a guilt complex and an apparent nymphomaniac who actually hates men. John has the same sort of complex and Constance is a mirror image of the female patient, appearing asexual and almost frigid but capable of falling instantly and deeply in love with "Edwardes" and ignoring every rational principle of her profession to flee with him in pursuit of the truth. Her mentor, Dr. Alex Brulov (Michael Chekhov), the "good" analyst in contrast to Murchison's corrupt one, rails against the irrationality of love and its uselessness in making clear, objective judgments. He sounds just like his counterpart, in fact; Murchison praises

Dr. Petersen as an excellent psychiatrist but a "stupid woman." As screwball comedies like *Mr. and Mrs. Smith* had perhaps demonstrated to Hitchcock, however, Americans don't see anything wrong if love makes people a little crazy, a concept these European rationalists don't quite get. As Norman Bates, the epitome of the director's homegrown mental cases, observes, "We all go a little mad sometimes. Haven't you?"

The Selznick years, and indeed the whole of the 1940s, do not represent the peak of Hitchcock's artistry. They were a transitional period and a learning experience whose most important dividends appeared only in *Strangers on a Train* and thereafter. These lessons included two major ones: the English thriller formula did not travel well to another continent and a wartime environment; and the only way for Hitchcock to deal with American masculinity was to render it neurotic or psychotic. Ironically, these realizations redirected his career, after a long detour into women's melodrama and romantic espionage adventures, into a magnificent fulfillment of the promise and premise of his foundational British film, *The Lodger*.

Works Cited

Allen, Richard. *Hitchcock's Romantic Irony*. New York: Columbia UP, 2007.

Allen, Richard. "Hitchcock, or the Pleasures of Metaskepticism." Allen and Ishii-Gonzáles 221–37.

Allen, Richard, and S. Ishii-Gonzáles, eds. *Alfred Hitchcock: Centenary Essays*. London: BFI, 1999.

Beebe, John. "The *Notorious* Postwar Psyche." *Journal of Popular Film and Television* 18.1 (1990). 28–35.

Deutelbaum, Marshall, and Leland Poague, eds. *A Hitchcock Reader*. Second ed. Chichester, UK: Wiley-Blackwell, 2009.

Elsaesser, Thomas. "The Dandy in Hitchcock." Allen and Ishii-Gonzáles 3–14.

Freedman, Jonathan. "From *Spellbound* to *Vertigo*: Alfred Hitchcock and Therapeutic Culture in America." Freedman and Millington 77–98.

Freedman, Jonathan, and Richard Millington, eds. *Hitchcock's America*. New York: Oxford UP, 1999.

Hark, Ina Rae. "'We Might Even Get in the Newsreels': The Press and Democracy in Hitchcock's World War II Anti-Fascist Films." Allen and Ishii-Gonzáles 333–47.

Koppes, Clayton R. and Gregory D. Black. "Blacks, Loyalty, and Motion-Picture Propaganda in World War II." *Journal of American History* 73 (1986): 383–406.

Leff, Leonard J. *Hitchcock and Selznick: The Rich and Strange Collaboration of Alfred Hitchcock and David O. Selznick*. New York: Weidenfeld and Nicolson, 1987.

Lehman, David. "Hitchcock's America." *American Heritage* 58.2 (May 2007): 28–36.

McGilligan, Patrick. "Hitchcock Dreams of America." *Hitchcock Annual* (2002–03): 1–31.

McLaughlin, James. "All in the Family: Alfred Hitchcock's *Shadow of a Doubt*." Deutelbaum and Poague 143–55.

Michie, Elsie B. "Unveiling Maternal Desires: Hitchcock and American Domesticity." Freedman and Millington 29–54.

Naremore, James. "Hitchcock on the Margins of *Noir*." Allen and Ishii-Gonzáles 335–47.

Rohmer, Eric, and Claude Chabrol. *Hitchcock: The First Forty-four Films*. Trans. Stanley Hochman. New York: Ungar, 1979.

Rossi, John. "Hitchcock's *Foreign Correspondent* (1940)." *Film and History* 12.2 (1982): 25–35.

Rothman, William. *Hitchcock—The Murderous Gaze*. Cambridge: Harvard UP, 1982.

Truffaut, François, with the collaboration of Helen G. Scott. *Hitchcock*. Rev. ed. New York: Simon and Schuster, 1984.

Wood, Robin. *Hitchcock's Films Revisited*. New York: Columbia UP, 1989.

Wylie, Philip. *Generation of Vipers*. New York: Farrar and Rinehart, 1942.

17

From Transatlantic to Warner Bros.

David Sterritt

According to the Producers Guild of America website, producers are powerful people who initiate, coordinate, supervise, and control all aspects of the motion-picture production process – creative, financial, technological, and administrative – on their own authority or that bestowed on them by studios or production companies. For movie directors and screenwriters, becoming a producer allows one, at least in theory, to preserve the artistic vision of a project by overseeing the creative and technical personnel who bring it to life. The list of major producer-directors during Hollywood's studio era is impressive: D.W. Griffith, Charles Chaplin, John Ford, Ernst Lubitsch, Orson Welles, Howard Hawks, and many more. So it is not surprising that Alfred Hitchcock, whose meticulous preplanning and attention to detail are legendary, would want to become one too.

Hitchcock achieved this goal in the late 1940s, first by starting his own production company, Transatlantic Pictures, and then by acquiring a contract with Warner Bros. Pictures that allowed him to produce his films with unprecedented liberty in matters of material, writers, and cast. Curiously, however, Hitchcock's greater independence did not immediately result in critically and commercially outstanding films. His first and only Transatlantic productions, *Rope* in 1948 and *Under Capricorn* in 1949, were bold in conception, unconventional in execution, and disappointing in box-office appeal. While his subsequent Warner Bros. projects were more successful, only *Strangers on a Train* (1951) could be called a full-blown hit; the other three – *Stage Fright* (1950), *I Confess* (1953), and *Dial M for Murder* (1954) – were profitable but not resoundingly so. Even so, the half-dozen years of Transatlantic and Warner Bros. productions were crucial ones in Hitchcock's career, for this was when he acquired

A Companion to Alfred Hitchcock, First Edition. Edited by Thomas Leitch and Leland Poague.
© 2011 Thomas Leitch and Leland Poague. Published 2011 by Blackwell Publishing Ltd.

the skills that successful producer-directors always need, and needed with special urgency in the middle of the twentieth century, when Hollywood was moving from the classical studio era to a new age of modernism and innovation.

Shifting Currents

Using the conventional milestone of 1939 as the dividing point between Hitchcock's vivacious British phase and the weightier American phase that began with *Rebecca* (1940), John Orr finds the latter period marked by the modulation of narrative suspense into psychodrama and by the recurring theme of bourgeois order being violated from within (11). The six Transatlantic and Warner Bros. pictures are grounded in precisely these concerns in ways that both confirm and complicate Orr's account of Hitchcock as a "matrix-figure" in three senses – as a conjoiner of "cinephile authorship and ... Hollywood genre" by means of preexisting stories modified to suit his purposes; as a creator standing "at the [authorial] centre of everything he filmed" as fully and commandingly as possible; and as a towering artistic force inhabiting the very "centre of cinema as such" (8–9, 10).

All of the films from *Rope* through *Dial M for Murder* are adapted from other works – three are based on novels, three on plays – and in most of them Hitchcock used his recently gained independence to amplify the existential tension and psychological suspense that audiences recognized as his trademarks. The matrix figure reworks the genre system with the vigor of an untrammeled auteur, guiding the efforts of creative and technical collaborators to align them as closely as possible with his intentions. Yet even as they affirm his presence at the center of each project, his authorial interventions have sometimes put off the audiences they were meant to attract, and some of them (*Rope* and *Under Capricorn* especially) have retrospectively displeased Hitchcock himself. The six Transatlantic and Warner Bros. productions reveal a Hitchcock still absorbing hard lessons imparted by his thorny experiences with producer David O. Selznick at Selznick International, and not quite primed for the sustained excellence he would achieve in his Paramount years. Accordingly, these films are as fascinating for their faults and miscalculations as for their many bold and brilliant moments. To play this down – to take too literally his uncompromising courage, his alchemical genius, his centrality to cinema as such – risks turning the matrix-figure metaphor into a variant of traditional auteurism, replicating auteur theory's overvaluation of the Great Director figure. The years from 1948 to 1954 provide salutary evidence of Hitchcock's fallibility along with ample confirmation of his extraordinary cinematic gifts.

Art and Entertainment

Hitchcock was still in his twenties when he began frequenting the Film Society of London, which was founded in 1925 and included among its members such luminaries as author H.G. Wells, playwright George Bernard Shaw, and economist John Maynard Keynes. As a leading force in London's "minority film culture," to use historian Tom Ryall's term (23), the society tended to privilege documentaries and European art films over popular American and English movies. At its screenings Hitchcock broadened his knowledge of Soviet montage, French avant-garde impressionism, and the German expressionist style he had been exposed to while working briefly at UFA, the prodigious German studio.

At the same time, however, Hitchcock's social background was quite different from that of the high-toned cineastes who frequented the society. His fascination with filmmaking had been sparked by the very Hollywood entertainments that the minority film culture actively opposed, and he keenly appreciated the magnetic appeal of crime and sex in British popular culture. Without denying Hitchcock's interest in artistically ambitious cinema, Ryall finds the clearest roots of his 1930s thrillers in a line of British popular culture that runs from Gothic literature and nineteenth-century crime novels to spy stories by the likes of John Buchan and "Sapper," not to mention ceaseless reports of rampaging sex and violence in the sensational British press (23–24, 179). Hitchcock's uniqueness as a filmmaker is inseparable from his ability to fuse elements of art-minded cinema with subjects and stories that (usually) comport well with current mass-media trends.

Working to realize cinema's potential as art and entertainment within Britain's stratified film community, Hitchcock found himself "a marooned figure, too businesslike and commercial to be an 'artist', yet too 'artistic' to be fitted comfortably into the British entertainment cinema of the time" (Ryall 183). Much the same can be said of his Transatlantic and Warner Bros. years, when he taught himself how to avoid perceived imbalances between his conceptual-artist side and his snappy-entertainer side (between the tones of *Rope* and *Stage Fright*, as it were) so that he could emerge as the triumphant auteur who captivated aesthetes and amusement seekers alike through the rest of the 1950s and beyond.

America and Selznick International

Hitchcock was not entirely new to producing when he and his partner, Sidney Bernstein, went about establishing Transatlantic Pictures in the middle 1940s. By the time he launched his so-called classic thriller sextet with the 1934 version of *The Man Who Knew Too Much*, he had "already begun to function as his own de facto producer" (McGilligan 160), with a particular knack for blending contributions from multiple writers into scripts that ultimately bore his own stamp.

But these producer credentials were unofficial; in the 1920s and 1930s those credited with producing Hitchcock's pictures included John Maxwell at British International Pictures, Michael Balcon at Gaumont British, Edward Black at Gainsborough, and Erich Pommer at Mayflower Pictures.

The sextet's rollicking success enabled Hitchcock to leave the undernourished British film industry and move to Hollywood, surely the most important event of his career. He took great pleasure in the creative and technical resources available to him in the United States, but he also discovered that he would not be functioning as his own de facto producer, at least when Selznick was in the picture. Selznick was one of Hollywood's most famously hands-on executives, and Hitchcock's first American contract was with Selznick International Pictures.

Rebecca, Hitchcock's first Selznick film, launched the American phase of his career with a flourish, earning eleven Academy Award nominations, including Best Director, and winning two of them, including Best Picture. The two filmmakers clashed frequently during the production, though, and Selznick's unceasing interference in creative matters irked Hitchcock even when he proceeded to implement the producer's ideas. They collaborated on three more films over the next seven years: *Spellbound* for Selznick International in 1945, *Notorious* for Selznick's recently established Vanguard Films and then RKO in 1946, and *The Paradine Case* for Vanguard in 1947. Each project caused discord and tension between the two, and while the outcome for *Notorious* was triumphant – it became a smash hit and a key film in Hitchcock's canon – an important reason, along with its ingenious screenplay and inspired casting, is that Selznick was absent from the production after its early stages, having sold it to RKO so that he could concentrate entirely on his 1946 Western *Duel in the Sun*.

Selznick returned to looking over Hitchcock's shoulder when *The Paradine Case* started up, barging into everything from casting decisions to scriptwriting, and this time the resulting film was a disaster for all concerned. As certain as a break between Hitchcock and Selznick appeared to be, however, each had reason to steer away from the prospect. Unsettled by changes in the industry, Selznick recognized that Hitchcock was a valued link with the past as well as a great asset in terms of publicity and prestige. He also realized that his new Selznick Releasing Organization would need a reliable flow of films to stay in business – films that might come from Hitchcock, either made for Selznick Productions or released through his distribution arm (Leff 268–69, 254–55, 243). On the other side of the equation, Hitchcock was eager to get Transatlantic up and running, and the time seemed right. In 1947 the British government instituted a punishing tax on money earned by American distributors in British theaters, and this made Transatlantic (a predominantly British enterprise) a potential tax-free conduit for money made by US companies in their strongest overseas market. Negotiations with such companies could be difficult, however, and whatever the drawbacks of bargaining with Selznick, his readiness to back Hitchcock's work – the publicity campaign for *The Paradine Case* was larger than for any other Selznick release – made

Hitchcock reluctant to burn the bridge between them, wobbly though this was (Leff 261–62).

Ultimately, the force of circumstances overrode the inertia of indecision. Badly in need of rest and reorganization, Selznick stopped producing films in 1948, and his releasing company ceased operations the following year. By then Hitchcock and Bernstein had signed with Warner Bros. to distribute Transatlantic's pictures, greatly pleasing Jack L. Warner, who expected Transatlantic to supply ample amounts of product in return for a modest investment of capital (Leff 271). What this formula left out was the possibility that an independent Hitchcock – especially a newly independent Hitchcock – might be less practical, prudent, and productive than a Hitchcock in steady dialogue with able producers, however bothersome that dialogue might seem during the throes of the creative process. Transatlantic soon put this possibility to the test.

Hitchcock and Bernstein

Hitchcock and Sidney Bernstein met in 1923, when Hitchcock was a rising newcomer in the English film industry and Bernstein was a film distributor, movie-house proprietor, and London Film Society council member. A pragmatic socialist who rose to power in the British media during the 1920s, Bernstein had co-founded the multimedia Granada Group in 1934; in later years he would be a founder of Granada Television. In the immediate postwar period his sights were set on international filmmaking. As he and Hitchcock planned it, Transatlantic would live up to its name by being equally British and American in its creative pool even as it remained primarily British in its business operations. Discussing the venture after Hitchcock wrapped up *Spellbound*, the partners realized that multiple tasks awaited them: obtaining low-interest loans from British and American banks; signing up investment partners; finding a Hollywood studio to take on financial risk and distribute the company's films; lining up properties that would attract bankable stars and directors; and do all this as a team with only two members (McGilligan 365–66).[1]

Major banks in Los Angeles and New York responded favorably to the pitches Hitchcock and Bernstein made as soon as *Notorious* was finished. As their studio partner they chose Warner Bros., which offered a deal allowing Hitchcock to work on Transatlantic as well as Warner Bros. pictures, paying him $3000 a week to produce and/or direct four of the latter over the next six and a half years, plus percentage points if their earnings were high (Krohn, *Hitchcock* 114). He and Bernstein then continued their hunt for narratives upon which Warners – and the banks that controlled Transatlantic's purse strings, and the stars Transatlantic would need to sign – could smile. Hitchcock had no shortage of ideas, but he and Bernstein did have shortages of time and money that lowered their chances of developing a project with substantial dramatic and stylistic impact.

Hitchcock kept plugging away at Transatlantic issues while working on *The Paradine Case*, even recruiting his celebrity friends Ingrid Bergman and Cary Grant to attend some of his New York business meetings. Up to this point the planned company was kept secret from those not directly or potentially involved, but it became public knowledge in spring 1946 when unauthorized press reports declared that Transatlantic was on the way, that its first picture would be an adaptation of Helen Simpson's 1937 novel *Under Capricorn*, and that its second would be a modern-day *Hamlet* with Cary Grant in the title role. The latter appears to have been more of a whimsical notion than a genuine prospect – dreamed up by Hitchcock, agreed to provisionally by Grant, and probably not pondered very seriously by either of them.

A film version of *Under Capricorn*, by contrast, was a realistic and interesting possibility, especially with Hitchcock's dream star, Ingrid Bergman, as the heroine. To start work on the screenplay, Hitchcock approached the renowned Scottish playwright James Bridie, who initially turned down the project. His recalcitrance became moot when Bergman proved unavailable, though when the project reemerged later he changed his mind. Still hoping to inaugurate Transatlantic with a Cary Grant movie, meanwhile, Hitchcock started thinking seriously about *Rope*, a 1929 play by Patrick Hamilton that had impressed him on the stage. It had a perversely grim subject that was very much up the director's street.

Rope

Hamilton's primary model for *Rope* was the well-known 1924 murder case centering on Nathan Leopold and Richard Loeb, two exceptionally intelligent Chicago youths who kidnapped and murdered a younger boy for reasons that never became entirely clear beyond an apparent desire for "thrill killing" and the challenge of pulling off a "perfect crime" as a demonstration of intellectual superiority. Their defense attorney, Clarence Darrow, saved them from the death penalty, but both were sentenced to life in prison.

Hamilton took various elements of the Leopold and Loeb case – the narcissistic perpetrators, their homosexual relationship, their vulgar Nietzschean philosophy, and the misstep that incriminated them – and wove them into a chamber play set immediately after the murder. The action unfolds in a room of the house shared by the killers during a party they hold to celebrate their secret crime. Among the guests are their victim's father and aunt, and the murderers serve refreshments from the trunk containing David's unseen corpse. Their macabre merrymaking goes smoothly until suspicions of wrongdoing start nagging at a guest named Rupert Cadell, who was once their teacher at school. Returning to their home after the party, he exposes the crime and summons the police.

Hitchcock had spoken of *Rope* in the early 1940s as a vehicle for an experimental technique he was considering, whereby scenes would be filmed in "real time," as opposed to cinematic time, by means of moving-camera sequence shots lasting as long as the camera's film magazine allowed.[2] Selznick had spoiled his first serious efforts along this line in *The Paradine Case*, but Bernstein opened up another chance when he remarked that since significant theatrical productions are important events in British culture, they should perhaps be filmed exactly the way they were presented on the stage (McGilligan 400). While conserving the legacy of English theater would have been in approximately last place on Hitchcock's artistic agenda, adapting motion-picture methods to an inherently theatrical subject – and vice versa – was a challenge he anticipated with pleasure. Acquiring, developing, and filming Hamilton's play became Transatlantic's top priority, ideally with Cary Grant playing Rupert, the friend and mentor who unexpectedly brings about the murderers' undoing. This role ultimately went to James Stewart, a romantic leading man whose grim experiences as a combat flyer in World War II had made him question the rightness of continuing in a profession as insubstantial as acting. While he did so continue, he turned to darker and more psychologically complex roles, of which Rupert was one of the first.

Hitchcock and Hamilton had divergent but overlapping interests. Born to "a strange and unhappy family" (Mepham) in 1904, Hamilton was permanently disfigured after being run over by a car in 1932, and took increasingly to alcohol in his private life and his novels, which are peopled by hopeless characters and preoccupied with "the perils and pleasures of drinking" ("Hamilton" 446). He was only twenty-four when he wrote *Rope*, his first theatrical success. Hitchcock, of course, was also strongly attracted to narratives of psychology and crime. As a filmmaker, however, he had learned to embed malign and morbid material in stylish, accessible stories that could be – and generally were – widely accepted as mass-audience entertainments.

The big studios had shown no interest in Hamilton's play, but Hitchcock felt it tapped into areas of human pathology that he could explore and embellish with tactical contributions of his own. After commissioning his actor friend Hume Cronyn to write a motion-picture treatment and the budding Hollywood writer Arthur Laurents to compose the screenplay, Hitchcock made various changes that tended to increase the ghoulishness of the story, as if there weren't already enough ghoulishness in Hamilton's concept. The finished film is a palimpsest in which Hamilton's play remains visible beneath Hitchcock's alterations, which provide revealing clues to his artistic personality at roughly the midpoint of his career. In keeping with Hitchcock's interest in theatricality, for instance, he adds a scene where Brandon (John Dall) and Phillip (Farley Granger) create a key part of the "set" for their "production" before our eyes. In the play, it is understood from the outset that the party's food will be served from the trunk containing the corpse, while in the film, the food is ready to be served in the dining room until Brandon has his new idea and rearranges things. In another change, the play begins in the dark as the murderers complete their crime, associating darkness with death; following the credits, the film opens on a clear close-up of the victim with the rope tight around his neck, plunging us into visual horror. These and other alterations display Hitchcock's distinctive authorial personality.

Many critics rightly regard *Rope* as one of Hitchcock's most intriguing projects, partly because of its unorthodox style, and also because Hitchcock dares to portray gay characters at a time when even implied homosexuality was taboo in American entertainment; to do this in his first film as an independent producer was a notably bold intervention in the complicated matrix of mid-century American values. The picture made Jack Warner so nervous that he put the brakes on his marketing campaign when audiences did not warm to it. While the lukewarm reception did not make for the rousing Transatlantic debut that Hitchcock had hoped for, at least its production marked the most decisive step in his troubled separation from Selznick and his hyperactive management style. According to Leonard J. Leff, auteur critics tend to regard this as a "momentous ... liberation" for Hitchcock, but others point to weaknesses in *Rope* and its immediate successors as proof that Hitchcock needed first-rate collaborators, even if they were as quarrelsome as Selznick, to "provide the context or the aura that made the 'business and tricks' resonate with meaning" – to stimulate him, even to complete him as a creative artist (Leff 277–78). Undaunted by the iffy reception of *Rope,* he proceeded with plans to shoot *Under Capricorn* with the same long-take strategy. This time Ingrid Bergman would be present to ensure a prosperous result.

Under Capricorn

Under Capricorn had been edged out as Transatlantic's first production because Bergman was not available, but Helen Simpson's novel kept percolating in Hitchcock's mind. Simpson had Hitchcock connections; she and Clemence Dane had co-written the 1928 novel *Enter Sir John,* on which Hitchcock's 1930 thriller *Murder!* was based, and Simpson had contributed dialogue to *Sabotage* (1936), Hitchcock's adaptation of Joseph Conrad's novel *The Secret Agent* (1907). Although she was born in Australia, she had lived in France and England from her teenage years until her death in 1940; she did research for *Under Capricorn* while visiting her native country in 1937.

Set in 1830, the story begins when Charles Adare, impecunious Irish nephew of the colony's new governor, arrives in Sydney and makes the acquaintance of Sam Flusky, an erstwhile stable groom and convicted murderer. Sam has served out his sentence, become a wealthy gentleman, and married Charles's beautiful cousin Henrietta, who is now an alcoholic shunned by society and secretly supplied with drink by Milly, a jealous housekeeper. Charles sets about restoring Henrietta's confidence and good name, sparking the climactic revelation that it was she who committed the murder for which adoring, protective Sam paid the penalty. In the end their marriage is revitalized, Milly's machinations are exposed, and Charles heads back to Ireland because even Australia isn't big enough to contain both him and the happily married cousin he has tacitly come to love.

To adapt Simpson's novel, Hitchcock approached the same writers who had worked on *Rope*. Hume Cronyn agreed to do the treatment, but Arthur Laurents refused to sign on as screenwriter this time. "What Hitchcock and Ingrid saw in [this novel] was a mystery to me," he remarked later. "I felt it was wrong for *all* of us" (Chandler 176). James Bridie had reservations as well, but capitulated to Hitchcock and went to work on the script. Bergman's schedule cooperated this time, and Hitchcock was delighted at the prospect of placing her under the Transatlantic banner. Ironically, however, she caused trouble for the production. Her high salary helped push the budget to $2.5 million, and she was uncertain how to twist her Swedish accent into an Irish brogue. Along with costar Joseph Cotten, moreover, she hated the demands of the long-take filming technique. "And of course the audience couldn't care less," she said in retrospect (Spoto 310). She was right about this – few critics, let alone moviegoers, had noticed the sequence-shot structure of *Rope* – but Hitchcock was not prepared to budge. On top of all this, *Under Capricorn* opened just as Bergman's out-of-wedlock pregnancy by Italian director Roberto Rossellini became a headline-grabbing scandal, inducing theater owners to cancel bookings and Bergman to refuse all interviews and promotional activities for the film.

Hitchcock said later that he had made multiple mistakes with *Under Capricorn*, but some critics have been kinder to the picture. Robin Wood argues for its "centrality ... to the Hitchcock canon," citing its intertextuality with other Bergman films, its connection with the tradition of woman-centered melodramas, and "the multiplicity of its influences, determinants, and anticipations" (335, 326–27), thus construing it as a matrix film *avant la lettre*. Other critics, including Florence Jacobowitz, have linked *Under Capricorn* to an array of earlier and later Hitchcock movies – *The Paradine Case*, with its upstairs-downstairs theme; *The Manxman* (1929) and *Blackmail* (1929), with their concern for class differences; *Rebecca, Suspicion* (1941), *Spellbound*, and *Notorious*, with their women's-film formulas; *I Confess*, with its confession scene; *Lifeboat* (1944), *Rope*, and *Rear Window* (1954), with their use of enclosed space; and *Vertigo* (1958), with its motif of a male protagonist who reconstructs a woman's image in the terms of his own desire. Looking beyond these connections and conventions, however, Jacobowitz finds in the denouement of *Under Capricorn* a belief in redemption, recovery, and hope that move in a new direction, toward "a post-war world in need of reinvention" (27). This aptly summarizes the film's position as a work of narrative and thematic transition.

Despite its commercial failure, *Under Capricorn* affirms Hitchcock as a matrix figure in a double sense. Cinematically, it combines elements of traditionalism (studio mise-en-scène, classical screen acting) and modernism (montage sequences juxtaposed with bravura moving-camera shots) in ways that revise and refresh the costume-picture and historical-romance genres. Sociologically, it links a fading order and an emerging one – the wartime order of sabotage and suspicion on one hand, the postwar order of desire and expectation on the other – with a lucidity unsurpassed by any other Hitchcock film of this period. All of this notwithstanding, its American reviews were tepid and its English reviews worse, with even the moderate *Times* saying it "lasts far too long and has far too many loose ends." Such poor opinions cast a pall on attendance, inducing the banks that backed Transatlantic to repossess the film and turn it over to Selznick's operation for one last try at profitability – a sad finish for a picture that, McGilligan reports, "Hitchcock himself never lost his fondness for" (438).

Stage Fright

Transatlantic had produced two pictures so far in its young life, and its financial track record – a box-office disappointment followed by a severe box-office disappointment – was not of a sort to inspire Hollywood's respect or to ensure a healthy future for Hitchcock's independent producing activities. Chastened by these realizations, he and Bernstein became more cautious as they assessed their options and plotted their next moves. They had pitched *Rope* to Warner Bros. as a "run-for-cover crime film" (McGilligan 401), but as we have seen, it was Jack Warner who wanted to hide out until controversy over the movie died down. Now his studio was having trepidations about *I Confess*, a proposed project in which Hitchcock wanted a Roman Catholic priest to be revealed as the father of an out-of-wedlock child. Postponing that production in favor of a plainly commercial vehicle seemed prudent and responsible, since this would calm Warner's anxieties, give his studio an in-house production ahead of schedule, and gain time for working out a feasible treatment of the "wrong priest" story.

Hitchcock had been developing just such a project since late 1948 – a sprightly mystery based on *Outrun the Constable* by Selwyn Jepson, a successful British author and occasional movie and TV scriptwriter. Serialized in *Collier's* as *Man Running* in 1947, published by Doubleday as *Outrun the Constable* the same year, and reprinted by Bantam as *Killer by Proxy* in 1950, this was one of several Jepson novels featuring Eve Gill, an ingénue sleuth who cracks mysterious cases by virtue of her appealing personality and youthful energy. In this adventure she comes to the aid of a man who is wanted for murder, ferreting out clues by infiltrating a famous actress's house disguised as an ignorant maid, and coping all the while with her eccentric father, a boatman with a mild criminal streak of his own. Hitchcock crafted the scenario with his wife, Alma Reville, their playwright friend Whitfield Cook, and screenwriter Ranald MacDougall, and then went to scout locations in London and on the English coast, where he had decided to shoot *Stage Fright*, as the picture was now called. The casting went well in most respects. The ingénue sleuth was played by Jane Wyman, fresh from her Academy Award for *Johnny Belinda* and from her split with husband Ronald Reagan, which made her especially pleased to leave the country for a while. The famous actress in the story, Charlotte Inwood, was played by a famous actress in real life, Marlene Dietrich, who had learned so much about lighting, lenses, and angles from her seven Josef von Sternberg pictures that Hitchcock instructed cinematographer Wilkie Cooper to do whatever she wanted him to do.

Discussion of *Stage Fright* is often freighted with the disparaging remark Hitchcock made to Truffaut about the so-called lying flashback near the beginning of the film, when Jonathan hops into Eve's car and tells her about the murder that just took place – an event that is visualized as a flashback while Jonathan describes it, but later turns out to have transpired in ways very different from Jonathan's duplicitous account. Truffaut parses Hitchcock's conclusion that he "never should have done" the scene (Truffaut 189) in a way that makes it seem a lie thrice over. Yet it is entirely suitable in a film that is about incessant slippages between truth and fiction, honesty and mendacity, identity and disguise, professional performance and the "presentation of self in everyday life," to borrow sociologist Erving Goffman's famous phrase. Hitchcock explores these ambiguities not only through the experiences of his characters, moreover, but also through the broad idea of the urban environment as a living, pulsing body with its own susceptibility to confusions of fact and falsehood, history and myth. The film begins with an old-fashioned theater curtain slowly rising to reveal a view of London, still bearing visible wartime scars that inject an echo of Italian neorealism (at an international high point as *Stage Fright* was made) alongside the masquerades and machinations that dominate the picture. Three quick shots later, Eve's car is zooming along in front of a patently rear-projected backdrop – reinforcing the theme of artifice versus actuality – as Jonathan launches into the notorious flashback, introducing motifs that will be repeated and varied throughout the story.

Truffaut seems unhappier with the flashback, and with the picture as a whole, than Hitchcock does in their interview, but the French director eggs on the British-American one until he says that he adapted Jepson's novel because several book reviewers mentioned it as potentially "a good Hitchcock picture. And I, like an idiot, believed them" (189). For many observers this is indeed a good Hitchcock picture, however, albeit less provocative than it might have been if Hitchcock had been allowed to use its theatrical ambience as a vehicle for sexy visuals. According to Krohn, the director planned on having Dietrich take off a bloodstained dress in front of the Richard Todd character, but desisted because of censorship problems. Hitchcock also angered Hollywood censor Joseph Breen by suggesting that the star who played a vulnerable deaf-mute in Johnny Belinda would appear in "short panties" (Krohn, *Hitchcock* 111). Mischievous moments such as these suggest that *Stage Fright*, dismissed by Truffaut as "simply another one of those little British crime movies in the Agatha Christie tradition" (189), was conceived by Hitchcock in more interesting, and potentially subversive, terms. Even as it stands, this fast-moving film offers enjoyable echoes of the classic thriller sextet while carrying the Agatha Christie tradition into new and unusual terrain.

Strangers on a Train

Hitchcock told Truffaut that *The Lodger: A Story of the London Fog*, his great thriller of 1926, was "the first true 'Hitchcock movie'" (43). On the first day of photography for *Strangers on a Train*, his great thriller of 1951, he gathered the cast and crew to announce that "none of his previous pictures counted – today was the real beginning of his film-making career" (Krohn, *Hitchcock* 114). Though the director still needed to present Warner Bros. with an unqualified success – *Stage Fright* had earned mostly lukewarm reviews, and the studio was still edgy about the *I Confess* project– his high expectations for *Strangers on a Train* were more than wishful thinking. Patricia Highsmith's first novel, the rights to which Hitchcock acquired for just $7,500 after instructing his agents not to mention his well-financed name, contained a wealth of Hitchcockian material: the indeterminate nature of good and evil, the transfer of guilt from one person to another, characters who are quasi-doubles or doppelgängers, and a supple overarching structure that prompted Hitchcock's often-quoted comment, "Isn't it a fascinating design? One could study it forever" (Truffaut 195).

The film draws its basic ingredients from Highsmith's 1950 book. In the novel, Guy Haines, a rising young architect, makes the acquaintance of Charles Anthony Bruno, a pushy and peculiar man who suggests that they swap homicides: He will murder the wife who keeps Guy trapped in a bad marriage, Guy will slay Bruno's hated father in return, and neither will be caught because nobody knows that the two men ever met, much less that they planned a pair of ostensibly motiveless crimes. Guy dismisses Bruno as a mere eccentric, but shortly afterward Bruno carries out the first killing and demands that Guy fulfill his part of the bargain. Hitchcock rings important changes on Highsmith's plot, however, some to avoid censorship problems and many more to build the grand design of which he was so proud. Beyond streamlining the narrative and altering details – alcoholic Charlie Bruno becomes madman Bruno Anthony (Robert Walker), for instance, and the architect becomes a tennis player with political ambitions (Farley Granger) – the film tones down the brooding savagery of Highsmith's original. In the book, Bruno sees the murder swap as a thrilling experiment, not particularly expecting Guy to follow through on his part of the deal, and his growing obsession with the issue is a side effect of his growing obsession with Guy himself; in the movie, Bruno stalks and intimidates Guy almost from the start. In the book, Guy has a confirmable alibi for the time of his wife's murder; in the film, his lack of one amplifies his vulnerability to Bruno's pressure tactics. In the book, Guy does eventually break into Bruno's family home and kill Bruno's father in his sleep; in the film's corresponding scene, Guy enters the father's bedroom to warn him of Bruno's evil scheme, only to find Bruno waiting for him in the father's place. Most sweeping and important, the book's Bruno and Guy are fixated on each other with increasing force throughout the story, unmistakably gripped by a perverse homoerotic attraction. The film changes this resonant overtone to a low-key undertone, transforming the story from a long crescendo of psychopathology into an elegantly crafted pattern-picture.

The outstandingly high quality of *Strangers on a Train* is surprising when one considers how hard adapting Highsmith's novel proved to be. No fewer than eight writers turned down offers to do the screenplay, either because they "couldn't visualize the story," as the director told Charles Thomas Samuels (Hitchcock 149), or because they simply didn't like the story, grounded as it was in perversity and unpleasantness. Hitchcock then hired the famous crime novelist Raymond Chandler, who took the job despite misgivings over the story's plausibility, and then rankled Hitchcock by fussing over narrative logic at the expense of the director's visual ideas. Having already dumped a good deal of Highsmith's novel, Hitchcock now dumped just about everything in Chandler's script (although Warners insisted on having his name in the credits) and brought in the little-known Czenzi Ormonde and Barbara Keon, a former Selznick colleague and now Hitchcock's associate producer. Ormonde and Keon finished their screenplay when the production was already under way, and an anecdote about Ormonde speaks volumes about both the high value of Hitchcock's collaborators and the authorial vision that makes the films distinctly his. Discussing her work for McGilligan's biography, she declared that she was not conscious of "the slightest homoerotic undercurrent between Bruno and Guy," that Hitchcock never mentioned it, and that, as far as she is concerned, "it doesn't exist in the script or the film" (449). Where, then, did the widespread impression of that undercurrent come from? The answer must be sweeping: from Highsmith, who invented the characters and their mutually obsessed relationship; from Whitfield Cook, who transposed these elements into cinematic terms; from Ormonde and Keon, whose contributions preserved the underlying ethos of the materials Hitchcock gave them; and most of all from Hitchcock, an ever more seasoned and self-assured artist who usually knew what he wanted and increasingly knew how to obtain it, even when the helpers he relied on were not entirely aware of what they were delivering.

This said, it must be added that Hitchcock transmutes the unambiguous homoeroticism of Highsmith's novel into an unrequited mania on Bruno's part, and that the extraordinary emotional charge of Bruno's fixation stems to a great extent from Robert Walker's justly acclaimed performance– easily the most fully realized of his career, which was cut short by his death at age thirty-three, less than two months after *Strangers on a Train* debuted. It was daring of Hitchcock to choose Walker for this role, since the actor was mainly known as a boy-next-door type. Krohn speculates that Hitchcock saw beyond his generally bland image because of a "famous jailhouse photo of [Walker] looking mean after his arrest on a drunk driving charge" (*Hitchcock* 118). More broadly, *Strangers on a Train* again displays Hitchcock's cinema as a matrix of romantic and modernist culture. Spoto traces the film's demented-fairground theme to such sources as Thackeray's novel *Vanity Fair* (1848), Goethe's epic drama *Faust* (1808/1832), and Robert Wiene's expressionist film *The Cabinet of Dr. Caligari* (1920); he also finds antecedents for the doppelgänger motif in Poe's story "William Wilson" (1839), Dostoevsky's novella *The Double* (1846), and Oscar Wilde's novel *The Picture of Dorian Gray* (1890), among other works. One may extend these lineages to later Hitchcock films, noting such examples of carnivalesque violence as the attempted drunken-driving murder in *North by Northwest* (1959), the insane masquerade in *Psycho* (1960), and the attack on the children's party in *The Birds* (1963), and of the doppelgänger motif in everything from *To Catch a Thief* (1955) and *The Wrong Man* (1956) to *Vertigo* and *Frenzy* (1972). In the intricate weave of *Strangers on a Train*, as Spoto writes, the "literature Hitchcock read … merged with the fears and lineaments and demons of his own soul" (329–30).

I Confess

Warner Bros. was naturally pleased when *Strangers on a Train* emerged as a box-office winner. At the same time, the studio remained on edge about *I Confess*, which Hitchcock was still developing despite the red flags it would almost certainly wave before Production Code censors. The source text was a stage drama called *Nos deux consciences*, or *Our Two Consciences*, which had appeared in 1902 under the name of Paul Anthelme, the pseudonym of Paul Bourde, a reputable author and journalist. Written in occasionally florid French, it limns the sacrificial ordeal of a Roman Catholic priest who submits to execution rather than reveal an exonerating secret that he learned in the confessional. Here was the anti–capital punishment theme that Hitchcock held dear, and also the transference-of-guilt motif, as the cleric undergoes humiliation and then condemnation for a murder that was actually committed by a peasant disguised in religious garb. According to John Russell Taylor, Hitchcock had been "haunted" (218) by the play since seeing it in London during the early 1930s and was able to buy the motion-picture rights from playwright and filmmaker Henri Verneuil, who had acquired the play from Bourde's nephew, and who wrote the first treatments for Hitchcock's version. Hitchcock expected to make *I Confess* as a Warner Bros. production, but as his visual and narrative ideas took shape he decided to exercise more control by doing it independently for Transatlantic, promising to make an additional film for the studio, free of charge, in return (Krohn, *Hitchcock* 128).

Though Krohn's "*I Confess* and *Nos deux consciences*" details the tortuous process by which the 1902 Paul Bourde play became the 1953 Hitchcock film, the eventual outcome, if not dramatically or emotionally seamless, was highly suggestive in its implications for Hitchcock's evolving thematic concerns. This is especially so when *I Confess* is considered in tandem with *Strangers on a Train*, which also centers on the twin themes of guilt transference and confession. More intriguingly, Krohn speculates that since Hitchcock saw *Nos deux consciences* in the early 1930s, the play might have served as an archetype or template for the appearances of those themes in such sophisticated thrillers as the original *Man Who Knew Too Much* and *The 39 Steps*, made in the middle 1930s. Unlike those films, however, *I Confess* was to be a tragedy, with the protagonist unjustly put to death and only then being publicly absolved. In addition, the priest would be burdened not only with the confession he cannot reveal but also with his own secret of having fathered a child before taking on his vocation.

Like the development process, the casting of *I Confess* was not free of problems. When it became clear that neither Cary Grant nor James Stewart would play Father Michael William Logan, the protagonist, Hitchcock thought of Laurence Olivier, who was ruled out by Warner Bros.' demand for an American in the lead. He then went successfully for Montgomery Clift, now a much bigger star than when Hitchcock had wanted him for *Rope*. When he arrived in Quebec for filming, however, Clift was disappointed to learn that the final shooting script was considerably less bold than the version he had read with enthusiasm. At the studio's insistence, the priest's secret offspring had been replaced by a one-night love affair in his pre-clerical days, and his execution was now averted by a not-guilty verdict. For his part, Hitchcock had little patience with Clift's fussy habits and Method acting techniques. To play Ruth Grandfort, a politician's wife pining for the man she loved before he became a priest, Hitchcock wanted an unfamiliar actress with a European accent. He happily accepted Bernstein's recommendation of Anita Bjork, a Swedish actress, but gossip columnists had a field day when she arrived with a lover and their out-of-wedlock baby. Jack Warner was at the end of his rope. This was bad publicity; he wanted no illegitimate children on his radar after arduously erasing one from Hitchcock's screenplay; and the potential scandal was far too reminiscent of the one Ingrid Bergman caused when *Under Capricorn* came out.

Reasoning that the best way to control *I Confess* was to buy it from Transatlantic and make it as an in-studio production, Warner Bros. offered this arrangement to Bernstein, who decided to remove his name from the production, take leave of Transatlantic on amicable terms, and let Hitchcock carry *I Confess* forward as he wished. Bowing to necessity, Hitchcock proceeded to principal photography, swallowing his regret at losing Bjork and his greater disappointment with yielding this intensely personal film to Jack Warner and company. Perhaps this late-breaking development motivated Hitchcock's decision to make his cameo appearance one of the first images after the opening titles: he is seen crossing the screen in distant profile, followed by a montage emphasizing road signs bearing arrows and the word "Direction," indicating one-way streets – which might be the director's way of presenting himself "in his independence" as author of *I Confess*, as V.F. Perkins suggests in his essay on the film (34).

Worries about censorship of *I Confess* arose almost at the beginning. Upon reading the treatment, Bernstein's secretary warned him it would be "classified as both anti-social and amoral by all the Associations, Societies, Borough and County Council and hospital after-care welfare workers" (Moorehead 192). Hoping to head off such problems, Hitchcock and Bernstein traveled to Quebec with scriptwriter George Tabori to test the waters vis-à-vis possible religious objections. Catholic authorities liked the project, even with the out-of-wedlock child and the unjust execution, because the cleric never lost his dignity and gravitas; covering themselves anyway, Hitchcock and Bernstein hired a Catholic theologian to be their technical consultant (McGilligan 457). By early 1952, Martin Quigley of the powerful Catholic Legion of Decency had started a furious correspondence over aspects of the film that seemed to him beyond the pale, and by summer the PCA chief, Joseph Breen, was embroiled in the fray. One matter that exercised him was Michael's one-night stand with Ruth (Anne Baxter), which occurs despite their shared knowledge of her marriage and his plan to enter the priesthood. Another was the idea of Michael literally dying for his faith by upholding the sanctity of the confessional to the bitter end, followed by a dramatic revelation of the real killer's identity – a conclusion that allegedly insults the criminal-justice system and might rile Montgomery Clift fans to boot. The only way to get around such disputes was to fall back on ambiguity and compromise in key areas of plot and character. As Amy Lawrence's research shows, "at every point … the film's producers, advisors [sic], and critics … opted for an opaque propriety over a fully-realized sainthood" (70). Although the movie turned a profit after its March 1953 release, the most Hitchcock could say for its American and British reviews was "not bad on the whole" (McGilligan 466). This independent Transatlantic picture had turned into a Warner Bros. studio picture, dividing Hitchcock and Bernstein in the process, and then paid unimpressive critical and commercial dividends to all concerned.

Dial M for Murder

Hitchcock's enthusiasm for technical experiments yielded many fascinating results – the bathroom monologue of *Murder!*, the confined environment of *Lifeboat*, the long takes of *Rope*, the long-shot logistics of *Rear Window*, the zoom-in/track-out shots of *Vertigo*, and the electronic sounds in *The Birds* (1963). In addition there was *Blackmail*, England's first feature with synchronized sound. So it is little wonder that the idea of making a 3-D movie intrigued him – even if the process itself, steadily reminding the audience of its presence, struck him as inherently anti-cinematic (Spoto 342).

Hitchcock wanted to start a new picture immediately because Transatlantic appeared to be going down for the third time. Bernstein had resigned from the production of *I Confess* because of the multiple problems it was presenting, and in early 1953 he returned from a project-scouting trip to Asia with the plan of resigning from Transatlantic altogether, even though this would unquestionably end the venture. Since forming his association with Hitchcock he had seen too many changes for the worse in the American film industry, including the antitrust actions that separated production companies from their theater chains, the political witch hunts that set studios and employees at one another's throats, and the rapid rise of TV competition (Moorehead 195). Taking into account also Transatlantic's many debts and the strain of being away so often from England, he decided the logical solution was to head for the exit as a movie producer. Hitchcock had probably felt this coming, and he may have thought Bernstein would change his mind before their company shut down completely. Shooting a modestly-budgeted adaptation of Frederick Knott's popular 1952 play *Dial "M" for Murder: A Collage for Voices* would solve or defer a number of problems – giving Hitchcock a sure-fire hit, giving Bernstein time to reconsider his resignation, and giving Jack Warner the most anomalous of gifts, a prestigious 3-D production.

Knott's play centers on a scheme by former athlete Tony Wendice to get rid of his wealthy wife, Margot, who has been having an affair with Max Halliday, a writer of television mysteries who becomes Mark Halliday in the film. Tony uses blackmail to coerce an old schoolmate named Charles Alexander Swann, alias Captain Lesgate, into murdering Margot, but she gets the drop on Lesgate and foils the plan, whereupon Tony twists the evidence around to pin a murder charge on *her*. The case is eventually cracked by dutiful Inspector Hubbard, who becomes one of the most creditable police characters in any Hitchcock film. Hitchcock might easily have opened up the stage-bound action, perhaps turning the lengthy exposition of the first act into scenes that lay visual groundwork for the meatier material to come. Instead he changed the action in only a few strategic ways, such as altering dialogue and introducing an element of delay, and a cinematically stunning excursus into the mechanics of the English telephone system, into the pivotal murder scene. Hitchcock's decision to retain the play's structure and setting, which meant confining almost the entire film to a single room, suggests that he saw *Dial M for Murder* as another step in the exploration of enclosed-space aesthetics that began with *Lifeboat* a decade earlier and culminated with *Rear Window* shortly afterwards. All of these endeavors attest to Hitchcock's fondness for stage-play adaptations, and to the multifaceted interest in theatricality that has a central or supporting role in nearly all of his movies.

Despite the presence of marquee stars Ray Milland and Grace Kelly, Hitchcock sometimes gave the impression that *Dial M for Murder* was a potboiler, and that the ponderousness of 3-D filming relegated it to minor status from the start. "A play is seen in 3-D normally," he said to biographer Charlotte Chandler, "and within the confines of a stage set it's much easier to control the added complications of shooting" with the bulky camera needed for the process. When he made this picture, he continued, "I was running for cover while waiting for the muse. A play is a safety net picture" (207). Yet he told Truffaut that he had *wanted* to "emphasize the theatrical aspects," and his comments reveal definite pride in what he was able to accomplish, however imperfect the results had often been. "All of the action ... takes place in a living room," he said, "but that doesn't matter. I could just as well have shot the whole film in a telephone booth. ... You might say that a filmmaker can use a telephone booth pretty much in the same way a novelist uses a blank piece of paper" (213).

Even as he worked on *Dial M for Murder*, Hitchcock worried "that 3-D might be a fad that would fade and that [the picture] would go out as a 'flattie'" (Chandler 207). He was correct – the movie reached the screen exactly two days after the trade paper *Variety* ran a front-page report proclaiming the 3-D craze officially dead (Krohn, *Hitchcock* 130). Movie houses showed it flat in 1954, but in 1980 new 3-D prints were shown in assorted theaters equipped with the necessary two-projector system. The revival demonstrated to critic J. Hoberman that Hitchcock's venture "was by far the most visually compelling of studio stereoscopic movies[,] … rivaled only by Jack Arnold's half-underwater *Creature From the Black Lagoon* [1954]." This is well-deserved praise, although Hitchcock might not have relished that particular comparison.

Paramount and Beyond

Hitchcock was not the only Hollywood filmmaker to learn the difficulties of independent production from first-hand experience. Among the others was Howard Hawks, also a favorite of the French New Wave's feisty "Hitchcocko-Hawksian" critics in the 1950s. He and Hitchcock had plenty of company in their bids for independence, since high tax rates in the late 1940s gave "any [successful] artist in Hollywood the motivation to form a corporation," as Hawks biographer Todd McCarthy writes (451). But these two made their boldest moves at about the same time – Hitchcock with Transatlantic and *Rope*, Hawks with Monterey Productions and *Red River*, both films released in 1948 – and each failed to sustain his company for long. Budget and schedule overruns on *Red River* undermined Monterey, sending Hawks back "into the clutches of the studios from which he had spent years working to free himself" (McCarthy 428). Transatlantic faded as well, but its waning was more gradual and the consequences less severe. Hawks waited for years before producing his pictures again on a steady basis. Hitchcock produced all of his subsequent films, and they constitute the most illustrious phase of his career.

Although he was well into his fifties when Transatlantic closed down, Hitchcock stepped up his production pace and worked harder than ever at promoting his pictures and his image. His income rose nicely, thanks partly to Lew Wasserman, the agent who advised him on business dealings much as Bernstein advised him on art collecting. Wasserman had been monitoring Paramount's transition from a traditional system, with studio bosses overseeing staff producers, to a production-unit system, with top creative personnel brought to the studio by offers of independence and profit-sharing arrangements. The executives in charge of this shift were Hitchcock fans, and Wasserman was able to broker excellent terms for five Hitchcock films as producer-director and four as director only. Hitchcock brought cinematographer Robert Burks with him and chose the rest of his team from Paramount's talent pool, including George Tomasini, who went on to edit nine of his pictures, and Hal Pereira, whose gifted crew devised many of Hitchcock's most memorable production designs (McGilligan 479, 483–84).

After the false starts, non-starts, and let-downs that peppered the Transatlantic and Warner Bros. years, Hitchcock's four successive Paramount projects came off smoothly and successfully: *Rear Window*, one of his finest creations; *To Catch a Thief*, one of his most fun; *The Trouble with Harry* (1955), arguably his most personal; and *The Man Who Knew Too Much* (1956), revisiting a favorite story from a new perspective. In a more modest version of the Transatlantic venture, Hitchcock established another independent company, Alfred J. Hitchcock Productions, which worked with Paramount on *The Trouble with Harry* and *Vertigo*, with Universal on *The Birds*, and on episodes of *The Alfred Hitchcock Hour* from 1963 to 1965. Wasserman engineered a profitable move to MGM later in the 1950s, resulting in the spectacular *North by Northwest* in 1959. Hitchcock made *Psycho* with his own television company, Shamley Productions, and then returned to Universal for all of his subsequent films. In sum, the Master of Suspense both produced and directed every feature from *Rope* through the 1976 thriller *Family Plot*, his last completed picture. The actual extent of his independence waxed and waned, but no Hollywood filmmaker enjoyed more consistent creative control. For all the challenges he faced during the Transatlantic and Warner Bros. years, they were the crucible in which he refined the extraordinary talents that made the films of his last quarter-century the most Hitchcockian of them all.

Notes

1. Unless otherwise indicated, factual material about Transatlantic and Warner Bros. in this chapter comes primarily from McGilligan, Leff, Spoto, and other standard sources.

2. Numerous critics have misdescribed the "ten-minute" takes of *Rope*. In fact, the shots vary between 4 minutes, 37 seconds and 10 minutes, 6 seconds.

Works Cited

Anthelme, Paul [Paul Bourde]. *Nos deux consciences: Pièce en cinq actes, en prose*. Paris: L'illustration, 1902. *Google Book Search*. Web. 18 July 2010.

Chandler, Charlotte. *It's Only a Movie: Alfred Hitchcock: A Personal Biography*. New York: Simon and Schuster, 2005.

Goffman, Erving. *The Presentation of Self in Everyday Life*. New York: Doubleday, 1959.

"Hamilton, (Anthony Walter) Patrick." *The Oxford Companion to English Literature*. Sixth ed. Ed. Margaret Drabble. Oxford: Oxford UP, 2006.

Hamilton, Patrick. *Rope: A Play*. 1929. London: Constable, 1994.

Highsmith, Patricia. *Strangers on a Train*. 1950. New York: Norton, 2001.

Hitchcock, Alfred. Interview by Charles Thomas Samuels. *Alfred Hitchcock: Interviews*. Ed. Sidney Gottlieb. Jackson: UP of Mississippi, 2003. 129–55.

Hoberman, J. "The Stunt Men." *Village Voice*. Village Voice, 6 Apr. 1999. Web. 29 Apr. 2009.

Jacobowitz, Florence. "*Under Capricorn*: Hitchcock in Transition." *CineAction* 52 (June 2000): 18–27.

Jepson, Selwyn. *Outrun the Constable*. New York: Doubleday, 1948. Rpt. as *Killer by Proxy*. New York: Bantam, 1950.

Knott, Frederick. *Dial "M" for Murder: A Collage for Voices*. New York: Dramatists Play Service, 1953.

Krohn, Bill. *Hitchcock at Work*. London: Phaidon, 2000.

Krohn, Bill. "*I Confess* and *Nos deux consciences*." *Casting a Shadow: Creating the Alfred Hitchcock Film*. Ed. Will Schmenner and Corinne Granof. Evanston: Mary and Leigh Block Museum of Art and Northwestern UP, 2007. 49–61.

Lawrence, Amy. "Constructing a Priest, Silencing a Saint: The PCA and *I Confess* (1953)." *Film History* 19 (2007): 58–72.

Leff, Leonard J. *Hitchcock and Selznick: The Rich and Strange Collaboration of Alfred Hitchcock and David O. Selznick in Hollywood*. New York: Weidenfeld and Nicolson, 1987.

McCarthy, Todd. *Howard Hawks: The Grey Fox of Hollywood*. New York: Grove, 1997.

McGilligan, Patrick. *Alfred Hitchcock: A Life in Darkness and Light*. New York: HarperCollins, 2003.

Mepham, John. "Patrick Hamilton." *The Literary Encyclopedia*. Literary Dictionary, 12 Nov. 2001. Web. 16 April 2009.

Moorehead, Caroline. *Sidney Bernstein: A Biography*. London: Jonathan Cape, 1984.

Orr, John. *Hitchcock and Twentieth-Century Cinema*. London: Wallflower, 2005.

Perkins, V.F. "*I Confess*: Photographs of People Speaking." *CineAction* 52 (June 2000): 28–39.

Producers Guild of America. "Frequently Asked Questions." 2009. Web. 3 Apr. 2009.

Ryall, Tom. *Alfred Hitchcock and the British Cinema*. Urbana: U of Illinois P, 1986.

Simpson, Helen. *Under Capricorn*. London: Heinemann, 1937.

Spoto, Donald. *The Dark Side of Genius: The Life of Alfred Hitchcock*. Boston: Little, Brown, 1983.

Taylor, John Russell. *Hitch: The Life and Times of Alfred Hitchcock*. New York: Pantheon, 1978.

Truffaut, François, with the collaboration of Helen G. Scott. *Hitchcock*. Rev. ed. New York: Simon and Schuster, 1984.

"Under Capricorn: Mr Hitchcock's New Film." *[London] Times* 5 Oct. 1949. *Alfred Hitchcock Wiki*. Web. 16 Apr. 2009.

Wood, Robin. *Hitchcock's Films Revisited*. New York: Columbia UP, 1989.

18

Hitchcock, Metteur-en-scène: 1954–60

Joe McElhaney

Between 1954 and 1960 Alfred Hitchcock directed seven films, four of them now widely regarded as masterpieces: *Rear Window* (1954), *Vertigo* (1958), *North by Northwest* (1959) and *Psycho* (1960). Three others have not acquired the same canonical status but are thought to be major works: *The Trouble with Harry* (1955), *The Man Who Knew Too Much* (1956), and *The Wrong Man* (1956). The remaining film, *To Catch a Thief* (1955), while popular at the time of its release and still widely shown today, is considered comparatively minor. "It was a lightweight story," Hitchcock later said (Truffaut 223). During the same years in which Hitchcock made these films, his celebrity status grew to an extraordinary degree, created in no small part by the success of his television show *Alfred Hitchcock Presents*, which began broadcasting in 1955, as well as by the various mystery anthologies and magazines that began to bear his name. Such a scale of creativity and self-promotion was substantially fostered by the gradual decline of the traditional Hollywood studio system and, along with it, the "classical" cinema so central to its output. This decline created a space within which Hitchcock was given an increasing degree of autonomy over his films and over his own image, controlling both production and exhibition of these films on a scale rarely granted him upon his arrival in Hollywood a decade earlier.

The 1950s also saw Hitchcock's films becoming central to the formation of auteurism, particularly as it was practiced at *Cahiers du cinéma* – although the auteurists cannot claim to have discovered him, as he had already been a much-publicized filmmaker even before his arrival in Hollywood. Nevertheless, the kinds of arguments they made about his work were highly original. Crucial was the importance given to mise-en-scène as the clearest expression of the auteur's vision. But auteurism was also more than this. Mise-en-scène could, at its highest state, be the

A Companion to Alfred Hitchcock, First Edition. Edited by Thomas Leitch and Leland Poague.
© 2011 Thomas Leitch and Leland Poague. Published 2011 by Blackwell Publishing Ltd.

essence of the cinematic and, implicitly or explicitly, become a meditation on the very nature of cinema. "What is cinema," Jacques Rivette rhetorically asked in a 1954 review of Otto Preminger's *Angel Face* (1952), "if not the *play* of actor and actress, of hero and set, of word and face, of hand and object?" (135). For Rivette, Preminger was fundamentally a metteur-en-scène rather than an auteur in that the mise-en-scène in Preminger, however skillfully employed, preceded a set of thematic obsessions, whereas a true auteur of the "possibly more naïve conception of the old school" (134) first possesses a vision of the world out of which he then constructs his mise-en-scène. Rivette includes Hitchcock, along with Fritz Lang and Howard Hawks, in this "old" school, and throughout *Cahiers du cinéma*'s writings on Hitchcock in the fifties there is little question that Hitchcock is an auteur.

In calling this essay "Hitchcock, Metteur-en-scène," my intentions are not to diminish Hitchcock's auteur status – a formidable task under any circumstances – but simply to use Hitchcock's mise-en-scène as the centerpiece of my analysis and to treat Hitchcock as though his methods are not necessarily all that different from those of someone like Preminger. In fact, the distinctions between auteur and metteur-en-scène are never quite clear either in Rivette's essay or throughout traditional auteurism, the categories often becoming polemical weapons allowing some critics to favor one filmmaker at the expense of another – the "aesthetic personality cult" of which André Bazin warned *("Politique"* 257).

My calling Hitchcock a metteur-en-scène has another value here. Much of the mythology surrounding Hitchcock's working methods is bound up with his rigorous pre-production, in particular the importance given to storyboarding, with both the shooting and the editing becoming a more or less mechanical process of giving life to something tightly constructed long before the sleepy-eyed director arrives on the set. Bazin indelibly captured this image of Hitchcock after visiting a location set for *To Catch a Thief.* Bazin described Hitchcock as "settled in his armchair" and conveying "the impression of being prodigiously bored and of musing about something completely different" *(Cruelty* 144). Bill Krohn's research in *Hitchcock at Work* has successfully challenged this myth, showing a director actively engaged in a production and post-production process that underwent almost continual modification and even, at times, improvisation. In what follows here I would like to retain Krohn's image of Hitchcock rather than Bazin's, although this will not be a simple process.

Conversation Pieces

At the most basic level, to be a metteur-en-scène is to be someone who stages scenes, blocking the actors within a specific setting, and ideally doing so in a compelling manner, integrating this staging with an expressive use of décor, costuming, and lighting. At its origins, this practice is related to stage and not film direction, the term, like mise-en-scène, having its origins in theatrical vocabulary. Though Hitchcock had no background in the theater, his fascination with theater as a literal space of performance and with the theatrical as both a metaphor and a mode of being is apparent from the beginning of his career. This fascination does not dissipate in the period covered by this chapter but if anything intensifies. The theatrical metaphors that pepper the dialogue of *Rear Window* underline the film's theatricality even while the film equally suggests an experiment of a deeply cinematic nature. *North by Northwest* repeats the same kinds of metaphors in its dialogue but extends their implications much further than its approximate 1935 counterpart, *The 39 Steps*, thus becoming a film largely *about* role-playing, masks, and shifting identities. A key element of the transformation of *The Man Who Knew Too Much* from its 1934 incarnation to its 1956 remake is turning the wife, named Jo McKenna (Doris Day) in the remake, into a performer whose husband, Ben (James Stewart), has forced her into a professional retirement that has become a clear source of tension within the marriage.

While Hitchcock repeatedly expressed his contempt for films that were "photographs of people talking," anyone with even a cursory awareness of his work will recognize that the films themselves are up to something more complicated than a simple pursuit of "pure film" (Truffaut 61, 283). For a start, the films are filled with long dialogue scenes, perhaps never so relentlessly as in the period between 1954 and 1960. *Rear Window*, a film that is so often celebrated for its cinematic nature, is composed almost entirely of one dialogue sequence after another. *The Trouble with Harry* is virtually a series of extended conversations. *The Man Who Knew Too Much*, *Vertigo*, and *North by Northwest*, for all of their accomplished montage, are also heavy on talk. However, the dialogue sequences in these three latter films are not purely expository but are notable for their visual and dramatic tension, causing these sequences to be no less rewarding on repeat viewings than the films' more obvious montage set pieces, such as the Albert Hall sequence in *The Man Who Knew Too Much* or the crop dusting sequence in *North by Northwest*.

The concentrated power of the dialogue scenes in these films no doubt represents the distillation of years of filmmaking. But more immediately, I would argue that it was the experience of directing the film version of Frederick Knott's 1952 play *Dial "M" for Murder* in 1954 that prepared Hitchcock for the expressive blocking and staging in the films that followed. In explaining his techniques in handling the film adaptation of this play, Hitchcock told Truffaut that he wanted to avoid the conventional mistake most films make in "opening up" such material for the screen. For Hitchcock, what cinematic adaptations of theatrical texts too often ignore is that "the basic quality of any play is precisely its confinement within the proscenium" (Truffaut 212). *Rope* (1948), an earlier theatrical adaptation also not "opened up," anticipated these possibilities for expressive confinement. But the confinement in *Rope* is complicated by other challenges the film sets itself. Most notable in this regard is what Hitchcock later dismissively referred to as the "stunt" (Truffaut 179) of building the film upon one extended take after another. Through these long takes, the film attempts to convey a sense not only of real time unfolding but of deductions and interpretations also unfolding as party guests speculate on the non-appearance of David, a major character murdered by the two hosts just before the party begins.

Hitchcock's interest in the mobile long take in his late-forties films, begun hesitantly in *Notorious* (1946) and *The Paradine Case* (1947) before reaching extreme proportions in *Rope* and *Under Capricorn* (1949), was consistent with the work of a number of other Hollywood filmmakers of the period: George Cukor, Vincente Minnelli, Max Ophuls, Edmund Goulding, Robert Siodmak, Orson Welles, and Preminger (as well as Kenji Mizoguchi in Japan). But in *Rope* and *Under Capricorn* Hitchcock seems under external pressure, as if the forties fashion for long takes and the mobile camera has created in him a desire to produce the ultimate examples of this trend. For all of the masterful technique on display in these two films, Hitchcock's actors sometimes give the impression of being locked into a visual conception in which the camera, pushed to extreme levels of duration and mobile intricacy, overrides virtually all other concerns. Both the rhythms of the camera and the rhythms of the actors as they move in relation to one another are unnaturally slowed down, as camera and actors attempt to synchronize with one another. Hence the slightly drugged, woozy feeling both films have.

"I could just as well have shot the whole film in a telephone booth," Hitchcock said of *Dial M for Murder* (Truffaut 213). The complicated mobile frames of *Rope* and *Under Capricorn* are replaced in this film by an extremely tight focusing of the mise-en-scène. Almost the entire film is built around the extraordinary tension that can arise through the apparently slightest gesture and the most insignificant item of décor, with cuts and shifts of an actor's position within the frame producing unexpected effects in relation to the mise-en-scène. In an essay that directly followed his review of *The Man Who Knew Too Much*, Godard argued that "montage is above all an integral part of the *mise en scène*" and that staging relates above all to matters of space whereas editing relates to matters of time (39). I am less certain that Hitchcock himself would always have made such a distinction. Certainly the eccentricities of *Rope* and *Under Capricorn* show evidence that for Hitchcock staging, particularly in relation to the long take, may also address matters of cinematic time. This miraculous integration of the temporal and the spatial in *Dial M for Murder*, in which editing and staging are fully of a piece with one another, increasingly marks Hitchcock's approach, particularly in relation to the exploration of confined spaces.

"You might say that a filmmaker can use a telephone booth pretty much in the same way a novelist uses a blank piece of paper," Hitchcock said about *Dial M for Murder* (Truffaut 213). To use a blank piece of paper is also to start metaphorically clean, simplifying and purifying one's technique. In the film immediately after this, *Rear Window*, the scale of the setting of the previous film (a small one-bedroom flat) is reduced even further to a cramped studio apartment; and the injured tennis star of *Dial M for Murder*, walking hesitantly about with a cane, becomes the injured photographer L.B. Jefferies (James Stewart), confined to a wheelchair. To varying degrees, such figures increasingly populate Hitchcock's cinema. In *Vertigo*, the acrophobia of Scottie Ferguson (James Stewart) makes the very act of walking up and down a flight of stairs potentially traumatic. The result is a film in which, in sequence after sequence, sitting, standing, moving about a room become agonizingly, expressively slow and pointed, as in the first sequence between Scottie and Midge (Barbara Bel Geddes) in her apartment, the first sequence between Scottie and Gavin Elster (Tom Helmore) in Elster's office, the scene in which Pop Leibel (Konstantin Shayne) recounts the Carlotta Valdes story to Scottie and Midge in his bookstore, and the first extended dialogue between Scottie and Madeleine (Kim Novak) in his apartment after he has "rescued" her from San Francisco Bay. Each of these is remarkable for its compressed intensity in its use of the mobile frame as well as its costuming and décor, everything arrived at through a meticulous process of detail after detail, cut after cut, slowly building toward its ultimate effect. Bravura camera movements do not disappear during this period: the elaborate cranes around the courtyard at the beginning and end of *Rear Window*, for example, or the crane quickly pulling back from Scottie at the bar at Ernie's in *Vertigo* as he literally cranes his neck to look at Madeleine across the restaurant. But such movements are integrated into a more wide-ranging approach to mise-en-scène than in the more single-minded experimentation of *Rope* and *Under Capricorn*.

Throughout this period, we find Hitchcock returning to the possibilities of staging and cutting within the most limited of spaces. The extended kissing sequence between Roger Thornhill (Cary Grant) and Eve Kendall (Eva Marie Saint) in *North by Northwest* is clearly working within the framework already established by the kissing sequence between T.R. Devlin (Cary Grant) and Alicia Huberman (Ingrid Bergman) in *Notorious*. In the earlier sequence the camera focuses tightly on Grant and Bergman as they kiss and he talks on the phone in a continuous two-shot that moves them from the terrace of her apartment, into the living room, and over to the door as they say goodbye. The sense of enclosure that the viewer feels here is bound up with the extremely tight framing of the actors. But all this is taking place within an environment that is otherwise fairly spacious. In *North by Northwest*, Hitchcock not only places his two lovers in a train compartment but backs them against a wall as they kiss. The long take and mobile camera are abandoned here in favor of more standard alternations between master shot and over-the-shoulder shot/reverse shots. But this kissing sequence is no less impressive than the earlier one. In stripping the décor to the bare essentials, Hitchcock gives the compartment an unexpected intensity. Writing in 1954, Bazin would refer to the tension Hitchcock was able to create within his mise-en-scène, a tension equally dramatic and plastic, in which "it is always a question of creating in the mise-en-scène, starting from the scenario, but mainly by the expressionism of the framing, the lighting, or the relation of the characters to the décor, an essential instability of the image" (*Cruelty* 153). About two minutes into the sequence, the actors, in a surprising move in the master shot, twice roll against the wall toward the camera as they continue to kiss and converse. "The train's a little unsteady," Roger tells Eve. "Who isn't?" is her rhetorical response. Here Hitchcock does not move his camera to follow his actors but instead has the actors move toward the camera so that a sense of infinitesimal development in terms of composition and movement occurs within the master shot.

But the sequence also achieves much of its power through the handling of gesture. In fact, one could argue that our eyes are even more strongly drawn to the movements of the hands of Grant and Saint than to the act of kissing itself: the way Saint slowly slides her right hand and then her left up Grant's chest as her left hand then begins to play with his ear, and the way Grant's hands come around to the back of her head and lightly hold it on her line, "Maybe you're planning to murder me tonight," his palms almost flat against her hair. These gestures achieve a strong erotic dimension while carrying the slightest undercurrent of violence. Although Hitchcock had long understood the expressive possibilities of gesture, these are films in which the integration of gesture within the larger dynamics of the mise-en-scène reaches a very high expressive level.

The silent-era influence in Hitchcock of using large and small objects to play with scale – the gun firing into the camera near the end of *Spellbound* (1945), the poisoned coffee cup in *Notorious* – significantly declines now. As the forties fashion for the gothic that could comfortably allow for Hitchcock's use of these devices gradually begins to fade, Hitchcock's work reflects this shift. During the fifties, even while continuing to create tension and visual interest through props, Hitchcock begins to give more sustained attention to the naturalistic use of these props with a far less forceful underlining of effects that emphasize them. Much of this shift undoubtedly reflects the influence of various postwar realisms and their investments in increasingly naturalistic dramatic and performance styles, styles that nevertheless continue to be combined, deliberately or not, with more artificial and melodramatic approaches. In Hitchcock, even the more persistent uses of objects one finds across his body of work, such as the literal exchange of the object or its transformation from the benign to the violent and menacing, are downplayed. Jefferies's backscratcher in *Rear Window*, for example, while used inventively by James Stewart throughout the film, remains just a backscratcher. By contrast, the pre-Columbian figurine that contains microfilm in *North by Northwest* feels close to parody in its evocation of the fraught objects more traditionally pressed into espionage.

In *The Man Who Knew Too Much*, gestures and objects become not simply expressive tools for the actors but a structuring element to the film on both a large and small scale. Ben McKenna is a surgeon, and his hands become emblems of his displacement as he is traveling with his family in Morocco. In the sequence set in an Arab restaurant, he finds himself, unlike his wife and their impromptu dinner companions, the Draytons, unable to master the local custom of eating chicken with the thumb and first two fingers of the right hand as the left hand rests in the lap. The sight of the McKennas' original dinner date, Louis Bernard (Daniel Gelin), arriving at the restaurant with a beautiful woman after Bernard had lied to them about his social obligations for the evening, prompts a furious Ben to rip a piece of the chicken apart with both hands, causing a waiter's consternation at the sight of this action. In his review of this film, Godard writes of Hitchcock's more recent tendency to stress "with such fierce irony the ridiculousness of the most natural, everyday gestures" (38).

Far less everyday is the following sequence set in the market square as Bernard, disguised as an Arab and with a knife in his back, staggers and then falls toward Ben. As he falls to the ground, Ben's inadequate gesture of reaching out to hold up Bernard leaves Ben's hands stained by the brown make-up Bernard has been using on his face. Hitchcock emphasizes this staining through two close shots, one of Bernard falling as Ben's hands accidentally wipe a portion of the stain from Bernard's face and the other Ben's point-of-view shot as he looks at his stained hands, Bernard on the ground just below them. Such gestures are scarcely everyday in either their movements or their implications, and Hitchcock's fascination with the stained hand (repeated in his following film, *The Wrong Man*, when Henry Fonda's Christopher Emanuel Balestrero is fingerprinted) can be read in symbolic or figurative ways. However, what is most interesting here is how Hitchcock builds up to this moment of the staining by first drawing attention to McKenna's hands within more everyday contexts so that the symbolic and the figurative emerge out of the everyday.

If Hitchcock was such a central figure for the auteurists in the 1950s, at least some of their interest is traceable to their concern with both the real and everyday and the artificial and constructed. Hitchcock was certainly not the only filmmaker whose work lent itself to such concerns, but his films from this period explored this matter in highly varied and complex ways. At the heart of this fascination is the paradox of cinematic realism itself, one that, in the critical commentary of the period, was articulated most influentially by Bazin. Godard's review of *The Wrong Man* is immersed in such paradoxes, even as Bazin himself remained skeptical of Hitchcock's ultimate value. For Godard, *The Wrong Man* is a "lesson in *mise en scène* every foot of the way" (50) in which this mise-en-scène's "neo-realist notations" are connected to the most profound type of revelation about the world. It is not so much gesture in this film as the face that interests Godard, the manner in which Henry Fonda will engage in a "contraction of the eyelids" as he closes them (51) or the manner in which a "searching attention to the passage of time" occurs through Hitchcock's close-ups of Fonda and Vera Miles: "We are watching the most fantastic of adventures because we are watching the most perfect, the most exemplary, of documentaries" (49).

In reviewing *Vertigo*, Rohmer would write that the first half hour of the film could be seen as "a kind of documentary on the urban setting of San Francisco" (168) while also noting that the film was otherwise "bathed in a fairytale atmosphere" (170). In these documentary fairytales, we repeatedly find a meticulous attention to verisimilitude in the mise-en-scène co-existing with blatant artifice. The courtyard of *Rear Window* and the décor of the individual apartments are miraculously detailed in the service of realism even though the entire setting has clearly been constructed in the studio. *The Man Who Knew Too Much, Vertigo,* and *North by Northwest* alternate between the location work that is fundamental to much of postwar cinema and expressive, extremely obvious rear projection and matte work. (*The Trouble with Harry*, by contrast, is remarkable for its integration of location and studio work, a seamlessness entirely fitting for that film's extremely ironic utopia.) "I try to achieve the quality of imperfection," Hitchcock enigmatically told Bazin. Bazin took the statement to reference Hitchcock's interest in maintaining a "margin for liberty, imprecision and, shall we say, humor" that often went against the grain of the formal and "technical perfection" of much of American cinema (*Cruelty* 149). But such imperfection may also have to do with allowing for, if not encouraging, this dialogue between documentary and fiction, the real and the artificial, the theatrical and the cinematic. What such a dialogue potentially creates is a mise-en-scène capable of producing these "notations," these contingent, revelatory moments that strike at the heart of the cinema's indexical power.

Hitchcock refers to the immobilized protagonist of *Rear Window*, looking out from his apartment window while we then see what he sees and how he reacts to it, as "the purest expression of a cinematic idea" (Truffaut 214). The idea in this case is bound up with editing – in particular, the point-of-view, shot/reverse-shot formation – and with the issues of interpretation (the protagonist's as well as the spectator's) that arise from the organization of these shots. "Cutting on a look," writes Godard, "is almost the definition of montage, its supreme ambition as well as its submission to *mise en scène*" (39). But the staging within individual shots and across entire sequences may be no less "cinematic" than the montage. In any film, the movements of the actors are always being shaped and mediated by the intervention of the camera. This relationship between actor and camera is never, except at its most mediocre and inexpressive level, a neutral process, a "photograph" of someone talking.

Throughout the films following *Dial M for Murder* the Hitchcock so gifted in finding ways to stage scenes in a flamboyant manner is succeeded by a Hitchcock seeking to refine the ways in which most of the major directors of the period approach the question of staging. In *Beyond a Reasonable Doubt* (1956), Lang repeatedly tracks into and away from his actors as a method of reframing, sometimes following their movements, sometimes reframing based entirely on his own intervention. Such devices rarely occur in Hitchcock at this time. In *The Trouble with Harry*, the long dialogue scenes are staged with the utmost simplicity, the actors alternating between sitting and standing as they exchange pages of dialogue, sometimes in static shot/reverse shots, sometimes simply facing one another within a single two-shot and talking. Whereas in the late forties Hitchcock attempts to compete with the trend toward long-take, mobile frame shooting, by the mid-1950s he begins to react against it even though the trend itself does not show any signs of abating. In fact, in the period surrounding *Rear Window* we find some of the most superb instances of complex, long take and mobile camerawork the cinema had yet achieved: Preminger with *Carmen Jones* (1954) and *River of No Return* (1954), Ophuls with *Lola Montès* (1955), Mizoguchi with *Sansho the Bailiff* (1954), Minnelli with *Brigadoon* (1954) and *The Cobweb* (1955), and Cukor with *A Star is Born* (1954).

These filmmakers are able to create large-scale environments in which the staging unfolds in a fluid, virtuosic manner, the characters and situations often linked through the choreography of camera and actors. Preminger's *The Man with the Golden Arm* (1955) is, like *Rear Window*, shot entirely on studio-constructed sets representing a large American urban space (New York in Hitchcock's film, Chicago in Preminger's), and both films feature important characters confined to wheelchairs. But the wife's disability in the Preminger film is a false one, assumed by her in order to tie the male protagonist even further to her in his guilt. Throughout the film, Preminger's camera glides within and across his studio sets or suddenly tracks in an arc-like fashion as his actors likewise move intricately, the camera perpetually framing and reframing as the actors move left or right, enter or exit the frame, or move from the rear of the shot to its foreground. Hitchcock, by contrast, keeps most of the major characters in *Rear Window* boxed within a single apartment, looking out at other small apartment spaces, and the film maintains its strict adherence to Jefferies's physical distance from the various actions and apartments across the courtyard, our full views of the décor of the apartments frustrated even further by the use of window and door frames to restrict full access.

At the same time, this restriction of space can create an extraordinarily focused exploration of the possibilities of staging. When Lisa (Grace Kelly) comes to Jefferies's apartment, intending to stay the night, a visit also marked by a visit from Jefferies's police detective friend, Doyle (Wendell Corey), there is none of the bravura of *Rope*. What we have instead is arguably a more subtle and complex exercise in moving actors within the frame in a way that articulates the larger narrative and thematic issues at stake within the sequence. From the moment Lisa walks into the apartment, and over the course of nearly two dozen camera setups, Hitchcock explores a number of possibilities for placing his actors within the setting and then having them move and gesture in inventive ways. Jeff's comparative immobility is contrasted with the ways in which first Lisa and later Doyle move about the apartment.

Lisa insinuates herself into the space, turning on lights while removing gloves and hat, moving from one side of Jeff's wheelchair to the other in an intimate manner as she excitedly discusses the Thorwald murder. The alternations in her standing, moving, or sitting – first in Jeff's lap, then across his massage table – create a set of visual contrasts between background and foreground, movement and stasis, horizontal and vertical that embody and display the tense, erotic dynamic between the two.

Doyle's entrance produces another set of problems as he likewise moves about the space. Doyle's skepticism about Thorwald's guilt introduces a discordant element. His movements are more foreshortened than Lisa's and more often inter-rupted by point-of-view and shot/reverse shots as he talks to Jeff. Lisa's presenta-tion of the brandy to Jeff and Doyle as she joins them in a drink allows Hitchcock to introduce several subtle but ingenious two- and three-shots of the characters as they discuss the Thorwald case. Doyle repeatedly breaks the three-shot compositions as he moves away from Jeff and Lisa, putting into play an alternation of isolated shots of Doyle and two-shots of Jeff and Lisa, as well as additional three-shots as Jeff and Lisa move toward a reluctant Doyle while the couple unsuccessfully attempts to convince him of Thorwald's guilt. The alternation of these shots expresses the shifting of power in terms of persuasion and resistance. The handling of the brandy snifters by all three of the actors, who constantly swirl the snifters in order to warm the drink, constitutes a major point of visual interest. These drinks never assume any direct relationship to the narrative and yet create enormous tension, as though the repressed anger among these three polite characters is being displaced onto the gentle but ominous gesture of the warming. As Doyle gets up to leave and pointedly expresses his skepticism about Thorwald's guilt, he takes a large swallow of the brandy but spills some of it down his front. This may well have been an accident on the part of Wendell Corey that Hitchcock left in the film, although Corey does have a line ("I'm not much for snifters") to acknowledge the slip. But it is this ambiguous relation between accident and intent that gives the gesture its force, its "quality of imperfection," as though a bit of extra-cinematic "real life" has spilled over into the meticulous mise-en-scène.

Earlier in the film, when Lisa disappears into the kitchen to make coffee and pour brandy, the film does not show us this activity, even though it would involve only the tiniest violation of the film's formal conceit of focalizing the perception of events through Jeff. (We are periodically shown events outside of Jeff's consciousness in the film, but only when he has fallen asleep; other characters' point-of-view shots will be introduced only when Jeff is in the room.) Instead, the film sets itself an even greater challenge than is conventionally necessary in terms of creating visual interest through confinement. Compare *Rear Window* with an earlier experiment in a single setting, *Lifeboat* (1944). Once Hitchcock has given himself the challenge of confinement in the earlier film, his cutting and framing repeatedly open up the space of the boat so that it seems elastic, adjusting its scale in relation to various dramatic needs. Even in the films from *Rear Window* on, Hitchcock cannot resist the occasional "cheat" shot in which rooms suddenly gain a few feet of extra space through the camera being placed where a wall or window would logically be. (*The Wrong Man* has several examples along these lines.) Nevertheless, it is clear that the fascination during this period is increasingly directed toward an exploration of the expressive infinite within the finite. (If *To Catch a Thief* seems such a comparatively "lightweight" film in the midst of so many bold experiments, it is most likely because the film never gives itself these kinds of challenges in terms of space and movement.) In *Rear Window*, shortly before she goes into the kitchen, Lisa shows Jeff the contents of her small overnight case: a nightgown and a pair of slippers. "Compact," she says of the bag, "but ample enough," a fitting description of not only the object Lisa is holding but also of the interior spaces of many of these films and of the figures who move within them.

Drawing Rooms

In the films between *Rear Window* and *Psycho*, the professions of the protagonists are most often associated with the production of images. Jefferies is a photographer, and one of his neighbors is an abstract sculptor. In *The Trouble with Harry*, Sam Marlowe (John Forsythe) is a painter. In *Vertigo*, Midge's "first love" is painting. Roger Thornhill is an advertising executive and Eve Kendall an industrial designer. Moreover, the décor of these films is sometimes littered with images. Jefferies's photographs are scattered across his apartment. In *The Trouble with Harry*, the seafaring artifacts Captain Wiles (Edmund Gwenn) has collected fill the space of his tiny home. Midge's sketches surround her workspace. All of these interior spaces are cluttered like store window displays while simultaneously defining character – an approach to décor that obsesses Minnelli throughout this period. Moreover, costuming increasingly is actively worked into the dramatic action, becoming subject matter as much as decorative matter. The narrative of *The Man Who Knew Too Much* is set into motion when the young son of the McKennas (Christopher Olsen) accidentally pulls the veil from a Moslem woman on a Moroccan bus, causing an uproar that requires the introduction of Louis Bernard into the lives of the McKennas. But the veil itself also lays the foundation for the various conflicts of culture and gender that lie at the heart of the film. Lisa works as a buyer in the fashion industry, and Midge makes her living as a fashion sketch artist. In both instances, fashion is worked into the very fabric of the film as a whole. Lisa's insight into women's fashion leads her to surmise that Mrs. Thorwald could not possibly have left town without the "basic equipment" of jewelry and makeup. The transformation of Judy into Madeleine in the last third of *Vertigo* is essentially a fashion makeover, as Scottie's fetish for Madeleine's clothes, shoes, and hairstyle is meticulously recreated by Scottie even as such a makeover also functions as a striptease in reverse. For Hitchcock, sexual arousal occurs through dressing rather than undressing a woman (Truffaut 244).

And so we have all these mobile frames, all this elegant choreography of bodies and gestures. But if the notion of Hitchcock as a director fanatically attached to his storyboards is something of a myth, it is nevertheless also clear that his cinema is one in which the image quite often remains an image, seized, drawn, stilled. This sense of Hitchcock's graphic as well as mobile framing may account for the ways in which our eyes will often gravitate toward paintings that hang on interior walls as though they somehow hold clues to the larger puzzle of the film: the landscapes in the library of the Townsend estate in *North by Northwest*, the portraits in the gallery in *Vertigo*. Even if no profound revelation occurs through such a pursuit, these paintings manage to insinuate themselves deeply into the visual texture of the film. There is a sequence in *The Wrong Man* in which Manny Balestrero, falsely accused of robbing an insurance company, is twice asked by dictating police detectives to recreate the note given to the teller in the holdup. In both cases,

Manny makes the same mistake, writing the word "draw" when he hears one of the detectives say "drawer." It is a fatal slip on Manny's part but an interesting "slip" in relation to Hitchcock. For all of the importance of décor and the human figure in Hitchcock, the films retain a strongly graphic dimension, as though they also wish to be seen and experienced as images that are drawn. The most obvious instance of this ambiguity is Hitchcock's ongoing fascination with matte work. Purely in terms of technique, the mattes in *Vertigo* and *North by Northwest* – the bell tower at the mission in the former film, the entrance to the lobby of the United Nations in the latter – are of an extraordinarily high expressive level. But because such work is so often used in combination with live action, there is an almost constant sense of a painted image insinuating itself into the realm of this live action. The Saul Bass credit sequences for *Vertigo* and *North by Northwest* likewise operate on the principle of graphic design working in tandem with live action.

In and of itself, there is nothing new about such a tension in Hitchcock's body of work. What is new is the clarity with which the matter is enacted during this period. That Hitchcock's characters are increasingly artists during the fifties should hardly be surprising given the postwar fascination with such figures, a fascination fully present in its cinema. The cinema of this period is not only one in which the influence of realism and documentary increasingly manifests itself in the image; it is also one in which the image is increasingly influenced by things drawn or painted. (We see this tendency in the realm of documentaries on artists as well, as in Alain Resnais's early 16mm shorts or, most famously, Henri-Georges Clouzot's 1956 *Le mystère Picasso*, the latter a film that particularly fascinated Bazin.) In their films during this period Minnelli, Mizoguchi, Douglas Sirk, Roberto Rossellini, Luchino Visconti, and Michael Powell often create a mise-en-scène in which the image evokes the painterly or in which the film will overtly cite a specific painter or painting. Bazin's writings on Jean Renoir are not simply concerned with the ways in which such films as *The River* (1951) and *French Can Can* (1954) suggest the world of Impressionism. Bazin also addresses the manner in which the theatrical and decorative limits of the traditional picture frame, already being dissolved in Impressionist painting, are finding their logical extensions in the cinema to which he was so attracted. *French Can Can* "is like a painting which exists in time and has an interior development" (Bazin, *Renoir* 131); in *The River* Renoir discovers (in a typical Bazin argument) "the true nature of the screen, which is not so much that it frames the image but that it masks out what lies outside it" (*Renoir* 107). This is not, however, Hitchcock's conception of the image. Hitchcock needs something else, a frame with a graphic clarity to its composition, immediately readable so that it acquires an individual interest and autonomy while also forming part of a montage structure. Renoir's concern with the out-of-frame (or, at least Bazin's reading of Renoir in this regard) is too fluid and imprecise for Hitchcock. Hitchcock *needs* the frame, even if each cut simultaneously destroys our sense of it.

At the same time as the cinema more self-consciously adopts a painterly impulse, we may also speak of an increased importance of the animated image as it spills over into live action. The entrance of the animation director Frank Tashlin into live-action cinema during the 1950s is key here. Tashlin never completely forsakes his roots in animation, often treating his mise-en-scène and the human figures within it as an elastic, cartoon-like element, as in *Artists and Models* (1955), which casts Jerry Lewis and Dean Martin as artists and Dorothy Malone as the author and illustrator of a controversial comic book. (The film also contains a brief parody and citation of *Rear Window*.) Hitchcock, who is not working within the realm of farce and caricature, never subjects his human figures to the cartoon-like extremes of a Tashlin. But in the dream sequence the painter John Ferren designed for *Vertigo*, Madeleine's bouquet is represented as a drawing in which the petals loosen themselves from their arrangement and, in a startling development, fly outwards, like an image from Walt Disney's *Fantasia* (1940). The boldness of this device, with its evocation of Weimar art cinema (one may be reminded, in particular, of the intrusion of abstract graphic imagery into some of Lang's silent films) courts audience laughter. But what is principally fascinating about this moment is Hitchcock's need to make use of animation here, as though the concrete tools of mise-en-scène can no longer supply the film with adequate expressive resources.

Krohn has shown that during the production of *Strangers on a Train* (1951), the work of the cartoonists Milton Caniff and Charles Addams was used as research (119). Caniff had expressed his admiration for the visual sharpness and dramatic form of Hitchcock's films several years earlier (44), and Hitchcock's reciprocal interest is most likely traceable to the montage-like boldness and graphic clarity of Caniff's panels, whereas his admiration for Addams is doubtless based on Addams's emphasis on the comic incongruity, in each single *New Yorker* cartoon, between the ghoulish and the everyday. *The Trouble with Harry* is at times close to the spirit of Addams, even though its visual style does not particularly resemble that of Addams's drawings. (Hitchcock used another *New Yorker* cartoonist, Saul Steinberg, to design the childlike credits, which culminate with a drawing of Harry's corpse, surrounded by bucolic images of the natural world.) In *North by Northwest*, Thornhill refers to the sight of Eve, Vandamm (James Mason), and Leonard (Martin Landau), all three of them attempting to maintain their elegant poise while assembled together at an auction, as "a picture only Charles Addams could draw."

Throughout this period, Hitchcock frequently presents the literal act of drawing or painting, as in the attention given to Marlowe's need to sketch the portrait of the dead Harry, or the first sequence between Scottie and Midge, during which Midge works at her drawing table. A contrasting example, the Louis Bernard murder sequence in *The Man Who Knew Too Much,* is even more interesting. As the disguised Bernard runs through the streets, attempting to get away form his eventual assassins, he bumps into a man carrying a bucket of blue fabric dye. The dye spills into the street as Bernard falls, staining his hands and white outfit. The dye was part of an aborted narrative idea built around blue footprints that Bernard would have left behind, allowing his assassins to follow and catch up with him. In the final version, the blue dye is, as Truffaut put it, "mystifying" (229). But perhaps not. In the film as it now stands, the blue stain becomes a variation on the brown makeup on Bernard's face, makeup that leaves its own traces on McKenna's hands. These blue and brown stains evoke both the world of mise-en-scène, the artifice of makeup and costuming, and the world of painting through their evocation of the physical properties of paint. In *Lust for Life*, Minnelli's 1956 biopic, the paint that Vincent Van Gogh (Kirk Douglas) uses often functions as virtually a physical, tangible object within the mise-en-scène. And in much of *The River*, color likewise assumes tangible form, as dye, as makeup, as powder. In *The Man Who Knew Too Much*, the blue dye assumes a similar function. The failure of the dye to perform its original narrative purpose allows it to assume a far more evocative role, becoming the raw material both of painting and of mise-en-scène.

If filmmakers repeatedly invoke the world of painting and drawing in the cinema of this period, that may be because they wish to resist the possible limitations of mise-en-scène's ties to the decorative and theatrical. "I would like to believe," Rohmer wrote in 1956, "that the two conceptions, that of the painter and that of the filmmaker, are not irreconcilable" (70). Nevertheless, we find filmmakers of this period drawn back to the tools of mise-en-scène, back to the concrete, the staged, the theatrical, as though unable to ultimately resolve what it means to create an inherently cinematic image. For Hitchcock, *Psycho* will take up many of the issues discussed here and carry them to a new level.

Private Traps

Let us begin at the beginning. Saul Bass's credit sequence for *Psycho* is, unlike those he designed for *Vertigo* and *North by Northwest*, purely graphic in nature and avoids the interplay of live action and graphic motifs found in the credits for his two prior Hitchcock films. Within the context of Bass's body of work, this is not a singular moment. Most of his credit sequences for Preminger, for example, were based on this kind of purely graphic play, with minimal or no integration of live action. But there is a slight difference with *Psycho*. Here Bass constructs his credits on an alternating set of horizontal and vertical lines that rapidly enter the frame, carrying the credits with them, pausing for a moment as the credits are displayed (with the lettering sometimes broken up in a zigzagging fashion, a type of visual analogue to psychosis), and then just as rapidly exiting the frame. We find a similar idea in Bass's work for *The Man with the Golden Arm*, in which a set of thick white lines dance about the frame, sometimes horizontally stacked, sometimes leaning against each other in a vertical fashion. But in the Preminger film, these lines eventually come together at the close of the sequence in order to form an arm. In *Psycho*, on the other hand, the graphic contrasts never coalesce into a representational image. As the last set of vertical lines disappear out of the frame, we dissolve into a live-action panning shot of the Phoenix skyline, with Bass-designed lettering establishing location and time entering the frame from right and left. The camera executes a series of pans and cranes (linked through dissolves) down toward the window of the hotel room where Marion Crane (Janet Leigh) and Sam Loomis (John Gavin) have just finished having sex.

The last of the vertical lines of the credits over Phoenix could be seen as loosely corresponding to the verticality of this urban skyline. But the effect is considerably muted in comparison with a similar idea in the credits for *North by Northwest* in which that film's linkage of crisscrossing lines eventually gives way to the skyscrapers of Madison Avenue. What is most significant in this opening of *Psycho* is twofold. The credits prepare us for the importance of the rigorous attention the film pays to visual contrasts between what Hitchcock later referred to as the elements of "our composition: a vertical block and a horizontal block" (Truffaut 269) and create at the same time an atmosphere of violence not through representational images but through an abstract visual play with compositional forms. The sense of aggression is reinforced by the aggression of Bernard Herrmann's all-strings score, conducted at a very rapid tempo.

Much has been written about *Psycho*'s historical importance; its low-budget, multi-camera, television-style shooting method; its experiments with narrative form and spectator identification; and its emergence on the international film scene at a time when the classical methods of the traditional Hollywood system were being challenged on an unprecedented scale by various filmmakers and film movements throughout Europe, Asia, and the United States. *Psycho* seemed to be of a piece with these developments rather than a throwback, both low-budget exploitation shocker and art film. The nature of the film's production methods and indeed the film's entire aesthetic is of a lean, rigorous, and violent stripping down of the elements of Hitchcock's cinema, becoming both the culmination of the films of this period and their negation. "Audiences like *Psycho*," Godard stated in a 1965 interview, "because they think Hitchcock is telling them a story" (223). They *think* Hitchcock is telling them a story. If Hitchcock's statements to Truffaut are to be wholly believed, it is not the story or characters that were the motivating and driving force for the film. Instead, it was the possibility of a play with cinematic form, a "pure film" that "belongs to film-makers" (Truffaut 283). Part of this process, however, is a deliberate deadening and abstracting of the film's mise-en-scène, indeed of the film's entire environment.

If the Hitchcock films of the mid- to late-1950s so often extract their expressive mise-en-scène out of very small spaces, *Psycho* pushes this idea even further. Sequences set in interiors are marked by even less physical movement of the actors than in any of the six films leading up to *Psycho*. In the frequently analyzed parlor sequence between Marion and Norman Bates (Anthony Perkins), visual and dramatic tension is created not by attempts at complex blocking and staging of action, as in *Rear Window* or *Vertigo*. The only time the actors walk here is when they enter the parlor at the beginning of the sequence and exit it at the end. Instead, Marion and Norman sit and face one another as they speak, in a series of shot/reverse shots, the editing patterns forming part of the film's attempted linkage of these two figures. Much has been made of this mirroring of Marion and Norman as well as of the bird motifs in the décor of the office (and in Marion's room in the motel), motifs that draw symbolic parallels between these two characters in relation to birds, angels, and flight. The stuffed birds and paintings of angels that dominate the décor here make for an uncanny spectacle because they are images of stilled movement and describe a space wherein Marion and Norman themselves give the appearance of being just one step away from a similarly deathly rigor.

Their movements and gestures here are slight. For the first two-thirds of the exchange, Marion's gestures (first shown in a medium shot and then in a medium close-up as she sits on a couch across from Norman) are largely confined to cautiously eating a piece of bread; for the final third of the sequence, in a close-up, she hugs herself, leaning her body into the left-center of the frame in what could be seen as a self-protective gesture against the increasingly dark narrative that Norman recites to her about his mother's psychosis, a narrative she finds both terrifying and spellbinding. For the first third of this sequence, Norman is shown in a slightly low-angled medium close-up, nervously rubbing his hands together and only breaking from this pattern once in order to touch a stuffed bird perched on a dresser behind him. By the time Hitchcock has cut to the second setup on him, an even more low-angled medium close-up, this one framing him in three-quarter profile, Norman's hands are hidden below the frame. He raises these hands only once, soon after the first cut to this new angle. As he discusses the possibility of resisting his mother's power, he spreads both palms out in a gesture of imaginary defiance, before lowering them again. The second camera setup on him renders him both more powerless (he is moved to far right of the shot as the stuffed owls mounted above his head on either side of him appear to be capable of swooping down on him, as though in retribution for being stuffed) and more sinister and violent, in that he is also linked with these birds.

In the absence of much of anything in the way of conventional blocking and staging, one of the most forceful visual and dramatic ideas throughout this conversation is Norman's periodic movement of leaning his body forward in order to emphasize something, and then sitting all the way back in his chair again. He does this in each of the three camera setups and in each instance the act of leaning forward increasingly carries an implied aggression toward Marion. This effect is particularly strong in the final setup, in which Norman's forward movement creates a terrifying close view of his face, framed by the two birds on the dresser behind him. Norman never moves out of his chair. But each cut and the reframing that accompanies it creates an impression of Norman insidiously moving closer to Marion. Hitchcock refrains from using even the slightest camera movement into Norman for an effect in any of these shots. Instead, it is the expressive weight of the human figure, filmed from three distinct angles and engaged in the slightest of movements, that is capable of connoting the greatest amount of violence and psychosis.

Throughout *Psycho*, it is as though traditional problems of staging hold little interest for Hitchcock. His recent tendency toward economy and distillation in mise-en-scène is now put into the service of a film in which almost every space (motel rooms, offices, automobiles) is defined by its confinement and in which the human figure can barely move at all. It is no longer a question (as it was in *Rear Window*) of having a stationary protagonist around whom mobile figures elegantly circulate. Instead, the movements of virtually everyone in this film are somehow curtailed. "We're all in our private traps, clamped in them," Norman tells Marion. Within such a context, we may see Marion's trajectory – from hotel room to office to tiny bedroom to automobile to motel room to shower and, finally, locked up in the trunk of a car, the car submerged in a swamp – as the terrifyingly logical culmination of the film's treatment of the human figure in relation to space. Writing on *Psycho* for *Cahiers du cinéma*, Jean Douchet would argue that the image of Marion, "wrapped in a transparent shower curtain, really becomes what she represented for us, a form" (Douchet 21).

The central compositional motifs of the film (the vertical and horizontal blocks) find their most explicit articulation in the contrast between the Bates Motel, spread out at the foot of a hill, and the gothic, "California gingerbread" (Truffaut 269) architecture of the Bates home that sits at the top of that hill. But this does not come to represent the contrast between a dead past and a vital present. Instead, both the modern and the gothic in *Psycho* are decaying and embalmed, two dead worlds. In the traditional gothic, architecture and décor are often abundant with symbolic meanings. *Psycho* undoubtedly traffics in some of this symbolic visual language. But it does so in a manner that suggests this treatment of space and décor has reached the state of expressive ossification and cliché. When Marion's sister, Lila (Vera Miles), explores the Bates home, she picks up a book in the attic whose binding is so clean and severe that it contains no indication of the book's title or contents. She opens the book but Hitchcock never shows us its contents, never shows us what Lila sees. It is an object poised between significance and complete irrelevance. "He only half-existed to begin with" is the evaluation that the psychiatrist (Simon Oakland) offers of Norman in the film's penultimate sequence. We may consequently speak of a cinematic "half existence" going on in *Psycho*. Marion works for a real estate office whose fundamental concern is not with architecture and décor as aesthetic objects but with the purely pragmatic buying and selling of property. The walls of this office are covered either with photographs of properties for sale or images of desert landscapes devoid of any human figures. The only character in the film who comes close to being a creator is Norman. But his "art" is taxidermy and the images he creates are those of death.

Consequently, gesture, like all physical movement in the film, becomes not only more controlled and restricted than ever in Hitchcock. It is also more desperate, an agonized and most often failed grasp at something, epitomized by Marion's pathetic clawing of the tiles in the shower and then reaching toward the shower curtain (and the camera) after she has been repeatedly stabbed, her final gestures before dying. "We scratch and claw," Norman tells Marion in the parlor sequence immediately before this murder, "but only at the air, only at each other. And for all of it, we never budge an inch." The folded bronze hands that are such an essential element of the décor to Mrs. Bates's tomblike bedroom provide the most condensed image in the entire film of this notion of stilled or frozen gesture. In the film's final sequence, we see Norman in his prison cell, the surroundings reduced to a virtually abstract gray and white. As the camera slowly tracks toward Norman, the window to his left disappears from view and the effect created gradually is of a space with no floors or walls, a space with no beginning or end, a world in which décor has been effectively removed. But Norman himself, fully succumbing here to his psychosis and "becoming" his mother, is refusing to perform even the simple gesture of swatting a fly from his hand, as though this would serve as proof of his innocence in relation to the murders.

"In general," Douchet writes, "in Hitchcock the human body is the first vehicle" (23). In the first of the films of the period being covered in this essay, *Rear Window*, we have a protagonist, L.B. Jefferies, who is confined to a wheelchair. This confined, restricted body nevertheless serves as a pre-condition for the extremely active mental state of Jefferies and for the intense relationship the film sets up between eyes that see and a mind that puts into motion a narrative and its accompanying mise-en-scène. In *Psycho*, the central "character" confined to a chair is the rotting corpse of Mrs. Bates, and it is not an apartment courtyard filled with a vast stratum of human existence that she looks out upon. Instead, her view is that of the blank wall of a fruit cellar, her eyes hollowed-out sockets. In *Psycho*, the human body is both the first and the last vehicle of the film. It is the mise-en-scène's point of origin but also its point of negation, a body ripped apart or transfixed in the negative in order to create a "pure film" that is finally beyond mise-en-scène.

Works Cited

Bazin, André. *Jean Renoir*. Ed. François Truffaut. Trans. W.W. Halsey II and William H. Simon. New York: Dell, 1973.

Bazin, André. "On the *Politique des Auteurs*." Trans. Peter Graham. Hillier 248–59.

Bazin, André. *The Cinema of Cruelty, from Buñuel to Hitchcock*. Ed. François Truffaut. Trans. Sabine d'Estrée, with Tiffany Fliss. New York: Seaver, 1982.

Caniff, Milton. *Conversations*. Ed. Robert C. Harvey. UP of Mississippi, 2002.

Douchet, Jean. "Hitch and His Public." Trans. Verena Andermatt Conley. *A Hitchcock Reader*. Second ed. Ed. Marshall Deutelbaum and Leland Poague. Chichester, UK: Wiley-Blackwell, 2009. 17–24.

Godard, Jean-Luc. *Godard on Godard*. Trans. and ed. Tom Milne. London: Secker and Warburg, 1972.

Hillier, Jim, ed. *Cahiers du Cinéma, the 1950s: Neo-Realism, Hollywood, New Wave*. Cambridge: Harvard UP, 1985.

Krohn, Bill. *Hitchcock at Work*. London: Phaidon, 2000.

Rivette, Jacques. "The Essential." Trans. Liz Heron. Hillier 132–35.

Rohmer, Eric. "Of Taste and Colors". 1956. *The Taste for Beauty*. Trans. Carol Volk. Cambridge UP, 1989. 67–70.

Truffaut, François, with the collaboration of Helen G. Scott. *Hitchcock*. Rev. ed. New York: Simon and Schuster, 1984.

19

The Universal Hitchcock

William Rothman

After *North by Northwest* (1959) and *Psycho* (1960), Hitchcock was riding high, artistically and commercially. He hoped to follow up these successes by wooing Grace Kelly out of retirement and pairing her with Cary Grant in an adaptation of Winston Graham's 1961 novel, *Marnie*. When the people of Monaco expressed their wish that their Princess Grace not return to the screen (and certainly not as a psychologically disturbed kleptomaniac), Hitchcock signed Tippi Hedren, a model his wife had noticed in a television commercial, to an exclusive contract. Deferring *Marnie*, he chose to make *The Birds* (1963), based on a Daphne du Maurier story, his first film at his new home, Universal. Thanks to his friend Lew Wasserman, Hitchcock enjoyed an ownership share in the company, and it seemed an ideal setup for the last chapter of his career. Yet his years at Universal were filled with disappointments.

Production of *The Birds* was challenging. Perhaps too challenging. "Not enough story, too many birds," recalled Hitchcock (Chandler 272). On the whole, I find the bird attacks, heavily reliant on special effects, to be the least effective parts of a film that contains no lack of remarkable sequences. Far more impressive, in its quiet way, is the passage in which Melanie (Tippi Hedren) sits smoking on a schoolyard bench while waiting for Annie to send the children out for recess. We see, as she does not, that crows, one by one, are gathering. But when her eyes follow a single bird and the camera follows her gaze to a framing that reveals crows occupying every possible perch on the once bare monkey bars, we are as shocked as she is. We are struck by their sheer number, but also by their eerie stillness, which continues until they fly off as one, in a sonic burst of beating wings, just as the children leave the schoolroom. The following attack on the schoolchildren – an impressive montage that was far more challenging, technically – is something of an anticlimax.

A Companion to Alfred Hitchcock, First Edition. Edited by Thomas Leitch and Leland Poague.
© 2011 Thomas Leitch and Leland Poague. Published 2011 by Blackwell Publishing Ltd.

And yet the single greatest shot in *The Birds* is the one that posed the greatest technical challenge: the "bird's eye" view of the gas station in flames, the camera occupying an impossible position alongside the soaring seagulls, as if a bird of their feather. The birds that oversee this world are not gods or devils, this shot implies. They are just birds. Creatures of their appetites, they are *in* nature. This they have in common with human beings. But they are not human. Ordinarily, when the camera calls attention to itself in a Hitchcock film, the film's author is showing his hand, declaring that he is the God who presides over the world of the film. This shot is different. Here, the camera, surveying its domain at a great height, unafraid of falling, seems beyond the control, or ken, of a merely human author.

No doubt emboldened and challenged by the films of François Truffaut, Jean-Luc Godard, and his other young French admirers, Hitchcock experiments in *The Birds* with cinematic devices that at times give it the feel of a New Wave film. He uses jump cuts, for example, to dramatize the moment at which Mitch's mother, Lydia (Jessica Tandy), discovers the body of a neighboring farmer, his eyes pecked out. *The Birds*'s narrative, too, has something of the feel of a European art film. I am thinking, for example, of the film's refusal to attribute to the birds a clear motive for their violent attacks on Bodega Bay's human inhabitants (although the film repeatedly intimates that the birds have a special bond with Melanie); its refusal to provide a "scientific" explanation (on the order of the radioactive fallout science fiction films of the 1950s were wont to cite as causing the strange metamorphosis of ants, mantises, and the like) for the birds' changed behavior (although the film keeps reminding us of the outrages against nature humans unthinkingly perform every day); and, especially, its unresolved conclusion, from which the conventional "The End" is pointedly withheld. The conclusion refuses to assure us that Melanie, in shock after the birds' mass assault on her, will ever be herself again. Mitch (Rod Taylor) does all he can, but no man has the power to rescue her. And the film's ending refuses to assure us that the birds, having ravaged Melanie, have returned to normal, that the cluster of attacks was a localized occurrence, and that humans can go on, as before, giving little thought to our fine feathered friends – or to each other.

Hitchcock's films are always open to allegorical interpretation, but *The Birds* is unique in openly presenting itself *as* an allegory. How can we not ask ourselves what the birds represent, and what they really want (a variant of Freud's famous question about what women want)? And the question "What do the birds want?" takes on special urgency because the ending precludes our taking the projected world to be a "private island" (to invoke a phrase Marion Crane [Janet Leigh] uses in *Psycho*), a place we can go, separated from our world by the safety curtain of the movie screen, to escape the conditions of our existence. Like Michelangelo Antonioni's *L'avventura* (1960), *The Birds* implies that it means more than it literally says, that it is *profound*. In the film's open striving for profundity, too, I sense that Hitchcock was emboldened and challenged by films like *Jules and Jim* (François Truffaut, 1962) and *Vivre sa vie* (Jean-Luc Godard, 1962) made by the young French cineastes who first recognized that his work had always had unsuspected depths.

What I value most in *The Birds*, however, are the down-to-earth moments – such as virtually every moment Jessica Tandy or Suzanne Pleshette is on the screen – that reveal its characters' humanity with an emotional directness unprecedented in Hitchcock's work. The camera, caucusing with the birds, not the humans, achieves a separation from the film's merely human author. Detached from Hitchcock's ego, at least rhetorically, the camera is freed from the rancor (to borrow a word from Nietzsche) that afflicts all human beings. Acknowledging that he is the servant, not the master, of the art of "pure cinema" (Bogdanovich 476), Hitchcock no longer claims possession of the camera, no longer strives to impose his will over the film's world. In *The Birds*, the camera goes a little mad sometimes, to paraphrase Norman Bates (Anthony Perkins), who knows whereof he speaks. But it is also freed, as never before in Hitchcock's work, to allow its human subjects the freedom to reveal their own humanity. I am not suggesting that in earlier Hitchcock films the humanity of the camera's subjects was never movingly revealed. In *Rebecca* (1940), for example, when the Joan Fontaine character descends Manderley's grand staircase in that gown and preposterous hat, her face reveals to us what she is trying to hide from Maxim (Laurence Olivier), her desperate wish for acceptance. And in *Vertigo* (1958), when Scottie (James Stewart) points out to Midge (Barbara Bel Geddes) that she was the one who broke off their engagement, a cut to a high angle close-up reveals to us the pain she is trying to hide. At such moments, however, the camera exposes the vulnerability of subjects who are trying to mask, not reveal, their thoughts and feelings. But when Mitch's ex-girlfriend Annie Hayworth (Suzanne Pleshette) offers friendly advice to Melanie, her rival, or when Lydia confides her fears to Melanie, what the camera captures is what they openly reveal of themselves.

Lydia revises humanely the stereotype of the monstrous mother that plays a central (if ambiguous) role in *Psycho*. Annie characterizes Lydia as fearing that Melanie will give her son the love she has never given him. No woman played by Jessica Tandy can be a monster, but Annie understands Lydia's fear to be the source of Mitch's resistance to committing himself to another woman. Annie's characterization rings true, and she offers it as a friendly gesture. Lydia is so different from her own mother that Melanie is genuinely interested in understanding her. Melanie and Lydia both recognize that they are competing for Mitch's love. Yet they develop respect, even affection, for each other.

In the course of *The Birds*, we come to appreciate Mitch for his honorable efforts to juggle his career and his responsibilities toward his family, which require him to help raise his younger sister and minister to the emotional needs of a mother who sees him as a sorry substitute for her dead husband. Lydia makes it clear that she doesn't see her son as his father's equal when she blurts out "If only your father were here!" as the family braces for the birds' attack on their home. Rod Taylor isn't Cary Grant's equal, either. No one is. Taylor's rugged features, physical strength, and thoughtful demeanor would make him a plausible romantic hero, if a somewhat wooden and humorless one. In *Notorious* (1946) and

North by Northwest, a character played by Cary Grant rescues the woman he loves, but only after his actions helped place her in jeopardy. But in the world of *The Birds,* no man has the power to rescue Melanie, if only because no man has placed her in danger in the first place. Mitch does everything that can reasonably be asked of a man to keep his mother and young sister – and Melanie – safe. Nonetheless, he is asleep, exhausted by his labors, when a rustling awakens Melanie. Whether in reality or in her dream, the birds are calling her. As if entranced, she quietly ascends the stairs toward the bedroom of Cathy Brenner (Veronica Cartwright), even as everyone in the theater is silently screaming, "No! Don't go up there!"

Melanie must sense, as we do, that the birds are waiting for her. Why else would they be calling to her? But why have they singled her out? Why does only she hear the call? Why does she answer it? In the shooting script, according to Bill Krohn, Melanie locks herself in the bird-invaded bedroom to protect the Brenner family, as if inspired by Annie's earlier self-sacrifice in protecting Cathy from the birds (250). At the end of F.W. Murnau's *Nosferatu* (1922), a woman an intertitle characterizes as "pure of heart" offers her life's blood to the vampire, thus putting an end to the contagion of death. Without denying the nobility of her gesture, Murnau's camera reveals that this woman, for all her purity of heart, desires the vampire no less than the vampire desires her. In offering her body to the birds' beaks and talons, Melanie, too, however pure of heart, is driven by desire – a desire she believes no man can satisfy. What does she desire of the birds? What does she believe they desire of her? Whether it resides inside her world or outside it, she feels the presence of a mysterious "something" that rules the roost in her world. Something that is not human – is it the camera? – is calling seductively to Melanie, knowing she will be drawn by this call, the way in *Vertigo* Madeleine, or, rather, Judy (Kim Novak), is drawn to the spirit of Carlotta Valdes, a mother forever searching for the daughter cruelly taken from her. Whatever she may imagine to be calling to her, whatever she may imagine to be about to happen, Melanie is utterly unprepared for the sustained ferocity of the birds' attack.

It is only from a scene that Hitchcock took the unusual step of writing himself – he inserted it into Evan Hunter's screenplay although Hunter thought it was stupid and added nothing to the film (Hunter 70) – that we learn that Melanie's mother had deserted the family when her daughter was a young girl. In Hitchcock's mind, but evidently not in Hunter's, it is Melanie's defining feature that she is a woman who has never known a mother's love. In the scene Hitchcock wrote, Melanie asks Mitch, in light of his own difficult relationship with his mother, whether it might be better not to know the love of a mother. He answers thoughtfully, after a long pause, that it is better to be loved. Although *The Birds* dwells more on Mitch's fatherless family than Melanie's motherless one, Hitchcock's interest in Melanie is deeper than his interest in Mitch. Her knowledge that her mother abandoned her gives Melanie a personal interest in learning something about a mother's love that her own experience has not taught her.

Hitchcock's scene illuminates Melanie's otherwise inexplicable decision to walk into that attic bedroom, though in the film she blocks the door by accident while trying to fend off the attacking birds. It is as if Melanie had heard in the birds' quiet call the voice of the mother whose love she had never known. The scene also underscores the thought-provoking, emotionally resonant connections between *Vertigo* and *The Birds*, and between *The Birds* and *Marnie* (1964). Carlotta Valdes does not abandon her daughter; in a bygone world in which men had the power and freedom to do such things, her daughter was taken from her. Marnie's mother (Louise Latham), too, never abandons her daughter, despite being pressured to put her up for adoption. Yet Marnie grows to adulthood not knowing that her mother loved her, hence not knowing from her own experience whether a mother's love is worth having. These are Hitchcock's most heartfelt films, and it is this question that binds them together. When midway through the film Marnie (Tippi Hedren) asks her mother point blank why she never gave her love, it is among the most moving moments in all of Hitchcock's cinema.

When Hitchcock released *The Birds*, many viewers were disappointed that it did not out-*Psycho Psycho*. The world of *The Birds* is not loveless, like the world of *Psycho*. Nor does love fall victim, as in *Vertigo*, to a villain's sinister machinations. In *The Birds*, there are no villains. All the characters are presented with sympathy. The birds kill, but they are not murderers. Far more than earlier Hitchcock films, *The Birds* conveys the sense that it is human nature to hunger for love. Yet love is so painful, our appetite for it so voracious, that avoiding love is also human nature. In *North by Northwest*, Hitchcock grants Roger and Eve their wishes; Roger rescues Eve, their romantic dreams come true, and love triumphs. In *The Birds,* the characters we care about are too scarred by life, too wounded, for their romantic dreams to have survived intact. The only character who still harbors romantic dreams is Cathy, Mitch's young sister, who insists, when the little family group is about to drive off into an unknown, perilous future, that they not abandon the lovebirds that were Melanie's birthday gift to her. In his capacity as author, Hitchcock still possesses the power he has always had to preside over "accidents" within the projected world. He still possesses the power to grant wishes, to make a character's dreams (or nightmares) "magically" come true. But in a world where human beings no longer harbor romantic dreams or believe in them, no longer know how to wish or what they really wish for, Hitchcock's powers as author no longer guarantee that he can reward with love characters who are worthy of love.

Few viewers at the time appreciated the interest *The Birds* accords the relationship of Melanie and Mitch, Annie's moving death, or the haunting, haunted figure of Mitch's mother. Fewer still were prepared for the emotional directness and intensity, the heroic courage and the unbearable sadness of *Marnie*. In *Marnie*, as in *The Birds*, there are no murderous villains. Lil Mainwaring (Diane Baker) and especially mean-spirited Sidney Strutt (Martin Gabel) treat Marnie unkindly, but they are not villains. And Marnie's mother, who causes her daughter inestimable grief, is a tragic figure, not a monster. Her most poignant moment comes at the end of the film, when her daughter finally acknowledges that her mother has always loved her, and her mother responds by saying, "You were the only thing in this world I ever did love." Still, she holds back from fully expressing her love for Marnie, first, by referring to her not as a person but a thing (a thing she acquired when she let a boy have sex with her in exchange for his sweater); second, by not even now caressing Marnie, although her hand is poised just above her daughter's golden hair; third, by forcing Marnie to pull back from physical contact by saying, as she has several times in the film, "Get up, Marnie, you're aching my leg." As Mark (Sean Connery) leads Marnie out of the house, promising they'll return someday soon, she looks back at her mother, sitting alone in the gathering darkness, and says, "Goodbye." "Goodbye," her mother answers. Not holding back from expressing his love for this woman who is incapable of expressing the love she feels, Hitchcock's camera stays on her as Mark and Marnie exit. Only then, when Marnie is gone, does she add, in a loving voice her daughter will never hear, "... Sugarpop."

I refer to the camera here as "Hitchcock's" because in *Marnie* Hitchcock breaks with *The Birds*'s rhetorical strategy of identifying the camera with the awesome, mysterious "something" that the birds represent, a "something" that is specifically not human. *Marnie* is not a return, however, to Hitchcock's earlier practice of using the camera to declare that he is the all-powerful God who holds sway over the world of the film. It is Hitchcock's own humanity, as well as that of the characters in the film, that shines through. But this means that he must acknowledge, at least rhetorically, that there are limits to his power, that the camera has its own appetites, and awesome powers that no merely human author can claim for his or her own.

Today, *Marnie* has become a touchstone. I find Robin Wood's judgment to be only slightly hyperbolic when he says, "If you don't like *Marnie*, you don't really like Hitchcock. I would go further than that and say if you don't love *Marnie*, you don't really love cinema" (quoted in Bouzereau). *Marnie* is far from perfect, but it moves me more deeply than any other Hitchcock film. Unfortunately, the film's reputation has been doubly tarnished by Donald Spoto's claim (475–76) that toward the end of production there was an incident in Tippi Hedren's trailer in which Hitchcock made an inappropriate advance on his star, or at least propositioned her, and by the oft-repeated assertion that the film is flawed by an offensive rape sequence. I will not speculate here on what, if anything, transpired in private between director and star. But I do feel the need to explain why what transpires between Mark and Marnie that fateful night during their honeymoon cruise from hell cannot unprejudicially be called a rape.

The sequence in question is preceded by a passage that takes place the first night of the cruise. When Mark finally goads Marnie into emerging from the bathroom, he strokes her face, ready to kiss it, when she suddenly pulls away, shouting, "I can't! I can't! I can't!" Mark responds to her earnest "If you touch me again, I'll die!" by promising not to. "I'll feel the same way tomorrow, and the day after, and the day after that," she says, her gesture of turning away from him at this moment underscoring the ambiguity as to whether this is a prediction or a vow. "Let's try at least to be kind to each other," says Mark. "Kind!" she retorts, almost choking on the word. "If that's too much, I'll be kind to you, and you'll be polite to me." "You won't?" "I won't," he echoes her, as she had echoed him. Without irony, he adds, "I give you my word." She looks at him. "Well, let's try and get some rest. How about it? You, in your little bed over there. Me, light years away, in mine here." Recognizing that this sarcastic tone is not a disavowal of his vow, she says, sincerely, "Thank you." Mark quietly goes to bed, and there is an eloquent cut to a long shot of Marnie, melancholy in her solitude, followed by a slow fade to black.

The alleged rape takes place after Mark and Marnie have been on the boat for so many days – and nights – that their tempers are frayed. Looking up from his book, he watches Marnie go into the bedroom, slamming the door behind her. He barges in. "If you don't want to go to bed, please get out." "But I do want to go to bed, Marnie. I very much want to go to bed." She cries out "No!" (in what the flashback will reveal, in retrospect, to be her "little girl" voice).

Marnie is still staring at Mark, unhinged by what she sees in his eyes, when there is a cut to his grimly determined face. His eyes growing colder, he angrily purses his lips and, with a violently abrupt movement, raises his arms and – this is conveyed mostly by sound – yanks her nightgown from her shoulders. From her shocked face Hitchcock cuts to the gown falling past Marnie's now bare legs; cuts back to her face, wide-eyed and expressionless; then cuts back to Mark. He is mortified by what he sees in her face, the shattered look his own behavior – uncannily fulfilling her prophecy – has caused. For Mark – and for Hitchcock too, I take it – this is a moment of self-recognition. With sincerity he says, "I'm sorry, Marnie," acknowledging that he has broken his promise to be kind, as she had predicted he would. Never again will he be unkind to her. Never again will she say no to him.

Gently, Mark covers Marnie's naked shoulders, cradles her head in his hands, and begins tenderly kissing her face. That she offers no resistance seems to gives him grounds for believing she has learned to trust him, and gives us grounds for believing that. He goes on to make love to her, not rape her. She does not resist, even seems to move on her own accord to the bed, though backward, as if in a trance. And yet a cut reveals – a revelation hidden from Mark – that Marnie's eyes are wide open and staring fixedly, though not accusingly, in the direction of the camera. The sequence ends, mysteriously, with the camera, moving on its own, panning from her tearfully rigid face on the pillow to a porthole as circular as the camera lens itself, a frame-within-the-frame within which we see a vision of the sky and the calm sea – a vision as inhumanly still, and as timeless, as the sleep of death itself.

When Evan Hunter, whom Hitchcock originally hired to adapt Winston Graham's novel, urged Hitchcock to cut this scene and wrote an alternative for Hitchcock's consideration, Hitchcock peremptorily replaced him with Jay Presson Allen. The scene, as Allen wrote it, proves Hunter wrong. But the fact that so many critics, misreading the scene, continue to believe, wrongly, that it is offensive reveals the magnitude of the risk that Hitchcock, for the sake of his art, felt compelled to take.

Jay Presson Allen believes, as I do, that Mark thinks he is making love to Marnie, not raping her. But she also believes that Marnie thinks she is being raped (Allen 20). The fact that Marnie goes on to attempt suicide may seem to confirm that she feels violated. But it is also possible that her suicide attempt is less a serious effort to kill herself, or even a cry for help, than a conscious or unconscious effort to prove her point – to Mark? to herself? – that she will die if he touches her again. Her blank stare at the camera leaves open the possibility that she desires him no less than he desires her, but finds herself unwilling or unable to express her desire, the way her mother is unwilling or unable to express her love. It also leaves open the possibility that Marnie, in her deeply disturbed state, *wants* Mark to force himself on her, not because she wants to be raped – no woman does – but because she feels so desperate a need to prove to herself that all men are brutes and that he is no different from other men. But Marnie also feels the need to prove this to Mark. That it is a matter of life and death to her to win her argument with Mark (or perhaps, at a deeper level, to *lose* her argument) proves that she knows in her heart that he is not a brute, that she is denying the real feelings she has for him (as her mother denies the love she really feels). If this is the case – and if it is also the case that Mark loves Marnie and believes he is making love to her, not raping her, and also believes that making love will help her to awaken to her real feelings – is he raping her? I believe not.

Why am I defending Mark? Because I take him at his word when he says, "It seems to be my misfortune to have fallen in love with a thief and a liar." He is declaring his love. To be sure, he is declaring his love in Sean Connery's insouciant, almost sarcastic, manner. But Marnie acknowledges that he means what he says when she replies, "Oh, Mark, if you love me you'll let me go." When she adds, "I'm not like other people. I know what I am," he replies, "I doubt that you do, Marnie. In any event, we'll just have to deal with whatever it is that you are." Then he adds, "Whatever you are, I love you. It's horrible, I know, but I do love you." "You don't love me," she retorts with rising anger, not so much doubting his sincerity as frustrated by *his* lack of self-knowledge: "I'm just something you've *caught*." Mark may seem to be confirming Marnie's charge when he says, at once amused by the absurd situation and moved by the depth of Marnie's feeling and his own, "That's right. You are. And I've caught something really wild this time, haven't I? I've trapped you and caught you and by God I'm going to keep you!" But Mark is reaffirming, not disavowing, his love, I believe. He is "taking on the responsibility" for her, as he puts it, because he loves her. The film asks us to believe that Mark *knows* he loves Marnie. Indeed, it asks us to believe, in retrospect, that he already loved her, perhaps without knowing it, when he proposed marriage in the least conventionally romantic proposal scene in the history of cinema (if not of the human race).

Mark's understanding of what his love for Marnie entails – what "love" means, what the responsibility is that he is taking on, and what its limits are – deepens as

Marnie unfolds. It will bring him to the point at which, by knocking on the wall, he opens the floodgates and releases the memory that Marnie had been repressing at a terrible psychic cost. But once Marnie's memory begins to flood in, Mark accepts that all he should do, all he can do, is to act as a midwife, as it were, by asking questions whenever needed to prod her to describe what she is seeing and hearing. Over this scene, Mark has no control. By distorting the perspective, Hitchcock finds a way, technically, to shoot this scene that is happening at once in the past and the present, and at once inside and outside Marnie's mind, in a way that sets it apart visually from everything that comes before and after it in the film. It is as if this scene were filmed not by a camera responsive to Hitchcock's human feelings, but by a camera over which he has no control. This "flashback," if that is what it is, culminates in the child Marnie, recognizing what she has done or what has been done to her, staring in horror directly at the camera as the screen becomes awash in blood. Mark cannot see what we are seeing. And we cannot see what the child Marnie is seeing, what the adult Marnie is seeing in her "mind's eye." What does Marnie see when she is looking with horror directly at the camera? What she sees, I take it, is what Judy sees at the end of *Vertigo* when a shadowy figure, emerging from the blackness, so frightens her that she steps back and falls, or jumps, to her death. She sees what Lydia's friend sees before his eyes are pecked out. She sees what we see, at the end of *Psycho*, when a death's head appears superimposed over Norman Bates's grinning face.

When Marnie snaps out of her trancelike state, she is changed, She has learned, as we have, that as a child she had killed one of her mother's johns. Mark sums up the moral, as he understands it: "It's time to have a little compassion for yourself." Not a bad moral, as morals go. And yet, Mark has not seen what we have seen. And we have not seen what Marnie has seen. Having looked death in the face, Marnie now knows the value of love. She knows now that she is capable of loving Mark. She knows that she is worthy of Mark's love. And she knows that her mother has always loved her. She also knows that her mother has not changed, that she remains incapable of expressing her love. And Marnie knows that it is beyond her power to rescue her mother from her private trap. She does not need the children chanting "Call for the doctor, call for the nurse" to make her mindful of the fact that she and Mark can now face the future together in a hopeful spirit, but are condemned to exist within a world suffering a sickness they are powerless to cure

Reviewers savaged *Marnie*. The film's failure was a catastrophe from which Hitchcock never fully recovered. As an artist, he was never the same again. Never again would he probe so deeply into the mysteries of love and the avoidance of love. Never again would he marshal the courage to bring to the screen a woman with whom he identified so profoundly – a woman whose belief that she was not like other people, that she was different in a way that made it impossible for her longing ever to be satisfied, touched a raw nerve in Hitchcock himself.

Professionally, *Marnie*'s poor showing at the box office, following the disappointing reception of *The Birds*, put Hitchcock behind the eight ball. *Mary Rose*, which

Hitchcock commissioned Jay Presson Allen to adapt from the haunting 1920 J.M. Barrie play about a woman who escapes aging, was a project he passionately believed in. Its theme of the "private island" where we can escape our existence with others in the world resonates deeply with Hitchcock's cinema. The world on film lures us with the promise of being such a place. Had Hitchcock filmed *Mary Rose*, it would have been one of his profoundest meditations on the seductive lure of the projected world, on what we hope to gain or risk losing by heeding its call. Sadly, however, Universal vetoed the project, concerned that such a melancholy film would further diminish the box-office value of the Hitchcock brand.

With *Torn Curtain* (1966) and *Topaz* (1969), the bottom dropped out.

Hitchcock had done some of his most successful work under the aegis of David Selznick. It was by at once conforming to and subverting Selznick's dictates that he found his own *American* voice after emigrating to Hollywood from England. That he thrived on that kind of tension is clear from the personal appearances that bookended episodes of *Alfred Hitchcock Presents* in the 1950s. He relished reminding the public that his "sponsors" were tying his hands. At Universal, his hands were still tied. But his stake in the company meant that he was now in bed with his "sponsors." Wearing two hats, he couldn't simply dismiss, much less mock, Universal's growing worry that Hitchcock's art of "pure cinema," as he had practiced it, was no longer universal (to use the irresistible word), was incapable of connecting with the changed, and changing, audience.

Hitchcock was becoming an old man. And this was happening at the very moment the youth culture was in the ascendancy, the sexual revolution gaining steam, the so-called generation gap widening, the Production Code loosening its grip. In the 1950s, *Alfred Hitchcock Presents* was almost alone among network television programs in appealing to the sensibilities of those alienated young people who were marching to rock 'n' roll's different drummers. At a time when a thirtieth birthday meant one was on the wrong side of the generation gap and thus as "out of it" as Mr. Jones, of Bob Dylan's "Ballad of a Thin Man," who has no clue as to what is "happening here," how was Hitchcock, in his mid-sixties, to stay ahead of the curve, or even stay relevant? He must have realized that there was a real and growing gulf separating him even from a new generation of filmmakers, even those who aspired to emulate his work.

The stars with whom Hitchcock had collaborated so fruitfully had aged, too. Rod Taylor was fine in *The Birds,* but he was no James Stewart or Cary Grant. Sean Connery was – and is – a great star, but he so outshone Tippi Hedren that it is all but impossible to believe that his Mark is in love with her Marnie. How different the last chapter of Hitchcock's career might have been if fate – and Monaco – had allowed him to make *Marnie* with Grace Kelly and Cary Grant!

Compounding Hitchcock's problems, he lost key members of his creative team when his long-time editor George Tomasini died, his great cinematographer Robert Burks was killed in a fire, and – particularly devastating – Hitchcock and Bernard Herrmann had a traumatic falling out during the production of *Torn Curtain*.

Years earlier, Herrmann had composed music for *Psycho*'s shower murder, going against Hitchcock's explicit instruction that he wanted only natural sound. When Hitchcock heard those screeching violins, however, he recognized how greatly they enhanced the murder's impact. And yet he had not simply been wrong to have wanted no music for the sequence. He wanted the shower murder to be his ultimate demonstration of the power of the art of "pure cinema." But that was not the art to which Herrmann was dedicated. Herrmann swore allegiance to the art he called "melodram" (quoted in Smith 358), which restored to music what he felt was its rightful primacy. In the case of *Psycho*, Hitchcock allowed Herrmann to prevail, but the incident must have opened his eyes to the fact that he and his friend, whose genius was as undeniable as his own, did not ultimately share the same artistic vision.

Ignoring Universal's galling insistence that *Torn Curtain*'s music be in a style appealing to the youth audience and include a potential hit song, Herrmann composed a score in his usual musical idiom. As if spoiling for a showdown, he again composed music for a sequence – the killing of the oddly likeable Gromek (Wolfgang Kieling), who discovers that defector Michael Armstrong (Paul Newman) is a spy and thus must be stopped by Armstrong before he informs the East German authorities – that Hitchcock wanted accompanied only by natural sound. Hitchcock must have felt that Herrmann had betrayed him. Or perhaps Hitchcock had to interpret his friend's principled action *as* a betrayal in order to keep from admitting to himself that he was betraying his own art by siding with the studio. Breaking Herrmann's heart, Hitchcock jettisoned his score and commissioned John Addison – an accomplished composer, but hardly Herrmann's equal – to write a new one. With Herrmann's score, *Torn Curtain* would surely have been a film Hitchcock would have found more satisfying. But no score could have made it the critical and commercial success Hitchcock needed.

Torn Curtain's failure was inevitable, if only because Paul Newman and Julie Andrews, cast as scientists, have no chemistry with each other or with Hitchcock's camera. Hitchcock quipped to Charlotte Chandler that he should have paired Andrews, fresh from *Mary Poppins* (Robert Stevenson, 1964) and *The Sound of Music* (Robert Wise, 1965), with a "[s]inging scientist" (284). Instead, he had Newman, a gifted actor at an early peak of his stardom, but acting as if a sour stomach, not America's security, were paramount in his character's thoughts. Both Andrews and Newman are great stars who could not possibly be better in what they do well. That Hitchcock was unwilling or unable to take advantage of the singular qualities that made them stars, or to solve the script problems that Newman in particular felt were impediments to his getting "inside" his character, reveals the magnitude of Hitchcock's crisis of confidence.

Topaz has a strong opening, vivid performances in supporting roles by Roscoe Lee Browne among others, and one shot that ranks among Hitchcock's greatest. When Rico Parra (John Vernon), a Castro lieutenant, discovers that Juanita de Cordoba (Karin Dor), his lover, is having an affair with a French agent, he shoots her to death, knowing that she would otherwise be tortured. Cinematographer Jack Hildyard captures Juanita's death in a ravishing overhead shot in which, as she falls, her purple dress billows out like a spreading pool of blood, or like a rosebud opening. But the film suffers from uncharismatic stars and an unfocused screenplay with an anticlimactic ending. And the film's Cold War theme was an obstacle to winning the hearts and minds of the millions of antiwar youth inclined to view capitalist America, not communist Cuba, as the greater threat to world peace.

His confidence at a low ebb, Hitchcock sent Truffaut a detailed treatment for a new film he was contemplating, evidently seeking reassurance that it was worth making. Truffaut couches his comments in respectful language, but Hitchcock must have sensed that his friend was less than enthusiastic. Though Universal may have pulled the plug, I suspect Truffaut's lukewarm response caused Hitchcock to lose faith in the project.

The treatment was for a film, alternately called *Kaleidoscope* and *Frenzy* (not to be confused with the *Frenzy* that Hitchcock did release in 1972), that was to have been filled with shocking violence, its impact enhanced by the handheld camera Hitchcock intended to use to create a greater sense of immediacy, and by the daring device of having the film's protagonist be the serial rapist/killer – on the surface, an attractive, confident man, but really "just a little boy who can't cope with life," to quote Benn Levy (McGilligan 677), who collaborated closely with Hitchcock on the treatment. I am not sad that Hitchcock and/or Universal got cold feet and abandoned the project. It might have been taken as proof that he was a misogynist obsessed with violence to women, that he was a vile monster, or – perhaps worse for his reputation as an artist – that he was "just a little boy who couldn't cope with life."

Frenzy, far better written and acted than *Torn Curtain* or *Topaz*, is a class act. But it preserves something of the flavor of *Kaleidoscope/Frenzy*. Apart from the darkly hilarious exchanges between Chief Inspector Oxford (Alec McCowen) and his wife (Vivien Merchant), the strongest passages all revolve around violence against women. In *Frenzy*'s most grueling sequence, Bob Rusk (Barry Foster), a serial rapist/killer, visits Brenda Blaney (Barbara Leigh-Hunt), the ex-wife of the film's protagonist, Richard Blaney (Jon Finch), in the matrimonial agency she runs. Informed that her agency will not serve a man with his repulsive sexual appetites, Rusk avows that he wants *her*, that she is his kind of woman. He begins to rape her. When he comes too quickly, he is so angry and frustrated that his voice becomes strangely slurred. To borrow a phrase from Norman Bates, he is transformed before her eyes – and ours – into a "raving thing." As I wrote in *The Murderous Gaze*:

> In *The Lodger*, murder is invoked but not shown; in *Blackmail*, it takes place behind a curtain; in *Murder!*, *The Thirty-Nine Steps* and *Stage Fright*, it is still not shown; in *Psycho*, the murder in the shower is presented in a montage that withholds all views of the knife penetrating flesh; in *Torn Curtain*, with the killing of Gromek, *Blackmail*'s curtain is opened, but murder is still a theatrical scene; in *Topaz*, it is treated poetically

(a dying woman's dress, viewed from overhead, billows out like petals as she falls). Only in *Frenzy* is there a full revelation. We see the murder of Mrs. Blaney, in all its horror, from beginning to end, its presentation stripped of theater and poetry, and it is perhaps the most heartbreaking passage in Hitchcock's work.

(249–50)

Brenda believes that the rapist who is about to strangle her is not a monster, but a pathetic man driven mad by his sexual perversion and impotence. We, too, believe that Rusk cannot help doing this terrible thing, that he is "just a little boy who can't cope with life." We continue to believe this until he goes to the dead woman's desk and stands for a moment with his back to the camera. He picks up his victim's half-eaten apple and, turning slightly toward the camera, takes a hearty bite. Then he pockets the remainder and coolly departs the premises. From the moment he bites the apple, he no longer seems a tormented human being, as much a victim as his victim is. Now he has the insouciant air of one of those heartless Hitchcock villains who lack regard for human frailties – a Serpent, not an Adam.

In another of *Frenzy's* other brilliant passages, Rusk leads barmaid Babs Milligan – played by the immensely likable Anna Massey, who was so memorable in a similar role in Michael Powell's *Peeping Tom* (1960) – upstairs to his apartment. As he closes the door behind them, all background sounds fade out, his voice breaking the unnatural silence as he speaks the words that spell her doom: "You're my kind of woman." When the camera slowly pulls back from the door and down the stairs to the street below, the sounds of the city slowly fade back in. London's life goes on, oblivious of Babs's cruel fate.

This camera movement, its elegiac mood enhanced by the sound track's invocation of silence, is a tour de force. It is also a haunting and eloquent acknowledgment of the unbearable sadness of this woman's death, the utter senselessness of her murderer's cruel act. And it is an acknowledgment of the unbearable sadness of being human, the sadness inherent in the fact that we are mortals born into the world and fated to die, the sadness apart from which the art of "pure cinema" would not be possible. We do not witness this horrific scene, but can imagine it all too well, for we know Babs's death scene will be a repetition of Brenda Blaney's. We are not indifferent to Babs's fate. But our lives too go on. The camera inexorably goes on, as is its fate, to the next scene, and then the next, moving ever closer, as it must, to the film's inevitable ending.

Why do Brenda Blaney and, more heartbreakingly, Babs Milligan have to die, or rather, why do their lives have to be senselessly cut short? Their fate is in Hitchcock's hands. Why does he sign their death warrant? Not because he hates them. We feel no special affinity with Brenda. But when Rusk kills her, it is murder, plain and simple, and Hitchcock hates murderers. Babs, by contrast, is a warm, caring woman. I cannot imagine Hitchcock taking pleasure in her fate. Violence against women, in Hitchcock's films, is never justified. Babs has done nothing to make us, or Hitchcock, want her to suffer. Then why, in a world on film over which he presides, does he at least tacitly endorse her murder? Perhaps there is no other answer than that Brenda and Babs have to die to enable *Frenzy* to be born. Then what justifies the film's creation? A work of art, it has been said, is of value in and of itself. What is *Frenzy*'s value? Is there a moral purpose Hitchcock's art serves?

In David Freeman's screenplay for *The Short Night*, the film Hitchcock was preparing for production when his failing health forced him to announce his retirement (as perhaps he always knew it would), there is yet another scene that depicts an act of brutal violence against a woman. It takes place early in the story. Rosemary, a young communist described as "[s]tudious looking" (86), finds herself alone in a small apartment with Gavin Brand, 39, who has just escaped from prison, having been locked up for five years for spying for the Soviet Union. Brennan (who had helped Brand escape) and Rosemary's husband are due to return soon with a truck to spirit Brand away, ultimately to be reunited with his wife, who is living with their two young boys on a secluded island off the coast of Finland (again the "private island" theme).

When she tells Brand – with a *"hint of coquettishness,"* the screenplay specifies (86) – that she is glad to have him to herself for a moment, he looks her up and down. She explains that she wants him to tell her about the amazing things he did for the Party in East Berlin. Her studiousness notwithstanding, Hitchcock would surely have filmed Rosemary so that she would appear attractive in a way that Brenda and Babs (and even Melanie and Marnie) do not. She goes to the sink to make tea. She can feel his eyes on her back. Growing increasingly uncomfortable, she starts chattering nervously as she prepares the tea. He draws her to him and kisses her. She doesn't kiss back, but she doesn't push him away, either. She says, "Please. ... Don't. ... They'll be back very soon [. ...] You know I respect you so much. We all do." "You know how long I've been in prison?" "You'll be seeing your wife soon [. ...] She'll be so happy ..." (88). Brand strokes her breasts. "Don't. Please don't do that. They'll be back any time now." "So soft," Brand says, "It's been five years since I felt anything so soft." "Don't do that. ... Please stop. ... I'll yell out ... really I will" (89).

The screenplay communicates, clearly, the possibility that Brand, who has not been with a woman for five years, interprets Rosemary's every "No" as a "Yes." She repeatedly tells him to stop, but the reasons she gives – that the others will soon be back, that he is a married man – do not rule out the possibility that she thinks he *should* stop, thinks she *should* want him to stop, but that she really wants him to go on. She keeps saying "please," keeps saying how much she respects him, keeps appealing to the better angels of his nature. Even when she says, "I'll yell out ... really I will," she does not "yell out," leaving open the possibility that she has no real wish to do so.

As if he were waiting for an excuse to do so, the moment Rosemary threatens to "yell out," Brand squeezes her cheeks to silence her. This is the moment he reveals his murderousness – to her and to us. The violence of his gesture forces her to try desperately to "yell out." Angrily telling her to stop "babbling," he "pushes his mouth at hers, kissing her and running his hands along her body" (89).

Her struggles to keep him at bay are what turn him on, provoking more violent efforts to silence her. Everything he does to stifle her voice forces her to react in ways that arouse him more. She throws scalding tea at him; scratches his face, drawing blood; bites deep into the flesh of the hand covering her mouth. Caught up in a cycle of escalating violence, his words, too, escalate, from "Stupid cow. You'll do as I say" to "You stupid bitch. Shut up" to "What do you think of that?" to "Oh damn you to hell" when her body goes limp in his arms (89–90). He forcibly stops her from speaking, then punishes her for "babbling." He commands her to do what he says, yet gives her no choice but to struggle. He squeezes the life out of her for not shutting up, then, as she is dying, mocks her for her silence. And when he realizes she is dead, he curses her for his own frustration, and calls upon God to damn her to hell for what he himself has done.

There can be no doubt that the screenplay is condemning Brand, damning him to hell, reminding us that we must never take even the smallest step in the direction of forfeiting our humanity, the way this misogynistic rapist/murderer does. And yet, this scene as written, had Hitchcock filmed it, would surely have had a powerful erotic impact by conveying viscerally the escalating intensity of Brand's arousal, and of Rosemary's, too, as her romantic dream turns into a nightmare from which she never awakens. Our view of him squeezing the life out of her would have been the scene's climax, its "money shot." Our horror at what we were witnessing, and our arousal by it, would have been inextricably intertwined. That human beings have an appetite for violence, that killing can give us pleasure, is a dark truth about our nature. And it is a dark truth about the art of "pure cinema" that this sequence would have acknowledged, more starkly than any other in Hitchcock's cinema, even as it was arousing us.

Within the screenplay as a whole, this scene has a crucial function. The film's protagonist, Joe Bailey, is the aggrieved brother of an American CIA agent killed in the line of duty by Brand. Encouraged by the agency to seek revenge, Bailey follows the trail of Brand's wife and children from London to Finland in the hope of intercepting the traitor before he can reach the Soviet Union. As the narrative unfolds, Joe falls in love with Carla Brand. Because we know the kind of brute Brand is, we are entirely on Joe's side when he declares his love for this man's wife even as he seeks to avenge his brother at her husband's expense. The final showdown between Joe and Brand – unlike the more ambiguous showdowns between young Charlie (Teresa Wright) and her Uncle Charlie (Joseph Cotten) in *Shadow of a Doubt* (1943) and between the Americans and Willy, the German (Walter Slezak), in *Lifeboat* (1944) – is that rarity in Hitchcock films: a Manichean conflict between absolutely opposed moral forces. Hitchcock wants us to feel no ambivalence, to wish with all our heart for Joe to prevail. The film needs the scene in which Brand murders Rosemary so that we will judge, not wrongly, that Brand has forfeited his humanity, that if Joe were to kill him, it would not be an act of murder, morally speaking.

In Hitchcock's films, evil is not an occult supernatural force. Brand is not an agent of the Devil. He is a human being, not fundamentally different from Joe, from Hitchcock, or from us. Joe knows that Brand is human, just as he is, and that he himself is capable of forfeiting his humanity the way Brand has. That knowledge motivates Joe to kill Brand and gives him the power to do so. It does not make Hitchcock immoral that he finds it possible, and necessary, to show us a monstrous act of violence through the eyes of the murderer. Hitchcock is a *moral* artist. At the core of his moral vision is the paradox, the sad truth, that to keep faith with the better angels of our nature, we have to be willing to kill. But we also have to be willing to love. Is this a happier truth? Not if it is also a truth – as Hitchcock was torn between wishing to believe, for his art's sake, and wishing to deny, for the sake of humanity – that, as Oscar Wilde put it in "The Ballad of Reading Gaol" (1897): "Each man kills the thing he loves" (quoted in Hitchcock 51).

If Mark Rutland is a definitive counterexample – an exception that *disproves* the rule of Wilde's maxim about the destructiveness of love – then Joe Bailey is another. Although Joe is prepared to kill Brand if that is necessary to keep Carla safe, in the event he does not kill at all. Brand escapes, but not before Joe rescues Carla's sons at gunpoint just before reaching the Soviet border. Nonetheless, *The Short Night* revolves around killing, not loving. That is why it does not make me sad that Hitchcock never filmed the screenplay. It makes me happy – I like to think that it made him happy – that *Family Plot* (1976), not *The Short Night*, was his swan song.

Family Plot is a playful twist on *Psycho*, with its plot set in motion when elderly Julia Rainbird (Cathleen Nesbitt) tries belatedly to wipe the slate clean by granting his rightful inheritance to the nephew she forced her sister to abandon when he was a child. What she does not know is that this child murdered his adoptive parents and has grown up to be a scheming crook (William Devane) who is anything but Mr. Nice Guy. Blanche Tyler (Barbara Harris), a fake (or perhaps not so fake) medium, sets out with her boyfriend, George Lumley (Bruce Dern), to locate the wayward nephew.

With a beauty and wackiness reminiscent of Shirley MacLaine, who had made her movie debut in *The Trouble with Harry* (1955), Barbara Harris is the most delightful Hitchcock leading lady since Grace Kelly. She has real chemistry with Dern, whose George is as likeable as Blanche. Both are unglamorous, unpretentious, well-meaning, only slightly larcenous characters with whom people like us can readily identify. They are not legally married, but theirs is a true marriage. For all their bickering, they love each other. Theirs is a relationship worth having. Is it a relationship of equals? That's a judgment call. He comes to her rescue and helps keep her safe. But she possesses powers he does not.

After they have locked the villains safely away, George points out to Blanche how much more their reward would be if they somehow found the stolen diamond that is the film's MacGuffin. Suddenly, Blanche seems to go into a trance, as if this were one of her fake séances. This trance, George believes, is for real. Intrigued, he follows her up the stairs. When she pauses and slowly raises her finger to point at something, the camera follows her cue and moves in the direction she is pointing. Lo and behold, there is the stolen diamond hidden in full view in a crystal chandelier. Seeming to awaken from her trance, Blanche acts as surprised as George that she has found the diamond. He beams with pride that the woman he loved even when he believed she was a fake psychic is actually a real one. The moment this man whom she loves leaves her side, she looks directly at the camera – at us, it seems – and her face lights up in a great big grin. Then she winks.

Some commentators have taken the secret she shares with us, the secret she withholds from George, to be that she was only faking her trance, that she possesses no magical or supernatural powers at all. (She must have overheard the kidnappers say where the diamond was hidden.) But that discounts the extraordinary powers she has to possess to be able to reveal her secret directly to the camera – directly to us.

Who is this woman? She is the proverbial enigma wrapped in a mystery. She is Blanche Tyler. But how can a fictional character, a woman who has no real existence, wink at us? She is Barbara Harris. But how can an actress who as I write is almost as old as Hitchcock was when he made *Family Plot* be this vibrant young woman who, like Mary Rose, does not age with the passage of time? She is a medium through whom Hitchcock, the film's author, communicates directly to us from beyond the grave. But how can Hitchcock wink at us if he has been dead and buried for thirty years?

To us, the flickering shadows projected on the movie screen are insubstantial phantoms possessing only an illusion of life. But to the denizens of the projected world, we have no more tangible reality than any ghostly spirits. Our world is not Blanche's world. In our world, *The Short Night* and *Mary Rose* are films that might have been; not everything possible is real. But there are no "might have beens" in Blanche's world. She cannot but wink at the camera every time *Family Plot* is screened. In the world on film, nothing is possible that is not real. But this projected world does not really exist. The world on film, a world in which all possibilities are real, and all are unreal, is itself at once real and unreal. That is, the medium of film overcomes or transcends our distinction between real and unreal, between the real and the possible, between reality and fantasy. Such is the nature of the projected world. But its nature is also its magic. Or, rather, our distinction between nature and magic, between the natural and the unnatural or the supernatural, is yet another distinction the film medium overcomes or transcends.

When Blanche grins and winks at the camera, it seems she is bridging the great divide between our two worlds so as to share a secret with us. Her wink seems to cue the film's closing shot, over which the final credits roll, of the priceless stolen diamond filmed head on. And yet, this shot of the diamond is not from Blanche's literal point of view. She was winking at us, not at the diamond. That the diamond is no mere object located on her side of the divide is a secret that Hitchcock, not Blanche, is sharing with us. This twinkling diamond is a multifaceted jewel, just as *Family Plot* is. As this shot frames it, the diamond appears strikingly like an eye – an eye looking directly at the camera. Thus the shot suggests, retroactively, that the preceding shot – of Blanche winking at the camera – was from the diamond's point of view. It is as if this diamond/eye is the camera that captured her wink at us, or the projector that is at this moment beaming onto the screen the very image we are viewing. Viewer becomes viewed, viewed becomes viewer; Blanche's wink becomes the diamond's twinkle; the past becomes the present; the projected world – the "private island" that keeps this woman safe from the ravages of time even as the film that grants her eternal youth moves inexorably on to its inevitable ending – becomes the world into which we are born and in which we are fated to die. The ending of *Family Plot* shares with us the secret, or, rather, the mystery, of Hitchcock's art of "pure cinema," that the two worlds are also one. There is no such thing as a "private island." Or, rather, if we live our lives, as Hitchcock's villains do, in such a way as to try to make the world our "private island," we forfeit our humanity.

Psycho also ends with a grin at the camera. But Norman's (or is it his mother's?) grin is a murderous one. It announces that we are the butt of the film's cruel joke. Blanche's wink – or is it Barbara Harris's? or Hitchcock's? – intimates that the ending of *Family Plot,* too, may be a joke. If so, it is not a joke at our expense. And the joke is anything but cruel. Whoever or whatever this woman is, we love her. And we trust her. We know that she wishes us well. Her wink at the camera – a medium's salute to a medium – is the happiest, most heartening, most life-affirming gesture in all of Hitchcock's cinema. Whatever else it may be, it is an acknowledgment of our love for Hitchcock, of his love for us, and of his gratitude to the art of "pure cinema" for having made such a relationship possible. It is better to be loved.

Works Cited

Allen, Jay Presson. "An Interview with Jay Presson Allen." By Richard Allen. *Hitchcock Annual* (2000–01): 3–22.

Bogdanovich, Peter. *Who the Devil Made It*. New York: Knopf, 1997.

Bouzereau, Laurent dir. and prod. "The Trouble with *Marnie*." 1999. Universal Studio Home Video. Special feature included with *Marnie*. Universal, 2000. DVD.

Chandler, Charlotte. *It's Only a Movie: Alfred Hitchcock: A Personal Biography*. New York: Simon and Schuster, 2005.

Freeman, David. *The Last Days of Alfred Hitchcock: A Memoir Featuring the Screenplay of "Alfred Hitchcock's The Short Night."* Woodstock, NY: Overlook, 1984.

Hitchcock, Alfred. Interview by Ian Cameron and V.F. Perkins. *Alfred Hitchcock: Interviews*. Ed. Sidney Gottlieb. Jackson: UP of Mississippi, 2003. 44–54.

Hunter, Evan. *Me and Hitch*. London: Faber and Faber, 1997.

Krohn, Bill. *Hitchcock at Work*. London: Phaidon, 2000.

McGilligan, Patrick. *Alfred Hitchcock: A Life in Darkness and Light*. New York: HarperCollins, 2003.

Rothman, William. *Hitchcock—The Murderous Gaze*. Cambridge: Harvard UP, 1982.

Smith, Steven C. *A Heart at Fire's Center: The Life and Music of Bernard Herrmann*. Berkeley: U of California P, 1991.

Spoto, Donald. *The Dark Side of Genius: The Life of Alfred Hitchcock*. Boston: Little, Brown, 1983.

PART VI

Auteurism

20

French Hitchcock, 1945–55

James M. Vest

In the wake of World War II, Alfred Hitchcock's movies surged into French consciousness with the force of the gushing waters in *Foreign Correspondent* (1940). During the decade following the Liberation, those pictures made from 1940 to 1944 and banned under the Occupation were finally screened, interspersed with new releases, reissues, and retrospectives. Consequently, between 1945 and 1955 French audiences had access to twice as many Hitchcock films as did many of their counterparts elsewhere, including the United States.

This inundation provoked much discussion among young French cinephiles inspired by film society debates and influenced by renowned critic André Bazin. Several of them – notably Eric Rohmer, Jean-Luc Godard, Jacques Rivette, Claude Chabrol, and François Truffaut – would soon write for a new film magazine edited by Bazin, *Cahiers du cinéma*. In the late 1940s Rohmer voiced positive opinions about Hitchcock in *Cahiers*'s predecessor, *Revue du cinéma*, and other publications. Rohmer's views were seconded by Rivette but countered by Godard and others, including Bazin, who critiqued Hitchcock's films in the pages of a popular weekly devoted to cinema, *L'écran français*, and elsewhere. The *cinémanie* in which Hitchcock films old and new were shown and debated gave way to what some called *Hitchcockomanie*, an effect heightened by three films – *Rope, Under Capricorn*, and *Stage Fright* (released in America in 1948, 1949, and 1950 respectively) – that premiered in France in rapid succession over the course of a relatively few months in 1950 and 1951.

In January 1950 Hitchcock traveled to Paris for the French premiere of *Rope*. Would-be French filmmakers were attracted to the experimental, economical approach to filmmaking advocated by this successful producer-director. Critical responses to *Rope*, however, diverged wildly, ranging from laudatory to sarcastically

A Companion to Alfred Hitchcock, First Edition. Edited by Thomas Leitch and Leland Poague.
© 2011 Thomas Leitch and Leland Poague. Published 2011 by Blackwell Publishing Ltd.

dismissive.[1] *Paris-Presse* reported that *Rope* confirmed Hitchcock's place among avant-garde filmmakers, whereas *Arts* saw the commotion as a bluff that needed deflating. *Combat* called *Rope* a brilliant example of filmed theater, while *Le monde* decried the tendency in certain circles to be impressed by cinematic technique at the expense of subject matter. The leftist *Drapeau rouge* labeled *Rope* a nauseating reflection of the tragic realities of capitalism. More emphatically negative responses greeted *Under Capricorn* and *Stage Fright*, which came to Paris in September 1950 and April 1951 respectively. When *Cahiers du cinéma* began publication in spring 1951, several of its feistier young writers – including Alexandre Astruc, Rohmer, and Rivette – were primed to respond vigorously in Hitchcock's defense.

Cahiers du cinéma arose after the demise of France's premiere monthly film magazine, *Revue du cinéma*, in 1949 and of *L'écran français* in the early 1950s. *Cahiers*'s particular emphasis on Hitchcock was prompted, in part, by the opinionated stances of two newcomers to the ranks of serious film commentary: a small student publication, *Raccords*, and a larger-format newsletter, *Gazette du cinéma*. These bootstrap operations left an indelible mark on the Hitchcock debates. Cultivating an activist stance in their short lifetimes, they laid the groundwork for more tenacious film magazines, among them two that persisted into the twenty-first century, *Cahiers* and *Positif*.

Raccords started life in February 1950 as an unadorned collection of thoughts on current cinema. Cobbled together by students at Latin Quarter schools, its prime mover was Gilles Jacob, who half a century later would preside over the Cannes Film Festival. The little magazine, whose stated goal was to rejuvenate outdated principles, soon gained a reputation for pith, pluck, and promise. Among its favored directors were Charles Chaplin and John Huston, lauded for their idiosyncratic approach to cinema and apparent commitment to social issues. Negative judgments were hurled against those who seemed less radical, notably Hitchcock.

The first issue featured an article by Oswald Ducrot intriguingly titled "Après *Le Procès Paradine*, le cas Hitchcock" (24–28). Dismissing *The Paradine Case* (1947) as extravagant Hollywood fluff, Ducrot pictures Hitchcock as a "frozen" director (28), as a "case" to be prosecuted and eventually closed. Subsequent issues of *Raccords* panned *Rope* as claustrophobic and summarily condemned *Notorious* (1946) as not worth the bother. Rising paper costs that contributed to the disappearance of *L'écran français* crippled *Raccords*. By Christmas 1951 it was defunct, but hardly forgotten.

Raccords's dismissals of Hitchcock were resoundingly countered by *Gazette du cinéma*, which began publication in spring 1950. It provided news of film club and Cinémathèque screenings as well as special features, including Jean-Paul Sartre's "Le cinéma n'est pas une mauvaise idée / Cinema is Not a Bad Idea." Among its contributors were Astruc, Rivette, Rohmer, and Godard. Emphasizing formal and creative issues rather than realism, Astruc would proclaim filmmaking the most wide-ranging kind of artistic expression while Godard would appeal for politicized cinema.

In the *Gazette*'s May 1950 debut issue, Rohmer's front-page analysis of *Rope* ("Étude technique / Study in Technique") praised Hitchcock for his creative use of camera movement, light, and color. For Rohmer, these were calculated artistic touches that constituted the heart of cinema and qualified Hitchcock as a master of his medium. Subsequent issues included several favorable reflections on Hitchcock's work. Vaunting *Under Capricorn*'s symbolic power, Rivette (in the October issue) defended Hitchcock's use of long takes, which he considered appropriate to depicting periods of mounting tension and confession. In these observations he anticipated several major contentions that would become rallying cries of Hitchcock's partisans: formal ingenuity, thematic integrity, and symbolic profundity especially in terms of transferred guilt. In the *Gazette*'s fifth and final issue (November 1950), Rohmer favorably compared *Under Capricorn* to Rossellini's *Stromboli* (1950). In a memorable assertion that, once modified in light of biographical facts, would inspire numerous commentaries on Hitchcock, Rohmer contended that, just as *Stromboli* was a major Catholic film, *Under Capricorn* was thoroughly Protestant in inspiration. When Rohmer subsequently readjusted his sights to center on Hitchcock's Catholicism, the qualifier "Protestant" had only to be recast as "Jansenist" – invoking a radical preoccupation with issues of transgression and guilt – to create the central thesis of the book-length 1957 study *Hitchcock* (Paris: Editions Universitaires), which Rohmer would co-author with Chabrol, major elements of which were articulated in *Gazette du cinéma* in 1950.

Countering negative assessments in *L'écran français* and *Raccords*, the *Gazette* presented Hitchcock as a technical innovator and committed artist who effectively communicated the essential nature of cinema. Its ardent cinephiles would move to *Cahiers*, while negative views of Hitchcock would be pursued in *Positif*, a new magazine from Lyons that would perpetuate *Raccords*'s legacy. Thus a pair of evanescent publications set the stage for the two longest running and most influential French cinema magazines, largely through their opposing views concerning Hitchcock.

Lamenting the dearth of respected publications that treated cinema as art and welcomed serious film criticism, veteran film critics associated with *Revue du cinéma* – notably Bazin and Jacques Doniol-Valcroze – set about creating a new monthly magazine whose reputation would exceed all its predecessors' and whose fortunes would be intimately connected to those of Hitchcock: *Cahiers du cinéma*. In the debut issue, Astruc rhapsodized over *Rope* and *Under Capricorn* ("Au-dessous de volcan / Under the Volcano," *Cahiers* 1 [Apr. 1951]: 29–33). This inventor of the phrase "caméra-stylo" claimed Hitchcock had proved himself capable of writing cinema with the camera, with style and internal unity. Astruc noted themes of grace extended and refused, linking Hitchcock's films with metaphysics. In the next issue Astruc defended *Stage Fright*'s much maligned flashback, insisting that Hitchcock was a master artist and storyteller ("Alibis et ellipses," *Cahiers* 2 [May 1951]: 50–51). With *Cahiers*'s characteristic openness to varied points of view, Astruc's two pieces were countered in short order by others more critical of

Hitchcock, including a carefully-argued analysis by Godard ("Suprématie du sujet/ Supremacy of the Subject," *Cahiers* 10 [Mar. 1952]: 59–61). Such critiques inspired the creators of *Cahiers*'s acerbic rival, *Positif*, founded in 1952.

As self-proclaimed heir apparent to *Revue du cinéma*, *Cahiers* was pigeonholed by adversaries as too effete, too conservative, too Parisian, too Catholic, or too Hitchcockian. Its ideological counterpoint, *Positif*, originated in working-class Ciné-Clubs of Lyons and took a more proletarian tack. In his statement of purpose its editor-in-chief, Bernard Chardère, proclaimed *Positif* to be a youth-oriented magazine devoted to aggressive writing modeled on *Raccords*, whose predisposi-tions against Hitchcock it adopted. Through the writings of Georges Sadoul, Louis Séguin, and Chris Marker, *Positif* embraced Third World cinema while downplaying Hollywood directors. Its tone was caustic, and its writers often adopted the free-associative style of surrealism. In an effort to deflate what they considered *Cahiers*'s pompous arrogation of the term *auteur de films*, *Positif*'s writers used it broadly, vaunting under its banner socially committed directors including Buñuel and Huston while castigating such *Cahiers* favorites as Hitchcock.

Until the mid-1950s, *Positif* waged a campaign of dismissive silence against Hitchcock, while Sadoul and other *Positif* contributors simultaneously lambasted him in large-circulation Parisian dailies and weeklies. From 1952 through 1955 *Cahiers* offered its readers twenty-six articles on Hitchcock, but in the same period *Positif* published only one, a diatribe in which Séguin summarily dismissed *Dial M for Murder* (1954) and *Rear Window* (1954) as Jesuitical drivel and concluded that Hitchcock deserved only scorn.

In 1952 the well-established weekly *Arts* upgraded its previously weak cinema coverage and leapt into the maelstrom of Hitchcock controversy. Under new man-agement, it became *Arts-Lettres-Spectacles* and turned first to Nino Frank and Henri-François Rey, then to Bazin, and eventually to Truffaut for commentaries on current films and cinema trends.

It was in this context of expanding cinema coverage that Godard, Chabrol, Truffaut, and their contemporaries began to formalize their views in print. They quickly became involved in the Hitchcock debates, especially over issues concerning moral and metaphysical themes in his films. Such discussions became increasingly focused after the re-release in summer 1951 of *The 39 Steps* (1935) and *The Lady Vanishes* (1938). They intensified upon the French release of *Strangers on a Train* (1951) in 1952 and of *I Confess* (1953) the following year.

While French critics were honing their opinions of Hitchcock, he was exhibiting on screen his attraction to France and Francophone culture. In *Strangers on a Train* the banter of Bruno Anthony (Robert Walker) with a French-speaking couple would establish important aspects of his character and social context. Several lines in French evidence Bruno's command of the language, serving to confirm him as educated, sophisticated, privileged. That sense of cultivated distinction, and with it the emerging issue of Bruno's manipulation of social norms and façades, was underscored through the reactions of Barbara Morton (Patricia Hitchcock) to this French-speaking milieu. These features would not be lost on French observers, who would see in this film's apparently motiveless killing a representation of a nonchalant *acte gratuit*, as described by Gide and Camus.

Francophilic tendencies were given full rein in Hitchcock's next film, *I Confess*, based on a French play by Paul Bourde, under the pseudonym of Paul Anthelme, *Nos deux consciences* (1902), which emphasized conflicts of conscience deriving from a priest's dilemma upon learning, in confessional, the identity of a murderer. Scenting an appealing prospect for a growing international market, Hitchcock would produce *I Confess* himself, based on an adaptation set in Quebec, upon which both he and his wife, Alma Reville, labored, along with several other writers.

Major portions of *I Confess* were made on location because of the appeal of Quebec's scenery, ecclesiastical iconography, and French language, as well as economic and personal incentives. French Canadian actors were cast in prominent roles, and local clerics and policemen became extras. By choosing untrained performers, natural lighting, and real-life settings, Hitchcock was electing to make a film along lines recently promoted by *L'écran français* and pursuing an ideal associated with Italian neorealism, which would later inspire the French New Wave as well.

The French-speaking backdrop offered ample opportunities for incorporating Francophone motifs, including signage, place names, characters' names, and salutations. Throughout *I Confess*, spoken French was authentic and untranslated, anchoring the film in its social and linguistic context while portraying the protagonist, Abbé Michael Logan (Montgomery Clift), as a man attached to two cultures without fully belonging to either. The same might be said of Hitchcock himself, who retained his British citizenship more than a decade after his wife had become an American, who delighted in French food and wines, and who visited French-speaking lands as often as possible.

When *Strangers on a Train* opened in Paris in January 1952, Nino Frank opined in *Arts* that Hitchcock's film conveyed neither an overarching worldview nor a meaningful personal message, thus attempting an end-run around emerging auteurist theories by denying to Hitchcock the personalized vision usually attributed to an auteur. Soon thereafter Georges Charensol took up the sword in *Nouvelles littéraires* (24 Jan. 1952), lambasting those he disparagingly characterized as *Rope*-partisans while claiming that Hitchcock's insincerity and lack of psychological depth forbade esteem.

Bazin soon joined the attack in a pair of articles. In a review for *Le parisien libéré* (10 Jan. 1952), he spoke of the macabre irony exercised by Hitchcock, irony that undermined effective characterization. Bazin would grant only that Hitchcock was an exceptional technician capable of delivering the precise dosage of emotion desired at a precalculated instant who nevertheless showed the effects of constraints imposed by Hollywood's cookie-cutter approach to filmmaking. In *L'observateur*

(17 Jan. 1952), Bazin argued that Hitchcock's attachment to clever, acrobatic effects far outweighed any interest he might have in humanity.

In his March 1952 *Cahiers* article (cited above), Godard distanced himself from those given to unwavering admiration for a director whose work others accused of lacking plausibility. Comparing *Strangers on a Train* to *The 39 Steps* and *Shadow of a Doubt* (1943), he called Hitchcock's latest effort superficial, stylized fluff. Godard asserted that Hitchcock's films could contain no metaphysical subject matter because Hitchcock himself was the subject of all his films. A battle of opinions, he accurately predicted, was likely to ensue.

Rohmer weighed in with an article ("Le Soupçon/Misgiving") praising Hitchcock's handling of psychological themes in *The Lady Vanishes* (*Cahiers* 12 [May 1952]: 63–66). In Rohmer's view, Hitchcock qualified as a genius through his depiction of suspicion and his distinctively metaphysical treatment of the absurd. Rohmer pronounced *The Lodger* (1926), *Blackmail* (1929), and *The 39 Steps* brilliant portrayals of abnormal psychology and called Hitchcock one of the most original and profound of cinema's auteurs.

Notable in these critiques by Godard and Rohmer was their tendency to cite evidence from a number of Hitchcock films made years apart in support of an overarching, unifying claim. That breakthrough was facilitated by contemporaneous screenings in France of Hitchcock films from three decades. It would soon lead Godard to reconsider his position. It would also prompt several writers at *Cahiers* to develop a comparative method that would emphasize themes and images iterated across the filmmaker's career, viewed as an interrelated whole.

Adding fuel to the growing conflagration was a 1952 Hitchcock retrospective in Toulouse that featured his silent films *The Ring* (1927) and *Champagne* (1928). The event was reported by Raymond Borde and Etienne Chaumeton, who highlighted the dominance of certain themes, motifs, and physical objects, which they identified as constants in Hitchcock's work across decades. Their article ("Flash-back sur Hitchcock," *Cahiers* 17 [Nov. 1952]: 55–58) exemplified a critical stance that Rohmer subsequently labeled (in "De trois films et d'une certaine école," *Cahiers* 26 [Aug.–Sept. 1953]: 18–25) a "mode analogique" (22), which involved gathering data from numerous films for comparison. Noting drinking glasses conspicuously positioned in *Champagne*, *Suspicion* (1941), *Spellbound* (1945), *Notorious*, and *Under Capricorn*, for example, led to speculation on Hitchcock's use of such objects to concretize morally supercharged contexts. This procedure produced a coherent theory supporting claims for underlying unity across a number of films that collectively could be viewed as a cohesive corpus created by an *auteur de films*. Their observations piqued further interest in the director's lesser-known work, and their methodology would flourish for decades to inform notable turn-of-the-century studies of Hitchcock's motifs by Laurent Bourdon, Michael Walker, Tom Cohen, Richard Allen, and others.

Countering charges that the Hitchcockians represented a small, voluble coterie of young critics rebelling against Bazin, Rohmer went on the offensive. His landmark article "Of Three Films and a Certain School" reviewed claims for cinema as art that had propelled postwar discussions of film theory while it excoriated critics too blind to see the innovative character of *Under Capricorn* and *Strangers on a Train* or the value of *I Confess*. Rohmer reinforced the Hitchcockians' central claim to have discerned throughout Hitchcock's oeuvre a clear, coherent pattern connecting Hitchcock's films across the years. Rohmer articulated this dual thesis: form was ineluctably linked to content for Hitchcock, and his films consistently depicted the spiritual at odds with the material.

Several currents coalesced in 1953 as critical controversies spilled over into the popular press and converged at the Cannes Film Festival. There, two months after its American release, *I Confess* competed head-to-head with Henri-Georges Clouzot's *Le salaire de la peur/The Wages of Fear* (1953), which garnered two top awards. Many French critics ignored *I Confess* or mentioned it only in the context of also-rans. *France-Soir* lamented that it proved disappointing to those who came expecting to be frightened. In *Arts*, H.-F. Rey branded *I Confess* a celluloid monster, comparing it unfavorably with Clouzot's gripping masterpiece. Most of the French reviewers at Cannes agreed with Rey, who would continue to blast the film when it went into general release in France that summer.

In the meantime Rey penned for *Arts* (26 June 1953) an impassioned appeal to aspiring filmmakers that would have considerable impact on the Hitchcockians. Rey encouraged would-be directors to undertake experimental filming practices, following the example of Jean Cocteau, who had recently made a movie without professional actors or crew. Such a tactic could, Rey argued, reenergize French cinema.

Though avid Hitchcockians could agree with Rey on the latter point, they still resented his continued aversion to Hitchcock. Soon after *I Confess* opened in Paris in June 1953, Rey hurled more vitriol at its creator. *Arts* (3 July 1953) ran Rey's critique under the headline "Le cas Hitchcock." That article's tone and approach echoed the invective published in *Raccords* under a similar title three years earlier: Rey asserted that Hitchcock was a prolific master of technique, but nothing more, and had never been an auteur.

Other French critics soon joined forces with Rey, with greater or lesser vehemence. Among them was Bazin. In a review for *Le parisien libéré* (2 July 1953) he proclaimed *I Confess* disappointing because Hitchcock never moved beyond the cerebral to address the heart. Even more radically disposed against *I Confess* was the acerbic Georges Sadoul, who in *Lettres françaises* (2 July 1953) took *I Confess* to task for its confessional mode. Sadoul maintained that Hitchcock had once again allowed his talents to be submerged by melodrama and only rarely succeeded in creating an atmosphere that made audiences forget the unbelievable nature of the stories he recounted.

In counterbalance Doniol-Valcroze noted in *L'observateur* (16 July 1953) that, despite a cool reception at Cannes, *I Confess* enjoyed box-office success and that ardent Hitchcockians accorded it a place of honor among the works of one they considered a top-tier director with moral vision. Doniol-Valcroze detected in its visual audacity tendencies strikingly at odds with claims for spirituality. For him, the concluding scenes showed the mark of an accomplished merchant who knew how to peddle a product. Doniol-Valcroze noted preemptively that assertions of a metaphysical intention in Hitchcock's work remained to be demonstrated.

Truffaut soon raised the stakes through his earliest writings. This twenty-one-year-old cinephile, a former juvenile delinquent and dropout, expressed his opinions forcibly, disagreeing vehemently with those who suggested that *Strangers* would assure Hitchcock a place in the purgatory of bad directors with good intentions. In "Du mépris considéré / On Contempt" (*Cahiers* 28 [Nov. 1953]: 51–54), he parried, suggesting that Hitchcock qualified as a worthy example to French filmmakers. Such remarks led to the drawing of definitive battle lines. Gradually Rohmer, Rivette, and Truffaut solidified a sweeping thesis centered upon their conception of Hitchcock as an *auteur de films*, by which they meant a director who, by virtue of a uniquely personal artistic style and the will to impose it creatively, could be viewed as the unifying force behind a body of cinematic work.

By the end of 1953 the Hitchcockians' position was gathering momentum. The analogical method and the vocabulary of guilt and grace were becoming commonplace in the writings of younger *Cahiers* contributors. All that was lacking for a massed attack on Hitchcock's disparagers would be Chabrol's entry into the fray, Godard's conversion, a rousing call to arms by Truffaut, and an opportunity to test the Hitchcockians' theories on the director himself. Those were all soon to come.

Hitchcock applied lessons learned at Cannes in a series of career-redefining moves. While filming *Dial M for Murder* at Warner Bros., he was planning his next picture, his first for Paramount. Upon engaging John Michael Hayes to create a preliminary treatment and screenplay for *Rear Window*, Hitchcock set about instructing Hayes in French gastronomy, using his own wine collection as a stimulus to give authenticity to French references in his next two projects, the second of which would be set entirely in France (see DeRosa 7, 31–44, 110).

Despite *Rear Window*'s all-American source, a 1942 short story by Cornell Woolrich, references to France abounded in the adaptation scripted by Hayes. Those allusions included not only comments on fine cuisine and fashion but also references to contemporary political situations involving France. The introductory panning shots ended inside the studio apartment of L.B. Jefferies (James Stewart) with a lingering look at samples of his photographic work, including an explosion at Frenchman's Flat and the cover of a magazine with an eye-catching heading proclaiming "Paris Fashions." Juxtaposed images of violence and fashion, with France as a common point of reference, set in motion *Rear Window*'s curious blend of love and conflict, a powerful mélange reinforced in the screenplay through dialogue concerning the impending crisis in French Indochina.[2]

The affection-struggle dynamic associated with Francophone culture was concentrated in Jeff's dealings with a woman who reflected another side of France, the reigning center of haute couture and viticulture. Numerous French connections were embodied in Lisa Fremont (Grace Kelly), whose character was defined largely by her taste for French apparel, by her acquaintances bearing French names, and by her appreciation of select French wines. The theme of French fashion was developed from the moment of Lisa's arrival. Her eye-catching gown, "right off the Paris plane," held special appeal because it was Parisian and thus set her apart from others in Jeff's Greenwich Village milieu (see Street 103–04). Lisa announced that their gourmet dinner would be accompanied by a bottle of Montrachet, which she pronounced in the French manner, like a connoisseur. Throughout the following discussion that bottle and foregrounded wine glasses served collectively as a point of reference, a shared pleasure of French origin, while Lisa talked about her life in the world of Parisian imports. Her day had been punctuated by a "quick drink with Madame Dufresne – just over from Paris, with some spy reports" concerning Parisian fashion trends. The dress, the wine, and her conversation all pointed to France as a source of glamour and intrigue.

Rear Window was conceived for projection on both traditional and wide screens (Gavin 78), and as Hitchcock moved toward a new vision, optically and creatively, a major technological advance strengthened his relationship with France. While *Rear Window* was in production at Paramount in the fall of 1953, that studio was launching a new process to compete with CinemaScope: VistaVision.[3] French cinephiles, intrigued by news that VistaVision's exceptional optical clarity involved a French invention, the Angénieux lens, were delighted to learn that Hitchcock's next picture, which would exploit that new technology, was to be filmed in France.

French Hitchcockians glimpsed patterns invisible to others partly because of the many Hitchcock films available to them, partly because of a growing interest in his projects focusing on French culture, and partly because of a distinctive set of predispositions uniting technological and theoretical interests with intense personal commitment. In advancing their theories Rohmer and his colleagues invoked empirical methodology and inductive reasoning in conjunction with a keen sense of personal experience and conviction, thereby alloying conventional Cartesian paradigms with eruptions of radical existential choice. When they recorded interviews with filmmakers, or harped on the optical advantages of VistaVision, or analyzed a film in terms of geometry, the Hitchcockians were in league with Descartes. However, when they emphasized directorial independence, insisted on the potency of the gaze, or heralded the cinematic metteur-en-scène as creator and the critic as transformer, they were allied with existentialists. Exercising a productive blend of tradition and innovation, they fused aspects of Cartesianism and existentialism into a polemic that Truffaut and friends labeled *la politique des auteurs*.[4]

Truffaut's film criticism was anchored in Cartesian practices invoked with idealistic intensity. It was undergirded by detailed observations achieved by repeated viewings of films and careful data checks facilitated by his personalized cataloguing system for classifying films by directors and movements (see de

Baecque and Toubiana 32–38). Truffaut brought to his critical writings extensive moviegoing experience reinforced by a commitment to factual detail and a propensity for seeing directors as central to the cinematic enterprise. That perception prompted Truffaut and his *Cahiers* colleagues to interview filmmakers in order to document their thought processes. To that end Truffaut took advantage of a recent invention, a reel-to-reel tape recorder, which he lugged to interviews. He also brought along carefully-prepared questions intended to elicit reflections on the practice of directing. This method was, he thought, both scientifically sound and useful in advancing understanding of the true nature of cinematic creativity, an understanding that would be crucial to aspiring filmmakers, including himself and his contemporaries. His procedures would be put to an extreme test in interviews with Hitchcock.

Soon after going on staff full-time at *Cahiers* in winter 1953–54, Truffaut assumed responsibility for distributing writing assignments and overseeing their progress into print. No one at *Cahiers* was surprised when he encouraged Bazin to solicit from Hitchcock, while conducting on-location interviews during production of *To Catch a Thief* (1955), the director's response to the Hitchcockians' theories about him; nor when Truffaut reserved the company tape recorder in preparation for Hitchcock's return to Paris after the Riviera shoot and assigned Chabrol and himself to cover that event; nor when he proposed a series of related articles that would result in an entire issue of *Cahiers* being devoted to Hitchcock. Thus Truffaut marshaled forces for an unstoppable counteroffensive.

His committed ally, Claude Chabrol, was two years Truffaut's elder. They became part of a group known as cinemaniacs, a close-knit clique including Rivette, Jean Douchet, Charles Bitsch, Suzanne Shiffman, Godard, and Rohmer. After completing his military service, Chabrol landed a job at Fox's publicity office in Paris that gave him access, as an insider, to valuable information and contacts. Chabrol was known for his conviviality and sensitivity to nuances of gesture and emotion. His training in pharmacology, literature, political science, and law enabled him to categorize structures and themes. He also knew English. Those traits would serve admirably in his dealings with Hitchcock.

Chabrol would become a major chronicler of the Hitchcockians' exploits and a principal defender of their idea of Hitchcock as Catholic *auteur de films*. The Hitchcockians perceived in Hitchcock's films both authorial creativity and a coherent collection of motifs, a "figure in the carpet," that had ethical as well as aesthetic significance.[5] Those motifs, they claimed, revolved around the central, related issues of binomial pairings and identity transfer, particularly the transfer of guilt, a subject much debated in postwar France.

While Astruc, Rohmer, Rivette, Chabrol, and Truffaut persisted in lauding Hitchcock, old-guard French critics, among them Charensol and Sadoul, continued to view him as a mere technician who had sold out to the American studio system. Because of the younger writers' unremitting insistence that Hitchcock should be taken seriously, Bazin labeled them "Hitchcockiens fanatiques" (30) in

"Hitchcock contre Hitchcock" (*Cahiers* 39 [Oct. 1954]: 25–32). Those "fanatics" convinced themselves that they detected throughout Hitchcock's works a pattern of consistent formal and conceptual traits that qualified this director as a bona fide *auteur de films*. Such issues had been intensified by an incendiary essay by Truffaut that *Cahiers*'s editors only reluctantly agreed to publish.

In "Une certaine tendance du cinéma français/A Certain Tendency of French Cinema" (*Cahiers* 31 [Jan. 1954]: 15–29), Truffaut condemned traditional French filmmaking for relying heavily on stilted adaptations from novels or stage plays with the goal of impressing film festival juries. Decrying as a travesty what was known in France as the *tradition de qualité,* Truffaut indicted prominent directors and screenwriters as snobbish perpetuators of formulaic movies. Like Zola's *J'accuse* (1898), Truffaut's denunciation named names, implicating in the crime of denaturing French cinema such renowned directors as Claude Autant-Lara, Christian-Jaque, and even Clouzot, as well as prominent screenwriters. In contrast Truffaut proposed a dynamic, personalized cinema of *auteurs de films* who were responsible for their screenplays as well as other aspects of mise-en-scène. Chief among the models for Truffaut's proposed reform were Cocteau, Jean Vigo, Jean Renoir, and other directors who imposed their unique vision upon their work. Truffaut could easily have been thinking of Hitchcock as well. Through his railings against *le cinéma de papa,* Truffaut anticipated the birth of New Wave filmmaking and articulated standards against which it would be judged.

This searing polemic unleashed a torrent of responses. *Cahiers*'s co-editors took the preemptive precaution, via an editorial in that same issue, of distancing *Cahiers* from Truffaut's sensationalist invective. Soon thereafter Doniol-Valcroze returned to the subject in a thinly-disguised damage assessment. Noting the hesitation that the editorial staff had experienced about printing Truffaut's article, he acknowledged the flood of responses on the subject, many negative. After recounting the rancorous reactions at professional meetings and allegations that *Cahiers* was anti-French, he reiterated the magazine's commitment to freedom of expression.

The seething controversy over *la politique des auteurs* and especially its application to Hitchcock was quickly taken up in the popular press. Well-established critics and neophyte movie reviewers alike defended positions on one side or the other. In the melee the vocabulary of cinematic debate was altered. In *Arts, France-Observateur,* and elsewhere, Cocteau and Clouzot, Bresson and Becker were now regularly referred to as auteurs in the Truffaldian sense. Even *Positif* snapped at the term and spat it out with a snarl. The concept of creative control was accentuated at a time when the movie industry and film theory were undergoing drastic changes and Hitchcock was preparing to spend a month filming in France.

The Hitchcockians' theories would soon be tested in critical essays and in interviews with Hitchcock in which issues concerning the concept of the independent producer-writer-director were raised. These young critics and potential cineastes noted with interest his efforts at autonomy. They followed reports of Hitchcock's new contract with Paramount, which would allow for an unprecedented degree of control and permit him eventually to retain rights to the films themselves. In their minds, this quest for authority over his films signaled Hitchcock as a true auteur.

Hitchcock's plans for filming in Provence led these *Cahiers* critics to contemplate possible contact with the person best qualified, they thought, to validate their hypotheses concerning structural and thematic coherence in his works, the filmmaker himself. In an ironic twist worthy of a Hitchcock film, the theorists at *Cahiers* were keen to refine and assay their hypotheses at the same time Hitchcock was preparing to initiate major enhancements to his public image. In these encounters, evolving French critical sensibilities would confront the emerging Hitchcockian persona that was essential to new professional ventures, including weekly television appearances as well as publications and paraphernalia bearing his name and image. In this unsettled atmosphere there was ample room for maneuverings, misunderstandings, and growth on all sides.

Location photography for *To Catch a Thief* was concentrated around Cannes and Nice, the Corniche above Monaco, the village of Tourettes-sur-Loup, and a villa at Saint-Jeannet that served as his protagonist's retreat. Hitchcock's French shoot began on 31 May 1954 and was completed on 25 June, at which time Hitch and the principal cast members set out for Hollywood. That intense period in France was preceded by extensive pre-production activities and followed by several weeks in which second-unit crews remained until on-site photography was completed (see DeRosa 101–24).

From the beginning, Hitchcock was intent on creating an authentic French ambiance in this film. He insisted that writer John Michael Hayes and his wife travel to Provence to absorb local color and customs. Concerned for both the sound and the look of his first VistaVision feature, Hitchcock determinedly took advantage of his French-speaking milieu. He provided French script-girl Sylvette Baudrot with a list of ambient sounds to record at specific intervals from 9 p.m. until 4 a.m., for a final product that would contain a number of those sounds and over 120 lines of French dialogue. Hitchcock determined that dubbing of French performers' voices should be completed at the Saint Maurice Studios at Joinville near Paris, a decision that would bring him back to France in January 1955 and exert a long-term influence on Truffaut and Chabrol.

Hitchcock engaged a large number of French actors for this production. Heading the list was veteran Charles Vanel, who had established himself as a major player in important films, most notably *The Wages of Fear*. Hitchcock's production included Brigitte Auber, Roland Lesaffre, Georgette Anys, René Blancard, Jean Hébey, Dominique Davray, Adèle Saint-Maur, and Gérard Buhr. Performers and crew members who worked on *To Catch a Thief* retained vivid memories of their experiences that summer. One was Grace Kelly, who, upon returning to the Riviera the following year, fulfilled her wish to meet Prince Rainier of Monaco. Another was crew member Baudrot, who published excerpts from her diary for that period in the October issue of *Cahiers* and returned to these sites for a souvenir visit in 2006, shared online.[6]

A mystery-romance involving two Americans in an enticing French setting well suited for dramatic chases appealed to Hitchcock. Whereas David Dodge's 1952 novel gave substantial coverage to French customs and institutions, Hitchcock's version emphasized the difficulty of assimilation experienced by foreigners. *To Catch a Thief* portrayed that sense of cultural disparity cleaving both ways.

British and American characters were represented as having mixed feelings for the French. When Mrs. Stevens (Jessie Royce Landis) voiced her disapproval of the practice of "service compris," the Englishman H.H. Hughson (John Williams) replied sarcastically, "that's France." The idea of inter-cultural tensions was highlighted in dealings of the protagonist, known as Le Chat, with his Resistance confrères and reinforced in the back seat of a bus, where Le Chat found himself squeezed between a French woman with a birdcage and Hitchcock. The vision presented was that of someone situated between two cultures, observing them both but connecting to neither.

Hitchcock was quite comfortable with the extensive use of foreign speech and indigenous sounds to create an authentic international ambiance. Having made two short films with actors speaking in French, *Bon Voyage* (1944) and *Aventure Malgache* (1944), Hitchcock was accustomed to that linguistic situation and maintained that it made little sense for films to show foreigners speaking in English. The opening sequences of this film (shots 1–92) were scripted to contain no English at all. Creating the desired multilingual environment required a precarious balancing act, and *I Confess* provided a useful model. Hitchcock saw to it that throughout *To Catch a Thief* conversational French marked the cadences of Provençal life and propelled the narrative in ways that would vivify the storytelling without resorting to subtitles.

The fact that *To Catch a Thief* was made in France with French performers and crew continued to intrigue the French media long term. *Cahiers*'s "Petit journal intime" section, featuring personal reflections on cinema by diverse observers, provided a record of day-by-day responses in June and July by Truffaut and Bazin respectively. On 28 June Truffaut briefly noted his participation in Hitchcock's Paris press conference, stating that the forty-five minute interview was so momentous that *Cahiers* readers should expect to hear more about it in subsequent issues (*Cahiers* 37 [July 1954]: 36). The "Petit journal" for July was written by Bazin from his summer retreat in the Provençal village of Tourettes, featured in the film's chase scenes (*Cahiers* 38 [Aug.–Sep. 1954]: 36–40). On 4 July Bazin reported on activities of Hitchcock's second unit team. Aerial photography involved a noisy helicopter. On the ground, a black Citroën pursued a reddish Delahaye. This chase was repeated several times while normal traffic was suspended until the desired results were obtained. Bazin noted that for three more days the helicopter fought air currents that made filming difficult. Hitchcock's telegrams from Hollywood indicated that the footage shot thus far should be redone. Crew members gave the impression that, at a distance of 6000 miles, Hitchcock made them feel that he was watching them.

Bazin also penned two accounts of his reactions to his exclusive interviews with Hitchcock in June, on location at the flower market in Nice and at the Carlton Hotel in Cannes, with the bilingual Sylvette Baudrot serving as interpreter. Despite her aid, the results of his attempts to test the Hitchcockians' theories on the film-maker were so disquieting that they provoked weeks of reassessment. Bazin first composed a lighthearted commentary for *Radio-Cinéma-Télévision* (18 July 1954) that allowed him to collect his thoughts, vent some steam, and begin to put a dif-ficult situation into perspective. It also permitted him to reassess the Hitchcockians' auteurist claims in a publication intended for a broad audience. Here Bazin admit-ted that Hitchcock consistently returned to certain themes and conceded that he might actually be a greater director than his superficial thrillers suggested.

For his better known and more extended essay, which appeared in *Cahiers* 39 (cited earlier), Bazin chose a title that suggested a well-known icon at odds with itself while pointing toward a major theoretical reappraisal: "Hitchcock contre Hitchcock." Bazin began with a contextualizing nod to the director's wildest partisans, then admitted with exemplary humility that critics could make mistakes and that artists' works could surpass their creators. Bazin resorted to vigorous metaphors of conflict to describe his exasperation at Hitchcock's entrenched defensiveness, at his "pirouettes" and "camouflage" tactics that tended more to obscure than to clarify (26, 27, 30).

The centerpiece of this article was an account of the crucial moment when Bazin presented the Hitchcockians' thesis for Hitchcock's consideration. Bazin laid out their claim to have discerned a theme common to Hitchcock's works, the identification of a weaker character with a stronger one through guilt and confes-sion, citing examples from *Shadow of a Doubt*, *Strangers on a Train*, and *I Confess* (30–31). Bazin noted that his interlocutor listened attentively and smiled broadly as the import seemed to sink in. When Bazin tried to advance the case for Hitchcock as a Catholic filmmaker, he changed the subject, and the interview concluded with Bazin unable to turn the conversation back to essentials.

Bazin's *Cahiers* article provided a vehicle for assessing both his own role as intermediary between the Hitchcockians and their exalted auteur and also docu-menting Hitchcock's off-putting demeanor and evasions. The first to confront Hitchcock with their ideas, despite his own strong reservations, Bazin saw himself as a messenger charged to deliver potentially explosive news. He concluded that, if Hitchcock's films really did exemplify that thematic unity, then he was indebted to the Hitchcockians for discovering it. Bazin's assessment revealed his commitment, despite lingering doubts, to the possibility that they might be right.

When his protégés learned of Bazin's efforts on their behalf, they resented the disrespect they sensed Hitchcock had shown to their mentor.[7] Bazin's accounts of Hitchcock's mocking attitude led the "Hitchcockiens fanatiques" to troubled reflec-tions that culminated in a collection of articles in a special issue of *Cahiers* devoted to Hitchcock that would feature Bazin's essay, Baudrot's diary of the Riviera shoot, and several other reflections on the director. As they prepared for that October issue, a sense of embattled entrenchment coupled with their own determination to be worthy of Bazin produced strong reactions in both Chabrol and Truffaut, reactions intensified by their own encounters with the reluctant auteur.

Two weeks after Bazin's interviews, when Hitchcock stopped over in Paris on his way back to California, Chabrol and Truffaut attended a long-awaited press conference at the Hôtel George V. Chabrol described that frustrating event in his "Histoire d'une interview" (*Cahiers* 39 [Oct. 1954]: 39–44). The two young Frenchmen felt disadvantaged by their inexperience and by problems with their tape recorder that delayed proceedings. They were also disappointed by the attitude of their interviewee, who talked about the fickle Mediterranean weather rather than giving thoughtful answers to their probing questions. After one of Hitchcock's oft-told anecdotes, Chabrol blurted out: "Do you believe in the devil?" (41). Hitchcock looked at him fixedly with what Chabrol registered as a somewhat astonished air, replied that the devil was in each of us, then shifted the conversation back to *Rear Window*. Chabrol asked how closely the director worked on the preparation of his screenplays. Very closely indeed, was the answer, from beginning to end including the layout of individual scenes. Just as Chabrol and Truffaut thought they had something of substance to support their auteurist views, the session concluded. The gnawing feeling of being manipulated lingered.

Truffaut convinced Chabrol to telephone Hitchcock and ask whether he would entertain a few more questions. Hearing the first one, "What is the figure in your carpet?" (42), Hitchcock invited the inquisitive Frenchman up for five minutes. Face to face with Hitchcock, Chabrol asked about the theme of a search for God that he and his colleagues had perceived in Hitchcock's works. Perhaps because of translation difficulties or perhaps because Hitchcock heard what he wanted to hear, the director replied, "*Good?* Oh yes." When Chabrol clarified his meaning, "Not good; God Himself," Hitchcock looked rather surprised and added, "God! … Maybe, but it is unconscious" (42–43). Taken aback by this apparent lack of self-reflection, Chabrol persisted, citing cases of Hitchcock characters ensnared by evil who escape only through confession. His questions elicited agreement – sincere confession, yes, contrition – and an unsettling smile as Hitchcock added that he became aware of such things only after the fact.

Chabrol countered this disclaimer with specifics, including the (to him) obvious symbolism of destiny in the sound of a train that obscured Guy Haines's threatening words in *Strangers on a Train*. Hitchcock replied that he was certainly aware of such things during the planning stages but that for him the screenplay was secondary to form and that he made the film correspond to the holistic impression in his head. Hitchcock added that he saw things "larger than life" (44). Chabrol translated that phrase back to him as "Métaphysique?" to which Hitchcock replied "Thank you" and went on to explain why he preferred melodrama to realism. As Alma Reville latched the last suitcase, her husband escorted Chabrol to the door.

Accompanying Chabrol's description of this unsettling encounter in *Cahiers*'s October 1954 issue was his interpretative article, "Hitchcock devant le mal/

Hitchcock Confronts Evil" (18–24), where Chabrol applied Catholic doctrine and existentialist tenets to Hitchcock's works, asserting that the director consistently showed characters who were, in both the Augustinian and Sartrean senses, free and who chose to do evil. Their crime, he argued, was not so important as their struggle and their choices. What mattered was their decision to accept responsibility as in *Under Capricorn* and *I Confess* or reject it as in *Shadow of a Doubt* and *Strangers on a Train*. Chabrol's awkward experience of those interviews and the writing of that article constituted the hothouse in which his contributions to the first book-length study of Hitchcock's films germinated.

The same issue of *Cahiers* contained Truffaut's provocative article, "Un trousseau de fausses clés / A Trousseau of False Keys" (45–53). Whereas Bazin registered Hitchcock's defensiveness and Chabrol spoke of his disingenuousness, Truffaut bluntly accused Hitchcock of lying. Expressing his discomfort with Hitchcock's portrayal of himself in his recent interviews as a willing victim of his own lack of comprehension, Truffaut asserted that Hitchcock was playing with Bazin, but Bazin was not his only dupe. Truffaut's tirade acknowledged the embarrassment of the Hitchcockians who wanted no part of an unreflecting genius.

In support of their assertion that Hitchcock's American films developed the theme of identity transfer through paired characters and situations, Truffaut offered an extended analysis of *Shadow of a Doubt*, showing how it consistently exhibited this theme through plays on the idea of duality, thus giving expression to the extraordinarily balanced construction of a film whose creator surely must have been conscious of this pattern. Therefore, in claiming that such structures were unconscious, Hitchcock lied. Truffaut claimed that Hitchcock had built his career and indeed his life on misunderstandings, choosing to be known as the master of suspense rather than as a Catholic auteur, and preferring a perverse form of modesty to self-acclaim. Consequently, concluded the former truant who had himself endured juvenile detention for concealment and misrepresentation, Hitchcock was indulging in rank lies.

Truffaut's argument took a peculiar twist that would have profound long-term impact. According to Truffaut, Hitchcock, like his characters, was a Hitchcockian construct and therefore extremely reluctant to explain himself. Nevertheless, Truffaut claimed, one day the director would have to act like other Hitchcock characters who sealed their salvation, *leur salut,* through confession (51). Origins of the famous 500-question interview that Truffaut would conduct with Hitchcock eight years later lay in that seemingly outlandish proposition, couched as a sacred threat.

These commentaries by Bazin, Chabrol, and Truffaut were published in the highly touted "Hitchcock issue" of *Cahiers*. That October 1954 number also included opinion pieces by Astruc, Rohmer, and Jean Domarchi. In "Quand un homme ... / When a Man ...," Astruc discerned in Hitchcock's work a distinctive cohesiveness revelatory of a universe at once aesthetic and moral (5). In "À qui la faute? / Whose fault?," Rohmer saw Hitchcock as a consummate formalist whose rhythms and skilled use of metaphor testified to his artistry (6–10). Moreover,

Rohmer reasoned, while it was natural enough for the creator to claim to be unaware of his design's ambitiousness, it was the task of critics to show how the creator's comments might illuminate the secret essence of his art. Under a title borrowed from Balzac, "Le chef-d'œuvre inconnu," Domarchi averred that Hitchcock effectively combined classical narrative techniques with a modernist emphasis on the subconscious, uniting universality with subjective particularity (33–39).

Scattered throughout that issue of *Cahiers* were some thirty photos from Hitchcock's films and various comments by Hitchcock himself, collected from published interviews, as well as documentary and archival items intended to provide additional evidence pertinent to "le cas Hitchcock." Completing the collection were Chabrol's translation of a 1941 essay by Hitchcock titled "Lights! Action! ... But Mostly Camera!" plus an eleven-page filmography compiled by Rivette, who listed Hitchcock as uncredited producer for every film after *The Paradine Case*, followed by a bibliography of articles about Hitchcock published in *Cahiers*.

This sixty-page compendium of opinions, theories, observations, and documentation constituted a concerted show of strength. The heftiest sampling of Hitchcockiana to date, it advanced the concept of Hitchcock the creator, capable of significant thematic consistency as well as stylistic brio. It tackled a major objection of the anti-Hitchcockians – implausibility – by arguing that discussions of Hitchcock's realism were anchored in subjective, emotional, and spiritual rather than geopolitical domains. This collective manifestation of the Hitchcockians' determination to push to the fore both their director and their own theories met with remarkable success. The intellectual and polemical traits revealed in the October 1954 issue became increasingly identified with a pro-auteur stance associated with *Cahiers*. The "Hitchcock issue" was reprinted in 1980 on the occasion of the director's death as a testimonial to the conjunction of Hitchcock and France.

Intense critical reaction to the Hitchcockians' claims ensued. *Cahiers* printed dissenting comments by Jean Desternes, a highly skeptical editorial by Bazin, Chabrol's rebuttal, and Gérard Genette's impassioned defense of what he called Hitchcock's Jansenism.[8] Genette's prediction that exegesis of Hitchcock's cinema had just begun proved more than accurate. Several critics admonished *Cahiers* for devoting an entire issue to such an unworthy subject. In *France-Observateur* (30 Sept. 1954) Doniol-Valcroze continued to blast the Hitchcockians, opining that Clouzot had come on the scene to make films worthy of a tradition that Hitchcock himself had abandoned. In *Lettres françaises* (2 Dec. 1954) Sadoul labeled Truffaut and company snobbish *précieux* and expressed pleasure that Bazin seemed more or less immune to the contagion.

While in Paris in 1955 to supervise the dubbing of *To Catch a Thief*, Hitchcock granted Chabrol and Truffaut in-depth, tape-recorded interviews, which saw immediate publication (*Cahiers* 44 [Feb. 1955]: 19–31) and prompted intense critical debate. During the next two years *Cahiers* frequently included articles about Hitchcock and published two more issues devoted primarily to his work.

Controversies continued as passionate points and counterpoints resounded in various media. In 1956, a major retrospective of Hitchcock's British films at the Paris Cinémathèque prompted Rohmer and Chabrol to produce the first book-length study of this auteur's oeuvre. Responses were heated.

The ruckus in France echoed across the Channel. In "French Critical Writing" (*Sight and Sound* 24.2 [Oct.–Dec. 1954]: 105) Lindsay Anderson extolled the seriousness and verve of his French colleagues, but castigated *Cahiers* for shortchanging analysis in favor of dithyramb. The younger critics in particular struck him as "short on analytical capacity, anxious to establish themselves as *littérateurs*," and engaged in "perverse cultivation of the meretricious."

Hitchcock himself initially pooh-poohed the French critical enterprise. Interviewed by *Sight and Sound* (25.3 [Winter 1956]: 157–58) at the time of the London premiere of *To Catch a Thief*, he claimed not to recognize himself in the Frenchmen's claims – "I must admit that some of those articles made me wonder 'Is this really me they're discussing?' " – and asserted that the inclusion of Catholic themes in his films must be purely "instinctive rather than deliberate" (157). During another interview he claimed that he preferred to leave certain things unexplained and that there was "nothing more stupid than logic," adding pointedly, "Descartes can go boil his head" (Fallaci 61).

Convinced of their insights, the French Hitchcockians persisted. In time Hitchcock, who shared with them a strong interest in reputation building, welcomed the flurry of international notice and warmed to the epithet *auteur de films*. When he was in Paris, representatives from *Cahiers* enjoyed exclusive interviews. Hitchcock's own claims to auteur status became more overt and categorical. In the *Cahiers* 44 interview with Truffaut and Chabrol he acquiesced to their assertion that most of his American films depicted paired relationships (21) and stated emphatically that he had never filmed from anyone else's script (29). Was Hitchcock confirming these critics' claims, or pointing them toward his own image-enhancing goals, or both?

Aftershocks were felt for decades. The controversies that raged in France in the 1950s laid the foundations for numerous studies of Hitchcock by French critics, among them *Cahiers* contributors Jean Douchet, Raymond Bellour, and Bill Krohn, as well as others from diverse cultural perspectives who have examined Hitchcock's creations in terms of preponderant themes and variations, of nuanced differences within a coherent vision.

The firestorm quickly spread beyond France. In 1963 Penelope Houston took the *Cahiers* writers' ideas to task in a point-by-point attack ("The Figure in the Carpet," *Sight and Sound* 32.4 [Autumn 1963]: 158–64), and 1970 saw the publication in *The American Scholar* (39.2 [1970]: 295–304) of Charles Thomas Samuels's "Hitchcock," a carefully articulated blast against the position articulated by Rohmer and associates. Robin Wood revisited Truffaut's assessment of Hitchcock as consummate liar and made it a point of departure for his "Alfred Hitchcock: Lost in the Wood" analysis of Hitchcock's later films (*Film Comment* 8.4 [Nov.–Dec. 1972]:

46–53). The Truffaldian thesis has been retested by scholars who studied Hitchcock from cultural, psychological, sociological, and thematic perspectives, serving as a springboard for major critical contributions by Tania Modleski, Thomas Leitch, Robert Kapsis, Susan Smith, Richard Allen, and many others.

The final word has yet to be uttered. "Auteur theory" squabbles, often reflexively invoking the perspective of French Hitchcockians, continue to thrive. Ultimately commentaries from all sides, including recent revisionist efforts, owe a major debt to those French writers who initially formulated a cohesive conception of Hitchcock's films as an oeuvre and the creator himself as an *auteur de films.*

Notes

Portions of this chapter are based upon materials published in my earlier scholarship on Hitchcock and France, including my essay "The Emergence of an Auteur: Hitchcock and French Film Criticism, 1950–1954" in *Hitchcock Annual* (2001–02): 108–24 and my chapter "To Catch a Liar: Bazin, Chabrol, and Truffaut Encounter Hitchcock," which appeared in *Hitchcock: Past and Future,* edited by Richard Allen and Sam Ishii-Gonzáles (London: Routledge, 2004, 109–18), both used and modified here with permission of the copyright holder and publishers. Portions are also derived from *Hitchcock and France: The Forging of an Auteur,* by James M. Vest. Copyright © 2003 by James M. Vest. Reproduced with permission of Greenwood Publishing Group, Inc., Westport, CT. I am indebted to Rhodes College for Faculty Development Endowment Grants supporting these projects and to my wife, Nancy Foltz Vest, for her assistance.

1. Full bibliographical references for periodicals mentioned in this chapter may be found in Vest, *Hitchcock and France,* Chapters 1–3. Principal monthly and quarterly sources will be documented parenthetically herein.

2. Scripted allusions to France's colonialist situation were removed from the released version of *Rear Window* for reasons of concision and politics.

3. Two notable widescreen processes relied on French optical innovations. Henri Chrétien's anamorphic lenses, essential to CinemaScope, debuted in France in 1927; Fox obtained proprietary rights to them in 1952. VistaVision, which used high-quality lenses crafted by French optician Pierre Angénieux, became the basis for IMAX.

4. The noun *politique* conjured rhetorical tactics for swaying public opinion, i.e., marketing strategies. The phrase *politique des auteurs* might be rendered into English as *campaign for promoting the idea of filmmakers as the chief creative force behind their films.* The French term became a catchphrase on the Continent and in England. Attempts to transpose it into the American idiom as "auteur theory" missed the mark widely.

5. One of the Hitchcockians' touchstones was Henry James, the title of whose 1896 story "The Figure in the Carpet" became a rallying cry for these seekers of concealed patterns.

6. References to Sylvette Baudrot in this section are to *Cahiers* 39 (Oct. 1954): 14–16 and her summer 2006 visit to the Riviera, with commentary and photos, presented by Kerzoncuf and Bokor.

7. In response to Bazin's query about pre-planning, Hitchcock replied snippily: How could he have given a French journalist an hour during shooting if he had to think

about his movie at the same time? (*Cahiers* 39 [Oct. 1954]: 32). Baudrot noted that Hitchcock concluded his interview with Bazin by saying *Au revoir, Monsieur,* purposely pronouncing the last word as "manure" (16n).

8.   All published in *Cahiers*: Desternes, "L'amour en couleurs" (42 [Dec. 1954]: 27+); Bazin, "Comment peut-on être Hitchcocko-Hawksien?" (44 [Feb. 1955]: 17–18); Chabrol, "Les choses sérieuses" (46 [Apr. 1955]: 41–43); Genette, "Courrier des lecteurs" (52 [Nov. 1955]: 59–60).

Works Cited

de Baecque, Antoine, and Serge Toubiana. *Truffaut.* 1996. Trans. Catherine Temerson. New York: Knopf, 1999.

DeRosa, Steven. *Writing with Hitchcock: The Collaboration of Alfred Hitchcock and John Michael Hayes.* New York: Faber and Faber, 2001.

Fallaci, Oriana. "Alfred Hitchcock: Mr. Chastity." 1963. *Alfred Hitchcock: Interviews.* Ed. Sidney Gottlieb. Jackson: UP of Mississippi, 2003. 55–66.

Gavin, Arthur E. "*Rear Window.*" *American Cinematographer* 35.2 (1954): 76+.

Hayes, John Michael. "Rear Window." Screenplay, final version. 1 Dec. 1953. Hollywood: Script City, 1953.

Hayes, John Michael. "To Catch a Thief." Screenplay. 1 July 1954. PDF accessed via Script City. 29 May 2010.

Kerzoncuf, Alain, and Nándor Bokor. "Location Trip to the French Riviera." Web. 23 Dec. 2007.

Street, Sarah. "The Dresses Had Told Me." *Alfred Hitchcock's* Rear Window. Ed. John Belton. Cambridge: Cambridge UP, 2000. 91–109.

Vest, James M. *Hitchcock and France: The Forging of an Auteur.* Westport, CT: Praeger, 2003.

21

Lost in Translation? Listening to the Hitchcock–Truffaut Interview

Janet Bergstrom

Hitchcock to Truffaut, discussing Notorious *(1946):*

From the recorded interview: "It's like killing a person with arsenic. It's the conventional method of a man killing his wife."

(ht14.mp3)[1]

As published in Hitchcock by Truffaut:

"Claude Rains and his mother try to kill Ingrid Bergman very slowly with arsenic. Isn't that the conventional method for disposing of someone without being caught?"

(122)

François Truffaut called the tape recorder a lie detector (de Baecque 141). That was based on years of experience interviewing people for the *Cahiers du cinéma* and elsewhere. In June 1962, he was making plans for his weeklong career interview with Hitchcock, which would take place in Los Angeles beginning on 13 August, the director's sixty-third birthday.[2] Truffaut wrote to Helen Scott, his New York–based translator and the person who facilitated every stage of the project, asking her to research the best recorder to bring with them (20 June 1962, *Letters* 184). The best one would be portable enough for him to carry easily (these were the days of reel-to-reel machines), and it should have the longest recording time per reel, because during the tape-changing intervals the only guarantee of fidelity to Hitchcock's words, hence to the way he formulated his thinking, would be her handwritten notes. Truffaut forewarned her, too, that

A Companion to Alfred Hitchcock, First Edition. Edited by Thomas Leitch and Leland Poague.
© 2011 Thomas Leitch and Leland Poague. Published 2011 by Blackwell Publishing Ltd.

she would need to write down what Hitchcock said if he continued their discussion before or after the machine was recording.

Hitchcock was prepared to do better than that. This was a director for whom sound was of paramount importance. He would soon explain to Truffaut how he had implemented sound strategically ever since his first dialogue film, *Blackmail* (1929), often delighting in vivid shot- by-shot, sound-by-sound descriptions; not only could he see his films in his mind many years later, he could hear them too. Hitchcock was then at Universal working on post-production for *The Birds* (1963). He was in the midst of planning the most experimental sound design for any of his films to date: instead of music and realistic noises (to represent the birds, for instance), he would use electronic sounds and effects, working with Oskar Salas and his Mixtur-Trautonium in Germany. (The credits for *The Birds* list Hitchcock's longtime composer, Bernard Herrmann, as "Sound Consultant." Remi Gassman and Oskar Salas are credited for "Composition and Production of Electronic Sound.") For his interviews with Truffaut, Hitchcock arranged for a recording engineer at the studio (*Hitchcock* 15). Nothing would be left to chance, and the audio quality would be professional. *Life* (and Magnum) photographer Philippe Halsman would take pictures of the group in their recording room, as published in Truffaut's resulting book, *Hitchcock*. One of Halsman's strikingly artistic, even audacious, promotional photos for *The Birds* made the cover of *Life* magazine on 1 February 1963: three big crows have perched on Hitchcock, who presents them, as the master of ceremonies, with Bodega Bay in the background.

In December 1957, Truffaut published a review in *Arts* of Eric Rohmer and Claude Chabrol's new book, *Hitchcock*, under the title "Hitchcock is the Greatest 'Inventor of Forms' of Our Day." Truffaut wrote, "He was referred to with condescension, as a solid technician with a great sense of humor who didn't need to make the audience think." His essay demonstrated that, on the contrary, Hitchcock had made some serious critics think a lot. "I hardly need to point out that my conclusion is the same as that of Rohmer and Chabrol [Truffaut's fellow *Cahiers du cinéma* editors]: 'Hitchcock is, we would say, one of the greatest inventors of form in the entire history of the cinema. ... Form is not used to embellish the content: IT CREATES IT. All of Hitchcock is contained in this formula'" (7).

Truffaut's defense of Hitchcock was similar to the way in which he would describe the necessity for his trailblazing interview book some five years later – first, in his letter to the director himself to persuade him to take part in this venture, and then to publishers. On 2 June 1962 Truffaut wrote to Hitchcock outlining a detailed proposal for a weeklong, tape-recorded interview designed to have him speak systematically about every film he had made, in chronological order (*Letters* 177–79). He would bring "the ideal interpreter" with him – Helen Scott, from the French Film Office in New York: "she carries out simultaneous translations at such a speed that we would have the impression of speaking to one another without any intermediary" (178). Truffaut had seen all of Hitchcock's films five or six times.

Now that he had made three films himself – *Jules and Jim* (1962) had opened in New York – he saw Hitchcock's films "more from the perspective of how they were made" (*Correspondance* 232).[3] If Hitchcock agreed, he would gather the materials he needed to prepare the 400 to 500 questions he would like to ask him. The result would be a full-length book – not magazine articles, as would have been expected – to be published in both the US and France. The text would be transcribed, edited, and corrected several weeks after the interviews took place. Then Truffaut would send Hitchcock the English-language version for review and correction, and the book would be ready toward the end of the year. His introduction to the book, Truffaut's letter concluded, would reflect his guiding passion and conviction:

> If, overnight, the cinema had to do without a sound track and become once again a silent art, then many directors would be forced into unemployment, but, among the survivors, there would be Alfred Hitchcock and everyone would realize at last that he is the greatest film director in the world.
>
> (*Letters* 179)[4]

Upon reading this letter, Hitchcock, tears in his eyes, cabled his grateful agreement – in French: *"Cher monsieur Truffaut, votre lettre m'a fait venir les larmes aux yeux et combien je suis reconnaissant de recevoir un tel tribut de votre part"* ("Dear Mr. Truffaut, your letter brought tears to my eyes and I am so grateful to receive such a tribute from you," de Baecque 140–41; "Hitchcock-Truffaut" 5).

Truffaut thought that the book could be published very quickly because the simultaneous translations would be recorded. As he wrote to Helen Scott on 5 July 1962, "I realize now that our bilingual recording method will enormously facilitate publication since, as soon as the tapes have been transcribed, we will have a book in two languages requiring practically no translation (simply a scrupulous revision of the French text)" (*Letters* 191). That estimate turned out to be off by four years for the French edition – *Le cinéma selon Hitchcock* (Paris: Robert Laffont) appeared in October 1966 – and five for the American edition, *Hitchcock* (New York: Simon and Schuster), which came out a year later, in November 1967.

Truffaut's interview book with Hitchcock is one of the best known, widely read and beloved books on the cinema. It has long been a standard source of information about the director's career. For many, it is the only book they will ever read about Hitchcock. His statements to Truffaut have been quoted endlessly. Reading the conversation encourages an affinity with the way Hitchcock expresses himself – how he thinks, the associations he makes – from memories of his early days designing graphics for the intertitles of silent films up through his latest works. Naturally, the reader assumes that Hitchcock's words on the page correspond to what he said to Truffaut. I used to be that kind of reader.

My point of departure for this study was simple. Truffaut stated in his introduction that fifty hours of discussion had been recorded. The relatively modest length of the published text could not possibly have included everything Hitchcock said, even after eliminating the translations back and forth, and allowing for ordinary copyediting to reflect changes he made himself as he was talking, to delete false starts and filler words ("and," "but," "well," "um"), and so on. I knew that the complete interview was available on cassettes to researchers in the Margaret Herrick Library in Beverly Hills.[5] Why not compare the two? I wanted to find out what had been left on the cutting room floor and gain insight into the experience of the exchange.

And so I sat down with the book open to the beginning of the interview, headphones in place, and pressed "play" on the cassette machine, ready for the pleasure of listening to Hitchcock – whose voice it seems to me I have always loved – as I read his words on the page, and heard even more words that wouldn't be on the page. The book begins exactly as Truffaut had outlined its structure in his original letter to the director: a short biographical section leads into the beginning of his career in the film industry.

But that's not what I heard on the tape. Hitchcock was talking about *The Birds*, and then more and more about *The Birds*. Small wonder – he was still in post-production when the interview week commenced, weighing decisions about the final form the soundtrack would take. His excitement was palpable. The group had just come from a screening of the latest cut of the film. The way Hitchcock described what he was doing, and why, corresponded exactly to what Truffaut most admired about him: "His talent isn't instinctive like Preminger's, for example; he is really the guy who has given the most thought to cinema as both spectacle and style [*écriture*]" (Truffaut to Scott, 20 June 1962, *Letters* 184).

I paged ahead in the book to the section on *The Birds*, only to find bits and pieces of what I was hearing. The wording was almost never the same; often I saw an approximation or even a summary of what Hitchcock had said. For instance, he was eager to talk about substituting electronic sound for music. So far, he told Truffaut, the only scene with electronic sound was the "external attack sequence on the family in the boarded-up house."

HITCHCOCK (AS SPOKEN):	That's electronic sound and it was made in Germany. I sent the reel over to Germany and they copied the ideas I suggested. And I'm doing the whole film with that sound all the way through … no music.
TRUFFAUT:	There'll be no music?
HITCHCOCK:	Only those electronic sounds all the way through.

(ht24.mp3)

Hitchcock's way of thinking about electronic sound – and he continued at length – cast a different light on Truffaut's flattering statement that if it were no longer possible to use sound in film, Hitchcock would be recognized as the greatest filmmaker in the world. That was meant as an appreciation of his visual style or, as Hitchcock put it repeatedly in the interview, "making the point visually." But Truffaut was not prepared for "no music." He protested that music had been such an important component of Hitchcock's films, especially his American ones.

In the published interview, this exchange was transformed. Truffaut, not Hitchcock, stated: "There's no music, of course" (295).

In the recorded interview, after a few more remarks, Hitchcock continued:

> I don't think we should put music in this. I don't think music is good enough. I think sound is so much more important. For example, I'm hoping when the young man, at the end of the picture, goes out to get the automobile and we see birds everywhere for the first time […] to get electronically a strange murmur. No bird sound, but a hum of some kind that you feel that if he disturbs them too much this murmur will become a loud sound of attack. And yet it should be silence. It will be silence made of sound.
>
> (ht24.mp3)

In the published version, Hitchcock said that after Rod Taylor opens the door of the house and sees birds everywhere, "I asked for a silence, but not just any kind of silence. I wanted an electronic silence, a sort of monotonous low hum that might suggest the sound of the sea in the distance." Comparing the birds to "an engine that's purring," not yet ready to attack, he concluded: "All of this was suggested by a sound that's so low that you can't be sure whether you're actually hearing it or only imagining it" (297).

Hitchcock's conviction that music was inadequate compared to what he could do with electronic sound had lost its radical edge. "An electronic silence" does not do justice to a concept as strong as "silence made of sound."

Why were Hitchcock's words changed? As I continued to listen, I realized that Hitchcock kept coming back to *The Birds* all week long. At about the point that Truffaut's chronology finally caught up with the film in question, they had just seen another rough cut. By then, Truffaut had heard a lot about Hitchcock's preoccupation with sound, and so he could pose his questions differently, although he never did say what I quoted from the published text. Most of Hitchcock's published remarks were taken from their later conversation, but they included parts or paraphrases taken from earlier points in the interview as well. When he returned to the soundtrack during the bird attack on the house, Hitchcock told Truffaut that he had sent that reel over to Germany, "and they put their new electronic sound on it. It's not entirely correct at the moment. But what I'm going to hope, I'm hoping to make a deal with Bernard Herrmann, who's done music before, of course he's a very temperamental fellow, you know, VERY temperamental, to SUPERVISE the sound of the whole picture" (ht24. mp3). In the published text, this was boiled down to asking the composer to "supervise the whole soundtrack" (295). No longer does it sound like a momentous decision, a turning-point, as Hitchcock experienced it at the time.

The published text devoted to *The Birds* is a montage of fragments taken from different parts of the recorded interview. Making that montage read coherently came at the price of cutting, summarizing and synthesizing what Hitchcock had actually said and the context within which he had spoken.

It was understandable that Truffaut didn't want *The Birds* to take over the interview as Hitchcock's creatures had invaded Bodega Bay. And because the book was not ready for publication until some four years after the interview, *The Birds* had to be put in the past tense. The editors – by that time, Helen Scott was fully an editor – were doubtless trying to respect Hitchcock's thought, but rearranging and reformulating his statements had the effect of sacrificing his very particular way of expressing himself and of veiling his enthusiasm. *The Birds* was a special case only in that it entered the discussion so often. However, the lack of correspondence between the interview as spoken and the interview as published seemed to be so pervasive that I began to wonder how many sentences in the entire book had survived intact, or even how many phrases?

We can trace much of how, when, and why this happened through Truffaut's correspondence during the long years it took to produce the book, because Truffaut and his editing partner for the US edition, Helen Scott, were not in the same place: Truffaut was usually in Paris, working from a French translation; Helen Scott was usually in New York. For the same reason, letters also chronicling the vicissitudes of the project were exchanged between Truffaut and his American agent (Don Congdon) and his publisher (at Simon and Schuster, Elizabeth Sutherland, then Michael Korda, son of the art director and production designer Vincent Korda, nephew of directors Alexander and Zoltan Korda). During this period, Truffaut, with Helen Scott assisting him in many ways, was also absorbed with his films. He expected to shoot *Fahrenheit 451* at the end of 1962, but after a history of problems and delays, it was not released until 1966 (the same year as the first publication of the book, in France, which had been delayed exactly as long). During the hiatus created by *Fahrenheit 451*'s funding problems, he wrote and directed *The Soft Skin* (1964) and wrote the script for *The Wild Child* (1970). By the time *Hitchcock* was released in the US in November 1967, he had also written and shot *The Bride Wore Black* (1968).

Truffaut originally intended to publish Hitchcock's statements with few changes. He wrote to Helen Scott on 20 July 1962:

> [T]he text will necessarily be better in English since Hitchcock will be speaking in English; all he has to do is correct the text that we'll be sending him after an initial correction that you and I will make. The question of the translation into French is more problematic, in so far as your simultaneous translation of H.'s answers will perhaps need to be revised by you on paper to make it more faithful to Hitch.
>
> *(Letters 195–96)*

Over time, this approach gave way to the difficulties inherent in simultaneous translation, and to other pressures and considerations related to publishing and a changing vision of how the project's vocation, which remained unchanged as outlined in Truffaut's original letter to Hitchcock, could best be fulfilled.

Helen Scott was more than Truffaut's loyal assistant and translator. For good reason, she ended up with almost equal billing as co-author/editor of the Hitchcock book.

Born in New York and raised in Paris, where her father was a journalist for the Associated Press, she had to leave France in 1943 because she was Jewish. She went to Brazzaville, Congo, where she did radio broadcasts for the Free French. After the war, she was press attaché for Chief Justice Robert Jackson at the Nuremberg trials, became a senior editor at the United Nations, and then director of public relations for the French Film Office in the US. In that role, she had been instrumental in helping the French New Wave – and Truffaut in particular, ever since *The 400 Blows* (1959) – become known to the American press ("Helen G. Scott"; Toubiana xvi).

On 29 August, Peggy Robertson, Hitchcock's close assistant, sent one set of the tapes to Helen Scott in New York and another to Truffaut in Paris (Robertson to Truffaut). An American student began transcribing the English part of the interview in Paris, while Truffaut's assistants at his production company transcribed Helen Scott's French translations of Hitchcock's statements. But her French proved impossible for them to follow because of "strange diction" (de Baecque 143), combined with anglicisms, "franglais" (English words pronounced as if they were French), and occasionally inaccurate wording (the perils of simultaneous translation by non-professionals). Sometimes her voice was almost off-microphone or became incomprehensible when more than one person was speaking. Instead, the French team began translating the English transcription (de Baecque 143). On 18 October, Truffaut wrote Helen Scott that he never saw the American transcriber because she didn't speak French (*Letters* 203).

On 16 November, Truffaut wrote Don Congdon that an 800-page transcript was finished in both languages and he had started editing the French translation. He would reduce the length, but expand some paragraphs to clarify the discussion for a general audience. The editing process went on for a very long time. Periodically Truffaut communicated changes he was making to Helen Scott, with instructions to adjust the English manuscript accordingly, including moving statements ([Apr. 1963], *Letters* 215). Not until eight months later, on 13 July 1963, had Truffaut finished editing the book in French, so that Helen Scott could work on the American version in New York (Truffaut to Peggy Robertson).

Signs of the changes being made emerged in letters between Helen Scott and Truffaut. On 7 September 1963, she berated him for going too fast, sometimes missing Hitchcock's meaning. That created more work for her because she had to correct his text, with the understanding that he in turn would have to incorporate the changes he accepted into the French version. She had just seen *Rope* (1948) and regretted not having seen the other films earlier.

It was one thing for Truffaut to have reviewed Hitchcock's films scrupulously in preparation for the interview – and he continued to do so afterwards while he was editing – but he had not realized that the simultaneous translation would be affected negatively by not having brought Helen Scott into that part of the process. He replied that he was going to revise the text thoroughly, add more interventions of his own in the first section, as she suggested, and add a summary of each film (15 Oct. 1963, *Letters* 225).

The summaries were intended for readers who did not know Hitchcock's films. Both publishers were concerned that the book would be too technical and specialized to justify the cost of the many photographs that Truffaut insisted had to be placed where they came up in the text, which meant using a photo-offset process rather than the less expensive practice of grouping them in a separate section. Truffaut believed that the success of the book depended on integrating the discussion with its iconography, and he was probably right. He had to fight for this all along, and eventually he put a great deal of time into gathering photos, having frame enlargements made, and working on the pictorial composition of the book. That issue should have had nothing to do with the fidelity of Hitchcock's words as published compared to what he actually said. But as time went on, Truffaut was pressed more and more to reduce the text to make room for the photographs.

Meanwhile, Truffaut's film career was claiming his attention. During the many problems and revisions delaying *Fahrenheit 451*, Truffaut was working on *The Soft Skin*. On 17 December 1963, he wrote Helen Scott that he would finish shooting by Christmas (*Letters* 228). The film would be ready in time for the Cannes Film Festival in May 1964.

Editing the Hitchcock book was by no means over, but the project entered a new phase at the end of January 1964, when Truffaut's agent Don Congdon wrote that he should consider showing Hitchcock a draft as soon as possible because he would probably want changes, and Congdon needed his approval in writing before he could go to the magazines about serialization, which would be good publicity and pay well (Congdon to Truffaut, 31 Jan. 1964).[6] Truffaut could show this version to Simon and Schuster, but he needed Truffaut's introduction before coming to Paris in March. On 4 March, Congdon wrote Truffaut that he had still not seen the manuscript or the introduction, and that Helen Scott was not answering her telephone. Truffaut directed her to let Congdon see the manuscript, but he was far from ready to send it to Hitchcock (Truffaut to Scott, 10 Mar. 1964).

About six months after Cannes, Truffaut had completely revised the manuscript. He wrote to Helen Scott on 27 November and again in December, alerting her that there would be a lot for her to do quickly to adjust the English version: perhaps twenty-five typed pages to translate, many corrections to translate and enter, structural changes and cuts (*Letters*, 27 Nov. 1964, 256; [Dec.] 1964, 258). But it was not until 3 May 1965, five months later, that he replied to the substance of Congdon's request of 4 March 1964, more than a year before. He thought that Helen Scott had just finished the English version, he was writing his introduction, which he would send her to translate, and then everything would be sent to Hitchcock. If all went well, that text would go to both publishers. But Truffaut also needed another interview with Hitchcock to bring the manuscript up to date: *Marnie* (1964) had been released and Hitchcock was working on *Torn Curtain* (1966).

Soon after, Truffaut, while writing the script for *The Wild Child*, finally sent his introduction to Helen Scott for translation and suggested that she write to Hitchcock to ask when he could read the complete text and when the second interview could take place (Truffaut to Scott, 19 May 1965, *Letters* 270). Truffaut and Helen Scott had not stopped revising the text. On 28 July, she wrote to Truffaut asking to be paid for her considerable work, which, she pointed out, included editing that she had to do herself, above and beyond what Truffaut asked her to do, because the interview rambled and material had to be reorganized.

Not until 5 October 1965 did Truffaut write to Hitchcock directly to ask if he approved of the manuscript so that it could be given to the editors in New York and Paris (*Letters* 283–84). If not, he asked whether it would be possible for Hitchcock to dictate changes to Peggy Robertson or whether he would prefer to go over them at their next interview (Hitchcock had still not responded to Truffaut's request), to be scheduled in view of Truffaut's start date for shooting *Fahrenheit 451* at the beginning of February, when he believed Hitchcock would be finishing *Torn Curtain*. Hitchcock did not respond immediately (he was, after all, in the middle of production), and Truffaut became worried. He asked Helen Scott to contact Peggy Robertson, with the result that Hitchcock returned the manuscript on 22 October 1965 with notes for changes (de Baecque 145). On 18 November, Truffaut thanked him, assuring him that his changes would be made, and again requested a follow-up interview (*Letters* 289–90).

After this urgent exchange, it took Truffaut more than six months to send his introduction to Michael Korda at Simon and Schuster, along with a copy of the interview that did not incorporate Hitchcock's revisions because the manuscript had not yet been retyped (Truffaut to Korda, 1 June 1966). Considering how much time had passed since receiving Hitchcock's corrections, more than typing may have been involved. That same day, Truffaut also wrote to Odette Ferry, his French intermediary with Hitchcock, explaining that he needed Hitchcock's written approval of the layout and the introduction and an additional meeting with him, and suggesting a date.

Two weeks later, Korda wrote Truffaut that Hitchcock's agent, Herman Citron, had called him to say that Hitchcock was not happy with the translation (15 June 1966). Congdon, who had spoken with Korda, wrote to Truffaut about the same thing the following day. They were not sure which draft Hitchcock was referring to (they had not received the corrected English version themselves), but they reminded Truffaut that they could not proceed without Hitchcock's written approval. Congdon suggested that it would be best for the two men to meet to iron out any problems. Korda reminded him that Simon and Schuster needed time for copyediting after receiving Hitchcock's written approval – copyediting had already been done by the French publisher, Robert Laffont – which meant introducing even more changes in the published text from the interview as spoken nearly four years earlier. In view of this turn of events, Truffaut wrote again to Odette Ferry on 17 June asking her to intervene (*Letters* 292–93). He said that when Hitchcock had returned the manuscript with indications for changes six months before, he had included a note with these words: "I think you have done a wonderful job." It wasn't until two months later that Peggy Robertson had telephoned from

Pinewood, saying that "Hitchcock found the style insufficiently colloquial." Would Truffaut lose all the time and money he had invested (which he detailed, asking Ferry not to mention it to Hitchcock)? He hoped it wasn't that serious, "and that Hitchcock merely wants the style to be thoroughly revised." If so, the French edition could move ahead (he believed that the first five chapters were already being typeset), but the American edition would be stalled. Who would revise the text and when? The book should come out in time for Christmas to justify the cost of the photos and the offset printing. Would all this work be for nothing? He wanted Hitchcock to be satisfied.

Odette Ferry responded immediately to Truffaut's gun-to-the-head letter. She had translated the relevant parts for Hitchcock and he would approve them, with several small changes (17 June and 20 June, 1966). One word definitely had to be replaced, because neither of them knew what it meant: "non-adequation." Hitchcock set the dates for the second interview. Truffaut replied to her with great relief on 20 June 1966 but stressed that nothing could go forward without Hitchcock's approval in writing, and therefore indicated that he needed to ask again whether Hitchcock wanted one of his assistants to revise the final version or whether Hitchcock himself would do it (*Letters* 293, 295). Truffaut would send the manuscript incorporating the corrections he had just received to Michael Korda within forty-eight hours; a second copy would be sent to Hitchcock.

Apparently there was no more discussion of a thorough revision of the English text. Hitchcock's written agreement was definitively promised after the second interview was held in London in July 1966. On 28 July, Truffaut notified Don Congdon that they had cabled Korda to draft the agreement letter, which Hitchcock would sign as soon as he received it (*Letters* 296). Congdon replied on 4 August that after so much indirect communication about Hitchcock's opinion of the interview text, it would be good to know if he had discussed it with Truffaut directly. Indeed, had Truffaut talked to Hitchcock about it? It would appear not. Almost a year later, on 31 March 1967, Truffaut wrote to Hitchcock to say that several people had mentioned that he worried the English-language version was not "sufficiently colloquial" (the phrase had come up numerous times by then, for instance, in his letter to Odette Ferry on 17 June 1966, *Letters* 292). The reason, Truffaut explained, might be the montage he had created by ending many chapters with quotations from his writings, such as excerpts from an essay Hitchcock had published in the *Encyclopedia Britannica*.[7] Of course, the montage created by Truffaut, Helen Scott, and possibly other editors had been much more comprehensive than that.

Truffaut began his book with questions about Hitchcock's childhood, his education, his first jobs and formative experiences, and how he had entered the film industry. Unlike the case of *The Birds*, where much interview material was cut, this part was built up. Some embellishments seem harmless; probably they were taken from other interviews. Rewording, rearranging, and compressing Hitchcock's statements is the common denominator.

Throughout the interview, one finds countless examples of one word replaced with another when the original was usually more precise. Why, for instance, in a discussion of *Blackmail*, replace "If I were committing a murder, I'd hit him over the head with a brick [rather than use a knife]" (ht3.mp3) with the pallid "If I had killed him, I might have struck him over the head with a brick" (65)? (In the film, the woman says: "A good clean honest whack over the head with a brick is one thing. There's something British about that.") Regarding *Spellbound* (1945), why change "chase story" (ht13.mp3) to "manhunt story" (165)? Why, talking about *Lifeboat* (1944), substitute "nasty Nazi" (ht13.mp3) for "bad German" (156), or in the section on *Notorious*, change "villains" (ht14.mp3) to "spies" (170)? This last example involved more small, typical changes. Hitchcock stated during the interview, "I did make an attempt here to make the villains behave with reasonable evil"; as published, this became: "there was an attempt to make the spies behave with reasonable evil" (170). In this instance (and it is hardly unique), Hitchcock's way of putting it, "I did make an attempt," was changed to the passive voice, "there was an attempt to make," thereby deleting his role as decision-maker as well as weakening the sentence stylistically.

Other word substitutions changed Hitchcock's meaning more significantly. He said that *The Lodger* (1926) "was the first picture POSSIBLY influenced by my period in Germany. The whole approach to it was instinctive with me. It was the first time I had exercised any style" (ht2.mp3). In the book, his last phrase reads "my style" (44), following Helen Scott's translation during the interview, "*mon style.*" Soon afterwards he said, "I took, shall we say, pure narrative and presented for the first time ideas in purely visual form." In the book, "pure narrative" became "a pure narrative" (44). And again, describing his anxious walk though London with his future bride awaiting the verdict after the first screening for the studio bosses, he made a point of saying, "Mrs. Hitchcock and I were not married then, but we were going to be married in about three to four months time." In the book, it's "Mrs. Hitchcock and I couldn't bear to wait" (49).

Similarly, there are relatively small deletions with significant meaning. Truffaut asked Hitchcock about lynching in connection with the handcuffs that the Jack-the-Ripper suspect at the end of *The Lodger* got hung up on, literally, as he tried to climb over a fence to escape from the mob chasing him. Hitchcock then asked him a question he didn't expect, and the rest of their discussion did not end up in the book:

HITCHCOCK: The handcuffs, of course, were (pause) a thing, an idea that goes, I don't know, psychologically, fairly deep. I don't know what you, François, think of the psychological, almost psychotic, attitude towards tying up (pause). It's somewhere in the area of the fetish, isn't it? Isn't that so?

TRUFFAUT: I don't know (laughing). It's very much impressed me in your films.

HITCHCOCK: But I think that somehow, I don't know what it is, that handcuffing has a deeper significance to people.

TRUFFAUT: Yes, because it's the most immediate symbol of the deprivation of liberty.

HITCHCOCK: Well, but it has sex connotations.

TRUFFAUT: Maybe. I don't get this idea [*sens*] at all. [Helen Scott translated this as "a psychological attitude at all."]

HITCHCOCK: He doesn't, ah?

(ht2.mp3)

As published, this exchange is quite different:

HITCHCOCK: Psychologically, of course, the idea of the handcuffs has deeper implications. Being tied to something ... it's somewhere in the area of fetishism, isn't it?

TRUFFAUT: I don't know, but I have noticed that handcuffs have a way of recurring in your movies.

After departing from sex for a few moments, Hitchcock mentioned a "sexual connotation" and then talked about the Vice Museum in Paris (47).

Neither Truffaut nor Helen Scott was well-informed about silent film history. Hitchcock emphasized seeing films made by Decla-Bioscop, explaining how Decla-Bioscop came before Ufa, which would make a natural bridge to his own early work in Germany. But this information fell on deaf ears. Hitchcock began by designing art for the intertitles of silent films. Truffaut asked him to explain. Hitchcock replied that all title cards were "illustrated [....] You had, in those days, narrative titles and spoken titles" (ft1.mp3). As published, this became, "On each card you had the narrative title, the dialogue, and a small drawing" (27), thereby erasing Hitchcock's distinction between the two kinds of title cards.

Discussing *Spellbound*, Truffaut admired the kiss followed by seven doors that open (165), but Hitchcock's reply was cut: "I got that from the research. I said, what is the best symbol for people falling in love for the first time, and it was the opening of doors" (ft13.mp3). He wanted David O. Selznick to hire Salvador Dali to design the dream sequences so that they would be sharper and more clear than the rest of the film, unlike the usual technique of filming dreams with a blurry, hazy look (165). Hitchcock told Truffaut why he couldn't get that effect from his cinematographer, but it was cut: "I had, as I told you, George Barnes the cameraman, and the photography would be soft because he is a woman's photographer" (ft13.mp3).

While the truth value of Hitchcock's statements in a general sense was usually not significantly affected by all the small changes for the nonspecialist reader for whom the details might not be important, what got lost for everyone was a sense of the experience of the exchange and the opportunity to witness how this director thought of, and remembered, his logical, step-by-step process of seeing problems and then solving them in a way that combined narrative, emotion, and mise-en-scène – exactly why Truffaut had chosen Hitchcock in the first place.

From innumerable possible examples, take the way Hitchcock talked about *The Lodger*. Just after Hitchcock told Truffaut that he had found a style, he described opening the film with the head of a screaming blonde girl and I remember the way I photographed it. I got a sheet of glass, I laid the head of the girl on the glass, and spread the hair until it filled the frame, and underneath the glass, lit it from behind. And then I cut from the big head to an electric sign, which was advertising a musical play. It said, *ce soir*, TONIGHT, GOLDEN CURLS, TONIGHT, GOLDEN CURLS, and panned from the sign to the water, and it's flickering on the water, and out of the water comes the dead head of the drowned girl—pulled ashore, consternation, murdered, and ... no titles ... no titles. ... Police, crowd, reporter, notebook, reporter to telephone.

Hitchcock continued in the same way to chart the progress of four more sequences, until the main character finally came into the story fifteen minutes after the film began (ht2.mp3).

In the book, the first part is similar, except that "I" was changed to "we" and "big head" (which Hitchcock used repeatedly instead of "close-up") was changed to "head." Then Hitchcock's staccato, telegraphic style was normalized: "Then we cut to show an electric sign advertising a musical play, *Tonight, Golden Curls*, with the reflection flickering in the water. The girl has drowned. She's hauled out of the water and pulled ashore. The consternation of the bystanders suggests that a murder has been committed. The police arrive on the scene, and then the press. The camera follows one of the newsmen as he moves toward a telephone" (44–45).

It's odd that Truffaut wasn't more interested in conveying the visual manner in which Hitchcock framed his responses, like a series of images that, as he said (and that is omitted from the book), didn't need "titles" to explain them. The photographs that Truffaut included in the book go a long way toward making the argument for Hitchcock as a visual director, but the combination of his verbal means of expression along with the images would have been much more powerful.

Hitchcock had been interested in sound at least since *Blackmail*. In the interview, he explained that it had been planned as a silent film, but then he had been asked to prepare the last reel with sound so that it could be advertised as a part-talking film, given the novelty and box-office importance of dialogue in 1929. Hitchcock decided to do more than that: he would re-shoot the entire film with sound. Hitchcock was trying to move ahead with his own ideas about filmmaking by using sound psychologically, focalized through one character, Alice (Anny Ondra). She had stabbed a man to death with a knife the night before to escape being raped. A neighbor came in when the family was at the breakfast table and couldn't stop talking about the murder. She wouldn't have used a knife. In the interview, this is how Hitchcock made the point about how he tried to use sound experimentally:

As her dialogue went on, it became a sound of talk, talk, and the talk became less clear except one word: Knife. Knife. Knife. Knife. And I played it on the girl's face. And you hear this neighbor, and it dies away, goes a long way away, and all you can hear is KNIFE, KNIFE. Suddenly the voice of the father: "Pass the bread knife, would you please, Alice?" Normal voice. And she has to pick up the same knife she's just committed the murder with. But it was a contrast (pause) to the normal voice coming back. That was the first experiment with sound.

(ht3.mp3)

For Hitchcock, it was an important step forward in building up sound to be realistic psychologically. He had started the discussion of *Blackmail* by calling it "the next Hitchcock picture," after *The Lodger* (ht3.mp3).

In the book, this reads:

> And the talk goes on and on, becoming a confusion of vague noises to which the girl no longer listens. Except for the one word, 'Knife, knife,' which is said over and over again and becomes fainter and fainter. Then suddenly she hears her father's normal loud voice: 'Alice, please pass me the bread knife.' And Alice has to pick up a knife similar to the one she's used for the killing, while the others go on chattering about the crime.
>
> (65)

Throughout the interview, Hitchcock talked about specific ways he tried to control the audience's emotions by channeling them through a character's psychology. Here, his choice of camera position – "I played it on the girl's face," one of his big points – was deleted. Here, she "no longer listens," but Hitchcock's idea was more important than that: she *can't* listen, because she has no control over this focalization of sound. It has been rendered, precisely, subjective, subject to her state of mind. "The same knife" was changed to a "similar" knife, presumably because it couldn't have been the same knife. That one had been left at the crime scene. The more important idea, for Hitchcock, now speaking from Alice's perspective, was that it might as well be the same knife. There is no mistaking his meaning.

When he came to *Young and Innocent* (1937), Hitchcock enthusiastically described – as if reliving the scenes – how he orchestrated the narrative by manipulating point of view and giving the audience information that the characters didn't have. For him, this last part was another step forward in his goal of involving the audience in figuring out how the dilemma would be resolved (ht7.mp3). Unfortunately, this is an excellent example of how Hitchcock's train of thought got lost in the copyediting, even though a long (redacted) extract was included in the book.

The interview and the book are relatively close at the beginning of Hitchcock's example (114–15, ht7.mp3). A young girl is searching for the murderer. The only person who can recognize him is a tramp who knows that his eyes blink uncontrollably. The tramp observes that it is ridiculous for them to try to find those eyes in the crowd. His statement triggers one of Hitchcock's most elaborate camera movements, one that took two days to achieve: starting high above the hotel lounge, the camera advances through the crowd to the performers in a band, in blackface, to a close-up of the drummer until his eyes fill the screen. Then the eyes twitch, and Hitchcock returns the camera to the girl and the tramp.

Here is how he continued, in the interview, to make the point that to him was the most important:

> NOW the audience had the information. NOW the question was: how is this girl and this old boy going to discover the man? NOW came a progress of the police. A policeman sees the girl, goes on the phone and tells her father, who is the head of the police. The band breaks up for a smoke. They go back to the toilet—*cabinet*—where […] the drummer strolls into the alleyway and there he sees

at the far end approaching a group of three men, two in uniform and one not. He ducks back, he's guilty. Ducks back in the doorway and the band resumes. NOW the nervous drummer sees [at] the other end of the ballroom the policeman who is keeping his eye on the young girl. NOW the drummer sees the father, who's in civilian clothes, with the two uniformed men, move round back into conversation with the other watching policemen. Of course, it's all about the little girl, but the drummer doesn't know this, he thinks they're for him. NOW his nervousness is reflected in the drum beat. AND THE DRUMS AREN'T DOING WELL AT ALL. The orchestra's being thrown out of time, of rhythm. And he gets worse and worse.

(ht7.mp3)

In the book, not only has the language been normalized, but the steps were lost by which Hitchcock took such pleasure describing how the narrative moved ahead through the alternation of the characters' perceptions, based on what we see them see.

A policeman outside sees the girl, who is the daughter of his chief. He goes to the phone. Meanwhile, the band has stopped for a break, and the drummer, having a smoke outside in the alley, sees a group of police hurrying toward the rear entrance of the hotel. Since he's guilty, he quickly ducks back inside, to the bandstand, where the music resumes. Now the jittery drummer sees the policemen talking to the tramp and the girl at the other end of the ballroom. He thinks they're looking for him, and his nervousness is reflected in the drumbeat, which is out of tune with the rest of the band. The rhythm gets worse and worse.

(115)

What could top "the drums aren't doing well at all?" More than a loss of the colloquial, Hitchcock's analytical train of thought, the way he had worked through both sound and image, and the rhythm of his points of emphasis had been lost or rendered matter-of-fact.

Certain categories of information seem to have been omitted from the published interview for reasons over and above the need to keep the page count down or omit Hitchcock's slightly off-color jokes and descriptions of individuals that might offend them or even prove libelous. Information was dropped that would be considered precious today, particularly by film historians: explanations of technique were greatly limited compared to the original, references to television and the film industry as such, including observations about people who were not necessarily well-known and what they did, as Hitchcock remembered this or that film or phase of his career. When it came to unusual films that Truffaut understandably had not seen (although he did try to see them later), such as the two 1944 propaganda films Hitchcock made in England to contribute to the war effort (*Bon Voyage* and *Aventure Malgache* – Truffaut might have seen *Bon Voyage* as a boy), his descriptions were condensed to such an extent as to misstate or eliminate much that would be of great interest today. Jean Renoir's *A Salute to France* (1944) was part of the same group as Hitchcock's, short semi-fictional films created for the French populace at the time of the Allied invasion of northern France to show them that the Allies respected them and that they were working with the French Resistance for the liberation of the country.

Unlike the text in the book, Truffaut was going to pass over them, but they were important for Hitchcock to discuss (ht13.mp3, 159–61). Like everything else in the interview, this passage is full of interest – both for what was said and for clues that point toward other avenues that could not have been developed at length at that time or accommodated within the limitations of either the interview or the book.

In conclusion, lest my undertaking be misunderstood, my analysis of some passages showing the differences between Hitchcock's statements during the interview and as published amount to an homage to the enterprise of creating this resource and to its contemporary usefulness, a tribute to the efforts of Hitchcock, Truffaut, Helen Scott, and everyone else who worked so hard to record, edit, publish and save the original documentation and make it available to researchers. The book in its entirety – Truffaut's introduction, the main discussion, the photographs, and the filmography, as well as the chapter Truffaut wrote after Hitchcock died for a "definitive version" – fulfilled Truffaut's intended purpose beautifully. Together, Truffaut and Hitchcock demonstrated the undeniable importance of Hitchcock's body of work and showed how it integrated mise-en-scène, narrative structure, film technique, emotion, and psychology. The book has never stopped sparking interest in studying films and in making films.

Now, almost fifty years later, shouldn't it be possible to reproduce the entire interview exactly as it was spoken – English, French, translations back and forth, exchanges in between languages, a full written transcript accompanied by a CD or audio files? Truffaut stated in his introduction that the interview was fifty hours long. The complete set of tapes from the original interview at the Herrick Library is nearly twenty-six hours long. (Perhaps Truffaut added the time from the second interview or time he might have spent in discussions over the years.) In the summer of 1999, as part of the Hitchcock centennial celebrations, a selection of eleven hours and fifteen minutes was broadcast on the French radio station France Culture. Those programs are readily available on the internet as mp3 files. I challenge anyone to listen and not become thoroughly intrigued by the impression of presence when hearing the intonation of those voices and realizing the difference it makes compared to reading a transcript, even if the transcript were entirely faithful to the original. This is a project for a team of Hitchcock workers who could provide reliable annotations, as has been the practice for comparably significant critical editions of literary works.

Notes

All translations are my own unless otherwise indicated. Occasionally I have modified a published translation. I am grateful to the staff of the Bibliothèque de la Cinémathèque Française, especially to Valdo Kneubühler, and to Barbara Hall at the Margaret Herrick Library, Academy of Motion Picture Arts and Sciences, Beverly Hills.

1. My quotations from the recorded interview come from the eleven-hour-and-fifteen-minute selection edited for French radio broadcast on France Culture in the summer of 1999, "Alfred Hitchcock avec François Truffaut," by Serge Toubiana and Nicolas Saada. The programs are available at a number of internet sites in twenty-five MP3 files. I have identified quotations using these file numbers (e.g., ht1.mp3). My study was based on the full set of tapes available at the Herrick. I do not know whether recordings of the second interview, on *Marnie* and *Torn Curtain*, were preserved, nor do I know whether the first manuscript that Hitchcock returned to Truffaut with his annotations still exists. In my quotations from the mp3 files, I have used italics and capital letters and indicated pauses in order to capture the tone and rhythm of the conversation.

2. My chronology of the events leading to the publication of Truffaut's Hitchcock is indebted to Antoine de Baecque's "Hitchbook," which is based on Truffaut's *Hitchcock* Introduction and on materials held by Les Films du Carrosse, Truffaut's production company, many of which are now located at the Bibliothèque de la Cinémathèque Française. An abbreviated account appears in de Baecque and Serge Toubiana's Truffaut biography. My chronology does not always coincide with de Baecque's.

    I also benefited from the Bibliothèque du Film (BiFi) exhibition of documents and photographs titled "Hitchcock-Truffaut: Secrets de fabrication," which was on display in the library from 7 October 1999 to 7 January 2000, as well as the BiFi's exhibition booklet, which reproduced some of the documents on display. A shorter version of the booklet, with some differences in the text, is online at http://www.bifi.fr/public/ap/article.php?id=200. For a time, a slightly different version of the documents and texts from this exhibition was available online in the library.

3. This statement is absent from the published English translation.

4. Truffaut published a similar statement in the Introduction to *Hitchcock* (18).

5. In 1984, Patricia Hitchcock O'Connell donated a complete set of the tapes of the August 1962 interview (fifty-two thirty-minute reels, a maximum of twenty-six hours) to the Margaret Herrick Library as part of the Hitchcock Collection.

6. Congdon to Truffaut, 8 Sept. 1966 and 13 Sept. 1966. Congdon had contacted *Life* and *Playboy* after the interview in 1962, and both had expressed interest (Congdon to Truffaut, 24 Aug. 1962). Ultimately, however, all the magazines Congdon suggested – *Playboy, Life, Look, Ladies Home Journal, Esquire* – lost interest or turned down publication. The project was regarded as an insider book for film and Hitchcock aficionados, with too little about his personal life to appeal to a general audience.

7. Hitchcock's essay "Film Production" was published in the *Encyclopedia Britannica*, 1965 ed., 15: 907–11, as part of an eight-part entry "Motion Pictures," and reprinted in Gottlieb 210–26.

Works Cited

With the exception of Helen Scott's letter of 7 September 1963 to François Truffaut, all unpublished letters cited parenthetically in the text are listed by correspondents, date, and source: "BiFi" for the Bibliothèque de la Cinémathèque Française (formerly the Bibliothèque du Film/BiFi), "Herrick" for the Margaret Herrick Library, or both, for items in both collections.

Congdon, Don. Letters to François Truffaut. 24 Aug. 1962; 16 Nov. 1962; 31 Jan. 1964; 4 Mar. 1964; 16 June 1966; 4 Aug. 1966; 8 Sept. 1966; 13 Sept. 1966. BiFi.

de Baecque, Antoine. "'Hitchbook'. Ou comment fut écrit le plus célèbre livre de cinéma." *Vertigo* 17 (1997). 139–48.

de Baecque, Antoine, and Serge Toubiana. *Truffaut*. Trans. Catherine Temerson. New York: Knopf, 1999.Trans. of *François Truffaut*. Paris: Gallimard, 1996.

Ferry, Odette. Letters to François Truffaut. 17 June 1966; 20 June 1966. BiFi and Herrick.

Gottlieb, Sidney, ed., *Hitchcock on Hitchcock: Selected Writings and Interviews*. Berkeley: U of California P, 1995.

"Helen G. Scott, 72, Writer for Truffaut and Other Directors." Obituary. *New York Times* 24 Nov. 1987: B11.

"Hitchcock-Truffaut: Secrets de fabrication." Exhibition booklet. Bibliothèque du Film, 1999.

Korda, Michael. Letter to François Truffaut. 15 June 1966. BiFi.

Robertson, Peggy. Letter to François Truffaut. 29 Aug 1962. BiFi and Herrick.

Rohmer, Eric, and Claude Chabrol. *Hitchcock: The First Forty-Four Films*. Trans. Stanley Hochman. New York: Ungar, 1979. Trans. of *Hitchcock*. Paris: Editions Universitaires, 1957.

Scott, Helen. Letter to François Truffaut. 7 Sept. 1963. Displayed in the exhibition "Hitchcock-Truffaut: Secrets de fabrication" (7 Oct. 1999–7 Jan. 2000) and reproduced in the first online presentation of the exhibition. BiFi.

Scott, Helen. Letter to François Truffaut. 28 July 1965. BiFi.

Toubiana, Serge. "Hélène Scott, l'intrépide." *Cahiers du cinéma* 402 (Dec. 1987): xvi.

Toubiana, Serge, and Nicolas Saada. "Alfred Hitchcock avec François Truffaut." Summer 1999. France Culture radio. http://www.hitchcockwiki.com/wiki/Interview:_Alfred_Hitchcock_and_Francois_Tuffaut_%28Aug/1962%29

Truffaut, François. *Correspondance*. Ed. Gilles Jacob and Claude de Givray. Paris: Hatier, 1988.

Truffaut, François. "Hitchcock est le plus grand 'inventeur de formes' de l'époque." *Arts* 647 (4–10 Dec. 1957): 7.

Truffaut, François. Letter to Alfred Hitchcock. 31 Mar. 1967. BiFi and Herrick.

Truffaut, François. Letters to Don Congdon. 11 Nov. 1962; 3 May 1965; 28 July 1966. BiFi.

Truffaut, François. Letter to Michael Korda. 1 June 1966. BiFi.

Truffaut, François. Letter to Odette Ferry. 1 June 1966. BiFi.

Truffaut, François. Letter to Peggy Robertson. 13 July 1963. BiFi.

Truffaut, François. Letter to Helen Scott. 10 Mar. 1964. BiFi.

Truffaut, François. *Letters*. Ed. Gilles Jacob and Claude de Givray. Trans. and ed. Gilbert Adair. London: Faber and Faber, 1989.

Truffaut, François, with the collaboration of Helen G. Scott. *Hitchcock*. Rev. ed. New York: Simon and Schuster, 1984.

22

Robin Wood's Hitchcock

Harry Oldmeadow

In 1960 two neophyte critics on either side of the Atlantic were writing on *Psycho*. Andrew Sarris's review was his first for the *Village Voice* (see Kapsis 64), while Robin Wood submitted his first critical venture to *Sight and Sound*. Penelope Houston rejected it on the grounds that Wood failed to understand that the film was intended as a joke; in a word, he had taken the film too *seriously* (Wood xliii). The article was subsequently published in *Cahiers du cinéma* (Nov. 1960). The rest, as they say, is history; Sarris and Wood soon became the two most influential English-language exponents of the critical auteurism pioneered by the French cinephiles.

Hitchcock's artistic reputation and significance in film studies derive, in part, from the quality of the criticism his work has attracted. Wood's *Hitchcock's Films* (1965) and *Hitchcock's Films Revisited* (1989) stand as conspicuous landmarks in this crowded landscape. To understand Wood's achievement in his first book we need to consider briefly Hitchcock's standing at the time. The early films had established his reputation as a superior suspense-film craftsman. Following Hitchcock's 1939 move to America, most transatlantic and established French critics preferred his British films "for their visual speed, comic realism and varied social canvases" (Durgnat 22). Hitchcock was appreciated primarily as an *entertainer,* "the world's best director of unimportant pictures," according to John Grierson (72). As late as 1967 O.B. Hardison could write, "Nobody would seriously compare Hitchcock to a dozen directors and producers who have used the film medium as an art form" (137–38).

In 1954 Claude Chabrol interviewed Hitchcock for *Cahiers*. Perhaps mindful of Sartre's maxim that every technique reveals a metaphysic, Chabrol remarked, "Some of my colleagues and I ... have discovered in your works a carefully hidden theme, and that is the search for God" (Chabrol 41) – *la métaphysique de Hitchcock*.

A Companion to Alfred Hitchcock, First Edition. Edited by Thomas Leitch and Leland Poague.
© 2011 Thomas Leitch and Leland Poague. Published 2011 by Blackwell Publishing Ltd.

Here, suddenly, was a serious approach indeed! Truffaut, Chabrol, and Rohmer, in the vanguard of both critical auteurism and the *nouvelle vague* cinema, were *aficionados* of Hitchcock's work. The first major turning-point in Hitchcock criticism was the 1957 publication of Rohmer and Chabrol's *Hitchcock*, reading him as a Catholic moralist, preoccupied with themes such as the transference of guilt, the ambiguous commerce of good and evil, temptation, sin and redemption, and the like. No less a Hitchcock partisan, François Truffaut took a more secular approach, finding Hitchcock to be "among such artists of anxiety as Kafka, Dostoevsky and Poe" (*Hitchcock* 20). No lack of seriousness here either! In what Raymond Durgnat described as a "delirium of interpretation" (23), Jean Douchet saw in Hitchcock's films an occult "duel of Light and Shadow, therefore of Unity and Duality" (Douchet 24). For Douchet the wellsprings of Hitchcock's art were neither Catholic morality nor existentialist angst – per Durgnat, at least – but an arcane occultism encompassing both neo-Platonism and Manicheanism (Durgnat 23–24).

The wider acceptance of auteurism in the 1960s much enhanced Hitchcock's reputation. By the early 1960s American critics like Sarris and Peter Bogdanovich were exalting Hitchcock as auteur. The British reappraisal was initiated in *Movie*. Ian Cameron (*Movie* 3 and 6) anatomized Hitchcock's "mechanics of suspense," particularly in *The Man Who Knew Too Much* (1956) and *Psycho* (1960), and highlighted the "remarkable obsession with motherhood and maternal relationships" ("Hitchcock 2" 10) in the 1950s films. V.F. Perkins opened his *Movie* 7 analysis of *Rope* (1948) by observing that Hitchcock, although working primarily in one genre, set himself an immense variety of self-imposed technical and formal problems. Cameron and Richard Jeffery (*Movie* 12) offered an extended analysis of two recent and highly controversial Hitchcock films, *The Birds* (1963) and *Marnie* (1964). For all the seriousness of the French critics, the real forerunners of Wood's study were these articles in *Movie*, less concerned with abstract metaphysical themes than with meticulous textual analysis that took account of the way in which Hitchcock's cinema worked its effects. The *Movie* critics "emphasised, not a hidden symbolism, but an overt level of dramatic and moral experience" (Durgnat 24).

"Why should we take Hitchcock seriously?" The opening line of *Hitchcock's Films* was to become justly celebrated. (See, for example, Deutelbaum and Poague 1.) In his sustained response to that question Wood rendered it obsolete, and thus changed the face of Hitchcock criticism thenceforth. The question, Wood told us, would hardly need asking "if the cinema were truly regarded as an autonomous art, not as a mere adjunct of the novel or the drama" (55).

Firstly, Wood insists, we must understand that the cinema's effects are felt on many levels, not only the conscious. Of a particular scene in *Marnie*, Wood writes:

> The point, like so much that is important in the film, is *felt* rather than registered consciously by the spectator. … It seems to me a fair representative specimen of that local realization that one finds everywhere in recent Hitchcock films. … The cinema has its own methods and its own scope.

(56–57)

Secondly, we must overcome the prejudice against popular cinema. From the popularity of Hitchcock's films there "arises a widespread assumption that, however 'clever,' 'technically brilliant,' 'amusing,' 'gripping,' etc., they may be, they can't be taken seriously as we take, say, the films of Bergman or Antonioni seriously" (57).

In a passage soon to be widely ridiculed, Wood compares Hitchcock's cinema to Shakespeare's immersion in a "'commercial' – and at the time intellectually disreputable – medium, the Elizabethan drama" (57). British criticism, says Wood, is typified by Houston's 1963 *Sight and Sound* article:

> Miss Houston appears to include herself in that "general agreement that (Hitchcock) is a master"; yet nothing she finds to say remotely supports such a valuation. There is continual evasion of critical responsibility, a refusal to follow any line of enquiry rigorously to its conclusion. …
>
> Most of Miss Houston's article seems to rest on two supports, both critically insufficient to say the least: what Hitchcock has said, and what she herself assumes to have been his intentions in this or that film. … The whole article … is typical of the dilettantism that vitiates so much British film criticism.
>
> (59–60)

Though Wood extols the pioneering work of Rohmer and Chabrol as "a very serious attempt to account for the resonances his films can evoke," their book is not altogether satisfactory: "depriving the films of flesh and blood[,] reducing them to theoretical skeletons… [,] they play down the suspense element and the comedy, and strip each film down to some bald intellectual postulate" (62). Wood finds Douchet's readings, "for all their interpretative excesses and, again, a tendency to reduce things to abstractions, more generally persuasive (63).

Earlier Wood warned against the critical excesses of Hitchcock's French admirers and rejected their "spirit of uncritical veneration," stressing the need to "make the necessary discriminations between different works, or admit occasional failures of realization within works" (58). Nonetheless, whatever the deficiencies of the *Cahiers* analyses, they "are so far beyond anything the British 'Establishment' has given us in intelligence and critical rigor" that "[e]ven their moments of lunacy seem more intelligent than the relentless triviality of 'Establishment' reasonableness" (64).

Now Wood returns to his initial question. The short answer reveals the Leavisite position to which Wood at that time adhered: we must take Hitchcock seriously because he is a creative artist with a complex but coherent moral vision whose art explores "themes of profound and universal significance" (66). Wood adduces four general points in favor of his argument: there is a *unity and consistent organic development* in Hitchcock's work; within this unity there is an arresting *variety*, especially evident in his last five films – *Vertigo* (1958), *North by Northwest* (1959), *Psycho*, *The Birds*, and *Marnie* – which are each different in "tone, style, subject matter, method" (65); thirdly, *the inseparability of theme, form and style* that we find in Hitchcock's later films is one of the hallmarks of the artist; and lastly, there is the *disturbing quality* of Hitchcock's cinema, a characteristic it shares with much other great art.

One of the functions of art, writes Wood, is to *disturb* us, "to penetrate and undermine our complacencies and set notions" (67). No doubt Wood would have endorsed Susan Sontag's dictum: "Real art has the capacity to make us nervous" (99). Far from being a simple matter of "suspense" (important though that is), Hitchcock's films discomfort the spectator through a "disconcerting moral sense, in which good and evil are seen to be so interwoven as to be virtually inseparable, and which insists on the existence of evil impulses in all of us" (67). If Hitchcock tells us that "a good six or seven reels of worry is what I aim for" (quoted in Kapsis 24), Wood argues that this "worry" is actually deeply rooted.

Hitchcock's Films offers us close readings of *Strangers on a Train* (1951), *Rear Window* (1954), *Vertigo, North by Northwest, Psycho, The Birds,* and *Marnie* (*Torn Curtain* [1966] was added for the 1969 edition). Why these particularly? Of the early British films, Wood writes that "they are so overshadowed by his recent development as to seem, in retrospect, little more than 'prentice work, interesting chiefly because they are Hitchcock's" (73). The last five more or less choose themselves, seeming to Wood "to constitute an astonishing, unbroken chain of master-pieces and the highest reach of his art to date" (72). Moreover, these highly varied and accessible works have received meager critical attention in Britain. *Strangers on a Train* and *Rear Window* are included because of their "intrinsic merit" and popularity (73). After paying homage to the Hitchcock criticism of his *Movie* colleagues, Wood also offers fragmentary but illuminating comments on Rebecca (1940), Spellbound (1945), Lifeboat (1944), Notorious (1946), Rope, I Confess (1953), and The Wrong Man (1956).

At the time, *Strangers on a Train* was critically neglected (see Kapsis 257). Wood finds its governing assumption to be that "subversive, destructive desires exist in all of us, waiting for a momentary relaxing of our vigilance" (93). This foreshadows themes that Hitchcock will elaborate over the next decade:

> [W]hat Conrad calls the "sickening assumption of common guilt" (developed especially in *Psycho*); the theme of the search for identity (*Vertigo*); the theme of the struggle of a personality torn between order and chaos. ... We find here, too, the characteristic Hitchcock moral tone: the utterly unsentimental and ruthless condemnation of the forces that make for disorder, coupled with a full awareness of their dangerously tempting fascination; a sense of the impurity of motives ... [in which] good and evil are inseparably mixed. And, running through the film, there is that Hitchcockian humor ... [,] the manifestation of his artistic impersonality, of his detached and impersonal attitude to themes which clearly obsess him.
>
> (98–99)

Despite its thematic density the film is, in Wood's view, ultimately unsatisfactory, partly because of the inadequacies of two of the leading players, Farley Granger and Ruth Roman, whose screen personalities cannot carry the weight of Hitchcock's themes. The consequent effect is somewhat two-dimensional, "like watching the working out of a theorem rather than of a human drama" (99).

Rear Window was immediately popular with the critics and almost universally praised for its humor and suspense – "exhilarating," "full-bodied," "the most roundly enjoyable Hitchcock film in years," exclaimed the critics, "more laughs than chills." Bosley Crowther toyed with the notion that *Rear Window* might be a "significant" film – but he soon trashed the idea: "Mr. Hitchcock's film is not 'significant.' What it has to say about people and human nature is superficial and glib" (quoted in Kapsis 26–28). The *Cahiers* critics, on the other hand, found the film very "significant" indeed (see Truffaut, *Films* 77–79).

Wood opens his account by disavowing two extreme readings, both centering on voyeurism. *Rear Window* is neither the "whole-hearted condemnation of curiosity, prying, voyeurism, *libido sciendi* and *delectatio morosa*" argued for by Rohmer and Chabrol, nor a "corrupt, distasteful" film that "shamelessly exploits and encourages" these impulses: "the morality of the film is far subtler and more profound than either suggests" (100). Wood finds the readings given by Douchet (*Cahiers* 113) and Paul Mayersberg (*Movie* 3) helpful, but pays more attention to the film's treatment of marriage and sexual relationships. He also comments in some detail on Hitchcock's use of space and its role in forging the spectator's identification with L.B. Jefferies (James Stewart).

In the 1970s and 1980s, *Rear Window* became a privileged site of theoretical contestation. Wood partially anticipates Laura Mulvey's celebrated 1975 theorizing of "the male gaze" when he alerts us to the role of Lisa (Grace Kelly) as spectacle for both Jefferies and the (male) spectator. He also refers to the camera symbolism and suggests that the murder "represents, in an extreme and hideous form, the fulfillment of Jefferies' desire" (104). Wood resists any facile reading of the film's last sequence by registering the irony implicit in the narrative resolution and the precariousness of its closure. Far from being simply a "light comedy thriller" (the prevailing view in Britain and America), *Rear Window* is a film of "disturbing undercurrents" (106).

Vertigo was a commercial flop that provoked considerable critical consternation. Audiences and reviewers alike were upset by the early disclosure of the mystery, the film's ending, and its failure to re-establish an unambiguous moral order and equilibrium. Critics in "highbrow" publications like the *New Yorker, Time,* and the *Nation* were generally unsympathetic, but some of the more popular reviewers, including Crowther, acclaimed the film as a successful romantic thriller (Kapsis 53–54).

Early in *Hitchcock's Films* Wood had compared *Vertigo* – in "form" and "content" (inseparable in the Leavisite lexicon) – with Keats's poem *Lamia* (1819) and Kenji Mizoguchi's *Ugetsu Monogatari* (1953), finding it, "in maturity and depth of understanding as in formal perfection, decidedly superior to Keats' poem if not to Mizoguchi's film" (66–67). Now Wood launches his textual analysis with a Big Statement:

> *Vertigo* seems to me Hitchcock's masterpiece to date, and one of the four or five most profound and beautiful films the cinema has yet given us. This is a claim that may surprise, even amuse, the majority of my readers; but I think an analysis of the

film, by revealing an entirely satisfying and fully realized treatment of themes of the most fundamental human significance, can justify it.

(108)

Boileau and Narcejac's novel *D'entre les morts*, writes Wood, was a formulaic and "squalid exercise in sub-Graham Greenery ... saturated with that easy pessimism that is as much a sentimental self-indulgence as its opposite" (108). Hitchcock transmutes this grimy literary material into a cinematic masterpiece. Wood notes the significance of the changed locale, the use of the sequoias, the transformation of the characters, and the introduction of a new character, Midge (Barbara Bel Geddes). The "ignominious worms" of the novel become fully human characters "whom we are permitted to regard – for all their weaknesses and limitations – with respect and sympathetic concern" (109). *Vertigo* is shaped by "a simultaneous awareness of the immense value of human relationships and their inherent incapability of perfect realization" (109).

Wood then embarks on the most thorough textual dissection in *Hitchcock's Films*, beginning with the credits and prologue, working through the three "acts" or "movements," and ending with the final shot of Scottie (James Stewart) looking down on the dead Judy (Kim Novak). Aspects given especially intensive analysis include the opening rooftop chase scene ending in Scottie's literal and metaphorical suspension, the mise-en-scène of the sequences in Midge's apartment and Elster's office, the presentation of Madeleine, the use of spiral and flower motifs, the significance of the dream sequence, and the shattering alienation effect of Madeleine's "suicide" (an effect repeated in the shower murder in *Psycho*).

Vertigo is an *organic* film, which is to say that its structure, plot, characterization, and style are all subordinated to the development of its central themes. Wood again deploys Shakespearean comparisons to insist on the *complexity*, *unity* and *coherence* of Hitchcock's film, concluding: "In complexity and subtlety, in emotional depth, in its power to disturb, in the centrality of its concerns, *Vertigo* can as well as any film be taken to represent the cinema's claims to be treated with the respect accorded to the longer established art forms" (130).

This passage will not, perhaps, strike today's reader as exceptional. In 1965 these were brave words indeed. Along with his analysis of *Psycho*, Wood's treatment of *Vertigo* stands as the most impressive chapter in the book. All too often we find occasion to recall Sontag's maxim that interpretation is "the compliment that mediocrity pays to genius" (99–100). Not here. Wood's essay provides the kind of criticism *Vertigo* had richly deserved and been denied, and it was crucial to the canonization of both film and filmmaker.

Critics and audiences gave *North by Northwest* a much more uniformly enthusiastic reception than *Vertigo*. It conformed more closely to the perceived Hitchcock formula: a captivating blend of humor, romance, and suspense. Wood wants to dispel the prejudices associated with the view that Hitchcock is "a polished light entertainer," with its debilitating corollary that we therefore need not take him seriously as an *artist*. But "*[a] film, whether light entertainment or not, is either a work of art or it is nothing.* And the basic essential of a work of art is that it be thematically organic" (131; my italics). Wood stresses the thematic unity of *North by Northwest* and foregrounds "its charms, its deftness, the constant flow of invention, its humor and exhilaration," which is "not to turn a light comedy into an unsmiling morality play, but to suggest why *North by Northwest* is such a very, very good light comedy" (141).

Many fans were deeply offended by *Psycho,* and the reviews were mixed. Crowther wrote of "a blot on an honorable career" (quoted in Rebello 165); Houston called it "that sick joke in a Gothic horror format" (*Contemporary* 69); Dwight Macdonald dismissed it as no more than a padded-out television show, and "a reflection of a most unpleasant mind, a mean, sly, sadistic little mind" (quoted in Rebello 165). Sarris, on the other hand, had no doubt that he had seen something extraordinary – "the first American movie since *Touch of Evil* [1958] to stand in the same creative rank as the great European films" (quoted in Kapsis 64). Wood's account of *Psycho,* "perhaps the most terrifying film ever made" (142), is a re-working of his *Cahiers* review. Like many Hitchcock films, it takes us on a journey from the "normal" to the "abnormal" (142–43), making us experience the continuity between them. This, along with "the dominance of the past over the present" (143), is the film's organizing theme.

Wood accents the identification techniques used to implicate the spectator in the situation and psychology of Marion Crane (Janet Leigh) and subsequently of Norman Bates (Anthony Perkins). "That we all carry within us somewhere every human potentiality, for good or evil, so that we all share in a common guilt, may be, intellectually, a truism; the greatness of *Psycho* lies in its ability, not merely to *tell* us this, but to make us experience it" (148).

Wood concentrates not on the "incomparable physical impact" of the shower scene ("probably the most horrific incident in any fiction film") but on the traumatic effect on the spectator of the shattering of the identification: "so engrossed are we in Marion, so secure in her potential salvation, that we can scarcely believe it is happening; when it is over, and she is dead, we are left shocked, with nothing to cling to, the apparent center of the film entirely dissolved" (146).

Psycho is Hitchcock's "ultimate achievement to date in the technique of audience participation." The minor characters "are merely projections of the spectators into the film, our instruments for the search" (146–47). (The treatment of the scene in which Lila [Vera Miles] searches the Bates house furnishes another example of Wood's highly accomplished techniques of textual exegesis, particularly of mise-en-scène.) Wood's summation is unequivocal:

> *Psycho* is one of the key works of our age. Its themes are of course not new – obvious forerunners include *Macbeth* and Conrad's *Heart of Darkness* – but the intensity and horror of their treatment and the fact that they are here grounded in sex belong to the age that has witnessed on the one hand the discoveries of Freudian psychology and on the other the Nazi concentration camps.
>
> (150)

Whether, like David Bordwell, we find such formulations "hyperbolic" is a matter of judgment; certainly, "Wood's style reemphasizes the colossal artistic and moral stakes Hitchcock is playing for" (Bordwell 228–29). For Wood, *Psycho* is a work that can "contemplate the ultimate horrors without hysteria, with a poised, almost serene detachment," achieved in part by the "detached sardonic humor" (151).

There is much more that might be said about Wood's treatment of *Psycho*. Bordwell, whatever his localized disagreements with Wood, has rightly written that

> Wood's essay on *Psycho* is fairly brief, but its clarity and fecundity have made it, and indeed his entire book, an exemplar for the Anglo-American interpretive community. The essay's careful explication of how the film enacts its semantic fields makes it a pedagogic model, and its rhetorical control remains instructive.
>
> (229)

The scope of the present chapter does not allow us to recapitulate Wood's no less interesting treatments of *The Birds* and *Marnie*. His recuperation of these "varied and disconcerting" (152) texts, both frequently maligned by the critics, encouraged a more sensitive reading of their peculiar tensions and ambiguities. The account of *Marnie* was especially salutary. Contrary to claims that it represents some kind of "falling-off" in Hitchcock's creative output, a symptom of impending creative senility, Wood argues that *Marnie* is "one of Hitchcock's richest, most fully achieved and mature masterpieces" (173). In Wood's view, three kinds of objections need to be addressed: that the film is marred by "absurdly clumsy, lazy, crude devices, used with a blatant disregard for realism"; that the film is psychologically naive, inconsistent, too schematic and generally unpersuasive; and that Marnie's case is "much too extreme for the film to have any universal validity" (173–74). Wood's essay on *Marnie* is rather like the film itself – dazzling in parts but unsatisfactory as a whole. His defense of the film's expressionistic devices is ingenious but not always persuasive: the production history of *Marnie* suggests that many of the techniques used in the film were, uncharacteristically, indeed *ad hoc* and opportunistic (see Kapsis 128–31). Moreover, those critics who discerned in *Marnie* a diminution of Hitchcock's creative powers were vindicated by what was to follow.

Hitchcock's Films was widely reviewed in the film journals. Here, I give a cursory sample only. In the light of earlier jousting, it is perhaps worth returning to Penelope Houston, whose *Sight and Sound* review was surprisingly friendly, though one sees exactly what the *Movie* critics found so infuriating about her mode of criticism. Wood's book, she says, is "an eccentric but not unappetizing hors d'oeuvre" to Truffaut's impending book on Hitchcock. (How wrong she was! Truffaut's amiable book is a mere confection next to Wood's magisterial study.) Though she understandably resents Wood's arbitrary dismissal of the British films, she finds the claim that the five films from *Vertigo* to *Marnie* constitute an "unbroken chain of masterpieces" to be "[b]rave [and] cantankerous" without saying why.

She describes Wood's chapter on *North by Northwest* as "schoolmasterly," finds the *Marnie* chapter "the most obviously strained," and reproaches Wood for downplaying "the consistent and fascinating element of cruelty" with which the director treats his "immaculate blonde heroines." And despite the potential insightfulness of the latter claim, Houston *still* finds Wood to be taking Hitchcock too *seriously*!

In *Film Heritage* Robert Haller regretted the fact that "until recently the literature on Alfred Hitchcock has been incomplete, esoteric, or generally uncritical"; Wood's book is "more comprehensive and less esoteric (if not much more critical)." Haller finds the discussion of the thematic continuities in Hitchcock's films more cogent than "the airy constructions of Claude Chabrol and Eric Rohmer" (37), concurs with the estimate of *Vertigo*, applauds Wood's defense of *Marnie* but regrets his extravagant praise of *The Birds* – whose central conception, he says, Wood refuses to question. Nonetheless, Haller concludes, "Wood's book remains the best piece of scholarship ever devoted to Hitchcock" (38).

In 1971 Foster Hirsch reviewed Wood's monographs on Hitchcock, Hawks, and Bergman for *Film Comment*. Auteurism had by now become the reigning orthodoxy in many film journals, and Hitchcock's reputation had risen rapidly in the few years since *Hitchcock's Films*. Hirsch acknowledges Wood's preeminent position as a film critic, comparing his work to Eric Bentley's pioneering role in drama criticism in the 1950s. He notes Wood's indebtedness to F.R. Leavis, situates him in the auteurist camp, and commends his detailed textual analyses, commenting also on Wood's "quite remarkable visual memory." He hails many aspects of the book: Wood's attempts to validate film as "a suitable subject for rigorous investigation" (74), his "absolute familiarity" with the texts, "his cultural background, his eye for visual detail, his literary acumen, his love of subject" (75). What is most likely to strike today's reader of this otherwise intelligent review is the way in which Hirsch still manages, apparently, to miss one of the main points of the whole book: Hitchcock's mastery of the cinematic medium.

In his 1992 study Robert Kapsis exposed the concatenations at play in the making of Hitchcock's reputation, including the biographical "legend" that the portly Englishman and his publicists created, changes in expectations amongst audiences and critics, the politics of canon formation, and the influence of popular and scholarly studies. Conventional wisdom had attributed the rise in Hitchcock's reputation to the French auteurists who "initiated a sincere but hardly disinterested campaign culminating in Truffaut's book, *Hitchcock* (1967)" (69). This book, according to Donald Spoto, "established Hitchcock's status as the quintessential *auteur,* or movie 'author,' a director who exerted unprecedented creative control over each of his films" (495). Kapsis, on the other hand, wants rather to emphasize changes in critical discourse and film aesthetics in accounting for the elevation of Hitchcock's reputation since the early 1960s (70). But both accounts downplay Wood's book. The *élan* of the *Cahiers* critics and the *nouvelle vague* cinema held a romantic allure for many later English-language critics; thus it was easy to overestimate their contemporary impact on transatlantic film criticism. Truffaut's early articles (from 1954 onwards) and the Rohmer-Chabrol book (1957) were not translated into English until very much later and, as Truffaut himself conceded in a letter to Hitchcock, they had little impact beyond a handful of cinephiles (Kapsis 71).

Moreover, auteurism – what Kapsis calls "the broad shift in film aesthetics" – was not some exotic creature that appeared out of the clouds; it was a movement generated by particular works – reviews, essays, articles, books. It was precisely studies such as Wood's that gave the auteurist approach to film criticism intellectual legitimacy. *Hitchcock's Films* demonstrated just what fruits this critical approach could yield. It also made out the most cogent case hitherto for regarding Hitchcock as a master of the medium. Interestingly, Kapsis himself dates the turning point in Hitchcock's reputation as a "serious artist" to 1965: he does not tell us precisely why, but it hardly seems coincidental that this was the date when Wood's book first appeared.

As Kapsis has observed, while *Hitchcock's Films* went largely unnoticed by journalistic reviewers, academic critics were quick to recognize the book as a pioneering textual exegesis. Indeed, since 1965 *Hitchcock's Films* has been widely read, anthologized, debated and cited. It remains an *exemplar* of auteurist criticism – in David Bordwell's terms, "an essay or book which influentially crystallizes an approach or argumentative strategy":

> The exemplar instantiates "what the field is about"; if it is progressive, it shapes future work; if it has been superseded, it still must be acknowledged, attacked, quarreled with. Essayistic and academic critics write in the shadow of exemplars.
>
> (24–25)

Bordwell has also pointed out that film criticism has been carried out within three "macro-institutions": journalism, *belles lettres*, and the academy (19). Wood's book performed a signal role in the infiltration of the third of these "macro-institutions." A veritable mountain of academic Hitchcock scholarship now exists – as the present volume attests – much of which, at the very least, took as axiomatic those central claims for which Wood had argued so passionately in *Hitchcock's Films*. Even those many later critics who diverged sharply from Wood were beholden to his book, often in ways of which they were doubtless unaware.

Among Wood's many subsequent reconsiderations since *Hitchcock's Films*, three stand out: "Alfred Hitchcock: Lost in the Wood," under the pseudonym "George Kaplan"; the Retrospective in the 1977 edition of *Hitchcock's Films*; and the lengthy Introduction and eight new essays, written over a period of eleven years, which comprise the new part of Wood's 1989 book *Hitchcock's Films Revisited*, further augmented in 2002 by a new Preface and a substantial essay on *Marnie*. "Lost in the Wood" wittily exposes his earliest doubts about some of the more inflated claims he had made for Hitchcock's work. The Retrospective is chiefly interesting for three reasons: the revised assessment of specific texts (most interestingly, *The Birds*); notes on post-1968 films; and Wood's changing critical/theoretical orientation. The Retrospective also explores the influence on Hitchcock's work of Soviet montage theory and German Expressionism, as well as situating the American films much more firmly in the Hollywood matrix.

By the time of *Hitchcock's Films Revisited*, Wood sees his early work as belonging "firmly to a certain phase in the evolution of film theory/criticism [i.e., auteurism] whose assumptions are no longer acceptable without qualifications so drastic as effectively to transform them" (1). But he goes on to claim that "those assumptions, even today, do not seem to me entirely untenable and cannot simply be swept aside contemptuously" (2). He concedes that *Hitchcock's Films* was innocent of any concept of ideology and certainly uninformed by his current feminist concerns. He distances himself from the axiomatic "coherence" of the earlier book, which he now attributes to an unproblematic auteurism centered on the personal creativity and vision of the director, an approach that ignored the many commercial, systemic, generic and ideological determinants of Hitchcock's films. It is toward assessing the influence of precisely these factors that much of the new work is directed. Nevertheless, Wood also wants to rehabilitate something of the Leavisite notion of art and associated notions of "intelligence, sensibility, complexity, a sense of value" (26) that have been declared "invalid," "bourgeois" and the like by structuralist-semiotic-materialist-psychoanalytical theory (SSMP hereafter).

The originality of Wood's critical position now lies in his attempt to fashion a rapprochement of SSMP and a humanistic-Leavisite criticism. This goes hand-in-hand with Wood's resistance to certain theoretical tendencies that he attacks as obscurantist (the mystificatory jargon and oracular "authority" of the French poststructuralists), abstract (the apparent imperviousness of much film writing to concrete political realities and life-experiences), and essentialist (positing some new variant of the Human Condition – e.g., Lacan on "Woman"). He also resists the reductive tendencies of contemporary theorizing that jettisons the idea of personal creativity altogether.

The Introduction to *Hitchcock's Films Revisited* confronts a range of theoretical issues: authorship and the signification/expression debate; the utility of semiotic deconstructionism; the potential relationship of an evaluative criticism (drawing on Leavisite criteria) and SSMP. The circumscriptions of auteurism are unexceptionally rehearsed by Wood. What is more interesting is Wood's effort to rescue the notion of authorship, albeit in severely modified form, from the oblivion to which SSMP has ostensibly consigned it. To recognize that Hitchcock's films "belong to the culture, its institutions, its values, its ideology, its internal conflicts and struggles" (5) and that they are constrained by the conventions of various systems does not oblige us to deny the creative "intelligence and control" that Hitchcock exercised as an individual filmmaker (23). Thus Wood disavows both a simplistic auteurism and the poststructuralist discourse that conjures the author out of existence altogether. He navigates the troubled waters between a conservative "apoliticism" and an ideological reductionism, between the naïve notion that film criticism can ignore political determinations and the equally constraining idea that everything can be reduced to the level of ideology. In *Hitchcock's Films Revisited*, Wood honors his own dictum that it is desirable for the critic to draw on the perceptions of many different theories while refusing to be the prisoner of any.

The most interesting and innovative aspects of the book can be examined under three headings that flag some of Wood's newer interests: structural formations; the Hollywood complex of ideology-genre-star-auteur; and sexual politics.

In 1965 Wood had peremptorily dismissed Hitchcock's British films as interesting primarily in their anticipations of later films (73). He subsequently regretted this "embarrassingly ignorant and supercilious dismissal" (230), which had been motivated by an exclusivist preoccupation with "artistic value" (231) and also, perhaps, by a subconscious abhorrence of the stifling and "depressingly familiar" (260) British middle-class milieu in which most of the films are set, and which Wood himself had found so oppressive. By 1989 Wood is no longer concerned only with "artistic value" but with a network of previously neglected issues. Wood now discerns a "continual recurrence and variation of a number of simple embryonic structures, separately and in combination," from which the corpus derives "its essential unity" (240). He typologizes Hitchcock's films into five basic plot formations (each, of course, being especially amenable to particular thematic concerns). Here is an abbreviated version of Wood's schema.

1. **The Falsely Accused Man.** *The Lodger* (1926), *The 39 Steps* (1935), *Suspicion* (1941), *Young and Innocent* (1937), *Spellbound, Strangers on a Train, To Catch a Thief* (1955), *The Wrong Man, North by Northwest, Frenzy* (1972). The "falsely accused man" films usually exhibit the "double chase" structure in which the hero, pursued by the police, hunts the real villain/s. The hero is always innocent of the crime of which he is accused but usually guilty (perhaps ambiguously) of something else (often sexual). These films "move unanimously toward the protagonist's rehabilitation/restoration to society" (242). The (implicit) critique of the hero is more trenchant in the American films, thus requiring a more radical transformation to effect his redemption.

2. **The Guilty Woman.** *Blackmail* (1929), *Sabotage* (1936), *Rebecca, Notorious, The Paradine Case* (1947), *Under Capricorn* (1949), *Stage Fright* (1950), *Vertigo, Psycho, The Birds, Marnie.* The "guilty woman," by way of contrast, "is *always* guilty." This "sexist imbalance" is partially redressed by "the sympathy the films extend to their transgressive women" (242). With the striking exception of *Blackmail*, these films belong overwhelmingly to the American period. Where the falsely accused man's destiny is typically restoration to the social order, the guilty woman's fate is suffering and punishment, often quite "disproportionate" to her "crime." But "[i]n no single case ... does the film invite us to view the punishment with complacence or satisfaction: typically, we are left with a sense of unresolved dissonance that relates, at bottom, to the fundamental strains produced by our culture's organization of sexuality and gender" (243). Wood sees "an intricately dialectic relationship of complementarity/opposition" between the "falsely accused man" and "guilty woman" films that is "the lynchpin of the entire Hitchcock oeuvre" (243).

3. **The Psychopath.** *The Lodger, Shadow of a Doubt* (1943), *Rope, Strangers on a Train, Psycho, Frenzy.* The psychopath story often overlaps with the first category, the pathology being embodied in a villain who is often the "center of fascination" but never, unlike some of the guilty women, "a primary identification figure" (245). The psychopath/villain often also functions as the hero's "double" in the "exchange of guilt" motif.

4. **Espionage/Political Intrigue.** *The Man Who Knew Too Much* (1934 and 1956), *The 39 Steps, Secret Agent* (1936), *Sabotage, The Lady Vanishes* (1938), *Notorious, North by Northwest, Torn Curtain, Topaz* (1969). The espionage story often amounts to no more than a MacGuffin rather than a plot formation. It sometimes takes on more density and thematic resonance in those films (including the last four listed above) in which the corruptions of political intrigue are seen to contaminate personal relationships and in which the victimization of women occurs "within the domain of masculinist politics" (246).

5. **Marriage.** *Rich and Strange* (1931), *Sabotage, Rebecca, Suspicion, Under Capricorn, The Man Who Knew Too Much* (1956), *Marnie,* and, with some qualifications, *Rear Window* and *Frenzy.* The "marriage" films give us a remarkably "bleak and skeptical" picture of that institution, despite the Motion Picture Code and the idealization of marriage in patriarchal ideology. Conventional "happy endings" – for example, "the expected construction or reconstruction of the heterosexual couple" – are "presented without much evidence of engagement or conviction ... or with overt skepticism" (246).

Blackmail provides Wood not only with a case study of Hitchcock's structural formations but an avenue into the debate about the "classic realist text." Wood articulates two conventional premises this way:

1. The function of classical narrative has been, overall, to reinforce and appear to validate the patriarchal order and its subordination of women.
2. The fundamental principles that govern the structuring of classical narrative include symmetry ... and closure. (249)

Wood argues that these two theoretical postulates are too often collapsed so that symmetry and closure, *in themselves,* are seen as inevitably reaffirming the patriarchal order. Not so, says Wood. Hitchcock offers us many "closures" in which the apparent resolution is subverted by an ironic dissonance that allows the spectator a critical distance.

Wood's interest in *Blackmail* derives, in part, from its privileged status as the first of the "guilty woman" films and from its pervasive principle of symmetry – a symmetry not only between the narrative opening and closing but of sequences within the film's segments, within individual sequences, single shots, and even particular frames. The complex patterns that Wood uncovers generate a series of effects through an interplay of sameness and difference. The primary function of this symmetry is captured with "exemplary clarity" (265) in what is improperly called the "murder" sequence, here closely analyzed.

Blackmail's many visual and narrative pairings, doublings, anticipations and reminiscences severely problematize spectatorial identification and render various motifs and themes disturbingly ambiguous. A complexity and ambiguity of tone precludes any complacent reading of a "transparent" text: the "dominant reading" (i.e., one conforming to the narrative's ostensible purposes) is everywhere thrown into question by the discordant meanings and the unsettling tone generated through symmetry. Similarly, the cultural code (conventional clusters of meanings and associations attached to particular images, symbols, institutions, etc.) and the authorial code often collide in Hitchcock's films, creating levels of further ambivalence and discord.

Wood's 1977 "Ideology, Genre, Auteur" signaled a range of new critical concerns, particularly the complex interactions within Hollywood texts of ideology, genre, stars and authorship. Reprinted in *Hitchcock's Films Revisited*, Wood's essay compares two small-town domestic comedies, *Shadow of a Doubt* and Capra's *It's a Wonderful Life* (1946). The lessons of this critical exercise are clearly stated: "The strong contrast the two films present testifies to the decisive effect of the intervention of a clearly defined artistic personality in an ideological generic structure" (293). Wood found himself dissatisfied with the prevailing view of *Shadow of a Doubt* as an affectionate, mildly satiric family comedy (the early Anglo-American consensus) or as a rigorous working out of Hitchcock's "Catholic" themes (Rohmer-Chabrol). Each of these readings does, of course, answer to certain elements in the film but each is "false and partial" (296). Wood sees the film as completely dominated by Hitchcock, but the ideological and generic determinants nevertheless remain crucial: "the Hollywood ideology ... is shattered beyond convincing recuperation. One can, however, trace through the film its attempts to impose itself and render things 'safe'" (297). Wood traces the various ideological subversions to Hitchcock's presence, "to the skepticism and nihilism that lurk just behind the jocular facade of his public image" (298). The fact that many viewers have been deceived by the overt project testifies to the strength of the prevailing ideology. No one will be surprised to hear that Wood finds the key to *Shadow of a Doubt* in its psycho-sexual pathologies, embedded in the implicit double incest theme that Wood teases out of the narrative and that the film shows to be the product of sexual repressions and sublimations characteristic of the American family – the worm in the apple, so to speak.

Wood's extended consideration of Hitchcock's work with Ingrid Bergman opens with the observation that "[a]rguably the most important recent development in film theory/criticism has been the radical opening up of discussion of stars: the construction of the star image/persona, the intricate interrelationship of acting/presence/image, the ways in which a star functions, and the complex of meanings she or he generates, within a given filmic text" (303). Wood has written several times on the career of Ingrid Bergman, nowhere more incisively or more affectionately than here, addressing her first Hollywood period from *Intermezzo* (Gregory Ratoff, 1939) to *Under Capricorn*, and particularly her collaborations with Hitchcock. Wood's examination of the Bergman films serves at least three purposes: it challenges the hegemony of a Lacanian psychoanalytical model in recent Hitchcock criticism, especially as it relates to "the look" and to identification; it traces Bergman's trajectory as a Hollywood star; and it examines the meanings that the Hitchcock–Bergman interaction engenders in *Spellbound, Notorious,* and *Under Capricorn.*

Wood had more than once expressed irritation at the widespread influence of the Lacanian model of the Hollywood cinema elaborated by Laura Mulvey in 1975. He had also voiced some skepticism about the critical "gains" made by Raymond Bellour in his analyses of Hitchcockian texts. In his campaign against the reductive and constricting applications of psychoanalytical theory (to which he had no objection in principle) Wood here chooses as his stalking-horse a 1980 article in *Wide Angle* by Michael Renov. Clearly influenced by both Mulvey and Bellour, Renov argues that *Notorious* takes us from "identification" with the male gaze to the "ideology" that subordinates women and reinforces patriarchal myths and oppressive gender roles.

Wood concedes that Renov's argument is "plausible, closely argued, up to a point convincing" (305). But more needs to be said. Renov's model of identification is not so much wrong as inadequate and "far too simple, its insufficiency deriving from the strategy, *inherent in the very premises of the semiotic tradition,* of reducing the complexities of signification within a text to those aspects that are 'scientifically' demonstrable, *but which are not necessarily the most important determinants of its meaning and effect"* (305; my italics).

The construction of identification, Wood argues, is far more delicate and subtle than most semioticians acknowledge, and can never be reduced to the mechanics of various "looks" (of characters, spectators, camera). Indeed, the term "identification" is itself problematic, covering as it does a very wide spectrum of spectatorial responses (sympathy, empathy, total involvement). Illustrating his case through reference to *Notorious,* Wood isolates six cinematic strategies of identification:

(1)   *identification with the male gaze* (as theorized by Mulvey *et al.*);
(2)   *identification with the threatened or victimized,* powerfully, frequently and self-consciously exploited by Hitchcock;
(3)   *the varied degrees of sympathy* that films evoke for different characters, often modulated by various techniques, including symmetry;
(4)   *the intellectual identification* that derives from the construction of a scenario so as to limit the spectator's awareness to that of one of the characters;
(5)   *the use of cinematic devices* such as point-of-view shooting (its effects recently "greatly exaggerated"), editing, camera distance and angles, music and sound effects;
(6)   *identification with the star* (a commonplace of virtually all theories of the Hollywood cinema).

Wood's general conclusion is one that many contemporary critics might well ponder:

> [I]dentification in the cinema is an extremely complex, multilayered, intricate phenomenon which absolutely prohibits reduction to a simple formula such as the "male gaze" or the use of POV shots. Identification may not be total or nontransferable;

it can flicker sporadically and partially in the play of sympathies, shift from character to character, operate in relation to two different (and perhaps antagonistic) characters at once, be encouraged, qualified, or denied altogether. Most important, it can function on different levels simultaneously, developing tensions and contradictions in a complex dialectic.

(310)

Since Eric Rohmer and Claude Chabrol pointed out that *Murder!* (1930), *Rope,* and *Strangers on a Train* form a kind of "homosexual triptych," there has been a great deal of interest in Hitchcock's representations of (homo)sexuality. Wood brings to Hitchcock's homophobia the same primarily Freudian conceptual apparatus that was so brilliantly deployed in his widely acclaimed analysis of *Raging Bull* (Martin Scorsese, 1980). He recapitulates the key concepts: constitutional bisexuality, gender as social construction, repression, the castration complex, the oedipal trajectory, homophobia as "the return of the repressed," sexual fear/anxiety as the seedbed of misogyny, the contradictions and tensions inherent in the sexual ideology of patriarchy.

Wood uses Donald Spoto's *The Dark Side of Genius* (1983) as a gateway to the director's sexual repressions/anxieties/projections, which can be traced in both his biography and his films. Resisting any simplistic "psychoanalysis" of Hitchcock, he points instead to the "complex and contradictory" (342) evidence we find in both the life and the oeuvre. Among the aspects Wood highlights: the director's deeply ambivalent attitude to both his female and gay collaborators and the suggestive reverberations in his relations with Ivor Novello and Montgomery Clift; his life-long fascination with "deviancy," and the simultaneous impulses of attraction and repulsion; and certain sadomasochistic and hysterical traits in Hitchcock's personality. Wood provides the master key to Hitchcock's extremely tangled attitude to both women and gays in this passage:

> The violence against women and the homophobia must be seen as the products of a terror and panic that are the logical response, within the terms of our culture, to its construction of gender, of one of its most "unsuccessful" graduates. Against these phenomena must be set Hitchcock's frequently passionate identification with his female characters, and his more troubled and ambivalent, partial identification with his gay characters.

(345)

Wood ruminates on Hitchcock's treatment of a whole chain of "fascinating, insidiously attractive Hitchcock villains who constantly threaten to 'take over' the films in which they appear" (347) and who "enact that obsession with power/ domination/control and the dread of its loss (impotence) that pervades his work at every level" (348). The textual explication informs Wood's general thesis that "[d]omination—power/impotence as two sides of the same coin—is clearly the central concern (one might say the driving obsession) of Hitchcock's work on all levels, methodological, stylistic, thematic; the distinction of that work—its importance for us today—lies in the ways in which that obsession is pursued to the point where its mechanisms, its motivations, its monstrousness, are thoroughly exposed" (360–61).

The closing essay in *Hitchcock's Films Revisited* gives us rereadings of *Rear Window* and *Vertigo*, so highly prized in *Hitchcock's Films*. To these can be added the formidable 2002 essay in which Wood returns to the "complexities and perplexities" (388) of *Marnie*, now less concerned with a defense of the anti-realist devices than with a more coherent and self-consciously Freudian reading of the film's sexual politics. Earlier valuations and insights survive intact, but Wood now argues for the significance of these films not primarily in terms of "artistic coherence" or "moral complexity" but in reference to the ways they dramatize and expose "certain compulsive drives of the male ego as constructed within our culture" (376).

A question lurking behind much of Wood's later work surfaces in these late essays: "Can Hitchcock be saved for feminism?" (371) – a question that has haunted recent Hitchcock criticism. Wood arrives, via a somewhat different route, at more or less the same conclusion reached by Tania Modleski, who was writing *The Women Who Knew Too Much* (1988) at the same time Wood was assembling *Hitchcock's Films Revisited*. Although Modleski wants to foreground her disagreements with Wood, her general view is altogether consonant with his: "[W]hat I want to argue is *neither* that Hitchcock is utterly misogynistic *nor* that he is largely sympathetic to women and their plight in patriarchy, but that his work is characterized by a thoroughgoing ambivalence about femininity" (Modleski 3).

To see Robin Wood's formative role in the history of Hitchcock's critical reception as beyond dispute is not to deny that Wood's work is marked, inevitably, by certain limitations. On the debit side of the ledger are the sometimes blinkered preoccupation with certain psycho-sexual themes, understood within a constrictive Freudian frame; an ideologically fueled tendency to excessive allegorizing and schematizing (such as the relentless identification of marriage and "castration"); the intermittent intrusion of facile and sometimes belligerent proselytizing on behalf of an ill-defined Marxist-feminist cause; the defensive but somewhat incongruous persona of a maverick "outsider," evident in the sometimes dismissive attitude to his academic colleagues who, by and large, have treated Wood's own work with considerable respect. (The insecurities masked by the persona can be discerned in Wood's sometimes painfully self-revelatory writings, such as the lengthy 2002 Preface.) Yet these are paltry foibles when weighed against his achievements, not only in the field of Hitchcock studies but in the evolution of film-critical discourse more generally. And it as a critic that Wood really counts.

Whatever may be the fashions of the day, and whatever riches might be yielded by different theoretical perspectives and critical methods, the qualities evinced in Wood's work can hardly be "outdated": an incisive but flexible intelligence focused on the often elusive particularities of the film text itself; an emotional sensitivity and a visual receptivity attuned to the most subtle nuances and inflections of both image and narrative, capable of registering even the most fugitive of effects; a prose style that is both supple and lucid, free of the turgidities, pomposities, and obscurations of much contemporary film writing; a warm human sympathy, fine-grained moral sensibility, and considerable imaginative reach. Informing his critical practice there is also an awareness of larger cultural traditions on which the modern cinema draws and in which it is situated.

Given Wood's own critical trajectory and his recently reaffirmed claim that F.R. Leavis is "the greatest of all critics" (xli), it is perhaps appropriate to recall George Steiner's words about the Leavisite critic's engagement with the text: "[The critic] aims at complete responsiveness, at a kind of poised vulnerability of conscious-ness in the encounter with the text. He [or she] proceeds with an attention which is close and stringent, yet also provisional, and at all times subject to revaluation" (Steiner 230).

How apt a description of Wood's practice! The phrase "poised vulnerability of consciousness" takes on a sharper edge when we recall how Wood's own painful search for self-identity has further sensitized his perceptions of the Hitchcockian psycho-sexual problematics of "male desire, male anxiety." Here was a critic pecu-liarly suited to the challenges of Hitchcock's enigmatic and disturbing oeuvre. Woody Guthrie once said that a good poet or songwriter tells you something you already know. It might be said that the better class of critic tells you something you may have already sensed or felt but that you had only partially understood. Granting Sarris's observation that "[n]o critic, no scholar, no doctrine or dogma can provide the last word on Hitchcock" (Foreword 12), it remains true that, better than any other critic, Wood has explained why we continue to be fascinated, often grimly, by Hitchcock's films.

Works Cited

Robin Wood's *Hitchcock's Films* was first published by A. Zwemmer (London) and A.S. Barnes (New York) in Peter Cowie's "Tantivy Press" series in 1965. Subsequent paperback editions appeared in 1969 and 1970, and an augmented third edition hardback appeared in 1977. Columbia University Press published *Hitchcock's Films Revisited* in 1989 and a "revised edition" in 2002. Because the most recent edition incorporates all of the previous iterations of the book, all parenthetical references in the text are to this edition.

Bellour, Raymond. *The Analysis of Film*. Ed. Constance Penley. Bloomington: Indiana UP, 2000.

Bordwell, David. *Making Meaning: Inference and Rhetoric in the Interpretation of Cinema*. Cambridge: Harvard UP, 1989.

Cameron, Ian. "Hitchcock 1 and the Mechanics of Suspense." *Movie* 3 (Oct. 1962): 4–7.

Cameron, Ian. "Hitchcock 2: Suspense and Meaning." *Movie* 6 (Jan. 1963): 8–12.

Cameron, Ian, and Richard Jeffery. "The Universal Hitchcock." *Movie* 12 (Spring 1965): 21–24.

Chabrol, Claude. "Histoire d'une interview." *Cahiers du cinéma* 39 (Oct. 1954): 39–44. Trans. by James M. Vest as "Story of an Interview." *Alfred Hitchcock: Interviews.* Ed. Sidney Gottlieb. Jackson: UP of Mississippi, 2003. 38–43.

Deutelbaum, Marshall, and Leland Poague, eds. *A Hitchcock Reader.* Second ed. Chichester, UK: Wiley-Blackwell, 2009.

Douchet, Jean. "Hitch et son public." *Cahiers du cinéma* 113 (1960): 7–15. Trans. by Verena Andermatt Conley as "Hitch and His Public." Deutelbaum and Poague 17–24.

Durgnat, Raymond. *The Strange Case of Alfred Hitchcock, or The Plain Man's Hitchcock.* Cambridge: MIT P, 1974.

Grierson, John. *Grierson on Documentary.* Rev. ed. Ed. Forsyth Hardy. London: Faber, 1966.

Haller, Robert. Rev. of *The Films of Alfred Hitchcock,* by George Perry, and *Hitchcock's Films,* by Robin Wood. *Film Heritage* 1.4 (Summer 1966): 37–38.

Hardison, O.B. "The Rhetoric of Hitchcock's Thrillers." *Man and the Movies.* Ed. W.R. Robinson. Baton Rouge: Louisiana State UP, 1967. 137–52.

Hirsch, Foster. Rev. of *Hitchcock's Films, Howard Hawks,* and *Ingmar Bergman,* by Robin Wood. *Film Comment* 7.4 (Winter 1971–72): 74–75.

Houston, Penelope. "The Figure in the Carpet." *Sight and Sound* 32.4 (Autumn 1963): 159–64.

Houston, Penelope. *The Contemporary Cinema.* Harmondsworth: Penguin, 1963.

Houston, Penelope. Rev. of *Hitchcock's Films,* by Robin Wood. *Sight and Sound* 35.1 (Winter 1965): 49.

Kaplan, George [Robin Wood]. "Alfred Hitchcock: Lost in the Wood." *Film Comment* 8.4 (Nov.–Dec. 1972): 46–53.

Kapsis, Robert E. *Hitchcock: The Making of a Reputation.* Chicago: U of Chicago P, 1992.

Mayersberg, Paul. "The Testament of Vincente Minnelli." *Movie* 3 (Oct. 1962): 10–13.

Modleski, Tania. *The Women Who Knew Too Much: Hitchcock and Feminist Theory.* New York: Routledge, 1988.

Mulvey, Laura. "Visual Pleasure and Narrative Cinema." *Screen* 16.3 (Autumn 1975): 31–39.

Perkins, V.F. "Rope." *Movie* 7 (Feb. 1963): 11–13.

Rebello, Stephen. *Alfred Hitchcock and the Making of* Psycho. New York: Dembner, 1990.

Renov, Michael. "From Identification to Ideology: The Male System of *Notorious.*" *Wide Angle* 4.1 (1980): 30–38.

Rohmer, Eric and Claude Chabrol. *Hitchcock: The First Forty-Four Films.* Trans. Stanley Hochman. New York: Ungar, 1979.

Sarris, Andrew. Foreword. *Hitchcock's Rereleased Films: From* Rope *to* Vertigo. Ed. Walter Raubicheck and Walter Srebnick. Detroit: Wayne State UP, 1991. 11–13.

Sontag, Susan. *A Susan Sontag Reader.* Baltimore: Penguin USA, 1982.

Spoto, Donald. *The Dark Side of Genius: The Life of Alfred Hitchcock.* Boston: Little, Brown, 1983.

Steiner, George. "F.R. Leavis." 1962. Steiner, *Language and Silence: Essays on Language, Literature, and the Inhuman.* New York: Atheneum, 1967. 221–38.

Truffaut, François. *The Films in My Life.* Trans. Leonard Mayhew. London: Allen Lane, 1980.

Truffaut, François, with the collaboration of Helen G. Scott. *Hitchcock.* Rev. ed. New York: Simon and Schuster, 1984.

Wood, Robin. *Hitchcock's Films Revisited.* Rev. ed. New York: Columbia UP, 2002.

Wood, Robin. "Ideology, Genre, Auteur." *Film Comment* 13.1 (Jan.–Feb. 1977): 46–51.

Wood, Robin. "Psychanalyse de 'Psycho.'" *Cahiers du cinéma* 113 (Nov. 1960): 1–6.

Wood, Robin. "Raging Bull: The Homosexual Subtext." *Movie* 31–32 (Winter 1986): 108–14.

PART VII

Ideology

23

Accidental Heroes and Gifted Amateurs: Hitchcock and Ideology

Toby Miller with Noel King

Attention, teachers, parents and other educators! The 39 Steps is not just funny. It's highly educational! Take advantage of our wonderful and thorough STUDY GUIDE.

http:// www.39stepsonbroadway.com / study.html

If the British public had been asked in the late Forties to name a famous beauty spot, a majority would have named Margaret Lockwood's rather than, say, the Lake District.

Ronald Bergan

Hitchcock was not prone to constative remarks about class struggle, the state, or imperialism; he did not refer to technology and value as motors of economic and hence social and cultural transformation; nor was he an historical determinist, measuring change via successive modes of production; and rather than analyzing the exercise of power by the ruling class and the state, he told entertaining stories that were presumably blind to ideology critique.

In short, Hitchcock was not a good Marxist. But can his work be addressed from beyond itself, from a materialist perspective? After all, he may have had Frankfurt School tendencies. Consider this impeccably Adorno-like simile to describe the culture industries: "Television is like the American toaster, you push the button and the same thing pops up every time" (quoted in Wasko 10). And Hitchcock's decades of oscillation between adoration and detestation for the ruling class are

A Companion to Alfred Hitchcock, First Edition. Edited by Thomas Leitch and Leland Poague.
© 2011 Thomas Leitch and Leland Poague. Published 2011 by Blackwell Publishing Ltd.

matched by a *Leitmotif* in his films: again and again, trustafarian-like protagonists are accused of crimes they did not commit, and must come to terms not only with the unwarranted and unwanted condition of criminality, but also its corollary of hyper-competence.[1] Naïfs are lifted up from their ordinary lives to adopt the subject position of skilled spies and desperate fugitives.

Their accidental heroism is constructed through Hitchcock's MacGuffins, narrative alibis that set in train supposed quests where the getting of knowledge matters more than the knowledge itself. The sheer meaninglessness of these plots is sometimes said to subvert mainstream film, because it destabilizes the convention that spectators have perfect knowledge of what matters on the screen in a way that is analogous to the perfect knowledge of the studious and loyal consumer or citizen (Beckman, *Vanishing*; Cohen). Symptomatic interpretations, whether undertaken through Marxist criticism or the psy-function, have understood Hitchcock's texts seemingly against their orthodox formal and stylistic grain – even as form and style are invoked to anchor criticism in originary texts. This theory is deployed to argue for the defamiliarizing impact of MacGuffins, which supposedly make it obvious to viewers that the alibis for their attention over an hour and a half have been just that: mere avatars of form, style, character, and subplot. Put another way, while Hitchcock may appear to be a genre filmmaker dedicated to the artistic conventions of the continuity system and the commercial conventions of the studio system, he actually subverts them artistically through the implausibility of his plots. Such accounts echo Baudrillard's dialectically utopic and dystopic account of the empty triumph of signs as sources and measures of value under capitalism. Beginning as reflections of reality, commodity signs such as screen texts are transformed into perversions of reality, because representations of truth are displaced by false information. Then these two delineable phases of truth and lies become indistinct. Underlying reality is lost. Signs ultimately refer to themselves, with no residual correspondence to the real, because they have adopted the form of their own simulation (Baudrillard 10–11, 29, 170).

Such arguments replay debates from three decades ago about the ability of realism to radicalize audiences by laying bare complex social issues in a clear and cogent way that highlights the shallowness of loyal consumption and citizenship, versus the ability of the avant garde to radicalize audiences by undressing dramatic norms that position spectators as perfectly knowledgeable in order to reveal the reactionary nature of the studious and loyal consumption and citizenship that is supposedly analogous to filmgoing.

The realist-text debate thrived in the columns of *Screen* and *Edinburgh '77 Magazine* (see Bennett *et al.* 305–52). These claims and their descendants have not been backed up by studies of how audiences process information, or with due attention to the material careers of the texts being scrutinized. They represent narcissography at work, with the critic's persona a guarantor of assumed audience resistance (see Morris). The debates are as venerable as they are irresolvable absent ethnographic and questionnaire research. Rehearsing the controversy, or assuming that it has been resolved in favor of realism or defamiliarization, takes us nowhere.

We are using a different optic here, via cultural materialism, and (ironically) going against the textual grain to do so: symptomatic readings are encouraged and interpellated by much of Alfred Hitchcock's oeuvre – what the *Guardian* haughtily but memorably dismisses as his "railway-bookstand Freudianism" (Sweet; but cf. Almansi). Rather than reclaiming Hitchcock for a skeptical modernism, for instance, we prefer an approach that finds ideological workings and reworkings in the materiality of originary texts and their popular commentaries and uptakes. Rather than engaging in self-endorsed acts of academic interpretation, we apply materialist ideas to Hitchcock's work through the prism of ideology. That still runs the risk of endowing criticism with a special privilege, but we hope to elude such privilege by drawing on actually-existing signage to back up our claims.

First, we'll consider the nature of our other subject here, ideology, explain our methodology, and address the espionage genre's relationship to economy and empire. Then we'll focus on *The 39 Steps* (1935) and *The Lady Vanishes* (1938), the texts that established Hitchcock as unique in the eyes of François Truffaut, among many others.

Ideology

When it was first coined in the eighteenth century, "ideology" was a neutral term of observation that referred to a corpus of ideas. By the mid–nineteenth century, the notion that an entire governing system of ideas could exclude dissonance and difference and privilege the holders of material advantage and prevailing social relations had switched that around (Macherey, "Idéologie"). In Marx's words: "it is impossible to create a moral power by paragraphs of law." There must also be *"organic* laws supplementing the Constitution" – which is to say, ideology (27, 35). These organic laws and their textual efflorescence represent what Althusser called each "epoch's consciousness of itself" (*For Marx* 108). Gramsci theorized this supplement as an "equilibrium" between constitutional law ("political society" or a "dictatorship or some other coercive apparatus used to control the masses in conformity with a given type of production and economy") and organic law ("civil society" or the "hegemony of a social group over the entire nation exercised through so-called private organizations such as the church, the unions, the schools, etc.") (204).

Althusser maintained that a society's economic base is composed of productive forces and relations of production. Its superstructure consists of the law and the state plus ideology, the latter comprising religion, ethics, and politics. The state is a critical component. It has two chief characteristics. The first involves the threat or use of force to elicit obedience to authority. This characteristic is typical of the military, the police, the courts, the bureaucracy, and prisons – "the (repressive)

State apparatus," or (R)SA. Its work is done by sanction and interdiction. The second characteristic is formed by numerous "Ideological State Apparatuses," or ISAs. These include religious and educational institutions, the family, the polity, the trade union, and the communications and cultural ISAs. Their work is done by persuasion (*Lenin and Philosophy*). In Hitchcock's case, spy agencies, part of the (R) SA, are represented by cinema, an ISA, which communicates perspectives on gender, class, race, region, socialism, capitalism, and empire.

Althusser theorized ideology as "a 'Representation' of the Imaginary Relationship of Individuals to their Real Conditions of Existence." He argued that to criticize an ideology, for example religion, is to presume that it is illusionary, but *alludes* to reality, and hence has grounds which are both true and germane to itself on which it can be criticized: "(ideology = illusion/allusion)" because it is an "imaginary transposition of the real conditions of existence." Art has the capacity to detach itself from conventional ideology, but must at least reference ideology in order to make sense to its public. In a sense, art can function like a spy, working within a system to undermine it (S. Miller 22–23; Althusser, *Lenin and Philosophy*).

The idea of an ideological underpinning to film is not the exclusive province of Marxism, of course. Marcel Mauss built his famous paper "Les techniques du corps" ("Techniques of the Body") on the way that different peoples learn to move and gesture. The cinema was his crucial modern record of how societies think about and represent themselves ("Fragment"). Borrowing from Mauss, Norbert Elias constructed a figurational sociology of the civilizing process, with film an index of change: the medium's international mobility and mimetic impact saw people start to walk and talk as if they were members of cultures they had never experienced personally.

In this context, we might recuperate Hitchcock's films, arguing that they form part of a new popular culture that represents an inclusive modernity. Such a position would maintain that far from being supremely alienating, the popular expands civil society, providing the first moment in history when political and commercial organs and agendas are receptive to, and part of, the popular classes – when the general population counts as part of the social rather than being excluded from political-economic calculations. At the same time, there is a lessening of authority, the promulgation of individual rights and respect, and the development of intense but large-scale human interaction. This supposed flattening-out of social difference informs Daniel Bell's 1960 thesis in *The End of Ideology* that polarized political positions are no longer appealing, a position still argued by a large number of straight white male Yanqui intellectuals – a precondition for Robert Putnam's utopia of social capital forty years later.

One might apply this logic to Hitchcock's films of the 1950s and 1960s. But there are limits to these myths of modernity. The ongoing public endorsement of capitalism, despite its manifest injustices and inefficiencies, plus contemporary polling's indication of huge polarizations of political opinion, has cast serious doubt on the end-of-ideology thesis (Mészáros; Jost; Jost *et al.*). But we applaud the notion that one cannot fruitfully make ideological interpretations of every moment and activity, and acknowledge the liberatory aspects of the modern and its inclusive ethos.

Of course, in the 1930s, ideology was especially – and quite overtly – important because of the grand scale of its material conflicts: the rise of fascism, the development of state socialism, challenges to the British Empire, and the Great Depression. Given the topics of Hitchcock's movies, and the times, several ideological queries inevitably arise: was he an appeaser, a jingoist, a warmonger, an entertainer, a critic of old class mores, a conservative, or a radical?

Methodology

Rather than attempt to unlock Hitchcock's political thinking from his texts, we're concerned to see the shifting relations among the novels he drew on, the films he directed, and the subsequent career of his work – its legacy, its aftertexts. We can discern tendencies in his key British output and its impact at the time and since that give clues to the work's ideological freightage in ways that are fresher to us than slotting home attitudes to a particular authorial figure, not least because they challenge notions of coherently stable texts that are then read against themselves through symptomatic interpretation.

Our approach derives from several sources, starting with Roger Chartier's tripartite historicization of books. Chartier aims to reconstruct "the diversity of older readings from their sparse and multiple traces," focusing on "the text itself, the object that conveys it, and the act that grasps it," and identifying "the strategies by which authors and publishers tried to impose an orthodoxy or a prescribed reading" of it ("Texts" 157, 161–63, 166). We also find value in Pierre Macherey's work ("Culture"; "The Literary"). Like Chartier, Macherey turns away from reflectionism, which argues that a text's key meaning lies in its overt or covert capacity to capture the *Zeitgeist*. He also rejects formalism's claim that close readings can secure definitive meanings, because texts accrete and attenuate meanings on their travels as they rub up against, trope, and are troped by other fictional and social texts and are interpreted by readers. Such readings may reflect, refract, or ignore social tendencies, including ideological ones, as Alec McHoul and Tom O'Regan show in their "discursive analysis of particular actor networks, technologies of textual exchange, circuits of communicational and textual effectivity, traditions of exegesis, [and] commentary and critical practice" (5–6).

Engagements with texts must therefore be supplemented, or perhaps supplanted, by an account of the conditions under which they are made, circulated, received, interpreted, and criticized. The life of any popular film is a passage across space and time, a life remade again and again by institutions, discourses, and practices of distribution and reception – in short, all the shifts and shocks of a commodity, as per Tony Bennett and Janet Woollacott's exploration of James Bond through different incarnations and Toby Miller's research investigating the career of *The Avengers*. The goal is to erase "the tenacious division that for so long separated sciences of description and sciences of interpretation, morphological studies and hermeneutical analysis" and recognize that the "'world of text' ... [is] a world of objects and performances" (Chartier, "Crossing" 38–39).

Our analysis is a materialist one, then, not in the sense that we seek a clear reflection of ideology in Hitchcock, but that we track both what happens *in* his movies and what happens *to* them as they travel, attenuating and developing links and discourses across their careers. In other words, we trace "their different and successive materialities" (Chartier, "Crossing" 40) in all their open, malleable, polyphonic qualities (Chartier, "Le droit").

Genre

Espionage involves surreptitiously conveying information about a country, company, or union to its enemy or rival. Much of this information is "official"; it has national-security significance or economic value. Along with the glamour and romance of undercover work, a blend of fabrication and fact has long characterized espionage in a complex interplay of art and life. For example, Nicholas Hiley argues that the period up to the 1930s saw "most British intelligence officers [take] the greater part of their ideas of secret service directly from fictional sources" (57).

At an ideological level, espionage fiction's nexus of "spectacular violence and social vacuousness" has led to Marxist accusations that it models anti-social conduct, heroizes the capitalist state, and delights in base consumerism (Westlake 37; Kerr 2; Morrison 21). But it also has champions. Reactionaries argue that the genre models struggles between bad and good and displays democratic values. For centrists, the success of espionage fiction demonstrates that citizen-readers approve of their governments acting covertly in the interest of state security. Other critics find a romance of citizenship in it, a drama where readers and viewers test and enjoy the limit cases that are regularly presented by the comparative anarchy of international relations. Loyalty, patriotism, and even the mundanity of public employment are entertainingly rehearsed as plays with death and doom (Der Derian 53–54, 57–58). It is worth interrogating the genre's history in some detail in order to consider these claims and situate Hitchcock's contributions alongside them.

Espionage fiction took off in the decade following *L'affaire Dreyfus* in late–nineteenth century France, when a Jewish officer was falsely accused of espionage in what became a racially charged case that pitted an emergent group of progressive intellectuals against the state and the right. Wesley K. Wark traces connections at that time in Britain between cheap popular fiction, journalistic and governmental xenophobia, shifts in class formation and the division of labor, and the emergence of moral panics about foreigners and spying:

The enemy could be the Jew, the foreigner, the not-quite gentleman, the corrupted, the bomb-throwers, the women. Why the day needed to be saved was very much a product of national insecurities that began to mount at the turn of the century. At their heart were fears about the pace of technological and societal change caused by the impact of the industrial revolution. In the wake of its manifold upheavals, traditional measures of the international balance of power were threatened and the domestic structures of government upset.

(275)

Ernest Mandel's compelling socio-historical account of such fiction describes the period between the two World Wars, when our two Hitchcock films were made, as an epistemological watershed. Crime fiction was transformed to allow for a new force, directed against the sovereign-state rather than property or individuals. These were crimes by one state against another, with governments personified by shadowy undercover figures. Since that time, the element of mystery in espionage fiction has derived from identifying and sabotaging an enemy's alliances, supporters, methods, and reasons (61–62).

Mandel explains that espionage plots usually follow a plan devised and executed by an opponent that is foiled in the lonely hour of the last instance by a lone operative inside the enemy's own sphere of action, who is successful because of superior beauty, physique, and technology. Mandel ties these developments to the split subjectivity and increased alienation produced by consumer capitalism. Superheroes must be raised to a higher level with the general development of bourgeois society: mechanization and diversification of commodity production, hyper-consumerism, and alienation of the individual (65).

The appealing quality of many early espionage heroes was their accidental, almost ironic emergence; rather than hardened professionals, they were gifted amateurs thrust into a role as protagonists of history. Such figures have a long lineage. The "diminished claim of affective ties on the heroic adventurer" dates back to ex-spy Daniel Defoe's *Robinson Crusoe* (1707) and the anomic male subject who must forage alone and govern himself until his historic destiny to control others can reactivate itself. This trope also relates to the utilitarianism of sovereign consumers and the alibi for empire that sees gallant adventurers happening upon "possessions" while looking for their authentic selves (J. Thompson 74).[2]

In nineteenth- and twentieth-century espionage, this amateurism had exclusive economic and social preconditions. A clubbish male atmosphere was evoked by the nicknames that early members of the British secret service used to refer to one another: "Woolly, Buster, Biffy, Bubbles, Blinker, Barmy, [and] Tin-Eye" head one list (Porter 169). Apart from attesting to the claim that English public schools produce children rather than develop them, this roll call signifies *joie de vivre*, not taking things too seriously, and never losing a sense of self that can transcend its environment – the stereotype of the phlegmatic all-rounder, accompanied by a righteousness implicitly informed by race, class, and gender. Think of the moment when Nigel Havers clears hurdles adorned with champagne glasses in *Chariots of Fire* (Hugh Hudson, 1981).

Not surprisingly, espionage fiction was much loved by Theodore Roosevelt, A.J. Balfour, Clement Attlee, George V, and Robert Baden-Powell, while Woolly and Co. overtly modeled themselves on characters in novels, and wrote racist "yarns" based on their own experiences. They also engaged in public self-mythification via autobiographies that saluted their role, for example in World War II, in the style of espionage-fiction heroes; several said they had volunteered for perilous missions based on their desire to emulate the heroism of *The 39 Steps* (Porter 171–72; Knightley 122; Trotter 52; Stafford). Such tendencies conditioned the moment when a talented lower middle-class professional (Hitchcock) heroized talented ruling-class amateurs.

The 39 Steps

> Mr. Hannay, would you be so very kind and turn that mirror with its face to the wall?
>
> Annabella Smith (*The 39 Steps*)

The 39 Steps was the most popular British film of 1935. It brought Hitchcock his initial acclaim by New York critics (who regarded him as the only significant foreign director), spawned more than thirty stage adaptations in Manhattan over the next three years, and encouraged Hergé to write a chase sequence for Tintin (Ryall 105, 175; Infiesta; Kapsis 23). The movie was fondly remembered by 1930s cinemagoers looking back sixty years on (Kuhn), when it also featured in numerous *fin-de-siècle* plebiscites establishing a public-intellectual canon of movies. The British Film Institute named it the fourth-best British film of all time after polling a thousand industry mavens (*The Lady Vanishes* was 35th); *Time Out* voted it 76th of the hundred best; *Movieline* positioned it on an equivalent list; the *Arizona Republic* ranked it 87th out of the "Top 100 Foreign Films"; the *Star Tribune* placed it number 38 of *all* films; the *Herald* of Glasgow named it best British film; and the Ed McMahon Mass Communications Center rated it amongst "100 of the Best Films of the 20th Century." The egregious *National Review* put it amongst the "100 Best Conservative Movies," and a dramatization for the stage left the high-Tory Auberon Waugh, who thought the hero was based on his maternal grandfather, "proud to be English again" (T. Miller, *SpyScreen*). This achievement is as dubious as they come.

The raft of latter-day screen homages, adding to film remakes in 1959 (Ralph Thomas) and 1978 (Don Sharp), includes endlessly deferred plans for a Robert Towne–directed version, which led to loud protests from the Scots (despite the original film's depiction of Scotland) when Australia offered cheaper location shooting (Dupuis); the use of the storyline in *12 Monkeys* (Terry Gilliam, 1996); spoofing citations in *High Anxiety* (Mel Brooks, 1977) and *Foul Play* (Colin Higgins, 1978); and a 2008 made-for-TV BBC movie starring Rupert Penry-Jones, from the British TV series *Spooks* (2002–).[3] The original continues to attract viewers on television and other formats. A 2000 DVD release of the movie included an audio essay, a documentary, and a 1937 radio adaptation released on audiotape in 1998 (T. Miller, *SpyScreen*). The acclaimed exhibition "Hitchcock et l'art: Coincidences fatales" at the Georges Pompidou Centre in Paris and Montréal's Musée des Beaux Arts opened in 2001. Visitors began their tour in a dark room. Fumbling in the half-light, they came upon twenty-one quotidian objects turned into fetishes through Hitchcock, notably the silk stockings wound around handcuffs from *The 39 Steps* (Grigor; Conrad).

Re-released with a new print in 2008, the film was welcomed by Jim Hoberman as "the movie with which Hitchcock became Hitchcock." Followers of Hulu could watch it online gratis and *de jure* from 2009. A theatrical pastiche (originally called *John Buchan's The 39 Steps*, then renamed *Alfred Hitchcock's The 39 Steps*), with four actors playing all the parts and the script borrowing generously from 1935, became a worldwide success in 2007–09. It played up the original movie's humor to generate what the *New York Times* referred to as a "fast, frothy exercise in legerdemain" (Brantley). Penguin Books offers readers both the original novel and an interactive digital rewrite by Charles Cumming, complete with maps and *21 Steps* (wetellstories.co.uk/stories/week1/). *The 39 Steps* has been eponymized by a hotel in Edinburgh and a bar in Barbados, and metaphorized by *Health Economics* and the Acheson *Report* to explain inequalities in Britain (Birch) and by *Drug Discovery Today* and *Toxicology Letters* to update readers on gene-expression profiling, while *L'information psychiatrique* finds that a schizophrenic patient ("Louis") has delusions based on it (Imbeaud and Auffray; Thompson and Pine; Guyard *et al.*). *Psychological Science* cites the film as proof that "a pattern of waves that course through a temporal signal and are independent in phase" encourages spectators in best cinemetric, anti-ideological style to focus on narrative by offering large amounts of spectacular action (Cutting *et al.* 4).

The movie stands out among Hitchcock's British films for its worldwide public esteem, perhaps because it is available for uptake from a variety of perspectives; its cultural politics are all over the place. John Buchan, who wrote the 1915 literary antecedent *The Thirty-Nine Steps*, was an anti-gay, anti-Semitic, and generally racist class snob. These tendencies are on clear display in the novel, where women are almost entirely absent (T. Miller, *SpyScreen*). The film is different, not surprisingly given Hitchcock's views on imperialism (he was skeptical) and women and spying: "The international spy has multiplied a thousand fold. Scientists or street sweepers may act as spies, for money, for patriotism, for adventure. Women, with their eye for detail and their acting ability, make excellent spies" (Williams; Hitchcock quoted in Atkins 9).

There is an added element to the *Steps*, a distance from privilege that derives from the colonial status of the hero, Richard Hannay (Robert Donat). He stands to one side of the English ruling class because he hails from the colonies and Old Dominions: Rhodesia in the Buchan novel, Canada in the Hitchcock film.[4] In the novel, Hannay ascribes his capacity to escape danger to the fact that "I'm a colonial and travel light" (83). This connects him not only to colonialism, of course, but to masculine freedom of movement, the two combined under the sign of tourism (Kirby). But that freedom paradoxically renders him an outsider to the world of Tin-Eye and Bubbles. He would have been welcome to share a snifter with them, but would never truly have "belonged." Each time he excused himself to the rest room or departed the group at the end of an evening, eyebrows would be raised and additional confidences exchanged.

Donat's fresh-faced beauty and asthma-aspirated voice are crucial to capturing the "dispassionate amusement" (Rothman 114–15) that comes with being not quite English. In London, Hannay is a lost soul. He needs to leave the capital and go back to the land, perhaps because he made his money in the Dominions and locates his subjectivity there. The countryside allows him to track the secret he must unravel while providing the space in which he can avoid capture. That doubleness merges in an Edenic return, a kind of reverse Bildungsroman, that places Hannay in the wilds of Scotland. In Buchan, this is a choice made out of familiarity and consanguinity, paralleling the flight from the city to redemption-through-peril in John Bunyan's *Pilgrim's Progress*: romance meets Protestant morality and muscular Christianity in a quest for salvation through good deeds (Panek 52). In Hitchcock, the choice is born of necessity, because the few clues to the mystery Hannay must solve lead him there. But again, he seems at home in a way that he was not in London. Rurality brings freedom, as rugged Dominionist self-possession overrides unsettled urban indolence. At the same time, agrarian life holds hidden dangers, and he must in any event end up in the metropole in order to thwart the plot against British security he has uncovered.

Hitchcock's distaste for urban life is visually thematized in the panic of the music-hall crowd out of control in the film's opening sequence. The scene expresses the leery, proletarian aura of such spaces, which were frequently adjacent to breweries (Devas 46). In the novel, the audience is full of "capering women and monkey-faced men" (Buchan 12). City crowds were figures of great anxiety in the early twentieth century, which saw the emergence of élite theory in sociology and pessimistic proto-social-psychology. Vilfredo Pareto, Gaetano Mosca, Gustave Le Bon, and Robert Michels argued that newly literate publics were vulnerable to manipulation by demagogues, while the founder of the "American Dream," the Latino James Truslow Adams, saw "[t]he mob mentality of the city crowd" as "one of the menaces to modern civilization" and disparaged "the prostitution of the moving-picture industry" (404, 413). These critics were frightened of socialism, democracy, and popular reason (Wallas 137). They shared a terror of mob rule, which they deplored and, quaintly, doubted – for behind every public tumult of mass energy supposedly lay a group of agitators, ready to displace existing rulers with their own power-mongering. For élite theorists, the demotic side of audiences was a sham; the herd mentality was ultimately orchestrated.

Buchan's Hannay finds that "the talk of the ordinary Englishman made me sick" (9). Throughout the novel, he disparages the first-person narration he is giving us for pandering to popular taste, likening it to "wild melodrama," "a penny novelette," and "pure Rider Haggard and Conan Doyle" (Buchan 169, 170, 65). In the film, Hannay reacts to revelations about "a certain foreign power" with an incredulous "it sounds like a spy story," and later explains being saved from a bullet by a hymn book as something he's never witnessed "except in the movies," while an initially hostile interlocutor calls his version of events a "petty novelette spy story." Just after the picture came out, Hitchcock acknowledged in *Sight and Sound* that he "made only thrillers ... the equivalent merely of popular novelettes." His alibi was the absence of good screenwriters in the UK, which meant that his own abilities and his collaborators' determined his choices.

Popular taste's susceptibility to rhetoric is also articulated to imperialism. When Hannay addresses a political gathering, he rouses stolid Scots into collective frenzy with demagoguery, not policies and programs, while the second and ultimate music-hall sequence sees further chaos and a riot. These scenes also place Hannay squarely in the tradition of Empire. He carries the full burden of the civilizing impulse in his body against ill-informed hordes (Panek 44) – in the novel, one character refers to him approvingly as "a white man" (Buchan 26). Britain's putative goal in World War I – the liberation of Europe from Prussian militarism – was structurally homologous to the putative goal of its Empire – to displace barbarism with a "higher" form of life (Kiernan 181). Same discourse, new object, with Hannay the model subject who helped bring capitalism and government to Africa / North America, and would protect civilization in Europe. In each case, deliverance from demons within would come from angels without. Hannay is privileged, even if he is an outsider, through class, race, gender, and empire. They give him the confidence and the will to triumph (Devas).

And yet. The speech to the Scots is for all the world an example of New Deal rhetoric:

> I've known what it is to feel lonely and helpless and have the whole world against me. Those are things that no man or woman ought to feel. I ask your candidate and all those who love their fellow men to set themselves resolutely to make this world a happier place to live in. A world where no nation plots against nation, where no neighbor plots against neighbor, where there is no persecution or hunting down, where everybody gets a square deal and a sporting chance, and where people try to help and not to hinder. A world from which suspicion and cruelty and fear have been forever banished. That is the sort of world I want! Is that the sort of world you want? Fine! That's all I have to say.

And there was also a steely side to this speech ("I'm not rich and I've never been idle"). Taken together, these empathetic and disciplinary words encompass some of the contradictions of imperialism.

Just after World War I, British Prime Minister David Lloyd George told the Imperial Conference that the Empire was "the most hopeful experiment in human organisation which the world has yet seen," because its *modus operandi* was ethical rather than coercive, "based not on force but on goodwill and a common understanding. Liberty is its binding principle" (quoted in Mansergh 158). This sense of mission was crucial to Hannay's life in the colonies, and it explains his unease when presented with the lack of a challenge "at home." The goal fitted Buchan's firm Calvinism, which found the dystopic in the utopic and vice versa. Sloth lay around the corner from pleasure. This restlessness presumably took Hannay across class lines and into the film's opening music-hall sequence. While the setting is partly a narrative device, it is also an index of Hannay's liminal status and his ability to identify with those excluded and downtrodden by class politics at the metropole.

Before he can adopt the mantle of an Imperial hero transposed to Europe, Hannay must undergo a transformation. When he encounters the dying, then suddenly lifeless Franklin P. Scudder in Buchan or Annabella Smith (the noted operetta singer Lucie Mannheim) in Hitchcock, Hannay is aroused from his ennui and skepticism by Scudder's/Smith's sacrifice, realizing he has simultaneously become a suspect and a target, because the police will believe him to be a killer and the spies will take him for a confederate of the corpse. The change of gender from novel to film in the character of the dying spy is crucial, part of Hitchcock's adaptation of Buchan's homosociality into a story-world where female characters are powerful figures on whom men rely for direction, ideas, and succor.

The mysterious femme fatale who displaces the novel's male spy sports husky Teutonic tones, an olive complexion, high emotion, and dark hair. These mark her out as a woman with a "past," unlike the "ladylike and self-righteous" blonde Pamela (Madeleine Carroll), who has all the confidence of her leisured, gendered fraction of the ruling class (Landy 126). The foreign woman spy knows on sight that Hannay can be trusted, but is too full of desire and mystery to be a suitable partner. She accosts Hannay during the riot with "May I come home with you?" When he inquires why, she replies, "Well, I'd like to," before going to his rooms for what he flirtatiously, but presciently, calls "your funeral." Hannay assumes Annabella is an actor, to which she enigmatically responds, "Not in the way that you mean." By contrast, Pamela's hauteur invites Hannay in even as it seems to push him away. She mistakenly categorizes him as a villain, not least because their first meeting finds him forcing himself on her sexually in order to avoid arrest on a train. Her sanctimonious reaction blinds her to his desperate goodness, even as it marks her as desirable. A perfectly legitimate objection to sexual harassment becomes a double sign – that she is quick to judge, and is wifely material. For *Libération* seven decades later, their first meeting may be like premature ejaculation, because it almost concludes the film before it has begun – but in a pleasurably poetic way; while *Le parisien* sees it as a fitting preliminary to a world about to enter the revolutionary chaos of war (Skorecki; Leguèbe).

The interplay of gender, sex, and potentially deadly violence repeats. Hannay escapes Portland Place by persuading a milkman to exchange clothes so the "bachelor" Hannay can escape a cuckolded husband and the latter's brother-in-law undetected; when he anxiously enters a railway carriage, his fellow occupants are discussing the ladies' underwear they sell; and his landlady screams on discovering the initial murder, which Hitchcock articulates with the whistle of Hannay's train heading north in one of the most famous match-on-sound cuts in cinema. Then we meet a crofter's game and sexy wife (Peggy Ashcroft), who hides and romances Hannay at great personal cost – retributive domestic violence. A disturbing edit again contrasts sound and image. After Hannay has been shot by the spymaster and taken a tumble, Hitchcock cuts to the crofter's cottage where the fugitive hero had spent a night and where we now learn that the overcoat he had been given to aid his escape contained a life-savingly thick Scottish hymnal. We then cut to a close-up of the bullet-stopping volume, accompanied by the offscreen laughter of the local sheriff and Hannay, from a shot of the empty coat hook, accompanied by the offscreen sounds of a blow struck and a woman's scream, as the crofter beats his wife for giving Hannay the coat. This is interpreted by Derridoids as "the logic of hospitality[,] … sexual access to the master's women" (Schantz 12). More benignly, when Hannay and Pamela are handcuffed together, he complains: "There are twenty million women in this island and I get to be chained to you." This apparently unwelcome bracketing becomes a sign of their transformation into a couple, as an innkeeper's wife opens the way for them to be alone together. And the film's final shot, from the rear, sees Hannay's cuffed hand reaching for Pamela, all in black satin – a moment of paradoxical, kinky romance.

Gender is subtly foregrounded whenever Hannay is absent from the action because we either know or are later shown that he is asleep or unconscious – a classic warning about men letting down their guard, failing to be alert, and showing vulnerability. Lastly, the famous camera movement in on the spymaster's missing fingers – quoted in Hitchcock's own television work (Kapsis 41–42) and in exchanges between Holden Caulfield and his kid sister in *The Catcher in the Rye* (Salinger 67–68) – references the need to compensate for lacking a "normal" masculine body via political machinations – just the opposite of a guileless, virile subject from the Dominions like Hannay.

The man with no identity is typical of spy-genre protagonists, nowhere more fully than in Hannay's memorable utterance, "I'm nobody." From there, he proceeds to be, serially, a milkman, a mechanic, a parade marcher, a politician, and a criminal – a perfectly depthless figure who can be anyone and be inconspicuous anywhere. Paradoxically secure in his shallowness, he passes as ordinary – a truly insidious, albeit accidental, agent of the ISA, if you like. At the same time, this shallowness sets up the conditions of possibility for comedy, as a series of misunderstandings produce disasters followed by a happy resolution. Supposedly joyous settings that go wrong, such as a music hall, a party, or meeting a gorgeous woman, nevertheless show that the space for happiness exists somewhere, a lost pleasure that can be regained if Hannay can keep reasoning while all around him appear mad.

Hitchcock's gift in *The 39 Steps* is, in contradictory fashion, to create a *bricolage* that denigrates the masses but has affection for them, touches on the wholesale ambiguity of the colonial subject returned and disappointed, and allows gender play to substitute for xenophobia. It is as though the director, like so many audience members, yearned to be like Hannay, but knew that he belonged with the *polloi*.

In addition to these tendencies, the film's historical backdrop matches Buchan's novel. For while the book was published during World War I, the film came out just as Germany was rearming and powerful debates were being waged within Britain over the need for military preparation. In this sense, Hannay's despair in the face of repeated bureaucratic mistrust of his intentions and disbelief in his explanations might be said to mirror the desperation felt by anti-appeasement forces at the time. Of course, Hannay stands as an inchoate prophet, unclear of what he is revealing, so the analogy is incomplete. But that naïveté generates his charm and guarantees the truth of his message. Those qualities make him – and his director – a more contradictory subject than ideology critique can normally encompass, even as they touch on ideological issues of the day, and have been troped to do the same ever since.

The Lady Vanishes

You are a spy! – Iris Henderson
Oh, I always think that's such a grim word. – Miss Froy

Also a comedy-romance-thriller, *The Lady Vanishes* (1938) traces the adventures of cross-European train travelers who variously befriend, lose, imprison, conceal, seek, ignore, deny, rescue, and chase a little-old-lady English governess who happens to double as His Majesty's spy – no charming amateur she. The film stands alongside *The 39 Steps* as the high-water mark of Hitchcock's post-silent cinema British filmmaking, displaying again his quaint mix of affection and contempt for imperial and ruling-class hypocrisy and insouciance. It also marks the commencement of an agreement whereby MGM engaged in co-productions with Gaumont-British and Gainsborough, which allowed Metro to distribute the picture in the UK – a key moment in Hollywood's use of the New International Division of Cultural Labor to exploit resources and schemes across the globe ("Anglo-American"; Miller *et al.*). Production of the film, originally entitled *Lost Lady,* was disrupted when the Electrical Trades Union went on strike ("Film Studio"). So the text was dripping with ideological issues before it was even made: US cultural imperialism meets UK industrial action.

In the seven decades since it appeared, this little film has provided innumerable intertexts and tropes. *Slate* contests Hoberman's view of *The 39 Steps* in identifying *The Lady Vanishes* as "Hitchcock's First Hitchcock Film" (Rich). In a *Sight and Sound* piece written for a 2008 screening, Graham Fuller alerts readers that the event "coincides with the centenaries of Michael Redgrave and Sidney Gilliat, who wrote the screenplay with his partner Frank Launder" (Fuller 37, 40). When Fuller mentions that "2008 is also the anniversary of the film itself, and of Neville Chamberlain's disastrous 'peace for our time' speech, which he made on returning from Munich on 30 September 1938, three months before *The Lady Vanishes*'s Christmas day premiere," he joins the many commentators who have understood the movie in terms of intertexts: the London *Times* in 1938 reported that audiences responded, "'Mr. Hitchcock is right. We must shoot down these foreign blighters'" ("New Films"). Seventy years later, the *Guardian* listed it as "the most political film Hitchcock ever made" (Sweet) because the moment when a "cringing pacifist coward" is shot "carried an irresistible message to 1930s Britain – and to 1930s America" against appeasement (Bradshaw). The *Evening Standard* goes so far as to say that it was "possibly designed to show Hitler that the British had more in them than met his eye" (Malcolm).

There had to be a certain subtlety in handling such issues at the time. Prior to the outbreak of war in September 1939, the British Board of Film Censors was ill-disposed to films that deviated from appeasement or criticized the Nazis (Webster). On reflection, the movie has been seen as "Hitchcock's guilty farewell to his homeland – the work of a man who suspected war was coming, and had already decided to sit it out in Hollywood drinking orange juice" (Sweet); the British film producer Michael Balcon (who had been involved in *The 39 Steps*) derided Hitchcock and other English wartime expats in Hollywood as "cowards" and "deserters," reserving particular opprobrium for the "plump young technician" (quoted in Trumpbour 148).

Set in and between the fictional nation of Bandrika and the (quasi-)factual nation of Britain, *The Lady Vanishes* has traveled a long way since its maiden voyage, leaving a mark on everything from twenty-first-century politics to contemporary transportation. The *Independent on Sunday* troped "The Lady Vanishes" to describe French First Lady Cécilia Sarkozy's mysterious absences from state functions (Poirier), the *Independent* to ask what happened to Fenella Fielding (Chalmers), the *Sun* to attack Margaret Thatcher for inaction during her first days as leader of the Conservative opposition in 1975 ("First 100"), and the *Guardian* to mark the (supposed) end of Thatcherite neoliberalism and authoritarian populism twenty years later (Rawnsley). For the *New Yorker*, it referred to the impenetrability of Hillary Rodham Clinton's character (Kolbert). When she became Secretary of State, *Slate* insisted she watch the film in order to master the art of diplomacy (Kaplan). The *Scotsman* trivialized the country's Education Secretary, Fiona Hyslop, with the same referent (Maddox), the *Monterey County Herald* used it to account for the unexpected arrival of painted lady butterflies that resemble monarchs and confuse northern California residents (Agha), *Newsweek* to engage the films of Roman Polanski and Peter Yates (Kroll), the *New York Times* to explain trends in fashion (Swidler), *O: The Oprah Magazine* to describe what it feels like for women when they cease to draw the male gaze ("Other People's"), *The Age* to uncover racist Australian immigration policy (Marr), the *Economist* to write about Myanmar/Burma's detention of Aung San Suu Kyi ("The Lady"), and *The Wrap* to account for Rachel Uchitel canceling a press conference slated to detail her links to Tiger Woods (Mikulan).

For the *Journal of Bioethical Inquiry*, *The Lady Vanishes* encapsulated the absence of women from debates about somatic-cell nuclear transfer and embryonic stem-cell technologies (Dickenson), while the *Journal of Organizational Change Management* troped it to account for obstacles to women becoming leaders (Höpfl and Matilal), the *Journal of Lesbian Studies* to specify the complexity of identifying who is a lesbian (Weston), the *Australian Law Journal* to note the gendered workings of the law (Chatterjee), the *International Journal of Work Organisation and Emotion* to examine affective labor (Bolton), the *Australian Journal of International Affairs* to explain the subjectivity of the noted international-relations scholar Coral Bell (Taylor), *Contemporary South Asia* to describe the Marxist historiography of India (Mitra), *Church History* to discern the impact of semiotics and post-structuralism on feminist scholarship (Clark), and *Film Quarterly* and *Camera Obscura* to identify a deep-seated fear of women (Fischer; Beckman, "Violent").

This complex, troping mélange of fact and fiction forms the backdrop to our argument: that like *The 39 Steps*, *The Lady Vanishes* is a conservative text because of its faith in the "talented amateur" and, in this case, the "Little Englander," but is equally a liberatory one in the contradictions of gender, class, sexuality, and national difference that it discloses – hence the film's talent for invocation in so many different social and cultural contexts.[5] This is not an instance of spy fiction allegorizing or adequating to the real, of indexing or undermining ideology, but of contributing to it in a contradictory way that makes subsequent tropes possible. To explain this, we engage *The Lady Vanishes* by considering the play of gender, class, and sexuality in the text and its source – Ethel Lina White's 1936 novel *The Wheel Spins,* where the vanished lady is prized because she is "against the Red element" rather than the Nazis (White 105).[6]

Michael Redgrave's Gilbert the ethnomusicologist plays the muddling, talented amateur whose unsullied Englishness makes him closer to clubland than Hannay. A charming, cheeky, raffish, almost rakish, naughty-but-nice scholar, Gilbert moves whimsically between recreating and recording bizarre folk rituals and romancing, ironizing, doubting, aiding, comforting, and directing his love interest. Gilbert is equally at home in comedy and crisis, amity and action, emotion and intellection. He embodies a structural homology to international politics in the light touch he applies to everyday life, which can rapidly transmogrify into fierce aggression as required. For example, he says of "British diplomacy – 'Never climb a fence if you can sit on it.' It's an old Foreign Office adage." That flexibility both hides and enables the play of diplomacy and its shadowy alter arts.

Margaret Lockwood plays Iris Matilda Henderson, the young woman who meets and subsequently loses the vanishing lady, Miss Froy (May Whitty). Her feminist counter-public sphere galpals, Googie Withers as Blanche and Sally Stewart as Julie, resist any notion of passive, decorous womanhood through their overbearing occupancy of each hotel room they enter while voyaging across "the Continent." As a group, they are indomitable, using their wit and sex throughout the first part of the film to dominate seemingly any context: "Bandrika may have a dictator but tonight we're painting it red."

Effortlessly, endlessly flirty, moneyed, sophisticated, and self-confident, at one point Iris stands in her underwear on a table addressing the hapless hotel help. She is to be married back in London later that week. Her friends ask why her bridegroom can't change *his* name. After all, she's played baccarat at Biarritz, not to mention eating "caviar at Cannes" and "sausage rolls at the dogs." Able to shift easily between cosmopolitan international elites and organic intellectuals of the working class, the girls pick up and discard cultural signage as easily as pie.

There are some restrictions to their gleeful, giddy independence. Despite "that little thing called love" evoked by Blanche, Iris is downhearted in asking "What is there left for me but – marriage?" Certain limits are set to their lives by gender and class. Iris's fiancé is referred to as a "blue-blooded cheque-book chaser." In other words, he is an aristocrat whose wealth is gone, though his social standing remains. By contrast, she plaintively confides, "Father's simply aching to have a coat of arms on the jam label." For despite the hauteur with which she and her gay friends address the international proletariat ("Don't tell me Cook's are running cheap tours *here*," Blanche witheringly moans) their self-confidence plainly derives from commerce and industry rather than formal station. They are spending daddy's new money, and the quid pro quo is the respectability their marriage into a peerage will bring his household. The *nouveaux riches* crave lineage – an endless *arriviste* quest for history – and can get it by associating with genteel folk whose decadent lifestyles need refinancing by a new and vigorous class.

White's novel spends some time exploring what constitutes "ladyness" among the group, a concept and social type that involves particular codes of behavior and dress – avoiding "bad form" and "abandon." Some fellow passengers explain why they wear evening attire for dinner on the Continent: "If we didn't dress we should feel that we were letting England down" (White 26). By contrast, the galpals are derided as "a party of near-nudists, who drank all day and night" (White 112). They are the frothy superstructure of empire's bite.

Iris's extraordinary self-confidence relies on a casual imperialism, as when the novel finds her convinced of the rightness of her cause thanks to an image in her mind's eye – "the Union Jack fluttering overhead" – and a sound in her mind's ear – "the strains of the National Anthem." Even if she "can't speak a word of this miserable language," all will be well because "*I* expect foreigners to speak English" (White 87, 72, 59). At an early point in her adventure, exasperated by her inability to master European languages, Iris thinks "of Basel on the milky-jade Rhine, with its excellent hotels where English was spoken and where she could be ill intelligibly and with dignity" (White 40). Melbourne's *The Age* newspaper greeted the film upon its initial release in a similarly giddy yet anxiously confident way that juxtaposed the sense and sensibility of empire with the difference and threat of "foreignness," explaining that most of the film's action takes place "in Central Europe, where almost anything is liable to happen nowadays (and things do happen)" ("Brilliant").

Gender and nation cut multiple ways, of course. Gay issues form a recurrent theme in Hitchcock's work, drawing both on the heady sex of English public schools and his own violently Catholic background (Wollen). A queer account might see Redgrave's private life of bisexuality referenced when Gilbert says, "We've got to search this train. There's something definitely queer in here." And this was the first of several films, perhaps most notably *Night Train to Munich* (Carol Reed, 1940), in which Basil Radford and Naunton Wayne played homosocial cricket obsessives. Wayne opines that Redgrave's story about abduction "seems a bit queer" just minutes after he and Radford are seen in bed together. Contemporary viewers may well read this rather differently from their 1938 counterparts. Or not. But we should also interpret the two buffoons as representatives of middle-class Englishness who travel, slowly then quickly, from uninterested disinterest to alarmed action in the face of fascism's rise, captured here in a train ride that is also a journey from lying about a potential kidnapping to safeguard their arrival in time for a Test match through to staying put and fighting the enemy (Sweet). In the process, the characters ultimately put aside the pseudo-anonymity offered by first-class travel, forsaking their "private mentality" in favor of "fighting the anti-democratic hordes" (Kirby 21).

These destabilizing moments and characters emerge in environments of flux, a hotel and a train, where bodies and things are on the move, unmoored from norms and ready for crisis as much as pleasure – notably an adulterous couple (Cecil Parker and Linden Travers). It seems as though each middle-class subject stands ready to fabricate a story, for reasons (cricket scores or philandering) that point to gendered British suburban hypocrisies and falsehoods. They are home-counties counterparts to "European" duplicity, which is at least driven by the desire for geopolitical advantage. Disappointed by her barrister boyfriend's inconstancy, Laura Parmiter, who is traveling as Mrs. Todhunter, sees through class distinctions to gendered similarities: "a professional man did not differ so greatly from a tradesman in essentials. ... [T]hey looked much the same before shaving and without their collars" (White 130).

As Wolfgang Schivelbusch explains, the expansion of rail lines across the world in the nineteenth century brought new relations of space and power that joined industry, science, and the body in a complex of power and knowledge that pathologized railway workers and passengers. Hitchcock was certainly fascinated by the train's bizarre amalgam of imprisonment and mobility. It is a key player in many of his most famous texts, from *The 39 Steps* to *North by Northwest* (1959), perhaps because there are multitudinous places to hide (Wollen 82; Greenspun). In White's novel, train travel is compared to horse-riding and flying, but her most memorable descriptions are more disturbing: "screaming through darkness," "monstrous metallic," "scorching," "rushing," "jerking," "shooting," "explosive," "ripping," "rattling," "sweeping," and "insensate, maddened" (White 30, 150). The train in both novel and film is a paradoxical object, a source of both prison and liberty, incarceration and flight.

For Fuller, *The Lady Vanishes* is predicated on "speed – of narrative, wit, motion and emotion." He suggests that the element of the film most likely to resonate with viewers today "is Hitchcock's manipulation of Iris' consciousness and, through the use of the train as a vehicle for dreaming, the idea that she, not Miss Froy (the literal disappearee) is the lady who vanishes" (38). Iris is pathologized by her fellow-passengers as an amiable but disturbed young woman. The seemingly definitive diagnosis comes from a scheming brain surgeon, Egon Hartz (Paul Lukas), whose duplicity embodies the railway's ambiguity, simultaneously facilitating the speed and freedom of modernity and the truth-claims and discipline of the psy-function. In the novel, travel gives Iris a "sense of nightmare." Her travails are augmented by "maniac shrieks of the engine and the frantic shaking of the train" and the confusion surrounding Miss Froy's whereabouts – and her very identity – in the flux of motion. As if trapped in a mechanical vortex, Iris finds herself "in the grip of an insensate maddened force, which, itself, was a victim to a relentless system" (White 150–51). At the same time, the railway turned "the everyday business of transport" into "a temporary rapture" (White 43).

The sign is truly disarticulated from its referent in *The Lady Vanishes*: Was there a lady? Can Iris ever become one? Which lady vanished? The sense of mobility and destabilization, of opportunity and constraint, are ever-present because the condition of their frippery existence for the English aboard is empire, which relies on the secret services of Miss Froy. Bundled together on a cross-class, cross-continental train, they depart unsure of anything but their unshakably jolly chauvinism.

Conclusion

Just as train tracks laid out new forms of dominion in *The 39 Steps* and *The Lady Vanishes*, they delivered difference and newness, where vanishing points could be resumed as new metaphorical baggage. The train that took Hannay north to Scotland to clear his name and find out the truth and the train where Miss Froy disappeared and was rediscovered were vehicles of modernity, with many points of embarkation and disembarkation on the way to their destinations. The two films depicting them have had similarly complex and even chaotic itineraries, touching on the grand ideological issues of their day, even as they referenced quotidian life – mega-themes of geopolitics alongside micrological details of speech.

In the inevitably conflictual drama of such small stories, as well as in his adaptation of jingoistic works, Hitchcock's British espionage movies managed to be both of their time and beyond it, laying down trackwork that has led to their own palimpsestical recoding again and again by audiences and producers. In doing so, they manage to pose prevailing ideological questions and transcend them, through a dedication to observation and quixotry as much as position-taking and politics.

Notes

This chapter borrows from Toby Miller's "39 Steps to 'The Borders of the Possible': Alfred Hitchcock, Amateur Observer and the New Cultural History," which appeared in *Alfred Hitchcock: Centenary Essays*, edited by Richard Allen and S. Ishii-Gonzáles (London: BFI, 1999): 316–31. The passages are reproduced here with the kind permission of Palgrave Macmilan. These involve Non-exclusive Print and Electronic rights in the English language for distribution in the following territory: World for one edition. We thank the editors and Edward Buscombe for their thoughtful comments.

1. The *New York Times* refers to a trustafarian as a "heavily subsidized 20-something" (Haughney).
2. Edward Buscombe reminds us that one might apply a similar notion of the talented amateur to Hitchcock's *The Man Who Knew Too Much* (1934/1956), *North by Northwest*, and *Torn Curtain* (1966).
3. The program has been screened in North America as *MI-5* and *MI5*, because of locally-racialized connotations associated with the original title.
4. Rhodesia was not technically a Dominion, because it was originally colonized by private enterprise, but was informally administered through the Dominion Office. Buchan ended his days as Governor-General of Canada.
5. We acknowledge but doubt the claim that because these texts do not see their protagonists turn into permanent operatives, they are paeans to active citizenship (Hark).
6. The novel has attracted very little scholarly analysis (but see Homberger; van Seters). It was republished as *The Lady Vanishes* by Bloomsbury (London) in 1997.

Works Cited

Acheson, Donald. *Independent Inquiry into Inequalities in Health Report*. London: The Stationery Office, 1998.

Adams, James Truslow. *The Epic of America*. New York: Triangle, 1941.

Agha, Laith. "The Lady Vanishes." *Monterey County Herald* 2 Apr. 2009. Web. 28 Dec. 2009.

Allen, Richard, and S. Ishii-Gonzáles, eds. *Alfred Hitchcock: Centenary Essays*. London: BFI, 1999.

Almansi, R. J. "Alfred Hitchcock's Disappearing Women: A Study in Scopophilia and Object Relations." *International Review of Psycho-Analysis* 19 (1992): 81–90.

Althusser, Louis. *For Marx*. Trans. Ben Brewster. Harmondsworth: Penguin, 1969.

Althusser, Louis. *Lenin and Philosophy and Other Essays*. Trans. Ben Brewster. London: Verso, 1977.

"Anglo-American Film Agreement." *Times* [London] 11 July 1938. Web. 28 Dec. 2009.

Atkins, John. *The British Spy Novel: Styles in Treachery*. London: John Calder; New York: Riverrun, 1984.

Baudrillard, Jean. *Selected Writings*. Ed. Mark Poster. Stanford: Stanford UP, 1988.

Beckman, Karen. "Violent Vanishings: Hitchcock, Harlan, and the Disappearing Woman." *Camera Obscura* 13 (1996): 77–103.

Beckman, Karen. *Vanishing Women: Magic, Film, and Feminism*. Durham: Duke UP, 2003.

Bell, Daniel. *The End of Ideology: On the Exhaustion of Political Ideas in the Fifties*. Cambridge: Harvard UP, 2000.

Bennett, Tony and Janet Woollacott. *Bond and Beyond: The Political Career of a Popular Hero*. Basingstoke: Macmillan, 1987.

Bennett, Tony, Susan Boyd-Bowman, Colin Mercer, and Janet Woollacott, eds. *Popular Television and Film*. London: BFI, 1981.

Bergan, Ronald. "Margaret Lockwood – The Lady Vanishes, or Rather, Fails to Appear." *Guardian* [London] 19 July 1990. Web. 28 Dec. 2009.

Birch, Stephen. "The 39 Steps: The Mystery of Health Inequalities in the UK." *Health Economics* 8 (1999): 301–08.

Bolton, Sharon C. "The Lady Vanishes: Women's Work and Affective Labour." *International Journal of Work Organisation and Emotion* 3.1 (2009): 72–80.

Bradshaw, Peter. "The Lady Vanishes." *Guardian* [London]. 11 Jan. 2008. Web. 28 Dec. 2009.

Brantley, Ben. "Spies, Blonde and a Guy Go North by Northwest." *New York Times*, 16 Jan. 2008. Web. 28 Dec. 2009.

"Brilliant Comedy: *The Lady Vanishes* at Athenæum." *The Age* [Melbourne] 19 June 1939. Web. 28 Dec. 2009.

Buchan, John. *The Thirty-Nine Steps*. 1915. Boston: Houghton Mifflin, 1919.

Chalmers, Robert. "The Lady Vanishes: Whatever Happened to Fenella Fielding?" *Independent* [London] 24 Feb. 2008. Web. 28 Dec. 2009.

Chartier, Roger. "Crossing Borders in Early Modern Europe: Sociology of Texts and Literature." Trans. Maurice Elton. *Book History* 8 (2005): 37–50.

Chartier, Roger. "Le droit d'auteur est-il une parenthèse dans l'histoire?" *Le monde* [Paris] 17 Dec. 2005. Web. 28 Dec. 2009.

Chartier, Roger. "Texts, Printings, Readings." *The New Cultural History*. Ed. Lynn Hunt. Berkeley: U of California P, 1989. 154–75.

Chatterjee, Bela Bonita. "The Lady Vanishes: Gender, Law and the (Virtual) Body." *Australian Law Journal* 29 (2008): 13–30.

Clark, Elizabeth A. "The Lady Vanishes: Dilemmas of a Feminist Historian after the 'Linguistic Turn.'" *Church History* 67.1 (1998): 1–31.

Cohen, Tom. *Hitchcock's Cryptonymies*. 2 vols. Minneapolis: U of Minnesota P, 2005.

Conrad, Peter. "The Tainted Saint." *Observer* [London] 22 Apr. 2001: 10.

Cutting, James E., Jordan E. DeLong, and Christine E. Nothelfer. "Attention and the Evolution of Hollywood Film." *Psychological Science* (2010). Web. 6 June 2010.

Der Derian, James. *Antidiplomacy: Spies, Terror, Speed, and War*. Cambridge: Blackwell, 1992.

Devas, Angela. "How to Be a Hero: Space, Place and Masculinity in *The 39 Steps* (Hitchcock, UK, 1935)." *Journal of Gender Studies* 14.1 (2005): 45–54.

Dickenson, Donna L. "The Lady Vanishes: What's Missing from the Stem Cell Debate." *Journal of Bioethical Inquiry* 3.1–2 (2006): 43–54.

Dupuis, Jérôme. "Sur les traces de Hitchcock." *L'express* 20 Sept. 2006. Web. 28 Dec. 2009.

Elias, Norbert. *The Civilizing Process: The History of Manners and State Formation and Civilization*. Trans. Edmund Jephcott. Oxford: Blackwell, 1994.

"Film Studio Strike: Cinemas Open as Usual." *Times* [London] 20 Apr. 1938. Web. 28 Dec. 2009.

"First 100 Days: Margaret Thatcher." *BBC News*. BBC, 16 Mar. 2006. Web. 28 Dec. 2009.

Fischer, Lucy. "The Lady Vanishes: Women, Magic and the Movies." *Film Quarterly* 33.1 (1979): 30–40.

Fuller, Graham. "Mystery Train." *Sight and Sound,* Jan. 2008: 36–40.

Gramsci, Antonio. *Selections from the Prison Notebooks.* Ed. and trans. Quintin Hoare and Geoffrey Nowell-Smith. New York: International, 1978.

Greenspun, Roger. "'Beats Flying, Doesn't It?': The Train in Hitchcock." *MoMA* 8 (1991): 14–19.

Grigor, Murray. "Paris Match: Braque, Duchamp … Alfred Hitchcock?" *Guardian* [London] 13 Aug. 2001: 12.

Guyard, Hubert, Robert Le Borgne, Michel Morin, and Frédérique Marseault. "Schizophrénie et distribution des compétences: À propos de l'histoire clinique d'un patient." *L'information psychiatrique* 80.5 (2004): 371–78.

Hark, Ina Rae. "Keeping Your Amateur Standing: Audience Participation and Good Citizenship in Hitchcock's Political Films." *Cinema Journal* 29.2 (1990): 8–22.

Haughney, Christine. "Parental Lifelines, Frayed to Breaking: Parents Pulling the Plugs on Williamsburg Trust-Funders." *New York Times* 7 June 2009. Web. 28 Dec. 2009.

Hiley, Nicholas. "Decoding German Spies: British Spy Fiction 1908–18." *Spy Fiction, Spy Films, and Real Intelligence.* Ed. Wesley K. Wark. London: Frank Cass, 1991. 55–79.

Hitchcock, Alfred. "My Own Methods." *Sight and Sound* 6.22 (1937): 61.

Hoberman, Jim. "*The 39 Steps* and *Shoot the Piano Player* Blow Up Conventions of the Comic Thriller." *Village Voice* 3 Sept. 2008. Web. 28 Dec. 2009.

Homberger, Eric. "English Spy Thrillers in the Age of Appeasement." *Intelligence and National Security* 5.4 (1990): 80–91.

Höpfl, Heather, and Sumohon Matilal. "'The Lady Vanishes': Some Thoughts on Women and Leadership." *Journal of Organizational Change Management* 20.2 (2007): 198–208.

Imbeaud, Sandrine, and Charles Auffray. "'The 39 Steps' in Gene Expression Profiling: Critical Issues and Proposed Best Practices for Microarray Experiments." *Drug Discovery Today* 10.17 (2005): 1175–82.

Infiesta, Conde-Salazar. "Suspense, sus penas, sus labores." *ABC.es.* 9 Jan. 2009. Web. 28 Dec. 2009.

Jost, John T. "The End of the End of Ideology." *American Psychologist* 61.7 (2006): 651–70.

Jost, John T., Christopher M. Federico, and Jaime L. Napier. "Political Ideology: Its Structure, Functions, and Elective Affinities." *Annual Review of Psychology* 60 (2009): 307–37.

Kaplan, Fred. "Hillary Clinton, Watch These Movies! *High Noon, Godfather II, Grand Illusion,* and 22 Other Indispensable Movies for Understanding War and Diplomacy." Slate. com. 4 May 2009. Web. 28 Dec. 2009.

Kapsis, Robert E. *Hitchcock: The Making of a Reputation.* Chicago: U of Chicago P, 1992.

Kerr, Paul. "Watching the Detectives." *Primetime* 1.1 (1981): 2–6.

Kiernan, V.G. *European Empires from Conquest to Collapse, 1815–1960.* N.p.: Fontana, 1982.

Kirby, Alan. "Holidays with the Hun: The Male Tourist and His Murderous Itinerary." *Journal of Tourism and Cultural Change* 5.1 (2007): 17–27.

Knightley, Philip. *The Second Oldest Profession: Spies and Spying in the Twentieth Century.* New York: Penguin, 1988.

Kolbert, Elizabeth. "The Lady Vanishes." *New Yorker,* 11 June 2007. Web. 28 Dec. 2009.

Kroll, Jack. "The Lady Vanishes." *Newsweek,* 7 Mar. 1988: 68.

Kuhn, Annette. "Cinema-Going in Britain in the 1930s: Report of a Questionnaire Survey." *Historical Journal of Film, Radio, and Television* 19.4 (1999): 531–43.

"The Lady Vanishes." *The Economist* 7 June 2003. Web. 28 Dec. 2009.

Landy, Marcia. *British Genres: Cinema and Society, 1930–1960*. Princeton: Princeton UP, 1991.

Le Bon, Gustave. *Psychologie des Foules*. Paris: Alcan, 1899.

Leguèbe, Éric. "Histoire d'amour sur fond de revolution." *Le parisien* 8 May 1998. Web. 28 Dec. 2009.

Macherey, Pierre. "Culture and Politics: Interview with Pierre Macherey." Trans. and ed. Colin Mercer and Jean Radford. *Red Letters* 5 (1977): 3–9.

Macherey, Pierre. "Idéologie: Le mot, l'idée, la chose." *Methodos* 8 (2008). Web. 28 Dec. 2009.

Macherey, Pierre. "The Literary Thing." Trans. Audrey Wasser. *Diacritics* 37.4 (2007): 21–30.

Maddox, David. "The Lady Vanishes." *The Scotsman* 25 Sept. 2009: 14.

Malcolm, Derek. "Classic Cast to Die For." *Evening Standard* [London] 10 Jan. 2008. Web. 28 Dec. 2009.

Mandel, Ernest. *Delightful Murder: A Social History of the Crime Story*. London: Pluto, 1984.

Mansergh, Nicholas. *The Commonwealth Experience*. London: Weidenfeld and Nicolson, 1969.

Marr, David. "The Lady Vanishes." *The Age* [Melbourne] 23 June 2005. Web. 28 Dec. 2009.

Marx, Karl. *The Eighteenth Brumaire of Louis Bonaparte*. Peking: Foreign Language, 1978.

Mauss, Marcel. "Fragment d'un plan de sociologie générale descriptive." *Annales sociologiques* a1 (1934). Web. 28 Dec. 2009.

Mauss, Marcel. "Les techniques du corps." *Journal de psychologie* 23.3–4 (1936). Web. 28 Dec. 2009.

McHoul, Alec and Tom O'Regan. "Towards a Paralogics of Textual Technologies: Batman, Glasnost and Relativism in Cultural Studies." *Southern Review* 25.1 (1992): 5–26.

Mészáros, István. *The Power of Ideology*. Rev. ed. London: Zed, 2004.

Michels, Robert. *Political Parties: A Sociological Study of the Oligarchical Tendencies of Modern Democracy*. Trans. Eden and Cedar Paul. London: Jarrold and Sons, 1915.

Mikulan, Steven. "The Lady Vanishes: Rachel Uchitel Press Conference Canceled." *The Wrap* 3 Dec. 2009. Web. 28 Dec. 2009.

Miller, Stephen Paul. *The Seventies Now: Culture as Surveillance*. Durham: Duke UP, 1999.

Miller, Toby. *The Avengers*. London: BFI, 1997.

Miller, Toby. *SpyScreen: Espionage on Film and Television*. Oxford: Oxford UP, 2003.

Miller, Toby, Nitin Govil, John McMurria, Richard Maxwell, and Ting Wang. *Global Hollywood 2*. London: BFI, 2005.

Mitra, Subrata K. "The Discourse Vanishes: Revolution and Resilience in Indian Politics." *Contemporary South Asia* 9.3 (2000): 355–65.

Morris, Meaghan. "The Banality of Cultural Studies." *Logics of Television: Essays in Cultural Criticism*. Ed. Patricia Mellencamp. Bloomington: Indiana UP, 1990. 14–43.

Morrison, Grant. "Un Monde de Miraculeuses Métamorphoses." Trans. David Fakrikian and Bruno Billion. *Chapeau Melon et Bottes de Cuir*. Ed. Alain Carrazé and Jean-Luc Putheaud. Paris: Huitième Art, 1990. 21–22.

Mosca, Gaetano. *The Ruling Class*. Trans. Hannah D. Kahn. Ed. Arthur Livingston. New York: McGraw-Hill, 1939.

"New Films in London: *The Lady Vanishes*." *Times* [London] 10 Oct. 1938. Web. 28 Dec. 2009.

"Other People's Glances." *O: The Oprah Magazine*, 1 Mar. 2009: 180.

Panek, LeRoy L. *The Special Branch: The British Spy Novel, 1890–1980*. Bowling Green: Bowling Green U Popular P, 1981.

Pareto, Vilfredo. *Sociological Writings*. Trans. Derick Mirfin. Ed. S.E. Finer. Oxford: Blackwell, 1976.

Poirier, Agnès Catherine. "Cécilia Sarkozy: The Lady Vanishes." *Independent on Sunday* [London] 24 June 2007. Web. 28 Dec. 2009.

Porter, Bernard. *Plots and Paranoia: A History of Political Espionage in Britain 1790–1988*. London: Unwin Hyman, 1989.

Putnam, Robert D. *Bowling Alone: The Collapse and Revival of American Community*. New York: Simon and Schuster, 2000.

Rawnsley, Andrew. "The Lady Vanishes." *Guardian* [London] 25 Apr. 1999. Web. 28 Dec. 2009.

Rich, Nathaniel. "*The Lady Vanishes*: Hitchcock's First Hitchcock Film." *Slate.com*. 4 Dec. 2007. Web. 28 Dec. 2009.

Rothman, William. *Hitchcock—The Murderous Gaze*. Cambridge: Harvard UP, 1982.

Ryall, Tom. *Alfred Hitchcock and the British Cinema*. Rev. ed. London: Athlone, 1996.

Salinger, J. D. *The Catcher in the Rye*. 1951. New York: Little, Brown, 2001.

Schantz, Ned. "Hospitality and the Unsettled Viewer: Hitchcock's Shadow Scenes." *Camera Obscura* 73 (2010): 1–27.

Schivelbusch, Wolfgang. *Railway Journey: The Industrialization of Time and Space in the 19th Century*. Trans. Anselm Hollo. Berkeley: U of California P, 1977.

Skorecki, Louis. "*Les 39 marches*." *Libération* 2 Feb. 2007. Web. 28 Dec. 2009.

Stafford, David A.T. *The Silent Game: The Real World of Imaginary Spies*. Rev. ed. Athens: U of Georgia P, 1991.

Sweet, Matthew. "Mustard and Cress." *Guardian* [London] 29 Dec. 2007. Web. 28 Dec. 2009.

Swidler, Amy. "The Lady Vanishes." *New York Times* 21 Jan. 2001. Web. 28 Dec. 2009.

Taylor, Brendan. "Coral Bell's Contribution to Australian Foreign Policy." *Australian Journal of International Affairs* 59.3 (2005): 257–60.

Thompson, Jon. *Fiction, Crime, and Empire: Clues to Modernity and Postmodernism*. Urbana: U of Illinois P, 1993.

Thompson, Karol L., and P. Scott Pine. "Comparison of the Diagnostic Performance of Human Whole Genome Microarrays Using Mixed-Tissue RNA Reference Samples." *Toxicology Letters* 186 (2009): 58–61.

Trotter, David. "The Politics of Adventure in the Early British Spy Novel." *Spy Fiction, Spy Films, and Real Intelligence*. Ed. Wesley K. Wark. London: Frank Cass, 1991. 30–54.

Truffaut, François. "HITCHCOCK 100: Al maestro con cariño." Trans. Cecilia Beltramo. *Clarín* 13 Aug. 1979. Web. 28 Dec. 2009.

Trumpbour, John. *Selling Hollywood to the World: U.S. and European Struggles for Mastery of the Global Film Industry, 1920–1950*. Cambridge: Cambridge UP, 2002.

van Seters, Deborah. "'Hardly Hollywood's Ideal': Female Autobiographies of Secret Service Work, 1914–45." *Intelligence and National Security* 7.4 (1992): 403–24.

Wallas, Graham. *The Great Society: A Psychological Analysis*. Lincoln: U of Nebraska P, 1967.

Wark, Wesley K. "The Intelligence Revolution and the Future." *Queen's Quarterly* 100.2 (1993): 273–87.

Wasko, Janet. Introduction to *A Companion to Television*. Ed. Janet Wasko. Malden, MA: Blackwell, 2005. 1–12.

Webster, Wendy. "'Europe Against the Germans': The British Resistance Narrative, 1940–1950." *Journal of British Studies* 48 (2009): 958–82.

Westlake, Mike. "The Classic TV Detective Genre." *Framework* 13 (1980): 37–38.

Weston, Kath. "The Lady Vanishes: On Never Knowing, Quite, Who is a Lesbian." *Journal of Lesbian Studies* 13 (2009): 136–48.

White, Ethel Lina. *The Wheel Spins.* 1936. Harmondsworth: Penguin, 1955.

Williams, Tony. "Alfred Hitchcock and John Buchan: The Art of Creative Transformation." *Senses of Cinema* 43 (2007). Web. 28 Dec. 2009.

Wollen, Peter. "*Rope*: Three Hypotheses." Allen and Ishii-Gonzáles 74–85.

24

Hitchcock and Feminist Criticism: From *Rebecca* to *Marnie*

Florence Jacobowitz

Can Classical Hollywood Cinema Be Saved for Feminist Criticism?

I agreed to write this chapter on the significance of Hitchcock to feminist film theory and criticism following the completion of a course I taught on women and film that included films by Hitchcock and other classical-era Hollywood directors, including Dorothy Arzner. The students' ambivalence toward these films extended beyond a particular auteur; for them, the problem with seeing any value in classical realism overrides a problem with specific directors like Hitchcock. Students are familiar with the basic tenets of feminist theory established in "Visual Pleasure and Narrative Cinema" and hold firm to them: classical realist films construct a male viewer and women, symbolizing castration "and nothing else," are investigated, saved or punished, or fetishized as pure spectacle (Mulvey 305). Although Laura Mulvey concedes that Hitchcock's *Vertigo* (1958) foregrounds the problems of voyeurism and fetishistic romantic fantasy that are the perverse results of masculine insecurity, the argument remains that the film activates and reinforces the very processes that it ostensibly foregrounds in the narrative. Not surprisingly, Mulvey advocated a rejection of classical cinema.

Though feminist theory radicalized criticism in the way it foregrounded the concepts of power and oppression in narrative entertainment films, where women are often objectified or punished, it did so at the cost of reducing all realist films to the same formula, and thus diminished the value of critical readings and distinctive

A Companion to Alfred Hitchcock, First Edition. Edited by Thomas Leitch and Leland Poague.
© 2011 Thomas Leitch and Leland Poague. Published 2011 by Blackwell Publishing Ltd.

works that challenged the assumptions at the base of feminist theory. Many of the caveats and modifications that followed Mulvey's presentation of feminist film theory adopted and maintained the basic premise that realism locks the viewer into a fixed position based on identification with the protagonist, thereby downplaying the complicating significance of reading conventions, metaphor, tone, irony, and star personae, all of which are inherent to a genre-based form of entertainment. Feminist theorists like Mary Ann Doane compounded the problem of women's ability to produce a feminist reading by arguing that women lack the necessary distance to do so; their inability to fetishize their castration results in their overidentification with the image, the "textual body."[1] The possibility of a female spectator who can engage actively with a given film, intellectually and emotionally, on a variety of levels, is not an option. Students therefore resist the idea that viewer positions are not locked in place, that identification and point of view are complex and can be subverted intentionally to question the viewer's reliance on gender stereotypes (as in *Vertigo*), that realism in its more sophisticated forms demands an understanding of a complex language that was nurtured by the studio system and challenges the theoretical picture of classical realism solidified in the last thirty-five years.[2]

Before offering a close reading of *Marnie* (1964), Hitchcock's last great woman-centered film, it seems fitting to begin with *Rebecca* (1940), Hitchcock's first American film, which inaugurated a cycle of women's films drawing from psychoanalysis, the gothic, and women's fiction, most notably *Jane Eyre* (1847). Both films address a woman's difficulty in negotiating the expectations that define normative heterosexual relations and the loss of the mother. Both demand a complex form of identification where one can empathize and identify with the heroine without sharing her often limited understanding of the world.

Rebecca and Feminist Film Theory

Rebecca is rooted in a long tradition of women's fiction. Selznick's insistence that Hitchcock stay close to Daphne du Maurier's popular novel is well-documented. The Hitchcock/Selznick *Rebecca* is now recognized as having been a seminal film that inspired a number of other women's films that followed, reworking the story of a young woman's induction into marriage, haunted by the presence of another woman and unable to gauge the desire of her volatile husband. It is also credited with having an influence on Hitchcock that persisted throughout his career.

Because *Rebecca* is a woman's film, made for a largely female audience, it has attracted the attention of feminist theorists interested in the responses of female viewers. Feminists who subscribed to the idea of the cinema as a male discursive system that relies on the female to allay fears of sexual difference were particularly interested in films that solicit a female viewer, unusually offering the female spectator the power of the investigating gaze. One of the most influential feminist attempts to analyze films directed to a female audience is Mary Ann Doane's discussion of *Caught* (Max Ophuls, 1949) and *Rebecca*. Both represent a strain of the gothic that she classifies as "the paranoid woman's film," and Doane sees them both as exemplifying her thesis regarding the impossibility of female spectatorship. They both contain scenes, she claims, that illustrate the repression and ultimate erasure of the woman's voice, presence, and desire. The male usurps the narration and the look is transferred to the male protagonist. Since the cinema is dependent on masculine structures of seeing, it cannot "sustain a coherent representation of female subjectivity," and the shift provokes a crisis (Doane 147). Because they have no distance from the castrated maternal body, women cannot fetishize and thus displace their fears of sexual difference: "Female scopophilia is a drive without an object" (141). The woman therefore cannot derive pleasure from being a voyeur or consequently a spectator: "The image as mirror/window takes on then the aspect of a trap, whereby her subjectivity becomes synonymous with her objectification" (33). Instead, Doane argues,

> [a] certain despecularization takes place in these films, a deflection of scopophilic energy in other directions, away from the female body. In this particular cycle of gothic films, the very process of seeing is now invested with fear, anxiety, horror, precisely because it is objectless, free-floating. The aggressivity which ... is contained in the cinematic structuration of the look is released or, more accurately, transformed into a narrativized paranoia.
>
> (129)

According to Doane, Joan Fontaine's character in *Rebecca*, the second Mrs. de Winter, lacks the ability to differentiate herself from Rebecca. She is doomed to duplicate her identity (and possibly her fate) in her desire to attract and please her husband, Maxim (Laurence Olivier); as a result, she experiences the terrifying loss of her own subjectivity. The woman, whose voiceover introduces the narrative, loses her voice and her ability to see (the power of the gaze). The home movie scene is used by Doane to demonstrate that "even as she spectates, the force of the tendency to reduce the woman to an image is inexorable" (156). The scene begins with Fontaine dressed in black satin and pearls, realizing the magazine image, an image of desire she hopes will attract her husband's gaze despite his earlier warning against it; the scene ends with Maxim's imposition of an image he wants to hold on to, of the insecure young girl, an image that proclaims his mastery over her. The scene demonstrates Fontaine's failure to replace Rebecca (highlighted in her discomfort with addressing the servants regarding the missing Cupid), but most important for Doane is Maxim's blocking the image and his aggressive look back at the spectator, "turning Fontaine's gaze against itself" and inciting terror (166). The scene ends with a cut that absorbs the home movie into the diegesis of the film (sealing Maxim's desire and obliterating hers). The paranoid woman's film promises subjectivity but delivers aggression, demonstrating the impossibility of women's spectatorship and agency, both in relation to the image and, presumably, within marriage. All the woman is offered is a masochistic identification with her own immobilization and erasure.[3]

The Women Who Knew Too Much

Tania Modleski's study of "Hitchcock and Feminist Theory" was groundbreaking on many fronts. Unlike Doane, she attempts to include the female spectator who had been "excluded from the terms of the film's address" (Modleski 24).

> While it is not at all accurate to say that I wanted to "save Hitchcock," to recall the words of Robin Wood, I did indeed aim to save his female viewers from annihilation at the hands not only of traditional male critics but of those feminist critics who see woman's repression in patriarchal cinema as total, women's "liking" for these films as nothing but masochism.
>
> (122)

Modleski's thesis opens up a space for articulating women's mixed, anger-tinged response to Hitchcock. She notes Hitchcock's obsession with "exploring the psyches of tormented and victimized women," which has been identified as a kind of sadism (25), but also remarks "that the obsession often takes the form of a particularly lucid exposé of the predicaments and contradictions of women's existence under patriarchy." This sympathy for and identification with his "outlaw heroines," as Modleski makes clear, is not intentional on Hitchcock's part. "Obviously, it is not necessary to assume conscious intention on the director's part; as a matter of fact, there is virtually decisive evidence that Hitchcock was oblivious to the interest and sympathy he created for his heroine" (25). Modleski explains Hitchcock's unintended sympathy and identification by theorizing that women's bisexuality unconsciously reminds men of their own innate bisexuality, which undermines their ability to distance themselves fully from women. Modleski, like other feminist theorists, acknowledges that women overidentify with the mother, but illustrates how identification with the feminine is even more problematic for the male. She sets out to demonstrate how "men's fascination and identification with the feminine continually undermine their efforts to achieve masculine strength and autonomy and is a primary cause of the violence toward women that abounds in Hitchcock's films" (8).

Although Modleski's insistence on the unconscious aspect of this masculine identification precludes the possibility of the films offering a fully articulated critical analysis, she does offer a theory of spectatorship that is not locked into identification. "[W]hile on the surface *Blackmail* [1929] seems to offer an exemplary instance of Hitchcock's misogyny, his need to convict and punish women for their sexuality," she writes, the film, like so many of his other works, actually allows for a critique of the structure it exploits and for a sympathetic view of the heroine trapped within that structure. This means that the female spectator need not occupy either of the two viewing places typically assigned her in feminist film theory: the place of the female masochist, identifying with the passive female character, or the place of the "transvestite," identifying with the active male hero.

(23)

Here Modleski invites a reading of the socially trapped heroine that is not directly reliant upon identification and thus allows the female viewer an analytical position beyond identification with an image of immobility. The woman's tendency to overidentify with the mother is therefore not collapsed into an overidentification with the text. At times, however, Modleski's reading of *Rebecca* still relies on the idea that "overidentification" describes the viewer's relationship with Fontaine. "It might thus be said," she writes about the scene in which Mrs. Danvers (Judith Anderson) tempts Fontaine to commit suicide, "that the *spectator* is here forced to undergo an experience analogous to that of the heroine: both she and we are made to experience a kind of annihilation of the self, of individual identity, through a merger with another woman" (47).

Modleski reads *Rebecca* as a film dramatizing the woman's oedipal story, her inscription into patriarchy, made for a largely female audience. Fontaine overidentifies with the mother (primarily Rebecca, but also Mrs. Danvers) in the mistaken belief that she will attract the father. She learns that what the father wants is for her to give up the mother and accept her difference, her devalued, "vacuous self. In the film's fantasy, a *woman's* fantasy par excellence, the hero highly prizes the woman's insignificance" (47). Modleski is not that far from Doane's reading, in which the female viewer identifies with the woman's experience of the annihilation of her own subjectivity and her assimilation into patriarchy. The huge difference is that Modleski addresses the film's emphasis on the difficulty of this trajectory for women, and the importance of women's desire for other women. The attraction to Rebecca produces a resistance that disturbs the film's ideological intentions of subduing and silencing the woman. Rebecca flaunts the male's fear of castration through her inability to be seen, the power of her mocking laughter, and her "own multiplicity – her remarkable capacity to play the model wife and mistress of Manderley while conducting various love affairs on the side" (51). This conception of Rebecca mitigates against the idea of woman as lack. "[D]espite this apparent closure, the film has managed in the course of its unfolding to hint at what feminine desire might be like were it allowed greater scope" (51).

This hint is taken up and developed by queer theorists like Rhona Berenstein who argue that *Rebecca* acknowledges a woman's sexual desire for another woman beyond the oedipal context of desire for the mother. Although queer theorists foreground the specificity of the lesbian experience, it seems logical that the maternal could be broadened to include desire for another woman. The significance of Berenstein's analysis is that it implies the ability of a female viewer to produce a reading that is not bound specifically to a close identification with the female protagonist and the absorption of her perceptions. Most importantly, it elaborates a more positive pleasure that the film offers women, one derived from Rebecca.

Although the film (largely via Maxim) presents Rebecca as being monstrous and demonic, she opens up an underground space for the circulation of taboos (her disruptive sexuality) that are profoundly attractive to the young woman who desires her. For example, Berenstein places great emphasis on the presentation of Rebecca's bedroom as a sexualized space beyond Maxim's control. Mrs. Danvers's reminiscences and gestures are overly pronounced, laden with sexual innuendo that fascinates the Joan Fontaine character. The viewer might identify with Fontaine's feelings of inadequacy, but as Berenstein notes, quoting Harriet Hawkins on the novel, "the character most female readers would most *like* to be is, of course, the confident, the fearless, the popular, the accomplished, the adored [and, Berenstein adds, the queer] Rebecca" (quoted in Berenstein 95). The flashback structure of Fontaine's voiceover describing her dream and obsession with Manderley and the past, coupled with the film's final track-in on the case embroidered with Rebecca's initial, supports this privileging of Rebecca. Berenstein concludes that Fontaine's description of herself at the start as a spirit possessed by a "sudden supernatural power" aligns her with Rebecca and introduces the possibility of two couples from the start. She goes on to argue that "not only do the doubling and coupling indicate the primacy of the women's relationship throughout *Rebecca*, but they also attest to the power of their bond to survive the end of the narrative" (87). The film thus offers the female viewer the pleasure of a woman-identified experience that subverts the unconvincing happy ending of the couple's survival. It also contradicts the trajectory of a woman forced to discover her own insignificance. The female viewer enjoys a profound pleasure beyond anger that undoubtedly complicates and deepens the experience of the movie. Although the film cannot overtly promote the woman's attraction to another woman, its presence, under the oneiric guise of the gothic, suggests its potency as a fantasy.

The Critique of the Male Fantasist

Whereas Doane concludes that the "paranoid" woman's film lures women with a promise of subjectivity only to demonstrate their erasure, Ed Gallafent's reading of *Gaslight* (George Cukor, 1944) and *Rebecca* suggests that the gothic offers a critique of the male fantasist that might also account for its appeal to women. Gallafent adduces Charlotte Brontë's *Jane Eyre* to illustrate certain patterns familiar to the educated viewer: the young bride's entry into a house; another woman who has lived there and died; the bridegroom's relationship with the other woman, which is a mystery to his bride; the doubling of the dead woman and the bride, with the dead woman representing the bride's "repressed possibilities and desires" (86). Gallafent's reading, however, is not dependent on the viewer directly identifying with the female protagonist or her desires. He argues that the film also presents the male as fantasist, whose fantasies and needs conflict with those of the heroine. Fontaine's desire, to become sexually sophisticated like Rebecca, threatens the husband's fantasy, which follows from his need to control his wife. His masculinist fantasy demands that she demonstrate how unlike Rebecca she is; he is attracted to her unsuitability to be mistress of Manderley, which secures his dominance.

This emphasis changes one's reading of key scenes, like the viewing of the home movie. Beyond demonstrating Fontaine's "failure to assert herself" as mistress of the house, the scene demonstrates Maxim's need to declare her difference from Rebecca publicly, contradicting his own advice that she handle the servants herself. He prefers her humiliated self to a mistress of "real domestic authority and power" (95). Fontaine's articulation of this preference, that he has married her because she is gauche and will never generate gossip, unwittingly hits a nerve and triggers Maxim's aggressive response, for it challenges his fantasy of himself as "Byronic master." He regains his composure by presenting himself as "the crushed romantic": "Happiness is something I know nothing about" (96). The scene depends upon an ironic layering of meaning: it registers both Fontaine's desire to present herself as a mature, sexually confident woman and Maxim's immersion in his own fantasy of himself, which this image threatens. The final shot of the honeymoon home movie is presented, Gallafent argues, in ironic contradiction to the tensions dramatized in the scene. The scene places Maxim's rage and invites a critical understanding of his outburst and his disingenuous, self-flattering excuse for it. Maxim's aggression is presented in terms of his narcissism: his need to control Fontaine and prevent her from acquiring the power associated with Rebecca. The final image of the film, which refers the viewer back to Rebecca, is a commentary on the film's critique of the volatile male fantasist and the woman's motivation by a fantasy of her own.

Gallafent's reading presumes a viewer's sensitivity to the inflections of the film's generic sources, where the ambivalent presentation of the husband is a familiar trope. The film's critique of Maxim is crucial to understanding how we are invited to read *Rebecca*. It implies a privileged understanding denied Fontaine. Maxim is a qualified hero, and one's trust in his authority is intentionally undermined and disturbed. He bullies and patronizes Fontaine, regrets his decision to marry, humiliates his wife in front of the servants, rationalizes his violence against Rebecca, and conceals his role in her death. This ambivalence is complicated by the complex identification with Fontaine that the film constructs. Despite the often indulged immersion in Fontaine's subjective perspective (feelings of insecurity, of being overwhelmed), one is invited to identify both with the desire to be a good wife and build a happy marriage and with her fascination with Rebecca's sexuality, sophistication, and power. At times the viewer, like Fontaine, is startled by Maxim's outbursts (at the ball), and at times the outburst is placed against an ironic commentary (the home movie sequence). This reading shifts the emphasis of the film from a story about a couple and the dead woman who comes between them to one that presents a critique of patriarchal sexual relations and marriage.

Andrew Britton makes this point with regard to what the Freudian-feminist melodrama offers the female viewer:

> *Rebecca* and *Gaslight* and *Notorious* [1946] are so distressing because our involvement with the heroine is so complex. We "identify" with her very closely, but we are also the spectators of a symbolic drama which makes critically present to us the determinants and conditions of existence of the experience with which we are identifying. … [In these films] the most intense kind of participation in the *subjectivity* of a particular character co-exists with a heightened awareness of the *objective* social forces in relation to which that subjectivity is organised.
>
> (41)

One retains a deep feeling of empathy for the protagonist along with the opportunity to analyze that involvement intellectually within a broader social context.

Feminists are wary of crediting a classical realist film, and particularly Hitchcock, with articulating a critique of dominant gender norms. Wood's question whether Hitchcock can be saved for feminism needs to be understood in the frame of a more open approach to classical realist cinema, one that places Hitchcock in the context of an art form with a developed vocabulary for articulating, under the right conditions, concerns profoundly relevant to women.

Reading *Marnie*

Like *Rebecca*, *Vertigo*, and *Psycho* (1960), *Marnie* is a film that evolves from a classical realist tradition, but its greatness is attributable to the manner in which it creatively redefines the conventions from which it draws. *Marnie*'s sources are the woman's film and its gothic variant. Hitchcock described the film as a character study and a psychological mystery (Truffaut 238). It is a character study of a woman traumatized as a child by an event involving her mother, a single parent and prostitute, and one of her clients, a sailor. Marnie harbors this trauma as a repressed memory; as an adult, she is a compulsive thief and terrified of sexual contact with men. One of her employers falls in love with her, blackmails her into marriage, has sex with her against her wishes on their honeymoon, and finally insists that she confront her mother about the past as a step toward her recovery. (One of the things she learns is that she was conceived as a result of a barter – sex exchanged for a basketball sweater.) It is not surprising that *Marnie* was unpopular with audiences and critics alike; even on the surface level of plot, it is a challenging film.

The film is structured as a mystery, revealing the details of the traumatic incident as a key to understanding Marnie, and as such demands that the audience assemble its meaning in a sophisticated manner. The romance between Marnie (Tippi Hedren) and Mark (Sean Connery) is also notably problematic. That the deep affection Marnie develops for Mark remains distinct from a suggestion of sexual desire may, in part, be attributable to casting. Hitchcock's original choice for the role of Marnie, Grace Kelly, might have resulted in a work more consistent with the traditions of classical Hollywood and would have created a different relationship with Sean Connery, one potentially more sexually charged. The star image Tippi Hedren developed in *The Birds* (1963), her only film prior to *Marnie,* is entirely different. She manifests vulnerability beneath the veneer of the competent, assured young woman, as well as a façade that is more private and inscrutable. Tippi Hedren's Marnie is less accessible to Mark, and one might argue that this reserve hampers the romantic formation of the couple. Marnie safeguards and disguises herself, creating as a result a character that is less assimilable. Hedren's Marnie moves the film away from Mark, toward the mother/daughter relationship (a theme hinted at in *The Birds*), emphasizing her resistance to reliving her mother's oppressive experience instead of her integration into society.

Marnie can be read as a variant of *Rebecca* that highlights a woman's difficulty (with Marnie, her failure) in negotiating the oedipal trajectory and her problematic attachment to another woman, here the mother. A feminist interpretation might suggest that the criminal heroine is saved by the hero who renders her safe (cured of her transgressive independence) and available to him. A closer reading of *Marnie* suggests a film more significantly about the daughter's intense commitment to the mother, about the difficulty of separating and of forming a viable adult identity. *Marnie* elaborates on these issues in a manner that contemporizes them, exposing the pain that underlies them while emphasizing Marnie's sense of herself as an outsider. The film's thematic, the study of a woman alienated from both the social world and her own sexuality, aligns *Marnie* with a modern, postwar cinema of characters marked by trauma, without a place and in need of healing. Critics have addressed the film's formal audacity (or what was at first considered its misguided stylization) in more modernist terms, but given its remarkable relevance to women, and the fact that it was Hitchcock's last woman-centered film addressing questions of identity and desire, it is disappointing that it has not received more of the feminist revaluations it so richly deserves.

The repressed memory that reappears in Marnie's haunting dreams, the murder of the sailor, reveals metaphorically the way her experience of the oedipal moment defines her: she defends the mother and herself from the male who intrudes, separates the daughter from the mother, and thus threatens them both. Marnie actively protects the mother, usurping the phallus and eradicating the need for the father. In the scene where Marnie gives her mother the symbolically loaded gift of the fur collar, she states, "We don't need men, Mama – we can do very well for ourselves." Her mother (Louise Latham) agrees: "Look at my girl, Marnie. She's too smart to go gettin' herself mixed up with men – none of 'em." In this Marnie and her mother are like-minded partners who have both written men out of their lives. Marnie struggles to sustain a relationship with her mother that insists upon this rejection. The problem for the mother is that Marnie, who has become a sexual and desirable adult, is no longer as trustworthy in this bond as was the child.

The fantasy of self-sufficiency, the erasure of the phallus (the expulsion of men), draws on a number of women's films. As Britton notes, it is "something the woman's film *does* but to which it seldom *refers*" (45). *Blonde Venus* (Josef von Sternberg, 1932), *Queen Christina* (Rouben Mamoulian, 1933), *Stella Dallas* (King Vidor, 1937), and *Now, Voyager* (Irving Rapper, 1942), however different and distinct, dramatize variations of this theme; the men's function in these films is to demonstrate that they are ultimately not necessary to the heroine.

Sternberg ventures furthest in articulating this theme. The Dietrich character's capitulation to the family at the end of *Blonde Venus* attests to the difficulties of sustaining a fatherless family unit, despite the evidence that the mother and child are satisfied and fulfilled alone. Helen's independence, self-reliance, and ability to survive with the child radically contradict the idea that men are necessary to the family or to her survival and happiness. The opening scene of the women performers swimming together happily before the intrusion of the "father" sets up a homosocial environment and a sense of plenitude that is highly significant in framing what follows.

In addition, *Blonde Venus,* like *Marnie,* foregrounds the issue of women's commodification in a society that gives their roles and bodies an exchange value. Marnie has worked hard to resist this fate by reinventing herself as a respectable young woman who can pour tea, ride horses, dress elegantly, and mask her accented speech, yet she still moves in a world where she is objectified sexually and valued accordingly. Dietrich's Helen understands the system and exploits it to her advantage. Marnie's actions are similarly motivated – her robberies can be read as her refusal to be exploited – but are less available to her on a conscious level.

Stella Dallas (Barbara Stanwyck), like Helen, is socially branded an unfit mother, so she sacrifices the love of her life, her daughter, to improve the young woman's social opportunities. The pathos at the end is a result of the ambivalence this sacrifice generates, as the film supports Stella as being a good mother. Marnie's unhealthy relationship with her mother must also be sacrificed, but the film is similarly ambivalent about the justice of this outcome. Mark will attempt to cure Marnie by forcing a confrontation and separation from the mother.[4] The tone at the end, in some ways similar to that of *Stella Dallas,* is unmistakably bleak, conflicted, and heartbreaking. Assimilating Marnie into society as a "healthy" woman demands her sacrificing the one relationship she wants most. As in many women's films, this separation doesn't fix the social problems in which the relationship is embedded.

Marnie draws from the fantasy of independence dramatized in the woman's film and demonstrates its impossibility in a particular culture. The film doesn't blame Mrs. Edgar; it places her in relief. Both Marnie and her mother are victims of a society that perceives women in a particular way. Marnie's illness is an unconscious response to a society in which prostitution is a defining metaphor for both gender and sexual relations. Despite the failure of the mother/daughter relationship, Marnie's intense commitment to it expresses a longing with which many women can empathize. Mark is, in some ways, like the other erased phalluses of the woman's film – Ned Faraday (Herbert Marshall), Stephen Dallas (John Boles) – in the way he functions, as Britton points out, to unleash the struggle in which heterosexuality becomes, from the woman's point of view, a "site of conflict" (44). Mark is also different in his progress toward understanding Marnie, which makes him a more multidimensional character who can ultimately be generous toward her. Mark is confident in his sexuality (and the casting of the Bond star underlines this), and Marnie's rejection of him sexually is coded as *her* illness. For the film to make sense, Mark's concern for Marnie must extend by the end beyond self-satisfaction (i.e., making her available for him). Like *Rebecca,* however, the film ends by emphasizing the loss of the women's relationship, a loss that exceeds the formation of the couple, emphasized in the little girls' jump-rope song. The girls pointedly stop their singing to look at Marnie when she emerges from her mother's house at the end, as if acknowledging her, before continuing to proclaim the child is still ill.

Marnie also draws from the melodramatic variant of the gothic, a genre concerned with "the horror of the normal" (Britton 41) that allows a cultural space for the critique of the Cinderella myth. *Marnie* analyzes the myth of marriage to a wealthy, handsome man as the answer to what women want. After a hasty marriage, Marnie will be locked in the house, Wykwyn, a symbol of male power and privilege not unlike Manderley, as well as on the cruise ship on an enforced honeymoon, held captive by a combination of blackmail and good intentions. The honeymoon bedroom will become a site of terror for the wife, and, as in *Rebecca*, the suppression of her close relationship with another woman will be the cost of her recuperation into patriarchy. The overstatement of these conventions underlines the unnaturalness of what is required to produce normality. *Marnie*'s roots in the woman's film / gothic melodrama provide a context for the film's modern thematic of a woman's alienation from herself and the culture. As a character struggling with her identity (Marnie acts out different roles but doesn't embody any) and lacking an understanding of what she experiences and how this defines her, she presents a challenge for the audience in terms of identification.

Marnie's subjectivity is marked by impasses, blockages, and compulsions that elude her. Marnie is a character who responds to the world from various levels of consciousness. She often fluctuates between an adult woman and a childlike young girl. At times she is in control and safeguards her privacy and motivations, appearing cynical, harboring resentments and a kind of inner rage. Other times – for example, during her panic attack in Mark's office – she is vulnerable, almost transparent, and lost in a state disconnected from events around her. Her subjective experience is interrupted by moments of intense fear (triggered by the thunderstorm) or anger (the red gladiolas) or distress (the hunt), extreme emotions that contradict Marnie's veneer of control. The narrative is similarly interrupted by moments that bear a dreamlike emphasis exceeding narrative explanation (the shoe that drops in the Rutland office and the anxiety it generates about getting caught or the remarkable spillage of the pecans that dramatizes a violence neither Marnie nor her mother is willing or able to address). *Marnie* demands a distinctive kind of viewer participation; it asks one, on the whole, to empathize with Marnie (she defies identification, as she is presented in puzzle pieces) in a manner that is at once visceral and detached. Identification with Mark is thwarted by his partial perspective (he doesn't, as Mrs. Edgar points out, "know the whole story") and by moments of self-serving domination (the proposal, the "rape") that keep him at a distance. The two crucial visits to Mrs. Edgar's house in Baltimore, Marnie's other home, qualify and undermine Mark's self-proclaimed role as the detective / doctor who will expose the truth and help cure Marnie. These two scenes carry the emotional weight of the film. Marnie wants her mother without boundaries or conditions, and her mother is blocked from reciprocating or responding in kind. This is the tragic impasse that the film can neither resolve nor repair. The viewer is asked to assemble parts of a story that none of the characters fully understands.

As is typical of Hitchcock's economical and precise form of storytelling, the scenes prior to Marnie's first visit home introduce her as a character who appears to be very much in control and empowered, establishing a fantasy of independence: Marnie is the outlaw who robs men who seem, on some level, to deserve it. The scenes also initiate *Marnie*'s complicated address to the viewer.

(1)   The film's stylized, oneiric landscape is introduced in the opening scene. A woman walks away from the camera, very precisely along a painted line, toward a completely empty platform in a train station. As in a dream, time and orientation are unclear; it is a public space that seems oddly deserted. One is directed to notice details: the stuffed yellow purse, the too black wig-like hair, the receding line on the platform.

(2)   There follows an abrupt cut to a medium close-up of a businessman, Sidney Strutt (Martin Gabel), proclaiming almost directly to the audience: "Robbed!" The abruptness is highlighted by a change in style from an oneiric silent landscape to a more traditional form of narrative storytelling. The scene derides Strutt's self-righteous indignation. He objectifies the vanished secretary in his sexualized description of her, over which he lingers, which reveals why he hired her despite her lack of references. This suggests that Strutt got what he deserved, a conclusion that is critical to the development of the story, both to the introduction of Marnie as the thief and later when Strutt reemerges as a threat to Marnie's freedom. The scene introduces the male hero, Mark Rutland, who like Strutt recalls the secretary in terms of her body ("the brunette with the legs") and is also amused by the robbery and Strutt's claims of victimization.

(3)   The enigmatic thief is then partially revealed with her new purchases, rifling through her various identity cards and choosing a new one, and then rinsing the black dye out of her hair. Only then does a medium close-up introduce the female star, Tippi Hedren, looking triumphant, blonde hair tossed back.

(4)   The scene in the station builds on the preceding one, establishing the theme of the woman's ability and control: stowing her luggage, disposing of the locker key.

(5)   This culminates in her checking into an inn where she is warmly greeted as a familiar guest before leaving for the stables. The sequence ends with her exhilarating ride on her horse, Forio, a visual expression of power, satisfaction (which is also sexual, evident in her comment to Forio, "If you want to bite somebody, bite me"), and release.

This introduction to Marnie presents a woman who is self-sufficient, organized, and completely independent, a woman who can take care of herself. Her outlaw credentials are supported: it is altogether a fantasy of power, one that not only excludes the male, but addresses and responds to woman's subordination in the workplace, where objectification is status quo and an expected part of the job. Marnie uses her sexuality as a means to an end, undermining her exploitation. The scenes are disquieting in the way Marnie is presented as a loner, outside of social groups; she is as alone in the busy terminal as she is on the empty train platform. She is a figure of identification that one can't easily get to know; even her identity seems fluid and interchangeable.

The First Visit

This initial impression of Marnie is severely challenged when Marnie visits her mother. The woman who arrives in a taxi, impeccably dressed and coiffed, regresses to a point where she becomes a little girl, insecure, without control over the emotions that direct her, competing for her mother's affection with Jessie Cotton (Kimberly Beck), a young rival who recognizes the level playing field (Jessie's first volley is the announcement: "She's making a pecan pie *for me*"). Marnie secures her claim on her mother through money, thus replacing the father: "I send you plenty of money. You don't have to be a babysitter." Marnie's gift of the fur collar also connotes a husband's possession and claim of ownership. Mrs. Edgar's relationship with Marnie is characterized by contradiction. She enjoys receiving extravagant gifts, despite her half-hearted protestations to the contrary, and is proud of Marnie's financial independence and status as "private secretary to a millionaire"; but she is suspicious of Marnie's sex life and the possible role it plays in securing this status.

Mrs. Edgar's ambivalence is dramatized through references to Marnie and Jessie's hair. Marnie is chided for lightening hers because "too blonde hair always looks like a woman's trying to attract the man." Mrs. Edgar thus replaces the sexual adult with the preadolescent child. The displacement is explicitly referred to in the comment that Jessie's hair reminds her of Marnie's when she was little (and in her calling Jessie the endearment she uses for Marnie, "Sugarpop"). Marnie interprets her mother recalling her hair as a sign of affection, and when she sits down, complaining that her leg aches, Marnie places her head on her mother's lap (an awkward gesture for an adult), invoking the child through the memory she and her mother share.

The mother, however, rejects her, saying, "Marnie, mind my leg," and replaces her with Jessie, who can sit on her lap without causing discomfort. While the mother enacts the displacement by stroking Jessie's hair, she continues, "I never had time to take care of Marnie's hair." The result of the substitution is poignantly evoked by the slow track in to a close-up of Jessie's hair from Marnie's point of view and the sad, lost look on Marnie's face. Jessie's subsequent question ("Didn't you all have a Daddy, either?") and Mrs. Edgar's reply ("We surely did not") together pinpoint the underlying issue. Marnie and her mother can enjoy the exclusion of the father only as long as Marnie denies her identity as a sexually mature adult. The mother, who prefers the pre-sexual child, transfers her desire to Jessie.

When Marnie and her mother move into the kitchen to prepare Jessie's pie, Mrs. Edgar confirms the choice she's made. Her preamble suggesting that Mrs. Cotton and Jessie move in with her is immediately countered by Marnie's pointed clarification that she wants Jessie to move in. Mrs. Edgar admonishes her for her jealousy, and Marnie's tone of voice changes suddenly, as if the adult has been banished and the child emerges in the slow deliberate voice with which she asks, "Why don't you love me, Mama?" She follows the plaintive question, dredged from another part of her psyche, with an attempt to touch her mother and again is rebuffed by her mother, who automatically recoils. When Marnie notices, she snaps out of the child voice and demands, in an adult voice, "Why do you always move away from me? ... What's wrong with me?" She then answers her own question by reference to the "things" she has done on her mother's behalf: "What do you think they are, things that aren't decent? ... Why, you think I'm Mr. Pemberton's girl. Is that why you don't want me to touch you? Is that how you think I get the money to set you up?" Her articulation of what blocks their relationship triggers a violent response from the mother who cannot touch her. She strikes Marnie, the bowl falls, the pecans disperse, and the music crashes, signaling the significance of Marnie's question.

This remarkable exposure of what stops the mother from reciprocating in a relationship with Marnie is quickly repressed. The division marked by puberty (alluded to in the film's recurring images of blood stains and the fear they trigger), the assumption that the daughter will find another love object, threatens and permanently alienates the mother from her daughter. Mrs. Edgar is experienced in the way the system works; women will always be susceptible to trading their sexuality for money, security, marriage. The part of the story Mrs. Edgar doesn't know is that Marnie circumvents the exchange by ingratiating herself as a passive object of the gaze before punishing men for their exploitation through robbery. Marnie's contempt for the sexual system is summed up later in the film in a striking comment she makes to Mark that "women are stupid and feeble and that men are filthy pigs." The irony is that she hasn't slept with any Mr. Pemberton, a far worse crime in the Edgar household (a complete capitulation to the demands of exchange signified in prostitution) than robbery. Marnie adopts her mother's contempt for patriarchy but cannot, as an adult, gain her trust. What Marnie doesn't consciously understand is that her adult self dooms their relationship, a problem that may account for her unconscious regressions to herself as a child. Mrs. Edgar veils her rejection of patri-archal gender relations behind a religious morality that Marnie rejects. The dilemma the film articulates extends beyond the specific event of the sailor's murder. It is rooted in a culture structured by a predatory system that victimizes women (par-ticularly impoverished single-parent families: as Marnie later states, "we were poor, grindingly poor") and prostitution signifies the limited choices available to them.

The scene in the kitchen is followed by Marnie's dream of intrusion and separa-tion, a subconscious reenactment of Marnie's fear of separation from the mother. The recurring nightmare is followed by a new train station, a new job, another robbery. Marnie tries to replace the father but never succeeds in achieving the validation she craves.

Reading the Symptoms

Symptoms of Marnie's inability to negotiate a stable, coherent identity emerge at various points in the narrative. The most blatant are the suffusions of red she sees, triggered by the color (though this is selective; the color red appears, for example, at the hunt before the panic attack begins) as well as the dreams of being forcibly removed from bed and having to separate from her mother. Less obvious are the personality shifts when Marnie seems to regress to a child, evident in changes in her voice and demeanor. Marnie's panic attacks indicate a loss of control; Marnie very much relies on the control evident in her skills at switching identities and pulling off robberies. The first attack, triggered by the sight of the red gladiolas, the gift of Mrs. Cotton, indicates the threat Marnie feels at being supplanted by Jessie.

A number of Marnie's panic attacks that take place with Mark – at the workplace, in Mark's office, at the races – indicate her fear of losing control, in part because of a growing attraction to Mark that is threatening to her. The first of these occurs when Marnie begins work at Rutland's. It is difficult to gauge exactly what unnerves Marnie, but the spilled red ink on her sleeve is an indication that Marnie is not as precise and controlled as she appears. Her concentration and preoccupation is with the safe, but she must also be aware on some level that Mark is watching her, evi-dent in her intense annoyance at the "fuss" he makes over her rushing to the wash-room to wash out the ink. Marnie's loss of composure attests to cracks in the façade and introduces tension and suspense regarding her ability to execute her plans.

The most significant of the attacks with Mark occurs when Marnie agrees to meet Mark alone on a Saturday to help him with his work. Mark's pointed com-ments on instinctive animal behavior, and how "lady animals figure very largely as predators," tells her that he suspects her. Following this episode, Marnie becomes frightened by the storm and sees red flashes. Her voice changes back to a young girl's when she cries out, "Stop the colors!" After the dead tree crashes through the window, Mark comforts Marnie, gently kissing her head and then her lips. Only when Mark tells her it's over does Marnie return to her adult self, though she denies mentioning colors and dismisses her terror as fear of thunder and lightning. The storm and the crashing tree dramatize Marnie's fear of sexual contact, which Marnie's attraction to Mark, along with his suspicions about her, have triggered. Mark's comment that she hardly seems a woman "who'd be terrified of anything" indicates how out of character Marnie's panic attack appears.

When Marnie feels threatened or at risk of losing control, she robs as a means of reasserting power. It is logical that she first robs Rutland's immediately after her first visit to Wykwyn with Mark. Though surprised by Mark's insistence that she meet his father, Marnie does not express reluctance or displeasure. The visit, which ends with their kiss in the stable and plans for another weekend together, is directly followed by the scene in which Marnie robs the safe. The editing of the scenes suggests that the robbery is a response to Marnie's feelings for Mark, and that their relationship threatens her.[5] The scene that follows, of her riding Forio, suggests that Marnie is sublimating the sexual energy aroused or usurped by Mark.

Marnie will experience three more psychic intrusions in the film: her second dream, the panic at the hunt, and the "lived" memory in the final scene of the film. Marnie's dream returns at Wykwyn, in the scene following her surreptitious call to her mother upon her return from the honeymoon cruise, primarily to assure her that she will send money soon. The first dream, in Mrs. Edgar's house, emphasizes Marnie's unwillingness to move and be separated from her mother. The dream at Wykwyn reinforces the anxiety that Marnie must protect her mother from being hurt: "Please don't cry, Mama. … Don't hurt my Mama!" When Mark tries to wake Marnie, still in her dream state, she tells him in her childlike voice that they will hurt her mother and that she hears "noises." When she fully wakes up she returns to her guarded, protective self, adopting her sardonic tone with Mark and rejecting his interest in analyzing her trauma. Despite Marnie's astringent sarcasm ("Talk about dream worlds. You've got a pathological fix on a woman who's not only an admitted criminal but who screams if you come near her"), her willingness to free associate is revealing, as are the associations. She links Mark to the male predator of her nightmare: "I'll slap your filthy face if you come near me again, Jack." Her response to "death" is "me," and it is her first conscious articulation of feeling deadened; it is followed by her plea for help, Marnie's first full admission that she is far from the image she cultivates of someone self-sufficient and in control.

The Honeymoon: If You Touch Me, I'll Die

In *Marnie*, love, marriage, and a honeymoon are presented in terms of predation, abduction, and blackmail – and the husband's right to assert his claim of ownership through sex. If the desire for the mother brackets the narrative, the honeymoon/

rape/suicide is its traumatic core and turning point. It dramatizes all of Marnie's fears about a woman's place in the social world – of entrapment and enforced separation from the mother enacted through the male who intrudes and demands sexual relations.

Mark's actions are informed first and foremost by his desires and needs, and he rationalizes these under the guise of moral responsibility: "Somebody's got to take care of you and help you." He argues that he is protecting Marnie from other sexual predators who will inevitably demand sexual payment for the robberies: "It's down to a choice of me or the police, old girl." Mark indulges his fantasy of marriage without Marnie's consent, and the ceremony is pointedly elided in the narrative. (Ironically, Lil [Diane Baker] interprets the hasty marriage in terms of predation but inversely, as Marnie blackmailing Mark.) Mark is surprised by the intensity of Marnie's response the first time he attempts physical contact: "For God's sake, I can't stand it. I'll die." Some nights later Mark is less patient and more belligerent and demanding. He has been drinking and is far less understanding of what he per-ceives as Marnie's indifference to his sexual needs. Mark's first move, to rip Marnie's robe off her, is met with Marnie's scream, "No." He apologizes, tenderly covers her nakedness, and begins to caress her as she looks past him. The following shot, from Marnie's point of view (and the viewer is aligned with her), is of Mark lowering himself toward her. There is a cut to Marnie lying prostrate, frozen, followed by a pan to the porthole shot of the sea. Marnie seems to be in another state of con-sciousness, still, deathlike. In part, Marnie has made her preference clear; in part, Marnie is attracted to Mark and is also painfully aware of her difference ("I'm not like other people"). She responds to Mark's caresses as she does in earlier scenes, by unconsciously disengaging, which Mark may read as her consent. Marnie perceives sexual relations in terms of self-annihilation (evoking fears of separation, loss, and suffering), and the pan to the sea alludes to the sailor, her mother's pain, and Marnie's attempt to save her. Marnie ends up floating face down in the pool; if not a full-fledged suicide attempt, it is a statement to Mark that he has not understood her terror and her inability to reciprocate sexually. Mark does learn that he has caused her to suffer, and shortly after their return to Wykwyn, Mark delivers Forio to her. This is an important gesture of conciliation, kindness, and love, as Mark understands Marnie's deep commitment to Forio and the pleasure she derives from riding him. It is a sign that Mark is finally respecting her needs regardless of his own and is reaching out to her, and it is a turning point in their relationship.

Marriage and the Outsider

Mark and Marnie settle into married life at Wykwyn and celebrate with a party conceived to officially introduce and initiate Marnie into Mark's social world. Marnie's comment that she is "not a bit nervous" signals her increasing acceptance of the marriage. Lil's strategy of inviting Strutt to the party is intended to undermine Marnie's newfound security and emphasize her status as an interloper. Mark's counterattack, his insistence that Marnie participate in the hunt, is a response to Lil, designed to validate Marnie's right to membership in his community. Marnie's anxiety attack is not simply triggered by the color red; it follows her witnessing the fox being savaged and the participants' resulting amusement. It is then that she experiences her anxiety, breaks away from the group, and rides off on Forio, as if she is identifying with the prey and sees herself as an outsider who will be exposed and savaged.

When Forio fails to clear the fence and is seriously injured, Marnie takes the gun and kills Forio herself, rejecting Lil's offer with a pointed question: "Are you still in the mood for killing?" Marnie thus attributes the disaster to Lil's resurrection of Strutt, which, from Marnie's perspective, is an attempt to destroy her life. She shoots Forio and offers words of consolation, "There, there, now," the words Marnie will utter when remembering the killing of the sailor. Using a parent's words to a child, Marnie is comforting herself and realigning herself with her mother. Forio's death is a result of her capitulation to Mark and the fantasy he offers of fitting into his society as a normal person – an intrusion that threatens her self-sufficiency and allegiance to her mother. "There, there, now" returns Marnie to a self-protective role and is a rejection of complaisance and life with the father. Because Marnie's usurpation of the phallus is relived through robberies, she proceeds from there to rob Rutland's and reestablish her outsider identity and independence. The subjective zoom-in/track-out during the robbery implies that Marnie has interrupted her pattern of behavior through her relationship with Mark and hesitates to destroy it. Mark's offer to take her back to Wykwyn is met by her lunging for the gun; the hunt has proved her alienation and exclusion from society.

The Second Visit: Symmetry, Repetition, Difference

Mark insists that Marnie's recovery depends upon her confronting her mother and fully remembering the past. The stormy day points to Marnie's subjective state and the regression Marnie experiences in her mother's home. Ironically, Mark is unaware of how his intrusion restages the trauma; it is because he threatens Marnie's bond with her mother that she warns Mark, "If you tell my mother about me I'll kill you."[6] Having carefully and selectively created a persona that is acceptable to herself and her mother, Marnie safeguards their tenuous relationship. She has negated and eliminated the threat of the male intruder by replacing him. Marnie's choice regarding what and whom she wants is clear. Mark's ignorance of the dynamic underlying their relationship is evident in one of his opening volleys to Mrs. Edgar: "Your beautiful young daughter can't stand to have a man touch her, any man" (pointing to himself). She responds, "She's lucky to feel like that. Just plain lucky." The comment incites Mark to point out the contradiction that Mrs. Edgar "made [her] living from the touch of men." He fails to understand, because it is beyond his privileged experience, that trading sex for money was related to survival. Mrs. Edgar connects Mark to the other male intruders – "You get out. I don't need any filthy men coming in my house no more" – and her struggle with him restages the past. Regressing, Marnie responds in her little-girl voice, "Let my Mama go. You're hurting my Mama," explicitly connecting Mark to the sailor: "You're one of them. One of them in the white coats." She explains that the tapping signifies that "they want in, them in their white suits."

The scene dissolves into the event relived and remembered by Marnie. Marnie's memory is subjective and reflects her interpretation, but the presentation of the past at times contradicts her recounted memory or offers information beyond Marnie's understanding. Marnie remembers the displacement, having to move from the bed to the couch. As in the present, Mrs. Edgar's desire to repress the reality of the circumstances is her attempt to protect her daughter, as she did in the past when she told her, "Go on back to sleep, Sugarpop," as if Marnie weren't seeing or hearing what takes place. But the scene implies that the child does hear and is aware of the sexual activity close by. When Marnie is frightened by the noise of the thunder, the sailor, oddly, emerges first to comfort her. Hitchcock's presentation of the sailor's prolonged caress is deliberately ambiguous. The significance is in Marnie's perception of the kiss as crossing a line. Marnie and her mother perceive the sailor as a threat because of their feelings of unease with the situation of prostitution in the home. They unite in a hysterical rejection of the sailor's intrusion and crossing of boundaries: "He come out – to me!" Marnie's mother reacts in response to her daughter's plea, "Make him go, Mama. I don't like him to kiss me," by striking the sailor with the poker. He appears to be protecting himself, while Marnie perceives their struggle in terms of her fears: "He hit my Mama!" The sailor falls on Mrs. Edgar and, entwined and entrapped in his legs, Marnie's mother calls for Marnie to help her. The pose suggests intercourse, something Marnie has likely heard or imagined and feared, and Marnie responds to her mother's cries for help by repeating her mother's actions. She picks up the poker and strikes: "I hit him with a stick!" Her subsequent "There, there, now" – echoing her last words to Forio – is spoken to console both mother and daughter. Marnie's words in the present are edited against the individual shots of the terrified faces of the young Marnie and her mother. There is a cut back to the spreading blood against the white fabric of the sailor's shirt, the shot condensing the lethal and sexual implications of Marnie's protective act, and both mother and daughter scream.

In the present, Mrs. Edgar's cane is a visual reminder of the suffering and subsequent elimination of men from their lives. She explains that she interpreted Marnie's repression of the event as a sign of forgiveness and rationalizes her silence as a strategy of maternal love and protection and a means to prevent losing her. The statement is a revelation to Marnie, who says, "You must have loved me, Mama." Her mother's tender admission, "Why, you're the only thing in this world I ever did love," is precisely what Marnie wants, a reciprocation of her intense love. After her explanation of Marnie's conception, as a result of bartering sex for a sweater, she tells her, "I still got that old sweater and I got you, Marnie," which is an important acknowledgment of a positive end result of a system both women have come to reject. She reaches out and touches Marnie's hand, momentarily signifying a breakthrough and an inversion of the reflex withdrawal of the pecan scene. Mrs. Edgar has chosen to protect herself and Marnie by banishing all heterosexual relations and their implications of prostitution under the guise of "decency," and Marnie articulates the irony and her resultant status as an outsider: "I certainly am decent. Of course I'm a cheat and a liar and a thief, but I am decent."

The problem that the film can't resolve is that the mother's bond with the child and pledge to keep her safe and "decent" break down when the child becomes a sexually mature adult. Marnie's desire for her mother's love is expressed in her repeated gesture of placing her head on her mother's lap, and though her mother's hand hovers over Marnie's hair, she cannot fully love the adult and rejects her, using the excuse of the injury and its implications of sexual violence, "Marnie, you're achin' my leg." At best, she calls out of earshot, as if admitting the impasse to herself, "Goodbye, Sugarpop." Mark's understanding and compensating gesture of stroking Marnie's hair replenishes her self-esteem and is a profound gesture of consolation. Mark's recognition of Marnie's needs is also expressed in his response to her question, "What's going to happen?" He doesn't suggest, as he did earlier, that he'll take her home; instead he asks, "What do you want?," thus transforming the narcissistic male fantasist into a partner who acknowledges her identity and her needs. Many have commented on the awkwardness of Marnie's response, "Oh Mark, I don't want to go to jail; I'd rather stay with you," underlined by the repetition of the young girls' "Mother, mother, I am ill" jump rope rhyme. Marnie is a little less alienated, but hardly cured, and still estranged from normality. The melancholic end caused by the impasse with the mother and the difficulty of developing an identity that is whole and sexually satisfying are familiar to the traditions of the woman's film. *Marnie* offers women the pleasure of acknowledging and dramatizing a painful loss that is mandatory in the culture and resists implying that marriage to the "ideal" male is satisfactory compensation.

Notes

1. Doane addresses the problem of overidentification by recommending a strategy of masquerade, as a reminder that femininity is a role, a social construction, thus creating a distance between character and role, and between viewer and character.

2. Robin Wood's reading of *Notorious* (1946) in "Star and Auteur: Hitchcock's Films with Bergman" (303) is exemplary in showing how the viewer's empathetic identification with Ingrid Bergman's Alicia challenges politicized readings that situate Alicia as the victim of competing male systems of domination. Hitchcock is equally precise in his use of Cary Grant's star image, playing with and against type, foregrounding his

shortcomings as he does those of Maxim in *Rebecca*, Scottie (James Stewart) in *Vertigo*, or Mark in *Marnie*. Arguing that Alicia is the film's conscience and moral center produces a coherent argument for the film's feminist value. Wood's perspective on identification and stardom is confirmed in Susan Smith's claim that "films are capable of offering us a much more independent, coherent, critical outlook upon their narrative worlds than that available to most characters within them" (155).

3. Under this theoretical rubric, the meaning of Ophuls's *Caught* is dramatically emptied of its political import, despite Doane's admission that "in *Caught* there is an unconscious acknowledgement of the economics of marriage as an institution" (173). Since Ophuls couldn't have intended the remarkable analysis the film offers of the commodification of women and its reification through marriage, the film is reduced to one that supports a patriarchal silencing of the woman.

4. The ending of *Now, Voyager* is, in some ways, similar: "[T]he film begins, as it will end, with the staging of the Oedipal scene in which an ingratiating patriarch enters the 'woman's castle' in order to separate the daughter from the mother" (Britton 52).

5. In Hitchcock's November 1961 treatment, he notes Marnie's attraction to Mark. He describes her returning to Mark's house following a ride and seeing Mark in the bedroom. "He is stripped to the waist, standing before a mirror and trying to remove something from his eye. Her gaze lingers on his smooth, muscular torso. She goes to him, takes the towel he offers, and, standing very close, removes the particle. Aware of a sensual stirring within her, she immediately withdraws, angering Mark" (Auiler 227).

6. Marnie's threat echoes Charlie's in *Shadow of a Doubt* (1943). She too warns her uncle (a figure of desire), "Go away or I'll kill you myself." Charlie's actions are motivated by her relationship with the mother; there too the father is "erased."

Works Cited

Auiler, Dan. *Hitchcock's Notebooks: An Authorized and Illustrated Look Inside the Creative Mind of Alfred Hitchcock.* New York: HarperCollins, 1999.

Berenstein, Rhona J. "'I'm Not the Sort of Person Men Marry': Monsters, Queers, and Hitchcock's *Rebecca.*" *CineAction* 29 (Fall 1992): 82–96.

Britton, Andrew. "A New Servitude: Bette Davis, *Now, Voyager* and the Radicalism of the Woman's Film." *CineAction* 26–27 (Winter 1992): 35–39.

Doane, Mary Ann. *The Desire to Desire: The Woman's Film of the 1940s.* Bloomington: Indiana UP, 1987.

Gallafent, Ed. "Black Satin: Fantasy, Murder and the Couple in 'Gaslight' and 'Rebecca.'" *Screen* 29.3 (Summer 1988): 84–103.

Modleski, Tania. *The Women Who Knew Too Much: Hitchcock and Feminist Theory.* Second ed. New York: Routledge, 2005.

Mulvey, Laura. "Visual Pleasure and Narrative Cinema." *Movies and Methods.* Ed. Bill Nichols. Vol. 2. Berkeley: U of California P, 1985. 305–15.

Smith, Susan. *Hitchcock: Suspense, Humour and Tone.* London: BFI, 2000.

Truffaut, François, with the collaboration of Helen G. Scott. *Hitchcock.* Rev. ed. New York: Simon and Schuster, 1984.

Wood, Robin. *Hitchcock's Films Revisited.* Rev. ed. New York: Columbia UP, 2002.

25

Queer Hitchcock

Alexander Doty

"Queer Hitchcock." What does this mean? If we understand "queer" as an adjective, then it is about naming and analyzing what is "queer" about Hitchcock's life or his work. If we understand "queer" as a verb (as in "to queer Hitchcock"), then it is about reading his life or his work from certain cultural or theoretical positions. Queer Hitchcock, in the first instance, is concerned with (auto)biographical signs or textual codes that mark the man and his works as expressing queerness – or as "being" queer – in some way. In the second sense, the focus is upon how particular culturally- or theoretically-informed readers understand Hitchcock and his work in queer ways. In practice, most commentaries move between suggesting that queerness in Hitchcock is an inherent property of the text (whether the "text" is Hitchcock himself or his various cultural productions) and suggesting that it takes a reader attuned to queerness, in one way or another, to explain how Hitchcock might be understood as queer. In *Hitchcock's Bi-Textuality*, Robert Samuels enacts this coming together of textual and readerly approaches when he promises to "show how Hitchcock's films are extremely heterogeneous and present multiple forms of sexual identification and desire, although they have most often been read through the reductive lens of male heterosexuality" (1).

In order to consider the widest range of popular and academic work on Hitchcock's films – on which most of this Queer Hitchcock work has focused – this chapter understands, and uses, queer as (1) an umbrella term that includes all categories of non-normative sex, gender, and sexuality identities and practices, such as homosexual, gay, lesbian, bisexual, transgender, transsexual, non-normative heterosexual, genderqueer, intersex, and as (2) indicating positions and practices that are both non-normative and not clearly connected to, or contained by, existing sex, gender, or sexuality categories. I should add that, in the academy at least,

A Companion to Alfred Hitchcock, First Edition. Edited by Thomas Leitch and Leland Poague.
© 2011 Thomas Leitch and Leland Poague. Published 2011 by Blackwell Publishing Ltd.

queer has also become associated with work that conducts progressive or radical critiques of normative heterosexuality. Things get a bit tricky when deciding what to include within the non-normative in general and what constitutes non-normative heterosexuality. Should all non-normative sexuality practices be considered queer? Incest? Necrophilia? Bestiality? Sadomasochism? Pedophilia? When and how does the enactment of gender become non-normative? When a woman punches someone? When a man cries? When and how, exactly, does heterosexuality become non-normative and, therefore, queer? Is non-normative heterosexuality any sexual activity that is not conducted within marriage, in the missionary position, and for the purpose of procreation? Or does it happen whenever a woman is on top?

Since I don't consider queer as referring only to "positive" or progressive / radical non-normativity, all non-normative sexuality will be fair game in discussing Queer Hitchcock. As for non-normative gender and heterosexuality, while definitions of what "the norm" is for gender and heterosexual performance in Britain and the United States do not change radically during the period when Hitchcock is alive and making films – a consistency enforced by the British Board of Film Censors and the Production Code Administration, among other social institutions – there are consensual shifts throughout the twentieth century concerning "proper" masculine, feminine, and heterosexual behavior. There is also the experience of looking back at Hitchcock and his films from the vantage point of the early twenty-first century, with its considerably different notions of what falls within, and outside of, sex, gender, and sexuality norms. In deciding what we might consider expressions of queer gender or non-normative heterosexuality in Hitchcock and his films – as well as in what critics say about these films – I will keep one eye on history and one on the here-and-now. So what is queer about Hitchcock, the private person, the public figure, the artist? Who are the queer characters in Hitchcock-directed films? What, more generally, are the queer qualities of these films? What moral or ideological positions do Hitchcock and his films, individually or as a group, take on queerness? These questions lay out the major issues and concerns in popular and scholarly work when it comes to Queer Hitchcock.

Biographies and autobiographies are considered non-fiction, but, as we know, they offer interpretations of lives that give these lives narrative structure and thematic coherence. While they are not autobiographies per se, interviews often use autobiographical material to construct or support a desired public persona. Since Hitchcock didn't write an official autobiography, but was interviewed many times, we might take the collected interviews as providing an autobiography of sorts. Certainly these interviews have been a rich source of material for Hitchcock biographers, all of whom cite at least one of those classic anecdotes the director loved to repeat. For our purposes, the anecdote du jour, which takes place variously in Paris, Munich, or Berlin in the early 1920s, involves Hitchcock and his wife, "two innocents abroad" (McGilligan 143), being taken to either a brothel or to a sex party at which they watch two women having sex. Depending upon the interview,

Hitchcock reports that he either became a mesmerized voyeur in the face of queer sex (and filed the image away) or he exclaimed something like, "But this is a world of perdition!" (Fallaci 58).

Given the composite portrait the biographies paint of Hitchcock and sexuality, there is every reason to conclude that he was simultaneously appalled and enthralled by the woman-on-woman action. After telling his version of this anecdote, Patrick McGilligan remarks that "the Jesuit in [Hitchcock] was attracted by taboos and fascinated by sin – and sex ranked high in the Catholic pantheon of sins" (65). Suggesting that the greatest taboo – and therefore the most fascinating one – for Hitchcock was queer sexuality, McGilligan continues by making a brief excursion into the "Sapphic overtones" in Hitchcock's films "inspired" by the "lesbian" incident (65). Truffaut cites butch-femme coded couples in *The Pleasure Garden* (1925) and *The Lodger* (1926) as evidence that "from [his] very first pictures on, there is a distinct impression that [he was] fascinated by the abnormal." Hitchcock replies, "That may be true, but it didn't go very deep; it was rather superficial" before launching into the "lesbian" anecdote (39). The (auto)biographical fixation on this homosexual story should not obscure the fact that Hitchcock was also simultaneously disturbed and aroused by heterosexual sex, which he found "perverted in a different way" (Cameron and Perkins 51). Indeed, Robin Wood asserts that we can't fully understand Hitchcock's attraction-repulsion to homosexuality unless we consider it alongside his equally conflicted attitudes about heterosexuality ("Letter" 195).

Donald Spoto's *The Dark Side of Genius* provides the most consistently queer interpretation of the director's life, in part by using Hitchcock's off-the-set life to read his films and using the films to understand his life. More than once, Hitchcock said that through his films he expressed the desires and anxieties he was loath to reveal in his personal life, so Spoto's approach is understandable. In "The Murderous Gays: Hitchcock's Homophobia," Robin Wood analyzes Spoto's biography and concludes, "The testimonies and biographical data that Spoto presents, with reference to Hitchcock's attitude to homosexuality and homosexuals, add up to evidence that is characteristically complex and contradictory … suggesting an ambivalence that parallels and is closely related to the ambivalence toward women" and femininity (202).

Spoto's biography sets up its queer thematic on Hitchcock's life while discussing *The Lodger*. According to Spoto, Hitchcock was initially "shock[ed]," then "[f]ascinated," by "the darkly handsome and effeminate" star of the film, Ivor Novello, who was open about his homosexuality, at least within show business circles (*Dark* 86). Novello would be the first of a number of actors Hitchcock worked with – Esme Percy, Henry Kendall, John Gielgud, Charles Laughton, Judith Anderson, Tallulah Bankhead, Farley Granger, Cary Grant, John Dall, Montgomery Clift, O.E. Hasse, Anthony Perkins – who, for Spoto, offered the director vicarious queer thrills as they represented "the possibilities of life's alternatives" (86). Taking into account all Spoto and other biographers have to say about Hitchcock's interactions with queer performers, it appears that the director was both disturbed and compelled by these actors – and that he felt that they could lend a certain queer aura to their characterizations and to his films. According to *Rope* (1948) scriptwriter Arthur Laurents, "Hitchcock knew exactly what he was dealing with in this story" (Spoto, *Dark* 304). The homosexuality in *Rope* "never came up until we got to casting," Laurents said in another interview. Cary Grant and Montgomery Clift turned down the parts of Rupert and Brandon, respectively, because they wouldn't take the "risk"; John Dall (Brandon) and Farley Granger (Phillip), however, "were very aware of what they were doing" (Russo 94). According to Laurents, Hitchcock "wanted to be able to get away with" the "homosexual element of the script" (Spoto, *Dark* 304) and "was interested in perverse sexuality of any kind. ... But being a strong Catholic, he probably thought it was wrong" (Russo 94).

If we are to believe the unnamed actress Spoto cites "who knew [Hitchcock] well," the director's queer "instincts" extended to gender, as he "always told his actors that they really had to be part masculine and part feminine in order to get inside any other character" because "[s]ubjectivity ... and feeling ... transcended gender" (*Dark* 86). Spoto and others read many Hitchcock films – especially *Blackmail* (1929), *Rebecca* (1940), *Shadow of a Doubt* (1943), *Vertigo* (1958), and *Marnie* (1964) – as offering evidence of how Hitchcock's own "subjectivity" appears to "transcend gender" in the sense of empathetically representing women/"the feminine" and constructing complex characters who combine traditional gender qualities. Hitchcock also appears to have enjoyed more literal gender play. Spoto describes an "offbeat home movie" shot in the early 1930s in which the director appears in drag after spending "hours of preparation – sewing sheets, refining the makeup, making a wig" – for his performance (130). Although "[c]arefully guarded for decades after," Spoto contends that the film was "shown in Hitchcock's private screening room at Universal Studios in 1976" (130). The revised edition of François Truffaut's book-length interview with the director reproduces (without credits) a short 1950s article by John D. Weaver, "The Man Behind the Body," that places its text about Hitchcock "living the orderly nine-to-six life of a civil servant" next to a large picture of the director decked out as a dignified matron, complete with lace and pearls, looking demurely at the camera (321).

Certainly something queer had been building up in the (auto)biographical air over the years, if Georgine Darcy, who played Miss Torso in *Rear Window* (1954) could tell biographer Charlotte Chandler that, after Hitchcock's death, interviewers would ask her, "Was he gay?" (219). Patrick McGilligan cites an appearance by John Russell Taylor on a 1999 episode of *E! Hollywood True Story* during which Taylor drops a bombshell that he kept out of his Hitchcock biography. According to Taylor, the director told him that he might have become a "poof" if Alma hadn't come along (McGilligan 65). Perhaps as telling is *Out* magazine's quoting a note from Hitchcock to Joan Crawford: "In my very rare homosexual moments I often glance through the pages of *Vogue*, where the other day I saw a magnificent picture of you" (Duckett 8). Like the home movie, his "poof" comment to Taylor, and his picture as a matron, this statement reveals that Hitchcock, if not fully queer him-self, had his queer gender and sexuality "moments" that were pitched somewhere between serious engagement and comic detachment. The *Vogue* comment and the comment from that unnamed actress also reveal that Hitchcock seemed to under-stand that gender and sexuality identity / subjectivity are not monolithic or unified, but can be a many-splendored, if sometimes disconcerting, thing.

If Hitchcock the person only sporadically revealed his queerness, his films provided him with a more consistent outlet. "I think too much sex while you are working goes against the work and that repressed sex is more constructive for the creative person," Hitchcock told Charlotte Chandler, adding, "It must get out, and so it goes into the work. I think it helped create a sense of sex in my work" (7). If we follow Hitchcock (who followed Freud), "repressed sex" doesn't generally "get out" in normative ways. Popular and scholarly discourse over the years has pro-vided a striking guidebook for spotting how and where non-normative sexuality and gender seems to "get out" in Hitchcock films, as well as offering a handbook for reading Hitchcock queerly. If we use a definition of queer that includes all sex, gen-der, and sexuality non-normativity, the Hitchcock films with the most consistent critical and audience queer quotient have been (in chronological order) *The Lodger*, *Murder!* (1930), *Rebecca*, *Shadow of a Doubt*, *The Paradine Case* (1947), *Rope*, *Strangers on a Train* (1951), *Vertigo*, *North by Northwest* (1959), *Psycho* (1960), and *Marnie*.

For critics like Robin Wood, "compound[ing] the problem" of naming the non-heterosexual queer characters in Hitchcock films is that "it was impossible openly to acknowledge even the existence of homosexuality in a Hollywood movie; con-sequently, homosexuality had to be coded, and discreetly, and coding, even when indiscreet, is notoriously likely to produce ambiguities and uncertainties" (205). For example, should the male transvestism in *Murder!* and *Psycho* be understood as a code for a gender-inversion form of homosexuality, or are these instances of (queer) heterosexual cross-dressing, as they are connected to theatrical perfor-mances and to a personality "split" between a young man who looks at women through a peephole and his dead mother? Critics run the gamut in making cases for who, exactly, are the non-heterosexual Hitchcock queers. There is, on one hand, a Wood-like conservatism that concedes "supposed to be" homosexuality only to Handel Fane (Esme Percy) in *Murder!*, Brandon and Phillip in *Rope*, Mrs. Danvers (Judith Anderson) in *Rebecca*, Andre Latour (Louis Jourdan) in *The Paradine Case*, and Bruno Anthony (Robert Walker) in *Strangers on a Train*. On the other hand, there is the liberality of Theodore Price, who finds homosexual elements in most Hitchcock films and queer characters in many of them, often by understanding any sign of unconventional gender performance and all troubled relationships with women as evidence of male homosexuality or bisexuality. Give or take a character or two, most commentators seem to agree that, besides the characters on Wood's list, Hitchcock's major non-heterosexual queers would include Leonard (*North by Northwest*), Norman Bates (*Psycho*), and Marnie Edgar (*Marnie*). Less frequent or sustained cases have been made for the queerness of the

Lodger (*The Lodger*), the General (*Secret Agent* [1936]), Caldicott and Charters (*The Lady Vanishes* [1938]), Rebecca and the second Mrs. de Winter (*Rebecca*), Isobel Sedbusk (*Suspicion* [1941]), Uncle Charlie (*Shadow of a Doubt*), Alex Sebastian (*Notorious* [1946]), Rupert Cadell (*Rope*), Guy Haines (*Strangers on a Train*), Father Logan and Otto Keller (*I Confess* [1953]), John Robie (*To Catch a Thief* [1955]), Phillip Vandamm (*North by Northwest*), Lil Mainwaring (*Marnie*), and Bob Rusk (*Frenzy* [1972]). I would add to this list Louisa Windeatt (*The Farmer's Wife* [1925]), young Charlie (*Shadow of a Doubt*), and Herb Hawkins (*Shadow of a Doubt*).

Interestingly, if the Lodger, the second Mrs. de Winter (Joan Fontaine), Rebecca, Uncle Charlie (Joseph Cotten), young Charlie (Teresa Wright), Alex Sebastian (Claude Rains), Norman (Anthony Perkins), Marnie (Tippi Hedren), and Bob Rusk (Barry Foster) are not read as homosexual or bisexual, they are sometimes understood in relation to incest, and, therefore, considered queer in another way, whether heterosexually (the Lodger, his sister, and his mother; Rebecca and her cousin Jack Favell [George Sanders]; Uncle Charlie, his sister, and his niece; young Charlie and her uncle; Sebastian and his mother; Norman and his mother; Rusk and his mother), homosexually (young Charlie, Marnie, and their mothers; the second Mrs. de Winter and her mother substitutes), or bisexually (if we consider Rebecca, Jack, Maxim, and Mrs. Danvers; the second Mrs. de Winter, her mother substitutes, and Maxim; young Charlie in relation to both her mother and her uncle; Sebastian in terms of his mother and his comments about Prescott [Louis Calhern] and Devlin [Cary Grant] being "handsome" men; and Marnie in terms of her mother and Mark Rutland [Sean Connery]). Joan Fontaine's Lina McLaidlaw (*Suspicion*) and Rod Taylor's Mitch Brenner (*The Birds* [1963]) might also be considered under the queer sign of incest. Besides incest, other forms of queerness evoked – if never made explicit – in Hitchcock's films include necrophilia (most strikingly in *The Lodger*, *Rebecca*, and *Vertigo*), bestiality (*Marnie*, in which Marnie croons to her horse, "Oh, Forio, if you want to bite somebody, bite me!" and, arguably, *The Birds*, in which beaks most memorably penetrate Annie Heywood [Suzanne Pleshette], Melanie Daniels [Tippi Hedren], and a farmer, leaving the former in a suggestive position and the latter two prone on bedroom floors), and sadomasochism. Sadomasochism presents the challenge of (1) separating representations of more positive consensual S/M role-playing from its more negative "power struggle" forms, and (2) deciding what kind or degree of abusive sadomasochism would mark "non-normativity," particularly in representing heterosexual relationships, which in their normative forms frequently contain some degree of mental, if not physical, abuse. As far as I can tell, no one has made a case for the first kind of sadomasochism as being represented in a Hitchcock film, and *Notorious* would appear to be the model for separating garden variety heterosexual sadomasochism from its more pathological queer forms in Hitchcock films, while *Rope* offers the same model for homosexual relationships.

Part of making a case for the sexuality of characters in Hitchcock films is identifying, or rejecting, certain visual and aural codes or particular narrative constructions as signs of queerness or straightness. In establishing what he considers Hitchcock's homosexual "motifs," Michael Walker finds that "[h]omosexual undercurrents are one of the most persistent and significant features to Hitchcock films" (52). For Walker, these "undercurrents" can work to establish particular characters as homosexual, or they can create a more vaguely queer erotic atmosphere around characters and events. For example, Walker points out the frequency of such motifs as the same sex "cruising" scenario – as in *Rebecca*, *The Paradine Case*, *Strangers on a Train*, *North by Northwest*, *Torn Curtain* (1966), and *Topaz* (1969) – and offers extended analyses of the bedroom encounter between Andre Latour and Anthony Keane (Gregory Peck) in *The Paradine Case* and the hotel meeting between Philippe Dubois (Roscoe Lee Browne) and Luis Uribe (Don Randolph) in *Topaz* to show how they evoke "a gay pickup" (252–54, 257–58; see also Durgnat 388 on *Topaz*). Walker also considers the homosexual charge in episodes of male-male voyeurism, particularly in espionage films like *Secret Agent*, but also in such films as *Strangers on a Train* and *Rear Window*. One might expand Walker's discussion by considering the queer ménage à trois in which the one person, usually a woman, acts as the trigger or the diffuser for homosexual, bisexual, or incestuous desire, as in *The Ring* (1927), *Murder!*, *Rebecca*, *Shadow of a Doubt*, *Notorious*, *The Paradine Case*, *Strangers on a Train*, *I Confess*, *North by Northwest*, *Psycho*, *The Birds*, and *Marnie*.

Robin Wood makes a spirited case for not identifying characters as homosexual based on "heterosexist" cultural practices. For example, he takes issue with critics who seem "to assume that 'sexually disturbed' equals 'homosexual,'" or those who accept "popular" notions that a gay man "shows traces of effeminacy, had a close relationship with [his] mother, or hates and murders women" ("Letter to the Editor" 195; "Murderous" 197). However, Wood admits that Hitchcock may "have shared" these "heterosexist myths about homosexuals" ("Murderous" 205). Robert J. Yanal takes up this idea: "[I]t is just these [heterosexist] 'myths' which a heterosexual film director ... would have used to signal homosexuality to ... [a general] audience otherwise clueless about gay men" and other queer folks (105). Certainly Price's reading of widespread male homosexuality in Hitchcock films hinges on understanding the director and his films as working within mainstream conventions, including the idea that homosexual men hate or resent women. Implicitly, at least, most critics seem to agree that Hitchcock – out of prejudice, ignorance, or expediency – employed certain dominant cultural codes to represent homosexuality and other forms of queerness. However, not all commentators have the critical distance of Wood and Yanal. John Hepworth is particularly scathing about critics who unreflexively buy into the stereotypes Hitchcock employs and who seem unaware of the homophobia of their own remarks. Hepworth cites an example from Eric Rohmer and Claude Chabrol:

> When Hitchcock gets around to probing the problem of homosexuality ... we will become aware that his condemnation of homosexuality is justly based on the

impossibility of true homosexual love: since this love is only an imitation, it is condemned to nonreciprocity.

(27–28)

For Hepworth, passages like this reveal how certain critics are themselves guilty of the "idiotic prejudice" against homosexuals that he finds in many Hitchcock films (191).

With Hepworth's remarks about Hitchcock critics, we move from debates about merely naming queer characters or queer situations to examining the politics of Queer Hitchcock. Hepworth takes a very hard line, linking negative representation in the films to psychosocial flaws in Hitchcock:

> Whenever Hitchcock reaches for his pet theme of "psychological disorders" you can almost invariably expect him to deal with *sexual* disorders, and this in turn usually means crazy – and I mean crazy – dykes and faggots. …
> Any thoughtful examination of Hitchcock's cinema reveals that … gay sexuality was his supreme bête noir, and that Hitch was a supreme fag baiter. … The infuriating nastiness of Hitchcock's most homophobic films lies in his willingness – even eagerness – to strike low blows and hold up crowd-pleasing scapegoats.

(188)

In one interview, Hitchcock seems to resist readings like Hepworth's that understand many of his psychopathic murderers as homosexuals, by noting that "[n]ormally a psychopath is sexually impotent. He manages to make it with women only when he strangles them" (Nogueira and Zalaffi 127). But what does this mean, exactly? Is someone who can become aroused by women only by killing them unambiguously heterosexual? Should we consider this some horribly "queer" form of heterosexuality? Might we understand actions like these as signs of "repressed" or "latent" homosexuality? Revelations in later Hitchcock biographies, like McGilligan's and Chandler's, about the director's own impotence – he sometimes introduced himself as "Hitch, without a cock" (Chandler 35) – as well as promotional photographs of the director "playfully" strangling women, make his remark about sexual psychopathology all the more provocative, especially when we consider that many male–female strangulations (and stabbings, which would "read" similarly) in his films *are* committed by men who are marked as queer, if not as clearly homosexual: Ivor Novello's Lodger (if you see him as the killer), Uncle Charlie, Bruno Anthony, Norman Bates, Bob Rusk. And what might we make of those highly charged male-on-male strangulations in *Rope* and *Torn Curtain*? With the exception of *Torn Curtain*, the murderous men in these films are often decoded as both psycho and queer. So, while only a certain percentage of murders in Hitchcock's films are committed by characters who might be read as queer or homosexual psychopaths – and whose violent psychopathology could be understood as an expression of their queerness – the bottom line for many people appears to be that these killer queers represent a large percentage of all queer characters in Hitchcock's oeuvre.

But just how large is this cohort of killer queers in relation to all queer representation in Hitchcock? This gets us back to the question of how one goes about designating who or what is queer in Hitchcock films. Hepworth is one of the critics Wood thinks is too broad – and too set on using dominant reading practices – in naming queer characters, and therefore concluding that all psychotic murderers in Hitchcock films are queer. For his part, Wood understands characters like Uncle Charlie, Norman Bates, and Bob Rusk as straight psychopaths, and he suggests that we might consider Hitchcock's "supposed to be" queer characters, psychopathic or not, in relation to how the director represents heterosexuals and heterosexuality ("Murderous" 207). While he does see a "homophobic element" in Hitchcock films, Wood also points out that many of these films are highly critical of straight men and "patriarchal domination" ("Letter to the Editor" 195). That is, if queerness is sometimes phobically (re)presented in Hitchcock films, then straightness, particularly straight masculinity, comes in for its fair share of negative representation. "This doesn't *excuse* the homophobia," for Wood, but it can explain why a figure like Bruno in *Strangers on a Train* is presented both homophobically and as "a far more attractive and fascinating character than the shallow, bland, and opportunistic 'hero'" ("Letter to the Editor" 195). Wood also suggests that if we begin queerly reading outside of heterosexist and homophobic dominant culture conventions, we might discover queer characters in Hitchcock films who aren't linked to mental illness or to violence:

> Is Louis Jourdan in *The Paradine Case* supposed to be gay? He has none of the iconography of "gayicity," but gayicity has always been a heterosexual construction, one way or another. ... As a gay man, I find it easier to accept him ... as gay or bisexual than, for example, Joseph Cotten in *Shadow of a Doubt* or Anthony Perkins in *Psycho*. But if this reading is correct (or at least plausible), he is certainly the gay character in Hitchcock who is neither neurotic nor villainous.
>
> (205)

For the past two decades, most ideological analyses of Queer Hitchcock have taken Wood's middle road, which considers how the ambiguous coding of non-normative gender and sexuality in Hitchcock films frequently allows for readings that recognize the potential for homophobia (or a less specific queerphobia) along with the potential for readings of queer characters and narratives that might, for example, make a case for the attractive (queer) villain, or for a film such as *Rope* being more about how homophobic, heterosexist, patriarchal culture perverts Brandon and Phillip than it is about how queerness leads to psychopathology and murder.

Wood's call for reading practices less constrained by dominant culture's ways of seeing has also been taken up by a number of critics who, besides Andre Latour, have added Louisa Windeatt, Caldicott and Charters, the second Mrs. de Winter, Isobel Sedbusk, Herb Hawkins, young Charlie, and Lila Crane to an ever-growing list of what we might called Hitchcock's usually overlooked "stealth queers." These stealth queers are not necessarily "positive" representations, but are characters whose visual, aural, and narrative (re)presentation generally resists the easy, common dominant-cultural practice of equating things like "gender inversion," an artistic sensibility, and closeness to one's mother to queerness – and queerness to neurosis, psychosis, violence, criminality, sin, evil, and villainy. Granted, a character like Louisa Windeatt (Louie Pounds) is presented wearing a tweedy, tailored skirt, jacket, and tie ensemble, but the film clearly is on her side when this robust, independent landowner laughs uproariously in the face of a marriage proposal from egotistical widower Samuel Sweetland (Jameson Thomas). She gives him no reason for her refusal – but we can guess at one reason she laughs at her befuddled suitor. Similar sartorial coding again becomes "classic" rather than "clichéd" (or "typing" rather than "stereotyping") when placed in a benign narrative context in *Suspicion*:

> When Lina and Johnnie … go for dinner at the novelist Isobel Sedbusk's house, there are two other guests. One is Isobel's brother Bertram; the other is a woman who is dressed in a manner which is clear 1940s coding for a lesbian: jacket, tie, tightly drawn back hair. It is fairly clear that she is not Bertram's companion. Isobel calls her 'Phil' … and she in turn calls Isobel 'Izzy'; surely Hitchcock is implying that the two are a (completely unneurotic) gay couple.
>
> (Walker 249)

One might also note here that while "Phil" may be more obviously coded, Isobel (Auriol Lee) is not – though she is made legible as a lesbian by her association with Phil. But, again, even the "clear 1940s coding for a [mannish] lesbian" is positively presented – especially in relation to the dysfunctional heterosexual couple, Lina and Johnnie. Then there is Lila (Vera Miles), who also has a no-nonsense tailored ensemble to match her take-charge attitude. If *Psycho* were a conventional film, the narrative would make her more normatively feminine so that she could take her murdered sister's place as the girlfriend of Sam Loomis (John Gavin) – which is what happens in the novel. But this Lila has no interest in men, she doesn't like Sam, and she doesn't hesitate to step in as detective and avenger when Sam, Arbogast, and the local authorities seem too slow or too tentative in investigating her sister's disappearance. Gus Van Sant's 1998 remake was much more explicit in representing Lila (Julianne Moore) as lesbian hero, but clearly the signs were already subtly – and affirmingly – there in Hitchcock's film.

Shadow of a Doubt's soft-spoken Herb (Hume Cronyn), who lives with his mother and continually draws the father of the Newton family away from his wife and children, is made a sympathetic and warmly comic figure, particularly when he is juxtaposed with the incestuous Uncle Charlie–young Charlie–Emma Newton (Patricia Collinge) triangle. Herb also becomes a hero when he rescues young Charlie from succumbing to carbon monoxide poisoning in the garage. Rounding out this examination of Hitchcock's heroic queers are Caldicott (Naunton Wayne) and Charters (Basil Radford), from *The Lady Vanishes,* whose lack of interest in women, and appearance in a small bed sharing a pair of pajamas, codes them as a couple for some viewers. Initially, Caldicott and Charters are represented as comical and self-centered. But they are no worse than the antagonistic straight couples, and they save the day in a climactic gun battle.

One recent line of critical inquiry that takes in both controversial killer queers and stealth queers considers the dandy figure in relation to Queer Hitchcock. Richard Allen finds Hitchcock's use of dandyism an important part of the director's "romantic irony," which combines "ideal[ized]" and "perverse" representations of sexuality, whether straight or queer (118). In Allen's reading, the dandy is a "complex" figure, who, "[c]onsidered as a figure who is incipiently homosexual, though not explicitly so, ... can also be defined by the way that he combines feminine and masculine traits in accordance with the theories of gender that circulated in Hitchcock's youth, where homosexuality was conceived in terms of male femininity – a feminine soul in a man's body" (83, 84). For Thomas Elsaesser, "Hitchcock's dandyism" (both in the man and in his films) is "a combination of the aesthete, the rogue and the mountebank," representing "a mode of irresponsibility, playfulness, unseriousness and sexual ambiguity that combined the stance of the Oscar Wilde dandy with a more aggressive brand of schoolboy humour and a willful immaturity" (10). While he admits that most Hitchcock's villains are connected to a dandyism "often made 'sinister' by stereotypically homosexual traits or hints of sexual perversion," Elsaesser also contends that some of Hitchcock's protagonists are coded as dandies to a certain degree, and, therefore, are ripe for the queering, including Robert Donat's Richard Hannay (*The 39 Steps* [1935]) and Cary Grant's Johnnie Aysgarth (*Suspicion*) and John Robie (*To Catch a Thief*).

Marking a difference from Elsaesser's work on the Hitchcock dandy, Allen finds that "while there is only a thin line between the dandy" and certain gothic "Jekyll/Hyde hero figures (like Maxim de Winter in *Rebecca*)," Hitchcock dandies are always (a) criminals and (b) antagonists (and doubles) of the films' heroes, "demarcated from [the heroes] by their queer sexuality, which excludes them from entering into a normative heterosexual relationship" (106–07). While Allen's Hitchcock dandies can't enter into a "normative heterosexual relationship," one might follow Wood in considering these queer criminal dandies against the many straight-coded Hitchcock protagonists, like John "Scottie" Ferguson (James Stewart) in *Vertigo* or Mark Rutland in *Marnie*, who also are not part of normative heterosexual relationships. These characters – for better, but usually for worse – might also be said to inhabit queer representational spaces.

Heterosexuality is also queered in Hitchcock through what Lee Edelman calls Hitchcock's "attack on 'heteronormativity'" in many films (quoted in Allen xi). *Vertigo*, *Notorious*, and *Marnie* would top the list of films critics have read as scathing indictments of heterosexuality, as these films reveal how horrifying it is when heteronormative notions about gender roles, romantic love, and sexuality are taken to their "logical" conclusions. Of course, not everyone finds Hitchcock's take on heterosexuality all that progressive or radical. For all the elements of heteronormative exposé and critique in *Vertigo*, for example, there are aspects of the film that invite us to share Scottie's patriarchal romantic reverie. Mark Rappaport feels that even though "hell is the couple," for Hitchcock, and "[t]he relationships portrayed in [his] films are codependencies that are fueled by dovetailing neurotic needs," the director usually holds out "the notion of love, however damaged or distorted," as a possible means of redeeming these "flawed relationship[s]" (48–49). "In this respect, Sam [Joseph Cotten] and Henrietta [Ingrid Bergman] in *Under Capricorn* (1949) are the paradigmatic Hitchcock couple" for Rappaport (49).

Raymond Durgnat also finds that if the representation of heterosexuality in Hitchcock films "has its troubled streak, its variations from the norm are usually prudent, stylised and, if not exactly innocent, impersonal. ... [T]here is much teasing, much dissatisfaction, much involuntary tussling for dominance. ... [But] Hitchcock remains, prudently, within the limits" (53, 51, 53). However, Durgnat makes much of the moment in the Truffaut interview where Hitchcock, while discussing the heterosexual couple in *The 39 Steps*, insists that the handcuffing in this film (and, by implication, Joe's handcuffing Daisy in *The Lodger*) "has deeper implications. ... [I]t's somewhere in the area of fetishism, isn't it? ... When I visited the Vice Museum in Paris, I noticed there was considerable evidence of sexual aberrations through restraint" (Durgnat 52; Truffaut 47). A page or two earlier, Durgnat asserts that the "simplest yet most precise image" of heterosexuality in Hitchcock is in *The 39 Steps*, where "[h]andcuffs pull your limp hand over the silk-stockinged thighs of the girl who wants to hand you over to the police" (51). Setting aside Durgnat's heterocentric male description of the shot, I wonder how many people would consider the image heteronormative? This image also takes us back to Hitchcock's own admission of impotency, often signaled by his "Hitch, without the cock" introduction. While a man "without a cock" might be in a heterosexual relationship, would it be considered heteronormative?

Besides *The 39 Steps*, some of the Hitchcock films that feature signs of male impotence in the face of the (hyper-)feminine are *The Lodger, Rich and Strange* (1931), *Rebecca, Notorious, Strangers on a Train, Rear Window, Dial M for Murder* (1954), *To Catch a Thief, Vertigo, North by Northwest, Psycho,* and *Frenzy*. Of course, in order to conduct a queer heterosexual reading of a number of these films, you would have to understand certain male characters (the Lodger, Bruno Anthony, Guy Haines, Norman Bates, Bob Rusk) as straight and not as homosexual or bisexual. Not surprisingly, considering Hitchcock's pronouncements on impotence and psychopathology, a number of these male characters turn sadistic and become aroused by verbally or physically abusing women in attempts to control them. Since women in Hitchcock films are rarely complete masochists – they almost always fight back to some extent – Hitchcock's male sadists are seldom able to achieve the terrifying, full-blown queer sadomasochism of the heterosexual relationships in *Notorious* and *Vertigo*. *Rebecca* represents an interesting case of queer heterosexuality. While it is initially Maxim (Laurence Olivier) who torments his masochistically-inclined second wife, leading her to the brink of suicide (with the help of Mrs. Danvers), it turns out that his callous treatment of his second wife is the result of the equally sadistic treatment he endured at the hands of his first wife, Rebecca, who forced him into a position of impotent shame and fury, which he then takes out on his second wife. *Psycho* is another interesting case for a queer heterosexual reading, not only because the sadomasochistic heterosexual couple living beyond the pale consists of a mother and son, but because this couple has been internalized by the son, Norman, who most likely murdered his mother in a fit of jealousy and repented by preserving her body and taking on a version of her personality in which she is as intensely jealous of his being with other women as he was of her being with other men after his father died. Norman is both the sadistic mother who bullies her son and kills any woman he becomes interested in and the masochistic son who puts up with his mother's abuse and cleans up after her murders. Here is a gender-and-sexuality queer heterosexual couple contained in one psychotic body.

But a big part of what makes *Psycho* an endlessly fascinating film in the Queer Hitchcock canon is the way in which it becomes the locus of a number of queernesses: abusive heterosexual sadomasochism, incest, necrophilia, gender crossing or mixing, and repressed homosexuality – if you read as "repressed homosexuality" Norman's use of an internalized, murderous mother as a way for him to take on/in "the feminine," a way to remain permanently close to his mother, a way to avoid sexual contact with women, and a way to avoid dealing with what all this might mean. The most persistent queer focus on *Psycho* has been on its incest theme, which might include Lila and Marion living in their dead mother's house (and with her memory), Marion's co-worker, Caroline (Patricia Hitchcock), going on about the strain of dealing with the rivalry between her mother and new husband, the oilman Cassidy (Frank Albertson) coming on to Marion while telling her about his daughter, and Norman's relationship with his mother. All of these parent-child relationships are presented in sexually charged contexts that juxtapose normative heterosexuality with its queerly incestuous rival. Marion's boyfriend, Sam, is reluctant to come to her house for a date, feeling they'd have to send her sister away and "turn mother's picture to the wall." Caroline tells Marion how her mother provided her with tranquilizers to knock her out on her honeymoon. Cassidy uses an insinuating tone as he calls his daughter "my baby" and "my sweet little girl" while discussing her upcoming wedding. And Norman apparently killed his widowed mother after he found her in bed with a man.

Same sex and opposite sex incest turns out to be one of the most persistent forms of queer sexuality in Hitchcock films. As with homosexuality and bisexuality, the incest motif in Hitchcock films most generally takes the form of insinuating or suggesting incestuous desire rather than gesturing toward the physical act itself. Incest is often suggested in Hitchcock films by having a parent and child set up housekeeping together in ways that indicate the child is substituting for a physically or emotionally absent parent, while the parent becomes like a spouse or partner to his or her child. This formation occurs, for example, in *The Lodger, The Farmer's Wife, Shadow of a Doubt, Notorious, Strangers on a Train, North by Northwest, Psycho, The Birds,* and *Marnie.* Cases have also been made for incest-suggestiveness occurring in quasi-parent/child relationships, like those between Iris (Margaret Lockwood) and Miss Froy (Dame May Whitty) in *The Lady Vanishes* and the second Mrs. de Winter and her matronly employer, Mrs. Van Hopper (Florence Bates), in *Rebecca*. Then there are those instances where sibling or other close familial relationships are represented within intense, sexually-charged contexts: *The Lodger* (the Lodger and his sister), *Rebecca* (Rebecca and her cousin Jack Favell), *Shadow of a Doubt* (young Charlie and both her mother and her uncle, Uncle Charlie and both his niece and his sister), *Psycho* (Lila and Marion), *The Birds* (Mitch and his sister, Cathy [Veronica Cartwright]). No matter how the "family romance" is represented, there is usually a sequence set around a bed or in a bedroom, or involving some other intimate object or act (a ring, matching chairs near a fireplace, lovebirds, a manicure, dancing at a "coming out ball," the gift of a fur stole and flowers) that anchors incest readings of these Hitchcock films.

I will conclude this chapter with an analysis of *Strangers on a Train*, one of the films that everyone agrees is part of the Queer Hitchcock canon. Both Arthur Laurents and Farley Granger, who were lovers at the time, have testified that it was Robert Walker's idea "to play Bruno Anthony as a homosexual" (Russo 94). According to Granger, this idea was worked out between Walker and Hitchcock, but not mentioned to Granger at the time, because "[Hitchcock] wanted me to act kind of normal and not be aware of too much undercurrent" (Chandler 196). Granger's "act kind of normal" is telling, as the actor's "kind of normal" performance has led audiences and critics to understand Guy Haines as straight, as a "repressed" or potential homosexual, as bisexual, or as more vaguely queer, as is the case for Robert L. Carringer, who sees Guy as "a man of indeterminate sexual identity" (quoted in McGilligan 443). Robert J. Yanal makes a case for Guy as "heterosexual, staid, taciturn, athletic, a bit slow, self-satisfied, sane, but passively murderous," in contrast to Bruno, who for Yanal "is homosexual, theatrical, talkative, leisured, clever, envious of Guy, mad, and actively murderous" (104). Yanal finds that, in the context of mainstream American films and cultural codes of the early 1950s, Bruno "is best read as gay" (105). Among the items Yanal cites here are many things that would also code Bruno as one of Hitchcock's dandies: "[h]e is a dapper dresser," he and his mother "have tête-à-têtes during manicures," and he "speaks in italics" – for example, "I've had a *strenuous* evening" (105). McGilligan attributes much of Bruno's homosexual dandyism to writer Whitfield Cook, who "knew how to code the signals from his circle of friends" (442). For Robin Wood, however, it is just the kind of "evidence" for Bruno's homosexuality offered by commentators like Yanal that make him, at best, a "supposed to be" queer character whose "attribution seems to rest more on popular heterosexual myths about gay men than on any actual evidence the film (caught in the constraints of censorship) can provide: he hates his father, is overindulged by his silly mother, seems rather to enjoy murdering women, and dresses flamboyantly" ("Murderous" 207). On the other hand, Wood says, "It is probable that Hitchcock thought [Bruno] was gay" ("Murderous" 207).

While Hepworth makes an impassioned case for understanding Bruno as one of Hitchcock's vicious, homophobic creations, a number of critics read Bruno's narrative and cultural function as being more complex than a simply negative image. For Wood, "Bruno forms a link in a chain of fascinating, insidiously attractive Hitchcock villains" both straight and queer ("Murderous" 207). Richard Barrios offers what is perhaps the most affirmative reading of Bruno as homosexual:

> Witty, natty, and bright, Bruno could almost be a gay role model for the early fifties. He's not a stereotype, certainly, and he's more clever, funny, and likable than anyone else in this movie. Unfortunately, he's also a psychopathic killer.
>
> (227)

Mixing queerness and feminism, Robert J. Corber and Sabrina Barton explore the ways in which Bruno's homosexuality is paired with Miriam's transgressive female heterosexuality as threats to all-American Guy's gender and sexuality identity, as well as to his position as masculine, heterosexual narrative agent and bearer of the desiring gaze. Corber sets his reading of the film within the context of post–World War II hysteria about homosexual men and non-domestic women, while Barton's psychoanalytic reading considers how the film uses Bruno and Miriam (Laura Elliott) to expose the violence patriarchy uses against sexual women and homosexual men in order to maintain its tenuous hold on power and privilege, even while it justifies eliminating "the deranged homosexual" and "the voracious tramp" (218).

For Spoto, Guy and Bruno enact a "homosexual courtship" from their first scene together, "with Guy as the latent closet type and Bruno the flamboyant gay who attempts to bring him out into the open" (*Art* 212). "Guy is not wholly given to his relationship with Ann[e] Morton," Spoto says later, which is why he escorts her "*away* from the minister" in the final scene of the American version of the film (*Art* 218). In a more psychoanalytic vein, William A. Drumin also finds that "Bruno's attention to Guy can be construed as a homosexual courtship" and that Guy's ties to heterosexuality are tenuous, at best: "[T]he degree of Guy's love for Ann[e] is in considerable doubt. Guy intends to go into politics, and marrying a senator's daughter could be very helpful for making his way in this field" (194). For Drumin, Guy's estranged wife, Miriam, and Bruno's father "are the principal figures who can block a male homosexual relationship," so Bruno decides that they must die in order to open the way for his union with Guy. It is a "union" that is consummated on a fairground carousel that runs amok, killing Bruno – "latent" and passive Guy's more "flamboyant and aggressive" homosexual double – and returning Guy to Anne and to heterosexuality (206). Michael Walker, among others, takes this doubling a step further, suggesting that the film's narrative might be read as the dream/nightmare of "the repressed homosexual" Guy – a dream in which he conjures up a seductive and murderous Bruno to embody his darkest desires (150–51). Walker and Drumin are among those who find *Strangers on a Train* a terrifying representation of homosexuality juxtaposed with a picture of a troubled and troubling heterosexuality that is, however, good enough for Guy and the narrative to retreat to with a sigh of relief.

Bruno is also the center of *Strangers on a Train*'s representation of incest, whose proposed plot – Bruno wants his father killed so that he and his mother can live together in a big house – suggests a dry run for *Psycho*. Bruno's connection to heterosexual incest also provides a way of reading his affinity for strangling women as an expression of male heterosexual psychosis rather than of homosexuality or queerness. One of Bruno's most spectacular strangulations, which has him wrapping his hands around the neck of a society matron, might be read as a displacement of Bruno's simultaneously erotic and malign desires toward his mother. But perhaps the most famous strangulation in all Hitchcock involves Bruno cruising a flirtatious Miriam at an amusement park, just as he had cruised her husband on the train. If you read Bruno as a homosexual, then he is doing an excellent job of performing normative masculine heterosexuality here. However, if you see Bruno as (queerly) heterosexual, as bisexual, or as more vaguely queer, then he is being turned on by prospect of strangling Miriam after a long foreplay in which he seduces her away from her two boyfriends as they pass through the fairgrounds, into the Tunnel of Love, and onto the Isle of Love, where Hitchcock films the murder like an erotic embrace that ends with Miriam lying down where "smoochers" go for a tryst.

In speaking about Robert Walker–as-Bruno, Pauline Kael offers a pointed summary of the mixture of fascination, empathy, and aversion typical of Queer Hitchcock: "[D]ear degenerate Bruno. ... Walker's performance is what gives this movie much of its character and its peculiar charm" (352).

Works Cited

Allen, Richard. *Hitchcock's Romantic Irony*. New York. Columbia UP, 2007.

Barrios, Richard. *Screened Out: Playing Gay in Hollywood from Edison to Stonewall*. New York: Routledge, 2003.

Barton, Sabrina. "'Crisscross': Paranoia and Projection in *Strangers on a Train*." Creekmur and Doty 216–38.

Cameron, Ian, and V.F. Perkins. "Hitchcock." Gottlieb 44–54.

Chandler, Charlotte. *It's Only a Movie: Alfred Hitchcock: A Personal Biography*. New York: Simon and Schuster, 2005.

Corber, Robert J. "Hitchcock's Washington: Spectatorship, Ideology, and the 'Homosexual Menace' in *Strangers on a Train*." *Hitchcock's America*. Ed. Jonathan Freedman and Richard Millington. New York: Oxford UP, 1999. 99–122.

Creekmur, Corey K., and Alexander Doty, eds. *Out in Culture: Gay, Lesbian, and Queer Essays on Popular Culture*. Durham: Duke UP, 1995.

Drumin, William A. *Thematic and Methodological Foundations of Alfred Hitchcock's Artistic Vision*. Lewiston, NY: Mellen, 2004.

Duckett, Chip. "Out Front." *Out* June–July 1993: 8.

Durgnat, Raymond. *The Strange Case of Alfred Hitchcock, or the Plain Man's Hitchcock*. Cambridge: MIT P, 1974.

Elsaesser, Thomas. "The Dandy in Hitchcock." *Alfred Hitchcock: Centenary Essays.* Ed. Richard Allen and S. Ishii-Gonzáles. London: BFI, 1999. 3–14.

Fallaci, Oriana. "Alfred Hitchcock: Mr. Chastity." Gottlieb 55–66.

Gottlieb, Sidney, ed. *Alfred Hitchcock: Interviews.* Jackson: UP of Mississippi, 2003.

Hepworth, John. "Hitchcock's Homophobia." Creekmur and Doty 186–94.

Kael, Pauline. *Kiss Kiss Bang Bang.* Boston: Atlantic Monthly / Little, Brown, 1968.

McGilligan, Patrick. *Alfred Hitchcock: A Life in Darkness and Light.* New York: HarperCollins, 2003.

Nogueira, Rui and Nicoletta Zalaffi. "Hitch, Hitch, Hitch, Hurrah!" Gottlieb 119–28.

Price, Theodore. *Hitchcock and Homosexuality: His 50-Year Obsession with Jack the Ripper and the Superbitch Prostitute—A Psychoanalytic View.* Metuchen, NJ: Scarecrow, 1982.

Rappaport, Mark. "*Under Capricorn* Revisited." *Hitchcock Annual* 12 (2003–04): 42–66.

Rohmer, Eric and Claude Chabrol. *Hitchcock: The First Forty-Four Films.* Trans. Stanley Hochman. New York: Ungar, 1979.

Russo, Vito. *The Celluloid Closet: Homosexuality in the Movies.* New York: Harper and Row, 1987.

Samuels, Robert. *Hitchcock's Bi-Textuality: Lacan, Feminisms, and Queer Theory.* Albany: SUNY P, 1998.

Spoto, Donald. *The Art of Alfred Hitchcock: Fifty Years of His Motion Pictures.* Garden City: Doubleday, 1976.

Spoto, Donald. *The Dark Side of Genius: The Life of Alfred Hitchcock.* Centennial ed. New York: Da Capo, 1999.

Truffaut, François, with the collaboration of Helen G. Scott. *Hitchcock.* Rev. ed. New York: Simon and Schuster, 1984.

Walker, Michael. *Hitchcock's Motifs.* Amsterdam: Amsterdam UP, 2005.

Wood, Robin. "Letter to the Editor." Creekmur and Doty 194–95.

Wood, Robin. "The Murderous Gays: Hitchcock's Homophobia." Creekmur and Doty 197–215.

Yanal, Robert J. *Hitchcock as Philosopher.* Jefferson, NC: McFarland, 2005.

PART VIII

Ethics

26

Hitchcock and Philosophy

Richard Gilmore

Hitchcock intends to unveil reality.

Jean Douchet (18)

When Roger Thornhill (Cary Grant), in *North by Northwest* (1959), steps off the darkened bus and into the bright sunlight at the Prairie Stop crossroads on Highway 41, he blinks a few times and looks around, not really knowing what he is looking at or how to identify the person he is looking for. At a loss to make sense of the scene that surrounds him, he seems, for the first time in the movie, completely out of his element. This scene reenacts the most famous scene in the history of philosophy, that of the freed cave-dweller stumbling out of the darkened cave into the bright sunlight of the intelligible world in Plato's allegory of the Cave in Book 7 of *The Republic.*

Plato's allegory is meant to narrativize the appearance/reality distinction. The premise of the appearance/reality distinction is that things are not as they appear to us to be, or, in other words, there is more going on than we think. The job of philosophy is to see through the veils of appearance to the reality hidden behind them. Or, to stick with the cave allegory, it is to help people find their way out of the dark cave of mere appearances into the bright light of the truth. The political and ethical implications are that appearances enslave us and the truth sets us free.

If Roger Thornhill, dust-covered and confused, standing alone at Prairie Stop on Highway 41 is what freedom looks like, it does not look like much. Thornhill's world looks like a kind of wasteland, vast and sere. The "real" will look like a wasteland, at least at first, because it has been stripped of all of the familiar constructions with which we fill our environment in the world of appearances. In the case of Roger Thornhill, those constructions are the gleaming glass and steel

A Companion to Alfred Hitchcock, First Edition. Edited by Thomas Leitch and Leland Poague.
© 2011 Thomas Leitch and Leland Poague. Published 2011 by Blackwell Publishing Ltd.

buildings of New York City, the cabs and the girlfriends, the business associates and martinis, and most powerfully insidious of all, the oleaginous money that greases the way for him at every turn. Money seems to flow out of Roger Thornhill's pockets like fruit from a cornucopia, but it does not nourish and sustain; it detaches, divests of responsibility, and frees through disconnection.

The logic of late capitalism, in the phrase of Fredric Jameson, does precisely that: it disconnects us, fragments us, severs us from any sense of real responsibility (ix–xxii). In the city, the world of appearances, Roger Thornhill is extremely adept. He is also disconnected, fragmented, and irresponsible. The wasteland of the "real" is the last illusion to go. The real appears like a wasteland because it is divested of all that had seemed so important and real: the power of these buildings, these relationships, this money. Philosophy says that these things only appear important. As Socrates says at his trial in the *Apology*, "I go around doing nothing but persuading both young and old among you not to care for your body or your wealth in preference to or as strongly as for the best possible state of your soul" (*Five* 34). The great promise of philosophy is that there are great powers to be discovered outside the world of appearances. The "real" of philosophy is actually a beautiful world of possibilities outside the cave.

William Rothman has described Hitchcock's films as "philosophically serious" in the sense that "[t]hey are thinking seriously about their medium, thinking seriously about themselves, thinking seriously about such matters as the nature and relationships of love, murder, sexuality, marriage, and theater" (271). I agree with Rothman that Hitchcock is a serious thinker and that he thinks in film, primarily in images. I also agree that Hitchcock's seriousness as a thinker includes a considerable self-consciousness in his filmmaking. I am not sure anyone could interpret his films as wildly or complexly as he has already envisioned them. I would add that the nature of his thinking, the nature of his wisdom, is most closely aligned with that paradigmatic figure of philosophy, the ironic Socrates. It is Socrates who tells the story of the allegory of the cave in Plato's *Republic*. Socrates also compares his powers to those of the greatest Greek heroes – Heracles and Achilles. This claim seems laughable to his audience, the members of the jury at his trial, as it is related in the *Apology*, because they can judge power only in the world of appearances. Real power, the power possessed by Socrates, is as invisible to them as gravity. Hitchcock's power is similarly invisible to those "who have eyes but cannot see."

Hitchcock's philosophy of film is his theory of what he calls "pure cinema." Pure cinema derives from the power of montage. This is what Hitchcock tells Peter Bogdanovich about pure cinema and montage:

> I believe in pure cinema and montage. ... You take a shot of Jimmy Stewart, say, looking; then a shot of what he sees; then his reaction. But you see, it's like the old Pudovkin test. He took the same shot of an actor looking downward with a blank expression, and spliced it between a shot of a baby playing and a shot of an open grave. The audience that saw it marveled at the subtlety of expression and emotion

the actor's face had shown. But in reality it was the same identical shot of the actor after both the baby and the grave. Only montage has the power of audience suggestion. I'm very keen on this method of story telling.

(476)

Hitchcock goes on to remark, "As far as I am concerned, you see, the content is secondary to the handling; the effect I can produce on an audience rather than the subject matter" (476).

"The old Pudovkin test" was really an experiment conducted by Lev Kuleshov, Pudovkin's teacher, soon after the 1917 Russian revolution. Kuleshov alternated the identical shot of the face of the pre-revolutionary actor Ivan Moszhukin with shots of a plate of soup, a little girl in a coffin, and a woman on a couch. "According to Pudovkin, who later described the results of the experiment, audiences exclaimed at Moszhukin's subtle and affective ability to convey such varied emotions: hunger, sadness, affection" (Monaco 309). It was Pudovkin who seized upon the significance of the experiment for film theory. For Pudovkin, the essence of film was montage, and the essence of montage was "linking" images together to form a new meaning. That is what Pudovkin took the Kuleshov experiment to show. Put the image of an actor's face with a baby, we "see" tenderness. Put the same image of the actor's face with a coffin, and we "see" sadness. The meaning of the French word montage is "putting together," and in film this kind of putting together has the power to generate new meanings.

Pudovkin's putative opponent in film theory, Sergei Eisenstein, agreed that montage was the essence of cinema, but disagreed with the idea that the essence of montage was a "linking." For Eisenstein, "montage is conflict" (*Form* 38). It is about "collision": "from the collision of two given factors *arises* a concept" (*Form* 37). Two images put together by a cut are always in conflict; they always collide. But this "putting together" is, as Eisenstein says of the similar meaning-construction dynamic of hieroglyphs, a "copulation." As Eisenstein says, "the copulation … of two hieroglyphs of the simplest series is to be regarded not as their sum, but as their product, i.e., as a value of another dimension, another degree; each, separately, corresponds to an *object*, to a fact, but their combination corresponds to a *concept*" (*Form* 29–30). I understand Eisenstein's description of the copulation of two hieroglyphs to be describing something virtually, perhaps actually, sexual. The combination of the two facts generates a new entity altogether, a (new) concept. This is how montage works for Eisenstein; it is generative.

Eisenstein calls this, appropriately enough, "the montage of attraction." In his first published essay, "Montage of Attractions," Eisenstein talks about using "emotional shocks … to make the final ideological conclusion perceptible" (*Sense* 230–31). What I understand Eisenstein to be saying here is that in theater, as in cinema, there is power in aggressively juxtaposing elements that trigger complicated emotional responses in the members of the audience from which a new awareness can emerge. It is an "attraction" instead of a forced compulsion because it works with the audience's own emotional responses. The (ideological) conclusion, the acquired new knowledge, is generated in the spectator by the spectator, by means of an emergence from the spectator's own emotional and intellectual constellations. The director lays out the complex relation of parts that draws, "attracts," the audience to a particular interpretation of them.

"Montage" is a vague concept, used in many different ways by different people. In the United States, it is generally used to mean "editing" and is associated with "trimming" and "removal." In Europe it is thought of much more in this dialectical way described by Eisenstein, and so is associated with "building" and the construction of meaning (Monaco 183). In talking about Hitchcock's use of montage I will primarily have in mind Eisenstein's theory of montage, and so I will be using a somewhat stipulative definition of montage. I will also refer to a "montage sequence," which is also a vague term, but for my purposes will mean a sequence in which montage is used generatively to create new concepts in the minds of the audience. I will also use montage to describe the process of creating emergent meanings through juxtaposed images. I understand there to be a continuum between montage and mise-en-scène (literally "putting in the scene") since, as Eisenstein says, "conflict within the shot is potential montage" (*Form* 38). Mise-en-scène sets up the montage and montage makes manifest the potential of the mise-en-scène.

Eisenstein's theory of montage is philosophically rich. It essentially recreates, as a theory of cinematic montage, Charles Sanders Peirce's philosophy of the logic of Firstness, Secondness, and Thirdness. His theory of montage includes an ontology, what is real in the world; an epistemology, how we can know what is real; and an ethics, what we should do in the world. This is how Eisenstein describes his philosophy of montage:

> The foundation for this philosophy is a *dynamic* concept of things:
> Being—as a constant evolution from the interaction of two contradictory opposites.
> Synthesis—arising from the opposition between thesis and antithesis.
>
> (*Form* 45)

Eisenstein clearly has Hegel in mind here, but I think Peirce's philosophy is better suited to draw out the subtleties of Eisenstein's thinking. That is primarily the case because of the great importance that Peirce puts on the relation between particulars, and on the relation between particulars and universals or generals.

Peirce describes himself as a "scholastic realist" devoted to "objective idealism" (5: 53; 6: 20). Peirce's realism involves the idea that ideas are real, that they really operate in the world and are not just human projections onto the world. So, for Peirce, it is more accurate to say that we are "in ideas" rather than saying that we "have ideas." The real, for Peirce, is what is the case whether anyone thinks it or not. An example of an idea that appears to be a "real" idea is Darwin's idea of evolution. We are more in it than it is in us. If it is a real idea, and the reality of ideas must be approached fallibilistically, then it was real (operative in nature) before anyone had thought of it, and it is real whether anyone believes it or not.

Peirce identifies three logical categories he calls Firstness, Secondness, and Thirdness. Understood experientially, Firstness is like a mood, pervasive, complete, and self-contained. Secondness is like an intrusion of a new, unexpected, inexplicable element that disrupts our mood and creates in us the need for some kind of resolution to this disturbance. Thirdness is achieved when we solve the problem of the disturbance. Thirdness occurs when we understand what the problem is and what the solution is. It is the "Aha!" of discovery and the pathway to a return to Firstness. For Peirce this is how we think. We are in Firstness until we are disturbed, say when an attractive man or woman appears. We are compelled into Secondness by the unaccountable disturbance and we seek a resolution. We form many strategies, plan various courses of action to achieve our goal of resolving this disturbance, until we finally come upon a plan that works (Thirdness), then we implement it, and, if we are lucky, succeed. Our companion won, we eventually return to a state of Firstness. For Peirce, this is also how the world works. Evolution is perhaps the most active manifestation of this pattern in nature. A species or individual abides until there appears some competitor for its niche. A competition ensues in which different strategies are engaged. One species or individual happens upon a strategy that confers advantage. Then the competition winds down, until a return to a relative state of Firstness is once again achieved.

This is just the way Eisensteinian montage works. There is a shot – Firstness (with some potential tension, some potential Secondness perhaps already contained within the scene). There is a second shot – Secondness (a second shot means change, change means discord, "collision," the need to interpret, to resolve the tension that has been created). The interpretation, the "concept" that is created in the mind of the spectator, is Thirdness. This pattern will be repeated from montage to montage, and in the film as a whole.

Montage is how Hitchcock thinks in film. Hitchcock's relation to philosophy will be determined by what he thinks about and how he thinks about what he thinks about. What he thinks about is style. In "On Style" Hitchcock wrote: "I only interest myself in the manner and style of telling the story. But as for the story itself, I don't care whether it's good or bad, you know. If it serves my purpose" (299). What his purpose is, I take it, is a function, basically, of his philosophy. If content is what is represented, style is the way the thing is represented. The idea that the way a thing is represented is more important than what is represented is itself a kind of philosophy.

In *The Transfiguration of the Commonplace*, Arthur Danto attempts to give a comprehensive, universal theory of what makes art art, and his answer is, in short, style. As Danto says, speaking of the paintings of Giotto, "What I call 'style' must have been less what Giotto saw than the way he saw it, and invisible for that reason." Danto sums up this idea about style by saying, "It is as if a work of art were like an externalization of the artist's consciousness, as if we could see his very way of seeing and not merely what he saw" (163).

And why does the artist want to externalize his or her consciousness? Danto does not address this more ethical question, but I would suggest two and a half answers. The first reason is to show others something the artist sees, a way of seeing, that might help. As Nietzsche says, "there is one thing alone we really care about from the heart—'bringing something home'" (13). The second reason is to create, beyond the artwork, people who can understand and appreciate the artwork, which is itself an externalization of the consciousness of the artist. This amounts to the explanation that the artist creates art in order to create a community of people among whom he or she would like to live. This certainly seems to have been Socrates' motive for doing philosophy. A subset of this desire to create a community in which to live is the desire to find, to create, a partner with whom one can have sex.

Hitchcock is a very sexual director. The skimpy evening wear of Lisa Fremont (Grace Kelly) in *Rear Window* (1954), the "short fuse" of Jennifer Rogers (Shirley MacLaine) in *The Trouble with Harry* (1955), and the underwear of "Madeleine Elster" (Kim Novak) hanging to dry in Scottie's kitchen in *Vertigo* (1958) are but three instances of a pervasive eroticism in Hitchcock. His overt use of sex, however, is much like the recurrent interest Socrates shows in sex. It is a cover for his real interest, which is an emergent eroticism. If sex is the physical act, eroticism is the emergent reciprocal relationship of attraction that can develop between people. Socrates lures Alcibiades in with an apparent interest in sex, only to reveal that his true interest is in the erotic possibilities of ideas. Hitchcock too uses sex to draw us into his movies, to attract us, but then what emerges is a fascinating erotic core of compelling, and complicated, reciprocal desire.

Hitchcock says, "Pure cinema is complementary pieces of film put together, like notes of music make a melody. There are two primary uses of cutting or montage in film: montage to create ideas, and montage to create violence and emotions." The former form of montage he says involves "juxtaposition of imagery relating to the mind of the individual" (Bogdanovich 522). This is the immense power of montage, that we can get inside another person's mind. This is what cinema has a peculiar power to do in a way that no other art has. As Hitchcock says, "close-up of a man; what he sees; his reaction to it. And that ... can't be done in the theatre, can't be done in a novel. You put the audience in the mind of a particular character" (Bogdanovich 545).

There is an ontology here, a theory of reality, that emerges from a theory of what a human being is. The theory addresses the problem of the relationship between the universal and the particular. As Peirce says,

> we observe two sorts of elements of consciousness, the distinction between which may best be made clear by means of an illustration. In a piece of music there are the separate notes, and there is the air [the melody]. A single tone may be prolonged for an hour or a day, and it exists as perfectly in each second of that time as in the whole taken together; so that, as long as it is sounding, it might be present to a sense from

which everything in the past was as completely absent as the future itself. But it is different with the air, the performance of which occupies a certain time, during the portions of which only portions of it are played. It consists in an orderliness in the succession of sounds which strike the ear at different times; and to perceive it there must be some continuity of consciousness which makes the events of a lapse of time present to us.

(5: 253–54)

This sounds remarkably similar to what Hitchcock says about his use of montage in film. The ontology here is that there are "two sorts of objects." One sort of object is like the notes, and the other sort of object is like the melody. This distinction corresponds, in a person, to body and soul, or body and personality. The body corresponds to the notes, a kind of physical phenomenon, and the personality or soul corresponds to the melody, which is non-physical and emergent. The melody of a piece of music emerges over time. It cannot be identified in any given moment, but only as it emerges across time. The melody signifies "an orderliness in the succession of sounds." In another place Peirce will associate this "orderliness" with a feeling of unity (Peirce 6: 315–18; Gilmore 315–16). There are three things to say about this. First, the "orderliness" is where the meaning is. What the meaning of a thing is, whether it is a piece of music or a person or a movie, is determined by the principle of unity or orderliness that makes that thing, that piece of music or that person or that movie, what it is. The second thing to say is that this sense of orderliness or unity is something we first recognize by feeling. Once we have felt the unity we can think about it, analyze it, study it, but we must feel it first. It is literally invisible, so we can only see it if we feel it first. The third thing is that things like bodies and notes affect us by compulsion, what Aristotle calls "efficient causality." Things like personalities and melodies affect us by attraction, what Aristotle calls "final causality."

It is also important that these "two sorts of objects" are interdependent. For it to be music, there must be both notes and some sort of emergent principle of "orderliness," something like a melody. A corollary to this view of the universe as everywhere composed of "two sorts of objects" is the ancient wisdom of the relation of the microcosm to the macrocosm, specifically that the macrocosm is contained in the microcosm. This is an ancient Pythagorean wisdom. The idea is that any given system of relations reveals the way all systems of relations operate. Every system of relations has, at once, an orderliness and a counter-indication to that orderliness, a suggestion of something more going on, signs of a larger pattern subsuming this pattern.

This is true in the films of Hitchcock. Virtually every scene contains the essential elements of all the scenes. This is why Hitchcock's films have been so generative of interpretations. You can start anywhere and get to the largest ideas that characterize all of his films. That is because every small montage sequence is a kind of microcosm to the macrocosm of the film as a whole, and, beyond that, to all of

Hitchcock's films. The two fundamental features that are distinctive of Hitchcock's montages are the emergent orderliness and a remainder, an element that resists narrativization. In this way montage, as used by Hitchcock, is constantly leading us to conclusions that are themselves partial, hence themselves signs that lead us to still further conclusions.

The paradigmatic figure of the philosopher is the ironic Socrates. What is most characteristic of irony is that one means something other than what one says. Gregory Vlastos quotes Quintilian for the definitive definition of irony. "'Irony,' says Quintilian, is that figure of speech or trope 'in which something contrary to what is said is to be understood'" (21). Vlastos attributes to Socrates the invention of a new form of irony, what Vlastos calls "complex irony." Non-complex irony is akin to sarcasm in being both easily accessible and relatively determined. "That's brilliant" meant to mean "That's stupid" is an example of non-complex irony. Complex irony, on the other hand, both does and does not mean what it says, is and is not always accessible. As Vlastos says, "In 'complex' irony what is said both is and isn't what is meant: its surface content is meant to be true in one sense, false in another" (31). For example, when Socrates says, in the *Euthyphro*, "You, Euthyphro, surely are wise, but I have no wisdom. I should become your pupil" (*Five* 5), his remark is an example of complex irony. First of all, when Socrates makes this claim, Euthyphro takes Socrates literally, clearly does not recognize the irony. He just agrees with Socrates that he has knowledge and Socrates does not. Moreover, even for those who recognize such claims as ironic, that recognition is something initial rather than final. The recognition of the irony is only a beginning of understanding. It may take a lifetime to fully understand the complex irony of these claims.

This sense of irony is more powerful, and gets closer to the truth, than traditional notions of truth. This complex notion of irony preserves complexity in meaning in a way that traditional philosophical ideas of truth, truth as something static, determinate, univocal, do not. This complex form of irony can affirm, simultaneously, the tragedy and the comedy of human experience in this world. Which is nearly to say that the world is itself ironic, or, at least, our experience in it is, and to speak of our experience in the world without using such complex irony is always to say too much or not enough.

Hitchcock has said, "I like to exploit the fine line between comedy and tragedy; I like to take the ordinary and make it extraordinary. I believe in pure cinema" (Bogdanovich 476). I understand Hitchcock to be saying here that it is by means of pure cinema itself that he is able to sustain this balance between comedy and tragedy – that it is by means of pure cinema that he is able to simultaneously show the ordinary and the extraordinary. I understand him to be saying that pure cinema is inherently ironic. I understand him to be saying that his way of thinking and seeing the world is inherently ironic. Robert Frost gives a description of what a man, of what a human being, ought to be, that well captures the man Hitchcock seems to me to be:

The style is the man. Rather say the style is the way the man takes himself; and to be at all charming or even bearable, the way is almost rigidly prescribed. If it is with outer seriousness, it must be with inner humor. If it is with outer humor, it must be with inner seriousness. Neither one alone without the other will do.

(351)

This wisdom is reflected in Hitchcock's style of making movies. Any given movie might be serious or humorous, but his most serious movies have their comic side, and his most comic their tragic side.

That Hitchcock was ironic in some minimal sense seems beyond dispute. There has to be some irony in his claim that there are no symbols in *North by Northwest*, except maybe the last image of the train going through the tunnel, or in saying that *Psycho* (1960) is a "humorous" picture (Bogdanovich 532). On the other hand, is his irony of sufficient complexity to compare with that of Socrates? Does Hitchcock use irony in his thinking in film? Can the use of the camera and montage be ironic? Is there some sense in which Hitchcock cannot *mean* what he *shows*? Or that he can mean something other than or more than what he shows? Or that he can mean and not mean what he shows, as is the nature of complex irony? *North by Northwest* begins with dark lines, moving across a green background, that inscribe a kind of cage-like grid (the arrows in the words of the film's title, north and west, lining up exactly with grid lines) that montages (technically, this is a dissolve, but the effect is an Eisensteinian "collision" that is generative of a new concept) onto a concrete, steel, and glass modern high-rise building. After that comes a series of shots, a montage sequence, of teeming masses of people, first shown walking down a sidewalk and exiting a building, then descending into a subway station, then people crossing a street (with a street sign in the shot reading "No Turns"), then a shot of people descending two stairways inside a building, then a shot of two women fighting over a cab, to Hitchcock's cameo missing a bus, then to inside the office building and to some elevator doors opening to reveal Roger Thornhill with his secretary, moving forward fast and talking fast, amid a throng of people. All of this has Bernard Hermann's frenzied score in the background. That is what we see (and hear). Is there a complex irony communicated in this montage sequence? I think the answer has to be yes.

Why does it have to be yes? On the one hand, the montage sequence shows scenes of busy people in a city rushing from work at the end of their workday. A movie has to start somewhere. Why not there? That the sequence is about a busy city is already more than what is literally shown, and so it has some of the properties of irony, but it would be simple irony, at best, with a relatively specific, determinate meaning.

There are, however, some odd things, remainders, counter-indications to this simple, determinate reading of this opening sequence. One odd thing is the montage from the grid lines on the green background to the gleaming glass office building. What is odd about it is hard to say. Office buildings are places of business. This one, in particular, looks very modern, very expensive, like a place where very successful business people will be doing business at the highest level. The grid against the green background is schematic, dehumanized, cage-like. The two images do not seem to go together, and yet they are put together via montage.

The descent into the subway seems to refer to an almost identical scene, from the same camera angle, in Charlie Chaplin's *Modern Times* (1936) in which people going to work in a giant factory are shown coming out of a subway station. That shot is set up with a shot of a herd of shorn sheep jostling each other along with one black sheep in their midst. So in *Modern Times* it is sheep jostling one another, then people jostling one another coming out of a subway station, then a shot of the giant factory, then a shot inside the factory, with people jostling one another to get to their stations. This is pure montage in the Eisensteinian sense. The collision of these images works our emotions and produces a new concept, a concept not literally contained in any one of the shots. It is a concept that has to do with the dehumanizing social circumstances of "modern times." It is a concept about the way factories full of machines designed to improve human lives end up reducing some human lives to the mindlessly mechanical. Included in this concept, however, is the black sheep, the sign that sticks out, what Slavoj Žižek calls the "anamorphic spot" (88–91), which indicates a counter way for the narrative to go. The whole montage sequence in *Modern Times* is virtually recreated at the beginning of *North by Northwest*.

The irony in *Modern Times* is determinate. There is a pretty direct correlation between the shorn sheep and the workers, the workers and the giant gears of the machinery in the factory. The irony in *North by Northwest* is more subtle and more complex. First of all, one has to get that there may be some irony, get that there may be something more going on. Then, one has to get the specific reference to *Modern Times*. Once one sees that, then the irony is complex indeed. The movie essentially declares itself to be about not just Roger Thornhill and his misadventures, but about modern times, modernity itself. In this updated version, the scene of maximum import has moved from the factory building to the urban high-rise building, but ramifications of and correlations with the factory building get carried over. This complex irony is generative of meanings: the buildings are cages, the people are sheep, it is a state of Darwinian nature in which the strong get the cab, the serious busy-ness of business is not so much different from the mindless busy-ness of working on an assembly line, and about as meaningful.

In Chaplin's *Modern Times* the people are coming out of the subway, at the start of their day. In *North by Northwest* they are descending into the subway, presumably at the end of their work day.[1] It is as though Chaplin's montage in *Modern Times* signals the beginning, the emergence of, modernity in cinema, to which Hitchcock responds by signaling the end of modernity: this is what modernity has brought us to, a whole new level of alienation and self-ignorance. The descent into the subway is then a sign for the decline of the West.

What is the counter-indication, the "anamorphic spot," to this descent narrative in this opening montage sequence? It is the figure of Roger Thornhill himself, in his beautiful gray suit. He glides through the pervasive push and shove of the streets like a dancer. His very presence, the grace and the power of his movements, suggest a counter-narrative to the Darwinian state of nature on the street. It is also quite clear that he is unknown to himself, that his grace and power are directed to no ultimate aim beyond his own puerile self-indulgence. In that is announced (one aspect of) the plot of the movie: the creation of the adult Roger Thornhill.

The anamorphic spot is, in Žižek's Lacanian world, the return of the Real. It is a sign of the real inconsistency of the narrative one has been using to make sense of one's world. Everyone's narrative is always incomplete, or rather, its apparent completeness always covers over the elements that do not fit the narrative, the way the mind fills in the blank spot of the scotoma, the blind spot of the eye. For most of us most of the time, the counter-signs are best left unrecognized. It is the nature of the philosopher to be preoccupied with the counter-signs, to be disturbed by them. To be disturbed by the counter-signs takes a great deal of honesty and courage. It takes a willingness to have one's narratives, one's world, turned upside down. Hitchcock is concerned with the counter-signs, and there are plenty of them to complement Roger Thornhill's apparent success: his insincere relationships with his girlfriends, his dependence on his mother, his drinking, and the ultimate pointlessness of his frenzied rushing. What Roger Thornhill needs is some philosophical direction from a good, ironic, Socratic philosopher, which is exactly what he will get.

In *Shadow of a Doubt* (1943), the film Hitchcock said was his own favorite of all of his films, young Charlie (Teresa Wright) is just such a philosophical figure, with the requisite honesty and courage. The way the process works, however, is that in our first encounters with the countersigns, we resist the re-narrativizing that they suggest. Early in *Shadow of a Doubt*, Charlie, intrigued by the fact that her uncle (Joseph Cotten) has mangled her father's evening paper, tells him that she understands that there is something in the paper that he, Uncle Charlie, is trying to hide. She sees the piece of the paper in his jacket pocket, grabs it, and confronts him with it. Angered, he grabs her by the wrists painfully hard. He gets control of his anger and becomes more mollifying. It is a disturbing experience for young Charlie, but she loves her uncle, accepts his mollifications, and chooses to regard his violent outburst as an aberration.

Later, when the detectives who are searching for the Merry Widow Murderer are snooping around the house posing as journalists doing a story on the average American family, there is a scene in which Charlie is talking with one of the detectives, Jack Graham (Macdonald Carey). The exchange begins by Charlie saying, "You know, your picking us as an average family gave me a funny feeling." Charlie has a lot of funny feelings. She is extremely sensitive, in fact, to anomalies and often has such funny feelings about things that she appears to be almost telepathic. She quite suddenly has another funny feeling about the questions the supposed journalist is asking about Uncle Charlie. She is saying how wonderful he is, but the journalist seems to be pushing the idea that he may not be so wonderful. As she heatedly defends her uncle she unconsciously rubs her wrists where Uncle Charlie had previously grabbed her. Clearly, she is putting that earlier scene together with this scene of questioning by this man, but the inner connection remains occluded to her.

Later that night, after she has spent a very pleasant evening with Graham, there is a wonderful, bizarre montage that begins with them walking along laughing together and then quickly dissolves to a close-up of Charlie's face looking distraught. It is a big emotional jump for the viewer, as it must be for the character of Charlie. She says, "I know what you are really. You're a detective. There's something the matter and you're a detective." She is right about that. She has been working on the signs, consciously and unconsciously. There have been too many counter-signs to the story she was given about these two men being journalists doing a story about an average American family, including signs based on her own experiences with her Uncle Charlie.

When she finally goes to the library to investigate the missing newspaper page she becomes herself "the Hitchcockian hero, 'the [wo]man who knows too much'" (Žižek 88). When she returns home we see the price her knowledge costs her. Her entire home life is re-narrativized. Her mother's idle talk sounds like crazy chatter in the face of the horrific fact of the presence of her murderer uncle. The game her father (Henry Travers) plays with his neighbor Herb Hawkins (Hume Cronyn) of devising murders for each other, of each other, now seems all too horribly close to the truth she sees as a real possibility of the human world she inhabits. Just as the bucolic countryside is converted into a landscape of menace by the counter-turning windmill in *Foreign Correspondent* (1940), so is the Newton household for Charlie when she becomes one who knows too much.

A very interesting contrast with Charlie is her mother, no dupe herself, but no philosopher either. Right after Charlie has almost died in an apparent accident for the second time, we see her mother, Emma Newton (Patricia Collinge), saying to herself, "First the steps, then the garage …?" She is seeing the signs. She is wondering about them. She is not simply ignoring them. She has the sensitivity, the ability to feel something strange, but she is unable to see the pattern, the connecting link that reveals the "orderliness" underlying this disorder. Charlie is able to follow the arguments of the world, to see emerge from the particulars the larger patterns that reveal the truer narratives than the conventional ones that people ordinarily work with. She is able to see extraordinary possibilities in ordinary situations. This is what it takes to be a philosopher, not to mention an artist.

The experiences of Charlie and her mother replicate the experience of watching a Hitchcock movie. As one watches a Hitchcock film one cannot help but begin to wonder whether there might not be something else going on besides the simple plot. The films are so rich with provocative montage that we, as the audience, cannot help but have strange feelings stirred up in us that we cannot completely account for. Frequently these feelings have an aspect of the uncanny, a feeling Freud explains in terms of the return of the repressed. There is something slightly uncanny in the scene of young Charlie defending Uncle Charlie as wonderful to the pushy detective while simultaneously rubbing her wrists that Uncle Charlie had earlier grabbed with such force. What is the Hitchcockian answer – or at least part of his answer – to the question of what returns in the experience of the return of the repressed? It is the return of the signs of the counter-narrative that we are not yet prepared to confront, or are not yet able to see as a consistent alternative narrative.

If Hitchcock's style is so powerfully expressed in his use of montage, what about those films that downplay or eschew montage as far as possible, like *Under Capricorn* (1949) and especially *Rope* (1948)? These films, it seems to me, are his tests of the medium (and, perhaps, of his audience). If Eisenstein and Peirce are right, and the world itself works by a process that is like generative montage, it seems like it might be possible to do a film in which all the power of montage is contained in the mise-en-scène. Hitchcock describes *Rope* as "probably the most exciting picture I've ever directed" ("Exciting" 276). He does not, it seems to me, give up on Eisensteinian generative montage – the putting together of images that conflict, affect, and generate new concepts – in these films; he just attempts to create it in a much more subtle way, so that collisions are created via mise-en-scène. So there is the chest with the body while the people at the party chat. There are the looks between Brandon Shaw (John Dall) and Phillip Morgan (Farley Granger) that we see but the other party guests do not. There is Rupert Cadell (James Stewart) discussing the special moral privileges of the intellectually superior while we observe the form such intellectual arrogance can take. In *Under Capricorn* there is the long take of Lady Henrietta Flusky (Ingrid Bergman) walking barefoot and drunk into the dining room where some of the prominent local men are seated, their wives absent in protest against this very woman – a shot in which a tremendous amount of information is given, none of it explicitly, but generated from collisions of context and behavior, of what is said and not said, looks that are sympathetic and those that are not. Hitchcock himself decided that those films were failures. As he quipped, "films must be cut" (Truffaut 184). But it is not clear that the failure was all his. It is subtle, difficult work for an audience to track all the emergent meanings without the assistance of montage to make them more explicit.

Hitchcock's philosophy is in his style, and his style is his philosophy. His style is to be thoughtful about every detail he encounters, and to think through the details to the arguments they contain, and, through the arguments, to the conclusions they entail. What is discovered is that there is always an emergent unity or orderliness among the divergent parts, just as a melody emerges from the divergent notes. What is also discovered is that within every perceived unity, there are counterindications that suggest still larger patterns that are operative. The way to capture this combination of unity and incompleteness is with the trope – in Hitchcock's case, a visual trope – of complex irony. Complex irony has the wonderful property of simultaneously offering a relatively accessible, determinate narrative and a much less accessible, indeterminate, but generative counter-narrative. This means you can watch a Hitchcock film once and be well-entertained, or you can watch a Hitchcock film dozens of times in an effort to be, in Henry James's phrase, "one … on whom nothing is lost" (13), and be even better entertained. Douchet is right, per my epigraph, that "Hitchcock intends to unveil reality." And the reality Hitchcock unveils is a reality that is infinitely complex, and so infinitely subject to interpretation. Hitchcock does in his philosophical films what the best philosophy has always done. He offers us a vision of how complex a human being can be, and how this greater complexity exists out there like a better, as yet unrealized, but realizable version of our own selves. He critiques the forces of seriousness and unseriousness that oppress us, politically, socially, and personally. He frees us from our caves, and makes us feel how enjoyable such freedom can be. His project is truly Socratic: to create the community of more complicated people amongst whom he would prefer to live. It would also be a community, no doubt, of people who enjoyed a good martini and an eroticized, suspenseful story.

Note

1. My thanks to Tony McRae for the observation of this difference between *Modern Times* and *North by Northwest*.

Works Cited

Bogdanovich, Peter. *Who the Devil Made It*. New York: Knopf, 1997.

Danto, Arthur C. *The Transfiguration of the Commonplace: A Philosophy of Art*. Cambridge: Harvard UP, 1983.

Douchet, Jean. "Hitch and His Public." Trans. Verena Andermatt Conley. *A Hitchcock Reader*. Ed. Marshall Deutelbaum and Leland Poague. Second ed. Chichester, UK: Wiley-Blackwell, 2009. 17–24.

Frost, Robert. *Robert Frost: Poetry and Prose*. Ed. Edward C. Latham and Lawrence Thompson. New York: Holt, Rinehart, and Winston, 1972.

Eisenstein, Sergei. *Film Form: Essays in Film Theory*. Ed. and trans. Jay Leyda. New York: Harcourt, Brace, and World, 1949.

Eisenstein, Sergei. *The Film Sense*. Trans. and ed. Jay Leyda. New York: Harcourt, Brace, and World, 1947.

Gilmore, Richard. "Existence, Reality, and God in Peirce's Metaphysics: The Exquisite Aesthetics of the Real." *Journal of Speculative Philosophy* n.s. 20.4 (2006): 308–19.

Gottlieb, Sidney, ed. *Hitchcock on Hitchcock: Selected Writings and Interviews*. Berkeley: U of California P, 1995.

Hitchcock, Alfred. "My Most Exciting Picture." 1948. Gottlieb 275–84.

Hitchcock, Alfred. "On Style." 1963. Gottlieb 285–302.

James, Henry. *The Future of the Novel: Essays on the Art of Fiction*. Ed. Leon Edel. New York: Vintage, 1956.

Jameson, Fredric. *Postmodernism, Or, The Cultural Logic of Late Capitalism*. Durham: Duke UP, 2001.

Monaco, James. *How to Read a Film: The Art, Technology, Language, History, and Theory of Film and Media*. New York: Oxford UP, 1977.

Nietzsche, Friedrich. *On the Genealogy of Morals and Ecce Homo*. Trans. and ed. Walter Kaufman. New York: Vintage, 1989.

Peirce, Charles Sanders. *Collected Papers of Charles Sanders Peirce*. Ed. Charles Hartshorne and Paul Weiss. 7 vols. Cambridge: Harvard UP, 1931–35.

Plato. *Five Dialogues: Euthyphro, Apology, Crito, Meno, Phaedo*. Second ed. Trans. G.M.A. Grube. Indianapolis: Hackett, 1981.

Rothman, William. *The "I" of the Camera: Essays in Film Criticism, History, and Aesthetics*. Second ed. New York: Cambridge UP, 2004.

Vlastos, Gregory. *Socrates: Ironist and Moral Philosopher*. Ithaca: Cornell UP, 1991.

Žižek, Slavoj. *Looking Awry: An Introduction to Jacques Lacan through Popular Culture*. Cambridge: MIT P, 1997.

27

Hitchcock's Ethics of Suspense: Psychoanalysis and the Devaluation of the Object

Todd McGowan

Psychoanalysis in Suspense

In his interviews with François Truffaut, Alfred Hitchcock famously draws a sharp distinction between surprise and suspense. Surprise occurs when a film confronts spectators with the unexpected and thereby creates a momentary shock, whereas suspense involves confronting them with what they know is coming. Hitchcock insists on the difference between surprise and suspense in order to locate himself as a partisan of the latter and to distinguish his films from what commonly passes for suspense thrillers. As he points out, "There is a distinct difference between 'suspense' and 'surprise,' and yet many pictures continually confuse the two" (73). Hitchcock's justification for opting for suspense over surprise is primarily an economic one. The duration of suspense indicates its worth: if filmmakers keep spectators unaware, they can create "fifteen seconds of *surprise*," but if they inform them of the impending encounter, they can produce "fifteen minutes of *suspense*" (73). By sustaining more spectator investment in the events of the film, suspense produces more arousal than surprise does, even if it appears to pack less of an immediate punch. In the suspenseful situation, spectator enjoyment occurs through an extended experience of absence, whereas surprise locates enjoyment in the moment of presence.

Hitchcock's concern for locating spectator enjoyment in sustained absence rather than in momentary presence underlies his preference for suspense at the expense of surprise. This way of locating enjoyment places him in proximity to the psychoanalytic project. Both Hitchcock's films and psychoanalysis envision our existence as inherently suspenseful and at the same time as lacking in surprise, and they also conceive of the ability to endure suspense as the linchpin of ethical subjectivity. The psychoanalytic process might be seen as the attempt to convince analysands to abandon their faith in the prospect of being surprised. The implicit ethics of the Hitchcock film, like the ethics of psychoanalysis, says something like, "Don't give ground relative to the state of suspense."[1]

Perhaps the most persistent critique of psychoanalysis is its inability to accommodate the possibility of surprise. Psychoanalytic theory identifies a structure – that of the death drive – that underlies and informs our everyday activity, and it interprets variations in this activity as vicissitudes of this drive, not as possible ruptures from it. Since the drive defines subjectivity, there is no possibility of such a rupture and thus no possibility for surprise. The structure of the drive brooks no deviation because it incorporates all deviations within the satisfaction it provides. Jacques Lacan gives this idea a concrete form when he insists, in his *Seminar II*, that "a letter always reaches its destination" (205). That is, even if it follows multiple detours, a subject will always act in a way that procures its satisfaction. This absence of an exit, this occlusion of surprise, becomes the great psychoanalytic lacuna for critics from Karl Popper to Jacques Derrida. According to Derrida, there must be a possibility for dissatisfaction, a possibility written into the fact of satisfaction. As he puts it, "Not that the letter never arrives at its destination, but it belongs to the structure of the letter to be capable, always, of not arriving. And without this threat ... the circuit of the letter would not even have begun" (444). The capacity for a letter not to arrive – the possibility that it might surprise us – escapes Lacan in particular and psychoanalytic theory as a whole, and this oversight stems directly from the privileged place that the drive occupies within psychoanalysis.

The fundamental distinction for psychoanalysis is that of desire and drive.[2] As psychoanalysis theorizes it, the drive is not a biological instinct but the product of the collision between instinct and the social order. This collision creates a subject irreducible to either its biology or its cultural positioning.[3] The subject of the drive necessarily veers off course and encounters an obstacle in the pursuit of its goal, but this obstacle itself becomes the source of its satisfaction. As Joan Copjec notes,

> the death drive achieves its satisfaction by *not* achieving its aim. Moreover, the *inhibition* that prevents the drive from achieving its aim is not understood within Freudian theory to be due to an extrinsic or exterior *obstacle*, but rather as part of the very *activity* of the drive itself.
>
> (30)

The drive repeats the initial loss that founds it when the individual undergoes subjectivization, and the subject derives satisfaction from this repetition. The production of its own obstacles allows the drive to be self-sustaining and to operate outside the constraints of time.[4] It never has to wait on the presence of an object in order to achieve satisfaction but instead finds satisfaction through its own obstacles.

The problem with the subject of the drive is that it always emerges initially as a subject of desire because the confrontation with loss inevitably produces a misunderstanding on the part of the subject. The subject envisions the possibility of the ultimate enjoyment in the recovery of a lost object because it fails to see how the loss of the object has actually created the lost object. Subjects believe, in other words, that they have lost something substantial and that this partial object might be obtained again through the project of desiring. That is to say, they believe in the possibility of being surprised. The subject of desire is a subject with faith that surprise is possible and that the object might appear. But desire is the result of the retrospective illusion created by loss. Though the subject has in fact lost nothing – the loss is formal and has no content – through its subjection to language and the social order, it appears to have lost something. Fueled by this misconception, the subject of desire, in contrast to the subject of the drive, is unsatisfied.

Whereas the drive finds satisfaction through its repeated movement, desire seeks a different form of satisfaction through attaining its object. Desire puts its faith in the future presence of the object, while drive involves the acceptance of the constitutive nature of the object's loss. If the object were not lost, it would no longer be *the* object, as the structure of the drive inherently recognizes.[5] But desire is structured around the impossible goal of sustaining the object as lost and attaining it at the same time. The alternatives between drive and desire overlap each other within the subject, so that even the subject of desire continues to pursue the path of the drive. The serial failures of the subject of desire to attain its object function as the repeated successes of the subject of the drive. The project of psychoanalysis focuses on exposing the subject of the drive obscured by the subject of desire, and this is a project central to Hitchcock's cinema, which is why he insists on suspense with an ethical fervor. This ethical insistence on suspense places Hitchcock in a peculiar relation to mainstream cinema.

Hitchcock Contra the Mainstream

With much justification, most viewers and critics locate Hitchcock among mainstream filmmakers. He made films within the studio system; he confined himself primarily to genre films; his films were always aimed at a popular audience; unlike Sergei Eisenstein or Orson Welles, he was not responsible for any great cinematic innovation; and he never directed what most would call an art film. But what separates Hitchcock from most mainstream cinema and situates him in proximity to psychoanalysis is the way that his films negotiate the relationship between drive and desire. Psychoanalytically speaking, what defines mainstream cinema is its fundamentally ideological contention that desire has an object that can satisfy it. By proffering this claim through all different sorts of narrative and visual structures, mainstream cinema strives to convince spectators that their desires can be fulfilled with available objects and that these objects will remain sublime (and capable of producing enjoyment) even when one attains them.[6] This effort is ideological because it works to reconcile spectators to the social order and to depoliticize their position within that order. In order to function in this way, however, mainstream cinema must hide the evident contradiction underlying its structure: the object cannot be at once accessible and sublime, immanent in the social field and transcendent.

Hitchcock extracts himself from mainstream cinema through his refusal to abide this contradiction by making films that entice spectators with the possibility of accessing the lost object. Despite critical lamentations about its predictability, mainstream cinema is a cinema where surprise rules. Its surprises always involve access to an object that appears impossibly lost: the rediscovery of their "Paris" affections by Rick (Humphrey Bogart) and Ilsa (Ingrid Bergman) at the end of *Casablanca* (Michael Curtiz, 1942); the recovery of the self by the troubled Will Hunting (Matt Damon) at the conclusion of *Good Will Hunting* (Gus Van Sant, 1997); the return of peace to the disturbed community with the final sacrificial gesture of Walt Kowalski (Clint Eastwood) in *Gran Torino* (Clint Eastwood, 2008). What is predictable about mainstream cinema is precisely its ideological commitment to the unpredictable and to the possibility that the future will surprise us. It opts for the hope implicit in desire over the stubborn repetition of the drive and thus locates the spectator's libidinal investment in the ending – in the object of desire that the films finally recover.

The traditional conception of cinematic suspense, as developed by D.W. Griffith and theorized by Noël Carroll, focuses on the outcome of the suspenseful situation. Films create suspense, according to Carroll, through their manipulation of possible outcomes. As he puts it, "suspense in the film generally results when the possible outcomes of the situation set down by the film are such that the outcome which is morally correct in terms of the values inherent in the film is the less likely outcome (or, at least, only as likely as the evil outcome)" (101). Though Carroll allows that Hitchcock's suspense violates his general rule by creating suspense even when the morally incorrect outcome is less likely, this admission fails to register the break that Hitchcock effects between his form of suspense and that developed by Griffith. In a film such as *Way Down East* (1920), spectator desire coalesces, as Carroll's theory suggests, around possible outcomes: either Anna Moore (Lillian Gish) will go over the waterfall and drown or David Bartlett (Richard Barthelmess) will arrive in time and save her. Hitchcock's suspense, in contrast, works to direct the spectator's desire away from the final result. The focus in *Rope* (1948), for instance, is not on whether or not Brandon (John Dall) and Phillip (Farley Granger) will get away with murder but on how they expose their own culpability. When their mentor, Rupert Cadell (James Stewart), discovers their guilt at the end of the film, this denouement does not come as a surprise, nor is it structured as the object of the spectator's desire. Hitchcock eschews surprise because it engages all our desire on the outcome, and he refuses to allow his form of suspense to fall into this same trap.

Hitchcock's celebrated scorn for the whodunit stems from his attempt to turn the emphasis away from the outcome in his films. He tells Truffaut, "I generally avoid this genre because as a rule all of the interest is concentrated in the ending" (74). While watching a whodunit, spectators invest themselves in the solution and identify their satisfaction with the discovery of this solution. In this sense, the whodunit reflects and sustains a desiring subjectivity. The problem with the whodunit – and the problem with the structure of desire as such – is that it never provides the satisfaction that it promises and thus leaves the subject perpetually desiring something else. The ending of the whodunit reveals the solution to the mystery, but this solution is inherently unsatisfying for the spectator because it is not what desire actually desires.

Desire seeks a lost object that remains desirable only insofar as it remains lost. Though we attain many of the objects of our desire, we cannot attain the object that causes our desire; we cannot attain *the* object. This object that causes our desire is, as Lacan puts it in his *Seminar X*, "not only separated but always elided, elsewhere than there where it supports desire, and yet in a profound relationship with it" (291). Whenever we think that we have circumscribed or isolated this object, it escapes us, and we end up with nothing. The solution of the whodunit proffers the illusion of the truly satisfying object, and this is why Hitchcock disdains it for the suspense thriller in which the solution is already known. But even the thriller as it is most commonly conceived and constructed gives too much emphasis to the ending and thereby aligns itself with desire rather than with the drive.

The difficulty for Hitchcock lies in reconciling the repetition of the drive with the generic demands of the thriller. Typically, the thriller depends on the discovery of an object (a murder weapon, a code, secret plans), and this discovery corresponds with the spectator's experience of surprise. It is only a poorly-made thriller that permits an audience to know the hidden object before the denouement. Surprise seems intrinsic to the very functioning of the genre, and Hitchcock himself is responsible for the most celebrated instance of surprise in the genre's history – the shower murder in *Psycho* (1960). This surprise and other prominent ones over Hitchcock's career would appear to reflect an inability to fully adapt the thriller to the logic of the drive.

But even when Hitchcock does resort to surprise, he does so almost always in order to set the stage for a later upsurge of suspense. Just as the initial existence of the subject of desire is necessary for the emergence of the subject of the drive, some initial surprise is often required for the emergence of suspense. This is evident in the case of the murder of Marion Crane (Janet Leigh) in *Psycho* and in the case of the surprising kiss that Francie Stevens (Grace Kelly) gives to John Robie (Cary Grant) in *To Catch a Thief* (1955). The shock of Crane's murder creates in the spectator the expectation of a similar shock that looms over the investigation of Arbogast (Martin Balsam) when he enters the Bates house, and this expectation testifies to the development of suspense out of surprise. In his essay "'In His

Bold Gaze My Ruin Is Writ Large,'" Slavoj Žižek notes, "Hitchcock ... succeeded in intensifying the effect by presenting the second murder as something *expected*" (230). Whereas the murder of Crane takes the spectator by surprise, the murder of Arbogast involves the spectator in an experience of suspense that depends on the earlier surprise. The initial surprise does not function as an end in itself but works to increase the power of the later suspense sequence. A similar process occurs on radically different terrain in *To Catch a Thief*.

In the Truffaut interview, Hitchcock defends his preference for icy women rather than sensual ones because such women sustain "the element of *surprise*" in sex (224, Hitchcock's emphasis). One never knows, he claims, what sexuality the icy exterior hides. Hitchcock proceeds to document Francie's first kiss of John as a moment of surprise where the hidden sexual desire emerges. It is a self-confessed instance of surprise in Hitchcock's cinema. And yet, as is the case in *Psycho*, surprise here serves as a basis for later suspense. Because we know of Francie's desire for John, the moment of their third kiss in the film can play out as an extended suspense sequence in which we know the ultimate conclusion. As John and Francie sit on a couch in her hotel room, Hitchcock cuts between the image of them and the fireworks exploding outside the hotel window, and with each cut back to the couple, they come closer to kissing. As the moment of the kiss becomes nearer, the cuts become more rapid until they finally kiss. Here, Hitchcock prolongs the time before the kiss in order to create suspense, but this suspense relies on the previous surprise kiss, which allows us to know what the result of the suspense sequence will be. Surprise in *To Catch a Thief*, as in *Psycho*, functions as a necessary preliminary to suspense.

By employing surprise in the service of suspense, Hitchcock reveals precisely how the drive emerges out of desire. Even when his recourse to surprise appears indisputable, surprise, despite its central role in the thriller as a genre, is never the endpoint of Hitchcock's filmmaking. The thriller for Hitchcock must eschew surprise as an end in itself and remain faithful to the logic of desire. In order to accomplish this, Hitchcock must systematically devalue the object of desire in his films. The devaluation of the object corresponds to his adherence to the drive, and the different ways that Hitchcock works to devalue the object reveal his attempt to develop a cinema faithful to the drive that psychoanalysis uncovers.

The Empty Object

The type of object for which Hitchcock is most well known reflects perfectly his commitment to the object's devaluation. The MacGuffin is an object that embodies a wealth of apparently significant content but ultimately is important only insofar as it moves the narrative along. In the words of Mladen Dolar, Hitchcock's

MacGuffins "signify only that they signify, they signify signification as such; the actual content is entirely insignificant. They are both at the core of the action and completely irrelevant; the highest degree of meaning – what everybody is after – coincides with an absence of meaning" (45). What the MacGuffin really is doesn't matter, though the entire narrative turns on the pursuit of it. Its appearance of rich content functions as a lure for characters within the narrative and for spectators outside it. This lure acts as an engine for desire but can do nothing to satisfy that desire. The satisfaction must lie elsewhere, and experiencing the role of the MacGuffin as an object allows spectators to recognize this.

In his extended interview with François Truffaut, Hitchcock offers his most succinct and most famous account of the MacGuffin. He tells Truffaut,

> You may be wondering where the term ["MacGuffin"] originated. It might be a Scottish name, taken from a story about two men in a train. One man says, "What's that package up there in the baggage rack?"
> And the other answers, "Oh, that's a MacGuffin."
> The first one asks, "What's a MacGuffin?"
> "Well," the other man says, "it's an apparatus for trapping lions in the Scottish Highlands."
> The first man says, "But there are no lions in the Scottish Highlands," and the other one answers, "Well then, that's no MacGuffin!" So you see that a MacGuffin is actually nothing at all.
>
> (138)

Hitchcock's example of the MacGuffin emphasizes its impossible status: not only is the object that one has never it, but one cannot even isolate it as an idea. It remains necessarily empty, and yet it functions as an engine for the Hitchcockian narrative. The emptiness of the MacGuffin as an object permits spectators to locate their satisfaction in the striving that it unleashes rather than identifying satisfaction with the discovery of its secret.

Hitchcock's MacGuffins deflect attention from themselves onto the desire of the characters in the narrative. Though this object functions as an engine for the narrative, the narrative itself never evinces any concern for its content. Characters stress the importance of recovering it and act in order to do so, but they have no investment – and thus the spectator can have no investment – in what the MacGuffin offers. The libidinal investment of the narrative and the characters always lies elsewhere. Four exemplary MacGuffins are the plans memorized by Mr. Memory (Wylie Watson) in *The 39 Steps* (1935), the tune whistled in *The Lady Vanishes* (1938), the top-secret clause to the treaty in *Foreign Correspondent* (1940), and the microfilm hidden in the statuette in *North by Northwest* (1959). Though each object occupies a structurally crucial position in the narrative, the films devalue each object by giving it little narrative attention. In each case, the characters within the narrative act to retrieve the object, but the films do not permit spectators to invest themselves in it or in its retrieval. Roger Thornhill (Cary Grant), for instance, evinces no satisfaction with the recovery of the microfilm in *North* by *Northwest* because he has no investment in it. Its purely formal role for him gives it a purely formal role for the spectator as well.

The narrative centrality of the MacGuffin helps to produce a desire not oriented around the attainment of its object, which is to say, a desire that has taken on the form of the drive. Through its absence of any content, the MacGuffin naturally facilitates suspense rather than surprise. With the MacGuffin, there is nothing there to surprise the spectator. The emptiness of the MacGuffin reveals the emptiness of the object of desire that most films – and, most often, our lived experience – obscures. Awareness of the emptiness of the object is what allows the subject to pass from desire to drive. The idea of a satisfying object sustains desire and leaves it perpetually dissatisfied, while the drive finds satisfaction in its act of not attaining or failing to attain the object. As Adrian Johnston puts it, "drives come to enjoy the very failure to reach the impossible goal, whereas desire is permanently dissatisfied with the inaccessibility of its goal" (372). Insofar as it remains contentless, the MacGuffin facilitates the enjoyment of the drive that any meaningful object would vitiate.

The Delayed Object

The devaluation of the object is clear when it is a question of the inherently empty MacGuffin. But even when Hitchcock establishes spectator investment in an object, he still manages to devalue it through the way he allows access to it. One prominent way that he does this is by showing the object being attained after the point at which we expect it to be. That is, his films often build suspense around a specific object, and the suspense sequence appears to conclude without the attainment of that object. After a delay and the cessation of suspense, the object finally does appear. This delay has the effect of separating the act of desiring from the object, a separation that reveals the desire itself as essential and the object as merely a contingent occasion for the desire.

This separation of the act of desiring from the object to be attained belongs to the movement from desire to drive. The delay in Hitchcock's suspense devalues the object of desire in order to affirm the subject of the drive. When the object appears to be absent altogether and appears only after the suspense has seemingly ebbed, we can recognize the fundamental unimportance of the object. As with the MacGuffin, the delayed object foregrounds the object's strictly formal role.

The most famous of the delays in Hitchcock's films occurs in *Sabotage* (1936), where Stevie (Desmond Tester) is riding a bus while unknowingly carrying a bomb set to go off at 1:45. By acquainting the spectator with the expected time of the explosion (through showing a note) and constantly cutting back to a ticking clock, Hitchcock establishes the explosion itself as the object of desire in this case.[7] After building suspense, Hitchcock cuts from the bus to the clock with the minute hand moving to 1:46, as if to suggest that the bomb will not explode. It is only after we experience this letdown and assume that the bomb will not go off that it in fact does.

This same delayed effect operates on multiple occasions in the underrated *Topaz* (1969). Midway through the film, a French agent, Philippe Dubois (Roscoe Lee Browne), entices a Cuban secretary, Luis Uribe (Don Randolph), to allow him to photograph the secret Russian plans for Cuba that Cuban leader Rico Parra (John Vernon) has in a briefcase in his hotel room. After Dubois coaxes his way into Parra's room for an interview, Uribe must grab the briefcase and take it back to his own hotel room, where Dubois can meet him to photograph it. During the suspense sequence, Dubois lures Parra onto the balcony in order to take his picture waving to the crowd while Uribe stealthily grabs the briefcase from the hotel room. While Uribe is approaching and seizing the briefcase, Hitchcock shows Parra begin to look into the room and then attempt to return to it, but each time Dubois interrupts him and allows Uribe to escape with the briefcase.

After we see Dubois later enter Uribe's room undetected, the film seems to suggest that they have successfully obtained the plans. But Hitchcock cuts to another sequence in Parra's room that restores the suspense. Parra sits at his desk and works. While doing so, he reaches down and places a paper in a case that was next to the briefcase that Uribe took. As he does this, his face registers that something is wrong, and it appears as if he is on the verge of noticing the missing case. He rises from his desk and looks around the room, where he finds a paper that he was seeking, which he hands to an aide to retype. Again, it seems as if the suspense is over and as if Uribe's theft will go undetected. Parra sits down again at his desk and pours himself a drink. He grabs a key, and we see a close-up of his hand as it reaches for the missing red briefcase and doesn't find it. At this point, he recognizes the deception and goes to Uribe's room, where he discovers Dubois photographing the secret documents. Hitchcock thus delays the conclusion so that we think nothing will happen. Something happens only after we think the danger has passed, not at the height of the suspense.

Toward the end of *Topaz*, Hitchcock structures another suspense scene in the same fashion. Here, two French officials who are spying for the Soviet Union meet and discuss the threat of discovery. Henri Jarré (Philippe Noiret) comes to the house of Jacques Granville (Michel Piccoli) to express his fear that his identity has been compromised, but it is clear from the beginning of the scene that Granville views Jarré, his partner in espionage, as a threat to his own identity and as a danger that he must eliminate. It appears as if he plans on poisoning Jarré when he pushes a drink on his partner. He tells him, "Let me give you something to settle your nerves. A cognac?" Granville then refuses to have a drink himself, stating that he's expecting a guest. At this point, Hitchcock includes a shot of Jarré looking nervously into his drink and saying, "If I'm Devereaux's target now, how long before he will become a threat … to others?" As he says these last words, the film cuts to a shot of Granville, implying that he will be in danger. This seems to signal that Granville is poisoning Jarré in order to save himself, as even Jarré recognizes and articulates.

Jarré looks scared and suggests eliminating André Devereaux (Frederick Stafford). Granville doesn't respond to this idea, but instead urges Jarré to drink. He says, "Now, if you will finish that cognac." Hitchcock cuts to Jarré again looking nervously down into his glass and subsequently drinking. Here, the poisoning appears to occur, and the suspense concerns its effects becoming visible. Noting that his guest is coming, Granville hurries Jarré out, suggesting that he doesn't want the poisoned Jarré to die in his house. But when Jarré walks down the road, nothing happens to him. The entire suspense sequence ends up concluding with a whimper. Or so it seems. Later that night, we see Jarré perfectly healthy at home being interviewed by a journalist. It is only later that Devereaux discovers Jarré's dead body on the roof of a car below his apartment. Even here, Hitchcock initially suggests that the body is that of the journalist until Devereaux turns Jarré's head to reveal his face. Hitchcock creates the expectation that Granville will kill Jarré and then fulfills that expectation. But he does so only after he seems to assure the spectator that Jarré is no longer in danger.

This technique seems to suggest the introduction of surprise into Hitchcockian suspense: the object appears when we no longer expect it rather than when we do. The delayed object necessarily startles the spectator to some extent. But this delayed effect does not represent Hitchcock's attempt to smuggle some surprise back into his suspense and to thrill the spectator with a momentary shock. Instead, it follows directly from his valuing of suspense over surprise. By delaying the appearance of the object, Hitchcock detaches the experience of suspense from its resolution, which suggests that there is, properly speaking, no resolution. There is no moment at which desire has attained its object and can rest easily. Desire is constantly animated in the drive, and satisfaction exists in this constancy rather than in the momentary apprehension of the object.

The Unwanted Object

The object in a Hitchcock film is not always empty and not always delayed. There are times when it appears fully at the moment when the spectator expects to find it. But it is the act of giving spectators the object that they want that marks another of Hitchcock's methods for devaluing the object. That is to say, Hitchcock further devalues the object of desire by providing full access to it. Mainstream cinema functions ideologically not insofar as it simply gives spectators what they want and acquiesces to their desire but insofar as it does so only partially. The mainstream thriller shows the triumph of the hero but not the defeat of the villain; the mainstream romantic comedy depicts the union of the couple but not its aftermath. By refusing to give us fully what we desire, cinema paradoxically sustains the ideological fantasy of wholeness. One can continue to believe in heroic triumphs or in perfect romantic unions because one does not fully see them in a way that would allow their incompletion to become visible. But Hitchcock provides full access to the object of desire: he gives spectators what they want, and in doing so, he reveals the unsatisfying nature of the desired object.

This becomes most apparent in Hitchcock's treatment of the villain. On the one hand, the structure of the thriller almost always culminates with the hero's victory over the villain, a victory that realizes the desire immanent in the thriller's formal structure. But on the other hand, this victory represents not the satisfaction of desire but the elimination of it. Most thrillers work to pass off this disappearance of desire as its fulfillment through their emphasis on the hero's enjoyment of the victory. We see John McClane (Bruce Willis), fresh from the nearly single-handed defeat of a dozen criminals, embrace his formerly estranged spouse, Holly (Bonnie Bedelia), at the conclusion of *Die Hard* (John McTiernan, 1988), and the film presents this scene as the realization of both John's desire and ours as spectators. No Hitchcock film would end with such a complete realization of desire. Such a conclusion would mark a betrayal of the ethics of suspense (and the corresponding ethics of the drive) that Hitchcock develops in his cinema. As a result, his films often end by underlining our libidinal investment in the villain.

As is well known, Hitchcock sees the villain as the key to a film's success. A film without a compelling villain, he thinks, will inevitably fail because it will not capture the spectator's desire. Contrary to what we might initially assume, villains represent the key to our investment in a film because they provide the object that sustains our desire. Most films, of course, mask our libidinal investment in the villain by eliminating the villain in a denouement that focuses attention on the hero. Hitchcock, however, grasps the inextricable link between the villain and the spectator's desire. His suspense sequences often demand that we avow this connection by focusing more directly in their conclusions on the defeat of the villain than the triumph of the hero. By doing so, Hitchcock renders visible the undesirability of attaining the object of desire. We want the villain to be eliminated – this is the object of desire in most thrillers – but we want to want this result, not to see it come to fruition.

The turn toward the villain occurs in many of Hitchcock's films, but it is most pronounced in the conclusions of *Murder!* (1930), *Sabotage*, *Saboteur* (1942), and *Notorious* (1946). In each case, the filmic conclusion renders explicit the spectator's investment in the villain. The ending becomes more the horror of the villain's demise – apparent suicide in *Murder!* and *Sabotage*, a sympathetic downfall in *Saboteur* and *Notorious* – than a celebration of the hero's triumph.[8] As the villain experiences his demise, we experience it with him. We see, for instance, a close-up of the agony of Frank Fry (Norman Lloyd) as he literally hangs by a thread from the Statue of Liberty about to fall to his death. Fry remains the villain, but the filmic structure aligns our desire with him here.[9] The point is not simply that we have the ability to sympathize with the villain, but that the villain is the real locus of our desire. Though we consciously desire the villain's defeat, we sustain an unconscious investment in his continued presence as a creative obstacle. As spectators, we don't want the end that we think we want because we are subjects of the drive who can find satisfaction only in the drive's repeated failures and not in desire's successes. Hitchcock's suspense brings us to the point of glimpsing ourselves immersed in the drive.

The final scene of *Notorious* further demonstrates this pattern. American secret agent T.R. Devlin (Cary Grant) has convinced Alicia Huberman (Ingrid Bergman), the daughter of a prominent Nazi, to marry one of her father's former Nazi friends, Alex Sebastian (Claude Rains), in order to spy on the activities of his ex-Nazi group. After he learns that Alex and his mother (Leopoldine Konstantin) have become aware that Alicia is a spy and that they have been poisoning her, Devlin enters their house to rescue her. As Devlin walks a drugged Alicia out of the house, Sebastian and his mother confront them and attempt to stop their departure. At this point, the film seems to construct suspense according to the standard formula: our desire aligns itself with the hero and the victim trying to triumph over the villain.

However, Hitchcock shoots this scene so as to reveal complications in our desire at the very moment when we would expect our desire to become the most unambiguous. Because Alex and his mother have slowly poisoned Alicia and because of their Nazi allegiances, they fully occupy the villainous position. And when they enter the scene, they appear as a threatening force. The scene introduces Alex by cutting from a shot of Devlin and Alicia walking toward the stairs to leave the house to a shot of Alex coming up the stairs to stop their departure. When Alex confronts the couple, the threat that he represents for them becomes clear. But after establishing this opposition between Devlin and Alicia on the one side and Alex on the other, Hitchcock cuts to a long shot looking down the stairs in which we see one of Alex's fellow Nazi conspirators walk forward and say to Alex, "What's happening here?" It is clear that the Nazi colleague is growing suspicious of Alicia and Devlin, and we know that Alex would face execution if his colleagues learned that he had married an American spy. Given the angle of this shot and the effect that it creates, we can surmise that it comes from Alex's point of view. It highlights Alex's vulnerability. The shot is one of the most important in the film because it enacts a fundamental transformation of desire in this scene, dividing our desire between the couple and Alex.

We invest our desire in Alex at this point as a result of the threat that his colleague manifests toward him. Whereas until the entrance of the colleague Alex was the sole threat, this event introduces an additional threat, a threat that actually forms an antagonism with the earlier threat. It is not simply that there are multiple threats in the scene, but that the threat is at the same time threatened, placing the spectator in an impossible position. We want to see Alex and his mother punished for their attempt to murder Alicia (and for their Nazism), and yet at the same time we identify with them as potential victims of Nazi cruelty. As the scene unfolds, Hitchcock emphasizes the antagonism: as the four walk down the stairs toward the front door, we see alternating close-ups of Devlin and Alicia together, Alex, and Alex's mother. The film cuts from a close-up revealing Alex's anxiety to a long shot of the group of Nazis now assembled at the bottom of the stairs. Alex's behavior in this scene further induces us to invest our desire in his situation. We see him distracted and unable to respond to the simple questions of his colleagues. But Hitchcock's attempt to direct our desire toward Alex reaches its high point at the end of the scene, which ends the film as well.

When Devlin, Alicia, and Alex walk through the front door and arrive at Devlin's car, Devlin and Alex help the ailing Alicia into the car, and then Devlin slides into the driver's seat. As he does, the camera pans toward the lock button on the passenger-side door. We see a close-up of Devlin's hand locking the door and thereby leaving Alex to face the Nazi group and certain death. This close-up provides spectators with what they want in its full traumatic force. Throughout the film, we believe that we desire the demise of Alex and his mother, but when it comes, our desire aligns itself with them rather than against them. The film concludes by forcing us to experience a desire we don't want – our investment in the Nazis (Alex and his mother) about to be put to death. It thereby reveals the underlying nature of every desire: every desire is a desire that we don't want. The film ends with a tracking shot that follows Alex to the front door of his house and the awaiting Nazi group, and as Alex enters, the door closes on the camera, leaving the spectator on the outside with the certain knowledge of Alex's impending death. This final shot reveals that our desire can find no happy resolution.

As the example of *Notorious* suggests, Hitchcock constructs his suspenseful situations with an aim toward emphasizing antagonism rather than reconciliation. These situations include oppositions, but oppositions that cannot be reconciled with each other. They place us as spectators into the position of the desiring subject with the divided loyalties that come with that position. The villain is not simply a character to be despised, but also a source of attraction and sympathy, even at the moment when he becomes the most threatening. At the highpoint of Hitchcockian suspense, our desire becomes in part aligned with the villainous force and therefore divided against itself. In this way, Hitchcock departs dramatically from the kind of suspense developed by Griffith, where our attitude toward the villain can remain unambiguous throughout. Our alignment with the villain in Hitchcock's films is part of his overall project, which works to deprive the spectator of any potentially satisfying object. In order to find Hitchcock's films enjoyable, one must look elsewhere than in the objects that they provide.

The Disruptive Object

If the notion that Hitchcock devalues the object is hard to swallow, it is because his films seem so emphatically to privilege objects. In Hitchcock's films, objects stick out, like the tea label in *The Lady Vanishes,* the ring in *Shadow of a Doubt* (1943), the lighter in *Strangers on a Train* (1951), and the necktie in *Frenzy* (1972).

But even in the instances where Hitchcock highlights and privileges the object, the object's importance lies in what it tells us about the order of the world rather than in some intrinsic value. The Hitchcockian object that sticks out and arrests our attention demarcates a rupture in the order of the world and thereby reveals that our world – either natural or social – is not whole.

The protruding object reveals the limit of the world and in the process interrupts the attempt to discover meaning in that world. In *Looking Awry*, Slavoj Žižek notes how

> the fundamental constituent of the Hitchcockian universe is the so-called "spot": the stain upon which reality revolves, passes over into the real, the mysterious detail that "sticks out," that does not "fit" into the symbolic network of reality and that, as such, indicates that "something is amiss."
>
> (116)

The object is an indicator that there is a hitch in the functioning of the world, a disruption that acts as an ultimate barrier to our desire at the same time as it mobilizes our desire. It marks not the realization of desire but its interruption. As the indication that we cannot realize our desire, the protruding object is essential to Hitchcock's development of an ethics of suspense. It demands that we abandon the promise of desire for the repetition of the drive, though Hitchcock often depicts this object by arousing the spectator's desire for it.

Near the end of *Young and Innocent* (1937), Robert Tisdall (Derrick De Marney) and Erica Burgoyne (Nova Pilbeam) are searching at the Grand Hotel for the actual murderer of Christine Clay (Pamela Carme) in order to exculpate Robert, who has been falsely accused. Their only clue as to the identity of this man is that he suffers from an uncontrollable facial twitch. As the scene begins, a crane shot surveys the hotel restaurant and dance floor, before turning to the band playing, where it finally centers on the drummer (George Curzon). The shot moves in on the drummer's face in an extreme close-up, and when just his eyes are visible in the shot, they begin to twitch.

Here, the movement of the crane shot manifests the desire of the characters in the film and the spectator as it travels toward its object, the twitching eyes, but when the camera finally arrives at its object, it evinces the disjunction between the object and the surrounding world. Hitchcock's use of the extreme close-up to conclude the crane shot effects this separation.[10] In the same way, the reverse tracking shot down the stairs the tracking camera had just climbed in *Frenzy* makes clear the incongruity of the object that the shot encounters. In this case, the murder we imagine taking place behind the closed door at the top of the stairs seems utterly out of place within the normal world to which the camera subsequently retreats. The emphasis of both the crane shot in *Young and Innocent* and the tracking shot in *Frenzy* is on the disjunction between the object and what surrounds it. The object cannot realize desire because it remains irreducible to the framework in which desire manifests itself.

The windmill in *Foreign Correspondent* functions like the twitching eyes in *Young and Innocent*. As Huntley Haverstock, né Johnny Jones (Joel McCrea), looks for the car he has been chasing, which has mysteriously disappeared, he sees his hat blowing in the wind and a windmill turning in the opposite direction. The windmill sticks out because it appears to violate the order of nature. According to Pascal Bonitzer, "the whole fiction of *Foreign Correspondent* was based upon the idea of a windmill whose sails turned in the opposite direction to the wind. The-object-which-makes-a-stain is thus, literally speaking, an object which goes against nature. The object in question invariably shows up against the background of a natural nature – of a nature that is, as it were, too natural" (21). This object that sticks out of the natural world identifies the object that Haverstock seeks – the wrongly-turning windmill houses the car that he has been following and functions as a base for the agents who have kidnapped the diplomat Van Meer (Albert Bassermann) – but it also marks the impossibility of attaining this object. Though Haverstock does ultimately find Van Meer and thwart the fascist plot, the windmill represents a barrier that no one can overcome insofar as it reveals the ontological disconnection between desire and its object: the object exists on a different ontological plane than the desire that seeks it. The windmill makes evident the limit of the natural order and the impossibility of realizing desire within that order.

The obtrusive object that disrupts the order of the world becomes most apparent in *The Birds* (1963). In this film, the birds do not function as a symbol to be interpreted but as a fundamental barrier to meaning. As Lee Edelman puts it in *No Future*, "Hitchcock's birds, in the specificity of their embodiment, resist, both within and without the film, hermeneutic determination" (135). The film offers no legible meaning for the birds' attack, and even metaphorical readings collapse through their sheer proliferation. Because the birds might represent everything from ecological disaster to familial strife, they come to represent nothing, and it is through signifying nothing or an absence of meaning that they produce suspense in the film. Though Melanie Daniels (Tippi Hedren), Mitch Brenner (Rod Taylor), and Mitch's family might escape from the birds, neither they nor the spectator can figure out what the birds want or what motivates their attacks. The birds are an opaque presence in the film that testifies to the object's resistance to any signifying structure.

The irony of *The Birds* is that the flocks of birds become a natural object that derails the natural order. To put them in the terms of Pascal Bonitzer, the birds are Hitchcock's most extreme version of "an object which goes against nature." Hitchcock chooses a natural entity as this object in order to show that even the natural order derails itself. Even if we could exist as entirely natural beings, *The Birds* suggests, we would nonetheless encounter a barrier to realizing our desire. Insofar as it has the capacity to derail itself, the natural order is not a possible arena for the realization of desire. Hitchcock's film attests to the impossibility of returning to nature because there is no natural nature to which to return.

The disruptive and obtrusive objects in Hitchcock's films ultimately make apparent the object's unimportance in Hitchcock's world. Hitchcock forces us as spectators to stumble over objects, a process that illustrates what objects do *not* provide. The disruption that the object occasions reveals that one cannot attain the object. The protruding object remains at the end of a suspense sequence – as the birds remain, surveying the Brenner retreat, at the end of *The Birds* – in order to make clear that there can be no ultimate reconciliation of desire in the world. Satisfaction must lie in the movement of the drive rather than in the successful attainment of the object. Satisfaction must always remain in suspense.[11]

The Inexistent Object

Hitchcock's most explicitly psychoanalytic films – and the ones that have attracted the most attention from psychoanalytic film theorists – are those in which he takes the devaluation of the object to the point of revealing the object's inexistence. This is the case with the great films of the 1950s and early 1960s, in which the object of desire becomes exposed as a copy or a fraud that does not correspond to any original. The object attracts our desire because it appears to embody a substantiality that we can access, but Hitchcock's films lay the object bare in order to show that it is nothing but the power of our desire. What appears to be an object becomes revealed as the product of a desire that seeks an object, as Hitchcock's films from *Rear Window* (1954) to *Psycho* demonstrate.[12] In this way, they further develop the ethic of suspense that marks his entire career.

The inexistence of the object takes different forms in each of the films of this period. Though *Rear Window* initially casts doubt on the existence of the object (a murderer across the courtyard), it eventually appears to confirm its tangible presence when the private investigation that L.B. Jefferies (James Stewart) conducts allows him to ascertain the guilt of Lars Thorwald (Raymond Burr). Jeff's – and the spectator's – desire seems to find an object adequate to it as Thorwald himself comes to Jeff's apartment and implicitly admits to his guilt. But this admission is accompanied by a question about Jeff's own desire. As he provides an answer to Jeff's desire, Thorwald confronts it with a question in return, and this question reveals the reflexivity of desire itself.

When Thorwald assaults Jeff at the conclusion of the film, he confronts Jeff with the question of what Jeff wants from him. Hitchcock shoots their encounter in a way that flips the entire trajectory of the narrative. As Thorwald enters Jeff's apartment, we see a close-up of his face with light illuminating his eyes in the darkness. The subsequent reverse long shot of Jeff near the window in his wheelchair shows him completely in shadow. Here, Thorwald is desiring while Jeff is the inscrutable object. Thorwald asks him, "What do you want from me? Your friend, the girl, could have turned me in. Why didn't she? What is it you want? A lot of money? I don't have a lot of money. Say something. Say something. Tell me what you want." Though Jeff has sought to understand Thorwald throughout the film, this encounter reveals that there is nothing substantial to seek, which is why Thorwald merely reflects Jeff's own desire back to him. It is only when Thorwald leaves the terrain of pure desire to ask Jeff about a specific object (his wife's ring) that Jeff can offer a response to Thorwald's incessant questions. Thorwald forces Jeff to confront his own desire, which means that the mystery that Jeff discovers across the courtyard is nothing but the mystery of his own desire. His desire is its own object.[13]

The great revelation of the inexistence of the object occurs in *Vertigo* (1958), where Scottie (James Stewart) desires and falls in love with a woman, Madeleine Elster (Kim Novak), whose very existence is in question. After trailing and rescuing Madeleine from almost drowning, Scottie begins a relationship with her that apparently ends with her jumping to her death from a bell tower. This suicide, however, is part of an elaborate ruse organized by Gavin Elster (Tom Helmore), who hired Scottie to follow a woman playing his wife, Madeleine, whom he murdered just before the fake Madeleine pretended to jump. When Scottie mourns Madeleine's death and pines for his lost object, he mourns an object that never existed except as a lure for his desire. As he later spots Judy Barton (Kim Novak) on the street and notices her uncanny resemblance to Madeleine, he takes her as a promising substitute for his original love. Ultimately, however, his attempt to make this substitute into a perfect copy of the original leads him to discover that the apparent original was in turn only a substitute wife whose performance as Madeleine was staged exclusively for his benefit. Here, Hitchcock reveals that the lost object around which all our desire is oriented exists only as the result of misperception on our part. Our desire originates with an object that emerges only through its loss, an object that has no substantial existence.[14] As *Vertigo* shows, there is no lost object to recover, even though the lost object animates our desire.

A similar missing object animates *North by Northwest*, though the consequences are not nearly so tragic for the characters involved. Roger Thornhill becomes entangled in an espionage ring when spies take him for the agent George Kaplan. Thornhill spends much of the film trying to extricate himself from the ring by finding the real George Kaplan. After constructing the figure of Kaplan as an engine for the spectator's desire, Hitchcock subsequently reveals that Kaplan does not exist. American intelligence officials created Kaplan as a fiction to draw suspicion away from their actual undercover agent, and the foreign spies mistake Thornhill for this figure that doesn't exist. Thornhill's search for Kaplan necessarily founders because his object exists only as a fiction.[15]

Psycho organizes the spectator's desire around a missing object – the body of Mrs. Bates. While watching the film, we hear Mrs. Bates's voice but never see it clearly attached to a speaking body within the image. It operates as what Michel Chion calls an *acousmêtre*, which is a voice "'offscreen,' outside the image, and at the same time *in* the image: the loudspeaker that's actually its source is located behind the image in the movie theater. It's as if the voice were wandering along the surface, *at once inside and outside,* seeking a place to settle. Especially when a film hasn't yet shown what body this voice normally inhabits" (23). An *acousmêtre* is a voice that one cannot localize in the image, a voice that resists clear delineation. As such, this voice inaugurates desire. Chion notes that "it is the law of every offscreen voice to create this desire to go and see who's speaking, even if it's the most minor character (provided that the voice has the potential to be included into the image; it can't be the disengaged voice of commentary)" (141). When we hear the *acousmêtre,* desire forms around the impossible object – the object not included in the image – that is its source.

The fundamental desire that animates *Psycho* concerns localizing the voice of Mrs. Bates. We first hear this voice unattached when Mrs. Bates upbraids Norman (Anthony Perkins) for his idea of inviting Marion Crane to dinner. As we watch Marion hide the money she has stolen in her motel room, we hear the voice of Mrs. Bates from a distance proclaiming, "No, I tell you no. I won't have you bringing strange young girls in for supper ... by candlelight, I suppose, in the cheap erotic fashion of young men with cheap erotic minds." Even as the film cuts away from Marion to the origin of this voice, we see only a long shot of the house that contains it and a light in the bedroom – not even a shadow of the figure speaking. The film sustains this disconnection between the voice and the speaking body until its conclusion: we never hear Mrs. Bates speaking when we see her face, nor do we ever obtain a complete view of her body. This absence has the effect of focusing desire on the absent body of Mrs. Bates.

The final image of Norman sitting in the jail cell as we hear the voice of Mrs. Bates finally localizes the wandering voice. Here, the voiceover of Mrs. Bates's voice represents Norman's internal monologue, allowing us to recognize at last the origin of this mysterious voice. However, the film localizes the voice in a foreign body (Norman's) and in this way reveals that the object to which we might attach the voice does not exist. The suspense that the *acousmêtre* triggers finds its resolution in the image of Norman speaking, but this resolution highlights the object's inexistence. The missing object that animates suspense throughout the film turns out to have no substantial content. It is nothing but an aspect of Norman's psyche. One watches *Psycho* waiting for the body to which one might attach the wandering voice, and Hitchcock ends the film by showing that one only has the voice itself. As spectators, we must find satisfaction in the voice and not in the substantial body that it appears to promise. Through this insistence on the enjoyment of the voice without the body, *Psycho* continues the ethics of suspense that begins even in Hitchcock's silent films.

In order to be a suspense filmmaker, one must evince an interest in objects. By subtracting an object from the narrative universe, the filmmaker creates suspense around this object. Most filmmakers center the spectator's attention on the possibility of the object's recovery or its salvation. Will the Klan arrive in time to save the Cameron family at the conclusion of D.W. Griffith's *The Birth of a Nation*

(1915)? Will Indiana Jones (Harrison Ford) recover the Ark of the Covenant in *Raiders of the Lost Ark* (Steven Spielberg, 1981)? Will Jason Bourne (Matt Damon) discover the secret of his past in *The Bourne Ultimatum* (Paul Greengrass, 2007)? And so on. In each case, spectator engagement in the film depends on spectator investment in the missing object, whether it is material or psychic. But if Hitchcock is the master of suspense, it is because he departs violently from the essence of traditional suspense. Hitchcock's films allow us to locate our satisfaction not in the missing object but in our repeated acts of missing it. He is the suspense filmmaker for whom the object as such has no importance, and this indifference toward the object holds the secret to his ability to arouse the partisans of psychoanalysis, who rightly see in it the indication of a profound kinship.

Notes

1. In his *Seminar VII*, subtitled "The Ethics of Psychoanalysis," Jacques Lacan offers as a mantra for the ethical position that psychoanalysis demands a similar formula: "the only thing of which one can be guilty is of having given ground relative to one's desire" (319).
2. Though Freud himself never explicitly articulates the importance of the distinction between desire and drive, he envisions the analytic cure as giving up the idea that the ultimate satisfaction exists elsewhere, which is the attitude of desiring subjectivity.
3. The two opposed heresies in psychoanalysis are thus naturalism, which reduces the psyche to its biology, and culturalism, which reduces it to its societal conditioning.
4. In the *Four Fundamental Concepts of Psychoanalysis*, Lacan says, "The constancy of thrust forbids any assimilation of the drive to a biological function, which always has a rhythm. The first thing Freud says about the drive is, if I may put it this way, that it has no day or night, no spring or autumn, no rise and fall. It is a constant force" (165).
5. Lacan christens the lost object that causes desire the *objet petit a*. He insists on this term rather than "object of desire" because, although the *objet petit a* arouses desire, no subject can ever attain it. This distinction between the *objet petit a* and the object of desire allows Lacan to theorize the difference between drive and desire. Desire comes to name the act of mistaking the object of desire for the *objet petit a*.
6. For a fuller account of how mainstream cinema functions ideologically, see McGowan 113–59.
7. Hitchcock constantly places the spectator in the position of desiring the evil outcome, as with the bomb explosion in *Sabotage*. This pattern becomes especially apparent in *Psycho*, where Hitchcock aligns the spectator with Norman Bates (Anthony Perkins) in his efforts to cover up the murder of Marion Crane by cleaning the motel room and submerging her car in a swamp. The ultimate moment of identification with Norman's cover-up occurs when the car stops sinking, an event that appears to thwart his efforts.
8. Alenka Zupančič contends that the end of *Murder!* not only draws attention to the villain but goes so far as to portray the villain as the ethical center of the film. The suicidal act of Handel Fane (Esme Percy) that concludes the film rises to the status of an ethical act, in Kant's sense of the term, that dwarfs the presence of the film's hero Sir John (Herbert Marshall). At the end of the film, according to Zupančič, "Sir John emerges as nothing but Fane's pale shadow" (98).

9. The contrast between the endings of *Saboteur* and *Die Hard* is so striking that it suggests that the latter consciously alludes to the former. Like Fry, villain Hans Gruber (Alan Rickman) is hanging on precariously and about to fall from a great height. In contrast to Fry, however, Gruber is trying to pull Holly to her death instead of simply trying to save himself. When John unclasps her watch, which Gruber is holding on to, and thereby causes him to fall to his death, the film emphasizes the rescue of Holly rather than the demise of Gruber, who remains a threat until he begins to fall. McTiernan shoots a conclusion very similar to that of *Saboteur* that nonetheless completely rejects the earlier film's turn toward the villain.

10. In his *Theory of Film*, Béla Balázs notes – and this is later taken up by Gilles Deleuze – that the close-up isolates the face from the space that surrounds it. He claims, "Facing an isolated face takes us out of space, our consciousness of space is cut out and we find ourselves in another dimension: that of physiognomy" (61).

11. Gilles Deleuze contends that "in Hitchcock, actions, affections, perceptions, all is interpretation, from beginning to end" (200). The problem with this formulation is that Hitchcock's inclusion of the protruding object highlights what remains irreducible to interpretation. The hermeneutic project in Hitchcock's films always encounters a barrier that testifies to the limit of interpretation (which is simultaneously the limit of desire). This object stands out as a refusal of sense.

12. The exception is *The Wrong Man* (1956), which cannot demonstrate the inexistence of the object because the film's hero, Manny Balestrero (Henry Fonda), never appears as a desiring subject. Balestrero's complete innocence reflects a psychotic inability to desire. As Renata Salecl notes, "The truth behind his perfect image is not a simple weakness, but psychotic indifference manifested in the total absence of guilt – the ominous and uncanny character of his 'inner peace of mind' becomes palpable in the scenes where Manny, as indifferently as he reacted to his own misfortune, observes Rose's outbursts of madness with an impassive eye" (189–190).

13. As Miran Božovič explains, "Thorwald's window gazes back at him differently from any other because Jeff sees it in a different way: in it, there is something that intrigues him, something that all other windows lack, something that is 'in the window more than the window itself' and has always been of concern to him – in short, the object-cause of his desire. *Faced with this window, Jeff can see himself only as the subject of desire*" (169).

14. *Vertigo* not only shows that the initial object does not exist, but it also illustrates that in the process of performing as Scottie's object Madeleine gives the actual Judy more substance than she otherwise would have. The performance has a creative power. As Robin Wood notes, "in a sense, it is Madeleine who is the more 'real' of the two, since in Madeleine all kinds of potentialities completely hidden in Judy find expression" (123).

15. Though Kaplan as an object does not exist, the signifier "Kaplan" nonetheless has profound effects on the narrative. According to Raymond Bellour's reading of the film, this name functions as the paternal metaphor that makes possible the various relations in the film. He says, "Kaplan's name intervenes as the differentiating term that structures the imaginary according to the symbolic. It is, *par excellence*, the object = x defined as the phallus, always lacking and always in excess, which never ceases to be missing from its place, and which articulates out of this lack the structural series of the narrative" (105).

Works Cited

Balázs, Béla. *Theory of the Film: Character and Growth of a New Art.* Trans. Edith Bone. New York: Dover, 1970.

Bellour, Raymond. *The Analysis of Film.* Ed. Constance Penley. Bloomington: Indiana UP, 2000.

Bonitzer, Pascal. "Hitchcockian Suspense." Žižek, *Everything* 15–30.

Božovič, Miran. "The Man Behind His Own Retina." Žižek, *Everything* 161–77.

Carroll, Noël. *Theorizing the Moving Image.* Cambridge: Cambridge UP, 1996.

Chion, Michel. *The Voice in Cinema.* Trans. Claudia Gorbman. New York: Columbia UP, 1999.

Copjec, Joan. *Imagine There's No Woman: Ethics and Sublimation.* Cambridge: MIT P, 2002.

Deleuze, Gilles. *Cinema 1: The Movement-Image.* Trans. Hugh Tomlinson and Barbara Habberjam. London: Athlone, 1992.

Derrida, Jacques. *The Post Card: From Socrates to Freud and Beyond.* Trans. Alan Bass. Chicago: U of Chicago P, 1987.

Dolar, Mladen. "Hitchcock's Objects." Žižek, *Everything* 31–46.

Edelman, Lee. *No Future: Queer Theory and the Death Drive.* Durham: Duke UP, 2004.

Johnston, Adrian. *Time Driven: Metapsychology and the Splitting of the Drive.* Evanston: Northwestern UP, 2005.

Lacan, Jacques. *The Four Fundamental Concepts of Psychoanalysis.* Trans. Alan Sheridan. Ed. Jacques-Alain Miller. New York: Norton, 1978.

Lacan, Jacques. *Le Séminaire, livre X: L'angoisse, 1962–1963.* Ed. Jacques-Alain Miller. Paris: Seuil, 2004.

Lacan, Jacques. *The Seminar of Jacques Lacan, Book II: The Ego in Freud's Theory and in the Technique of Psychoanalysis, 1954–1955.* Trans. Sylvana Tomaselli. Ed. Jacques-Alain Miller. New York: Norton, 1991.

Lacan, Jacques. *The Seminar of Jacques Lacan, Book VII: The Ethics of Psychoanalysis, 1959–1960.* Trans. Dennis Porter. Ed. Jacques-Alain Miller. New York: Norton, 1992.

McGowan, Todd. *The Real Gaze: Film Theory After Lacan.* Albany: SUNY P, 2007.

Salecl, Renata. "The Right Man and the Wrong Woman." Žižek, *Everything* 185–94.

Truffaut, François, with the collaboration of Helen G. Scott. *Hitchcock.* Rev. ed. New York: Simon and Schuster, 1984.

Wood, Robin. *Hitchcock's Films Revisited.* Rev. ed. New York: Columbia UP, 2002.

Žižek, Slavoj, ed. *Everything You Always Wanted to Know about Lacan (But Were Afraid to Ask Hitchcock).* New York: Verso, 1992.

Žižek, Slavoj. "'In His Bold Gaze My Ruin Is Writ Large.'" Žižek, *Everything* 211–72.

Žižek, Slavoj. *Looking Awry: An Introduction to Jacques Lacan through Popular Culture.* Cambridge: MIT P, 1991.

Zupančič, Alenka. "A Perfect Place to Die: Theatre in Hitchcock's Films." Žižek, *Everything* 73–105.

28

Occasions of Sin: The Forgotten Cigarette Lighter and Other Moral Accidents in Hitchcock

George Toles

> As we read, we throw aside the trammels of civilization, the flimsy veil of humanity. *"Off, you lendings!"* The wild beast resumes its sway within us, we feel like hunting animals, and as the hound starts in his sleep and rushes on the chase in fancy, the heart rouses itself in its native lair, and utters a wild cry of joy, at being restored once more to freedom and lawless, unrestrained impulses. Every one has his full swing, or goes to the Devil his own way.
>
> William Hazlitt, *On the Pleasure of Hating* (107)

We have had many decades to absorb the Catholic problems (chief among them the rigors of Jansenism and the transfer of guilt) that Claude Chabrol and Eric Rohmer elegantly formulated in their landmark study of the "first forty-four" Hitchcock films. But we may not have sufficiently considered the implications of the claim they casually insert at the conclusion of their *Rear Window* chapter: "Hitchcock may be a moralist, but there is nothing of the moralizer about him" (128). Perhaps the director's perspective on his characters (including the viewer, who is invariably the hidden central character) is neither cynical nor judgmental, merely disappointed. And this disappointment comes out of an awareness that any represented crime or guilt or shame is already imaginatively Hitchcock's own. He addresses us, where sin is concerned, as a man who knows "too little" instead of too much. By forgiving his viewers in advance for their absolutely predictable failures of vision and imagination, Hitchcock reveals that no one is more

A Companion to Alfred Hitchcock, First Edition. Edited by Thomas Leitch and Leland Poague.
© 2011 Thomas Leitch and Leland Poague. Published 2011 by Blackwell Publishing Ltd.

in need of clemency, and less likely to deserve it, than the "master" he fearfully, presumptuously pretends to be.

For Rohmer and Chabrol, steeped in Catholic theology, Hitchcock does not have to moralize in individual cases because he accepts the reality and ubiquity of original sin. Since no one can be free of guilt, Hitchcock is never obliged to reproach characters for the deplorable state in which he typically finds them. Rohmer and Chabrol declare that for Hitchcock (and themselves) the "heart of man is 'hollow and a sink of iniquity'" (128). Because there can be no goodness without infusions of divine grace, it is futile to expect characters to become heroic by their own efforts. Yet for Rohmer and Chabrol, the cardinal virtue in a Hitchcock film is "exigence," which means, among other things, "that we can never be too hard on ourselves" (128). The singular ethical obligation is that we imitate, however haltingly and imperfectly, the sacrificial gesture of Christ.

Though Rohmer and Chabrol are alive to the ways in which we may vicariously participate in the crimes of Hitchcock characters and delight in our own disreputable desires, we do not seem enjoined to inquire into our individual moral and emotional experience as spectators. Where ethics are concerned, we are bound to a "one size fits all" Archetypal Sinner's vision. The differences among particular viewers' ways of partaking, being enticed, and trapped seem almost irrelevant. Consider the following description of L.B. Jefferies's inadequate response to Lisa's kisses in *Rear Window* (1954). The photographer's failing is implicitly tied to every spectator's inability to find the proper balance between erotic and spiritual love.

> Hitchcock is not a censor of the flesh but of the desire whose constitutive vice is to feed on itself and forget the love which must serve as its base. The world he denounces is, on the contrary, the hypocritical world of Victorian society. If the hungry kisses with which Grace Kelly covers James Stewart's bored face have something obscene about them, it is because the photographer, whose impotence is not so much physical as moral, is incapable of replying to them with equal ardor. In short, each of the characters – protagonists or those playing a minor role – is enclosed not only in the cell of his apartment, but in the stubborn satisfaction of something which when seen externally, partially, and from afar can only appear ludicrous.
>
> (126–27)

It is hard to reconcile the idea of Hitchcock "denouncing" Victorian hypocrisy with Rohmer and Chabrol's insistence that he does not moralize. What are we to make of Grace Kelly's "obscene" kisses and their capacity to expose James Stewart's moral impotence? The viewing distance in this representative passage is too far back for us to consider how the critics might "share" Stewart's culpability. Slipping away from their declared identity as fellow sinners with kindred human frailties, they render a "moralizing" judgment that they regard as appropriate for the offense. When the "ludicrous" *Rear Window* cell-dwellers arrive at a moment of recognition that is not foolhardy or morally deficient (say, in their response to the woman's outcry against her neighbors' callousness after her dog is killed), the chastened voyeurs briefly enter a circle of lucid guilt in which each "drinks the cup of his egoism down to the lees" (127). Rohmer and Chabrol go on to acknowledge that they too are egoists, "severely" and appropriately "scourged" by the director for an abstract, depersonalized, incurable proneness to self-aggrandizing sin (128), but their confession seems mechanical, lacking in conviction. The pose of confession is the reflex of a "serious" Catholic believer, something one can avow without giving anything personally incriminating away. For all Rohmer and Chabrol's emphasis on guilty participation in a Hitchcock narrative, I can think of no instance when they are emotionally or morally disoriented in their own response to a Hitchcock scene. They never lose their bearings or the security of their moral knowledge. They are not so "surprised" by sin that they fall into it (giddily or unthinkingly) the way so many Hitchcock characters do.

Robin Wood's seminal *Hitchcock's Films* (1965) sets out to provide a less dogmatic, more flexible account of Hitchcockian morality than the *Cahiers*-based French critics achieved. He describes Hitchcock's moral sense as "disconcerting" because "good and evil are seen to be so interwoven as to be virtually inseparable" (67). Hitchcock also "insists on the existence of evil impulses in all of us" and makes us "aware, perhaps not quite at a conscious level (it depends on the spectator), of the impurity of our own desires" (67). There is nothing in this characterization of Hitchcock's moral thinking that Chabrol, Rohmer, or Jean Douchet would take issue with, though Wood draws his value scheme from an exacting F.R. Leavis humanism rather than a Catholic acceptance of original sin. For Leavis, "seriousness" about life is essential to any major work of art. Instead of embracing an orthodox Christian preoccupation with patterns of redemption and sacrifice, Wood advocates with Leavis an art that ultimately embodies (as opposed to merely endorsing) "positive values." A work's aesthetic significance depends on how it achieves "affirmation through its feeling for and commitment to 'life'" (42). In the 1989 edition of his book, Wood quotes one of F.R. Leavis's favorite passages from D.H. Lawrence to describe how criticism, "properly handled," can best function. These two sentences nicely exemplify the whole process of morality "in motion," the testing flux of one's sympathies as one takes something in, or not: "It is the way our sympathy flows and recoils that really determines our lives. [The novel] can lead the sympathetic consciousness into new places, and away in recoil from things gone dead" (43).

I owe an enormous debt to Wood for first showing me in the 1960s what it means to fully submit to the demands of a complex scene. He demonstrated how one could see in a general way what was going on without actually having an experience of a scene's art or its life. One can easily miss the chance for genuine, sometimes hazardous, involvement and more easily still miss the summons to respond as a whole person. Wood knows that we must always be attuned to the details in an authentic exchange with art and patient in our discoveries of what is being asked of us. Equally deserving of patience is the working through of the feelings that images generate in their specific relation to the values of the spectator. Feelings and values may well fail to coincide, and on occasion be fruitfully at odds with

each other. Most impressive of all for me was Wood's refusal to artificially reconcile or sort out narrative passages where contradictory responses are in play. He
recommends that we strive to hold two separate, often opposite, ideas in our heads
at once. An especially memorable example of this salutary divided response
appears in his reading of the ending of *The Birds* (1963):

> The mother's cradling of Melanie in her arms and the shot of their interlocking
> hands: is it a gesture of acceptance (hence creative and fertile) or a new manifesta-
> tion of maternal possessiveness? Melanie's broken condition: does it represent the
> possibility of development into true womanhood, or a final relapse into infantile
> dependence? All these questions are left open: if we demand a resolution of them we
> have missed the whole tone and temper of the film.

(172)

What Wood does not do in his moral readings of Hitchcock is reveal how the
succession of acts of partial identification while watching the films and the sorts
of internalized delinquency and excess that flow from them put pressure on the
ethical ideals to which he subscribes and throw his own coherence as a moral being
into disarray. He does not, in other words, acknowledge the "wild beast resuming
its sway within us" that is William Hazlitt's model of the reader, the beast that
secretly releases us from the restraints of law and decency.

Charles Altieri has described the process of identification in a fashion that cuts
it loose from Wood's reliance on ethical accountability. According to Altieri, our
reading or viewing self need not worry about its own integrity or sufficiency as
we experience "the kinds of satisfactions" that occur when our desires "hook
onto what they seek" at a given moment (135). It is not a matter of gathering
oneself together as a viewer, but of recognizing how we are productively dis-
persed, as the involved mind "intensifies" while "finding places for its [chaotic]
energies" (135). As we try to reconstruct our viewing experience after the fact, it
is crucial that we acknowledge and try to reckon with the full extent of our dis-
persal. "Often what matters about feelings is the resistance they give to the terms
belief provides" (165). Wood often approaches such a position, but finally wants
to adjudicate matters so as to favor a suitably capacious rational belief. For Altieri,
the moral self, like the emotional self, is "expressed" and "reformed" as it "make[s]
all the turns and twists necessary to stay connected with where [identifications,
fantasies, disruptive desires] might lead it" (136). "[I]dentification is not a process
of comparing states [from an outside vantage point] to see which ones actually
belong to me. It is more like a process of extending the self by deciding that this
mode of activity engages me to take responsibility for it because of who I become
during the time I am engaged in it." We can be taken by surprise, and then, as we
fitfully regain presence of mind, find "how [our feelings are] modified by the
occasion, no matter what our [prior] vision of character [or proper conduct]" (139).
Altieri seems to hope for an "expansive turbulence" as we connect with images.
How else are we likely to lose ourselves? In a rather heedless manner, we try to

organize our "involvedness" with a fiction while being caught up in it. But we are not up to the demands of this labor, and for that we should be grateful.

We don't experience a Hitchcock film as the figure we know ourselves to be in advance – someone with sensible values ready to hand, which can be consulted and imposed on a narrative to some degree "foreign" to us. Rather we are "deformed" and "reformed" after giving our "I" the slip in the viewing process, drifting away from our professed affiliations in a fashion that our consciousness need not monitor. Robin Wood believes that what he terms the "lure of irresponsibility" is something directors and ethically sophisticated viewers alike do well to avoid. I would argue, instead, that all consequential moral engagement with film demands that we hazard the perils and unseemly pleasures of irresponsibility.

With *Dial M for Murder* (1954), for example, we might assume from reading a plot summary that viewers would be consistently opposed to the plans of Tony Wendice (Ray Milland) to have Swann (Anthony Dawson) kill Margot, Tony's wife. After all, Margot is not only warmly sympathetic from the outset, even in her handling of her adulterous relationship, but she is played by Grace Kelly. And yet the actual experience of following the seedy, somewhat repellent Swann into the darkened apartment to carry out Tony's elaborate instructions begins to "disrupt" the logic of identification in a morally "irresponsible" way that becomes ever more disorienting as the murder sequence proceeds. (Hitchcock's concern with "putting the audience through it" always depends on the lure of dubious attachments.) We can readily turn into Swann, for a brief interval, as we nervously wonder whether he (we) can remember all the meticulous counsels and warnings that Tony patiently laid out for him. Breaking into a stranger's home, especially at someone else's behest and against "our" will, can be a daunting, fearsome proposition. It is always enticing in movies to affiliate ourselves with the completion of a challenging task. We can split ourselves, without undue strain, between anxiety over the welfare of sleeping Margot, unaware of the murderous trespasser moving about in her apartment, and Swann's efforts to become adjusted to the menacing, unfamiliar terrain of the living room. We may share his puzzlement and relief at the presence of an incongruously cheery blaze bidding him welcome from the fireplace.

When we cut to Tony at his club, we can instantly partake of his apprehension over the fact that his watch has stopped without his having noticed. As Mark Halliday (Robert Cummings), the romantic rival who has been conducting an affair with Margot, gives Tony the correct time (and it is clear that the cold-hearted schemer is less late for his crucial phone call to waken Margot than he had feared), we may be grateful to Mark for improving Tony's chances of success in his crime. Hitchcock makes us worry that the suddenly confused and fearful Swann will assume that the plan has broken down and will rashly leave his assigned post behind the curtains before Tony manages to place his scheduled call. The call that we find ourselves "rooting for" is one that we know, in another sector of our consciousness, will cue Margot's strangling. We do not knowingly embrace the desire to see Margot assaulted, but we may temporarily forget about our "safe" sympathy for her as other identification claims intervene and briefly take hold of us. We may not be certain that we want Tony to place his call on time until he encounters the obstacle of an elderly gentleman occupying the single available phone booth. At that instant, Tony's desperate impatience and need to control his agitation become ours, and it suddenly feels a matter of the greatest urgency that Tony solve the problem facing us. Hitchcock's mammoth close-up of Tony's finger dialing the number once the old man has cleared the way highlights the fact that this is a moment of moral choice for the viewer as well. It is the point of no return. The viewer collaborates with Tony by willing his finger forward in a kind of blank exhilaration.

We somehow balance our desire that Margot be spared against our immense relief that Swann has not quite made it out the door before the telephone ring brings him back and allows Tony's elaborate scenario to proceed. Only when the light goes on in Margot's bedroom do we recall that she is our primary identification: an appealing but sexualized prospective victim. Perhaps we can blend sympathy at this juncture with prurient attention to her nightgown. In any case, as she walks, half-asleep, toward the phone, we readily choose her welfare over the suddenly sinister Swann's. But still another turn awaits us when she arrives at the position designated for her death. Swann stands poised behind her ready to take action, yet he seems, in both his physical stance and agitated expression, comically ill-prepared for the job at hand – a silly amateur, a bungler, obviously no match for the now comparatively alert Margot, who seems to rise above the danger looming just a foot or two to her rear. We may grant Swann a little assistance here by choosing the moment for him to spring forward and figure out how he might best get his fabric around her neck without getting entangled with the telephone. We might credit ourselves as well with the capacity for greater calm and focus than Swann displays were we in a similar predicament. It is possible that we are also mildly resentful of Margot for not being more attentive to so "open" a threat. Why does she allow herself to be a victim? When Swann does take the plunge, he becomes far more deadly and savage than we had anticipated, so we turn against him decisively and revise our attitude toward him so that it has always been antagonistic. We are now eager for him to be thwarted in his aim and will experience unalloyed satisfaction if he is not only defeated but destroyed.

It is conceivable, of course, that not every viewer enters these identification "traps" in the sequence I've indicated, or with an equally intense involvement. My description of the participation channels available and even likely in the episode is meant to clarify the idea of spectator fragmentation. We venture into ethical territory as moviegoers not by locating the most responsible position for appraising others' wrongdoing, but by being drawn into a series of "wrong" places ourselves. How does (should) our moral sense operate when we become equally intimate with everyone's colliding investments of energy and self-absorption in a manner that resists sorting? Our certainty that a given action is heinous and unjustifiable does not make our reading of ourselves in relation to it any simpler. We must undergo a degree of deformation as watchers first if our subsequent desire to see Margot save her innocent self by stabbing Swann with a pair of scissors is to amount to anything.

In what is perhaps the most moving and edifying paragraph on the challenge of Hitchcockian morality that any critic has yet given us, William Rothman ushers us into the real mystery at the heart of all of the director's work:

> *Murder!*, like every Hitchcock film, presents itself to us as a mystery, akin to the mystery of murder and the mystery of love. It declares itself to be no more mysterious, but also no less, than we are to ourselves. Its mystery is the mystery of our own being as creatures who are fated to be born, to love, to kill, to create, to destroy, and to die in a world in which we are at every moment alone even as we are joined in a human community that knows no tangible sign, a world we did not create and yet for which we are responsible. Or we might say that a film is made and viewed and a life is lived; yet both pass before us like dreams.
>
> (105)

I shall now offer a reading of Hitchcock's *Strangers on a Train* (1951) whose focus is on what I call moral accidents in the film, nearly all of which involve the plotted movement of a cigarette lighter owned by Guy Haines (Farley Granger). We tend to think of Hitchcock's control of his narratives as so rigorous that our moral experience of them will have a similarly determined character. Hitchcock knows, we have often been told, what moral decisions and dilemmas will confront his characters and how his imagined viewers are likely to relate to them. My insistence on the accidental or contingent nature of our moral participation in a Hitchcock film builds on my assumption that the telling moral moments purposely lack the clarity of the director's plot points. The visible moral framework in most Hitchcock films appears to confirm the sufficiency of conventional attitudes and the inescapability of familiar social and ethical judgments. But this framework is, more often than not, an elaborate decoy. The real ethical occasions awaiting us in a Hitchcock narrative are designed for awkward mental occupancy. They are not a good, natural fit, and why should they be? They possess, in contrast to social norms, an indefiniteness that is tantalizing and aggravating by turns. Hitchcock arranges his obscure testing places as mundane, initially reassuring sites that are somehow misted over. He intends that we stumble our way into them. We didn't mean to arrive at this moment in this fashion; our mind was elsewhere, half-wandering.

The question for the Hitchcock spectator is always what becomes of us when we are distracted (the condition, after all, of most living), when we mean no harm, when interest of a certain kind and degree happens to befall us. It's unfortunate that at the time of this befalling we are nearly always unprepared to think about it more clearly. These accidents are over (thankfully) before we have had adequate opportunity to dwell on them, to consider what precisely they have to do with us. They are occasions of sin in a fuller, more mystifying sense than the Catholic criticism of Rohmer and Chabrol managed to account for.

At the amusement park climax of *Strangers on a Train*, an elderly man operating a merry-go-round is accidentally shot by a policeman. His intended target was the film's "innocent" protagonist, Guy Haines. As the operator topples to the ground and presumably dies, he extends the accident by pushing down the lever controlling the merry-go-round, causing it to accelerate to an alarming speed. A second old man, perhaps the work partner of the first, emerges from the crowd, volunteering for the dangerous task of crawling beneath the rider-heavy merry-go-round to reverse the lever and bring the whirligig to a halt. He accomplishes his goal expertly, displaying admirable poise and mettle throughout. As a result of his heroic action, the merry-go-round collapses. It is impossible to determine how many riders have been killed or seriously injured. Besides, the viewer is distracted at this juncture by the dramatically more pressing question of whether Guy will successfully retrieve a lost cigarette lighter from his sinister double, Bruno Anthony (Robert Walker).

In the conceptual space between the two matching elderly amusement park operators and the double accident lies the cigarette lighter, which somehow replaces them as a locus of moral thought. The two men, respectively victim and hero, cancel each other out. The lighter is what permits the action to break free of this potential blankness and go forward, providing in the process a saving focus and a curiously charged ethical significance. In its taut relation to the chaotic energy surrounding it, the lighter achieves the characteristic form of Hitchcock morality, and perhaps its slippery substance as well.

The opening sequence of the film places great emphasis on a formal pattern that firmly ordains Guy's first meeting with Bruno even though the meeting itself is, strictly speaking, an accident. Hitchcock requires us to think of the movements of the two men, from the moment of their separate taxicab arrivals at Union Station, as yoked together somehow, and headed irresistibly for contact. The visual rhythm and close matching of mirroring shots in the opening montage invite us to regard the portions of the men that we are shown – carefully pressed, tailored pants and immaculate shoes – as progressing unwittingly toward an already fixed destination: the meeting point forecast in the film's title. We are urged to concentrate, for the sake of comparison, on the details of the men's below-the-waist appearances (most notably, flashy wingtips vs. conservative brogans) and the items of luggage and gestures of service that accompany the pair in transit.

All this preliminary detective work is justified by our swift grasp of the idea that the two men belong together, that we have strong if as yet unrevealed reasons to consider them in terms of each other. Before we came along, Hitchcock implies, a kinship of some special significance had been developed in their separate spheres of life, and it is our task to guess, from the visual pattern laid out for us, what the nature of that pre-existing connection might be. Even when we break away briefly from our trailing of the men's movements through the station to a train's-eye view of the tracks to indicate that a journey is now underway, the tracks themselves in their crisscross overlapping continue the language of symmetry: "like" things are brought together and form a single entity with one path and purpose. This shot dissolves into a train compartment where the men's feet complete their seductive search for the assigned dance partner. The as yet anonymous feet select seats for their respective owners facing one another. The more conservatively dressed man's leg, in the act of crossing, seems to hover indefinitely in the air for a moment, and then his shoe extends itself to touch the shoe of the man sitting across from him. The shoe's gesture slightly suggests a hand politely reaching out to tap a fellow passenger's arm or shoulder.

When Bruno, the man who has been touched, suddenly acquires a face and, by further chance, recognizes Guy as a tennis celebrity, he feels entitled to initiate conversation with him. The two men, once named and seen "whole," immediately take on the appearance of free agents who have met in this fashion without calculation or any clear advance notion of what their coming into contact might accomplish. Once Hitchcock inserts the idea of accident into the midst of his rigorous formal arrangements, what opportunity is there for contingency to interrupt the flow of determinism and make its own presence felt? As Bruno works himself up to proposing an exchange of murders with this "perfect stranger," our preliminary positive assessment of Guy's character is qualified by flickering suggestions of shadiness and culpability behind his affable social mask. Nevertheless, we may well decide by the end of their exchange that Guy has not been troublingly implicated in Bruno's dark thoughts. He has been a polite, occasionally stimulated audience for Bruno's wild tales and proposals, but he gives little sense of taking Bruno seriously, or giving his "murder plot" serious consideration.

Two small gestures in their scene together – one at the beginning, the other at the end – might, in spite of our commonsense evaluation of what has taken place, prompt us to consider the possibility of Guy's collusion at some sly, unvoiced, subterranean level. We can regard both gestures as unequivocally accidental. And yet Hitchcock's handling of them urges us to linger over these accidents and wonder about the likelihood of a hidden purpose. These gestures seem linked to the deterministic flow of the opening, which seemed to exclude any hint of contingency. The first is the shoe touching, which instigates their conversation. Can Hitchcock's visual pattern induce us to believe that Guy's foot instinctively knows what it is doing when it reaches out to brush against Bruno's? Is Guy's body ahead of his mind in signaling a readiness for Bruno's enamored attention and his subsequent malevolent offer? At the conclusion of their talk, after Guy gives Bruno strong behavioral cues that he is merely humoring him and has declined further involvement with his scheme, Guy leaves his cigarette lighter behind in Bruno's private compartment. Does Hitchcock want us to regard Guy's forgetting of his lighter as sheer absent-mindedness, or as a veiled declaration of sympathy with and tacit encouragement of a psychological double?

From the moment Bruno catches sight of the lighter, he strives, perhaps madly, to interpret it as a coded message from Guy. He swiftly, smilingly infers that Guy has relinquished it deliberately, as a secret handshake and pledge. Is Bruno's view of the lighter's significance utterly mistaken? Given our growing awareness of Bruno's psychopathic proclivities and our judgment that he is oblivious to Guy's amused, patronizing dismissal, we have sufficient grounds to decide that Bruno is making something out of nothing. Yet Hitchcock is no more prepared to let go of this seemingly negligible object than Bruno is. He will structure the film's entire narrative around the lighter's itinerary, as it weaves its way by a tortuous, murder-lit route back to Guy's possession. Or almost possession: Guy's and the spectator's last view of the lighter occurs when Bruno involuntarily opens his hand to reveal it in the act of dying.

One way of holding on to the accidental dimension of the lighter being left in Bruno's keeping is to regard the object as a mere plot device. We can readily categorize the lighter as among Hitchcock's many "MacGuffins." A MacGuffin is an arbitrary something which is of great concern to the characters in a story, but whose precise significance is of only slight concern to the viewer. The MacGuffin object – for example, spy plans – is a resonant blank, like the "O" that stands for nothing and fills the space of Roger Thornhill's middle name in *North by Northwest* (1959). I am not satisfied with this tidy method of curtailing the moral importance and expressive force of the lighter. If Guy's forsaking of the lighter is reduced to pure chance – an act in which volition and accountability play no part – then his emotional complicity in the killing of his wife, Miriam (Laura Elliott), is wiped out. He becomes, simply and hollowly, a victim of circumstance. To grant him this reliable status deprives him of any weight or suggestiveness in the elaborate system of doubling that, like the lighter, looms large in the film's opening sequence and establishes a dense network of imagery that parallels the lighter's journey through the narrative.

For Bruno to function meaningfully as Guy's double, there must be core affinities between their characters. They need to be bound together inwardly to an even greater extent than they are bound by the machinations of the external plot. The double-spawning protagonist, whether in the spectral tales of German Romanticism or the amnesia-saturated world of film noir, is not required to acknowledge, comprehend, or actively embrace the affinities he encounters in his secret sharer. But as the double's story proceeds, the topography on which his split figure moves acquires a volatile, dreamlike shiftiness. The man-with-a-double's capacity to hold fast to personal boundaries and oases of clear intention is treacherously impaired. What once seemed safely sequestered in a knowable and private inner life has somehow leaked outside, where it confronts us in the guise of an alien personage – formidable, slippery, menacing, opaque, yet peculiarly intimate as well. For Bruno to expand, with the shadowing double's license, until he has infiltrated every recess of Guy's psychological terrain, Guy must at some stage say yes to him. He must collaborate, at least in his thoughts, in the act of self-division. In mentally summoning Bruno, Guy will cross a line indicating that Bruno's subterranean services are indeed acceptable: "after one's own heart," as it were.

The line that Guy Haines crosses in Bruno's private train compartment, barely perceptible at the time of its occurrence but adequate to forge a binding pact with

Bruno, is his perverse desire to have Bruno make off with his lighter. It is an action that Guy might idly fantasize without having to witness or explicitly sanction. If Bruno wishes, he can pocket the lighter after Guy's departure – that is, once his back is turned. Guy will not have performed a visible, incriminating act in over-looking his lighter. This gesture has a beautiful air of latency, of a vagrant, mischievous thought that can flare to life in another's possession.

Whatever links to sin the carelessly abandoned lighter insinuates exist solely at the level of thought. The most compelling use of objects in movies is to make characters' thoughts and feelings visible. In a Hitchcock film, the viewers' thoughts, aligned with a character's, may tilt in a certain iniquitous direction. As they do so, a material sign emerges to focus them sharply, giving form and solidity to their otherwise ephemeral existence. The thoughts that most fascinate Hitchcock, whether they sprout up in his characters or (better still) his projected audience, are those that might turn out to be sins. If it is possible, as Catholic theology affirms, to sin not only in words and deeds, but with equal opprobrium in our thoughts, then there is no reason why movies could not afford a ripe and sticky occasion for this third, most impalpable mode of sinning. Hitchcock can pass contagious, half-formed thoughts from his own outward-looking, pattern-making consciousness – where images compose and follow each other in the clear, light, quick manner of vivid external impressions – to the more inward-looking, vulnerable consciousness of the viewer. We viewers complete Hitchcock's thoughts by attending closely to his images.

As we absorb these thought-pictures, the most arresting may prick us or spread within us like an ink blot. They may lodge in us as our own thoughts, even if we began by "borrowing" them, and we can potentially become "guilty parties" in our means of pursuing and elaborating them. The thought transfer is as subtle and difficult to pin down as Guy's reason for losing track of his lighter. A little space of awareness bids welcome to an unsavory impulse. The mind soon enough passes beyond that space as if leaving a room, disavowing its fleeting decision to linger there and traffic in the inadmissible. But suppose this flashing impulse sets off kindred vibrations in other sectors of consciousness and these vibrations prove strong enough to form an alliance. The thought that keeps echoing wants to verify its presence and demands closer attention. A literal object can be a kind of shorthand representation of the thought and all the associations that have accrued to it. The object is a material reference point for the amplifying thought, and a receipt for its first emergence. Think of the cigarette lighter as such a receipt: firm, compact, ready to hand.

The lighter belongs to Guy, who has received it as a lover's gift that he may not quite deserve. The lighter also belongs to Hitchcock, who covertly passes it to the viewer as something to notice in a manner that resembles in its deviousness Guy's "thoughtless" delivery of the lighter to Bruno. We are like Bruno in our subsequent use of the thought-object we have picked up after Hitchcock leaves it for us. Bruno takes the lighter to be Guy's clearest expression of authorization for Bruno to proceed with his ideas. After stalking Guy's wife in the amusement park, he will illuminate her face with the lighter just before strangling her. He ignites this flame in part so that he will see her by Guy's light before laying hands on her. As viewers, we employ Hitchcock's borrowed lighter as though it were our permission to transgress freely, Bruno-style, in our looking and thinking and emotional participation. As long as it is Hitchcock's lighter, not ours, we are exempt from the obligation to dwell uneasily on where mere thinking leads us.

The viewer becomes Hitchcock's cavalier emissary and agent, unwrapping his own sordid fantasies by the light of the director's images. But there is no automatic consequence for such indulgence. We can tell ourselves that we are doing what we are supposed to do with the images, that we are simply honoring, again like Bruno, someone else's wishes and implicit instructions. The authority for any giddy thought crimes in the movie's amusement park cannot fairly be traced back to us. No crime we witness is our crime, it is borrowed from someone else. We can participate vicariously or we can simply watch. It all comes down to what we might, in our real and bogus innocence, call the thoughtless simplicity of watching.

Julien Gracq, arguing for literature's incontestable superiority to film in the matter of graduated, shaded vision, notes that the "sensory distribution," in its assimilation of movie images, is "strictly egalitarian" or monocular:

> To grasp this singularity [and hence the superiority of written images to those photographed], just imagine a cinema where, alongside a scene unfolding right in the optical field, other scenes or landscapes, related or different, would be vaguely and simultaneously perceived, in secret or in lost profile, from the corner of the eye – now anticipating the future, now revisiting the past, and always qualifying, neutralizing, or reinforcing the scenes being played out on the main screen. This domain of margins distractedly but effectively perceived, this domain of the corner of the eye – in order to compensate for other infirmities, such as less dramatic efficiency, less of a sense of the present, the elastic vagueness proper to images born of literature – accounts for almost all the superiority of written fiction.
>
> (287)

Hitchcock's invariably cunning deployment of visual form, which aims for a productive ongoing tension with the surface story and its declared values, corresponds in many respects to Gracq's "domain of the corner of the eye." While the visual patterns Hitchcock elaborates are certainly noticeable – at times, as in the beginning of *Strangers on a Train*, so conspicuous as to be unavoidable – they recede from prominence as character and plot concerns move to the viewing foreground. Emotional interest more naturally flows toward character and conflict than it does toward rhyming images. The viewer is meant to be aware, but only lightly, glancingly, of formal devices and the continuing repetitions that punctuate and intensify character busyness. Hitchcock's play with form has an "elastic vagueness" of exactly the same sort that Gracq celebrates in literature. His patterns dwell on the optical margin, "distractedly but effectively perceived."

Gracq's "lost profile" conjures up the famous Hitchcock line-drawing self-portrait that introduces each episode of his television series, *Alfred Hitchcock Presents* (later *The Alfred Hitchcock Hour*). Hitchcock images often seem to give us the profile of something elusive but naggingly familiar, something powerfully glimpsed a short time ago but now most likely estranged from us. The lost image is like a shadow of something that briefly arrested our attention before its place in our mind was quickly usurped, "written over," by something else. Hitchcock emphatically does not want his images to prompt a full, rational accounting. He would rather have them "tease us out of thought" than reinforce those portions of his story that are emotionally and morally definite. The cigarette lighter, in its various manifestations, serves as a model Hitchcock image. We are never in doubt about what we're looking at or what its normative, automatic associations are. It never tries to elevate itself portentously to the status of a symbol, a metaphor in cement shoes. But as it craves to repeat and return in the narrative, as it becomes wittily rather than anxiously overdetermined, it gradually drives us away from a stable frame of reference. The more we look at it, the more it invites speculation, but we are never pressed to settle what it means. It opens up possibilities without coaxing us to bear down on them. We can always let the lighter go, allowing it to be reabsorbed by its present-moment plot function.

We do find ourselves periodically moving closer to it emotionally, most noticeably perhaps when Bruno attempts to retrieve it through the sewer grate. We are at such times briefly caught in a cage with it, through Hitchcock's montage and hypnotic emphasis, and we may be led to project thoughts and feelings onto it that seem "natural" and beyond our control. As with other key Hitchcock images, we remain on the hook with it long and intensely enough to be smudged or dirtied by contact.

We are given an opportunity, when Bruno is first handed the lighter in the train compartment, to examine it in close-up from his point of view. How might it first appear as we share the perspective of his shrewd gaze? Almost all the offers in Guy and Bruno's "getting acquainted" talk come from Bruno ("I'd do anything for you, Guy"). The lighter, shared by Guy early on when Bruno is unable to locate a match, is Guy's only tangible offering. He hands it over readily and seems curiously unconcerned, at any point in their lengthy discussion, about retrieving it. Bruno pronounces the lighter "elegant," then correctly identifies it as a gift of some value. Inscribed on the lighter is a camouflaged declaration of love: "A to G." The letters hint at a depth of affection that the gift giver is reluctant to express directly. A pair of crossed tennis rackets alludes to Guy's profession and transforms the rackets into an emblem of enduring attachment. Though Anne Morton (Ruth Roman), Guy's current lover, has no personal connection to tennis, she wittily insinuates herself into the game by her choice of the crossed rackets, and suggests by her "crisscross" that she is, or would very much like to be, in successful competition with his earlier commitments. In both career and marriage prospects, Guy can exchange tennis for something better.

Bruno swiftly deciphers Anne's secret message to Guy, claiming to have learned all about this well-fixed Senator's daughter and her relationship with Guy from the "society pages." But the larger task of interpreting the lighter's message to Bruno from Guy will take up the rest of the narrative. It is not, of course, Guy's conscious intention to re-gift the lighter to Bruno. Even if we are determined to find Guy guilty of some form of thought crime, we might reasonably conclude that he is at this point merely eager to have the legal loose ends of his relationship with Miriam cleared up and out of the way. Although she is a vexing embarrassment to him, to be sure, and someone who can easily rouse him to rage, he is still confident that she is willing to grant him a divorce. We can more profitably wonder what Guy's care-lessness with the lighter reveals about his new relationship with Anne. His action implies that there is already something stale and disingenuous about his dealings with his replacement lover. The fact that the lighter drifts so quickly from his atten-tion intimates that the woman who gave it to him has a meager hold on his heart.

Miriam and Anne become interestingly entangled here. The one that he wishes to be rid of and the one that he has recently taken up are alike dispensable, throwaway figures. In Anne's case he can rely on social forms and a self-deceiving habit of manipulation to do the work of loving. In some respects Anne matches Guy in cold-ness, and she exhibits a distress bordering on fear whenever he is forced in her pres-ence to answer accusations that others have brought against him. The gift lighter, beneath its surface riddle of romantic declaration, contains a second layer of equivo-cation and withholding. Guy is a man spoken for who has not fully or convincingly committed himself. Anne's reduction of their names to initials says, on the one hand, "we both know who the letters belong to and what they mean" and, on the other, more beseechingly, "fill me and yourself in, carry us further toward defini-tion. You will have to light the fire, Guy, if the residual barriers between us are to be removed, if the residual stranger (in you, in me) is to become an intimate."

As Bruno, left alone with the lighter, leans back in his seat and scrutinizes it, he softly repeats the word "crisscross." The sight of the tennis rackets no doubt pro-vokes the utterance, yielding a satisfying image for him of the murder swap, but the word serves equally well to confirm for Bruno the appropriateness of the lighter passing from Guy's hand to his. "A" gave a gift to "G" as an avowal of love and a cunning attempt to solicit a reciprocal response. The "G" to "A" return-of-serve was not forthcoming, at least not in a binding form. For Bruno, since Guy left the not yet precious gift in his care, he has, in effect, readdressed it: "G" to "B." The original letters were arbitrary place markers, subject to reversal and revision. Crisscross. Bruno does not regard the lighter he now holds as a solid proof of Guy's attachment to him. He rather conceives it, perhaps accurately, as a pleas-ingly indefinite overture. "The gift will be more fully yours, Bruno, when you have done something to make yourself worthy of it. Neither Miriam nor Anne has yet secured my love. The lighter is my invitation to you to divine and answer my needs. I cannot (or will not) tell you what those needs are. If the name blazoned on your tie clip is to replace these vague initials on my lighter, you must discover where my heart is and show it to me."

Patricia Highsmith, author of the 1950 novel *Strangers on a Train*, describes in one of her late stories "the flaw of life" as "a long, mistaken shutting of the heart" (417). Guy's lighter, an elegantly sealed container for an unstruck flame, embodies this basic flaw in Guy's character. What saves the film version of *Strangers on a Train* from being an intricately heartless virtuoso exercise is Bruno's lavish perseverance in seeking to win Guy's emotional acknowledgment and if possible his love. Bruno's major aspiration, as he proceeds to murder Guy's wife without a firm agreement in place, is to furnish unassailable proof to Guy of how well he knows him and how much he is prepared to do to strengthen their friendship. Nearly all of the emotion in the film is generated by Bruno's mad quest to woo Guy with the lures of danger, drastic excess, and irresponsibility. Bruno is repeatedly rebuffed, of course, but he responds with courtly disappointment. He is not patient by nature, but for Guy's sake he will try. Now and then Bruno's fuming momentarily gives way to surprising gusts of tenderness.

Guy's relationship with Anne Morton and her family seem peculiarly afflicted by the malaise of smiling aloofness, an incapacity – even when honestly discussing his difficulties – to open himself up. With Miriam, in contrast, Guy is unable to contain himself. But even in his outbursts of anger and self-aggrandizing frustration, he can't seem to lose his tightness. The emotional world of the film seems, on the whole, misshapen: under a spell that has to do with Guy's heart, "its long, mistaken shutting." In other words, Guy's closed heart rather than Bruno's immoderate and savage open one is the covert source of the ailment that seems to confront us. I am reminded of Nietzsche's lament: "The desert grows; woe to him who harbors deserts!" (248). In the inverted logic characteristic of the best tales of doubling, the more cautious, socially adept and respectable figure – wound tight with the strain of denial and the lack of self-knowledge – sets the terms for the double's conduct. Guy is the knot Bruno is summoned to untie. Effectively divorced from the life he feigns taking part in, Guy also seems divorced from the pronoun "I," which in his case no longer quite seems a personal pronoun. Bruno, of course, cannot be said to understand anyone's feelings except his own (and perhaps intermittently his mother's), but he has a gala assortment of "personal" feelings, which delight, pummel, and transfix him.

It is extremely rare in Hitchcock for the nominal villain to be so extravagantly caught up in feelings as Bruno is – with a child's need to give himself over completely to each one in turn, as though he were not yet master of any of them. His responses to the rush that emotion so often carries are inordinate, but he doesn't want to lessen the size and force of these responses, because he fears that an irreversible, perhaps lethal, grown-up boredom is lying in wait for him. Nor can I think of another male figure in Hitchcock who, for all of his depraved scheming, declares himself as fully as Bruno. The "desert" that is Guy is policed by exacting social forms, as Hitchcock's films are by his equally exacting visual forms. Guy is pursued and supplicated by the childish, childlike Bruno, who wants to break through and flood Guy's controlled but arid spaces with his own ungovernable messiness. Bruno's love for Guy has a doglike excess, which may account for the otherwise baffling appearance of the dog on Bruno's staircase when Guy attempts a secret nocturnal visit to Bruno's father. The Janus-faced dog at first appears fierce and aggressive, but as Guy moves closer to him he turns, on the instant, lavishly tender and licks his hand. The heedlessness – indeed, the brute thoughtlessness – of Bruno's chaotic attachment to Guy finds its appropriate home in an amusement park, to which Bruno naturally gravitates: a place where straight lines begin to waver and wiggle, where wandering replaces set routes and the workday commitment to pragmatic doing regresses to frivolous undoing.

Returning to our initial opposition of determinism vs. accident: Bruno, who initially appears to be in the service of fixed and fated action (his contract, his unstoppable plans), is covertly an agent of accident. Unlike both Guy and Hitchcock, Bruno is a confident improviser, as eager to surprise himself as he is to surprise others. While he makes meticulous preparations for incidents large and small, he typically has no idea what he is going to do next. He seems delighted rather than alarmed by detours, indefiniteness, and unexpected developments, and he makes maximum allowance for accident, smoothly incorporating the workings of chance into his operations. The murder of Miriam, for example, is from beginning to end an antic impromptu. He agreeably adjusts his plans for the evening to Miriam's whims and counts on circumstances working out unpredictably in his favor.

Guy's lighter, once in Bruno's hands, begins to mirror its new owner, poised teasingly between the imperatives of fate and the arbitrary pranks of chance. The current it conducts in its early appearances flows equally from both sources. Although Bruno comes to get it and keep it somewhat fortuitously, the lighter carries in its engraved markings Kafka-like evidence of Guy's failings and evasions. A stern eye appraising this lighter can turn its "marks of affection" into a judgment; its first recipient was unworthy of the romantic faith bestowed on him. It feels right somehow that such a throwaway possession will eventually come to stand for every suspicion that is rightly or wrongly directed against Guy. Those barely perceptible Jamesian particles of guilt that might finally make legible the portion of Miriam's murder that authentically belongs to Guy, along with all his other sins of thought and omission, seem to collect, like magnetized filings, on the body of the lighter. As it becomes increasingly clear that the movement of the lighter, more than any competing plot element, will determine the course and outcome of the narrative – and will do so by sure design – we are obliged to dwell more searchingly on what this protean object reveals and conceals.

One might reasonably wonder whether to deem the lighter itself guilty or innocent. If Guy, for example, were to retrieve it without mishap before Bruno succeeded in planting it incriminatingly at the scene of the crime, would it immediately be wiped clean? And would the accumulated implications of Guy's relationship with Bruno – including the film's heavy, relentless pattern of doubling – then dissolve like a dream? Were the lighter and the doubling subject to misreading all along? Perhaps they were empty categories from the outset, which we were pressured to interpret in the event that they might prove meaningful; their emptiness would incline us to erase our own narrative footsteps at the end of the film, as well as those of Guy and Bruno. Guy's innocence, if accepted, trumps a delusive, guilt-projecting visual determinism (they were never doubles!), and makes his original meeting with Bruno a bona fide accident after the fact. "Don't talk to strangers," as the movie's epilogue proposes with pointedly limp flippancy. Guy is ironically confirmed, if we take the epilogue as instructive, in his instinct to share nothing real with others. Everyone should properly remain strangers, it seems, if one is to defend and preserve one's innocence as an adult.

When Bruno dies in the amusement park, loosening his grip on the lighter and exposing it to public view (to moral consensus, if you like), does the thing itself prove to be a mere nothing, and a matter of no further concern? To whom does the lighter ultimately belong, Guy, Bruno, or the viewer, and does its meaning alter according to how we settle final ownership? One suspects that Guy would not want the tainted object returned to him. The gift is spoiled now; let the police dispose of it. Not claiming the lighter would make Guy resemble the vast majority of Hitchcock protagonists, who achieve their desired ends by complacent refusals of self-knowledge. The miserable business that one has been embroiled in is over, and it had no connection at all with the person one really is. For a murky interval others were confused or skeptical about one's vigorous assertions of innocence, but it can now be shown triumphantly that the wrong man had been accused. "From the beginning," Guy can tell himself, "I was doubted, mistrusted, held unfairly to be responsible. Privately I have always known myself, in the ways that count, to be in the right. Now others must ratify this view." And the viewer is exonerated by the same means, by the same self-validating stroke, at the same instant. We too are divorced cleanly, if we wish to be, from any further emotional, moral and thought investment in this film experience. Guy's innocence is matched by our own. Whatever we as viewers have given to Bruno – so he could run stirringly "naughty" errands as our surrogate self or double – is safely returned to us at the end, or better yet, disposed of.

Before Bruno manages to get to the amusement park to fulfill his intention of hiding Guy's lighter in plain view at the murder site, he experiences an accident of his own that nearly results in his losing it prematurely. The viewer is persuaded at this juncture that Bruno's continued control of Guy wholly depends on his retaining control of the lighter. In a moment of blind cockiness, he is jostled while holding the lighter too loosely. It slips from his fingers, then drops through a sewer grate. For a time the lighter seems at a recoverable distance on an upper ledge, but Bruno, too impetuous in his attempt to grasp it, nudges it to a lower level, where it lies, agonizingly, several stubborn inches past his outstretched arm's furthest reach. The emotional struggle to retrieve the lost object would seem rightly to belong to the questing hero at this late phase of the narrative. Bruno appears to be pitted in a moral struggle against the dictates of accident – a malign force that has unjustly intervened to sever both his ties and claim to the lighter. His hand's outreach, and near miraculous stretching, feels like a religious act of faith.

Bruno's solitary Arthurian test is intercut with Guy's atypically reckless style of play in the Forest Hills tennis tournament. The logic of this episode, where Guy is concerned, is that Guy deserves to win his match, since he is altering his tightly controlled, conservative, self-protecting tennis strategy. The loosening and simultaneous sharpening of his customary mode of attack in the game as he battles the clock (i.e., Bruno's timetable) is meant to suggest a corresponding elasticity in his approach to the human dilemmas confronting him. If the same logic were applied to Bruno in his "crisscross" contest with the lighter, he would not be rewarded with success, since the accident would be a fitting rebuke for his increasingly rigid, senseless persecution of Guy. It may be time for the double, whose harsh tutelage of Guy has served its purpose, to be tested himself and confronted with limits. He must transform his tactics and reverse course, or face humiliating defeat in his steadily diminished sphere of influence. Yet paradoxically the emotional force of the scene, as opposed to its conventional ethical sense, places the viewer, with bewildering fullness, on the side of Bruno and his dexterous strangler's hand.

This sewer grate scene is the third of three character-centered moments in the film with expansive, overtly emotional power, each of them involving Bruno's hands and linked to the lighter. The second episode of dauntingly obscure emotional power occurs during Bruno's involuntary strangling of the "stand-in" elderly society woman at the formal-dress party. Bruno's hands shift intention there from a playful bit of theater to a deadly squeezing action as his eyes are caught by a young woman's stare across the room. This second woman is Anne's sister, Barbara (Patricia Hitchcock), whose glasses reflect, for Bruno if not for us, the flame of the lighter that had illuminated Miriam's features just before he strangled her. The first fraught moment is Miriam's actual death, reflected in her glasses once they fall to the ground.

As in the sewer grate scene, Bruno at the party seems to enter a trance as his hands acquire a will of their own. The party and grate incident both involve Bruno's hands taking their cue and strength from the lighter flashing tauntingly from an unforeseen viewing distance. Bruno tightening his hold on the woman's throat seems in the party scene a proxy attempt to take the lighter back from his victim. The object seems to be part of the glasses that confront him. Previously a reflection in Barbara/Miriam's lens, the lighter has now transformed itself into the substance of Barbara's gaze. It is the thing that looks back at him. Barbara's glasses and her half-fearful, half-accusing eyes (in a disconcerting, viewer-implicating close-up) rather than the invisible Mrs. Cunningham beside him are what catch and hold Bruno's gaze until he eventually passes out. When Barbara was first introduced to him in an earlier scene, her glasses immediately cued a memory of Miriam, a memory marked by the reflection of his lighter's flame in her lenses. In the party scene, the lighter is not literally reflected for a second time, but the viewer's memory of it is awakened by the carnival music accompanying Barbara's fearful reciprocation of Bruno's suddenly transfixed gaze.

Although this party scene incident, like so many of Bruno's activities, is "out in the open," the viewer seems kept at several removes from the hypnotic object.

The lighter is perhaps even more insistently "there," as Slavoj Žižek would tell us, by remaining hidden from literal sight: a vanishing point in the image. Mrs. Cunningham (Norma Varden), whose neck has been eagerly offered to Bruno for his flirtatious use, is unseen and forgotten once his performance is underway. Barbara, the woman who replaces her as a potential object of vision, is equally missing from his view. She is mistaken when she solemnly declares to her sister after Bruno's departure that he was attacking her. Barbara's glasses, from Bruno's perspective, were the only living aspect of her face, the point of his helpless concentration, a reminder of another pair of glasses with an equally blurry owner. Remembered music from the amusement park returns Bruno, like a merry-go-round, to the spot where he killed Miriam. His re-enactment of the murder is experienced as a set of enigmatic dream fragments rather than a clearly retrieved memory. Bruno tries to focus his attention on the lit lighter as though it beckoned to him from behind Barbara's eyes. The object, like an obscured face behind a window, acquires here the human power to look back at him through the mediating lens of Barbara/Miriam's glasses.

As the viewer reaches back for her own memory of the murder, the face of Miriam vanishes there as well. We recall only a pair of enormous glass lenses in the grass, in whose ghostly light the body of Miriam leans slowly earthward and comes to rest there, reduced to a dim shapelessness. The lighter, at this human endpoint, has been transformed, as in the party scene, into Miriam's orphaned glasses – which is to say, into an act of disembodied viewing. The glasses are our replacement lighter, the sole available light to see by. Only the spectator is entitled to "wear" these glasses and peer through them. Doing so enhances our power of scrutiny and involvement. We authorize this sight of death by entering into it with such rapt fluidity. How deliriously close we are to Miriam's dying while still, it would appear, safely detached from it. The face that a short while ago belonged to the glasses, in a kind of supporting role to them, was lit up for us for a shy, surprised moment, then extinguished. After a graceful shift in perspective, the oval frame holds the entire, now faceless victim comfortably within its borders as Miriam passes from the light of life into a blind, destitute darkness. A ghostly light now literally inhabits the lens of the glasses. This soft afterglow replaces the flare of the lighter that earlier signaled Bruno's declaration of sexual readiness. The lens doesn't quite release its last touch of illumination. Dreamily ensnared still in the trance of Miriam's former arousal by Bruno, the glasses cradle the fading gleam of eros as Miriam reclines gently deathward. As the glasses become irrelevant to their even more deeply abandoned owner, they still seem to clutch the romantic prospect of her last thought: the anticipated fulfillment of an embrace. In her abrupt separation from the glasses, they become ours to see through.

The transfer of the glasses from Miriam to the viewer parallels the way in which Guy allows Bruno to claim the lighter that is "left for him" in the train compartment. By what authority does Bruno take hold of the forsaken object, look it over and pocket it? He cannot be sure what he is expected or meant to do with it, any more than we are. We seem to take possession of Miriam's glasses by accident. They fall haphazardly into our hands, so we might as well put them to use. Resting on the spot where accident has cast them, they take on the terrible calm of a sphinx in a Francis Bacon painting. Our matter-of-course viewing of the death scene is sharply disrupted the moment we "find" the glasses. Unavoidably, our watching turns self-conscious, but to what end?

The morality of a Hitchcock film is often tucked away in such odd object places as this one. We are suddenly given something to look at or through that we clearly recognize but have somehow lost our ability to interpret. The ease of looking – the entrancing force of our concentration – supplies a pleasure that works against our confusion. A sudden gap or tear in our normal, passive viewing perspective arrives without warning, brought about by a disrupted relation with a familiar object and its placement in space. We are temporarily estranged from our preferred, sanctioned thoughts, thoughts that square with our working notion of what the scene – indeed, what reality – is about (e.g., a murder involving a maniac and a hapless victim). When we enter this gap, we may attempt to close it by bearing down on the manifest beauty of the image until the confusion goes away. A potentially moral challenge is evaded by intensifying our absorption with the visual, which allows a kind of "blanking out" until our initial idea of the scene's straightforward meaning returns to us.

In these estranging episodes, we bear some resemblance to Bruno watching the screen of Barbara's glasses at the party, a screen that holds a flickering memory image of a nearly forgotten murder. He can't remember, for the time being, who or where he is. He doesn't know that he is doing actual injury to the woman sitting next to him. He loses sight of her and of his squeezing hands because of the half-formed thoughts that grip him. Bruno also loses sight of the fact that he is himself under scrutiny. Although he imagines he is hidden, he remains in the full glare of public disclosure. The playful strangling turns ghastly and real, a near-lethally stretched moment of blankness covering another thought that will not come clear. Bruno's buried thought authorizes his squeezing hands. He blindly indulges their action without making it into an act of volition or avowed knowledge. Bruno does and doesn't own his own thoughts in this embarrassing seizure. The woman struggling for her life in the seat next to him attests that he does own them, in ways that tell. He does not of course wish them to spill forth uncontrollably here, but the brutal thoughts are already in his memory-possession and, at this transitional moment, in his emotional possession. At the time of the murder, Bruno did not absorb or dwell on the thought that he actually extinguished Miriam's life in the process of strangling her. He approached the killing in the spirit of the "test your strength" game he played earlier in the amusement park while he was stalking Miriam. He indefinitely postponed taking on the death he brought about. Miriam's presence as suffering victim is a memory image he has dropped or left behind, as if by accident – like her glasses or Guy's lighter. An attentive stranger (Hitchcock) who has noted Bruno's slip returns the banished thought (in the form of glasses and lighter) to him at an appropriate later time: "I think this may be yours. I recognized you from before and made the connection."

In his 1873 essay "On the Optical Sense of Form: A Contribution to Aesthetics," Robert Vischer writes of how in actual experience

> there exists a state of pure absorption in which we imagine this or that phenomenon in accordance with the unconscious need for a surrogate for our body-ego. As in a dream, I stimulate, on the basis of simple nerve sensations, a fixed form that symbolizes my body or an organ of it. ... The way in which the phenomenon is constructed also becomes an analogy for my own structure. I wrap myself within its contours like a garment.
>
> (Quoted in Fried 37)

Later in this extraordinary, Hitchcock-prefiguring essay, Vischer combines the idea of projection with a metaphor of concealment, which contains (accidentally?) the notion of preparing for a killing. We have

> the wonderful ability to project and incorporate our own physical form into an objective form, in much the same way that wild fowlers gain access to their quarry by concealing themselves in a blind. What can that form be other than the form of a content identical with it? It is therefore our own personality that we project onto it.
>
> (38)

To extend Vischer's metaphors further, we can say that Hitchcock and the viewer are both concealed in their separate blinds. The viewer, like Bruno at the party, believes that he is too well-hidden from anyone's scrutiny to be in danger of getting caught, or caught out. In his game with Mrs. Cunningham, Bruno ventures into the open because he is confident that a deeper blind, impenetrable by anyone present except perhaps Guy (whom he confidently manipulates), is in place. And at the moment of maximum security, Bruno is transfixed and undone by an image form – akin to himself – that he had not anticipated. The viewer, in turn, is unmindful of the fact that he is himself the "quarry" of Hitchcock, who is concealed, almost in plain sight, in an adjacent "blind." We are the ones the director always has his sights on, and it is by means of our involuntary projections and physical and emotional entanglements with what we see that he will draw us out from cover and catch us unawares. We can be exposed, in the full glare of his knowledge of what we are imaginatively capable of, without ever losing the illusion that we have remained invisible and in control of our impulses. Our recognitions, our guilty thoughts connected by projection to our hands and eyes, will be strangers to us again almost immediately as we blank out the particulars of what we have assented to.

As Bruno reaches through the sewer grate, his mental state recalls the one he inhabited right before he found his perfect moment to strangle Miriam. He is not yet in a trance. He is fully alert, has the lighter firmly in view, and can "feel" exactly how much distance separates his hand from the all-important object. In this situation, he has no doubt about who owns the lighter. Guy may be its legal owner, but Bruno's right to it goes beyond any prior claim. The lighter is Bruno's authorization to control Guy and the most tangible proof of their enduring connection. If Bruno is entitled to retain his hold on Guy and expose his treachery, then he should get the lighter back. Bruno, like most of us, appeals to Providence, with our tacit support, in a crisis. The restoration of the lighter, in fact, seems animated by a miracle, as if accomplished through the cooperation of some sympathetic, occult power. As we watch Bruno strain beyond his customary physical resources and bodily limitations to recover the object, our initial detached amusement at his plight is exchanged, without our conscious approval, for impassioned identification. The hand of Bruno becomes an extension of our own. As our fingers at last feel the answering touch of the lighter, we may experience a sensation akin to ecstasy – the blessing of fulfillment. During that intense interval when it is nearly but not quite crowned with success, Bruno's quest seems as urgent, honorable and indeed meaningful as any that our actual life in the world has offered us.

Earlier, when another stranger on the train to Metcalf, having noticed the lighter in Bruno's hand, requested a light from him, Bruno refused to share it, offering matches instead. In the sewer grate scene, Bruno is required, as a result of Hitchcock's framing and cutting, to share the lighter with us. It is immensely important to Hitchcock – for moral as well as visceral reasons – to have us both will Bruno's success as we emotionally collaborate with him and at last feel the lighter pass into our own hands. A spectator's offhand judgment on Bruno's fierce exertions confirms as much: "It must mean a lot to him." The morality of Hitchcock has to do with making the lighter the repository and secret conductor of all the sinful thought energy in the narrative: everything that feeds the surface action illicitly and inadmissibly. Why is there so much pressure for the spectator to repeat Bruno's action in the train compartment opening and to make the lighter her own? Ideally, Hitchcock would like us to feel its significance, though we can't articulate what it is, as we burn to have it in our grasp, then assent to taking hold of it. In order to accomplish this goal, our hand must fuse with Bruno's. We form a secret pact with him as the lighter's current flows through both of us at once. Our saying "yes" to Bruno here seems almost obligatory. Our "taking Bruno's place" in the lighter exchange is what frees Guy to win his tennis match.

All of Bruno's previous sordid hand work seems, in the sewer grate scene, carried over to us as we projectively push our own hand into his as into a familiar glove. Think of Bruno's two fingers delicately closing over the lighter in its resting place of leaves and sewer muck and lifting it toward the light. Its taint instantly fades as Bruno's hand fully grasps it and returns the lighter to his pocket. Our temporary pact with Bruno appears once more to be repealed or set aside, though it is subject to renewal without advance notice. Our hands and minds, according to the standard Hitchcock dispensation, are wiped clean as the lighter disappears from sight.

There is no penalty for our thought embrace of Bruno at the sewer grate, just as there was none in sharing Bruno's and Hitchcock's mastery (along with an odd wince of the victim's pain) during Miriam's murder. We were there, on the spot, but not precisely in our own person, not in our own right. If we give in for a time to the naughty pleasure of thinking someone else's thoughts, we will soon find a clear and cleansed channel back to our own. The root of the word pain, Nigel Spivey reminds us, is the Latin *poena,* carrying the double burden of "penalty" and "punishment." The fugitive sinful thoughts Hitchcock would have his strongest images breed in us are usually on the oscillating shadow line dividing pain and pleasure. As we become connoisseurs of our visual relation to others' suffering, we deny both penalty and punishment for what we divertingly take in. Where is the harm in imagining, in indulging fleetingly the power of images to carry us out of ourselves? The direction of our thought hardly matters. The lively, childish greediness and messiness of the Bruno part of the viewer can always be disciplined and curtailed by the Guy part, with its wariness, carefulness, and social gift for saving face. As Bruno hastens away from the sewer to catch a cab, we are free to watch him, as we may imagine we always have, from Guy's distance, as though Bruno were eternally and reliably that "stranger" from the train, who has senseless designs on us, and whose actions and thoughts, in Guy's words, are those of a "crazy fool."

Hitchcock's intricately patterned visual form is the Bruno dimension of his films, extravagant and irrational, though relying on meticulous plans. Paradoxically, the subterranean pressure of form – the Bruno-like logic of the film's swiftly unfolding images – generates the authentic moral thinking of the narrative. Something illicit and elusive in the form always runs in opposition to the spurious, ready-to-wear morality articulated in the story proper. The imagery both doubles and unravels the story's conventional ethics. On Guy's behalf, Hitchcock takes very seriously the claims and dictates and expansive shaping influences of social forms, which provide most of what passes for safety and stability in our much too fragile lives. Hitchcock never loses sight of the fact that the social forms we sub-scribe to are substantial as well as arbitrary. To the extent that these forms prove comfortingly substantial, Hitchcock believes in them and relies on them. His plots, with their self-conscious, artificial closure, are closely aligned with social forms whose great virtue is that they can be endlessly tested, found wanting, and then restored without undue strain or fuss.

Hitchcock believes in Guy Haines, who is social form incarnate. But he is under no illusion that Guy's means of "making successful arrangements" has anything to do with self-knowledge or moral growth. Hitchcock believes in Guy in the same way that he believes in the movie spectator, arguably Guy's most abiding double. The visual form that is Bruno executes an intricate dance with the social forms of Guy's and the viewer's plot. To the extent that Bruno unset-tles this structure, showing how it requires more than its own terms for adequate, grown-up, culpable thinking, he is both the parodic conscience of social form and its exuberantly sinful tempter. If the viewer comes to acknowledge Bruno, by film's end, as deeply bound to the moral realm he flaunts and throws askew, she may gain the privilege of seeing beyond Guy, who steadfastly disavows kin-ship with Bruno's unseemly, unsharable world. The lighter, as the central image in Hitchcock's (and Bruno's) visual design, binds together all the film's shifty knowledge. When Bruno involuntarily shows it to us for the last time in his limp, outstretched hand, it is ours for the taking.

Yet Hitchcock is properly skeptical of our desire for real knowledge at the movies – certainly at his movies. He suspects that we will refuse to grasp the lighter if it carries any hint of residual taint. That we have "taken" it so often before, for brief intervals of furtive, shady, possibly sinful pleasure, can be dismissed as a viewing accident that we, like Guy, are allowed to forget. We leave such accidents behind in exchange for the socially determined ease of our affiliation with Guy and his determined innocence. After all, he has been fully exonerated by the mere sight of the lighter's reappearance. Try as we might, it is hard to hold on to the idea that "the innermost temporal rhythms," in Augustine's phrase, of our moviegoing and thinking could result in a meaningful guilt of any duration. Guy rather than Bruno will continue to be our surrogate, seeking his imitation of light and life in places where he is always a stranger to wrongdoing.

Works Cited

Altieri, Charles. *The Particulars of Rapture: An Aesthetic of the Affects*. Ithaca: Cornell UP, 2003.

Fried, Michael. *Menzel's Realism: Art and Embodiment in Nineteenth-Century Berlin*. New Haven: Yale UP, 2002.

Gracq, Julien. *Reading Writing*. Trans. Jeanine Herman. New York: Turtle Point, 1980.

Hazlitt, William. *On the Pleasure of Hating*. New York: Penguin Books—Great Ideas, 2005.

Highsmith, Patricia. "The Trouble with Mrs. Blynn, the Trouble with the World." *Nothing That Meets the Eye: The Uncollected Stories of Patricia Highsmith*. New York: Norton, 2002. 409–18.

Nietzsche, Friedrich. *Thus Spoke Zarathustra: A Book for All and None*. Ed. Adrian Del Caro and Robert Pippin. Trans. Adrian Del Caro. Cambridge: Cambridge UP, 2006. Cambridge Texts in the History of Philosophy.

Rohmer, Eric, and Claude Chabrol. *Hitchcock: The First Forty-Four Films*. Trans. Stanley Hochman. New York: Ungar, 1979.

Rothman, William. *Hitchcock—The Murderous Gaze*. Cambridge: Harvard UP, 1982.

Spivey, Nigel. *Enduring Creation: Art, Pain, and Fortitude*. Berkeley: U of California P, 2001.

Wood, Robin. *Hitchcock's Films Revisited*. Rev. ed. New York: Columbia UP, 2002.

PART IX

Beyond Hitchcock

29

Hitchcock and the Postmodern

Angelo Restivo

Asserting a relationship between Hitchcock and postmodernity might seem – especially to those scholars who hold a strongly historicist view of the development of aesthetic forms – a misguided project or yet another example of how "postmodernism" has become a term so all-encompassing as to have lost any critical efficacy. Hitchcock, after all, was decisively and thoroughly connected with modernity and the modern: we need only cite his onscreen fascination with such modern technologies as the railroad, the amusement park, and the telegraph; or his sympathy with surrealism; or his longstanding interest in psychoanalysis. And if the cinema is considered not just modernity's technology of vision but indeed its "central nervous system," then Hitchcock, as one of the supreme "masters" of this apparatus, must be seen as having provided modernity with some of its most compelling expressive forms. Accordingly, it would seem a serious mischaracterization to call Hitchcock a "postmodernist" or to assert his work is self-consciously "postmodern." For while the modernists clearly situated their work in relation to an era which thought of itself as "modern," the postmodern was only a nascent formation in the years of Hitchcock's later work and the term was not in wide use, even among cultural elites, until at least the mid- to late-1970s.

It is perhaps fitting that a chapter in this book dealing with postmodernism must immediately confront issues of terminology and periodization. For the purpose of this chapter, the surest starting point for conceptualizing the postmodern remains Fredric Jameson's structural, Marxist "definition" from what is now the canonical essay on the subject, "Postmodernism, or the Cultural Logic of Late Capitalism." Here postmodernism is characterized as equally a "cultural logic" and a "periodizing hypothesis," both of which imply that postmodernism is a super-structural phenomenon that is somehow expressive (as "cultural logic") of the emergence of

A Companion to Alfred Hitchcock, First Edition. Edited by Thomas Leitch and Leland Poague.
© 2011 Thomas Leitch and Leland Poague. Published 2011 by Blackwell Publishing Ltd.

some new formation of capitalism (hence the need for periodization). Though further specification is obviously necessary, we should note first that the privilege accorded here to Jameson's development of the concept of postmodernism follows from the way its reference points help us to assess what has become an ever-increasing inventory of "traits" or "characteristics" of the postmodern, ranging from styles of architecture and painting to characteristics of television to transformations of everyday life to fundamental shifts in affect and subjectivity – all the way to proclamations of the end of philosophy and/or history as it has been practiced since antiquity.

So to begin with, we would need to specify what this new formation of capitalism is and when it came into being. The shift is generally thought to have begun in the postwar period, overdetermined by a number of concurrent phenomena: the series of housing bills in the US in the immediate postwar period that shifted development away from the old urban centers and into the new suburbias; the development of the interstate highway system; the relatively quick adoption of television in the American household; fundamental shifts in strategies of advertising developed theoretically by social theorists at the University of Chicago and put into practice in Chicago advertising agencies; increased consumption of consumer durables and then non-durables as well – with this "consumerization" of the economy being repeated, in the 1950s in regionally specific ways, in the various economic miracles that occurred in Western Europe and Japan. One would expect such wide-ranging infrastructural changes to leave their marks on culture and everyday life, so that one could say that, in this early phase of infrastructural reorganization, the postmodern would manifest itself *symptomatically* in cultural production; whereas in a later period, we will see a more programmatic or self-conscious "-ism" come into being in relation to a now thoroughly transformed "life-world." Finally, however – and this will be especially important when we return to Hitchcock – it remains a matter of debate whether "full" postmodernity (whenever that may be said to have been achieved) represents a decisive break from modernity and its cultural logic or whether postmodernity is rather an extension and fulfillment of the project of modernity.

To move to the critical literature on Hitchcock and the postmodern, we can discern two different if interrelated critical strategies – the symptomatic reading of the films of the 1950s and 1960s, through which we uncover signs of an emergent culture of the postmodern; and the deployment of self-consciously postmodern theoretical positions regarding textuality – which are used to reread the entire Hitchcock oeuvre from a postmodern critical vantage point. An example of the first strategy could go something like this: the narrative trajectory of *Psycho* (1960) crucially depends upon the development of the interstate highway system, which the film images in its first movement (see Restivo, "Into"). Rather than putting Phoenix into the film's semiotic "bird series," it is thus more interesting to connect it to the transformation of urban spaces in what would become "the Sunbelt," which the interstate system, among other technologies and central planning strategies, made possible. That the limited-access interstate becomes "the road not taken" in the film is extremely significant because it places Marion Crane (Janet Leigh) into an "outmoded" spatial system, one which is reinforced by the Gothic house in the background of the Bates motel. Not without some humor, we could call the Bates motel a "mom and pop" operation – in other words, precisely the kind of small business threatened by the increasing standardization of the new, national markets, fostered by both the limited-access highway (with artificially constructed rest stops rather than the real towns of Route 66) and by television.

But after having done this groundwork, we could enter into the textual system of *Psycho* itself, not simply by noting that the endangered family business is the site of perversion but also by revisiting the myriad small details of the film, like the father Marion steals from – another pervert, by the way – who is buying his daughter a house as a wedding present (and "buying off unhappiness" as well) while Marion is stuck with a fiancé who cannot legitimize their relationship through marriage because he still believes in an outmoded (and gendered) work ethic that compels him to provide her with the equivalent of a "house" before they can be wed. Since we are not doing an exhaustive reading of *Psycho* here, but rather simply exemplifying the critical procedure of the symptomatic reading, we can conclude briefly. Film narrative necessarily takes as its raw material the stuff of everyday life, so it will be natural to expect signs of emergent relations of production to be visible in one form or another in films (e.g., the interstate highway system). But then, as narratives take on expressive form, certain social contradictions that are not necessarily apparent in the film's own historical moment nevertheless leave traces in the text, as symptoms. In the case of *Psycho*, for example, the symptom-trace involves the conflicted status of the Father (and by extension, the problem of perversion, which Lacan has slyly connected to the problem of the Father in his neologism *"père-version"* 'the version of the father') when the ethic of renunciation gives way to the immediate gratification of a consumption-driven economy, this latter transition having been rendered *allegorically* in the film via its protagonists and bit characters.

The most renowned exemplar of the first critical strategy is the Slovenian philosopher and cultural theorist Slavoj Žižek, who has mapped out the many markers of a shift from modern to postmodern in Hitchcock's work (especially in the films from *Psycho* onwards). In fact, Hitchcock played a major role in two of his key early books, *Looking Awry* (1991) and *Everything You Always Wanted to Know About Lacan (But Were Afraid to Ask Hitchcock)* (1992). Žižek is not primarily a film theorist. His project was fundamentally situated within debates in philosophy and critical theory, and his thinking was deeply influenced by psychoanalytic training at the Lacanian *Ecole freudienne* in Paris. By the late 1980s, when Žižek began his prolific publishing career, critical theory was faced with a number of impasses over issues of ideology and political agency, impasses that were mirrored in film studies by a sudden renunciation of the post-1968 theoretical paradigms – thought to be monolithic and totalizing – in favor of the study of more localized systems, whether coming out of cultural studies or new historicism. For Žižek, such a "balkanization" of discourses had all the markings of a symptom; and his unique position of being "in between" – between, on the one side, a failed totalitarianism and, on the other, the overheated phantasmagoria of the society of the spectacle – allowed him to develop a theory of ideology as held together by relatively intractable (and non-discursive or "Real") formations of fantasy. This analytical distance, which allowed Žižek to unmask the repressed libidinal workings of both Stalinism and late capitalism and show them to be profoundly similar, made Hitchcock an attractive figure for Žižek and allowed him to link Hitchcock with Jacques Lacan. Both were "absolute masters," and Hitchcock's droll and laconic stance toward publicly discussing the "deep messages" in his work could be seen as akin to Lacan's notorious silence during the analytic session. In psychoanalysis, the analysand reacts to this situation by turning the analyst into the "subject-supposed-to-know," and this transference is the very precondition for unleashing the plethora of unconscious raw material of the analysis. Žižek argues that Hitchcock is placed in a similar transference relationship to the critical establishment, which is what allows for the outpouring of interpretations of Hitchcock (and he is certainly one of the most interpreted of directors). This effectively removes the question of directorial authorship from the table: authorship is a transferential fiction and "the only way to produce something real in theory is to pursue the transferential fiction to the end" (Žižek, *Everything* 10).

Žižek's approach to periodizing Hitchcock starts in his very opening essay of the collection *Everything You Always Wanted to Know about Lacan (But Were Afraid to Ask Hitchcock)*, where he subsumes the procedure of symptomatic reading I described above under the notion of the historical mediation of form (1–12). He finds three major "periods" in Hitchcock's work, each with its own unique way of handling objects, social subjects (i.e., characters in the narrative), and sexual or romantic relations. Of course, anyone who has seriously watched Hitchcock films will know how critical particular objects are to the narratives of the films, from the keepsake ring in *Shadow of a Doubt* (1943) to the key, the wine bottles, and the coffee cups in *Notorious* (1946) to the pre-Columbian figurine in *North by Northwest* (1959). Looking at the Hitchcockian object through a Lacanian lens, Žižek divides these objects into types. The first is an object that functions as the Lacanian "object-a." Lacan's object-a is often described as the "object-cause of desire"; but we must be clear that the object-a has no positive content, is rather conceptually constructed to be a site that any number of objects will occupy and around which any number of desires will circulate. The MacGuffin, then, is the object in the Hitchcock universe that has the status of object-a: it is that "nothing," which could be any object whatever, around which the narrative is constructed and which mobilizes the desires and actions of all the characters (the uranium-filled wine bottles of *Notorious*, for example). A second type of object – epitomized by the ring in *Shadow of a Doubt* and the cigarette lighter in *Strangers on a Train* (1951) – functions differently and with more complexity. It is an object of exchange that binds the characters together into a Symbolic contract. In Lacanian terms, it is a scrap of the Real that breaks apart all the Imaginary doublings (of which there are many in the two films mentioned above, exhaustively inventoried in Hitchcock commentary) and throws the characters into symbolic relation. What is critical here is that this object stands in for a lack that is constitutive of the Symbolic, insofar as the Symbolic can never arrive at a signifier that "explains everything," for that would involve a leap outside the system itself into a metalanguage, which is impossible in any of the formations we call post-structuralism, whether Lacanian psychoanalysis or deconstruction. Thus, since what covers over this lack in the Symbolic is the Name-of-the-Father, one should expect to see the beginnings of a crisis in the paternal position in films where this object emerges. Finally, the third type of object is one that marks the eruption into the visual field of the traumatic Real; as such, it isn't so much an object as it is "the Thing itself," something that occludes the ocular field or that problematizes the boundary between surface and depth. Such objects include the swamp behind the Bates house in *Psycho*; the birds, taken together, in *The Birds* (1963); and the hull of the ship at the end of the street in *Marnie* (1964).

While Žižek evokes this typology of objects as confirming his division of Hitchcock's career into three periods corresponding to three formations of capitalism (see Žižek, *Everything* 5–8), I think it difficult to make the distinction between the first and second objects above in Hitchcock's work, as they tend to coexist; or to link those to a decisive historical break between national-industrial capitalism and imperialist-monopoly capitalism, a break that would have occurred much earlier historically. However, the shift between the first two types of objects and the third is a decisive and accurate critical intervention, for not only do we see the Imaginary-Symbolic objects giving way to the eruptions of the Real in Hitchcock's work by the late 1950s, but the theoretical implications of this shift in objects provide a strong reading of the shifts in subjectivity and the sexual relation as we move to postmodernity. For one thing, it provides conceptual grounds for understanding the shifts in the oedipal narrative so often connected to Hitchcock's work (as indeed to classical narrative more generally). If the oedipal is the ideological vehicle for social reproduction, then we see it most perfectly achieved in the films in which object-a is primary, where the Symbolic order is seen as a self-running automaton (e.g., "Mr. Memory" in *The 39 Steps* [1935]), and the couple is thrown together in a kind of arranged marriage (the handcuffs in the same film). In the narratives governed by the second type of object, the oedipal narrative ends up producing a suitable coupling, but not without having to overcome the obstacle of an "obscene" or perverse father-figure, whose hold over the characters is materialized in the object – the ring, the key to the wine cellar, and so on – that stands in for the ultimate lack in the big Other (which lack is never apparent when the object is a simple MacGuffin, like "The 39 Steps"). Finally, when the Real invades the image, we enter into an emergent postmodern organization of social reproduction in which the oedipal begins to fall apart. In Lacanian theory, the Real is that which escapes symbolization (a symbolization achieved, for example, through the second type of object above, the object that stands in for the process of symbolic interpellation itself). Thus this direct expression of the Real can be rendered only by resorting to the formless (e.g., the swamp) or the liminal (e.g., the surface of the screen). This tendency toward the eruption of the Real in the visual field is something that manifests itself in other visual arts. For example, Hal Foster has talked about the tendency of the postmodern painting to tear at the surface of the canvas or to problematize the border between inside and outside (Foster 141, 149). Finally, to make this description theoretically complete, we would need to note that the Real, in Lacanian theory, most properly pertains to the enjoyment, or jouissance, of the drives, which is precisely what the entry into the Symbolic (via the oedipal scenario) forever estranges us from. Historically, then, the society of consumption, or of the spectacle, is one in which the socially mediating role of the Symbolic is rent by an insistent injunction toward enjoyment, and it is this tension that gets expressed artistically via an eruption of the Real into the visual field, while it manifests itself in myriad other ways culturally.

The other, closely related, intervention Žižek made in his early work on Hitchcock and postmodernity has to do with a reformulation of the function of the gaze in film. (Žižek's work here thus has implications that go well beyond Hitchcock, as the Lacanian theory of the gaze is central to the psychoanalytic film theory of the 1970s and early 1980s.) The larger argument is that the gaze manifests itself in crucially different ways in Hitchcock as we move from the earlier to the later work (see Žižek, *Looking* 88–96, 116–122). In fact, this argument is closely connected to the arguments regarding the shifting depiction of objects as we move through Hitchcock, even if Žižek does not clearly connect these two developments in the books under consideration here. To begin to explicate this relation, let me make the initial claim: the signifier of the lack in the Symbolic (materialized in the second type of object mentioned earlier) has a profound connection to the phallus, and the phallus has a profound connection to the specular, and therefore to visuality in general. For just as the Symbolic must include within itself some signifier marking its own inability to totalize itself, so too must the Imaginary mark itself as such, and this mark is the phallus. Here we recall that the child's encounter with its image in the "mirror stage" is marked by a fundamental dissymmetry and ultimate failure, as the child's sense of command over its own body never fully coincides with the wholeness of the gestalt. It is the phallus that marks this fundamental failure, as it introduces a specular dissymmetry between presence and absence, connected to the real of sexual difference. Thus, a kind of "stain" is introduced into the visual field – an anamorphic blur that figures this oscillation between presence and absence – which Lacan will then connect to his concept of the gaze. The gaze falls on the side of the Other – so that, for example, the Brenner house is gazing at Melanie (Tippi Hedren) when she arrives with the lovebirds, and not the other way around – and is normally naturalized by fantasy. When it makes itself visible in the visual field, however, it is through a stain that "de-realizes" the rest of the visual field (Žižek, *Looking* 117): for example, the single spot of blood on Melanie's temple, where she herself cannot see it.

We can bring all this to bear on the periodization of Hitchcock by beginning with *Notorious*, where the wine-cellar key functions clearly as the second type of object described earlier. Around this key are occluded an array of symbolic relationships involving duplicity, jealousy, betrayal, duty, sacrifice, and love. In the bravura crane shot from the balcony to the close-up of Ingrid Bergman's hand holding the key, we could say that a "naturalized" gaze of the Other (i.e., the social formalities of the soirée) collapses into the "stain" of the key, which alerts us that the entire party is the backdrop for an entirely different drama invisible to most of the partygoers. The key, however, still "holds the visual field together," so to speak, which marks this particular stylistic device of Hitchcock as *modernist*: it self-reflexively presents us with the mechanism by which the gaze operates, rather than stages the breakdown of the gaze itself. In terms of visuality, something entirely different happens in *Marnie*, for example, when Marnie (Tippi Hedren) sees the red ink spot or the red spots on the outfit the jockey wears at the racetrack. These "objects" unleash a jouissance in the film that cannot be contained symbolically: the result is that the red flows over the surface of the screen, completely obliterating the illusion of depth the gaze works to preserve. This device, then, could be said to announce the properly postmodern. We can note that this was one of many devices in the film that was greeted by the critics with derision as a sign of Hitchcock's decline. However, the device is corny only to the extent that it is seen as an attempt to achieve a kind of "psychic point-of-view" shot. From a more recent critical vantage point, we can see the device differently, as a staging of the collapse of the visual field that comes about when the Symbolic order is no longer stitched tightly together by the kinds of objects that had previously served precisely that function.

To summarize, then, Žižek is able to interpret the stylistic and narrative shifts we see in Hitchcock's work as symptomatic of an emergent postmodernity. His procedure, importantly, is dialectical, with Lacanian theory as the mediator between the various "levels" – i.e., economic transformations, shifts in social relations, and aesthetic style. We have yet to address the second way in which Hitchcock's work has been discussed in relation to postmodernity, through the application of "postmodern" (or, more properly, post-structuralist) theories of textuality to his work as a whole. Even in Žižek's work, we can discern an approach to textuality that abandons the model of the self-contained work of art as an "organic whole" and instead problematizes the borders of the work of art by situating it within a more generalized intertextuality. While it is important to understand how the ring functions within the textual system of *Shadow of a Doubt*, for example, Žižek is less concerned with producing a reading of that film than he is with establishing the existence and functioning of a certain type of object in Hitchcock's work more generally.

Jameson has already identified, within the *modernist* work of art, an entropic tendency toward the episodic. He argues that insofar as the high modernist work charges itself with aesthetic autonomy, we find this autonomy manifesting itself in loosened narrative connections within the work (Jameson, *Signatures* 201–07). It is only when we reach the postmodern, we can infer from this essay, that the work becomes so deeply episodic that even the "sentences" become autonomous, so that pastiche becomes a dominant mode. (One need only recall an episode of *The Simpsons* to see this process at work.) This increasing autonomization of the signifier is arguably corollary to the "linguistic turn" in philosophy and theory. For if our only access to anything is through the signifier, then a work of art is a subset of a much larger discursive network. No longer a "well-wrought urn," the work of art is more akin to a "force field" that holds together all manner of discursive material.

Within this view of textuality, it is difficult to make the claim that any given work closes by arriving at some fullness of "meaning"; instead, works of art become polyvocal, like Umberto Eco's "open work." In his deconstructive approach to Hitchcock, Christopher D. Morris notes how the endless deferral of meaning that deconstruction claims is endemic to language is very much akin to "suspense," allowing him thus to claim a natural affinity between the procedure of deconstruction and Hitchcock's work. A recurrent emblem in Hitchcock's work is the hanging figure – the villain hanging from the Statue of Liberty in *Saboteur* (1942), Jefferies (James Stewart) from his window sill in *Rear Window* (1954), Eve (Eva Marie Saint) from Mount Rushmore in *North by Northwest* – and Morris notes how, etymologically, the root of the word "suspense" is connected to the verb for "hanging." Thus, the hanging figure in Hitchcock becomes the trope for suspense, not only as it occurs narratively in Hitchcock, but also in the way that Hitchcock tends to put denotative meaning itself in suspense. This deferral of meaning is announced in the very title of *North by Northwest*, for example, insofar as the title is a "shifter": it carries no denotative or referential meaning, but takes on meaning only in relation to the position of whoever might be speaking the phrase. But then, in the opening salvo of the film – and Morris shows us how truly "devious" this film is – the proper name (Thornhill) gets shorn from its referent (Cary Grant), thus giving a new inflection to Thornhill's quip to Eve that the "O" in his initials "R.O.T." stands for "Nothing." When we arrive at the climactic scene on Mount Rushmore, Morris notes how the contamination of figure and ground becomes fully operational, since the background to the image is itself a "figure," the heads of the founding fathers. And while a more literal interpretation of this climactic scene might make the claim that the founding fathers here announce the impassive bedrock of the Law (which will put Roger and Eve in the nuptial bed), the deconstructive reading allows us to see the way the Law is a kind of fiction, papering over the law of the jungle that lies underneath. Finally, Morris notes how the film's MacGuffin is called a "figurine," which shatters to reveal the microfilm it contains. But here, the secret that, once revealed, would promise finality and fullness of meaning is something we will never be able to read, something that turns out to be film itself. Morris does this kind of deconstructive reading of most of Hitchcock's films, but preserves the rather conventional critical strategy of separate readings for each film, moving forward in chronological order. In this sense, he seems less concerned with tracking a "break" in Hitchcock work than with asserting a continuity: there is something about Hitchcock's apprehension of modernity that makes his work particularly amenable to deconstruction.

In what is probably the most radical of the postmodern approaches to Hitchcock – Tom Cohen's exhaustive and difficult two-volume study, *Hitchcock's Cryptonymies* – we can see both of the two general strategies coming together. Cohen, like many others, sees a historical break in Hitchcock's work after World War II, while he deploys a reading practice strongly indebted to deconstruction (though heavily politicized through its inflection by the work of Walter Benjamin). Insofar as Cohen sees this reading practice as eminently congenial to Hitchcock's practice – so much so that he calls Hitchcock's films "weapons of mass (de)construction" – one can say that he argues for a continuity between the modern and the postmodern Hitchcock. But to begin with, we can ask how Cohen characterizes the break in Hitchcock's work. And while it may seem as if Cohen's division of his own study into two volumes – the first subtitled "Secret Agents," the second "War Machines" – might itself be structured around this break (as Deleuze's two volumes on the cinema are divided by a fundamental shift in the cinematic image around World War II), it is unclear whether this claim can be argued, as both secret agents and war machines traverse both periods of Hitchcock's work.

Cohen does argue, however, that the theme of espionage is aligned to the "modern" in Hitchcock insofar as this theme plays out against the backdrop of a "home state" whose citizens are part of a "mass," whereas in postwar Hitchcock the narratives become more "touristic" and situated in zones of "extraterritoriality," which would be much more in keeping with an emergent (postmodern) global system of production and consumption. In fact, the critical trajectory of the first volume of Cohen's work establishes this very shift, as Cohen moves from an initial engagement with *Sabotage* (1936) to a long analysis, at the end of the volume, of the second version of *The Man Who Knew Too Much* (1956). While his deconstructive approach to reading these two films will be considered in due course, here we can simply note that *Sabotage* is firmly situated within the horizon of a "national-imaginary" – "England," with all the local color of the bus trip to Piccadilly Circus. Indeed, the story is even based on a canonical work in the "great tradition" of the English novel. In contrast, in the second *Man Who Knew Too Much*, the action transpires in the transient zones of international tourism and the extraterritorial zone of the embassy. And if one were to object that, say, *North by Northwest* uses the espionage theme well into the post-break period – and here I am engaging in my own interrogation of Cohen's argument, rather than presenting one that he has set forth himself – we could counter that in *North by Northwest*, the Cold War raises the theme to a higher level of abstraction. The Professor (Leo G. Carroll) deflects Roger's query about his identity by saying, "FBI, CIA, ONI, we're all in the same alphabet soup," and one could easily imagine the KGB as one of the combinations floating around in this infernal brew. As Fredric Jameson implies in a brilliant essay on the spatial systems of this film, the iconic national locations in *North by Northwest* have none of the "density" of those in, for example, *Sabotage*. In fact, the area around Mount Rushmore has the sense of being the "Edge of the World" (Jameson, "Spatial" 57), as if the film were charged with imagining some new mediation of the relation between public and private space at a moment when this distinction has been blurred by an emergent postmodernity.

The cans of film hiding the bomb in *Sabotage* could be said to signal Hitchcock's awareness of the explosive potential of film, that "dynamite of the split second" (117) that Walter Benjamin famously talks about in his canonical essay "The Work of Art in the Age of its Technical Reproducibility." For Benjamin, the cinema offers us all the spaces of everyday life, but in images that are shorn of "aura." Because the camera registers the world with an inhuman lens, it (potentially) tears apart our familiar views of "[o]ur taverns and our metropolitan streets, our offices and furnished rooms, our railroad stations and our factories" ("Work" 117). In this way, film can fundamentally reconfigure our relation to history itself insofar as the juxtaposition of these images allows new constellations to emerge, giving us new possibilities for understanding the past and new potentialities for the future. Cohen pushes Benjamin's argument in a radical direction by arguing that the cinema's "de-auratic" properties are fundamentally connected to the non-mimetic quality of the photographic image: that is, before being a recognizable "tavern, street, factory," the cinematic image is first and foremost the inscription by light of abstract shapes on celluloid. As evidence that Hitchcock self-consciously mobilized this abstract quality of the film image, Cohen cites William Rothman's famous identification of the "bar series" that pervades Hitchcock's work – the inscription of parallel lines that we see, for example, in the impression the fork makes on the tablecloth in *Spellbound* (1945). Similarly, when Hitchcock calls *The Lodger* (1926) "a story of the London fog," he is making claims, Cohen says, about visibility and its relation to both the cinematic apparatus and to state power. For if the "story" is about "the fog," then Hitchcock seems to be asserting that first and foremost cinema is about the abstract patterns of light and shadow that strip the image of aura, and only secondarily about the ways in which these patterns are recognized to be mimetic of the world.

This is where Cohen's deconstruction comes in. If we immediately "mistake" the cinematic image for a mimetic representation of the world, it is because state power has pre-programmed us with our own internal image-archives. (From this comes Cohen's repeated critiques of the institution of film studies, for ratifying this mode of viewing the image.) For Cohen, perception and reference are not grounded in the Platonic system of model and copy, but rather in performative iterations that are mediated by bureaucratic apparatuses. This logic recalls Derrida's deconstruction of the signature. While ideologically the signature might be taken to point back to some originary "presence," in fact no such originary, authenticating instance of the signature can ever be found; one sees only a series of iterations, successively archived by the authority of the state. In order to break the power of the archival logics that govern our vision itself, Cohen argues that we must attend to the de-auratic qualities of the images, and so he tracks relentlessly the geometric shapes, phonemic scraps, numbers, and other "cryptonymies" that pervade Hitchcock's work. In this way, the cinema as an institution is "interrupted," in much the same way that the initial incident in *Sabotage* has the effect of interrupting the screening of a movie by knocking out the power. This interruption will put temporal succession into crisis and thus put history itself "in play," as *Sabotage* again illustrates. For one thing, the bomb in the film canisters goes off one minute later than it is diegetically supposed to; for another, Mrs. Verloc (Sylvia Sidney) can get away with killing her husband (Oscar Homolka) because a detective is unable to remember whether she said her husband was dead before or after the apartment blast occurred. Perhaps the best place to see where all these ideas come into play is in the Albert Hall sequence in the second *The Man Who Knew Too Much*. There, the symphony score, when seen in close-up, is a set of inscriptions or a bar series that takes on a communal (i.e., "mimetic") meaning only when it is performed in an iterative series that is part of the cultural and social archive. Even the sabotage of state power, in the form of the assassination, must be enacted through this archival script, so that musical recordings are used to "rehearse" the assassination, which is to occur when the cymbals crash (which, Cohen wryly notes, is also when the *symbols* "crash"). Doris Day's scream is what derails the performative iteration of the archive and thereby opens history to the unscripted event.

Finally – to cut short the present summary of Cohen's long and intricate argument, which I have treated at greater length elsewhere (Restivo, "Hitchcock") – in his nearly one-hundred-page analysis of the relatively neglected *To Catch a Thief* (1955), Cohen brings in the concept of the simulacrum, a key concept in theories of the postmodern. If the simulacrum is defined, at least colloquially, as the copy of a copy, then we can see how it is installed in the narrative of *To Catch a Thief* via the "copycat," the thief who is literally copying the "cat" burglar John Robie (Cary Grant). But Cohen brings into the analysis the postwar historicity of the French Riviera, which is seen as a touristic space, connected to an advertising poster, and which is dominated by "an economy entirely of service industries: insurance, restaurants, catering, gambling, hotels, police, that is, all theft and circulation *without production*" (2: 209). Cohen here is thus in agreement with such postmodern theorists as Jean Baudrillard, who claims that, in postmodernity, an image-economy has the effect of severing signs from referents and putting them into endless and seductive self-referential play. From this position, then, Cohen can read, for example, the circulation of the signifier "bourbon" in the film, whose reference short-circuits the distance between the simulacrum of the Bourbon court in the costume ball and the American commodity the mother consumes throughout the film. Finally, Cohen can note how the Mediterranean sun – which, from Plato's cave onwards, has been a metaphor for logos itself – is in this film not luminous but blinding, the "black sun" that throws into crisis the relation of copy to original. The famous fireworks scene is one example of this black sun, and while a standard reading might interpret the fireworks as the successful achievement of the sexual relation, a close reading of the sequence would show rather the failure of the relation, as the abyss of *double-entendres* renders everything as fake as the jewels in the room, pure seductive surface. The reading of this film comes at the end of the second volume of the work, and here Cohen hints that perhaps the thematic division "secret agents"/"war machines" might indeed point to a historical periodization. For Cohen argues that in the postwar period, what we see is the totalization of the state of war in a new (or emergent) global geopolitical regime.

With the introduction of the notion of the image-economy and the simulacrum, we can return to our initial definition of the postmodern and note the way that the conditions of postmodernity themselves disrupt traditional Marxism's neat separation of base and superstructure. For with the postmodernization of the economy, the principal energies of production in the most advanced economies become focused on the production and management of images (and, concomitantly, affect and fantasy as well), all of which had earlier been thought to be superstructural phenomena, or else locked within the privacy of the *bourgeois intérieur*. We thus see a kind of contamination or folding together of what had been thought to be separate and causally-related fields. This is why Nicholas Mirzoeff's definition of postmodernism is so resonant, provided we contextualize it within the economic periodization outlined earlier. According to Mirzoeff, "the postmodern is the crisis caused by modernism and modern culture confronting the failure of its own strategy of visualizing" (4). To be sure, Mirzoeff's definition has as one of its underlying goals the validation of the then new field of visual cultural studies, as is clear when he says that "it is the visual crisis of culture that creates postmodernity, not its textuality" (4). For the purposes of this chapter, what is useful in Mirzoeff's definition is the way in which it links modernity to postmodernity precisely on the terrain of the visual. Given Hitchcock's indisputable credentials as a "modern," we might still ask if, where, and to what extent we can discern in Hitchcock's work "modernism confronting the failure of its own strategy of visualizing." In the last part of this chapter, this is precisely what I will attempt to do, via readings of some motifs in *Rope* (1948) and *Vertigo* (1958).

Rope certainly presents us with an obsessive-compulsive strategy of visualization that was widely thought by Hitchcock and the critical establishment to have been a failure. Building on the brilliant work of D.A. Miller, I would like to argue that this film is premonitory of a new reconfiguration of the public/private opposition that would achieve its fullest expression in the films of Hitchcock's "great period" and that bears traces of an emergent regime of visuality more totalizing than that of the interwar period. In Miller's bravura reading of the film, the problem of the film's visual strategy – that is, its attempt to simulate something akin to real time against the technical constraints of the ten-minute film magazine – is directly connected to the problem of gay male visibility itself. Because the gay male figures every sort of social disaster from the disruption of the lineage of patriarchy to a breach in the gates of the security state, and because he can "pass" as straight, the camera must obsessively monitor the space of the penthouse lest any decisively telling sign escape from view. But nothing short of the presentation of the "spectacle of gay male sex" can ever decisively prove anything, and so the camera symptomatically enacts what it can never show, by "taking from behind" the men of the film as a way to preserve the simulation of surveillance. What I would add to Miller's analysis is something I've written about elsewhere: namely, that it is the emergent technology of television – as a medium of live transmission of images and sounds – that provides the visual strategy of *Rope* with its concrete technological-historical point of reference (Restivo, "Silence" 170). The promise (or fantasy) of television, then, was as a kind of anti-representation, a hyper-visibility that threatened the entire visual economy of the filmic system, while its connection to electromagnetic waves threatened a contamination of inside and outside that could fundamentally reconfigure notions of public and private.

At this point, it might be useful to bring in a ("modernist") film movement historically coincident with *Rope*, one that made a strong case for the cinematic image's fundamental connection to "truth": Italian neorealism. It turns out that André Bazin, neorealism's principal champion and theorist, left us with one very short, but profound, comment on Hitchcock's *Rope*, in an endnote to his essay on Vittorio De Sica. Bazin (implicitly) asks: Why don't the long takes of *Rope* produce the kind of cinema of duration that neorealism does? He explains: "The real problem is not the continuity of the exposed film but the temporal structure of the incident" (76). In *Rope*, that is to say, the event is already pre-programmed by the way in which the scripted action is structuring time; the temporality produced by the unrolling of the film is purely secondary. Though this description evokes the relatively commonplace charge that *Rope* is nothing more than "filmed theater," the implications of Bazin's comment are much more complex (something generally true about Bazin's work, which film studies is recently rediscovering). As we move forward in the commentary, Bazin says that the "artificial time" that *Rope* constructs contrasts markedly with the temporality constructed by *Umberto D.* (1952). There, he writes, "the problem of subject and script take on a different aspect. In these instances it is a matter of making 'life time' … take on the quality of a spectacle, of a drama" (76). Thus the first large conclusion we can draw about modernity and its regimes of visuality is that neorealism is fundamentally "at home" in the world, however devastated it finds its world to be: the neorealist event is "irrefutable," to use Bazin's word (78). Indeed, it would not be until the mid-1960s that directors like Antonioni and Godard would confront the failure of this (modernist) strategy of visualizing. *Rope*, however, stages its own failure of visuality, in part because the temporal structure of its events is at odds with the temporal structure enforced by the apparatus.

But what could be the meaning of this failure historically? Bazin's suggestive phrase "life time" might provide a clue to answering this question by leading us toward the concept of the "chronotope," and more particularly to the way Vivian Sobchak has deployed the concept in attempting to understand the historical significance of film noir (which, like neorealism, was contemporaneous with *Rope*). Bakhtin developed the concept of the chronotope in order to move beyond what he thought to be a too-limiting theory of genres: it can be defined as the matrix of spaces (in the sense of locations) and sequencings that provides a kind of generative principle for the narrative. Since the spaces of the world are permeated with historicity, we can see how the chronotope might allow us to anchor the novels (or films) of a certain period and genre to the specific historical world from which these works arise. Sobchak mobilizes the concept of the chronotope to help resolve certain vexing questions connected to film noir. As problematic as the generic label might be in relation to a set of films that are visually and narratively so diverse, we nevertheless sense that there is something real that holds these works together. Sobchak believes this something to be a chronotope (136, 148). To begin to uncover this chronotope, she notes that noir unfolds across a set of spaces – flophouse rooms and hotel lobbies, diners and nightclubs, train and bus stations, and so on – that were part of the fabric of the postwar environment but that noir hyperbolically intensifies, even as it banishes to the margins any stable notion of home. Permanence gives way to transience in a chronotope that Sobchak calls "lounge time" (156), which was expressive of a real, historically "lived" sense of being in transition for Americans of the postwar period.

Of course, film noir might be the last thing that would come to mind when thinking about a film like *Rope*, even if the film was made at the height of noir output. But I propose that the weight of the evidence compels the surprising conclusion that *Rope* takes the chronotope of "lounge time" and situates it within the domestic interior of the New York penthouse. It is this chronotope – along with the accompanying homosexuality – that allows us to understand why the event and its visualization in the film are so divergent as to throw its entire visual strategy into crisis. First of all, we can note how the dinner party Brandon (John Dall) and Phillip (Farley Granger) throw is a kind of "salon," and as Sobchak notes, the space of the salon has many affinities with the space of the nightclub in both gangster films and noir. For Bakhtin, the chronotope of the salon, as it appears in the nineteenth-century novel, is a space in which public and private become confounded, as, for example, political intrigue becomes entwined with adventures of the boudoir, and historical time becomes enmeshed with biographical time. As Bakhtin writes, the salon is the chronotope in which "webs of intrigue are spun, denouements occur... [and] dialogues happen" (quoted in Sobchak 154) – all of which seem uncannily applicable to the scene of *Rope*. Further, the chronotope of lounge time is diametrically opposed to the (ideologically normative) time of "home," with the latter's cyclical commemorations of birthdays, anniversaries, and important communal events. In noir, leisure is not restorative, but rather is "temporalized negatively as idle restlessness, as a lack of occupation, as a disturbing, ambiguous, and public display of unemployment" (158). In *Rope*, these particular figurations of leisure are signaled, positively, by the *jeunesse dorée* of the boys, and, negatively, by their implicit homosexuality and their dinner-party commemoration of their thrill-killing. Like their noir counterparts, Brandon and Phillip in *Rope* unleash within the social field an enjoyment that is ungovernable. And just as the noir chronotope is, in Sobchak's words, "quarantined" and "hermetically sealed" from traditional spaces of domesticity, so too the space of the penthouse is sealed off from the outside world, and the camera is forced to search relentlessly for something it will never find.

To summarize: "lounge time" is a chronotope of in-between-ness, expressive of the sense that something has been irretrievably lost and that something else – as yet unknowable – is emerging in its stead. As such, it leads us to the conclusion that noir itself is symptomatic, not simply of the earliest infrastructural reorganizations that would ultimately be connected to postmodernity, but, more interestingly, of the experience of "transition" itself, which we could argue is one of the principal affective registers of the postmodern sensibility itself, as waves of modernization become ever more rapid. This is perhaps why of all the genres of classical Hollywood, film noir seems the most resonant to a fully postmodern culture. Of course, noir stylistics and themes were foreign to the cinematic world Hitchcock constructed. In *Rope*, the signature stylistic features of noir appear in the film only as disconnected fragments or shards: the urban skyline, the neon sign outside the window, the "voice-off" and "flashback" when Rupert returns to confront the boys with his hypothesis of murder. But Hitchcock's deployment of the noir chronotope suggests that the notion of the transitional is central to understanding his work in the postwar period.

Vertigo also presents us with a novel visual device – the track-back zoom-in on the miniatures of the stairwell or street – which unlike the *Rope* trick is almost universally considered aesthetically successful. For our purposes, though, what is most interesting about this device is not only that it exhibits a kind of "static movement" but that it has no object except its own visual eruption. We are thus plunged into the image itself, in a way that Fredric Jameson says characterizes postmodernism and yet denies ever happens in Hitchcock (*Signatures* 216). To be sure, this visual device gets attached to a point-of-view shot cinematically and to a phobic subjectivity narratively. Still, there is something about this shot that suggests a more fully realized instance of Mirzoeff's notion of modernism confronting its own visual failure. *Vertigo*'s track/zoom shot might be arguably the (vanishing) mediator between the crane shot of *Notorious* (previously described as modernist) and the eruptions of red tint in *Marnie*. As we noted above, the crane shot to the key exposes the *mechanism* of the gaze without ever allowing the visual field to fall toward de-realization, as it would later do in *Marnie*. In *Vertigo*, we get the manifestation of the pure gaze, as object, the phallic anamorphosis that throws the subject into crisis and the object-world into incoherence.

The track-zoom shot, I would argue, is thus a crucial pivot that both links and separates the modernist works of Hitchcock from his later, transitional or symptomatically postmodern works. To understand why, we can begin with a consideration of Hitchcock's schematic construction of images. This, indeed, characterizes

Hitchcock's approach to the image generally, throughout his career. In his interview with Truffaut, Hitchcock explains his procedure in very specific terms:

A.H.   Some directors will place their actors in the decor and then they'll set the camera at a distance, which depends simply on whether the actor happens to be seated, standing, or lying down. It's never precise and it certainly doesn't express anything.

F.T.   In other words, to inject realism into a given film frame, a director must allow for a certain amount of unreality in the space immediately surrounding that frame. For instance, the close-up of a kiss between two supposedly standing figures might be obtained by having the two actors kneeling on a kitchen table.

A.H.   That's one way of doing it. And we might even raise that table some nine inches to have it come into the frame. Do you want to show a man standing behind a table? Well, the closer you get to him, the higher you must raise the table if you want to keep it inside the image. ... The placing of the images on the screen, in terms of what you're expressing, should never be dealt with in a factual manner. Never!

(263–65)

Thus to construct the cinematic image, the world is split apart into pieces and then reassembled, as a kind of "emblem." This is an eminently modernist procedure, one that Walter Benjamin would link to allegory, as that strategy most appropriate to an object-world fragmented by the commodity form.

But given the subject and themes of *Vertigo*, it would seem even more fruitful to move back to Benjamin's earliest development of his theory of allegory, in the *Trauerspiel* study, as *Vertigo*, after all, is a kind of "mourning play" steeped in melancholia. While space does not permit a full discussion of that study, we can note that, for Benjamin, the paralysis of melancholia is profoundly connected to the sense that the object-world has fallen into meaningless fragments. The paralysis of the melancholic emerges amid a more generalized crisis of the sign: pondered long enough, the lifeless remnants of the world's history can come to signify anything in the "book of the creation." That anything can come to signify anything else is naturally of enormous use to the allegorist, even if it means that there is no transcendent idea automatically to ground the play of substitutions. Ultimately, then, the allegorist works with endless fragments, piling them on with no specific goal in sight, "in the unremitting expectation of a miracle" (Benjamin, *Origin* 178).

Indeed, if we think back upon what makes *Vertigo* such an evocative experience as a film, we might think first and foremost of the many fragments that hold us in a kind of strange fascination. The film is filled with "signs" that point nowhere, like the "One Way Street" sign, or those of the Empire Hotel, the Argosy Bookstore, or the strangely mesmerizing lighted Fire Escape sign at the end of the corridor of Judy's room. This pointed lack of reference helps explain Jameson's remark that "[t]he hallucinatory San Francisco of *Vertigo* is undatable, out of time" ("Spatial" 59). All of these considerations, as we've said, mark *Vertigo* as very much continuous with the modernism of Hitchcock's work more generally. But the track-zoom shot, as phallic apparition of the gaze in the visual field, moves us beyond this modernist procedure. As the sound that accompanies this shot ratifies, there is about it something radically unassimilable to the rest of the filmic system. Here we do indeed see modernism confronting the failure of its strategy of visualization.

Works Cited

Bazin, André. *What Is Cinema?* Vol. 2. Trans. Hugh Gray. Berkeley: U California P, 2004.

Benjamin, Walter. *The Origin of German Tragic Drama*. London: Verso, 1998.

Benjamin, Walter. "The Work of Art in the Age of Its Technological Reproducibility." *Selected Writings*. Ed. Howard Eiland and Michael W. Jennings. Vol. 4. Cambridge: Belknap, 2006. 101–33.

Cohen, Tom. *Hitchcock's Cryptonymies*. 2 vols. Minneapolis: U of Minnesota P, 2005.

Foster, Hal. "The Return of the Real." *The Return of the Real: The Avant-garde at the End of the Century*. Cambridge: MIT P, 1996. 127–70.

Jameson, Fredric. *Postmodernism, or, The Cultural Logic of Late Capitalism*. Durham: Duke UP, 1991.

Jameson, Fredric. *Signatures of the Visible*. New York: Routledge, 1990.

Jameson, Fredric. "Spatial Systems in *North by Northwest*." Žižek, *Everything* 47–72.

Miller, D.A. "Anal Rope." *Inside Out: Lesbian Theories, Gay Theories*. Ed. Diana Fuss. New York: Routledge, 1991. 119–41.

Mirzoeff, Nicholas, ed. *The Visual Culture Reader*. Second ed. London: Routledge, 2002.

Morris, Christopher D. *The Hanging Figure: On Suspense and the Films of Alfred Hitchcock*. Westport, CT: Praeger, 2002.

Restivo, Angelo. "Hitchcock In Pieces." *Hitchcock Annual* 14 (2005–06): 157–73.

Restivo, Angelo. "Into the Breach: Between the Movement-Image and the Time-Image." *The Brain Is the Screen: Deleuze and the Philosophy of Cinema*. Ed. Gregory Flaxman. Minneapolis: U of Minnesota P, 2000. 171–92.

Restivo, Angelo. "The Silence of *The Birds*." *Hitchcock: Past and Future*. Ed. Richard Allen and Sam Ishii-Gonzáles. London: Routledge, 2004. 164–78.

Sobchak, Vivian. "Lounge Time: Postwar Crises and the Chronotope of Film Noir." *Refiguring American Film Genres: History and Theory*. Ed. Nick Browne. Berkeley: U of California P, 1998. 129–70.

Truffaut, François, with the collaboration of Helen G. Scott. *Hitchcock*. Rev. ed. New York: Simon and Schuster, 1984.

Žižek, Slavoj. *Looking Awry: An Introduction to Jacques Lacan Through Popular Culture*. Cambridge: MIT P, 1991.

Žižek, Slavoj, ed. *Everything You Always Wanted to Know About Lacan (But Were Afraid to Ask Hitchcock)*. London: Verso, 1992.

30

Hitchcock's Legacy

Richard Allen

Hitchcock's importance as a director is surely to be measured as much by the nature of his influence as by the quality of his accomplishments. Though there have always been those from Lindsay Anderson to Raymond Carney who have viewed him as a technically accomplished but essentially facile maker of popular melodramas, for many critics his accomplishments as a director rank him among the preeminent film artists. What remains indubitable, however, is his unparalleled and continuing influence in the history of cinema. In this chapter, I will suggest why Hitchcock's films have had such a sustained influence and assess that influence in the context of European and American cinema. Central to this ongoing reception is the canonical place Hitchcock occupies in the formation of the very idea of the film director as artist, and the way in which the idea of Hitchcock's auteurism informs the self-conscious directorial identity of filmmakers who are influenced by him. Accordingly, my purpose in this chapter is twofold: to explain the nature and character of Hitchcock's influence primarily in terms of the particular form taken by his work, and to describe the way in which the work of Hitchcock-influenced directors can be understood as adapting and transforming aspects of Hitchcock's idiom in a manner that is worthy of the epithet "Hitchcockian."

Hitchcock is not unique in the history of cinema in combining a modernist's self-consciousness with popular storytelling. Like the German expressionist filmmakers, Hitchcock combined an authorial and stylistic self-consciousness expressed in the ideal of a cinematic narration eschewing dialogue, which he dubbed "pure cinema," with an understanding of the "disreputable" origins of cinema in the fairground and its unique appeal as a form of attraction or spectacle that is linked to gaming or play and to the shadow world of forbidden desire. Also, like the

A Companion to Alfred Hitchcock, First Edition. Edited by Thomas Leitch and Leland Poague.
© 2011 Thomas Leitch and Leland Poague. Published 2011 by Blackwell Publishing Ltd.

German expressionist filmmakers, he embraced the idioms of popular romantic melodrama. Even before he arrived in Hollywood, however, Hitchcock was deeply committed to the "modern" storytelling techniques of popular Hollywood cinema that placed a premium on character agency and did not dwell on sentiment. Hollywood standardized the paradigm of the "double plot" that parallels the story of a formation of the couple with a second story, say, a plot of detection (see Bordwell, Staiger, and Thompson), and Hitchcock's contribution, via Buchan, was the wrong-man thriller in which "suspense" is attached to the formation of the couple. Furthermore, Hitchcock was particularly adept at inhabiting the protocols of narrative economy afforded by classical American cinema, which rigorously subordinates the parameters of film style to narrative causality and epistemic transparency, even as he consistently experimented with unreliable narration and the orchestration of point of view. Indeed, as John Orr points out, it is actually in his mature American work that Hitchcock's expressionism achieves its fullest realization, in films like *Rebecca* (1940), *Shadow of a Doubt* (1943), *The Paradine Case* (1947), *Strangers on a Train* (1951), *Psycho* (1960), and *The Birds* (1963), where it is seamlessly wedded to the classical idiom.

The source of Hitchcock's influence lies, then, in the particular synthesis of stylistic self-consciousness and popular storytelling achieved in his American films, which combines the conventional moral framework of the romantic suspense thriller with an orchestration, through form and style, of the allure of human perversity. As I have argued elsewhere, Hitchcock's idiom is that of the romantic ironist whose films are informed by a both/and logic that deliriously asserts the ideal of romance yet simultaneously embraces those forces of human perversity and nihilism that undermine and negate that ideal. As François Truffaut joked in his speech for Hitchcock's 1979 American Film Institute Life Achievement Award:

> In America … you respect him because he shoots scenes of love as if they were scenes of murder. We respect him because he shoots scenes of murder like scenes of love. Anyway, it's the same man we are talking about, the same man, and the same artist.

Hitchcock's films employ the idioms of classical suspense informed by conventional morality, yet they take ludic pleasure in prolonging and stylizing suspense in ways that subvert the customary alliance between emotional identification and moral allegiance. They conform to the imperative of entertainment cinema to keep the audience on a tight emotional leash yet display the more self-conscious, cerebral aspects of the artwork whose formal properties are mobilized by its creator to draw attention to his or her address to the audience.

The character of romantic irony accords a particular status to the figure of the author who hovers playfully above and within the text. Hitchcock's presence as the dryly witty, corpulent persona who walked into his own films and introduced his television show gives embodiment to the ludic narrator of the text, one who makes us think of the cinematic narrator as a particular person, the author "Alfred Hitchcock" as he is presented by the man Alfred Hitchcock. Hitchcock embodied the idea of the author in the age of mass media as one who fashions his own image for the audience and shapes his or her authorial intervention through the creative appropriation and transformation of the works of others. As Hitchcock adroitly realized, such self-fashioning through appropriative collaboration was indispensable for the film director who wanted to stamp his or her authority upon the relatively impersonal medium of film, whose source material was typically, in the studio system Hitchcock worked under, derived from others. Hitchcock-influenced directors do not always render literal their textual presence, but like Hitchcock they manifest a highly intertextual, appropriative approach to film authorship, most tellingly in the myriad ways they borrow from Hitchcock's own work and assert a self-conscious, playful control over the unfolding of cinematic narration, thereby visibly inscribing the presence and authority of the film director in the artifact of the film.

The nature of Hitchcock's influence depends on which aspect of his idiom is appropriated. Just as Hitchcock's romantic irony yields not only different but typically opposed critical understandings, so do different directors appropriate, intensify, or transform different aspects of his work. Some directors develop Hitchcock's complex evocation of guilt and innocence. Others amplify his representation of the shadow world of human perversity. Still others draw upon the expressiveness and articulateness of Hitchcock's style, or upon the way he sometimes turns the experience of film viewing into a game or puzzle. Hitchcock's influence manifests itself in myriad ways that are more or less pervasive, ranging from the wholesale appropriation of his idiom to the reworking and borrowing of specific wholes or parts of Hitchcock stories to the quotation or use of specific scenes, situations, or stylistic strategies.

European Art Cinema

Hitchcock's influence has been decisively framed by the historical factors that govern its reception. Of greatest importance was the canonization of Hitchcock as the paradigmatic auteur, or film director as creative artist, by the young French critics of *Cahiers du cinéma* – François Truffaut, Claude Chabrol, Eric Rohmer, and Jean-Luc Godard – all of whom wrote on the director. As James Vest makes clear, Hitchcock was not simply one of the American directors valorized by French cineastes of the 1950s; he was *the* auteur. In the hands of Rohmer and Chabrol, authors of *Hitchcock: The First Forty-Four Films* (1957; trans. 1979), and Truffaut, Hitchcock's famous interviewer, Hitchcock's films become a model for what we might term, after András Kovács, classical art cinema. This is a bourgeois cinema in content and address whose concern is with exploring serious themes of guilt and responsibility and the capacity for love and redemption, and it renders these themes in a manner that, while stylistically self-conscious, uses location shooting and is realist in its attention to everyday social milieus. Although they have been read as Hitchcockian (see Orr), Rohmer's films are so cerebral, realist in rendering, and lacking in drama and suspense that they might seem an antidote to Hitchcock's artifice, and it is Chabrol who more profoundly absorbs and exhibits the lessons of their study, that in Hitchcock "form does not embellish content, it creates it" (152).

In films like *La femme infidèle* (1969) and *Le boucher* (1970), Chabrol explores, like Hitchcock, the shadow world that lurks beneath the veneer of bourgeois values. While his everyday bourgeois milieu is one that lacks both Hitchcock's fascination with the sheen of romantic aestheticism and the perverse sense of humor that lends his cinema much of its entertainment value, it is marked by a profoundly Hitchcockian dialectic of surface and depth, by Hitchcock's expressionist style (especially his use of color), which serves to dramatize this dialectic, and by the doubling or triangulation of characters bound together by objects exchanged among them that mark their affinity, even when they are antagonists. Through this aesthetic, Chabrol makes explicit a logic, first defined by Robin Wood, that is central to Hitchcock's work: through an encounter with the shadow world the values of the ordinary are affirmed and redeemed, even as this encounter seems to turn those values upside down. *La femme infidèle*, a conventional drama of marital deceit, is given depth by its remarkable realization of bourgeois domesticity – a picture postcard of marital perfection, whose color design, framing, and mise-en-scène serves to delineate its artifice – and by its subtle turn of argument. The eruption of the shadow world into the everyday through the murder of the wife's lover by her husband, with appropriate references to *Psycho*, causes not the disintegration of the brittle artifice of normality but its affirmation as a bulwark against chaos, as the couple are bound together by the husband's action that affirms his love. *Le boucher* pushes this logic still further in dramatizing the relationship between a school-teacher, Hélène (Stéphane Audran), and a local butcher, Popaul (Jean Yanne), which imagines the continuation of the relationship between Norman Bates (Anthony Perkins) and Marion Crane (Janet Leigh) in *Psycho*. Perversely, Popaul kills in order to preserve the purity of the object he loves, and Hélène is drawn to him in such a way that she actually covers for his crime. Just as Charlie Newton (Teresa Wright) is emotionally bound to her Uncle Charlie (Joseph Cotten) in *Shadow of a Doubt* by shared knowledge, Hélène is emotionally complicit in Popaul's guilt. When he appears to turn upon her at the film's dénouement, Chabrol's ambiguous montage leads us to infer that she is prepared to sacrifice herself to him, as in Hitchcock's staging of Verloc's death in *Sabotage* (1936). In fact, Popaul has plunged the dagger into his own chest in what amounts to a final act of atonement that at once preserves and affirms his love, renders him deeply sympathetic, and seems, with finality, to bind Hélène to him (Neupert 140).

For Truffaut, too, Hitchcock is a model director because of the way he expresses narrative content through cinematic technique. Prior to *Le peau douce* (1964), his first major Hitchcockian work, Truffaut's films are haunted with references to *Vertigo* (1958). In *Jules et Jim* (1962), for example, Catherine (Jeanne Moreau) is identified with a sculpture just as Madeleine (Kim Novak) in *Vertigo* is equated with a painting. Like Madeleine, Catherine is rescued from water by the hero and falls to her death from a precipice. After *Le peau douce*, Truffaut will engage the Hitchcockian idiom in an increasingly heavy-handed way, as in *The Bride Wore Black* (1969), an austere black comedy that is almost cartoonish in its deployment of the Hitchcockian color system of blacks and whites and warning colors, in which a woman who recalls Hitchcock's Marnie (Tippi Hedren) systematically hunts down and kills her husband's murderers. While *Le peau douce*, with its thriller elements, is a departure from the airy romantic idiom of Truffaut's early work, it retains their lightness of touch, and the work is full of witty references to the master's films. A photograph that "frames" the protagonist with his flight-hostess lover Nicole (Françoise Dorléac) in the paper recalls the "framing" of Thornhill (Cary Grant) for the murder of Townsend (Philip Ober) in *North by Northwest* (1959), and Truffaut quotes from *Psycho*, as, driving with his wife from the airport, Jean (Pierre Lachenay) sees the co-pilot of Nicole's plane crossing the road – a visual reminder of his guilt, like the sight Marion Crane gets of her boss as she leaves Phoenix with the stolen money. While Truffaut seems to encroach on Chabrolian territory in peeling away the veneer of bourgeois propriety, the film, like others in Truffaut's canon, lacks Chabrol's emotional depth. Instead, Truffaut's Hitchcockian mode actually consists in dwelling upon the surface of things, his protagonist's blind and often comic pursuit of a rather trivial romance, the stubborn resistance of circumstance, his fleeting moments of pleasure, and the hand of destiny (or is it chance?) that dooms him. And even though Truffaut's touch is light, *Vertigo* governs the whole; *Le peau douce* is a tale of doomed love.

In contrast to realist art cinema, in modernist art cinema narrational self-conscious takes precedence over the construction of an unambiguously unified and objective narrative world. Supported by extended passages of "pure cinema," modernist Hitchcockians amplify the formal emplotment of ambiguity and the stylistic self-reflexivity of Hitchcock's work. Most typically, modernist art cinema takes the form of a reflection upon subjectivity and the subjective apprehension of space and time, as in the work of Resnais, which I will consider shortly. Jean-Luc Godard, by contrast, is a filmmaker who takes an experimental approach to cinematic storytelling as a process of intertextual assemblage that self-consciously flags its constituent parts as sound, voice, image, and story, fragmenting and then reordering these elements in a manner that privileges the manner of the telling over what is told, often in order to draw attention to how social meanings and social ideologies are created and re-produced. By comparison, Hitchcock appears a conventional filmmaker comfortably housed within a communicative style of filmmaking in which style and form are an expression of content, even as he subverts convention with his formal dexterity and self-conscious aestheticism. But this contrast between the classical and modernist filmmaker belies a fundamental affinity in sensibility that explains Godard's admiration of Hitchcock. For all Godard's celebrated deconstructive flair, his filmmaking practice from *Pierrot le fou* (1966) to *Passion* (1982) is parasitic not only upon the conventions he so thoroughly deconstructs but more specifically upon the romantic notion of the ideal or the absolute, whether conceived as the perfection of form, as the ideal of woman or romantic love, or as the ideal of absolute freedom so prevalent in sixties ideology.

Perhaps more than any other Hitchcock-influenced director, Godard most fully grasps the both/and logic of Hitchcockian romantic irony that at once asserts and subverts the ideal, thereby promoting the persona of the author as the figure who orchestrates this unstable universe. Whereas Hitchcock is preoccupied with plotting the formation and incipient destruction of the ideal of the couple, however, Godard returns us to the roots of romanticism in the idea that the work of art itself is the ideal, though it is an ideal that is undermined by the modernist realization that the artwork is but a representation or fiction. Godard is thus Hitchcock squared, or a post-romantic ironist, who applies both/and logic to the very art of cinematic storytelling rather than simply to the stories told, idealizing narrative and pictorial content and elements of style, such as color or camera movement, even while exposing their thoroughly derived, constructed, or artifactual status. Godard's films thus become, more than anything else, films about the figure of the author himself, who reveals his hand in each sound and every image.

The films of Chris Marker and Alain Resnais, arguably inspired by the philosophy of Henri Bergson, represent an alternative modernist film practice that uses the imagistic medium of cinema to represent the conflation of imagination and memory and to explore the subjective experience of time. Hitchcock might seem an unlikely source of influence upon these filmmakers were it not for *Vertigo*. In *Sans soleil* (1983), Chris Marker hints at the "creative misreading" of *Vertigo* that informs his appropriation of Hitchcock's film, and arguably that of Resnais too. During a sequence in which the narrator of the film revisits the locations of *Vertigo* in San Francisco, accompanied by images from the film, he recounts that "Hitchcock ... imagined Scottie [James Stewart] as time's fool of love. Finding it impossible to live with memory without falsifying it, he invented a double for Madeleine in another dimension of time, a zone that would belong only to him and from which he could decipher the undecipherable story that had begun at [the] Golden Gate when he had pulled Madeline out of San Francisco Bay." In this "creative misreading," Madeleine is Elster's wife, possessed by Carlotta Valdes, whose death she is condemned to repeat. In part two, Scottie, thinking himself responsible for her death, vainly tries to exorcise this loss by imagining her reincarnated in the figure of Judy, a fantasy that has all the reality of lived experience. Stripped of the rationalist framework of detection, truth, and explanation, a new version of the French Hitchcock emerges, a modernist Hitchcock who seeks to use cinema to explore the permeable boundaries of perception, imagination, and memory.

This "creative misreading" of *Vertigo* provides a key to understanding the manner in which *Vertigo* inspires Marker's *La jetée* (1962). *La jetée* is a science fiction film set in a post-apocalyptic concentration camp environment, hauntingly composed of (mostly) still photographs, in which a nameless man (Davos Hanich) is sent back to the past to retrieve supplies of food and energy. He is chosen for the mission because he has a peculiarly intense childhood memory fixation of a woman's face at Orly Airport before the catastrophe happened, a fixation scientists believe may provide the metaphysical force required to make the virtual reality of his memory actual. Sure enough, he finds himself seamlessly inserted into his mental pictures of the past, which temporarily become life itself in a timeless present. As in Marker's reading of *Vertigo*, but here by dint of time travel, a lost attachment from the past that cannot be relinquished is made real. But as Luc Lagier points out in his visual essay for French television, it is not simply that *La jetée* is like the story of *Vertigo*, because it also seems to inscribe Marker's fantasy, suggested in *Sans soleil*, of entering into Hitchcock's film. The hero, strapped in a seat and subjected to the experience of memory images, is like the film viewer of *Vertigo*, but the film he watches inside his head becomes the very world he enters. It is worth noting that Terry Gilliam's reworking of *La jetée*, *12 Monkeys* (1995), pays homage to *Vertigo* by directly quoting Hitchcock's film to frame the moment when the hero recognizes his female companion as the woman from his past.

Vertigo, conceived as a meditation on time and its illusory conquest, also seems to haunt the early work of Resnais, especially *Last Year at Marienbad* (1961). The analogies to the triangle formed by Scottie, Madeleine, and Elster (Tom Helmore) in *Vertigo* are apparent in the relationship between a man, a woman whom he may or may not have had an affair with a year ago, and her controlling husband. More striking still are the echoes of Hitchcock's visual style. The frozen postures of the figures amplify the sense of pictorial artifice attached to the figure of Madeline in *Vertigo*. The highly contrived mise-en-scène of the castle supplements the artifice of the figures as the space of Ernie's restaurant in *Vertigo* identifies the artifice of Madeline with the fiction of Hitchcock's film itself. And the relentless, *Vertigo*-like tracking shots through the corridors of the castle and across its elegant surfaces, accompanied by the narrator's voiceover, suggest not simply a penetration of space but a penetration of time – a journey of perceptual discovery that is also perhaps a memory or maybe just a figment of the narrator's imagination. At one moment, early in the film, as was Hitchcock's wont, Hitchcock's profile appears by the elevator, but here as a larger-than-life cardboard cutout. This joke in an ostensibly serious film indicates that, for all his metaphysical portentousness, Resnais in *Marienbad*, like Hitchcock in *Vertigo* and elsewhere, is enjoying a game with the film spectator.

Michelangelo Antonioni, like Resnais, inflects Hitchcockian ambiguity and stylistic reflexivity towards a modernist idiom. Antonioni's cinema, like Hitchcock's, narrates through orienting characters and character relationships in privileged spaces, through stasis or through movement, but whereas in Hitchcock the placement of characters in space is subordinate to story, in Antonioni it seems to become the substance of the work. *L'avventura* (1960), *Blow-Up* (1966), and *The Passenger*

(1975) each hangs its skeletal story on an idea inspired by a Hitchcock film: *Vertigo*, *Rear Window* (1954), and *North by Northwest* respectively. In *L'avventura*, a woman beloved of the male protagonist disappears, and he subsequently pursues a love affair with the woman's best friend, Claudia (Monica Vitti). As in the second half of *Vertigo*, it is an affair that is governed for both parties by the absence of the woman who has disappeared. Claudia even wears the blouse of her perhaps deceased friend. In *Blow-Up*, Antonioni creates a world full of surfaces and bodies shorn of meaning or human connection. Thomas (David Hemmings) is a highly successful and boorishly lascivious fashion photographer who casually shoots photographs of what he thinks is a couple who are kissing, but what turns out, in Hitchcockian fashion, to be a murder. Thomas is more of a rogue than Jefferies (James Stewart) in *Rear Window*; his casual voyeurism is without shame, he wields his camera, which is evidently a phallic prop, with abandon, and he dominates and controls his models with callous indifference. Yet burdened by their demands, he also, like Jefferies, betrays a sense of impotence and exhaustion. His camera, although a means of asserting himself within the world, is actually a symptom of his thorough alienation from it (Tomasulo).

If *Blow-Up* turns *Rear Window* into a meditation upon urban alienation, *The Passenger* renders explicit the theme of lost identity and self-alienation that lies at the heart of the picaresque narrative of *North by Northwest*, whose protagonist, Roger Thornhill, assumes the identity of another man and is threatened with extinction as he traverses the vast landscape of cold-war America. Unlike Thornhill, who struggles against death towards self-renewal and romance, David Locke (Jack Nicholson), once he deliberately assumes the identity of a dead man in *The Passenger*, gradually embraces it. Symptomatically, the image of Thornhill as George Kaplan, isolated at Prairie Stop in the midst of nothingness with his life on the line, is recalled at the *opening* of Antonioni's film as Locke stands alone in the desert by his Jeep waiting for a man on a camel: Antonioni's protagonist already begins at degree zero. The effect of the miraculous directorial intervention that saves the couple from the precipice in *North by Northwest* is inverted in *The Passenger*, where in a *tour de force* movement the camera abandons Locke in his hotel room, giving him space, as it were, to die, only to return inside to re-discover his corpse in the exact position of the man whose identity he had assumed, as if he had always already been dead.

Postclassical Hollywood

Following the French critical valorization of Hitchcock as an auteur, Hitchcock's films also achieved paradigmatic status among the so-called film school generation. In the context of the renewal of American cinema in the 1960s – in response to declining attendance on the one hand and the emergence of European art cinema on the other – the new American film directors were, like their French counterparts, deeply knowledgeable about film history, especially American film history, and self-conscious cinema stylists who nonetheless, like Hitchcock, sought to work within the commercial, entertainment idioms of Hollywood, in particular those of the psychological thriller and the horror film. Although Hitchcock made only two horror films, *Psycho* and *The Birds*, both films, especially *Psycho*, had a decisive influence on the mainstream emergence of the genre from the shadows of the B movie and exploitation film.

Two broad tendencies can be distinguished in the appropriation of Hitchcock's aesthetic in Hollywood. In the first, exemplified in auteurist terms by Steven Spielberg but manifest in the work of countless less accomplished mainstream directors, the vocabulary of Hitchcockian suspense is augmented and intensified, and sometimes merely rehearsed, while remaining firmly within the conventional, Manichean moral framework of popular melodrama, which seeks to preserve virtue and romance against villainy and human perversity. In this context, the subversive dimensions of Hitchcock's cinema threaten to become domesticated into the comforts of the middlebrow, as in Jonathan Demme's quasi-Hitchcockian *Last Embrace* (1979) and *Something Wild* (1986). In the second, exemplified in auteurist terms by the work of Brian De Palma and generically motivated by the modern horror movie under the spell of *Psycho*, Hitchcock's expressionism is intensified, through hyperbolic stylization, in a manner that is often wedded to an unreliably communicative narration that is flaunted to the point of self-parody. In this post-sixties cinema, the teasing allure of human sexuality is given a representational explicitness that Hitchcock's films lack until *Frenzy* (1972), but it still carries an aura of guilt and punishment, and the scandalous dimension of Hitchcock's cinema, while preserved, is carefully circumscribed within the generic framework of horror. The conventions of the horror genre motivated an extension and elaboration of Hitchcock's playful experiments with the control of narrational point of view. The horror film evolved into a forum for playing games with the audience around the provocation of their fear in a manner that was evoked in the original publicity campaign for *Psycho*, which prevented late-arriving patrons from walking in on the film during the screening and thereby primed them to anticipate the shocking death of the film's protagonist.

In a 1997 interview with the author, Patricia Hitchcock, Hitchcock's daughter and sometime actor in his films, said that Steven Spielberg was the true heir of Hitchcock, a claim that deserves to be taken seriously. Hitchcock's mastery of suspense consists in his development and perfection of a complex vocabulary of suspense that combines omniscient narration that creates anxiety about a known threat, like the bomb about to explode in *Sabotage*, with the restriction of point of view involved in "suspenseful mystery" that characterizes a film like *Vertigo*. Spielberg's filmmaking involves a remarkable augmentation of this Hitchcockian vocabulary of suspense in accordance with the logic of intensified continuity analyzed by David Bordwell (*Hollywood*). The elements of this vocabulary are already evident in *Duel* (1972), a made-for-television movie featuring the simplest of suspense narratives. An average Joe motorist (Dennis Weaver) is pursued and harassed by an oil truck. His only mistake lies in his initial effort to outrun it. Will he survive the attack? Spielberg's camera is at once omniscient and suppressive. The camera cuts from long shot, showing the truck looming up on the car, to point-of-view shots from the truck driver's perspective, to shots from the rear bumper of the car showing the truck rapidly approaching. In addition, Spielberg makes extensive use of the telephoto lens to inflate the size of the truck and make it look closer than it is. Suppressive narration keeps the truck driver anonymous, giving the truck the inhuman quality of a monster. Perhaps Spielberg's most important contribution to the rhetoric of horror and suspense in this film, one that he repeats in *Jaws* (1975) and subsequent films in the genre, is to provide the viewer with point-of-view shots of the truck bearing down on the hapless driver, shots that endow the monster with a fearsome kind of agency – though of course Hitchcock himself was arguably the first to pursue this strategy in the quasi-point-of-view shot he gives to the birds that hover over Bodega Bay in *The Birds*.

The proximity and distance of Spielberg from Hitchcock is evident if we consider *Jurassic Park* (1991), which reworks *The Birds* (Wollen). *Jurassic Park* emphasizes the avian kinship of the dinosaurs, and like Hitchcock in *The Birds*, Spielberg is supremely invested in giving realization to these monstrous beings. In both films, confrontation with the monster catalyzes a transformation in the family, human beings are compared to animals, and the "birds" take on figurations of a threatening femininity: Hitchcock's birds are the proverbial harpies, while in *Jurassic Park* the dinosaurs represent a fecund, self-reproducing nature. Even the idea of "Jurassic Park" as a dinosaur prison faintly echoes Hitchcock's representation of the caged lovebirds. In both films, the terms of entrapment between humans and creatures are reversed, and the directors go to great lengths to orchestrate what it feels like for the cinema viewer trapped in his or her seat (doubled in Spielberg's film as the theme park rider) to be attacked. And yet *Jurassic Park* is not a horror film but a kid's movie that partakes of the theme park mentality it criticizes. Family relationships are wholly sentimentalized and reconstituted at the film's close, and the film altogether lacks the ironic edge of *The Birds*, in which the spectacle is wholly focused upon the bird attacks and their killer instincts find a parallel in the emotionally destructive capacities of the human beings in the film. The closure of *The Birds* is profoundly ambiguous. At the end of *Jurassic Park*, by contrast, while T. Rex still rules the world, he is safely confined to the island of Jurassic Park, ready for the sequel, while the hero has overcome his child phobia and bonded with his new family.

Hollywood cinema also develops and augments Hitchcock's vocabulary of unreliable narration, to which the aesthetics of suspense is wedded. As Malcolm Turvey, drawing on David Bordwell, has pointed out, Hitchcock's narration can deceive us in two ways. It can seem communicative but retrospectively appear deceptive, like the aspersions cast by Hitchcock's visual expressionism upon the character of the Lodger in *The Lodger* (1926) or against Cary Grant's character Johnnie Aysgarth in *Suspicion* (1941), or else it can fail to communicate what it knows and only later fill us in on the facts, as in the scene from *Marnie* (1964) when the eponymous heroine drops her shoe after robbing the Rutland safe and we believe she will be found out by the cleaning lady, only to discover that the cleaning lady is deaf. This deployment of unreliably communicative narration to foster suspense is exploited and amplified by the psychological thriller and horror genres, in which the narration flaunts its control of the spectator's access to the whereabouts of the villain or the monster. Turvey discusses John Carpenter's *Psycho*-influenced horror film *Halloween* (1978), which develops the vocabulary of unreliably communicative narration by leaving it uncertain whether the camera's point of view does or does not conceal from the spectator the presence of the killer. What marks out Hollywood cinema of the recent past is that a communication that is pervasively unreliable and sometimes flatly deceptive has entered into the Hollywood mainstream in the form of the so-called puzzle film that systematically convolutes narrative ordering and deliberately plants false or misleading cues as to what is taking place in the story, as in *The Usual Suspects* (Bryan Singer, 1995), *Fight Club* (David Fincher, 1999), *Memento* (Christopher Nolan, 2000), and many of David Lynch's films (Buckland).

In Martin Scorsese's psychological melodramas, unreliably communicative narration and narrative suspense are wedded to the intensification of expressionist aesthetics in a manner that explicitly references the work of Hitchcock. The link between Scorsese and Hitchcock is perhaps best summarized by Bazin's comment that "each shot is for [Hitchcock] like a menace, or at least an anxious waiting" (69). In *Cape Fear* (1991), a Scorsese remake that reworks Bernard Herrmann's original score and employs the veteran art director and Hitchcock collaborator Henry Bumstead, a brutal rapist, Cady (Robert De Niro), terrorizes a family. In one scene husband and wife (Nick Nolte and Jessica Lange) make love to Herrmann's tremulous violins, washed with alternating red and violet "warning" colors caused by fireworks. As the camera draws toward the wife's pensive face, the screen fades to yellow. She puts on lipstick in a space otherwise washed of color, her face flashes to negative, and the screen fades twice to red (Scorsese here borrows from the aesthetic of *Vertigo* and *Marnie*). Then she approaches the blinds that cast the shadow of parallel lines across her face that mark the threat of the shadow world in Hitchcock's films. There follows a series of three quick point-of-view reaction shots as she sees the villain framed by exploding fireworks (recalling the point-of-view shots in reaction to the fire at the gas station in *The Birds*). Or is he merely an apparition, a figment of her fevered imagination? When the husband joins her in profile, looking through the slats and bathed in red light, Cady has disappeared.

In *Shutter Island* (2010), Teddy Daniels (Leonardo DiCaprio) arrives at an island housing the criminally insane in search of a missing female inmate presumed to have killed her children. He is interviewed by the head doctor, Dr. Cawley (Ben Kingsley), who reports that the female inmate is caught up in the extraordinary fantasy that her children are still alive and the inmates are her family. Just as Hitchcock used explicit references to expressionist film to cast aspersions on character motivation, Scorsese here uses a reference to Hitchcock's *Vertigo* – Dr. Cawley's smooth enunciation sounds like Gavin Elster talking to Scottie about Madeleine, and he is positioned like Elster talking to Scottie in the mise-en-scène – to prime the well-informed spectator to think that this a lie and snare. The twist in *Shutter Island* is that Dr. Cawley's story, though a lie and a snare, is designed to benefit rather than harm its victim.

However, it is Brian De Palma who has appropriated the Hitchcockian idiom in a more literal-minded way than any other director (Leitch). He adapts Hitchcock's plots willy-nilly: *Obsession* (1976) remakes *Vertigo*, *Sisters* (1973) reworks *Psycho* via *Rear Window*, *Dressed to Kill* (1980) reworks *Psycho*, *Body Double* (1984) melds *Vertigo* and *Rear Window*, and so on; his films are structured around Hitchcockian patterns of doubling, often in a very literal-minded way, as in *Sisters* and *Raising Cain* (1992); black comedy pervades his work; he is a master of unreliably communicative narration that is flaunted in his disguised dream sequences, such as the opening and closing of *Dressed to Kill* or the final scene in *Carrie* (1976), and in his "film" scenes that initially appear real, such as the opening of *Blow Out* (1981) or the closing scene of *Body Double*; and he obsessively quotes scenes from Hitchcock's works, especially the shower scene from *Psycho,* which is reworked in *Phantom of the Paradise* (1974), *Dressed to Kill, Carrie,* and *Blow Out,* not to mention the bathroom scenes in *Sisters* and *Scarface* (1983). He is also a learned student of Hitchcock's style. Characteristically he appropriates an element of Hitchcock style and intensifies its use in ways that seem gratuitously excessive given the sometimes banal, often overtly erotic contexts in which it is deployed. Examples are the reverse-field tracking shots that evoke the erotic allure of the mysterious stranger in the gallery pursuit in *Dressed to Kill*; the 360-degree pan in *Body Double,* where the passion of the hero for the woman he pursues suddenly bursts forth; and the hyperbolic deployment of Hitchcock's color systems, such as warning colors of yellow, orange, and red that appear in the corridor of the apartment of the female killer in *Sisters* just before her first murder. To these hyperbolized Hitchcockian idioms, De Palma adds his own, all of which are overt markers of narration: the split screen that often evokes parallelism or doubling; slow motion, which intensifies erotic suspense; and zoom shots, often in conjunction with point-of-view or reaction shot editing.

Through his pastiche, De Palma at once incorporates and transforms Hitchcock's aestheticism. Aestheticism in Hitchcock gives displaced expression to human perversity, as in the shower scene montage of *Psycho*. In De Palma's mannerist style, however, aestheticism no longer functions as an alibi for human perversity, but rather exists alongside the frank display of human sexuality. In the slow-motion shower scenes that open *Dressed to Kill* and *Carrie,* the shower is overtly phallic, female sexual pleasure is overtly exhibited, and the camera is shamelessly voyeuristic. There is a similar kind of frankness in the display and staging of violence in

De Palma. Whereas Hitchcock overtly withdraws his camera from the second murder in *Frenzy*, De Palma mimics this scene of withdrawal in *Scarface* only to return us promptly to the apartment to display the hell within. To this heady excess of aesthetic and sexual display is added self-reflexivity in the form of black comedy or the sick joke that is layered upon the Hitchcockian pastiche. The shower scene in *Dressed to Kill*, which begins in masturbation and ends in a sexual attack, is but a (wish-fulfilling?) dream; the coed sexual frenzy that opens *Blow Out* and ends in a shower murder is someone else's movie, for which the sound-man hero, in a parody of the sick joke, finds a scream that is of a real woman as she is murdered; even the bathroom killing scene in *Scarface* overtly parodies chainsaw horror (Hitchcock is a privileged source but by no means the only source). Combining sex, violence, style, and self-parody with a dose of sappy sentimentalism, De Palma's cinema, until he began making more conventional films like *Bonfire of the Vanities* (1990) and *Mission to Mars* (2000), gave delirious mainstream expression to the idiom of the exploitation film that finds its contemporary market niche in horror porn.

Postmodern Surrealists

Thus far I have proposed a rather neat dichotomy in the reception of Hitchcock between European art cinemas, whether classical or modernist, and the post-classical Hollywood of intensified continuity, which augments and amplifies the aesthetics of suspense and unreliable narration. However, the history of Hitchcock's influence in the post-New Wave environment is more complex. Some of the most important European Hitchcockians, while influenced by art cinema, have inhabited popular genres and idioms, from Roman Polanski to Paul Verhoeven, Dario Argento, and Pedro Almodóvar, while the films of the American Hitchcockian David Lynch, though genre-based, bear many of the characteristics of modernist art cinema. In the case of all five of these directors, their impulse, in a post-sixties environment (which comes belatedly in post-Franco Spain for Almodóvar), is to give expression to the Hitchcockian shadow world or the domain of human perversity in a way that brings it out of its occluded state. While inhabiting the popular genres and idioms of mainstream storytelling, all combine their interest in "human perversity" with self-conscious narrative gamesmanship and visual stylization that is more explicitly indebted than Hitchcock's own practice to art cinema narration. At the risk of constructing a critical category that is too baggy for its varied contents, all these directors might be described as postmodern surrealists: postmodern in the way their work combines the self-conscious narration of art cinema with popular genres, surrealist in the manner that their films privilege the representation of "human perversity" in a frank display of human sexuality and sexually motivated violence that is linked to the form and style of their work.

Roman Polanski's edgy, disturbing and darkly comic 1966 film *Repulsion* is one of the most influential of all Hitchcockian works, inspiring both *Psycho*-influenced Hollywood horror movies like De Palma's *Sisters* and the work of popular surrealists like Dario Argento and David Lynch. In Hitchcockian works like *Repulsion*, where Polanski tracks the progressive mental breakdown of his isolated female protagonist Carol (Catherine Deneuve) as if we were watching Norman Bates from the inside, art cinema meets exploitation, as the portrayal of deranged subjectivity is viscerally realized in guignol-like effects. Polanski adapts Hitchcockian expressionism in low-key lighting and intensified diegetic sounds, but he goes beyond Hitchcock in the manner in which the subjective perception frankly spills over into reality: cracks that the protagonist imagines break out over the house, hands appear through the walls to pull and grope at her body, and the rape she imagines appears to be literally enacted. *The Tenant* (1976) traverses the ground of *Repulsion*, but its debt to Hitchcock is more overt, and its black comedy is archly self-conscious in a manner suggesting that Polanski is now studying early De Palma as closely as his mentor. *The Tenant* reworks *Rear Window*'s theme of looking as the paranoia of being looked at by leering intrusive tenants, and like Norman Bates, its protagonist gradually assumes the identity of a dead woman. Here cross-dressing is a prelude to a staged suicide that recalls a number of scenes in Hitchcock, most of all the death of the "deviant" Handel Fane (Esme Percy) in *Murder!* (1930) cross-dressed in his feather costume and bedecked in his leotard of peacock eyes. Yet, unlike Hitchcock's finely-tuned handling of Fane's death-swoon, there is little pathos in the tenant's death. It is pure Guignol of the kind that Dario Argento would make his trademark.

In the films of Argento, known as the "Italian Hitchcock" and the creator of a very bad, made-for-television Hitchcockian pastiche, *Do You Like Hitchcock?* (2005), modernist art cinema is reduced completely to the exploitation idiom in a garish postmodern cinema of Grand Guignol and Steadicam "attractions." What distinguishes Argento's best work, if it can be put this way, is the thorough amoralism of his vision, a tendency already evident in Polanski. While in Hitchcock the presence of the shadow world always ultimately validates the world of appearances it is ranged against, in Argento's world moral hierarchy is thoroughly subverted and the surface coordinates of narrative melodrama are merely the occasion for staging attractions of stylish shock. For example, in *Opera* (1987) a young understudy, Betty (Cristina Marsillach), is being stalked by an anonymous man who ties her up and places needles under her eyelids so that she is forced to watch him commit brutal murders orchestrated to thrash metal and operatic arias (shades of *Psycho*). The killer is identified by swooping ravens (shades of *The Birds*), which are orchestrated by the opera director, Argento's double in the film, and released into the auditorium during an avant-garde version of Verdi's *Macbeth*. The killer confesses that Betty's mother made him kill young girls in her presence in a manner that he now reenacts in front of her. He is thus both victim and victimizer. But the status of Betty, the spectator's surrogate, is also ambiguous. Is she an innocent victim or co-conspirator? In the coda of the film, the killer pursues Betty after she has retreated with the film director to Switzerland and murders him. Betty immediately tells the killer that this is the outcome she wanted and they must run away, but then, when the cops appear, she betrays him. The moral indeterminacy of the conclusion points to the moral indeterminacy and circularity of the whole. Plot in *Opera* is a mere pretext for the staging of baroquely stylized scenes, often shot in garish red and/or jade green, which revolve around or culminate in murder. Recurring Steadicam point-of-view shots track what we assume to be the murderer's perspective, but they are consistently deceptive, and the murder scenes are at once gratuitously gruesome and highly stylized.

Lynch's work represents a less cynical confrontation with the realms of human perversity. Its increasingly fractured narration renders the status of the narrative world indeterminate in the manner of modernist cinema, even as it inhabits the popular idioms of the thriller. As with many directors, Hitchcock's influence is perhaps most keenly felt in his early work, most of all in *Blue Velvet* (1986), where the perverse, surrealist universe manifest in *Eraserhead* (1977) is contained within the anodyne small-town world of Lumberton. The film is a veritable Hitchcock anthology. Like Santa Rosa, which offers a home to Uncle Charlie in *Shadow of a Doubt,* Lumberton is a small town harboring a perverse killer, Frank (Dennis Hopper). The name of the hero, Jeffrey Beaumont (Kyle MacLachlan), the detective game he plays with Sandy (Laura Dern), and his voyeurism recall L.B. Jefferies in *Rear Window.* Trapped in the apartment of Dorothy Vallens (Isabella Rossellini), Beaumont watches sadomasochistic scenes of sex that make explicit the fantasy of the primal scene – the naïve little boy's perception of parental sex as a grotesque act of abuse and debasement – arguably underlying *Rear Window* itself. The emotional textures of the Hitchcockian shadow world that entwines desire with death are garishly amplified in *Blue Velvet.* Dorothy Vallens is associated with deep reds and blues that intensify the color scheme of *Vertigo* and suggest her quality as the femme fatale to whom, like Scottie Ferguson, Beaumont is drawn like a moth to a flame. By comparison, the everyday world is idealized in a manner that is lifeless, flat, and clichéd, as rendered in the opening montage of yellow tulips, white picket fences, and a friendly fireman on a red truck waving to the children at a school crossing that recalls the opening of *Rope* (1948). Bedecked in Hitchcock's warning colors, this is scarcely an ordinary normality but itself a kind of fantasy: the fireman has the quality of an automaton, echoed later in the figure of the mechanical robin at the finale. The "social reality" of the world as it appears is paper-thin and already so subject to irony that even authentic expressions of emotion cannot be trusted. The suffocating fantasy of the ordinary creates a kind of flatness; the two worlds, the everyday and the shadow world, are mirror images; nothing in this world is emotionally real. When Dorothy Vallens arrives naked and bruised at Sandy's home declaring, to Sandy's horror, that Jeffrey has "put his disease" in her, the shadow world erupts into the world of the ordinary in an alarming way, but our impulse is not to be appalled but to laugh.

Dutch director Paul Verhoeven belongs in the category of postmodern surreal-ists largely by virtue of his "erotic thriller" *The Fourth Man* (1983), which he unoffi-cially remade as *Basic Instinct* (1992) once he got to Hollywood. *The Fourth Man* is notable for rendering explicit the homosexual subtext that accompanies Hitchcock's depiction of masculinity in films like *Strangers on a Train* and linking it to Hitchcock's characteristic skepticism towards the formation of the couple. The narration is studiously ambiguous in the manner of Hitchcock's *Suspicion*: Christine (Renée Soutendjik) may or may or may not be a husband murderer who is out to murder her new lover, Gerard Reve (Jeroen Krabbé). *The Fourth Man* is also overtly reflexive – Christine films Gerard in just the same way that she has made home movies of her previous husbands (recalling the home movie in *Rebecca*), and when Gerard begins to think that she is a murderer, he imagines these movies concluding in their deaths. *The Fourth Man* effectively reverses the gender roles in gothic-influ-enced melodramas like *Suspicion* and *Rebecca*. The male protagonist becomes a female Bluebeard and Hitchcock's ingenuous heroine, ridden by uncertainty and guilt over her sexual agency, is now a homosexual man who sleeps with Christine as a means of getting to Herman (Thom Hoffman), a young man he has previously cruised. Also like Hitchcock's sexually insecure female protagonists and, in a more exaggerated and deadly form, Hitchcock's queer killers, Gerard suffers from para-noid fantasies about Christine's intentions. However, in the manner of the post-modern surrealists, these fantasies are hyperbolically inscribed, creating a sense that reality itself is cut to the measure of the protagonist's fears and desires. Yet, while in *The Fourth Man*, the queer subtext of a film like *Rebecca* – Joan Fontaine's charac-ter can have a "relationship" with a woman like Rebecca only under the veil of her relationship with Maxim – is thereby made oddly explicit, nonetheless, as Schneider and Sweeney (2005) have noted, it cannot imagine a space for homosexual desire outside the "murderous" institution of compulsory heterosexuality.

The most significant director in this diverse group is Pedro Almodóvar, the "Spanish Hitchcock," whose work is thoroughly informed by the Hitchcockian idiom – he regards Hitchcock's work as "visually the richest in the history of cin-ema" (Strauss 143) – even as it turns that idiom inside out. Hitchcock's surreal "warning colors" (yellows, oranges, and reds) that supervene on the world of the everyday, the sense of doubling that conflates the normal with the perverse, and the idea of self-identity as a performance, which, when linked to human perversity, as in *Psycho*, becomes deadly – all these elements of Hitchcock's shadow world also define Almodóvar's narrative universe. In Hitchcock's narrative world, the domain of human perversity, however much it is ambiguously valorized, is always marked out against sexually straight and narratively realist norms. In Almodóvar's films, by contrast, "human perversity" is not only rendered unambiguously desirable but ultimately comes to define what is normal via the conventions of popular melodrama, wherein heightened emotion and desire, self-performativity and disguise, coincidence and radical reversal of fortune all seem a normal part of everyday life.

Almodóvar's *Matador* (1986), though more schematic than some of his more well-known films, neatly illustrates the nature of his engagement with and transformation of Hitchcock's idiom. One half of the story tells of the formation of the nominally heterosexual couple. The brooding bullfighter Diego (Nacho Martinez), savaged in the ring, epitomizes machismo, yet this machismo veils an impotence and perhaps a repressed homosexuality that he compensates for by watching and engaging in sadistic acts of killing. His double, Maria (Assumpta Serna), who sometimes looks like a man in drag, kills her victims as they climax like a toreador impaling a bull at the moment of his charge, and then climaxes herself over each corpse. This couple, both turned on by death, become perfect partners. When their delirious consummation, bathed in hot colors, is invaded by the police, the audience is invited to root not for their murder-suicide to be thwarted but for their literal realization of the *Liebestod*. The other half of the story centers on Diego's pupil, the impotent, androgynous Ángel (Antonio Banderas), who is so lacking in machismo that, after spying *Rear Window*–like on Diego's young girlfriend Eva (Eva Cobo), he ignominiously fails in his attempt to rape her. Ángel literally suffers from performance anxiety; he lacks an identity that he can "perform." Ángel is endowed, like Hitchcock's dandies and Gerard in *The Fourth Man,* with a preternatural sixth sense that seems to have sprouted in proportion to his own lack of actual (sexual) power or agency. As if drenched in original sin (an all-too-willing wrong man), Ángel takes ownership not only of the rape of Diego's girlfriend, which she quickly refutes, but of the crimes that Diego himself committed. In his role as seer, Ángel functions, like L.B. Jefferies, both as the spectator and as the center of a film in which all the main characters function as his doubles. The world of *Matador*, which is equally that of cinema itself, is one in which the normal is perverse, the perverse is normal, and authentic identity is defined by the conviction with which is it performed.

By Way of Conclusion: Cinema and Gaming

The idea of the director as gamesman who plants deceptive cues to create suspense and shock highlights the control and manipulation exerted by the director upon the understanding and emotional response of the audience. Hitchcock conceived the work of the director as administering "healthy mental shake-ups" to an audience that had become "sluggish and jellyfied" (Hitchcock 109). Yet as Vera Dika points out apropos of horror film cycles like *Friday the 13th* (1980–2009) that were in part inspired by *Psycho*, the very mechanisms of narrative control and manipulation that cue suspense – Is this where the monster is? Is this the next victim? – are also those that actively engage the spectator's participation in the narrative. Overt control and orchestration of the viewer's expectations triggers the spectator's alert engagement in the narrative, which Dika compares to a user's participation in an interactive video game.

The salience of Hitchcock's films to gaming is not restricted simply to the kind of audience participation that is cued by unreliable narration and the orchestration of suspense but also to the mapping of space and the immersive aesthetics of the digital gaming environment (see Mamber). While he was at Universal, Hitchcock perfected an aesthetic of moving camera point of view in which the spectator, adapting the point of view of a character in the fiction, is given the feeling of entering into or penetrating the space of the film. While theatrical modes of identification are partially invoked by Hitchcock in these kinds of sequences, he also uses the human agent moving through space in the film as kind of placeholder for the spectator. We find in Hitchcock's cinema a remarkable anticipation of the immersive environment of the video game, especially when this aesthetic incorporates the threat of assault, as it does in Hitchcock's horror films. Of course, the situation is not one that is literally interactive. The film spectator cannot avoid assault; it is the camera rather than the spectator that controls looking; and the film, unlike the video game, will usually supply a reverse-field shot.

A different kind of game playing is also anticipated in Hitchcock's cinema – the kind associated with reality television, which we might call "reality gaming," where the voyeuristic spectator watches as contestants are restricted to a single location and subjected to a series of tests that will determine who stays and who goes. These shows are all versions of the lifeboat game that Hitchcock himself adapted in his film *Lifeboat* (1944). *Rope* provides a different kind of "reality game," one that is explicitly staged as a game by the protagonists within the fiction and is self-evidently perverse. The protagonists of the film invite the friends and family of their murder victim to a dinner party to see whether they are bright enough to notice that the victim's corpse is actually concealed in the chest that doubles as a dining table in the middle of the room. Furthermore, the staging in *Rope* is voyeuristic, as we peer, with the unblinking gaze of a long-take moving camera, upon the exotic lives of society homosexuals. *Psycho* and *The Birds* take the idea of the game environment into the realm of horror. Somewhere in the enclosed space of the *Psycho* compound there stalks a murderer. Who is it, and when will the killer attack? Bodega Bay in *The Birds* is likewise represented as an enclosed space where the protagonists wait to see when the birds will attack and whom they will kill, and at the end of the film they are confined to the darkened interior of a boarded-up homestead as they await in fear the final assault. Contemporary horror series like the *Saw* franchise (2004–08) fuse horror and reality gaming by placing characters in a closed and closed-circuit environment, where they are forced to fight to the death under the controlling eye of a sadistic, all-powerful psychotic gamesman.

Gus Van Sant, creator of the controversial 1998 remake of *Psycho*, uses a Hitchcockian gaming aesthetic to brilliant ends in *Elephant* (2003), his film about the Columbine school killings. *Elephant* is inspired by *The Birds* as filtered through a gaming aesthetic. As in *The Birds*, the audience is waiting in an isolated and closed environment, initially entered via a series of point-of-view tracking shots, for a random event of consummate evil to occur. As in *The Birds*, the attacks are leveled at once upon children, who represent the very idea of hope or future, and upon the human lovebirds – the school jock and his girlfriend. As in *The Birds*, while several social and psychological explanations are offered for the attack – parenting, video games, bullying, gun culture, repressed homosexuality – none are privileged. Like the bird attacks, this event defies human explanation. Finally, as in *The Birds*, *Elephant* creates an electronically processed aural envelope that includes bird sounds and serves to underscore the manner in which the school is transformed into a thoroughly alien, dehumanized environment.

Elephant's prolonged "following camera" long-take tracking shots evoke the gaming aesthetic of a first-person shooter game as well as the "liveness" of reality television. A gaming environment is implied by the film's opening sequence as, from an elevated angle, a car is perceived moving along the road, bouncing off the curb and other vehicles. A narrative game or puzzle is also evoked. Perceiving a father and son in the car, we assume the son is drunk, since we are already on the lookout for adolescent killers, but the drunk driver turns out to be his father. As in a first-person shooter video game, each character that is introduced is a potential killer who is flagged by a name, and the viewer randomly switches identities and perspectives so that random encounters in the corridor can be perceived from two different perspectives. The killings appear like those on a video screen – screaming is muted, the gun makes a light pop, figures run about randomly in the field of vision, there is no blood, and the bodies quickly disappear from view.

This sustained analogy does not suggest that video games caused the shooters' behavior; rather, it suggests that the shooters could have been any members of this teenage universe. In *Elephant*, high school is an environment of monadic isolation that lacks meaning, one in which a simple greeting in the school corridor seems as if it is a reaching out across an emotional void. The attacks, like the bird attacks in Hitchcock's film, seem a product of an emotionally desiccated and essentially mean-ingless world, and the act of making the film, like the photographs that one of the boys (a surrogate for the filmmaker) takes of his friends, becomes an effort to make sense from this absence of meaning. There is no better contemporary testament to the creative vitality of Hitchcock's influence thirty years after his death.

Works Cited

Allen, Richard. *Hitchcock's Romantic Irony*. New York: Columbia UP, 2007.

Anderson, Lindsay. "Alfred Hitchcock." *Sequence* 9 (Autumn 1949). LaValley 48–59.

Bazin, André. "Hitchcock contre Hitchcock." *Cahiers du cinéma* 39 (October 1954): 25–32. Trans. as "Hitchcock versus Hitchcock." LaValley 60–69.

Bordwell, David. *Narration in the Fiction Film*. Madison: U of Wisconsin P, 1985.

Bordwell, David. *The Way Hollywood Tells It: Style and Story in Modern Movies*. Berkeley: U of California P, 2006.

Bordwell, David, Janet Staiger, and Kristin Thompson. *The Classical Hollywood Cinema: Film Style and Mode of Production to 1960*. New York: Columbia UP, 1985.

Boyd, David, and R. Barton Palmer, eds. *After Hitchcock: Influence, Imitation, and Intertextuality*. Austin: U of Texas P, 2006.

Buckland, Warren, ed. *Puzzle Films: Complex Storytelling in Contemporary Cinema*. Chichester, UK: Wiley-Blackwell, 2009.

Carney, Ray. "The Seductions of Stylishness." Boston U. 2004. Web. 24 June 2010.

Dika, Vera. *Games of Terror: Halloween, Friday the 13th and the Films of the Stalker Cycle*. Rutherford: Fairleigh Dickinson UP, 1990.

Hitchcock, Alfred. "Why 'Thrillers' Thrive." *Picturegoer*, 18 Jan. 1936, 15. *Hitchcock on Hitchcock: Selected Writings and Interviews*. Ed. Sidney Gottlieb. Berkeley: U of California P, 1995. 109–12.

Kovács, András Bálint. *Screening Modernism: European Art Cinema, 1950–1980*. Chicago: U of Chicago P, 2007.

Lagier, Luc. "On Vertigo." Excerpts from *Court-curcuit (le magazine)*. Special feature included with *La Jetée/Sans Soleil*. Criterion Collection, 2007. DVD.

LaValley, Albert, J., ed. *Focus on Hitchcock*. Englewood Cliffs: Prentice-Hall, 1972.

Leitch, Thomas. "How To Steal from Hitchcock." Boyd and Palmer 251–70.

Mamber, Stephen. "Hitchcock: The Conceptual and the Pre-digital." *Stanford Humanities Review* 7.2 (1999): 128–36.

Neupert, Richard. "Red Blood on White Bread: Hitchcock, Chabrol, and French Cinema." Boyd and Palmer 127–44.

Orr, John. *Hitchcock and Twentieth-Century Cinema*. London: Wallflower, 2005.

Rohmer, Eric, and Claude Chabrol. *Hitchcock: The First Forty-Four Films*. 1957. Trans. Stanley Hochman. New York: Ungar, 1979.

Schneider, Steven Jay, and Kevin W. Sweeney. "Genre Bending and Gender Bonding: Masculinity and Repression in the Dutch Thriller." In *Horror International*. Ed. Steven Jay Schneider and Tony Williams. Detroit: Wayne State UP, 2005. 180–202.

Strauss, Frederic, ed. *Almodóvar on Almodóvar*. London: Faber and Faber, 1996.

Tomasulo, Frank. "'You're Tellin' Me You Didn't See': Hitchcock's *Rear Window* and Antonioni's *Blow-Up*." Boyd and Palmer 145–72.

Truffaut, François. Speech at American Film Institute presentation of Life Achievement Award to Alfred Hitchcock. 7 March 1979. Excerpted in *Alfred Hitchcock: The Masterpiece Collection*, Disc 15. Universal, 2005. DVD.

Turvey, Malcolm. "Hitchcock, Unreliable Narration, and the Stalker Film." *Hitchcock Annual* 16 (2010): 153–77.

Vest, M. James. *Hitchcock and France: The Forging of an Auteur*. Westport, CT: Praeger, 2003.

Wollen, Peter. "Theme Park and Variations." *Sight and Sound* 3.7 (July 1993): 7–9.

Wood, Robin. *Hitchcock's Films Revisited*. Rev. ed. New York: Columbia UP, 2002.

Index

All title references are to films unless otherwise indicated.
Principal discussions of particular people and titles are in **boldface**.

A Companion to Alfred Hitchcock, First Edition. Edited by Thomas Leitch and Leland Poague.
© 2011 Thomas Leitch and Leland Poague. Published 2011 by Blackwell Publishing Ltd.

ed and bound by CPI Group (UK) Ltd, Croydon, CR0 4YY

07/02/2023